This looks like a very good book — after the Intro & Conclusion Probably a #2

The Absent-Minded Imperialists

The Absent-Minded Imperialists

Empire, Society, and Culture in Britain

BERNARD PORTER

OXFORD UNIVERSITY PRESS

OXFORD
UNIVERSITY PRESS

Great Clarendon Street, Oxford OX2 6DP

Oxford University Press is a department of the University of Oxford.
It furthers the University's objective of excellence in research, scholarship,
and education by publishing worldwide in

Oxford New York

Auckland Bangkok Buenos Aires Cape Town Chennai
Dar es Salaam Delhi Hong Kong Istanbul Karachi Kolkata
Kuala Lumpur Madrid Melbourne Mexico City Mumbai Nairobi
São Paulo Shanghai Taipei Tokyo Toronto

Oxford is a registered trade mark of Oxford University Press
in the UK and in certain other countries

Published in the United States
by Oxford University Press Inc., New York

First published 2004

British Library Cataloguing in Publication Data
Data available

Library of Congress Cataloging in Publication Data
Data available

ISBN 0-19-820854-5

1 3 5 7 9 10 8 6 4 2

Typeset by Kolam Information Services Pvt. Ltd, Pondicherry, India

Printed in Great Britain on acid-free paper by
Biddles Ltd,
King's Lynn, Norfolk

Till min älskade Kajsa

Preface

Looking back, the empire seems an awfully big part of British history. Yet this is only recently coming to be acknowledged in Britain itself. Foreigners of course have known it for years. That is scarcely surprising. It was *as* an empire that Britain mainly presented herself to them. Some of them were caught up in it: as its victims or beneficiaries, according to circumstances or one's political views; as its subjects, anyway. Others used to compete with it. Americans encountered it both ways. This must go far to explain why it was her empire that mostly impressed these 'others' about Britain, and still tends to impress them in historical retrospect. Britons themselves on the other hand have usually downplayed it, comparatively. This is not just a recent phenomenon, a case perhaps of 'denial' born of post-imperial guilt or regret. The empire has always seemed to mean less to most British than to its admirers and critics abroad. It hardly features at all in any obvious way in British literature and art. It was usually neglected in English schools. (We shall be seeing the evidence for this later.) Why was this? Does it really reflect the reality of the empire's impact back home? Were those native historians who used to leave it out of their accounts of Britain's modern development entirely, or at least to marginalize it, justified in so doing, at any rate from the point of view of Britain's domestic history; or were they missing a trick here? Just what was the relationship between her experience as an imperial power—there can be no doubting that, of course—and her more inner being? In what ways can she be said to have been an imperial *society*, as well as an imperial nation?

This is the subject of this book. It has been written as a contribution to the current debate on Britain's imperial culture in the nineteenth and early twentieth centuries (*c.* 1800–1940), which in recent years has tended to give rather greater emphasis to the imperial factor in her domestic history than older-fashioned British historians used to. A number of influences have contributed to this, some of them political (the Vietnam war, for example, which extended the meaning of the word 'imperialism' for many), but two important books in particular. The first was John MacKenzie's *Propaganda and Empire* (1984), which showed the extent to which Britons were urged to become empire-minded from the 1880s onwards; the second was the late Edward Said's *Culture and Imperialism* (1993), which revealed actual imperial traits not only in the obvious post-1880 literary canon (Kipling, Conrad), but also in earlier authors (Austen, Charlotte Brontë, Dickens), where they had hardly been noticed at all before. (Said was not the first to do this, but he has been the most influential.) Both these books inspired 'schools' of followers, who then found even more imperialism embedded in nineteenth- and early twentieth-century British culture and society, sometimes in the most surprising places. So far so good (in the main). But this then gave rise in some quarters to the idea that Britain was permeated with imperialism at every level, to the exclusion of almost every other ideology or 'discourse' (using that word in its broadest sense), whether contemporaries realized it or not. That contemporaries did not always realize it was a reason for pointing it up where it did not appear overtly: *inserting* imperial references into television or film adaptations of nineteenth-century classic novels, for example, and into documentaries about other aspects of Victorian life, on the grounds that it was there *really*, even if not explicitly stated.[1] In this way, what before had been a 'merely' scholarly idea spread into more popular consciousness. It may have become the received wisdom by now; taking us a long way on from the time when imperial perceptions and influences were whitewashed out of domestic British history almost entirely.

That whitewashing was certainly reprehensible. It was also frustrating to historians like myself, who taught and wrote about imperial history, but were forced to do so in a kind of academic ghetto separately from the mainstream of 'British history', and were often misunderstood as a result. (For a start, we were widely assumed to be imperial*ists*. The presumption was that you studied what you empathized with. Most social historians, after all, were socialists.) This obviously gave a false view of the mainstream. To some outsiders it seemed incomprehensible. A favourite angle on British history for many years was what was called the 'Whig' one: a narrative of ever-growing 'freedom' through time. How could that be squared with the suppression of many freedoms which is a logical corollary of 'imperialism' by most definitions (*imperium* = 'power'), and was a pretty blatant effect of Britain's empire-building from the seventeenth century onwards—the period of the growth of this 'freedom'—both overseas and in Ireland? It just did not fit. You cannot judge a bully outside by the sweetness of his conduct in his home. (This is not to imply, incidentally, that either of those descriptions is necessarily a fair one for Britain in this period.) Quite apart from that, the whole implication of her worldwide dominance had to be that more people were involved in Britain's history than the 'British'—usually restricted to metropolitan white men—alone. Jamaicans, Punjabis, Ghanaians, white Canadians, Australian aborigines, and all the countless other peoples who got caught up in the web of the British empire at one time or another, women as well as men, were and are as much a part of Britain's story as the people who lived or originated in Britain itself. When the empire was lifted out of its ghetto and reintegrated in the mainstream by such as MacKenzie and Said, no one was more relieved and delighted than some of us old imperial history hands. At last the empire was coming home.

Many of the contributions of the MacKenzie-ites and the Saidists ('Saidist' is MacKenzie's mischievous neologism)[2] have hugely enriched our understanding, both of the nature of British imperialism and, on the other side of the equation, of Britain's culture and society. It is fascinating and important to realize the extent of the traces the former left on the latter, in particular: between the lines of Jane Austen's novels, for example, where one could easily miss them without Said's clever guidance; in more popular literature and music in the second half of the nineteenth century; on perceptions and constructions of gender; through sport; in shows, zoos, and museums ... and so on. This is an influence that was greatly neglected before. It is no longer. We have—I would guess—most of the materials available to us now to judge of the real impact and importance of the imperial factor in the domestic life of Britain in this period, and vice versa. That, however, has not yet been done properly. Effects have been discovered and described, but not evaluated. Sometimes—this book will argue—their value has been exaggerated. This is for a number of reasons. Semantic unclarity is one. Too much *concentration* on imperial factors is another; if you are only working on one aspect of a culture or society, its importance can seem greater than it is. The presumption that they *must* have been overwhelming is a third. This is the first study to tackle this question without any of these particular drawbacks. (It may have others.) It is a sober attempt to place the imperial factor in British domestic history in a broader context: to discover how great it was, what exactly it signified in different circumstances, and how it related to other influences, *overall*.

It also aspires to a more contemporary and practical purpose. Imperialism is not at an end. (This is being written in the immediate aftermath of the Iraq war of 2003.) This book will try to show what kind of support an earlier version of British imperialism required and received from the domestic culture of its time. That support, it will be also argued, may not have been essentially imperialist*ic*. This may be a general characteristic of certain kinds of imperialism, not just nineteenth-century British. If this is so, then it may help us to recognize the signs of it, better than if we are only on the lookout for 'imperial cultures', when it threatens to uncurl and strike again today. I shall be addressing this point in a brief foray into the post-1940 period, in the final chapter of the book.

* * *

It has become customary recently in works of this kind to describe the personal circumstances that may have influenced their authors both in their choice of subjects, and in the emphases they bring to them: 'where they come from', as it is sometimes put. Catherine Hall's long account of the various relevant influences on her childhood and after, in the Introduction to her subtle and illuminating *Civilising Subjects* (2002), is a model of this genre; as is the description of his 'Imperial Childhood' that David Cannadine published as an appendix to his stimulating *Ornamentalism* (2001). In much the same way, any reader of *Culture and Imperialism* ought also to read Said's revealing memoir, separately published as *Out of Place* (1999), which serves the same function. This must be a good idea. We are bound to be influenced by our backgrounds. The problem, of course, is that we cannot always know which aspects of our upbringings have most affected us. I shall be confining myself here, much more briefly than either Hall or Cannadine, to some of the most obvious ones in my case; they may, of course, not be the deepest.

In fact my (rather dull) background is closer to Cannadine's than to Hall's or Said's (class, type of schooling, dullness); but what struck me most on reading his account was how *different* were our experiences of the empire, including vicarious ones, when we were young. He remembers many such experiences; I can recall none. This is despite the fact that I am older than him, so the empire when I was a boy was still (just) a going concern. None of my relatives, so far as I know, emigrated to the colonies; none served there in the armed forces; we had no imperial books of any obvious kind on my parents' or grandparents' bookshelves; and I do not remember the empire ever being discussed or even mentioned at home as a child. My (Methodist) church was clearly not as keen on missionary work as Hall's (Baptist) one was. At school I studied no imperial history whatsoever. I can be pretty certain of this because I have checked in my old exercise books, which my mother kept. When I went up to Cambridge to read history in the 1960s it was virtually impossible to study it at all. British history was strictly 'constitutional'. There was a course on the 'Expansion of Europe' (what a telling title!),[3] but that was regarded—certainly at my college—as a second-best option, for undergraduates who could not cope with the alternative 'History of Political Thought' syllabus. I first came to the subject at postgraduate level, and then via my interest in political thought. My thesis—and first book—was on 'anti-imperialist' ideology. Before that I knew almost nothing of the empire, apart from being a member of the Labour party, from which it was supposed to follow (at that time) that I must be an anti-imperialist myself. That is what I certainly believed. My first acquaintance with people from the Commonwealth or colonies also came as a research student; my first visit to any ex-colony (the United States and Canada) was at the age of 29. Am I alone among my generation in this relative *non*-awareness of the empire, at any sort of conscious level (OK, I realize it could have affected me more subvertly), in my formative years? If not, it seems reasonable to suppose that the overt impact of the empire was *not* quite ubiquitous generally. At any rate, this is probably why I am more open to this possibility than those who were more steeped in it early on.

Another reason is that although I started off as an imperial historian—my second book was a general history of British imperialism, and I co-edited the *Journal of Imperial and Commonwealth History* for a period—I did not confine myself to this field. I wandered. Among other subjects I have researched and published on (all relating to Britain) are refugees, attitudes to Europeans, policing, the security services, diplomacy, architecture, and a general survey of nineteenth and twentieth-century Britain. That last book (*Britannia's Burden*, 1994) sought to integrate domestic and imperial history at the level of 'high' politics, though without much impact, apparently. (It bombed, probably deservedly.) I reckon this has given me a broader and deeper grounding in British history than those who have specialized more narrowly. There is nothing like getting away from the empire for a while to put it in perspective. As it happens, it also helped me to spot some other imperial influences on British life that I do not believe have occurred to other historians yet. (They will be mentioned later.) On the whole, however, the empire seemed to diminish in size; rather to my surprise, as someone who could not be suspected, I think, of being unlikely to spot the signs.

I should mention one last influence. I have twice spent substantial periods in Australia on study-leave. It is the country in which I feel most at home. (My grandparents *should* have emigrated.) One reason for this, as

I realized quite early on, was my feeling of identity with—or perhaps my wish *to* identify with—Australians as colonial subjects rather than with Britons as an imperial master race; which was how the Australians I met seemed to want to categorize me initially, especially when they were playing their favourite—and mostly quite amusing—game of 'Pom bashing'. I did not mind this personally (I gave the ex-cons back as good as I got), but it did give me the idea—a pretty obvious one, when you think about it—of how ridiculous it is to characterize whole nations in such terms: as being either one thing or the other. Empires are more complicated than this. One whole country does not rule another whole country. Each side contains its share of imperial masters and subjects. Some of the nastiest imperialists in the nineteenth century, by the worst definition of that term, for example, were émigrés, possibly even the ancestors of my Australian friends (though I hope not): the people, that is, who massacred the Australian aborigines. (That was not the doing of the imperial government.) There are also the 'collaborators'.[4] Likewise, in Britain in the same period there were millions of women and men—my grandparents among them—who were at least as much subjected and 'exploited' by the 'imperialists' there as almost anyone in the colonies, and far more so than those self-same émigrés, who were considerably more free (to slaughter their aborigines, for example) than ever my poor old granddad was. Britain was made up of imperialists and subjects, just like the colonies were. Her culture must have reflected this. It did, as we shall see.

Those are some of the influences on my thinking that I am aware of. Of course there may be others. I probably ought to mention that I am white, English (from Essex), middle-class, male, and with rather old-fashioned left-wing political proclivities. I have tried to escape from the obvious biases that these characteristics might imply. It will be up to my readers, however, to decide whether I have succeeded in this.

❦❦❦

In the final analysis, however, the truth or value of the argument I set out here will depend less on my own positioning, I hope, than on the quality of my argument. This will be based on four approaches, all of them historical. (I am a historian, after all, not a cultural theorist.) First, I shall be as semantically precise as I can be. Semantics are important; to a great extent, whether we want to regard a particular attitude or phenomenon as 'imperialistic' or not depends on the meanings we wish to assign to that word, some of which can legitimately be used to embrace almost anything. My use of the word may be more limited than some (though it is wider than many); but it will at least be a clear one, and I think more useful than some others. Obviously, anyone is at liberty to disagree with my thesis on the grounds that my definition is *too* restrictive. (It does not automatically embrace 'racism', for example.) We shall return to this, more than once. Secondly, I shall be examining the evidence for domestic imperialism *empirically and sceptically,* to see if it necessarily stands up if we do not *assume* that Britain was imperially 'steeped'. This, it seems to me, lies at the heart of the 'historical' method. Thirdly, I shall be examining the broader British social and cultural *context,* to see how the imperial factor appears when it is placed against that. Some recent scholars have paid insufficient attention to this. In the archeological site that is British society in the nineteenth and early twentieth centuries there are, of course, thousands of imperial shards to be found. Dug out and piled up at the side, they can be made to look overwhelming. Studied *in situ,* however, one gets a different impression. They appear widely scattered, and concentrated in certain layers and at particular spots. One misses an awful lot if one is not aware of where, exactly, they have been found. Some of them lie close to the remains of other structures or artefacts in a way that suggests that they may have broken off from them, and not from 'imperialism' at all. Between them there are also great expanses of *nothing*: of earth or rock whose barrenness may be as significant as the presence elsewhere of the shards themselves. This is where knowledge of the context is vital. (I shall be extending this metaphor later.) But even that cannot tell us everything. My fourth and final approach, therefore, will be to stand back and consider how the various sections of British society—for Britain did not have a single or even a dominant 'culture' at this time, but several entirely different and even contradictory ones: cultural scholars often appear unaware of this too—were *likely* to have responded to their empire, in view of their material situations and patterns of life, and the nature and requirements of the empire itself.

There will undoubtedly be flaws in the argument. Some may stem from my 'biases'. There are also gaps in my evidence. I make no apology, however, for this. There was no avoiding it. There is simply too much relevant material to cover all of it, especially if one wishes to take in the context and the barren patches too. Take newspapers, for example, a prime source for this kind of subject: I once idly calculated that just the London daily newspapers for a single year in the 1850s, say, must contain more than

20 million words. That figure may be wide of the mark; but with all the other sources I was presented with—Sunday and provincial newspapers, working-class prints, periodicals, comics, novels, autobiography, other non-fiction, poetry, plays, school textbooks, and so on, to mention only written materials—I was not going to waste valuable research time trying to get it right. So there are huge lacunae. I have tried my best to ensure that my *samples* of these materials are representative, by trying to pick them intelligently: broadly, for example, and from 'typical' places and 'likely' periods; but I may, of course, have missed some evidence which contradicts my thesis. (This is always the researcher's nightmare.) To alert readers to this possibility, I also spell out the exact range of my sources in the Endnotes, at the appropriate places, so that they – and the gaps in them – can be checked. I have also used the Endnotes to elaborate on and digress from points made in the text, I hope quite interestingly; which is why they are so gargantuan.

My samples are also limited in two other ways. First, I have largely confined myself to *English* sources, though in relation to 'British' imperialism, which is why the term 'British' is still used. That applies especially to what I have to say about the teaching of empire in English schools, none of which should necessarily be assumed to extend to the educational systems of the other nations of the United Kingdom. (This should not, of course, be taken to indicate any kind of disregard on my part for the 'Celts'. Like many English people, I wish I was Irish. Luckily my children are, half.) Scots, Welsh, and Irish responded to the empire in ways that paralleled the English in some respects, but also had peculiarities of their own. (The Scots, for example, may well have been *more* imperially aware and enthusiastic than the English.)[5] So I shall not be surprised if other scholars find differences here. It is up to them to find these out. Secondly, in dealing with the social and cultural differences between groups of Britons (or the English) that may have affected their responses to the empire, I have deliberately concentrated on *class* to the virtual exclusion of other divides. I believe I can show that this was crucial: that the working classes, for example, had an entirely distinct perception of the empire from the upper classes, arising from the peculiar material interests—*au fond*, their relationship to the dominant means of production—of each. (This will seem quite old-fashioned to some.) This, however, does not rule out other influences. The English were separated amongst and against themselves in other ways too: by region, for example, religious denomination, gender, and the urban–rural divide. These will also have had a bearing—possibly even a comparable one—on their views of the empire and imperialism. Again, I am not dismissing these, only leaving them aside for others to explore. (In the cases of religion and gender, the work has already begun.)[6] The main point I wish to make is that British opinion on this subject was far from monolithic. If it can be shown to have been unmonolithic in other than 'class' ways also, then that will only be grist to my mill.

The picture that will emerge from all this is that English people, and classes, related to the empire and imperialism in widely different ways. The empire probably affected nearly everyone materially. I should make it clear at the outset that I am not seeking to deny that. Later in this book (Chapter 12) I shall be discussing some of these possible effects. They include Britain's participation in two world wars, her economic rise and decline, the perpetuation of her class structure, and the state of her people's teeth. In all of these ways the empire impacted hugely on her culture and society. That should be enough material repercussions for anyone. But they were all *indirect*. (It was sugar from the empire, for example, not the empire itself, that helped rot people's teeth.) Direct effects—the impact of the empire or imperialism, that is, on the way people thought and behaved, and the latters' effect in turn on the empire, which are the main focus of this work—are more problematical. My argument here will be that they were in fact neither as ubiquitous nor as straightforward as is often assumed. My starting point (in Chapters 1–2) is that these effects did not *need* to run very broad or deep. The empire could have existed, and even expanded, as it did in the nineteenth century, with very little commitment towards it or even awareness of it at home. The degree of actual commitment and awareness were, of course, greater than that. The empire also undoubtedly affected people in ways they were not entirely conscious of. What is interesting, however, and significant for all kinds of reasons—not only for an understanding of British history, but also possibly for a true picture of what 'imperialism' is and how it arises and is sustained *in general* (present-day America inevitably comes to mind here)—is how uneven, complex, and changeable the relationship between Britons and their empire was. Chapters 3–11 will endeavour to demonstrate that. Imperial Britain was generally a *less* imperial society than is often assumed; and, for the rest, was far more ambivalently so.

This line will be more acceptable to some than to others. I anticipate that many reviews of this book may be combative. Some of this may be because I have not fully understood the counter-arguments. (I admit to be baffled by the works of certain 'postcolonial theorists'.)[7] Others may find nothing particularly original here. That is the other recurring nightmare of researchers: that what they have discovered must already be well known, simply because they have become so familiar with it themselves. Actually I know that this is not so of everyone. While I was completing this book I had the opportunity to test out some of its ideas on a conference of mainly American nineteenth-century historians and literary scholars at Bloomington, Indiana, many of whom told me it had never entered their heads before that Victorian Britain might *not* have been imperially 'steeped'. So this will be a revelation to some; or, at the very least, an alternative viewpoint that needs to be properly weighed—as I trust it will be—before it is found wanting.

❦❦❦

Now for the Acknowledgments. Like all historical researchers I have been reliant on various libraries and archives for help. The following deserve my special thanks: the Australian National University Library; the British Library and Newspaper Library; Cambridge University Library; Kungliga Biblioteket in Stockholm; Stockholm University Library; the Brynmor Jones Library, Hull University; the Newcastle Literary and Philosophical Society; the Public Record Office; the Robinson Library, Newcastle University; the Stirling Library, Yale University; the London Metropolitan Archive; and the Archive of Oxford University Press.

The following people (mostly friends) have helped me in various ways during the writing of this book, though some may by now have forgotten how: Tim Barringer, Gordon Batho, Chris Bennett, Jeremy Black, Jeremy Boulton, John Bourne, Peter Burroughs, Kathy Castle, Tony Clayton, John Derry, Janet Doust, Angela Gaffney, Ian Hancock, Phil Harling, Nick Hewitt, Anthea Hislop, Theo Hoppen, Chandrika Kaul, Zoe Laidlaw, Norman McCord, John MacKenzie, Peter Marshall, Martin Maw, Bob Moore, Deborah Morse, Finlay Murray, Bill Nasson, David Omissi, Jerry Paterson, Francis Plowden, Andrew Porter, Eliza Riedi, Benedikt Stuchtey, Max Tyler, Jim Walvin, Peter Yeandle, and Edith. (Strictly speaking Edith isn't a person. But she took me for walkies so that I could think.) I remember useful discussions on seminar papers arising from my early research for this book at London, Sheffield and Sheffield Hallam, Cape Town, Yale, California (Berkeley), and the Australian National Universities, from which I am sure I have taken on board useful points, whose authors, however, I did not always register the names of. They have my apologies. I also owe enormous debts to the four following institutions: the Leverhulme Trust, for financing two years of my research with a Fellowship; the British Academy, for the overseas conference grant that sent me to Bloomington in October 2003; the Research School of Social Sciences of the Australian National University, for the perfect academic environment in which I began this project (as well as the weather); and Corpus Christi College, Cambridge, for introducing me for the first time to the peculiarities of the English upper classes, which feature in this book, when I was a Fellow there many years ago. I must also record my thanks to my most recent *alma mater,* Newcastle University, mainly for letting me go. That enabled me to finish the book. It is difficult to do serious academic work at most universities these days, especially if one takes on administrative duties too (I had five years as a rather ineffective Head of Department), so early retirement was a boon. During the bad period my partner for the last eight years, Kajsa Ohrlander, who is no stranger herself to these kinds of stresses, managed to keep me relatively detached and sane. Since then she has helped enormously, both with intellectual stimulation (it is very invigorating for an old male fogey to live with a feminist postmodernist), and with love. This book will almost certainly be too 'positivist' for her liking, but is dedicated to her anyway.

Bernard Porter

Hull and Enskede
November 2003

Contents

List of Illustrations

Between pp. 234 and 235

I
Empire and Society

The British empire was one of the biggest things in history. At any rate that is the conventional view. In area it was immense. At its height, we are told, it covered a quarter of the world's habitable land area, and contained a fifth of its people: or it may have been the other way around. It intruded into every continent, every sort of terrain, and every climate; from the highest mountains (almost) to the broadest plains, from jungles to deserts, and from the Arctic to the equator. This was quite apart from the oceans, which it also effectively ruled. Its citizens and subject peoples together comprised a large cross-section of humanity, of almost all colours, ethnicities, religions, and what used to be called 'stages of civilization'. Only about a tenth of them looked and spoke and worshiped like the British, who had originally conquered and now ruled this immense conglomeration from a small, damp group of islands off the north-west coast of Europe. That seems extraordinary. It conjures up pictures of dedicated (or arrogant) proconsuls in plumed helmets, and brave (or bullying) redcoats forming in squares, supported by enterprising (or greedy) traders and self-sacrificing (or fanatical) missionaries, to exert a dominion over palm and pine (Kipling's phrase) which was unprecedented in the annals of mankind. Another image is of dense crowds of Britons back home cheering the process on—and warming the dampness out of them—at 'jubilees' held to celebrate the various stages in the long reign of the Queen-Empress who presided over the whole show. It was the greatest (or most exploitative) empire the world had ever seen.

It must have impacted on Britain. Such a huge enterprise could not fail to. 'No undertaking as far-flung as the British Empire', writes Edward Said, '. . . could have been sustained without the willing and perhaps implicit approval of the English "senso comune".'[1] It brought burdens and responsibilities, as well as opportunities, for most Britons, and will have fired the imaginations, at least, of the rest. This is bound to have been reflected in their economy, government, and social structure, which will have had to adapt to cope with it; and in their culture, which could hardly fail to be affected by so ubiquitous a project. Likewise, when the empire was lost it must have been a wrench. Britain's dominating feature for two centuries, her whole raison d'être, suddenly went. It was like a king losing his kingdom, or a hospital curing all its patients, or—this may be thought an apter metaphor—a prison warder whose inmates have all escaped. The disappointment will have been bitter, the disorientation traumatic, the adjustment cruel.

So one would expect. Appearances, however, paint a different picture. It has been pointed out many times that decolonization did not seem to have the effect on Britain that this scenario would suggest, and which France, for example, experienced when she gave up her smaller (though still considerable) empire in North Africa and Indo-China.[2] It caused no French-style constitutional convulsions, certainly not in the political structures and processes of the time. They went on as always, scarcely affected by this apparent revolution. The exception that inevitably comes to mind is the 1956 Suez crisis, but that only ruined one politician (Eden), and not even his government, which merely passed to another leader and remained in power for a further eight years. The only other rows over colonial questions simply isolated and enfeebled the Conservative right wing. Most politicians of all parties broadly accepted the general principle of colonial self-government, and went along with the unexpected pace of it with no great qualms. The general public seemed uninterested. Surely they would have been more concerned, and the politicians more passionate, if the empire had been important to them?

And if it *was* important, would we not expect to find more evidence of imperial involvement earlier, when they still had their worldwide possessions, and had no idea that this tragedy was to occur? Again, direct and overt signs of the 'imperializing' of Britain in the nineteenth and early twentieth centuries are elusive. Colonial issues rarely aroused any great interest in parliament, unless they involved major wars. The machinery of government was not affected, though some contemporaries feared it might be, by authoritarian habits acquired in places like India seeping back home.[3] The obvious connection between the empire and the economy—the Navigation Acts—was broken in 1849, and not resumed again—in the form of Imperial Preference—until 1932. For most of the nineteenth century British 'culture' at all levels avoided colonial subjects and settings almost perversely. Popular interest in the empire was not often—and never unambiguously—expressed. 'For the overwhelming majority in Britain,' wrote the Oxford imperial historian Frederick Madden as late as 1991, 'the empire had no everyday relevance. It was a fact—a peripheral fact, which rarely surfaced.'[4] There is an incongruity here. For most of the time that she was acquiring and ruling the greatest empire ever, Britain did not *look* particularly imperial.

There could be a simple solution to this. We may have got one or other side of the equation wrong. Perhaps the empire was not as important as it seemed. That would certainly explain its lack of impact at home. Alternatively, the evidence of impact may be there, but have been missed, or even covered up. That is a common belief among certain sorts of scholar today. There may also be ways of reconciling this apparent contradiction, one of which will be promoted in this book. But let us look at the easy answers first.

***

The first—that the empire was less significant than has been supposed—has had its advocates in recent years. They include several who have pointed out how much 'bluff' lay behind the empire—the impression of an all-pervading power that really did not exist, to cow its subjects and its rivals—which argument certainly has some merit. One or two have questioned whether the British empire even existed, which does 'sound eccentric', as the imperial historian Ged Martin, who raised the issue for discussion in 1972, put it then;[5] but was once seriously argued, by the Conservative politician Enoch Powell. Powell may be thought to be an unexpected anti-imperialist (in this sense). He is best remembered today as an extreme English nationalist and opponent of 'coloured' immigration. He first entered politics, in 1950, explicitly to put a stop to decolonization.[6] The transfer of power to India in 1947 traumatized him; later he remembered 'walking about the streets all night trying to digest it. One's whole world had been altered.'[7] This may explain his later volte-face. At the beginning of the 1960s, realizing that imperialism was a dead horse, he cut his losses and took another ideological tack. The main element in this—Powell's new shining ideal—was the free market. So far as the empire was concerned, he immediately began belittling it in retrospect. In 1961 he told an audience of fellow nationalists that it never had been significant, to Britain at any rate. Throughout the whole imperial episode 'the mother country remained unaltered... almost unconscious of the strange fantastic structure built around her—in modern parlance, "uninvolved"'.[8] Three years later the 'fantastic structure' itself had disappeared. In a remarkable speech in Dublin (of all places) he claimed that the British empire had been a 'myth', a 'deception', an 'invention', all along. It had originated as a ploy by the Conservatives in the 1890s to win votes. That people had ever believed in it was 'one of the most extraordinary paradoxes in political history'. It followed that if Britain had never had an empire, she could not have lost it, which made the *supposed* loss of it 'no very strong argument for national decline'.[9] Did Powell really believe this? In that same Dublin lecture he also argued that 'all history is myth' (he was ahead of his time here), and that 'the greatest task of the statesman therefore is to offer his people good myths and save them from harmful myths'.[10] This suggests that he was simply wanting to cheer ex-imperialists up. It may also have been his way of adjusting to his own personal post-imperial distress. The psychologists would call it 'denial'. It certainly does not seem objectively plausible, in this extreme form.

The other extreme probably needs to be taken more seriously, if only because it is a more widespread view. (You also don't have to be an unhinged politician to believe it.) This is that domestic British society was in fact broadly and deeply affected by the empire, but in ways that have not been noticed until recently. That would fit the view of the empire as something that was so big as to make it inescapable. There are two versions of this. The first suspects British historians of deliberately ignoring clear evidence of domestic imperialism, perhaps for Powell's sort of motive, or because they were (unlike Powell) ashamed.[11] Imperialism became deeply unfashionable in the last forty years of the twentieth century; British history textbooks, therefore, whitewashed over Britain's own colonial crimes and adventures. Imperial history was still taught, but in ghettoes of its own, separately from 'mainstream' British history (as at Cambridge in my day), and usually by imperial*ists,* which made more radical domestic historians want to keep their distance.[12] Imperialism was a 'ruling class' thing. Many social historians clearly felt ideologically uncomfortable with the idea that it could have been embraced by 'the people' too. A key study of the period—Richard Price's *An Imperial War and the British Working Class* (1972)—seemed to bear them out. This was 'denial', again. The other version is more charitable. It acknowledges that the marks made by the empire on Britain during the bulk of the nineteenth century, at least, are *not* all that obvious. That is why it needs clever people (like the adherents of this view) to tease them out. Traditional historians were looking for transparent signs—great debates about empire, pro-imperial demonstrations, novels and poems set on wild colonial frontiers—when in fact the proof of an imperial mentality comes in other, subtler forms. Only when scholars had become sensitized to these would the full impact of the imperialization of British society and culture become apparent. That finally happened from the middle 1980s onwards, when new approaches and techniques showed up imperial Britain for what she really was.

Every idea arises from a social or psychological context. We have seen how the 'anti-imperial' views of Enoch Powell and others probably did. That should not automatically discredit them, of course: people can get good ideas for wrong reasons—indeed, often do. The fact that this new 'imperialist' view of nineteenth- and twentieth-century Britain can also be partly explained in terms of extraneous factors and motives, therefore, should not be held against it too much. The social and political influences working on it are plain to see. One is the simple dying-off of the Powellite generation that had been traumatized by the fall of their empire, to be replaced by another that did not have the same motivation to deny it. For anyone born after—say—1950, the empire had nothing directly to do with them. It had become part of the comfortably distant past. Portrayals of it in contemporary films and television dramas both rose-tinted it (literally, in some cases), and emphasized its alienness. Few younger viewers of *The Jewel in the Crown* television series in the 1980s, for example, could possibly have identified with any of its characters. The new generation did not feel any particular *responsibility* for the empire: nor should it have. It no longer hurt, therefore, to admit that your forebears could have been imperialist. If you were a political 'modernizer'—as so many professed to be, from Harold Wilson's governments onwards—the imperial past might even be useful. Imperialism has furnished a convenient scapegoat in recent years to explain racism, economic decline, great-power delusions, Europhobia, and a host of other perceived old-fashioned failings in post-World War II Britain, in some cases possibly unfairly, but in a way that obviously strengthens the notion that Britain *used* to be soaked in the stuff. Denial is no longer the problem. Indeed, the pendulum may have swung too far the other way.

People began to see imperialism everywhere. In a way this was scarcely surprising: there *was* a lot of it about in the later nineteenth and early twentieth centuries, in certain forms. Propaganda was one. John MacKenzie was the first to study and take seriously the great amount of publicity that imperial causes generated at this time. His seminal *Propaganda and Empire* (1984) was followed by a flood of other studies on this and allied themes, many of them published in MacKenzie's own invaluable (if uneven) 'Studies in Imperialism' series for Manchester University Press. This seemed to suggest that imperialism penetrated much deeper into British society than had once been thought. Jeffrey Richards, one of MacKenzie's stable, claims that British popular culture was 'steeped' in it.[13] Catherine Hall thinks they were 'imbricated' with empire.[14] Antoinette Burton writes of imperialism's being 'an integral part of "British" social, political, and cultural history'.[15] It probably helped that none of these writers had any hang-ups over the notion of *working-class* imperialism; an idea which, indeed, soon found favour with some left-wing historians too. (It was one of the things that explained the failure of socialism in Britain.)[16] Of course, this very much depended on how persuasive one took the 'propaganda' to be. The MacKenzie school tended to assume that it must have been overwhelming because there was so much of it; an alternative reading, however, might be that it could not have been all that persuasive, if the propagandists felt they needed to propagandize so hard. One way to settle this might be to study the reception of all this propaganda: the 'demand' rather than the 'supply' side, as James Greenlee puts it.[17] In fact this is not easy; but a stab will be made at it in this book.

Another factor was a certain relaxation in some scholarly *definitions* of imperialism, which enabled more phenomena to be included under it. For example: if missionary prosyletism were to be counted; or foreign trade; or overseas travel; or—to take some of the more bizarre candidates that have been put forward—militarism, masculinism, zoo-keeping and 'England's social mission'[18]—then the scope for an 'imperial' impact on British society obviously expands enormously. (We shall return to this shortly.) A third factor may have been the course of US foreign policy in the final third of the twentieth century, and the sudden realization by many Americans that this could be said to fit some of these new definitions of imperialism too. That made the British variety immediately relevant to them. American scholars, in fact, have been very active in this field recently. (One or two of their studies of British imperial culture actually begin with the Vietnam war.)[19]

In any case, Americans and other ex-colonial subjects were almost bound to want to emphasize the imperialist elements in British society, because of the higher profile those elements inevitably presented from their viewpoint.[20] The face a nation presents to other peoples is always different from the way it feels inside. (A true picture, of course, will incorporate both.) In some cases anti-Britishness was a further factor. Imperialism has become a useful stick to beat Britain with, especially in comparatively innocent countries empire-wise, and if the wielders of the stick can persuade themselves that she retains imperial attitudes still.

For the cultural 'theorists', lastly, who were some of the most persistent 'imperialists' in these years, especially after Edward Said's *Culture and Imperialism* (1993), another motive may have come into play. Before Said they had scarcely noticed the empire. That was because the objects of their researches—the 'canonical' novels of the nineteenth century, for example—did not seem to do so either. The received opinion was that this was because the latter were élitist, divorced from contemporary society; from which it could be inferred that the researchers' study of them was élitist and irrelevant too. That may have been an incentive for them to discover some imperialism under the surface of these cultural productions. If culture could be shown to be *essential* to imperialism, it raised the importance of their field of study even more. This suspicion of the cultural 'theorists' is entirely unsubstantiated; but as the empirical evidence is so ambiguous in this area, as we shall see, and as none of them has yet produced a joined-up theoretical argument to justify this interpretation (hence the inverted commas around 'theorists'),[21] it may be worth floating. Fashion—bandwagons—also played a part. All this may help to explain the proliferation of imperial readings of British nineteenth- and twentieth-century society and culture that has taken place in recent years. This may be an unfair kind of criticism—the *ad hominem* one—but if we are to apply it to the Powellites we should do it to the imperialists as well. At the very least it will show that mixed motives can be imputed to both sides. Again, this does not necessarily make either side wrong.

❦❦❦

The word 'wrong' is an unhelpful one in any case. It implies that there are clear criteria we can use to determine definitely whether—in this instance—British society was 'imperialistic' or not. That is not so. Essentially, the issue comes down to a question of semantics: what do we mean by 'imperialism'?

Definitions could certainly be found or devised to justify either the Powellite view or its opposite. Each would be valid, as long as the authors defined their terms. (Many do not. Some appear to think that there is no need to. 'Imperialism' is taken as a 'given'.) The argument of this book will be that the first definition (Powell's) would be too narrow, and the second too vague and all-embracing, to be *useful*. 'Useful', however, is merely a practical, not a philosophical, criterion.

'Imperialism' has had a particularly chequered semantic history. Currently there is no general agreement over what the word means or covers; usually it is the authors who use the word most loosely who, for that reason perhaps, manage to discover the most signs of it. Whole books have been written simply on the way the term's meanings have changed.[22] Such changes have happened several times, and fundamentally, over the last two centuries (before then the word did not exist); often necessarily, the previous definition being too narrow and restrictive, but also in ways that can confuse. It has also been heavily laden with political baggage at most periods, but especially presently, when its negative connotations can make it difficult to use dispassionately or truly analytically.

This can be seen in Britain's case. One of the problems for the earlier nineteenth century—albeit a minor one—is that when Britons used 'imperialism' then it was usually to describe hated French Bonapartism, which is one reason why they denied its application to themselves.[23] It was only towards the end of the nineteenth century that the word became clearly attached to Britain's exploits abroad. That may have been one of the things that misled (or justifies) Enoch Powell. The word then stabilized briefly, but not altogether satisfactorily for anyone wanting to analyse the phenomena it described. 'Imperialism' became defined as a national policy of overseas territorial conquest and annexation. An 'empire' was the polity formed by that process. That definition seems straightforward; but even early on problems arose with it. The 'overseas' rider meant that it could not be applied to American and Russian expansion contiguous to their own frontiers, which seemed an anomaly. More serious, however, was the fact that it excluded the *effective* conquest of certain weak countries by more powerful ones, through means that stopped short of colonial annexation. A notorious example was Egypt after 1882, which was ruled in reality by a British consul-general who theoretically merely 'advised' a native Egyptian khedive. As a result Egypt was never coloured British red on contemporary world maps. That was an obvious fiction; but other, similar situations were only slightly less so. Even before 1882 Egypt had been in hock to foreign financiers, and governed—again, in 'reality'—by a committee of her creditors. Other countries too were dominated by European capital, even if they were *formally* governed by their own people. In some cases the degree of European control in these places was greater than in 'legal' colonies like those in Australia, which—despite their constitutional status—ran most of their own affairs. The problem this created was that a literal or constitutionally correct use of the word 'colony' did not necessarily indicate the true nature of any country's situation. As well as this, the term 'British empire' gave a false impression of the real scope and nature of Britain's power over other peoples. One or two contemporaries were aware of this: Herman Merivale of the Colonial Office, for example, who in 1871 described Britain's simple commercial dominance in east Asia as 'almost an empire, in all but name'.[24] Much later J. A. Gallagher and Ronald Robinson, in a seminal 1953 article, familiarized modern scholars with the concept of '*informal* empire', which was much the same thing.[25]

This approach was realistic, but it brought its own problems. The terms 'empire' and 'imperialism' no longer had clear bounds. It was difficult to know where to draw the line between 'colonies' and 'independent' peoples; largely it depended on one's assessment of how much 'freedom of action' the latter had. That issue could boil down to a question of ideology, with diametrically different ways of regarding the amount of 'freedom' any 'weaker' partner in a capitalist relationship might possess. The 'informal' approach also dissolved the bounds in another direction, undermining the concept of '*de*colonization', which was usually a procedure whereby formal rule was transferred from the colonial power to its colony, but without necessarily—in fact usually not—transferring economic power. This meant that part of the imperial relationship—arguably its essence—remained. The word often used to describe this was 'neo-colonialism', although it greatly resembled the much older 'informal imperialism' that was meant to have preceded the 'formal' stage. A third problem was that once the idea of informal economic imperialism came to be accepted, other 'informal' kinds of imperialism clamoured for consideration too. The most common was 'cultural' imperialism: a phrase first used to describe the effect of European religious proselytism in 'Third World' countries, and then American cultural expansion both there and just about everywhere else. As with economic imperialism, this did not involve (usually) the use of force or any other openly coercive method of control. On the surface both forms of imperialism seemed to be accepted willingly—indeed, in many cases were clamoured for—by the recipients.[26] As well as this: what if there was no conscious *intention* by the provider to 'dominate', either with the connivance of the recipients or not? Missionary activity, whether for the Christian God or for MacDonald's burgers, is often presented, on the contrary, as a means of *liberation*. So is the spread of the 'global market'. Are such activities properly characterized by a word or words whose Latin root ties it very firmly to the notion of 'power'?

The way to cope with all this confusion is not, of course, to decide how imperialism *should* be defined. There is no 'right' way. Imperialism is not a reality, in the philosophers' sense, but merely a convenient label. That is an important point to emphasize, because there is a tendency in some scholarly circles to reify the term as though it was a core and irreducible *cause* of events, on its own. It was not. Most of the phenomena to which we attach the word were complex mixtures of various factors, different in different circumstances, forever shifting, and always amenable to deconstruction in terms of other influences and interests. It would be perfectly possible to do away with the 'i' word altogether, and still find adequate ways of describing and accounting for what are supposed to be imperialism's characteristics and effects. It might even be a good idea, forcing scholars to look behind or inside the cushion they sometimes fall back on so lazily and uncritically. At the very least the great monolith would break up, and a *variety* of imperialisms come into view.

For example: it would become apparent how many of the defining qualities of modern 'imperialism' have existed independently of it, in other places and periods. Territorial expansion is obviously one of these. Peoples have spread out, emigrated, seized neighbouring territories, since the dawn of human time. If they had not, we would all still be crowded uncomfortably into the Rift valley of eastern Africa today. This process has usually been undertaken at the expense of other species and peoples, from the time that Cro-Magnon man wiped out the original (and by some accounts much nicer) Neanderthals of Europe, through the conquest of the real *indigènes* of the Americas by what are today called 'native' Americans, to the British and Irish and other European (and more recently Asiatic) takeover of Australasia, this time at the expense of the Aborigines. In modern days not all peoples expand, and not all people *within* 'peoples' wish to; but many have done so, and they are by no means confined to Europeans. The causes are usually practical and material, rather than—

though it is difficult to be sure about the Cro-Magnons—cultural or ideological. That is one thing. *Ruling* other peoples is something else. (It is very important to be aware of this distinction in the context of the subject-matter of this book, as we shall see; it is sometimes lost sight of.) This too is a common feature of most periods of human history. A stronger people overcomes a weaker neighbouring people, with varying degrees of force or consent, then dominates it, again in a variety of ways: enslavement, government, absorption. The tendency is as old as Adam. It is certainly not a peculiarity of modern imperialism. This should be obvious.

The same applies with even more force to the features that are often *associated* with imperialism. Peoples have traded outside their frontiers, for example, at least since they began to form settled communities some ten thousand years ago. That was the effective beginning of 'globalization'. A few—though this is rarer—have proselytised: not only Christians, but also Muslims, Buddhists, and Jews. These are common phenomena. This raises another issue. When ideologies like capitalism and Christianity are seen in cultural terms exclusively—as intrinsically 'Western' systems that 'imperialism' is seeking to force on the rest of the world—it rules out the possibility that they might in fact represent universal human values, albeit imperfectly (*very* imperfectly in the cases of those two). 'Modernization', 'liberalism', and 'scientific enlightenment' are three other phenomena sometimes regarded as imperialistic, because they are seen as starting in the West and then spreading out from there in the age of the European empires. In fact, as Jack Goody has shown, many of these were *not* of exclusive Western origin, but also arose independently in other cultures, making the identification of them with 'imperialism' patronizing as well as inaccurate.[27] Of course they could be used by imperialists—distorted—for purposes of domination. But the ideas themselves were not necessarily culture-specific, or merely relative. One particular example is the British banning of *sati*—the immolation of widows on the funeral pyres of their husbands—in India in 1829. The British objection to *sati* was undoubtedly ethnocentric, probably revealed a deep ignorance of Hindu culture, and may have been motivated by the desire to control. But it could *also* have represented an objectively more 'enlightened' attitude. This of course is controversial territory, especially since the philosophy known as 'post-modernism' began questioning the certainties inherent in the whole Western 'enlightenment' project. None of us can be so sure of those certainties today. (Neither, incidentally, as we shall see, were many British imperialists.) They may be no more 'true' than other outlooks. But they could be more *general* than is sometimes assumed, less characteristically Western; and so less necessary to be identified with imperialism, or even carried by it.

It goes without saying—or should do—that most of the other shards and fragments that have been excavated and pieced together, as we shall see, to indicate an imperial culture in Britain's case—which include racism, patriotism, militarism, masculinism, adventure stories, the study of geography, and so on—can exist equally independently. These features appear in many cultures all over the world, of all types. There is nothing inherently imperialistic, or necessarily contributory to imperialism, about any of them, unless you want to tailor-make your definition of imperialism to include them. The reason why they are widely assumed to be connected with imperialism in nineteenth- and early twentieth-century Britain, of course, is a better one than this. Britain did have an empire then. We know that from other than the archeological evidence. The likelihood, therefore, is that these pieces of culture used to attach to that empire when it was standing. But this is not a certainty. Other buildings existed then too. Some of the fragments may have broken off from *them*. Superficially they seem to fit those buildings better. If we did not know about the empire this is how the shards would have been reassembled—and were reassembled when we used to ignore or deny it. There are, in other words, other ways of reading the archaeological clues.

There are also other ways of reading the British empire that unambiguously existed: the irreducible core of British imperialism, if you like, before we have added on all these other features. Even that covered a multitude of phenomena which it is almost ludicrous to lump together in a single category, notwithstanding their common colour-coding on those famous red-besplattered British nineteenth-century maps of the world. Actually, as we shall see, that way of defining them came comparatively late in British cartography;[28] possibly because the early Victorians, too, saw little sense in identifying India, which had been conquered by arms and was ruled despotically (and also unevenly), with, say, the province of Nova Scotia or the colony of South Australia, which were regarded (we shall come on to the anomolies of this later) as extensions, via colonization—a different process from imperialism—of British radical freedoms in the world. The distinction between these is important for its own sake, and also to *perceptions* of the empire back in Britain. Until the end of the nineteenth century very few people identified with both. Some were for what Peter Marshall calls the 'authoritarian' empire, others for the 'libertarian' one.[29] There was no connection between them. If both these groups called themselves imperialists (and the latter, by and large, did not), this tells us little about them on its own. This is because their imperialism, such as it was, was rooted not *in* the empire, but in other sets of values which had no necessary connection with it. They constructed their various British empires in the light of their different, often conflicting, interests and ideals. That was when they took any notice of it at all; which was not often, as we shall see.

* * *

This is why it is imperative to look at the empire's impact on British society in *context*; to survey—to continue the archeological metaphor—the whole site. It will not do simply to look for 'imperial' evidence without being aware of what lies around it; or even, perhaps, to look for imperial evidence at all. People who look for things sometimes find them when they are not there; especially—in this case—if they are looking through distorting lenses. Even when you can avoid that, there is still the temptation to exaggerate the significance of what you have found. There *is* a lot of genuinely 'imperialist' material from this period, which if it is all coralled together looks impressive, and even overwhelming, but which really needs to be viewed *in situ* and against the background of other kinds of evidence if its real importance and meaning are to be adjudged. 'Imperialism'—by any 'useful' definition—was not the only characteristic feature of nineteenth- and twentieth-century Britain. It may not have been a dominant one. Only an awareness of the broader context can tell us how important it was, and how deeply, therefore, the fact of her possession of an empire sank its teeth into Britain's domestic society and culture.

One aspect of that context is of course the empire itself. One reason for thinking it exerted a great influence is that it *must* have done. It was 'one of the biggest things in history'. Whatever definition of imperialism we choose, it fits. The best—that is, most useful—definition is probably one that retains the notion of 'control' (*imperium*), which in the British case seems manifest. The plumed helmets and red coats were part of it. So were the great naval displays ('Reviews') and military parades of the time. In most colonies power was represented architecturally by government buildings that dwarfed those around them,[30] and although the same could not be said of the heart of the empire—India and the colonies were run from rather shabby London offices until they were given a great new palace in 1868—the formal centres of power could be picked out easily. Others, of course, lay elsewhere: in shipping-line offices, missionary society headquarters, the classrooms and dormitaries of the new public schools. Latterly those famous red-painted wall-maps were part of all this, leaving no doubt (except for the colour-blind) about the extent of British rule. This is the image that is supposed to have made a domestic imperial impact inescapable.

In reality it was not like this at all. In almost every way, as Ged Martin writes—it is his reason for at least considering the Powellite claim that the thing did not exist—'the pretensions of Empire outstripped its realities'.[31] If 'control' is the crucial factor in any imperial relationship, then the British empire—even the red-painted bits—must be problematical. Parts of it fit the bill; others clearly do not. The 'white dominions' of European settlement, for example, were very rarely 'controlled' by Britain in any practical way. Their settler inhabitants were free-er, generally, than their kin back home. (Transported convicts were obviously an exception, until they had served their terms.) Hence their attraction to some British radicals. This certainly applied to the American colonists before the War of Independence, the difficulty of 'controlling' whom was amply demonstrated by what happened when Britain tried to tax them—quite reasonably, one would think—to pay for their own defence. Of course things were very different for the *indigènes* of those colonies, most of whose oppression, however, came at the hands not of the imperial power but of its so-called 'subjects', who used their effective freedom from imperial restraint for that purpose. Britain tried to protect the natives (occasionally, anyway); often it was this that provoked her white subjects to rebel. This was apparently a second factor behind the American rebellion: the right of the colonists to grab 'Indian' territories;[32] it was certainly a major cause of the 'Great Trek' of South African Boers away from the anti-slavery British Cape Colony, in 1836. Strictly speaking—or is this too casuistical?—the exploitation and extermination that are often attributed to British imperialism could be said rather to be the results of a *lack* of imperial control. By the same token, they are likely to have had local and material, and not metropolitan and ideological, causes and motivations. This is another compelling reason for exercising caution over the word 'imperialism', and certainly for avoiding generalizing about it.

Elsewhere Britain exerted more power, but usually not much. It depended on circumstances. Some of the most limiting circumstances were metropolitan: Treasury parsimony, for example—the unwillingness to pour money into colonial government—and a certain liberal restraint. These are instances where other contemporary discourses overlaid more authoritarian imperial ones, and crucially modified them. Their effect on colonial rule on the ground was to compromise it nearly everywhere, with money and arms having to be substituted by tact and concession in order to *allow* the British to rule. Many of Britain's so-called subjects were left *un*ruled as a result, and even untouched. Vast numbers of them will not have known that they were British at all. It is this that gives the empire some semblance of a collaborative enterprise, though that description should not be taken too far. Prisons are collaborative too (warders have to defer to prisoner wishes to some extent). 'Hegemony' depends on this. But in the case of the British empire there was a very great deal of—for example—ruling through native elites, and tolerating, even artificially preserving, indigenous cultures, which was imposed by necessity and diluted Britain's freedom of action considerably. On one occasion, when she was too heavy-handed, it proved nearly disastrous: in 1857, when northern India 'mutinied'; from which the major lesson learned by the British thereafter was to exert a much lighter touch. Appearances are highly deceptive here. The governors' mansions and gorgeous uniforms really were little more than an elaborate bluff. The men inside them knew that they 'ruled' on suffrance, to a great extent.

None of this is meant in any way to 'excuse' Britain from responsibility for the tyrannies and atrocities that disfigured her empire so frequently throughout its history: slavery before 1833; the beginning of the virtual genocide of the native American people (before the Republic took over); the wiping out of the majority of the Aboriginal population of Australia, most of which was perpetrated while Australia was still formally British; the great nineteenth- and twentieth-century famines of India and Ireland (if one counts that as a colony);[33] the Jamaican, Denshawai, Amritsar, Hola, and other massacres; and so on. It could be said that Britain should have exercised more control over her emigrants, restrained her generals, intervened when the crops failed. She, after all, was supposed to be the government. Non-action in these circumstances is hardly less heinous than active crime. But that—so far as the present work is concerned—is by the way. The question of 'blame' is irrelevant. These circumstances are only mentioned for the bearing they have on the central issue of this book, which is the relationship between Britain's society and her empire. If the empire was not ruled very thoroughly—whatever the wider repercussions of that were—it means that it was not as enormous an undertaking as it is sometimes assumed to be. If that is so, then it may not have needed to touch British society so deeply. That opens up the further possibility that it did not in fact do so.

Other considerations support this. One is the way the empire was acquired. It looks as though this must have needed a great national effort, but it did not. Indeed, the idea that it did is a relatively recent construction, originating essentially in the late nineteenth century, in the minds of ideological imperialists who were alarmed at what they saw as the lack of national commitment to the empire in their day, and wished to paint a picture of its history that their fellow-Britons could take pride in. It was then that the 'builders' of the early empire were first raised to hero status, and the idea of an imperial 'patriotism' projected entirely anachronistically on to the past. In fact the empire before the ideologues' time had needed very little of either. It had fallen to Britain relatively easily. Most early colonies were acquired by small groups of individual settlers, or private enterprise companies, or incidentally, as spinoffs from other projects, like European wars. They were not the result of national initiatives, involved few British people, and needed little practical government support. They were marginal to the mainstreams of British society in nearly every way.

The broad reasons for Britain's overseas expansion are quite simple: enough to make explanations that root it in her 'society' or 'culture', for example, unnecessary. It happened (briefly) like this. In the seventeenth and eighteenth centuries Europe was more active than any other part of the world in overseas trade. She also became technologically superior, especially in the field of warfare. There may have been social or ideological factors contributing to that (the rise of Protestantism, for example), but none which had anything intrinsically to do with the outside world. This is why Europe colonized other continents, rather than the other way around. The first factor (trade) gave her the incentive, the second (weapons and ships) the ability. So, four or five European nations started building up empires, roughly—looking at these two centuries overall—equally. Then came another development. Towards the end of the eighteenth century what is called the Industrial Revolution really took off, and—for reasons that cannot be gone into here, but which include the capital amassed from her Indian and Atlantic trades[34]—in Britain ahead of the rest of Europe. That boosted the 'incentive' part of the equation in her particular case. Modern factory production increased the demand for materials to manufacture things out of (cotton, rubber, vegetable oils ...), and the amount of goods the factories then had to sell. Both domestic and foreign factors—limited markets at home, demand abroad—pushed many British manufactures into exports. So Britain became the leading commercial power in the world, by a factor of at least two over France, and many more over her other leading rivals.[35] It was this that accounts for what looks to be the quite amazing expansion of British economic influence in the wider world in the eighteenth and nineteenth centuries. It met with scarcely any resistance. Britain had no serious rivals—she was expanding into a relative vacuum. This laid the basis of her imperial expansion later. Virtually no historian dissents from this economic explanation today. (Some used to, before the collapse of communism, when it was thought to be tainted by 'Marxism'.) Other factors may have incidentally contributed to the process, but none is necessary to explain it. The ideology that later became attached to imperialism, for example, was not an original cause of it.

The transition from this to a more 'formal' imperialism is similarly (albeit more controversially) explicable in material terms. Of course, it may be that this transition is unimportant. Trading relationships between unequal partners are bound to be essentially dominating, runs one argument; or liable to become so, according to a milder version of it. In Britain's case there is one famous and grotesque example of an obvious imperialist act coming dressed in 'free trade' clothes—the Chinese Opium wars—and a hundred lesser or more ambivalent ones. The point about the Chinese case, however, for the present purpose, is that Britain's action in defence of her 'rights' there (selling opium) was limited to the minimum necessary to secure them—naval bombardment—and was consequently economical of money and men.[36] Elsewhere economy was also to the fore. Britain only traded where she could do so without great resistance, and only decided to overcome that resistance radically—that is, by colonial annexation—when it could (again) be done easily: with means that were sufficient to overcome the local opposition, but small enough to make only the slightest dent in her national resources. That is why she only went to war with weak reluctant customers, not with strong reluctant ones. It is also why she withdrew from as many colonial engagements as she persevered with, starting with America. This almost justifies the term 'reluctant imperialism'—which is sometimes mocked—to describe her annexations before the 1880s.[37] In very few cases—the Canadian rebellions and the Indian 'Mutiny' are the major exceptions before the final years of the nineteenth century—did she really put herself out. She did not need to

None of this should prevent us from characterizing Britain's foreign policy in the eighteenth and nineteenth centuries as 'imperialistic' if we wish to, unless 'imperialism' is to be restricted to its narrowest possible definition; but it does mean that her imperialism was of a kind that did not need to involve her greatly domestically. That was a distinctive feature of it, compared—probably—with most other 'imperialisms' the world has seen, both at other times and then. The empire was won and could be ruled by a relatively small number of Britons—precisely how many will be discussed in the next chapter—and without any significant commitment to it at home. Because it was so materially based, it required little cultural support from the metropolis either, apart from what was entirely consistent with other values, having nothing at all to do with empire, and stemming from other roots. Nor was there bound to be a substantial influence the other way: *by* the empire *on* British society; again because of its marginality. There might be. In fact, as we shall see, there were some repercussions. But they were not inevitable. They cannot be inferred from the vast size and the supposed importance of the empire alone. The evidence for them will have to be much more direct and unequivocal. The great British empire *could* have been acquired 'absent-mindedly', to quote the great historian J. R. Seeley (who meant it, however, sarcastically).[38] Hence the title of this book.

All this, it should be made clear, applies mainly to the period before the last years of the nineteenth century. After that things changed radically. The empire came under serious challenge, and as a result required—certainly in the opinion of its keenest champions—a more wholehearted domestic commitment. The problem *then* was that the nation had not been prepared for this, during these long years of relatively easy colonial pickings. Because the empire had been able to be maintained *without* a widespread and dedicated imperial culture prior to the 1880s, it was all the harder to construct one suddenly now. This was especially so in view of what had come to fill the place of that culture in the earlier nineteenth century: a variety of other concerns, priorities, value systems, and 'discourses', occasionally inimical to imperialism but more often irrelevant to it, jostling the latter in a way that had not harmed the empire then, but which might in these more trying times. Ultimately, this was—partly—why the empire declined and fell.

❦❦❦

The other reason for questioning the impact of imperialism on British domestic society lies in the nature of that society itself. That side of our equation requires definition and deconstruction every bit as much as the 'imperial' one. It too is more problematical than some scholars in this area appear to assume. It has taken—recently—the anthropologists to point out how oversimplified and reductionist many modern views of the 'West' are in relation to imperialism; how, if the generalizations that are commonly made in this quarter were applied to African or Asian societies, for example, they would immediately be dismissed as stereotypical and even patronizing.[39] Even the most sophisticated of the cultural theorists' accounts of the British 'culture' from which imperialism is supposed to have sprung in the eighteenth and nineteenth centuries tend to regard it as, if not homogeneous exactly, nonetheless a single entity of a kind: complex, admittedly, and even contested, but still 'dominant' and 'national', and static over time.[40] This is their reason for supposing that when they find evidence of 'imperialism' in one place (like the 'canonical' novels) it is likely to permeate the whole. In Britain's case, however, that is fundamentally wrong.

Not that it is very difficult to find people in Britain in the nineteenth and twentieth centuries who *believed* in a national culture. Sometimes they saw it as inclusive, or hoped it could become so. Our imperial zealots of the later nineteenth century—the ones who have also tried to mislead us about the significance of the empire—were among these. They wanted to bring the working classes in. But by then it may have been too late. The main tendency before this was to regard 'Britishness' (or 'Englishness', more often) in sectional terms. (This is a country, remember, unlike contemporary America and France, with virtually no concept of 'citizenship'. Britons were officially defined by their relationship not with each other but with the monarch. They were 'subjects', and remained so technically, in fact, until 1983.)[41] For the upper classes an 'Englishman' meant a 'gentleman'. The classes below them could not hope to aspire to that. It never occurred to most of the uppers to invite them. This is one of the reasons why the latter formed *alternative* cultures: they were deliberately excluded from this one. Some of those cultures also claimed a monopoly on Englishness, but of a very different kind. 'Patriotism', for example, was a word mainly used in the early nineteenth century by lower-middle and working-class radicals; it meant the defence of 'English' ('Anglo-Saxon') freedoms against the

essentially 'foreign' ('Norman') values that the 'gentry' represented. The gulf could not be clearer. Britons could not even agree on what being British meant.

Of course that did not necessarily preclude their agreeing on other things. Certain ideas, and especially perhaps the more visceral ones sometimes particularly associated with empire—pride, bellicosity, race prejudice—can bridge the broadest political divides. It is done through the media—news, images, schools, books—appealing to similar feelings and interests. The reasons for thinking that this may not have worked then in the case of the empire, however, are twofold. First, different sections of the British population had different media. The news they learned varied enormously; there was virtually no common literature: indeed, writes Natalie Houston, 'the publishing world... *aimed* to keep the reading of different economic classes completely separate';[42] and they were educated, again quite deliberately, as species apart. Even the images they were subjected to differed. (Only a privileged section of Britons before the very late nineteenth century, for example, will ever have set eyes on one of those famous empire maps.) It is important to grasp this: that Britain was a truly *multi*-cultural society in this period, albeit with the cultures in this instance being mainly predicated on class. Secondly, and more crucially: their *interests* varied, and accordingly many of their feelings. The sheer diversity of the British social scene in the nineteenth century is remarkable, and probably more significant for our purposes than the conflicts and antipathies. Where groups conflict—radicals, for example, against the gentry—there is usually some common ground, even if it is only a battlefield; as was the case in early and mid-nineteenth-century Britain, especially during Chartist times (*c*.1838–48). Usually, however, the various groups that made up what can really only very loosely be called British 'society' in this period went their separate ways. They had different material interests, different hopes and dreams, different gods. They did not—except in the ordinary business of daily living—meet. The gentleman had virtually no traffic with the manufacturer, the worker with the stockholder, the *agricultural* worker with the factory hand. They were virtual foreigners to one another. Benjamin Disraeli in 1845 famously described Britain as 'two nations',[43] but he could have made it many more than two. There were other wedges between the sections besides work: religion, for example; gender; region; language: many classes and areas could literally not understand one another; the urban–rural divide; and nationality in its strict (English, Irish, Scots, Welsh) sense.

It has already been suggested that some of these may have been nearly as important as the class divisions that this book will highlight. The main point, however, is that it is hard to believe that so disparate ('multicultural') a population could have shared many common ideals. The presumption has to be against it. This applies to imperial matters, as well as to anything else.

A glance at the broader history of Britain at this time—the early and mid nineteenth century—will reveal that this must be so. These were turbulent times (the cliché is almost unavoidable); especially the period between Waterloo and the collapse of Chartism around 1850. The country was being revolutionized, economically and socially, with fears of political upheaval too. There had probably never been a period of change quite like it, at any rate with so few precedents to guide those caught up in it: for this was, of course, the first transition to industrial capitalism that any country had ever gone through. The problems it gave rise to are well known, especially the serious social distress and unrest; and also the response of the authorities, which was (after attempts at repression) the piecemeal concession of reforms. This was really the 'biggest' thing that happened to Britain in this period, *pace* the empire; and it bore on her imperial relations quite profoundly.

The first way has been mentioned already. The Industrial Revolution led to an increase of foreign trade, culminating in foreign annexations in some circumstances. The imperial implications of that, however, were apparent to very few people at the time. Most in fact regarded trade as the antithesis of 'imperialism'. The second repercussion was to distract people *from* their empire. They had far too much on their plates at home. When you are caught in the maelstrom—starving, striking, getting rich, struggling with new working conditions, agitating for reform, anticipating utopia, fearing the mob, bemused or exhilarated by all the profound social and moral changes that are going on around you—you do not have the time or need to look to the margins, unless they relate specifically to your concerns at home. The colonies seemed to have very little bearing on any of this (with the exception of colonial emigration, to ease unemployment), and very little drawing power to take peoples' attention away from their domestic excitements, or—if they craved vicarious thrills—from the immeasurably more dramatic political happenings on the European continent. If the colonies had had more appeal, maybe the authorities would have tried to use them to stoke up patriotism in order to distract the people from their own problems, which has been alleged at other times; but there is little sign of this then.

The third repercussion is more positive. The Industrial Revolution was a time of intellectual ferment. (The fact that something is a cliché does not necessarily make it less true.) New ideas and outlooks were emerging, clearly suggested *by* the Industrial Revolution in many cases, and enabled to proliferate by the weakness of any other dominating national ethos (including an imperial one), which if it had been stronger might have channelled them in more authoritarian directions. They included ideas about liberty, for example; about the worth of the individual; science; work; God; morality; nature; peace; and about progress (this especially): all of which were much debated and developed during the course of the nineteenth century, and *some* of which came to be applied to the empire. That is a very definite link. The link was also mainly one-way: people applied lessons from home to abroad, rarely vice versa. 'Imperialism', as it manifested itself in Britain, was far more affected by what *happened* in Britain than by what happened or what was perceived to be happening in the empire. We shall see irrefutable evidence of this—and of the exceptions—in the following chapters.

But it was not even as simple as that. Industrialization did not affect Britain evenly. This was sometimes overlooked at the time. Observers—especially foreign visitors—tended to notice the new black industrial cities; but much of Britain remained embedded in a green and leafy past. This is well known today (it is sometimes blamed—even more than the empire—for Britain's economic decline).[44] It created a hybrid sort of society, where two stages of economic development lived side by side: the new industrial capitalist, and the old rural feudal. Neither can be said to have been 'dominant' over the other. They had separate spheres. How they managed to coexist is one of the most fascinating questions of modern British history, and yet more evidence of the lack of cultural homogeneity in this strange hotchpotch of a land. It required some mutual accommodation, of course. But this did not greatly affect each group's core values, which lay far apart. While the manufacturing capitalists and their offspring (workers, etc.) were beginning to regard society more 'freely' and 'progressively', the 'feudals' were desperate to preserve the hierarchical and paternalistic structures and values they felt that society still required. It is worth pointing out this disparity in particular, because it had an even more direct and vital bearing on the nature of domestic imperialism than most others. Its main significance at this point, however, is to reiterate the fact that Britain in the nineteenth century, and for some way beyond, comprised not one but a number of 'societies', each with its own value system and characteristic 'discourse'; the differences between which are far more important in relation to the impact of the empire on Britain (and vice versa) than any features that might have been common to them all then.

All this was in Britain itself. Abroad, of course, there were other British communities. Each had its own distinctive cultural characteristics.[45] They were influenced by the environments they had moved into, and their purposes in being there, which in most cases drastically modified the cultural inheritance they brought with them. This is normal; the Jesuitical idea that early conditioning always sticks is demonstrably false in this field. In new situations people's whole attitudes change. Britons who served in the colonies in the nineteenth and twentieth centuries were obviously affected by this, in ways that often put them out of step with the metropole. Race attitudes—to give one example—were more often moulded by the relationships these expatriates were placed in with other peoples, than by any cultural baggage they brought with them from home. This is why those attitudes differed so much between missionaries, for instance, and traders, and settlers. (Very broadly: settlers were the most 'racist', because they needed native labour and land; missionaries more 'culturist'—to coin a neologism—because their vocation was cultural transformation; and traders the most relaxed, because they treated with the natives equally.)[46] Function, rather than culture, or at the very least function acting powerfully *on* culture, determines these things. How otherwise to account for the notorious changes that can affect whole British communities when transplanted: into Northern Irish Protestant Unionists, for example, whose self-proclaimed 'Britishness' is scarcely recognizable as such to their mainland compatriots; or the largely mythical, preserved-in-aspic, 1940s suburban English society that white Rhodesians created for themselves in the 1970s under UDI;[47] or the alienation that so much of the British colonial-officer class felt from its British roots when it was repatriated after decolonization? From the latter's point of view, of course, it was Britain that seemed to have altered ('gone to the dogs' was the usual expression); but it is more likely that these are all examples of what the anthropologists call 'culture change' on the part of the transplantees.[48] This should be a caution, first against placing too much emphasis on metropolitan culture to account for colonial attitudes; and secondly against taking *any* of these people as as properly representative of 'Britishness'. They were certainly not.

All of which is only to say that there can be no *presumption* that Britain—the Britain that stayed at home—was an essentially 'imperialist' nation in the nineteenth and twentieth centuries. Of course she was, in the sense of acquiring and ruling an empire; but that empire (to recapitulate) might not have been as burdensome as it appeared. Consequently, it did not need to have had deep roots in British society—in its culture, for example—or to have affected it greatly in its turn. (This is what is meant here by Britain's being 'essentially imperialist'.) In any case 'British society' (singular) is a highly questionable concept, which obscures the country's enormous social, political, and cultural heterogeneity during most of this period, and the fact that different sectors of it could have reacted in entirely different ways, according to their own situations and interests. Of course imperialism *can* be regarded as ubiquitous, if it is defined broadly and loosely; but the more broadly and loosely it is defined, the less useful it becomes as a descriptive and analytical tool. This has been the argument of this chapter. Defined usefully, imperialism did not *have* to impact greatly on British society and culture. Of course this does not mean that it *could* not do so. The following chapter will explore the extent of this impact, at every level.

2
Participation

The early and mid-nineteenth century British empire did not need many people to run it. That would have offended against contemporary principles of low national expenditure and minimal bureaucracy. Those principles were adhered to by making the colonies pick up the tabs, and even do much of the ruling and policing themselves, through collaborators. That ensured that the number of native Britons taking on these duties was kept to a minimum. Most of these went to the dependent ('authoritarian') empire, with the settlement ('libertarian') colonies more or less running themselves, except in extraordinary circumstances, like wars. The ancillary agents of empire—sailors, traders, missionaries, and so on—were more numerous, but still just a tiny proportion of Britain's total population. As well as this, many of them tended to keep to themselves. This limited their impact on the stay-at-homes, which is what we are concerned with in this book. Of course there were other ways in which people could be said to have participated in the empire less directly. The wives and families of its primary employees obviously come into this category. So do those who serviced foreign missionary work at home; or helped manufacture goods made from colonial raw materials, or to sell in the colonies; or—to take an extreme example, which embraced nearly everyone—ate or drank products that came from there. These certainly involved large numbers of people with the empire; but not necessarily knowingly. That will have diluted the imperial impact on them. All this needs to be borne in mind when considering the relationship between the majority of the British people and their empire. It was not *necessarily* either close or obvious, or—as we shall see shortly—particularly warm.

***

The numbers can be computed precisely in some categories, more roughly in others. Those people employed to actually rule the empire formed a miniscule group. The Colonial Office had around 1,500 employees on its books in 1862; a figure that included clerks, messengers, porters, retired people, and a number of *indigènes*, like local mayors. By the end of the century that number had grown to 2,700. The equivalent India Office figures are 1,500 (1860) and 2,200 (1886).[1] Backing them up were between 65,000 and 100,000 soldiers in 'normal' times, which was a tiny army by comparison with many continental European ones. The Maori wars and Indian rebellion added 10,000 and 50,000 respectively to these figures. The navy—part of whose function, of course, was imperial defence—was about 40,000–50,000 strong, including boys.[2] (All crews, of course, were male.) Tagging along behind these people (or in some cases ahead) was a motley crew of missionaries, traders, explorers, planters, surgeons, lawyers, foresters, adventurers, and others who went out to the empire in the nineteenth century, and whose numbers are impossible to estimate accurately, but were probably not very large.[3] An intelligent guess for missionaries would be about 5,000 in the middle of the nineteenth century, though not all of these were serving in the colonies.[4] (Should *non*-colonial missionaries be counted? This is one of those instances where semantics come into play.) Taking account of these people's families, either accompanying them or remaining at home, and those who retired to Britain after service in the colonies (not all did: some stayed, or died abroad), this could bring the figure of those with direct or close vicarious experience of the empire up to half a million. This is in a total population (Britain and Ireland) of 27 million in 1851 and 35 million in 1881. It is not a huge proportion. Then there were the emigrants: 4 million British and Irish left Britain permanently to live in the colonies (mainly Canada and Australia) between 1815 and 1890.[5] This *is* a large number. But of course it cannot be added to the figure of British participants, because they ceased to be that when they left.

All of these people were indisputably acquainted with the empire; or at least with particular corners of it. It did not necessarily follow, however, that they were keen on it. Emigrants are a case in point. For a start, most of these did *not* go to the British colonies: two-thirds, in fact, made for the

United States. Even many of those whose first destination was British North America crossed the border soon afterwards. For the industrial poor of the north of England and Scotland especially, the burgeoning cities of the Republic seemed a far better option than the more agricultural colonies.[6] Obviously these people can have had no imperial feelings at all. Nor can the *involuntary* emigrants to the colonies: the hundreds of thousands of mainly working-class offenders who were transported to Australia and elsewhere before that form of punishment was stopped in 1869. Even after this Australia took some time to recover from the image that this had smeared it with. Its transformation from a living hell—the reputation it needed before 1869 to enable transportation to function properly as a deterrent—into a land of opportunity clearly presented difficulties.[7]

Voluntary emigrants may not have been much different, however. For a start, 'voluntary' may be the wrong word to apply to them. Most of them emigrated not out of true choice but because they were effectively forced to, usually to escape abject poverty. The great Irish emigration of the 1840s is the best example; but the same applied to the victims of the Highland Clearances, for instance, and the rural poor of the English east and south-west. Emigration was regarded as a hardship, a last resort, more than an opportunity; though it was that as well. Letters home are full of home-*sickness*.[8] Many resented the necessity of leaving. 'Oh Shame,' wrote one working-class *advocate* of emigration in 1844, 'that BREAD should be so dear and HUMAN LIVES so cheap.'[9] There was 'something rather damnable', wrote William Cobbett, '... to talk of *transporting* Englishmen on account of the *excess* of their numbers'. The English had a right to live in England.[10] (This was in response to middle-class movements to encourage emigration.) This feeling continued. The 1860s weekly *Working Man*, for example—motto: 'All Labour is Sacred'—blamed the iniquities of capitalism squarely for the need to emigrate: 'and a heavy penalty it is.'[11] This was the reason Joseph Arch, the agricultural workers' leader, gave for refusing an invitation to join the board of a 'colonization society' in the 1890s. 'If you are going to emigrate Bishops and Deans,' he wrote back to them, 'I would be on your Board of Directors tomorrow.'[12] Others suspected that the middle-class enthusiasm for working-class emigration was simply a ploy to defuse dangerous protest in favour of social and economic reform at home. There was something in this, as we shall see. A large majority of the British poor, of course, resisted the blandishments of those who were trying to get them to go. That may be an indication of the colonies' unpopularity.[13]

Letters home from emigrants were more often discouraging than not.[14] Even when emigrants did well, it was likely to make them look down even more on the country they had fled from. Letters are full of contrasts, explicit or merely hinted at, with the awfulness of things in Britain. 'Dear Brother, we have no overseers [here, in Australia] to tred [*sic*] us under foot.'[15] Many emphasize the 'independence' they have found abroad, in contrast with their British servitude.[16] For many emigrants—working-class radicals and democrats, for example, and the Irish—a large part of the attraction of places like Australia and Canada was their distance from effective imperial control. This helps to explain why there is almost no sign of any feeling of pride, either towards an entity called 'the empire' or even towards Britain, in this early and mid-Victorian émigré correspondence; though this may also have something to do with the fact that very few of the British working classes felt patriotic in any case. (This applies to the Irish too.)[17] You do not starve people out, forcing them from their homes and loved ones to the unknown extremities of the earth, and then expect them to feel proud of it. This is not the way imperialists are made.

The same applies to ordinary soldiers. Soldiering put thousands of ordinary Britons in touch with the empire, but not necessarily in a way that made them warm to it. You had to be pretty desperate to join the British Army for most of the nineteenth century, and very unfortunate to be posted abroad, as most infantrymen were, for at least some of their service. On some colonial stations in the early part of the century the mortality rate from disease—quite apart from any fighting that might be required—was around 50 per cent *a year*.[18] Only the lowest subjected themselves to this; including, for example, the three brothers of the working-class memoirist James Dawson Burn, one of whom died at the Cape and another (of cholera) in India; while the third tried deserting three times before being granted his discharge on finding an officer in bed with his wife in Demerara. The colonies had bad memories for Burn.[19] But he was lucky to survive long enough to *write* a memoir. Few other non-commissioned soldiers did, so we cannot tell how they felt about the empire typically.[20] The evidence we have does not indicate any particular affection for it; but this is impossible to quantify.

More to the point for the purpose of this book, however, is the impact these people's knowledge of the empire may have had on the wider population of Britain: the 98 per cent (probably) who never went there in any capacity. It may not have been very great. Such people were not *in*

Britain for most of the time. Emigrants, of course, never intended to return. Those few who did—usually ones who had made good in the colonies, to visit—tended to be ignored. He 'prowls around the streets,' wrote Edward Gibbon Wakefield in 1849, 'and sees sights till he is sick of doing nothing else, and then returns home disgusted... Nobody has paid him any attention because he was a colonist'.[21] Few Britons—unless they were professionally engaged there—went to the colonies simply to visit, or to keep in touch with relatives abroad. Not many could afford—or were willing to endure the discomforts of—the long return sea voyage to Australia, in particular. Partly for this reason, many working-class emigrants—possibly most—seem to have lost touch with their former homeland shortly after they left. Some kept up a correspondence for a while: there is a popular Victorian print depicting this,[22] and a few thousand of such letters surviving;[23] but in many cases the practice soon died out, except probably in areas of high and continuous emigration, like certain parts of Ireland. 'Letter writing between working class families then were [*sic*] practically non-existent', writes one urban autobiographer, explaining why his family heard so little from an uncle who emigrated to New Zealand in the 1860s.[24] Emigrants simply disappeared. 'A few boys and girls, more enterprising than their fellows,' wrote Thomas Hughes of his fictional village of Englebourn, to make a point about its entire ignorance of the empire, 'went out altogether into the world, of their own accord, in the course of the year; and an occasional burly ploughboy, or carter's boy, was entrapped into taking the Queen's shilling by some subtle recruiting sergeant. But few of these were seen again, except at long intervals.'[25] That is how emigration appears in most memoirs (and in one famous painting—Ford Madox Brown's *The Last of England*, 1860): as an exit, the end of the story, and certainly the end of their connection with their home communities, for the men and women involved. That may have been just as well for imperial enthusiasts: emigrants' letters were generally less than keen. In their absence, the emigration propagandists could full the gap with rosier views.[26]

We are left, then, with ex-colonial hands on furlough, and in retirement. Of all the different categories of these the ordinary soldiers and sailors were probably the least literate, and so the least likely to have left any marks that have endured. Surprisingly few working-class memoirists of the time recall coming across any of them before the 1900s. For the early part of the century, of course, this could well be because they served so long abroad—ten- to twenty-year continuous stints, sometimes[27]—and often did not survive to retire home. Evidence from the whole of the nineteenth century suggests that those who did were rather shunned. This was understandable in view of their reputation for brutality, which may have been justified. (The army was a brutalizing environment.) 'I have heard mothers solemnly declare that they would prefer to hear that their sons were dead, rather than that they were enlisted', a Royal Commission on recruiting was told in 1867.[28] It may be for the same reason that memoir-writers rarely went out of their way to meet such people. Whether they inspired those they did meet with tales of the wonders of the empire is unknowable. It seems unlikely.

Middle-class emigrants were almost certainly different, especially at the upper end. These were the classes of emigrant which were most likely to have kept up their correspondence with 'home', and for longest.[29] Young Frederic Trollope was even visited by his mother and father (Anthony) in Australia in 1871, resulting in a book from the pen of the famous novelist.[30] Officials, missionaries, planters, merchants, and army officers will also have made a more direct impact. Several worn-out missionaries, for example, returned to Britain as vicars or cathedral deans. Colonial and Indian officials enjoyed long periods of leave back in Britain while they were working (it was one of the perks of the job), and usually retired at around 50 years of age.[31] From the middle of the nineteenth century onwards there were little communities of these retirees scattered over much of Britain. Some entered public life, typically as local magistrates (keeping the lower classes in order: the sort of work they had often done in the colonies). A famous fictional one—an ex-Indian Army doctor—became Sherlock Holmes's assistant and chronicler. Dr Watson in fact represents a fairly stereotypical contemporary view of them: solid, decent, straight as a die, and a bit thick. There was probably at least one such ex-colonial in nearly every Home Counties village in the later nineteenth century, and whole clusters of them in favourite upper-middle-class retirement ghettoes, like Cheltenham and Tunbridge Wells, where they tended to keep themselves isolated from more 'ordinary' people. We shall be visiting them there later on.

* * *

Of course people could participate in imperialism without going to the empire, or bumping into those who had. One way was through their everyday work. The empire provided employment for large numbers of stay-at-home Britons. People who worked in factories and finance houses that provided goods and capital for the colonies, for example, or who made things out of raw materials imported from them, were all involved: factory workers, dockers, merchant seamen, bankers and professional investors, the clerks and cleaners they employed, and so on. This made practical imperialists out of hundreds of thousands—possibly millions—of ordinary British men, women, and (in the early nineteenth century) children, whether they were conscious of this or not.

It is tempting to regard this as a clear material benefit of imperialism for these employees; except that the picture is by no means so simple as that. For a start, only a minority of British production and investment involved the colonies during the whole of our period, and indeed for long afterwards. Much of it was purely domestic: businesses making goods out of Britain's own raw materials, for example, and then selling them on to other Britons. Even Britain's foreign trade and investment were not predominantly imperial. Figures for overseas commerce show the empire accounting for roughly a quarter of her imports and exports in 1850 and a third in 1900.[32] One estimate of Britain's investment in her colonies between 1865 and 1914 puts it at 25 per cent of her whole portfolio.[33] It might be possible, by means of some very simple arithmetic, to arrive at a crude estimate of the numbers of workers who depended on the empire by dividing total numbers by the proportion of their products that we know to have been empire-derived or bound. For example: between a half and three-quarters of all British cotton manufactures were sold abroad between 1820 and 1900, with around 20 per cent of these going to the colonies; which, if we divide the number of that industry's employees by this percentage, suggests that over 100,000 cotton manufacturing jobs relied on colonial markets in the middle of the century.[34] But that inference would be flawed, for two reasons.

The first is that it would take no account of markets that were not *strictly* colonies, but were either virtually so (Gallagher and Robinson's 'informal empire'), or were only available to Britain because of other colonies—especially naval stations, defending her wider world trade—that she possessed nearby. This is another of those questions that ultimately boils down to semantics. If imperialism is defined to embrace the whole of Britain's trading relationships with the rest of the world, for example (her 'commercial hegemony'), then huge numbers of British workers will have been involved. The second flaw works the other way. The mere fact that Britain ruled a particular market as a colony did not necessarily mean that she only traded with it *because* it was a colony. She might even have done *more* business with a country if it had not been: which would make the empire a *liability* for working people, if that were so. This was what ideological free traders argued at the time, and what the example of the United States—with whom Britain's trade actually rose after the War of Independence—was supposed to prove.[35] Later in the century the anti-imperialist economist J. A. Hobson argued that, in addition, imperialism depressed wages in Britain. Others claimed that it also cost middle-class people more than it benefited them, through the taxes they were forced to pay for imperial defence.[36] Later still it became fashionable to blame the empire for cushioning Britain from the need to 'modernize' her industry in a way that (it was implied) would have benefited its employees even more. The implication of all this is that working people were affected much less (or more adversely) by imperialism than their indirect involvement with colonial markets suggests; by imperialism, that is, as distinct from straightforward trade (if there is such a thing). This is still a matter of controversy.[37]

It does not, however affect the question of the *awareness* of the empire that people may have gathered through their work, whatever the reality of its impact on them was. This can only be conjectural, but it must be wrong to assume such awareness. There were some occupations whose imperial connections were unavoidable. City financiers specializing in colonial stocks should obviously be included here. Indeed, the whole of the financial community (and their clerks) must have been pretty imperially aware. The same is true of those who worked in dockyards, or for the great colonial shipping companies in the City of London, Liverpool, Glasgow, and elsewhere. At some of these the imperial message was rammed home by the names that were given to them: 'India Buildings', 'Africa House', and so on. (Needless to say, this could not be guaranteed to turn people into imperialists. Walter Citrine, for example, the great trade-union leader, remembered Elder Dempster's new 'Colonial House' in Liverpool mainly as the place where he was converted to socialism while working as an electrician in around 1900.)[38] In manufacturing companies with colonial connections the proprietors, purchasers, and salesmen will of course have been in touch with the empire, but the workers were probably not, unless there was some obvious way of telling where the materials they used originated from or where their finished products were bound for. Catherine Hall's claim that the fact that many of Birmingham's manufactures ended up in the colonies was one of the things that 'imbricated it with empire', therefore, is purely speculative.[39] (It is also not altogether clear what it means. The *Oxford English Dictionary* defines 'imbricated' as 'covered with tiles or scales'.) Britain's was a *mass*-production industrial system, which made it difficult to discriminate between destinations. (Pith-helmet makers must have had an inkling.) The fact that cotton cloth made in Lancashire was going to India, therefore, may not have impacted on the operatives. (On the other hand, they certainly knew where their raw cotton came from, when its supply was interrupted during the American Civil War.)

❦❦❦

There was little else in the ordinary lives of these people (the majority) that was likely to bring the empire home to them. They certainly will not have rubbed up against imperial subjects in their dingy streets and muddy lanes. Emigration from the colonies was never counterbalanced by any significant *im*migration until the 1950s. What there was mainly featured Irish (who of course were not counted as immigrants, because Ireland was part of the United Kingdom), continental European political refugees, and—towards the end of the century—Russian and Polish Jews. British workers *did* rub shoulders with these.[40] According to census reports only 33,688 people living in Britain in April 1851 came from the colonies, or 0.188 per cent of the total population. In 1901 the figure was 136,092, or 0.418 per cent. For most of this period they were greatly outnumbered by visitors from Europe and the United States.[41] In 1861, for example, there were nearly as many from the German speaking countries alone (30,313) as from the whole of the empire.[42] Europeans were also much more visible in other ways: because of their exoticism, and even the dangers they were thought to pose. For this reason they appear in contemporary fiction much more.[43] Most of the colonial visitors will have been white. (Unfortunately the early censuses do not break them down by colony.)[44] Non-whites must have been very thin on the ground in nineteenth-century Britain: far thinner, indeed, than in the previous century, when they had been relatively numerous as servants.[45] The only exceptions were in ports: 'Here the brown and yellow men of Asia are added to the stream of humanity. Loafing about, they talk in their high-pitched, sing-song voices; towards the white man, in this world of the white man's abasement, their attitude is half-cringing, half-defiant' (this is London's dockland at the end of the nineteenth century);[46] and in circuses and sideshows featuring 'tribal' Africans (we shall come to these later). Most working- or middle-class people probably never saw a single black face socially or at their work from the beginning of their lives to the end. This is why they scarcely feature in contemporary memoirs, by any class. (One curious exception is is the 'Beggar Boy' James Burn, who became the servant of a 'man of colour', probably an Indian, in Hexham in the 1810s. But that is very unusual.)[47] This is one clear way in which the dependent empire—the one Britain mainly ruled, as opposed to mainly settled—did *not* impinge on the masses until much later on.

Other ways in which it might have done so are sometimes suggested. Catherine Hall is one of those who feels the empire must have impacted on ordinary domestic lives.[48] For example, it was ingested. Tea and sugar are the examples usually given of foodstuffs that linked Britons with their empire in the most material way conceivable. Britain became a famous 'nation of tea drinkers' (replacing coffee for the middle and upper classes and small beer for the poor) through the enterprise of the East India Company, which had the monopoly of its importation from China. Towards the end of the nineteenth century Indian-grown tea began to supplant Chinese, which cemented the imperial connection even more.[49] Most people took it with sugar, which first became available as an affordable food item for the millions through its cultivation on colonial plantations using slave labour. Sugar made a huge difference to the dietary history of the British, and perhaps to other areas of their lives. (Sugar translates into energy, and also, of course, into obesity and dental decay. 'Der Mensch ist', as the ultimate materialist philosopher, Ludwig Feuerbach, put it punningly but neatly, 'was er isst.')[50] During the course of the nineteenth century the West Indies lost its primacy as Britain's main supplier of sugar, most of it coming from non-colonial sources by the 1870s;[51] but there is no denying the original Caribbean contribution, and hence 'the linkage of the consumption habits of Englishman to the world outside England, and particularly to the colonies of the empire' in these ways.[52] 'Not a washerwoman sits down to breakfast', Dr Johnson is reported as remarking, 'without tea from the East Indies' (by which he meant China) 'and sugar from the West.'[53] The empire—or at least Britain's global commercial dominance—flushed through their bodily systems every day.

Yet again, however, the question arises of how far they were aware of this. People are usually highly ignorant of the sources of their foodstuffs, unless they are clearly labelled. (A sample of inner-city Scottish children in 2002, for example, revealed that more than 50 per cent of them thought oranges and bananas grew in England, and 70 per cent that cotton came from sheep.)[54] Even if they were so labelled at this time ('Demerara Sugar'), this may have registered simply as a brand name, and not a place: whoever thought of the subcontinent, for example, in connection with 'India Pale Ale'? Tea in particular came to be associated with Englishness, not the exotic. Most foreign food imports had to be anglicized in this way before the British would touch them. David Burton's account of the introduction of Worcestershire Sauce into Britain could stand as a paradigm for the impact of colonial cultures generally:

> Despite its name, Worcester sauce was originally an *Indian* recipe, brought back to Britain by Lord Marcus Sandys, ex-Governor of Bengal. One day in 1835 he appeared in the prospering chemist's emporium of John Lea and William Perrins in Broad Street, Worcester, and asked them to make up a batch of sauce from his recipe. This was done, but the resulting fiery mixture almost blew the head off Messrs Lea and Perrins, and a barrel they had made for themselves was consigned to the cellars. Much later, in the midst of a spring clean, they came across the barrel and decided to taste it again before throwing it out. Wonder of wonders, the mixture had mellowed into a superlative sauce! The recipe was hastily bought from Lord Sandys and in 1838 Britain's most famous commercial sauce was launched.[55]

Colonial contributions were often disguised, therefore ('Worcestershire'), and adapted to British taste ('mellowed'). Kedgeree—a pale version of the original *khichri*—was another Anglo-Indian import.[56] Only one of the recipes in Miss Hill's *How to Cook or Serve Eggs in [One] Hundred Different Ways* (1825) suggests adding turmeric to them. Otherwise Eastern foods made surprisingly little impact in Britain, and probably only among 'ladies' (the word used for women of the upper and upper-middle classes), and possibly old India hands.[57] Curries in Britain are a post-colonial phenomenon (and still usually adapted to British taste).[58] Most of the spices imported into Britain in the nineteenth century were the milder ones—turmeric, for example, rather than chilli—consistent with the Briton's notoriously insipid culinary taste.[59] Bulk food imports (apart from tea and sugar) were mainly of wheat, and—when refrigeration made this possible in the 1880s—Argentine beef and and New Zealand mutton: breeds exported from Europe and husbanded to suit the British preference. Any outside influences, such as they were, came from the European continent, especially France. Occasionally Britons could read about more exotic alternatives: for example, an account of a 'breakfast consisting of turkey's eggs, biscuit... and cocoa-nut laced with brandy' sent from West Africa to *Household Words* in 1859;[60] but there is no evidence that any of them was moved to try these delicacies for themselves. It would probably have smacked of 'going native'—that awful phrase. Britons were well known for their intolerance of 'foreign food'; even those living in India insisted on their Sunday roasts.[61] Some were quite proud of the blandness of their own 'perpetual mutton chop and mashed potato', as English cooking was characterized by one (Scottish) writer, who believed it nonetheless placed Britain morally above nations with more sensuous palates.[62] It is possible—if tenuous—to read this intolerance as a sign of imperial arrogance. But it can hardly have helped to make people more imperially aware.

There were other ways to men's and women's imperial hearts—if they had any—than through their stomachs. Not all consumer items in the nineteenth century consisted of food, even for the poor. People had to clothe themselves. That, however, does not seem to have been a fertile field for acculturation either. Britons tended to dress conservatively. If they wanted to follow foreign fashions, then they looked to the European continent. Colonial materials were used extensively—Chinese silks, Indian muslin, Egyptian cotton, Australian wool—but usually only after passing through the hands of British tailors and dressmakers, who fashioned them in European styles. Two exceptions may have been 'cashmere' (Kashmir) shawls, retaining native designs, which apparently became fashionable among a small social circle in the 1860s and 1870s;[63] and decorative features such as ostrich feathers (from South Africa), when female couture reached one of its peaks (or troughs) of ostentation at the turn of the twentieth century. Again, any overt imperial references were usually washed out. The same applied to other colonial imports, few of which were easily recognizable *as* colonial in the forms in which they arrived in the shops. Subtropical timbers were shaped by English carpenters; opium found its way into very English patent medicines; and similarly Indian indigo, mother-of-pearl from the Celebes, African palm-oil products, and Malayan rubber and tin were all thoroughly domesticated. Likewise with housing—another basic necessity of life. The only colonial form of domestic architecture imported into Britain was the 'bungalow', originally a one-storey house for Europeans in India, usually with a thatched roof and a veranda all round. The 1894 edition of *Brewer's Dictionary of Phrase and Fable* reported that one or two had already been sighted 'at Birchington [near Margate] and on the Norfolk coast near Cromer'.[64] It is unlikely that these had thatched roofs and verandas, however; and very soon the Indian origin of the word (it means 'of Bengal') had been all but forgotten. (We shall come to public architecture later.) By the time they got into the hands of consumers, then, all of these exotic products had been thoroughly anglicized. The main exceptions were the mementos that old colonial hands brought back with them and filled their retirement villas (or bungalows) with: tiger skins, Afghan rugs, and the like. (The following inventory may be typical; it is part of the impedimenta that cluttered up the Elgars' home, and which Lady Elgar had inherited from her father: some 'Indian brass snuffers', a 'carved Bombay rosewood square footstall', a 'marble group of two elephants fighting', an 'elephant with howdah', an 'elephant and ram', a 'marble idol with dog', an 'octagonal game board', a 'salver decorated with peacocks and foliage', 'a brass vase', a 'stuffed antelope head', a 'general's sword in gilt scabbard', a 'trooper's sword in steel scabbard', sundry 'cavalry swords', a 'tulwar [Indian sabre] in sheath', a 'Sikh daggar [*sic*]', a 'Cingalese daggar', a 'fire lock damascened', and a 'Shield of hide'.)[65] It was in such homes that one would have smelled the kedgeree. Which might have been educative for other kinds of people if they had ever mixed with these colonialists. We shall see in the next chapter, however, that they generally did not. Lady Elgar was a rare exception. Certainly, few of the lower and lower-middle classes, the huge majority of people, will ever have had a glimpse inside houses like hers. The empire is highly unlikely, therefore, to have impacted on them in any of these material ways. That is the remarkable and significant thing.

⁂

Most Britons were certainly not bound to be imperialists, therefore, or to be interested in the empire, or even to be very much aware of it for most of the nineteenth century. It was entirely outside their experience and even knowledge. A tiny number of people worked for the empire directly; but few of those who could be said to have worked for it *in*directly—in cotton factories, for example—can have realized they were doing so. It had a minimal obvious effect on their ordinary material lives—work, shelter, food—until shortage of these forced some of them to emigrate to the colonies. Once there, such people were generally lost to those who had stayed at home. Neither emigration nor soldiering—the other main reason for people to visit the empire in substantial numbers—was likely to make them feel particularly fond or proud of it. The only exception was the small and closed caste of men who administered the empire, or officered the poor squaddies sent out there. The rest of the population had no need to be enthusiastic about the empire, or even particularly aware of it. So they may not have been.

There were other ways in which the empire might have appealed to them. They could have relished it vicariously. Just knowing that Britain ruled an empire might have made them proud. At the very least, it should have interested them. The empire was exotic enough, after all. Other things might have turned them on to it: books, newspapers, exhibitions, shows, songs, statues, and so on. Man cannot live by work, shelter, and bread alone. Or they might have harboured imperial feelings unwittingly: superior or racist or aggressive attitudes, for example, based on the mere awareness, however vague and ill-informed, that there was a British empire out there. These attitudes might not necessarily manifest themselves in a recognizable imperial*ism,* but could be imperialistic, by some definitions, nonetheless. So describing the limits of people's actual material participation in the empire only gets us so far. We also need to look at the cultural influences that worked on them. Because this was largely determined by which of the many social cultures people came from, it will be best to examine this in terms of *class.* This is how the next four chapters, therefore, will be arranged; beginning at the 'top'.

3
The Prefects

The most obvious imperialists in nineteenth-century Britain came from the upper and upper middle classes. These were the ones who seem to have felt the greatest pride in the empire, certainly early in the century; and in the strictly imperial aspects of it—the *ruling*, rather than, say, the trading or settling—most of all. This was for two main reasons. The first was that they were the people who actually *did* the imperial ruling: they comprised the great majority of those who were sent out to govern and officer places like India and the African colonies. That gave them practical experience of imperialism of this kind. But it was not the only thing that inclined them to it. They were already used to 'ruling' at home. By and large it was these classes, descended from Britain's old aristocracy, either literally or spiritually, that had dominated Britain's social and political life for centuries, and continued to do so even during the age of capitalism and liberalism, despite the antipathy of many of them to those ideologies, because they felt more comfortable with the idea of domination, or government, than most capitalists and liberals did. That was why they were chosen as colonial governors too. This has a bearing on the nature of their imperialism, the assumptions and values behind which were arguably more influenced by this—domestic—inheritance, than by any circumstances specific to the empire itself. Governing Indians was simply an extension of these people's government of the British working and middle classes. Even the most imperialistic classes in Britain, therefore, may not have been imperialists for strictly imperial reasons. This is another factor that limited the impact of the empire among the other classes of British society.

❦❦❦

Not all the upper classes were imperialists, even in this sense. The demands of the empire, as we have seen, did not require them to be. According to David Cannadine, the upper*most* classes of society tended to avoid the practical work of imperialism, at least, viewing 'such peripheral preferments in far-away places with scarcely concealed scorn'.[1] This may have had something to do with the empire's association with 'trade', or with hard work. If they did go to the colonies it was either as a temporary 'diversion',[2] or because they were hard up. Those whom genteel poverty forced to seek a new life in the settler colonies did not always fit in well there, among otherwise democratic communities who distrusted their 'airs' and accused them—not always fairly—of a reluctance to muck in with the rest.[3] '[W]hat the Cape of Good Hope does *not* want', wrote a contributor to *Household Words* in 1850, was 'young gentlemen with white hands and empty pockets, of no profession, and with very extensive notions of refinement.'[4] He wrote as if he had had experience of such wastrels. But this in any case was not really what the aristocracy were *for*. They did better when they were sent out to rule from the top: like the newly created Earl of Durham, who was famously sent to sort out British North America in 1838; or the majority of Indian viceroys, including the last, Viscount Mountbatten, who was the bluest-blooded of all of them; and the several lords (about 50 per cent) who served as Colonial or Indian Secretaries in British governments.[5] The aristocracy also supplied officers for the army, and a few colonial bishops;[6] and was one of the classes investing in colonial stocks.[7] The empire impacted on them enormously; but still not as much as it did on the upper middle class.

It is this class that has traditionally been seen as the main economic beneficiary of imperialism, through its involvement in the financial markets, subsidized (possibly) by the more heavily taxed classes beneath it.[8] But it also provided the bulk of the empire's rulers, both in Whitehall and in the colonies themselves. The Indian Civil Service (ICS), for example, recruited 76 per cent of its personnel from the 'professional middle classes' between 1860 and 1874, as against 10 per cent from the aristocracy and landed gentry, and 11 per cent from the lower middle class. This was in spite of the fact that it was the earliest of all government departments to adopt entry by competitive examination (in 1858), which in theory should have balanced things up. Thereafter little seems to have changed; notwithstanding the political and educational reforms that are supposed to have taken place in the meantime, writes Anthony Kirk-Greene, 'the social pattern of the ICS by 1870 was still easily recognizable in 1940'.[9] The Colonial Service (covering most of the rest of the empire) breaks down similarly.[10] Most recruits to both services were educated at public schools, which Kirk-Greene thinks were more important than social origins in creating a distinctive governing ethos.[11] It was certainly the minor public schools, and the grammar schools that aped them, that enabled those few lower-middles to claw their way into the governing club. This public-school bias also survived well into the twentieth century. Major (and from 1941 Sir) Ralph Dolignon Furse, who was head of recruitment at the Colonial Office from 1931 to 1948, believed quite simply that the public schools produced the best sorts of chaps. (Not necessarily the brightest, incidentally; the Colonial Office was suspicious of 'cleverness'.)[12] To prevent the wrong sorts coming in—his word was 'rubbish'—he refused to advertise vacancies, relying instead on 'personal contacts' and interviews. In his autobiography he acknowledged that this looked suspiciously like old-fashioned 'patronage', but defended it on the grounds that 'the English are conservative, and they know a good horse when they see one'. One way of telling, he found, was a handshake (or hoof-shake)—a limp one being a sure sign that a chap would not do.[13] This, of course, made for social cohesion; which was one of its aims.

In fact the true imperial classes were remarkably cohesive; almost a caste within a class. Imperial work ran in families, with every male member of some families becoming colonial officers, for example, and their friends being chosen from the same set. Indeed, this was why most young men joined any of the imperial services, according to Robert Heussler: '[t]he mere fact that ancestors, fathers, uncles, older brothers or friends were serving abroad or had done so in the past was enough.'[14] It was expected of them. Alaric Jacob tells of how his family—an ICS father, and a family tree thick with colonial governors and generals—never questioned that he was destined 'to a brave career in the East, with ribbons on the breast and warm pink brick and a tennis lawn up an English lane at the end of it'; though in his case he resisted, ending up as a left-wing journalist. (His mother even slipped an illuminated copy of Kipling's 'If' among the jars of gentleman's relish in his first school tuck-box to encourage him. His first act of rebellion may have been when he hid it until he could 'burn it in the lavatory'.)[15] 'No prosopographer of the servants of the Raj in India (the ICS, IPS, Indian Army, Indian Police, etc.)', writes Kirk-Greene, 'can fail to be struck by the recurrence and network of "Anglo-Indian" families, often reaching back to the Honourable Company.'[16] The family of Alice Elgar (née Roberts) is a case in point, with a father, six uncles, and two brothers all serving the East India Company in the early nineteenth century, most of them as army officers, and scarcely any close relative knowing any other sort of life. The composer Edward was a great disappointment to them as a husband for the general's only daughter; in response, they virtually cut her off.[17] Later, Field-Marshall Lord (William Riddell) Birdwood, an imperial soldier who rose to become commander-in-chief in India, and then (for some reason) Master of Peterhouse, Cambridge, could boast a full house of imperialists in his distinguished family: grandfather a veteran of the Bombay Army; father under-secretary to the government of Bombay; mother the daughter of a surgeon-major to the Bombay Horse Artillery; wife the daughter of a colonel-commandant of the Punjab Pioneers; an uncle at the India Office; four brothers all serving in India, and a sister married to another Indian officer; a cousin in the Bombay Lancers 'and later to be recognised as one of the finest judges of a horse in India'; another army cousin who retired to Australia; a son in the Indian Army (Probyn's Horse), and married to the daughter of an Indian political officer; one daughter married to a West Australian sheep-farmer, and a second who travelled around India looking after her father, as all dutiful spinster imperial daughters should.[18] Few families had as perfect a strike–rate as this; but the Birdwoods were not unique.

If they were not a caste apart at the beginning, these people's imperial experience made them so. It would have been surprising if it had not. Colonial service was not like other jobs; the climate, privations, danger, and responsibility could have life-transforming effects. Some it turned rotten;

one public schoolboy in 1891 noticed how often 'English gentlemen became ruffians out there'.[19] Only others subject to the same conditions and tempations could have empathized with them. The same was true of the more honourable among them; after a while they found they could only relate to men (and their wives) who had passed through the same fires. The effect was similar to that of the First World War on soldiers who fought in the trenches: the experience at once bonded them and cut them off from the bulk of society at home. 'Anglo-Indians'—in the nineteenth-century sense, of Britons who served in India—are the best example of this. India metamorphosed them; not into Indians, of course (although there are a few exceptions, of Anglo-Indians who took wholeheartedly to Indian lifestyles and cultures); but into a kind of hybrid creature, comfortable in no culture *apart* from this artificial, alien-dominant one. Rudyard Kipling was such a hybrid: one reason why he in particular cannot be taken as representative of English culture generally, though he may have influenced it. It is also the main reason why he felt so uncomfortable in his 'mother'—but no longer native—country when he returned to seek his literary fortune there in October 1889.[20] Britain did not live up to his expectations. This was a common reaction among returnees.

It became almost a cliché: old colonial hands complaining about how the Britain they found on their return there after a life of service in the empire seemed to have gone downhill. 'England seems quite a strange country nowadays,' Dennis Kincaid has an 'old Anglo-Indian' commenting in his classic 1938 study of British social life under the Raj. 'No one seems to have any manners and everyone is in such a hurry.'[21] In Virginia Woolf's novel *The Years* (1937) an imperialist returning from Africa remarks on 'how you've spoilt England while I've been away'.[22] That was how they saw it; but it is just as likely that it was *their* ideas that had changed. Other returnees found they could not take the drop in public esteem. 'He came back to England after ruling a district "about the size of Ireland", as they always said; and nobody had ever heard of him,' says another character in the same book.[23] This may say something about contemporary apathy about the empire, even among Woolf's own social class. (It is always dangerous to infer too much history from literature; but Virginia Woolf came from one of those very well imperially connected families, and so presumably knew what she was talking about.) It certainly indicates a sense of alienation of some sort.

Most returnees made little attempt to bridge the gulf. In retirement they mostly flocked together in ghettoes of their own kind. Cheltenham and Tunbridge Wells are the most notorious, but there were others; Norbiton in south-west London is an unlikely one.[24] This is a characteristic of immigrant groups anywhere. If they lived more scattered it was usually in old country villages, typically with names like Redmarley d'Abitot, which is where the Robertses holed out; where they were regarded as exotics by the other locals. Retirement age was comparatively young for the Indian and Colonial services—around 50—which left many years of active life to those who were not too worn out; some returnees employed this usefully in local voluntary work, often as unpaid magistrates, which seemed not too different from what they had been used to in the colonies. Otherwise most of them spent their leisure huddled together, typically in oak- and leather-bound London clubs, comfortingly reminiscent of the Adyar Club in Madras, for example; public-school Old Boys' reunions; Oxbridge senior common rooms; and the members' enclosures at Twickenham and Lords. They had almost no contact with the mainstreams of British society, apart from with those who thatched their country cottages, or came up before them in their magistrate's courts. Some of them were so successful in cutting themselves off that, as one observer put it in the 1890s, 'no one knows anything about them except themselves.'[25]

❦❦❦

Of course they were not isolated entirely. The clubs and common rooms they frequented gave them a broader social support than they would have found exclusively among their own kind, and a wider audience for their imperial ideas. Those ideas—what have been characterized here as the more strictly or narrowly imperial*ist* ones, implying formal rule and domination—were fairly widespread in this slightly larger community, and were debated in its media: *The Times*, for example, and the monthly and quarterly 'reviews' which are so distinguished a feature of British intellectual life in the nineteenth century: the *Edinburgh Review*, *Quarterly Review*, *Blackwoods*, *Fraser's Magazine*, the *Nineteenth Century*, and so on. Their ideas also surfaced in parliament. This is true even of the middle years of the nineteenth century, when imperialism (as a sentiment) used to be thought to have died under the onslaught of the rival doctrine of 'free trade'. That it did not do so is because, first, free trade had an 'imperialist' side of its own: we shall be coming to this in a later chapter; and secondly, because there were always those who resisted it, either wholesale—the protectionists—or for its supposed anti-imperial tendency. It was these two groups that contributed most of the recognizable 'imperialism', in the strict sense, to the debates of the time.

The third Earl Grey, colonial secretary from 1846 to 1852, was fairly typical of the latter category. He was a free trader, yet thought that Britain should still keep hold of her colonies. This was, first, because she had a duty to the people she already ruled: European settlers, but also, he insisted, *indigènes* and West Indian blacks; and secondly, because empire gave a nation 'power and influence' in the world.[26] A third strand in this skein of upper-class imperialist thinking was a mistrust of theory; of dogmas, that is, that had no regard for local human and social variations, national interests, 'common sense', morality, and so on. 'Tory imperialist economics', writes Anna Gambles, 'elevated history and experience over theoretical or abstract reasoning.'[27] That enabled them to justify paternalism and prestige, for example, in the face of the raging dogma of the day, which was 'political economy'. 'Professors and rhetoricians', Disraeli told the House of Commons in 1863, would always be able to find theoretical reasons for getting rid of the colonies: 'but you are not going, I hope, to leave the destinies of the British empire to prigs and pedants.' Common sense taught that 'the best mode of preserving wealth is power', which came with colonies.[28] Such arguments could seem rather defensive: '[t]here is neither extravagance nor impropriety', insisted the *Westminster Review* in 1870, clearly on the back foot, 'in realising for a moment the splendour of the empire';[29] and most proponents were at pains to emphasize that the imperial power being sought was for strictly defensive ends: 'not for the sake of domineering over other countries,' as Grey put it, 'but with a view to our own security.'[30] That might be seen as a gesture to contemporary liberal political correctness. In 1850 the *Edinburgh Review* dared to laud 'the sway of an empire on which the sun never sets'.[31] Ten years later one old India hand even proposed, in the *Cornhill Magazine*, to erect a monument to the not-greatly-lamented 'John Company' (the East India Company) on the site of its recently demolished headquarters: 'with a decorous inscription, setting forth that on that spot lived and died an English worthy, who contributed more, in his time, to the greatness of his country, than any man who ever lived.'[32] That would have been inconceivable to free-trade dogmatists (who hated the Company); but it shows that the spirit of upper-class imperialism was still alive.

It was also presented in terms of 'higher' motives. There was more to the life of great nations than mere profit, the imperialists claimed, if they wanted to concede the economists' argument (which not all of them did).[33] 'No nation', said Lord Carnarvon, another colonial secretary, in 1870, '. . . can afford to live a selfish life, wrapping itself up in its own miserable interests. If it does, it will inevitably come to disaster abroad and discredit at home.'[34] Political economists, claimed the *Westminster Review* in July 1870, often 'lose sight of [the] moral aspects' of the thing.[35] This was a reference to Britain's protective obligations. One or two speakers and writers pointed out the dangers of 'an internecine war of races' in several colonies (New Zealand, the West Indies) if Britain gave them up;[36] or of the reintroduction of slavery to a 'free' Jamaica if it then joined the United States.[37] (The MP Sir William Molesworth was one of those who pointed out how much better off America's own blacks would have been if they had still been in the British empire, and so subject to its Act of 1833.)[38] Britain had a 'duty' to look after her subjects. 'A solemn compact had been entered into between the mother country and her colonies,' Charles Ellis pointed out in 1825, which promised the latter 'every protection ... That compact ought never to be lost sight of.'[39] Ellis had West Indian planting interests—his own—in mind. But the same principle, duty, could be extended to other races. A major argument for keeping Britain in control of her colonies was that their non-European populations would otherwise deteriorate and even disappear:[40] either at the hands of unrestrained settlers, who had already been guilty of atrocities 'unworthy', as the philanthropist Thomas Fowell Buxton put it in 1835, 'of this great nation';[41] or because blacks were congenitally incapable of ruling themselves. 'A dominion of free negroes or coolies has, as yet, done nothing to inspire us with confidence', was how the *Edinburgh Review* put it in 1870, probably with Haiti in mind.[42] For one or two imperialists this was a prime reason for retaining the dependent colonies, even if they let their 'white' ones go.[43] Colonial 'freedom' was a recipe for anarchy and exploitation. The weak needed protection from this.

This was, roughly, the theory. It clearly stemmed from these men's class backgrounds; from their centuries-old function in *British* society, that is, based on power, and on an ethic—sometimes called paternalism—that stressed the duty of the privileged in society to guard and guide the less fortunate. During the nineteenth century that ethic was coming under challenge. The new liberal middle classes put more stress on personal responsibility. Paternalism was seen as a brake on enterprise. Government itself was distrusted. It was certainly not felt to be as worthwhile an occupation for the middle classes themselves—not as profitable, that is, either to themselves or to the community—as 'honest' industry. Ironically, this may have been why the old ruling class was allowed to carry on ruling in these new liberal and capitalist times: *some* government was necessary, and this class felt comfortable in the role; together with the fact that its members were so well rooted in Britain anyway. (The middle classes and their values never entirely displaced the uppers, as we have seen.)

The middle classes seem to have accepted this situation, on the understanding that the uppers should rule broadly in ways they approved of, which mainly meant not obstructing the progress of free-market capitalism at home. The upper classes agreed to that, eventually.[44] For the colonies this governing class was particularly useful. Most of Britain's colonies arose from the endeavours of her industrial and capitalist middle classes, who, however, were far happier exploiting them (in both the best and worst senses of the word) than actually running them. This was where the old upper and upper-middle classes came in. They actually *liked* governing, and were used to it, so they took over the running of the empire from them. They were the only ones who needed to be 'strict' (*imperium*) imperialists, therefore. The middle classes could fool themselves—as we shall see later—into thinking they were doing something else.

This role also influenced—possibly even determined—the *type* of their imperialism. It was this class, for example, that had the reputation of being the most 'bullying and insolent' of all Britons towards colonial peoples: an attitude which some feared might lose them India eventually;[45] but they behaved in the same way to their own social inferiors at home. Contemporaries noted how they tended to regard British workers 'as creatures of another species'.[46] Comparing upper-class reactions to the Jamaica revolt of 1865 to their response to the rioting in Hyde Park in favour of the parliamentary vote the following summer, Bernard Semmel writes that, despite 'ties of consanguinity, the "respectable" classes... regarded the London rabble much as the thirteen thousand whites of Jamaica regarded the 400,000 blacks. Like the Negro, the white rabble was tainted from birth and irredeemable, their unhappy condition an inevitable result of laziness, drunkenness, and want of thrift. And, like the whites of Jamaica, the "respectable" classes felt themselves a small and exposed and fearful minority.'[47] They had felt that, of course, ever since the French Revolution at the latest, and through successive stages of native British working-class unrest.[48] Revolts by underclasses, in other words, were not essentially novel, and did not require a radically different response—or even vocabulary—when blacks were involved. Whether this should be called 'racism' is a moot point; it comes very close to it. Only the 'ties of consanguinity', acknowledging the upper classes' racial identity with the Hyde Park rioters, should give us pause. (The general question of 'racism' will be discussed later.) It should also be emphasized that there was another side to aristocratic arrogance: the sense of *service* to one's 'inferiors', of *noblesse oblige*; the 'paternalism' that we have seen was so important an aspect of this kind of imperial theory. That could have happier results.

However we characterize it, this was essentially an extension of class feeling, rooted in the aristocracy's ruling function; and also—as one contemporary working-class writer interestingly suggested—in its peculiar training. 'Who, as a rule, are Mr Eyre's apologists', he asked in the wake of the Jamaica affair. 'The educated; those who have been drilled after classical models', and hence only knew Roman ways of doing things. 'Simple people who have not been taught to look upon the classical dictionary as a Bible, hate him [Governor Eyre], and, as I humbly conceive, justly.'[49] Born to rule, and trained in their public schools to feel superior (as well as to *oblige*), it is no wonder that the political elite of the day looked down on almost everyone. The only exceptions were *foreign* (including black) aristocrats and royals, who David Cannadine claims were treated on equal terms, so giving the lie, in his view, to the 'racist' slur.[50] That was another 'class' contribution.

❦❦❦

Many people—not only our working-class critic—attributed much of this superior attitude to the influence of the public schools. That of course is where most of the Prefects were taught. (The others were tutored privately.) In view of this it may seem surprising that so little was taught to them there *about* the empire; which supports the idea, however, that these people were rulers first, and imperialists second. They were also a ruling *class*, apart from the rest. That was how ruling in Britain was done. This helps explain why their imperialism, such as it was, did not filter down.

The concentration of most public school syllabuses on the Greek and Roman classics is well known. (We know less about private tutors.) That drove out subjects that might teach directly about the British empire, such as geography or modern history. There were a few exceptions. Haileybury, in its first manifestation as a training college for East India Company administrators (1806–58), included history—both British and Indian—and Sanscrit in its core curriculum;[51] but this ceased when it was refounded as an 'ordinary' public school, modelling itself on Rugby, in 1862. Haileybury was also one of the schools to introduce a 'Modern Side' (as an alternative to the 'Classical Side') for boys destined for the army or business.[52] Most Modern Sides were looked down on, however: in 1893 the Head of Harrow's Modern Side, Edward Bowen, felt compelled to resign when he found a new headmaster 'flooding' it 'with the worst boys on the Classical Side';[53] and in any case such courses were narrowly utilitarian, limited in most cases to English grammar, foreign languages, and mathematics. Occasionally boys were set history essays for holiday assignments.[54] Bowen claimed that despite history's being 'formally taught but little' at Harrow, 'it is incidentally taught all day ... In the upper forms an historical allusion is never remote from the purpose of any lesson', which may have been true in his own case. (Bowen had a keen amateur interest in historic battles.)[55] If so, however, it managed to pass over most boys' heads. 'I knew all about Heliogabalus,' wrote an Old Harrovian from Bowen's own time, 'but nothing about Peel.'[56] The historian H. A. L. Fisher remembers learning no modern history at all at Winchester in the 1880s: 'The vast field of modern knowledge was a closed book to us.'[57] Shrewsbury was 'aware of nothing later than the Roman Empire', according to the sister of one of its pupils, whose only brush with British literature and geography there came when he was told to translate some Milton into Latin, and to copy a map of Scotland, both as punishments.[58]

This neglect of formal imperial studies followed upper-middle-class boys (and later girls) to university. The classics ruled there too. (As late as 1960, if you wanted to read Natural Sciences at Cambridge you had to be qualified in Latin as well.) At the two ancient English universities there were no courses or even lectures in British imperial history—little enough in modern history generally—before the end of the nineteenth century. One Cambridge historian who deplored this was J. R. Seeley, who in 1883 published a famous book—*The Expansion of England*—to try to remedy this situation, but without apparently making much of an impact on his own university's curriculum: Ronald Hyam points out that the course of lectures that ultimately became *The Expansion* was delivered in only one of his twenty-six years (1869–95) as regius professor there.[59] Seeley's great complaint against the history teaching of his day was that it concentrated too much on the theme of the achievement of individual liberty, which he reckoned had been settled for good in the seventeeth century. Since then Britain's real history, he argued, lay beyond her shores: 'not in England but in America and Asia', and in the activities of Britain as 'a great organic reality' (as one commentator puts it) in the wider world.[60] Cambridge never accepted this. The core British history taught there until the 1960s, at the earliest, always remained 'constitutional'. Imperial history only reached Cambridge as a Tripos (that is, examined) subject in 1906, and then in the Economics—not the History—Faculty. The 'Expansion of Europe' paper—the title an obvious genuflection to Seeley—dates from 1945. It was an 'optional' paper only, and was regarded as marginal.[61] Oxford's experience was similar. Little colonial history was taught even as part of British history courses until 1905, when the the South African financier Sir Alfred Beit instituted a Chair of Colonial History there, and later a Lectureship.[62] The first Beit Professor, H. E. Egerton, was a chip off the Seeley block: 'The time has come', he said in his inaugural lecture, 'when the history of England should be identified with the British Empire.'[63] 'Yet within three years,' writes Frederick Madden, he 'was questioning whether Oxford was worthy of an imperial role.'[64] His undergraduate 'special subject' in colonial history attracted only seven takers (out of 142 possibles) in 1910, and was seen as an 'easy option' for mediocre students. As at Cambridge, imperial history at Oxford lacked 'prestige'.[65] London got its 'Rhodes' Chair of Imperial History only in 1919. At the 'red brick' universities there was apparently no imperial history teaching at all.[66] Most British history taught at all of these places remained obstinately domestic and whiggish, as though Seeley had never lived. Contemporary imperialists complained of this, and of Britain's neglect of imperial studies generally: a 'lamentable lacuna', wrote one critic, 'in the educational system of this the richest and most enterprising of the colonising nations'; especially when contrasted with Germany, with her Hamburgische Kolonial Institut and Deutsche Kolonial Schule, and France, with her prestigious École Coloniale.[67] The evidence suggests that Seeley's work may even have been more influential in academic circles in these countries than it was in Britain, possibly because it fitted so well with the nationalistic tradition of German history writing in particular.[68] It seems extraordinary that the classes from which imperial rulers were almost exclusively drawn in the nineteenth and early twentieth centuries should have been denied the opportunity to study the empire in their schools and academies.

There are a number of reasons why this was not supposed to matter. The first is that these classes could be trusted to know something about the empire anyway, from their own family connections or those of their chums at school. Certain schools were packed with the sons of colonial officers and soldiers.[69] Public schoolboys will have scarcely been able to avoid hearing about India in particular, quite apart from Edward Bowen's asides. Ex-schoolmates also provided links. School magazines[70] carried letters from Old Boys from as far afield as China, Japan, Canada, all parts of Africa, and even 'North Britain' (Scotland), which the *Wellingtonian* in 1889 included as 'Abroad'.[71] Readers were treated to exciting first-hand accounts of many of Britain's colonial wars, particularly from the late 1870s on.[72] (It is less in evidence before.) From the late 1880s there were also regular reports of Old Boys' reunions in various colonial venues.[73] Most of these items, incidentally (and significantly), feature Britain's dependent colonies, the ones she *ruled*; very few are about the settlement—democratic—ones. Fitting out public schoolboys as settlers was always a struggle, in part because they lacked the right attitudes and practical skills. In 1885 a 'Colonial College' was started up at Hollesley Bay on the Suffolk coast to remedy this, which flourished for a while, but then collapsed in 1905.[74] But there was also the question of esteem: at many schools emigration was seen as fit only for the 'brainless sons of gentlemen'. 'Many who were useless in England, because they had no brains,' said a Wellingtonian in 1889, 'would get on well in the colonies, where their physical powers would be appreciated.'[75] Debates on emigration centred around whether it should be subsidized (or even made compulsory) as a means of getting rid of working-class 'undesirables'.[76] In view of this it is unsurprising that letters in school magazines from Old Boys in places like Australia and Canada were greatly outnumbered by those from the dependent empire, especially soldiers, administrators, and big-game hunters.[77] These were the imperial roles—and the kind of imperial*ism*, therefore—that naturally appealed to the public schools.

Imperial influences could be brought to bear in other ways too. Public schools were boarding schools in the main, which gave them almost total—John Roach calls it 'totalitarian'—control over pupils' extra-curricular hours,[78] and therefore plenty of scope for imparting imperial propaganda, if masters were sympathetic. Many were, especially in the later period. J. E. C. Welldon, for example, headmaster of Harrow between 1885 and 1898, believed it was 'the duty of a teacher, to bring before his pupils, and not once in a way only, but habitually, the magnitude and dignity of the British Empire'. 'I believe, and I want my pupils to believe,' he went on, 'that the British race is the best in all the world.'[79] Welldon was probably the most zealously imperialistic of all the high-profile public school heads of the later nineteenth century, but there were others who saw it as at least part of their function to preach the empire cause.[80] Often this was done from the pulpit, with reverend headmasters (like Welldon) using imperial illustrations in their chapel sermons (usually the bravery of Christian soldiers), and at the very end of the century preaching from overtly imperialist texts. Many of these sermons might have seemed incongruous—somewhat bellicose—in other Christian pulpits, but not apparently at Cheltenham or Haileybury.[81] Visiting lay lecturers, presumably invited by the masters, gave talks on 'The Ascent of the Nile', 'School Life in India', 'My Tropical Experiences', and—especially—their missionary endeavours far and wide.[82] Towards the end of the century boys were treated to uplifting lectures on 'imperialism' *per se*, which were usually rewarded—though this was new—with 'immense', 'vociferous', or 'tumultuous' applause.[83] There were other ways of spreading the word. Personal advice may have been one; book requisitioning another. School libraries bought the latest imperial studies (like Seeley's) and military memoirs, for boys to read outside classroom hours.[84] The headmaster of one (minor) public school even donated popular novels by the ultra-imperialist G. A. Henty to his school library in the 1890s.[85] Public school novels also carried allusions to the empires. Thomas Hughes's *Tom Brown's Schooldays*, for example, describing one of the less 'imperial' schools, as it happens (Rugby in the 1840s), has many marginal ones.[86] School 'Volunteer' or cadet corps—proliferating around the turn of the century—may also have rammed imperial lessons home.[87]

The boys' response may be inferred from the contents of the magazines they produced for themselves, though doubtless subject to strict supervision and censorship from above. As well as reports from Old Boys in the colonies, these occasionally featured articles and reviews on broader colonial issues, mirroring the discussions in the elite periodicals outside.[88] They also carried accounts of school debating society meetings, which might be thought to reflect opinion fairly well. These sometimes discussed the great imperial issues of the day, and with more frequency from the 1880s, with the imperialist side generally winning handsomely.[89] Even stronger imperial feeling is probably indicated by reports of what the pupils got up to on 'Mafeking night' (18 May 1900), when public schoolboys seem to have been among the rowdiest of demonstrators. The *Wykehamist*, for example, described the Winchester pupils as a 'mob', rioting through the city streets before burning an effigy of the Transvaal president Kruger, apparently with the blessing of the headmaster.[90] Fledgling poets published doggerel on subjects like 'Central Africa' (Rugby, 1860, celebrating the Africans' past glories), 'The Captive Arab' (Haileybury, 1882),[91] and heroes slain in colonial wars. (Many were in Latin.)[92] Very occasionally pupils revealed an interest in Britain's colonial past, quite apart from battles, including in 1866 one of the first attempts to elevate Sir Walter Raleigh into an imperial hero after the 'centuries of vilification' he had been subjected to until then.[93] There can be little doubt of the main imperializing effect of all this, particularly around the turn of the twentieth century. Clement Attlee is only one of many ex-public school pupils who recalled that 'most of us boys were imperialists' at this time, 'with an immense pride in the achievements of our race'.[94] Bearing in mind the behavioural conformity that was notoriously and increasingly required of public schoolboys at this later time—the historian A. L. Rowse, who did not go to one, called the schools 'sausage machines'[95]—it must have been a difficult ethos to avoid.

Its impact should not be exaggerated, however. Imperial allusions in school magazines and other sources are often quite scattered, especially before around 1880. The empire clearly came low on most public schoolboys' scale of priorities until the time of the South African War. First among those priorities was usually sport, which dominated the pages of most school magazines at certain times: during the Ashanti War of 1873–4, for example, which, according to the editor of the Radley magazine, was pushed right out of the minds of Radleians by 'our chance of licking Bradfield; [and] what sort of Eight and XI we shall have next year'.[96] Budding poets were apparently very poor imperial material, if their failure to lend their talents to celebrating the empire, often regretted by school magazine editors, is anything to go by. 'We are proud of the patriotism of our Empire. Why does not some poet come forward with a sonnet on the Relief of Ladysmith, or the Heroes of Mafeking?'[97] (The best the *Marlburian* could come up with was a limerick.)[98] This attitude may have been a characteristic of the 'cultured set' generally (this will be discussed in Chapter 7). When a competition was run for a new school song for Haileybury in 1883, most of the entries were about games, and none at all referred to the school's famous Indian past.[99] Army cadet corps did not catch on everywhere: Brentwood, for example, despite calls for one from many of the boys in 1900, had to wait until the First World War for hers;[100] and much higher up the social scale 'Volunteers' at Eton were still contemptuously known as 'the dog-potters' in the early 1900s by 'quite a large proportion at the school'.[101] School debates on colonial issues were usually poorly attended, by comparison with favourite topics like Dickens versus Thackeray, women's suffrage (always defeated), whether ghosts existed (Radleians believed in them),[102] and—this comes up again and again—football versus cricket. Imperial events elicited nowhere near the same interest until the end of the century, when attendances for debates on them soared.[103]

Even then opinion could be divided. Imperialism was probably as 'natural' as it was often remarked Conservatism was to the sort of boy who attended a public school;[104] but it was never wholly dominant. A few masters had quite radical reputations, including Harrow's Edward Bowen, described by his biographer (and nephew) as 'a "peace at almost any price" man', despite his intellectual fascination with wars.[105] Edward Lyttleton actually flogged some of his boys at Haileybury (including Attlee) for overdoing their jingoism on Ladysmith Night,[106] and was forced to resign from the Headship of Eton over a sermon he had delivered during the Great War calling for reconciliation.[107] His imperialism was clearly a very different sort from, say, Welldon's of Harrow. The boys liked to think that they were even more mixed in their opinions. Among the editorial team that ran the *Harrovian* in 1878, for example, were said to be 'A Moderate Conservative, a Jingo Editor, a Peace-at-any-Price Editor, a moderate Liberal Editor, a Radical Editor, and last, but not least, an Irish Editor, who kept resolving himself into a Committee of Obstruction whenever the politics of "*The Harrovian*" was being discussed'.[108] That may have been a joke; but the existence—and tolerance—of dissent was very real.

School magazines, for example, occasionally carried pacifist, anti-imperialist and pro-Home Rule items.[109] Debates on imperial events invariably threw up solid minorities—between a quarter and a third—of (relative) anti-imperialists.[110] The main exception before 1899 was over the Gordon affair of 1884–5, which kept to this pattern while the hero was still alive in Khartoum, but switched when news of his death got through, and nearly everyone came over to the anti-Gladstone side (at Haileybury 'the Liberal members ... were evidently afraid to show their faces').[111] Powerful criticisms of colonialism were generally voiced, though they may not always have been fairly reported: 'He laid it down as a maxim', ran a summary of one Little Englander speech at Wellington in 1891, '...that strong nations ought not to rob the weak. He then went on to quote some interesting details about potatoes and market gardens.'[112] That was a neat put-down, and clearly intended—like the *Harrovian*'s swipe at the Irish—to be 'witty'. Wit may have swung votes in debates also, which were judged by performance as much as by principle. Not too much, therefore, should be read into the following, somewhat unexpected nineteenth-century public school debating society verdicts: a 9 : 8 decision against Napier's Abyssinian expedition at Radley in 1868; a dead heat over the Ashanti Wars at Malvern in 1873; a narrow defeat for pacifism at Haileybury in 1883; a vote against imperial federation at the same school in 1890; and a massive (40 : 10) defeat for the motion that 'the Partition of Africa is beneficial in every way' at Wellington in 1891.[113] Winchester seems to have been particularly prone to such transgressions, voting against imperial federation in 1900; censuring Cecil Rhodes in 1893 (probably out of anti-capitalist prejudice, which also worked against Joseph Chamberlain: one speaker dismissed him as all 'gas-works and screw-factory'); agreeing by 26 to 13 'that the Boers are a civilized and honourable people' just a month into the war with them: 'a chivalrous view of our enemy,' as the *Wykehamist*'s note-taker put it, 'which was hardly anticipated'; and very nearly accepting—the vote against was only 30 to 26—'that the unpopularity of England abroad is natural and justifiable' in April 1902.[114] Of course these votes were not necessarily representative, or even to be taken seriously. Nothing, after all, depended on them. But they do illustrate that different views about the empire could be aired. A number of boys were simply repelled by all the pro-imperial propaganda: like the future art critic Roger Fry, according to his biographer Virginia Woolf, for whom 'the whole Public School system . . . and all those Imperialistic and patriotic emotions which it enshrined' (at Clifton) merely stoked up a 'sullen revolt.'[115] Others who seem to have been put off imperialism by the schools' constant harping on it in the 1900s included 'George Orwell', the journalist Alaric Jacob, and the 'Cambridge Four' who became Soviet agents in the 1930s: Old Boys to a man.[116] These were some of the mavericks. They do, however, appear to have been a small number. Most public schoolboys happily followed the herd. There were certainly enough of them to run the empire; which was all that was required.

⁂

The way the schools prepared their pupils for this is well known. It was not by teaching them *about* the empire, or even to value it particularly, but by making them into good potential rulers—in any environment—through a concentration on what was called 'character'. That was the thing that Sir Ralph Furse was looking for, of course, when he shook the hands of all of them. Its main ingredients could vary slightly, but are pretty well encapsulated in the citation for Wellington's highest prize in the 1880s, the Queen's Gold Medal, awarded to 'the boy who has distinguished himself during the year by cheerful submission to his superiors, courtesy to those beneath him, fearless devotion to duty, and unflinching truthfulness'.[117] Respect for women was sometimes added to these;[118] together with sexual purity, and especially the avoidance of 'beastliness' (homosexual practices), though that was generally left unsaid. Hence the cold baths and corporal punishment. (At Eton that was called 'the sacrament of blood'.)[119] The fact that these ideals sometimes withered in alien climes does not make the pursuit of them any less genuine. This was what gave public-school men the *right* to lord it over others. It explained, as the Old Etonian Geoffrey Drage put it in 1890, why the British was 'the only empire known to history of which the rulers may proudly say, "we have loved righteousness and hated iniquity, and we have striven to do justice to all men without respect of persons"'.[120] The *ability* to lord over them was inculcated in other ways. Chiefly it was by building up 'discipline, authority, and team spirit',[121] all vitally necessary qualities for the job. As members of tiny ruling elites in distant, alien, and often unfriendly environments, they needed to trust each other, agree on fundamentals, and be relied upon to obey the call of 'duty' when it came. The schools helped them to do this.

This explains many of their notorious peculiarities in the nineteenth and early twentieth centuries, especially the undervaluing of classroom learning, explicitly and deliberately. The public school experience was meant to go much wider than that. 'The great public school,' wrote one authority in 1881,

> has much more to teach besides what is learned in the form of lessons, much which could not be learned by boys at home. It is a moral gymnasium, an arena for contest, a republican community in which personal rights have both to be maintained for oneself and respected in others; it should be a microcosm; a training ground for the business and struggle of life, and for the duties of a world in which men have to work with men and to contend with men.[122]

Many of the public-school system's champions took a positive pride in the 'ignorance' of its end-products compared, say, with its French and German counterparts. It left more room for the essential business of 'character building' to be carried out.[123] 'This ["cramming"] is not the way in which the rulers of a nation should be prepared for their great duties,' opined the *Edinburgh Review* in 1874; 'rulers who are to govern . . . as much by the force of the impalpable qualities which make up the English gentleman as by mere ability and book-learning.'[124] Games were an essential means to this; always popular, they actually became compulsory in many schools in the 1880s and '90s.[125] There was widespread contemporary criticism both of this and of the public schools' broader philistinism around the turn of the century, but it had little effect.[126] Masters clung to the ideas that, for example, 'England owes her Empire far more to her *sports* than to her studies', as Harrow's Welldon put it in 1894,[127] and that 'useful' knowledge was low or dangerous. 'Knowledge puffeth up', was the headline of a leading article in the *Marlburian* in 1888.[128] Rugger also had a moral value. 'You may think games occupy a disproportionate share of the boy's mind,' said the headmaster of Clifton. 'You may be thankful this is so. What do you think French boys talk about?'[129] But it was sport's contribution to 'character' that was valued most.[130]

Its value lay in teaching boys to subordinate their own wants to the general good; not the *very* general good—of society as a whole, for example—but that of their own competing groups. In games this was the team. It could also be their 'houses'; their schools; or—ultimately—their class. The 'loyalty' that was engendered in the schools very rarely went beyond that. National or imperial patriotism, for example, perhaps against expectation, almost never features prominently in public-school literature; and indeed is ridiculed at one point in Kipling's *Stalky and Co.*, published in 1899 but set in the 1870s; or at least the *expression* of it is, partly because in the story it is expressed by someone looking 'a bit of a bargee . . . born in a gutter, and bred in a Board-school, where they played marbles'.[131] That hints at one of the peculiar characteristics of upper- and upper-middle-class 'patriotism' where it does appear in this period. It was usually quite narrow. It did not take in 'bargees'. The favourite 'patriotic song' of public schoolboys appears to have been 'The Fine Old English Gentleman': a paean to old-fashioned feudal values.[132] That defined 'Englishness', at this level. Their own school songs (a striking genre of this institution) are singularly free of any broader patriotic content. Edward Bowen, who penned many of Harrow's famous ones, once expressed his positive dislike of 'patriotic songs' that were meant 'simply to stir up a warlike feeling'; nearly all of his are about the glories of the school.[133] 'Patriotism' may seem 'a large subject', said an article with this title in the *Wellingtonian* in 1891, 'but we intend to confine it to school patriotism'.[134] That was where it remained, for the upper and upper-middle classes, during the bulk of the nineteenth century.

Almost every aspect of the schools buttressed this. They were exclusive. Even when they took the middle-middle classes in, as many of the 'lesser' ones did, it was to mould them to the existing values of the upper-middle class. 'Boarding' helped. Not for these boys, as for the elementary or grammar school boy or girl, the corrective influence of the home when they arrived back at the end of the day for their tea. Indeed, this was the whole point of the system for some of its advocates, like the educationalist Nathaniel Woodard in the 1850s: 'The chief thing ... to be desired is to remove the children from the noxious influence of home.'[135] (Public-school headmasters were always railing against the corrupting effects of parents on children; especially widows, claimed Charles Vaughan of Harrow, who is said to have declared that his troubles with them had caused him 'to reconsider the objections to *suttee*'.)[136] Living together cemented their common values, as well as, of course, the intense personal friendships that sometimes gave cause for moral concern. 'That is why public-school men get on better than we do,' wrote A. L. Rowse in 1942: 'they accept, often without questioning, unconsciously, the same standards and assumptions: they understand each other—*and so they govern*.'[137] The uniformity may have been exaggerated. (Uni*forms*—the identical dress prescribed for public schoolboys—will have contributed to this.) We have just seen that political dissent was permissible within limits.[138] It was even more tolerated earlier in the century, when one of the qualities the Public schools were famous for encouraging was 'eccentricity'. Those earlier schools tended to be exhilaratingly rebellious places too. (The last Public school rebellion—the last, at least, that had to be put down by the military—was at Marborough in 1851.)[139] There can be no doubt that the pressure on boys to conform increased as the nineteenth century approached its end. (J. R. S. Honey attributes this to the changing demands of the empire in the later part of the century: 'Carving out an empire called for one set of values,' he writes, meaning the earlier, more enterprising ones; 'administering it required attention to quite another set.')[140] On being presented to an Old Etonian, wrote one 1901 critic (who was one himself, which might be thought to puncture his own generalization), 'you know exactly the kind of man to whom you are going to be introduced ... You know beforehand the precise point of view that he will take upon every conceivable topic, and the channels in which his conversation is certain to flow.'[141] Others too commented on the way the schools 'impress[ed] a uniform mark' on all their products.[142] But this is what strengthened them for the task of ruling that lay ahead.

Classroom education also bore on this. 'Classics' cannot be dismissed as entirely useless in this context, though some contemporaries—especially around the turn of the twentieth century—did criticize it on these grounds. 'I have long thought that we cannot face the competition of the world on Latin and Greek,' wrote Lord Rosebery to the head of his old school, Eton, in 1900; 'but I am afraid this is heresy to you.'[143] The first Viscount Cecil, son of the great prime minister Lord Salisbury and a leading League of Nations man after World War I, called his own classical education at Eton 'idiocy'.[144] Its champions, however, demurred; and not only because of the subject's intrinsic difficulty (and so the discipline it required). Greek and Roman history, claimed one, 'dealt with political problems which were just as much present in modern as in ancient life.'[145] Warre of Eton maintained that they were particularly handy for the understanding of 'Colonial affairs'.[146] Classical analogies were quite often brought into service in discussions of imperial questions: the ideal of 'imperial federation' being compared to 'Delos in its early days' by an Old Harrovian writing to his school magazine in 1869, for example,[147] and to Athens by a Haileyburian in a school debate in 1890.[148] The usual comparison, of course, was between the British and the Roman empires, despite the obvious sting that lay in the latter's tail. (Imperialists used that to show how the British might *learn* from Rome's decline and fall.)[149] Another advantage of ancient history may have been that it was all done with now, and so unchanging. There was no unsettling 'progress' *there,* of the kind so beloved by the middle classes. (As the next chapter will show, this was a crucial factor behind the difference in the two classes' imperial outlooks.) Instead, it could be quarried for timeless advice on how to rule. That, at any rate, was how it was used.

It was the advice on ruling that was most valued, not the imperial analogies. If colonial knowledge had been thought to be important for potential colonial governors, it would surely have been taught less analogously. But that did not matter. Such knowledge was not needed to engender support for imperialism, which in this environment could probably be assumed. Interest in *serving* the empire was generally passed down—as we have seen—in families. It was not, after all, necessary for *many* boys to be interested: only 2–5 percent of public-school leavers, depending on the school, actually joined the Colonial and Indian services, which was enough.[150] Even for these ones, their best preparation for imperial service was not necessarily imperial *knowledge,* of the kind that might have been gleaned from modern history or geography. Of course they would need some such knowledge eventually, if only to pass the exams for entry into the ICS. Provision was made for this at 'crammers' (private intensive teaching establishments) founded for precisely this purpose, and through special, empire-related 'extension' courses put on by Oxford and Cambridge universities from the 1880s on.[151] Special textbooks were prepared for these.[152] But that came after the essential training, in the schools; which was in the mysteries of ruling per se, not in imperial ruling especially. Those were the same for everywhere: for Britain, where most rulers turned out by the public schools were, of course, destined, as well as for the empire. The schools' perception of these mysteries owed less to imperialism than to the upper classes' old domestic feudal function, merely extended now to embrace another sort of villein. This can be clearly seen in the public-school literature of the time, where Asiatics and Africans are not presented very differently from the British working classes, or thought to require different treatment. Domestic 'louts' in *Tom Brown's Schooldays* become 'border ruffians' in the colonies.[153] This is why the empire featured so little in the upper and upper-middle classes' formal education; and why their perception of the empire was so distinct from nearly everybody else's in Britain; so feudal, essentially.[154]

* * *

No other class was likely to share this particular version of imperialism, which grew out of the upper and upper-middle classes' particular place in British society. The latter made little effort to spread it 'down' to the other classes, as we shall see later on. It depended on a view of British society that emphasized their own separation from the rest of it: the 'louts' and—even more—the bourgeois. There were two reasons for this. The first was purely functional. 'It could be argued', writes T. W. Bamford, 'that the simplest and easiest way of creating leaders . . . is to cut them off as a group from the rest of society.'[155] That, again, is what the public schools did. One of the purposes of their exotic uniforms was to distinguish Harrovians in the streets of Harrow, for example, from ordinary townees. The contempt they had for those townees ('burghers' at Harrow) was hardly disguised.[156] Public schoolboys developed their own esoteric customs and lingoes, to serve as secret codes in case the non-cognoscenti overheard. J. E. C. Welldon, headmaster of Harrow from 1885 to 1898 (and later bishop of Calcutta), compared these to 'a caste-mark in India'.[157] All public schoolboys shared a common private language, of course, in the shape of Latin, which Edmund Warre, head of Eton between 1884 and 1905, used purposely to shut the lower orders out.[158] Masters were hopelessly cut off; Montague

Butler of Harrow, for example, 'failed to understand the poor, and could not talk with them', according to one of his staff;[159] and when Welldon retired to the Durham deanery in 1918 he found himself totally at sea among the surrounding colliers.[160] But it did not matter. A ruling caste needs to be on a pedestal.

It was also, however, a question of ideology. The main hostility of the upper and upper-middle classes was directed not against the workers (whom they saw themselves as serving), but against the industrial and commercial capitalist class, which was coming to be the dominating influence in British society in almost every other—non-ruling—way. This—the upper classes' resistance to middle-class values, nurtured by the public schools—is a well-known phenomenon in other contexts. Some blame it for Britain's economic decline from the late nineteenth century onwards, through its undermining of the 'entrepreneurial ideal'.[161] There can be no doubting its wide currency. It pervades public-school literature, in ways we have met incidentally already: the prejudice at Winchester against even imperialists with commercial backgrounds, for example; the popularity of the 'Fine Old English Gentleman'; even, perhaps, the stress on team games, which might be thought to run intrinsically against the individualist ethic that is favoured by capitalism *pur* (there are almost no reports of public-school golf). The 'cad' of Vachel's Harrow story *The Hill* (1905) is the son of a boot-manufacturer, and so predictably weak, greedy, and lacking in school 'spirit'.[162] He is also fat. Attacks on the materialism, selfishness, and vulgarity of the middle classes more generally are legion.[163] Sometimes these are linked with imperial questions; public schoolboys, it was claimed, made the best colonial administrators precisely *because* they could rise above the sordid motives that were attributed to the commercial bourgeoisie, in particular 'acquisitiveness' and 'competitiveness'.[164] John Huntley Skrine, headmaster of Glenalmond in Scotland, saw the public school as a 'fortress', no less, for the idea of 'chivalry'—this was a common way at this time of bundling together this whole collection of old-fashioned values—'against the earthliness of money, fashion, luxury, selfish competition, sloth, cowardice, dread of pain, and all the other forces of materialism'; in order specifically to make Britain 'fit to keep the marches of an empire', which clearly 'money' and all the rest could not be trusted to do on their own.[165] The fundamental antipathy between these two ethoses could not be clearer.

The upper-class view of empire may not have been confined to the upper and upper-middle classes alone. Britain was a highly class-divided society in the nineteenth century, but not a totally rigid one. There were always those who worried about the divisions, and had ideas for repairing them. Some were to be found in the public-school system. One of Thomas Arnold's great ambitions for his regenerated Rugby, for example, was to heal the gulf between the classes that was widely seen as a phenomenon of dangerous import in the 1830s and 1840s (the Chartist age).[166] In the 1880s (with the revival of socialism) an attempt was made to return to this ideal, in the shape of the 'settlement' movement—missions run by some of the schools in slum areas;[167] but they were rarely successful, and accounts of visits to them in public-school magazines read like dispatches from foreign lands.[168] In 1890 Geoffrey Drage, an Old Etonian, urged public schoolboys to take up elementary-school teaching, in order to turn even the 'lower orders' into 'gentlemen, and I use the term in the highest sense'. A fear that there soon might not be enough 'born' gentlemen to run the empire was one of his motives for this.[169] In like manner, and for similar reasons, Robert Morant, who was permanent secretary of the Board of Education in the 1900s, advocated introducing public-school games—and their values—into inner-city schools.[170] None of this happened; but there was undoubtedly some seepage 'down' of values in other ways. One was through the conversion of boys taken from the less socially privileged classes, like the *nouveau riche*, into the public schools, where they could be soaked (as Skrine put it) in the 'tradition of manners which flower only in homes of leisure, and a standard of rank more delicate than the money-bag'.[171] (Obviously this did not work with Vachel's cad.) Another was through the new 'minor' and pseudo-public schools that mushroomed in Britain in the later nineteenth century, as a response to middle- and even lower-middle class demand for them, sometimes for educational reasons (though the grammar schools were arguably academically better),[172] but more often for the social cachet they bestowed; and of 'preparatory' schools (for 8–12-year-olds). Many ordinary secondary schools also aped the public schools' distinctive features, especially the 'house' system (even for day boys), uniforms, games, and the teaching of classics. W. D. Rubinstein calculates that as many as 25 per cent of the young British population could have been incorporated into the value-system of the elite in this way.[173] Another authority claims that public-school values 'filtered downwards and outwards until they permeated the *whole* of society'; but this is more questionable.[174] In any case, the 'permeation' is likely to have been uneven, thinner in some areas than in others.

It may have been thinnest of all in the area of empire; with the upper and upper-middle classes' *distinctive* imperialism filtering down less than their other values. The evidence for overtly imperialist propaganda in the 'prep' schools for example is meagre, perhaps because of the youth of its potential objects, or because—as at the senior public schools—their imperialism could be taken for granted.[175] In the 'lesser' public schools there is more evidence of imperial enthusiasm; but of a different kind. Their magazines are about as imperialistic, quantitatively, as the *echt* ones, but are far more focused on the settlement colonies, as one would expect from the functions of *their* Old Boys and readers.[176] Their sort of imperialism will be discussed in the following chapter. The 'ruling'—Indian—sort was mainly confined to Britain's traditional ruling classes, for the bulk of the nineteenth century at least. That, by and large, was how those classes liked it. It was *their* empire, not anyone else's. They had no desire to share it.

In 1919 the Austrian sociologist Joseph Schumpeter put forward the thesis that imperialism was basically an 'atavistic' phenomenon, a throwback to a pre-modern age and its values. At the same time he expressly exempted Britain from this, on the grounds that her society was too advanced.[177] He was right about this; the nineteenth-century expansion of the British empire took place for current (capitalist) reasons, not backward-looking (feudal) ones. On the other hand, there *was* something atavistic about how it was ruled: through these representatives of the backward-looking order, trained in neo-feudal ways in their public schools. It was this that made British colonial rule so successful (on its own terms), and so envied, incidentally, in countries that were not blessed with Britain's peculiar institution, or anything like it. It is probably unfair to quote here Adolf Hitler's admiring description of the British public-school system—in connection with India—as 'calculated to rear men of inflexible will and ruthless energy who regard intellectual problems as a waste of time but know human nature and how to dominate other men in the most unscrupulous fashion'; but there is a seed of truth there. Hitler also likened their products to a religious order.[178] This was what set them apart from most of their compatriots.

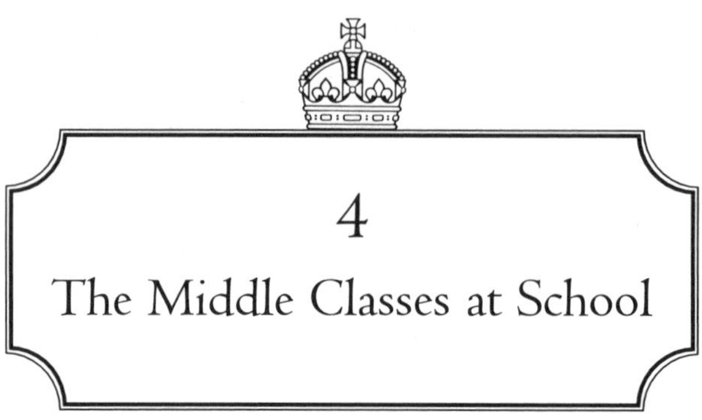

4
The Middle Classes at School

Middle-class imperialism was something else. For years the middle classes denied there was such a thing. A prevalent view in the early and mid-nineteenth century was that the bad old days of empire were all but over for Britain, about to be superseded by a brave new age of internationalism and freedom for all. Imperialism was associated with past régimes. (People would have agreed with Schumpeter on this.) Adam Smith had recently taught, persuasively, that it made no economic sense. The experience of the American War of Independence seemed to point the inevitable way ahead: soon all of Britain's other colonies must go. There was nothing to be gained by seeking to replace them. Though Britain still had an inherited empire, therefore, she was not imperial*istic*: not at all enthusiastic about it, or about adding to it. Indeed, many of her people regarded themselves and their nation as *anti*-imperialist in essence. This is where the historical 'myth' of early and mid-Victorian anti-imperialism originated.

Of course, as we now know, that was erroneous. As many new colonies were added to the empire during this period as at any other time.[1] This was quite apart from other forms of contemporary British expansion, that could be counted as 'imperialistic' by less rigid definitions of the word. For the early Victorian period this is generally called 'informal empire': the spread—however 'free' it may have been—of British commerce, culture, and people throughout the world. The nineteenth-century middle classes often took pride in this, even if they did not call it imperialism. They also had attitudes that undoubtedly carried imperialist potential; especially the belief that they were the most free and enlightened people in the world. It only needs a slight twist to use that as a justification for liberating and enlightening others. (It has worked with other empires too.) That makes them imperialists in a sense, or dangerously close to it, despite themselves. But they were a particular *sort* of imperialist, different from the classes we have just been considering: the ones that did their imperial ruling for them. These differences are significant. They may be so great, in fact, as to make it misleading to put the two classes in the same category in this connection; which is why they are separated here.

⁂

Schooling is a good place to begin in looking at the middle classes' attitude towards empire, as it was with their social superiors. It was here that the foundation of their view will have been laid. Unfortunately 'middling' schools present special difficulties, being far more diverse in character than the public schools, and less regulated and less well recorded than those for the working classes. They catered for a wide variety of social types, from the aspirant skilled working class to the less well-off professionals. Within these groups they could be socially quite mixed; too much so, in fact, for the 'Taunton' Commission of Inquiry into them (1868), which suggested they be formally segregated into three further 'grades' or sub-classes. (The crucial influence of class on education could hardly be better illustrated.)[2] They were very much market-led. Many of them consequently tended to be ephemeral: springing up at one moment in response to demand, only to collapse shortly afterwards, leaving little trace. Apart from these there were local day 'grammar schools', sometimes quite reputable; and at the other end of the spectrum residential schools where—in the words of a critic in 1837—'boys are sent out of the way to be boarded and birched at £20 a year'.[3] One contemporary called this whole sector 'a vast tract of howling wilderness and imposture'.[4] So it is difficult to know for sure what went on there.

They certainly provided broader curricula than the public schools (except for those which aped the latter), which could have made room for subjects like history, geography, and English literature: the potentially empire-friendly ones. The Taunton Commission thought they should do this, referring to French and German practice in this regard,[5] but that recommendation took a long time to seep through. In the case of the more aspirant grammar schools the public-school influence was partly to blame for this, together with the Oxbridge university requirement that every entrant took Greek.[6] Schools sometimes advertised history as a subject, but—as John Roach has pointed out—this cannot be relied on, as schools were often criticized by inspectors for listing courses that were not actually taught, just to attract customers. If any subjects were left out, it will have been the 'marginal'—that is, the least utilitarian—ones.[7] (Utilitarians had very set ideas about what should be taught in schools.)[8] 'History' in any case might mean classical or Old Testament history, and 'geography' the geography of the Holy Land. 'Modern' history often stopped with Elizabeth: just at the threshhold, that is, of the imperial age.[9] Reminiscencies from the time suggest that the quality of teaching in history was variable. At Arnold Bennett's Newcastle (Staffordshire) school it was 'preposterous: a silly system and tedious textbooks, resulting in knowledge both misleading and comically partial'.[10] English literature was given a boost when it was included as an optional subject for the Indian Civil Service examinations in 1855, though even there, as Richard Altick points out, it was mainly a memory test.[11] For Bennett 'Eng. Lit.' consisted of Shakespeare 'cut up alive into specimens of sixteenth century locutions'.[12] The decor of the schoolrooms themselves will have given little help. Those famous red-bespattered wall-maps that are such a part of their popular image cannot have appeared before the 1880s, at the very earliest.[13] The likelihood is, therefore, that history, geography, and literature, let alone *imperialistic* history and geography (there *was* no imperialistic English literature to speak of, as we shall see in a later chapter), were only patchily covered in even these middle-class schools.

Syllabuses though do not tell the whole story. The typical school day did not only consist of lessons. In between there were breaks: meal- or playtimes, when much of the 'real-life' education of the children took place. Unfortunately we know almost nothing of what went on here, though there is no empirical reason to suppose it had an imperial component. There are no known skipping rhymes or children's games that featured empire before the very end of the nineteenth century, unless it was very heavily disguised.[14] The precursor of 'cowboys and Indians' as the main playground war game appears to have been 'English and Romans', not 'settlers and Zulus', which would be the nearest imperial equivalent. ('Boers and Britons' replaced it briefly around 1900.)[15] Then again, we know very little of what teachers talked to their pupils about *aside* from the things they were supposed to teach. It would be surprising if that did not occasionally—with middle-class children at least—touch on burning public and colonial issues of the day, which might make up for the unevenness of formal education in this area. An example is H. G. Wells's dreadful Bromley Academy, which was one of those schools where history appeared on the official curriculum, but 'had dropped from the school outlook long before I joined it' (in the 1870s). Wells's account shows how empire knowledge could be put over in other ways. A normal school day, he recalls, had the boys at their desks surreptitiously reading 'penny dreadfuls', while the proprietor, Mr Morley, sat silent at the front. Nonetheless, Wells goes on, 'at times he [Morley] would get excited by his morning paper and then we would have a discourse on the geography of the North-West frontier with an appeal to a decaying yellow map of Asia that hung on the wall, or we would follow the search for Livingstone by Stanley in Darkest Africa'. Morley was a radical republican, and specifically anti-military, so it does not follow that the ideas that came down to Wells in this way were necessarily imperialist; but it does show that schoolchildren could be made *aware* of the empire even when they were not formally taught it.[16] Was this common? Unfortunately there were not many Morleys around with a Wells on hand to record their eccentricities.

All this has to be borne in mind when we look at the history and geography textbooks the pupils were given, in order to discover how the empire appeared to them. Hundreds of these were published. None of course was 'official'; unlike most other educational systems, the British has generally resisted prescribing particular texts. They were all the product of private enterprise, written—presumably—in response to market (teachers') demand. The sheer number of them can give the impression that they were more popular than was the case. In fact they were almost never used in the public schools, as we have seen, or in those for the working classes, which will be treated later. They were intended for these 'middling' school children: but they may only have been read by only a minority of *them*. That will have limited their impact; but they are the best evidence we have of the way the empire was *presented*, at any rate, to *some* middle-class children at this time.

❦❦❦

The first thing to strike one about these books is how low-key the treatment of the empire was in them. Few textbooks before the 1880s, especially, devoted much space to it, by comparison with other topics.[17] David Hume's great *History of England*, for example, written in the 1750s but still the leading text at advanced levels a century later, gave just fifteen of its 3,500 pages to the empire. Hume's account stopped at 1688, which partly explains this; but he could have made more of the early seventeenth-century 'origins' of the empire had he felt so inclined.[18] (The later Victorians did.) Books that covered later periods carried more imperial history, but not much more. This applies even to those with the 'e' word in their titles: like Dr Collier's *History of the British Empire* (1858), which has only seventeen of its 344 pages on the colonial side.[19] The usual practice was to mention the big imperial events—the settlement of America, the conquest of India, the American Revolution, and (if they got that far) Britain's various nineteenth-century colonial wars—perfunctorily and incidentally to other topics. Early emigration to America, for example, was treated as a footnote to the history of religious persecution in Britain.[20] India was a particular casualty. One or two textbooks did not even mention it.[21] Thomas Macaulay once marvelled at the fact that, whereas 'every schoolboy' knew something of the Spanish empire in America, they seemed entirely ignorant of Britain's eastern empire.[22] Even the textbooks that did feature the colonies never put them centre-stage. 'School books, as a rule,' wrote one commentator in 1870, 'supply every needful particular respecting the pettiest European state, but they are singularly reticent about the affairs of territories occupied by British citizens and subjects of incomparably greater size and importance.' He deplored this (he was an active imperialist himself).[23] Others—including presumably the teachers—did not seem to mind.

When the empire did come up, its treatment was not always flattering. Valerie Chancellor in her study of history texts has commented on the 'great variety of opinions' expressed in them about all kinds of matters, but about Britain's 'place in the world' in particular. Even where it is possible to discern common attitudes, she writes, 'they were rarely left unchallenged by other writers who disputed them'.[24] There was a great deal of criticism. Almost none of these texts, before the 1880s, holds up the empire as a matter for pride. This was partly because of the problem surrounding the word 'empire' during most of the nineteenth century, through its association with Napoleonic tyranny; but also because the empire itself was widely felt to be flawed. Hume, for example, was scathing about Sir Walter Raleigh's dishonesty and foolishness, and about the crimes of the early settlers towards the American *indigènes*,[25] and he was not alone in this.[26] One or two authors picked up on the British contribution to the slave trade.[27] Later, *every single* school textbook took the revolutionaries' side in the

American War of Independence.[28] The East India Company came in for much vilification, including attacks on Robert Clive and Warren Hastings, who were later to join Raleigh among the later Victorians' great imperial heroes. 'Vast as were the commercial advantages' accruing from Britain's conquest of India, wrote one anonymous author in 1875, 'it must be added that the triumphs of Clive were stained by those acts of cruelty, avarice, and breach of faith, which unhappily mark the whole history of our Anglo-Indian conquests.'[29] An earlier writer characterized the Company as a band of 'robbers', trampling perfectly good native governments under foot out of pure 'avarice'.[30] Another regarded 'the whole rise of the British empire in India' as 'one of our greatest national sins', in this case because of the Company's discouragement of missionary work there—the author was a clergyman.[31] Others, however, condemned it on entirely different—indeed opposite—grounds. Thomas Keightley's main reason for criticizing its agents' 'career of oppression and injustice' was their 'ignorance of the feelings, habits, prejudices, and institutions of those for whom they were legislating', and their 'unconscious application of European principles and analogies to a state of society so totally different from that of Europe'.[32] A minority of post-1857 works blamed British exploitation and arrogance for the outbreak of the Indian Mutiny, at least in part.[33] A geography textbook of 1863, focusing (unusually) on the empire, acknowledged that British colonization had 'not been an unmixed good—oppression, corruption and even destruction having been in many cases the consequence to the savage races of the approach of the whites'.[34] Examples were the genocide of the Caribs,[35] the slave trade from Africa,[36] and the traffic in alcohol.[37] The most widely criticized colonial policy, however—apart from Lord North's at the time of the American rebellion—was the first Chinese 'Opium' War (1839–42), 'undertaken on pretexts', wrote J. C. Curtis in 1860, 'which were largely, if not entirely, unjustifiable'.[38] (The second, in 1856–60, was thought to have a better excuse.)[39] A few writers worried about the morality of Britain's conflicts with the Afghans, and more about their wisdom.[40] Charles Knight deplored Britain's 'disrespect' towards Islam.[41] Others were put off imperialism by the wars it gave rise to. A number of history textbook writers were pacifists, or at least disapproving of the purposes for which past British wars had been fought, including in the colonies. 'They were undertaken to please the King,' runs one account of George II's wars, 'who cared more for honour than for England; they procured us no real advantage, cost us the lives of many brave men, and countless sums of money.'[42] All in all, the empire was at the very least an area for controversy in early and mid-nineteenth-century history textbooks. And the controversy nearly always took the forms of criticism or reluctant acceptance at best; almost never of adulation or patriotic pride.[43]

❦❦❦

One reason for this, and for the marginalization of the empire generally, was that it seemed incongruous in the light of what most of these textbook writers took as their main historical theme. That was the growth of peace and freedom in Britain from feudal times to the present day. This was their main 'patriotic' message, not the imperial one: to Seeley's displeasure, as we have seen. '[M]y desire has been', wrote the author of one of these books, 'to cherish that love of liberty which is best founded upon a sufficient acquaintance with its gradual development and final establishment amongst us.'[44] Most accounts claimed that this 'freedom' trend was unique to Britain and her offshoots (like America). 'The [British] Constitution,' wrote Miss A. Buckland, 'by which the rights of the people are secured, renders this country one of the freest and, at the same time most law abiding of all the countries of the world.'[45] The social-controlling function of this line is clear: if people believed they were free and getting freer, and that the world was becoming more peaceful, they would be content and politically docile. Imperialism sat uneasily with such a view. If Britain was the home of peace and freedom, what was she doing conquering other peoples and ruling them against their wills? It did not help that the origins of the empire—Tudor and Stuart colonization in America—were associated with the English régimes that these writers tended to deprecate most.[46] There was an ingenious way around this problem, as we shall see later; but for the moment—before the 1880s—the history of 'freedom' elbowed the history of 'empire' out.

There was, however, one big exception. British *settlement* colonies were different. Pride in them *was* allowed. Even David Hume, once he put the iniquities of their original conquerors behind him, regarded the British American colonies as 'established on the noblest footing that has been known in any age or nation'. That was because of the 'spirit of independency' they represented, reviving after the despotism (as he saw it) of the Elizabethan age.[47] They marked the flowering of English liberty, not 'imperialism' at all. Other historians used them to point the contrast between Spanish methods in the Americas, which was what *they* understood by imperialism—acquisitive, cruel, state-sponsored, exploitative; and Britain's—vigorous, hard-working, entrepreneurial, honest, and free.[48] Unlike other empires, claimed a geography text of 1863, 'the growth of the British Empire' had little to do with a 'love of conquest', but was 'the natural consequence of the growth of the commercial spirit, and of the ever-increasing wants of an energetic people confined to a comparatively small island home'.[49] Other early texts saw the colonies in much the same way: as an incidental offshoot of Britain's trading prowess, which was what really made her 'great'.[50] Nearly all the encomiums that are found to the empire—though it usually was not called that early on—dwell on these free and peaceful colonies: the United States, British North America, Australia, Canada, New Zealand—whether they were *still* colonies or not was irrelevant; and rather skated over the other (dependent) sort. One or two grasped the nettle and contrasted the former with the latter, to the latter's detriment. Which, asked one children's history book, 'was most worth having? The colonies of America ... had English feelings and spoke the English language: the inhabitants of our East India dominions ... are Hindoos and Moors, speaking the Hindoo, the Arabic and the Persian, and can be kept in subjection only by the sword.'[51] The two types were entirely distinct. 'In the old sense,' wrote the historian S. R. Gardiner later, in his later popular *Outline of English History*, clearly with the settlement colonies in mind, 'there is ... no Empire at all—for Empire means the government of a master—nor are there any colonies at all—for to be a colony is to be in some way dependent on the mother country. What we have now [*c*.1900] is an association of sister States proud of their common freedom.'[52] India was one thing; America, Australia, and the rest were quite another. You could be in favour of one while disapproving of the other; which is what many middle-class Victorians were.

Of course this distinction does not entirely correspond to reality. With regard to the 'free' settlement colonies, for example, it involves closing one's eyes to some inconvenient facts. One of these was the violence done to their aboriginal populations, which Hume had noticed in the case of North America, but which most later popular historians glossed over. For all the information they found there, readers of many nineteenth-century textbooks could have been unaware that continents like north America and Australia had any original populations at all. 'Beyond the sea', claimed one 1881 school history, 'were continents of rich land lying unused by man.'[53] Elsewhere readers were told that the original inhabitants simply disappeared, presumably with no pain. 'The savage men gradually melted away', wrote Charles Knight; which was a travesty of the facts, but a convenient one.[54] It was important for the champions of this kind of colonization to believe that these lands were virtually empty, available for new settlers to treat as they liked; it allowed them to distance themselves from the 'Spanish' kind of imperialism. There *was*, though, a crucial difference between the idea of the spread of liberty by peaceful means, and the forcible conquest and domination of other races: between the middle classes' imperialism, in other words, and that of the upper classes looked at in Chapter 3.

* * *

The problem was, however, that even the Victorian middle classes' libertarianism carried the seeds of imperialism within it. This is true of most political ideologies, very few of which are immune to being used to legitimize conquest and domination in certain circumstances. It does not mean that they are *necessarily* imperialistic, though; indeed libertarian arguments have as often been used against imperialism (for example, by Americans in America, 1776) as in favour of it (by Americans in Iraq, 2003). Later in the nineteenth century British liberals, too, used the rhetoric of 'liberation' to justify intervening forcibly in the affairs of other peoples to save them from despotism, war, or the tyranny of 'superstition', in a way that is reminiscent of US-led interventions in the Balkans, Afghanistan, and Iraq today. In both cases there may be suspicions of baser—more material—motives underlying the liberal rhetoric, which may or may not be justified, but which need not cast doubt on the sincerity of the rhetoric *per se*. One thing that may confirm this sincerity in the late Victorians' case is their confidence in the rightness of their way of doing things; their certainty that liberalism (and everything connected with it: parliament, the rule of law, capitalism, and so on) was objectively the best way for everyone, rather than just a matter of cultural preference: it was the summit of human endeavour, the 'end of history', to borrow an expression from a similar modern ideology.[55] One corollary of this view of liberalism is that it would be wrong *not* to intervene in order to impose it: a key move in the mutation from domestic liberalism to assertive imperialism. But this seems not to have been a factor in early and mid-nineteenth-century Britain, to judge from the views that were disseminated among her middle-class schoolchildren.

Few of these views actually *advocated* imperial expansion in order to 'enlighten' the world, or indeed for any other reason.[56] Occasionally enlightenment was presented as a mitigating factor, especially with reference to what was widely regarded as the least defensible of Britain's imperial exploits, the Chinese wars. 'But good sometimes comes of evil,' Jane is told by her Mamma in *Rodwell's Child's First Step to the History of England* (1844), 'and this war may be a good thing for the Chinese in the end; for they have already begun to know more about other parts of the world than they did before.'[57] 'War', wrote the author of an 1869 textbook, another critic of the Opium Wars, 'is one of the chief modes in which countries jealously sealed against foreign intrusion have been opened to the benign influences of commerce and religion.'[58] The same consideration could also justify colonial rule. Several textbooks that are otherwise lukewarm or even hostile towards Britain's eighteenth- and nineteenth-century annexations nonetheless make a point of admitting the good that is perceived to have followed from them. J. R. Green, for example, who generally deplores Clive's motives in India, still manages to persuade himself that Britain's subsequent good government there 'won the love of the Hindoos'; which leaves him at a loss for a historical explanation—it 'remains mysterious'—for the Indian Mutiny when it comes.[59] One highly critical account of British policy leading up to that Mutiny—'The English, rejoicing in their conscious superiority, had been habitually arrogant, overbearing, contemptuous'—still lists four positive gains from British rule for the Indians: education, social equality, women's liberation, and the spread of the Christian gospel.[60] One of the most critical of the geography textbooks of the period, the one that refers to the 'oppression, corruption, and even destruction' that the empire had brought to its victims, nonetheless concludes that 'the great aggregate influence from the progress of England's dominion has been sun-like; fertilising and productive to the earth itself, and diffusing the light of a higher intelligence, and the glow of a truer humanity to its inhabitants'.[61] That is not a bad plea of mitigation.

The other way of excusing British imperialism in retrospect—and an excuse was clearly felt to be needed at this time—was to present it as a sacrifice. Very few textbooks until the very late nineteenth century mentioned the economic gains that Britain got from the dependent colonies, or even that (apart from the widely discredited East India Company) she traded with them at all.[62] That may have been in deference to the free-trade dogma that colonies could not be profitable. It followed, however, that when Britain did attack or take over a non-European country, it was either a mistake (as in China), or had to be presented as a necessity. Sometimes the necessity was a broad one. 'So long as there remain such masses of ignorance over the earth, so long, *we are afraid*, force must be employed to preserve the little spots of civilisation from the flood of barbarism which might overrun them.' This was despite the fact that, as the same text avers, 'National war is the heaviest curse which affects humanity'.[63] It was all done out of duty. Almost every colonial war or annexation recorded in nineteenth-century textbooks is portrayed as having been 'forced' on Britain: by an act of aggression (the Chinese seizure of the *Arrow* in 1856, for example, which was reckoned to justify the second Chinese Opium War);[64] by native 'treachery', where indigenous rulers were judged to have reneged on agreements; or to protect either British subjects[65] or more innocent natives from cruelty and oppression. 'The kingdom of Oude, which was under the rule of its own princes,' averred one 1883 textbook, 'was so badly governed that it was found *necessary*, in 1856, to add it to our possessions.'[66] '[H]e was such a tyrannical ruler'—this is the king of Ashanti, according to an 1880s version of *Little Arthur's History*—'that our Government felt it *must* interfere.'[67] And from a 1903 text: 'As the native rulers were constantly fighting among themselves, we had been *forced* to conquer' [India]; 'the Government was *called upon* to interfere in Egypt' (by a 'religious fanatic'); 'we were *forced* to reconquer the Soudan';[68] and so on. Even the bad old East India Company, according to one 1881 history, 'bewailed, with pathetic earnestness, the conquests which were forced upon them'.[69] Overall, the empire was presented as 'a heavy burden for Britain to bear'.[70] Britons were 'reluctant imperialists' to a man (and the occasional woman). It must be here that this particular myth has its origin.

This plea was meant to sound imperially innocent—'we did not mean to do it'—but that was not its whole effect. It also legitimized imperialism, and in what might be regarded as a particularly unfortunate way: by blaming it on its victims. There are pre-echoes of Rudyard Kipling's 'white man's burden' here, in the sense of sullen duty towards inferiors—Kipling's 'fluttered folk and wild'.[71] That view was obviously demeaning to other peoples; but this does not necessarily imply imperialism, and indeed we shall find the opposite lesson being inferred from it in some circles in the mid-nineteenth century. It does mean, however, that any imperial feeling this attitude gave rise to was likely to be more arrogant and even angry than certain other kinds. To be forced into governing other peoples by their chronic misbehaviour was not likely to engender much love or respect for them.

The disrespect will have been exacerbated by the treatment of non-European colonial subjects that occasionally appeared in these books, most of which emphasized their 'primitiveness'. A particular area of criticism—curiously, perhaps, for as sexist a nation as Victorian Britain undoubtedly was—was the treatment of women. Muslims were a particular target here, but they were not alone. One geography text of 1852 paints a pathetic picture of Hindu women forbidden to learn to read or write, and condemned to a life of 'making curries and sweetmeats to please their husbands'.[72] Chinese foot-binding was frequently mentioned.[73] The *Wesleyan Juvenile Offering* claimed that: 'In heathen countries [woman] is the mere slave of men, ever oppressed by the stronger sex: not that her feminine qualities are different, and require that she be kept down; these are unaffected by the colour of her skin, or by the changes of the climate she lives in. Woman is the same all the world over—"soft, mild, pitiful, flexible"'.[74] (So it was not exactly a feminist view.) Non-Europeans were also demeaned in descriptions in the history textbooks of two particular historical incidents, both of them in British India: the 'Black Hole of Calcutta' of 1756, and the Cawnpore (Kanpur) massacre during the Indian Mutiny. J. R. Green described the first of these, when 127 captured Britons suffocated to death in a cell, as 'a crime whose horror still lingers in English memories': this was after 118 years.[75] The following is a typical description of the latter.

> Shrieks were heard and low groans, and the sound of blows as the savages hewed to death the unresisting women and little children who filled the room. Thrice a hacked and blunted sabre was passed out, and a sharper one received in exchange. Next morning the mutilated bodies were dragged forth and cast into a huge well.
>
> When, two days later, the avenging English, under Havelock, reached Cawnpore, the blood of the victims still lay on the stone pavement of the hall; fragments of ladies' and children's dresses, soaked in blood, were scattered all around...[76]

The problem here lies not in the depiction of the events (which did happen), but in the authors' morbid dwelling on them, and their attribution of them to—for example—'Oriental falsehood and treachery' (Green again),[77] as though there were something inherently treacherous about 'Orientals'.

❧ ❧ ❧

This, however, is not the whole story. Such accounts are by no means ubiquitous in the schoolbooks, and the racism found (or implied) in them never as perfervid as that expressed by certain literati of the time, for example over the Jamaica revolt of 1865.[78] Several textbook authors tried to be fair even to the perpetrators of those Indian incidents: '[t]here is no reason to suppose that the soobahdar designed their death', wrote one, of the 'Black Hole' incident;[79] and others balanced the Mutiny outrages with equally condemnatory accounts of British reprisals afterwards.[80] Presumably this was intended to show that cruelty was *not* only an oriental trait. (Readers of Charles Dickens's *Child's History of England*—a uniquely gruesome narrative of the crimes of Britain's own kings and queens—will already have been under no illusion as to that.)[81] A few textbooks managed to gloss over the Black Hole and the Cawnpore massacre entirely.[82] None stated openly that such conduct was particularly Indian in character; instead, most blamed the circumstances in which the Indians found themselves, and chiefly their superstition and ignorance. A few even blamed British racial arrogance.

These, in fact, were by far the most common approaches. Most geography schoolbooks from this period made a conscious effort, at any rate, to be non-racist. Many went out of their way to find things to admire in Asiatic culture, and in Africa's past. 'Hindoos', for example, were credited in *Chambers's Information* with being industrious, pacifistic, civilised, highly developed scientifically, and with great manufacturing and architectural skills.[83] One text of the time even ranks the University of Benares with Oxbridge.[84] The Chinese had a reputation among some for intelligence, inventiveness, commercial acumen, the fine arts, and literary scholarship.[85] 'Lower' cultures than these are seen as at least 'improvable'. Missionary educationalists in particular insisted on this, for reasons that are clearly spelled out in *The Wesleyan Juvenile Offering* in 1844: 'Our young readers have doubtless been led to believe that they are much more clever than the little Negroes of Africa and the West Indies; and the inference tended to be drawn is, that therefore it is to very little purpose to collect and give, in order that those may be taught who are so dull and slow to learn.' That would never do. So the *Offering* goes on to tell of a 'negro teacher', who obviously gives the lie to this.[86] Even 'Australian Negroes'—'even' because the aborigines were the one people that most Victorians gave up on—were, according to one geography schoolbook, 'a lively, good-humoured, inquisitive and intelligent race; [who]... acquire the knowledge of reading and writing almost as speedily as Europeans'.[87] The contemporary anti-slavery movement, with its powerful slogan, 'Am I not a man and a brother?', probably had much to do with this. 'But all men', declared the radical author of one influential early text, after categorizing the 'varieties' (not 'races') of humanity fairly conventionally, 'are the offspring of *one common parent*; and among these varieties, the swarthy negro and the delicate European are brethren, descended from the same ancestor', so making all differences 'accidental'.[88] 'And now, my young friends,' concludes an account of southern Africa in the *Juvenile Missionary Magazine* for 1866, 'you see that man, through all his varieties, has a common parentage, no matter how distant and how different may be the regions he inhabits, the complexion and the features which he possesses.'[89] That was the lesson the pedagogues wished to put over. It contrasts, incidentally, with the scientific racism that was systematically drilled into schoolchildren in some relatively non-imperialist European countries at this time; prompting the reflection that Britain's more direct colonial experience might have been a factor *diluting* the stronger racism found in more parochial lands.[90] Whether these more liberal attitudes took hold, of course, is anyone's guess.

In history books the same message was implied by one notable feature of nearly all of them: which was (if they went back that far) their depiction of Britons' own forebears some 2,000 years before.

> All the Britons went without any clothing, except the skins of wild beasts thrown carelessly over them; and they painted their bodies of a sky-blue colour, in rude forms of flowers, trees, and animals. Instead of houses they had little mean huts; they tilled no ground, their food being game and fruits. Their arms were, a shield and a short spear; to the lower end of the latter was fastened a bell of brass, in order to frighten their enemies, when they shook it...[91]

When middle-class Victorians thought of 'savages', therefore, it is likely to have been with reference their own ancestors rather than—or at least in conjunction with—any images they may have been presented with of 'barbarians' from other lands. This suggested not alienness but identity. Often the comparison was quite explicit. Thomas Keightley, for example, described his readers' ancestors as 'Nearly as low in the scale of humanity as her new colonists in after times found the aborigines of the New World'.[92] In at least one case the parallel must have been confirmed from the other side by an illustration of Australian aborigines which made them identical to Europeans in appearance and social conditions, if not in dress.[93] The implications of this were far reaching. In the first place it undermined the idea of an essential racial difference between 'Anglo-Saxons', say, and native Americans or Africans. Secondly, it suggested—though this was not an inevitable conclusion—that any people might 'progress'. If the Briton's woad-smeared ancestors had done so, then anyone could. It depended on environment, not on ethnicity.

This faith in human 'progress' was, in fact, far more central to the belief system of these early and mid-Victorian schoolbook authors than a view of the world divided into 'races'. Other peoples were categorized in terms of the 'stages' of progress they had reached, rather than as species; in chronological, that is, rather than spatial terms. They were seen as being 'behind' Britain, rather than different from her. (Just occasionally they were regarded as 'ahead'.)[94] Their cultures were frequently plotted against the graph of Britain's own historical development, with native Americans being put on a level with pre-Roman Britons, Africans located in the English 'dark' or 'middle' ages, and Indians and Chinese put somewhere around the sixteenth to eighteenth centuries. This was how Britain could be so certain of what was wrong with other countries; she too had been through all their stages—*Catholic* superstition, *Norman* tyranny, *feudal* wars, and so on. Generally the belief was that the transition through these 'stages' was inevitable, simply the product of 'enlightenment'; which also meant, incidentally, that imperialism was not *crucial* to it.[95] It was for this reason that almost the worst crime non-Europeans could commit was to deliberately cut themselves off from such enlightenment, as the Chinese and Japanese notoriously did.[96] The importance of environment (as opposed to 'race') seemed corroborated by the oft-observed phenomenon that civilizations could 'decline' as well as progress; as had clearly happened not only to Mughal India,[97] for example, and the Egypt of the Pharaohs, 'which was full of ancient learning when Britain was inhabited by savages';[98] but also to the Greeks, the Italians, and in one instance even the Brits.[99] There was hope, and a warning, for everyone in this.

It is worth reiterating the *non*-racist nature of this kind of world-view. 'Racism', strictly defined, means a belief in the impermeability of ethnic differences; but this was not implied here. If a prejudice was involved (which is surely the case), it was of quite another kind, based on a belief in the superiority of Britain's current 'civilization'. A possible word for this is 'culturism', though the distinction is not unproblematical. Stuart Hall regards both forms—he calls them 'biological racism' and 'cultural differentialism'—as simply 'racism's two registers'.[100] There is no doubt that one can be used to mask the other, and that people can slide from one to the other quite easily. On the other hand, it is also obvious that the *theoretical* difference between them is significant, and can have very divergent—indeed opposite—implications. At the very least, to refuse to recognize the difference—to reduce all of these attitudes to a general, all-purpose racism—must blunt any analytical tool we may wish to apply to this area of discourse; much as the reduction of all kinds of relationship with other countries to a simple irreducible 'imperialism' does. The distinction was important to contemporaries. To lose sight of it threatens to obscure at least one of the sources of their 'racial' attitudes; which was their arrogant but fundamentally liberal and optimistic belief in the advancement of everyone (or almost everyone), based *not* on their observations of or prejudices about those other peoples—not, in other words, on their imperial experience (even vicarious)—but on their understanding of their own nation's historical 'progress'.

There is a great deal to be said against this sort of attitude. It is culturally arrogant, at the very least. It can seem hypocritical, 'a bit steep' (as the saying goes), for nineteenth-century Britons to criticize other peoples for being sexist or caste-ridden, for example; or for believers in a virgin birth, miracles, and bodily resurrection to dismiss other faiths as 'superstitions'. Contemporary critics (like Dickens) raged at the double standard that had the middle classes weeping over poverty, tyranny, and immorality abroad, while being seemingly blind to them in Britain's own industrial cities. At the very least this 'culturism' indicates a lack of awareness of the effects on their own British culture of local environmental factors, and especially of capitalism, which clearly influenced their choice of admirable traits to select in other cultures, and probably blinded them to alternatives—the communitarian values associated with Islam, for example—which did not fit in with this. It also blinded them to some of the possible evils of their own system: capitalism, again, and especially its extension globally through 'free trade'. Then there are the question of real motives—were these 'progressive' ideals in fact just a cover for capitalist greed?—and the possibility that, despite protestations, racism lay at the root of them. But there was also another side. 'Culturism', if it *was* genuine, was not exclusive. It allowed for the possibility—indeed the likelihood, even the inevitability—that all peoples (or nearly all) could, like Britain herself, 'progress'. It at least gave the 'natives' the chance to 'catch up'. That could have a bearing, not so much on whether people supported imperialism or not, but on the kind of imperialism they were supporting, or thought they were.

❦❦❦

How much of all this got through to middle-class schoolchildren is difficult to say. It is worth reiterating that the views about the empire outlined so far in this chapter have been inferred from just a few minor references in school textbooks, where in almost every case they were overshadowed by other topics, and could well have been missed entirely by their young readers. Many school history books did not even cover the imperial age, stopping around 1500, while those that did made no great play of it. Every one of these texts concentrates on domestic rather than overseas history, and on domestic themes, typically the evolution of British liberties. Occasionally pupils were taught about continental Europe. (There are textbooks on that too.) The empire was marginal to all of this. One can understand Seeley's frustration in recalling these books, from which children could have gathered little of the importance (in his view) of the empire, or even of how it had come about. This final paragraph of an 1849 textbook, listing the great events of recent times, and Britain's part in them, is typical:

> The growth of the trade, colonies, and manufacturing wealth of England; the diffusion of knowledge among the lower classes; the increase of intercourse among nations, owing to the great development of steam navigation and the recent invention of railroads; and the intense interest excited by great political and religious questions throughout the whole of the civilised world, render the period of Her present Majesty's accession one of the most momentous in history. Great events have taken place, and there is much to hope and fear.[101]

'Colonies' are included here, but in context. (It is the 'settlement' colonies that are meant.) The 'empire' qua empire gets no mention. Children were almost never enjoined to be *proud* of it, and some books were downright critical, as we have seen. Patriotic pride *was* encouraged, but on the grounds of those 'liberties', and Britain's wealth, not because of her imperial power. The empire appears to have had an astonishingly low profile in most early and mid-Victorian 'middling' schools. It is difficult to see an imperialist frame of mind being nurtured in such an environment.

This may not be the end of the matter, however. First, there is the recurring problem that what children are taught in schools is not necessarily what they learn there. H. G. Wells's Mr Morley is an example of what a maverick teacher might do. There is also the matter of what pupils found significant. They will have decided this for themselves. One of J. R. Green's critics, stung by his condemnation of what he called 'drum and trumpet' history,[102] claimed that military history was 'the only side of history in which intelligent lads will or can take an interest'; Green thought this was wrong, and that his own sales figures proved it,[103] but the *Short History of the English People* is not entirely bereft of 'drum and trumpet', and it is at least possible that it was its more swashbuckling passages that many boys (and possibly even girls) found memorable. 'The time of peace is the truly *happy* time for a nation,' averred an early nineteenth-century history for 'cottagers'; 'but it is accounts of wars and battles that fill our books of history, and perhaps make them the more *interesting*'. (So the cottagers were treated to accounts of how Gibraltar was defended against the Spaniards, for example, by 'General Elliott, the governor, with his boldness and his red-hot balls'.)[104] Similarly, children could enjoy reading about Clive's scraps with the French and the Indians without bothering too much about the rights and wrongs of the conflict, however fair their authors tried to be to these. Single images could blot out paragraphs of even-handed analysis. The 'Black Hole' could very well have been one of these; it would take a great deal of reasoned argument to compete with an account of brave men struggling for breath in stifling heat, while their persecutors standing around jeering, as one version of that incident had it.[105] The same can be said of other thrilling set-pieces of British imperial history, however incidental to the main story these may have been. So it is possible that some imperial pride did get across, regardless of the attitudes of teachers and authors.

It could also creep through in other ways. Near the end of J. R. Green's *Short History* (1874), this stirring encomium to 'settlement' colonization appears. (Otherwise the book is as thin on the empire as most of its predecessors.)

> From the moment of the Declaration of Independence it mattered little whether England counted for less or more with the nations around her. She was no longer a mere European power, no longer a mere rival of Germany or Russia or France. She was from that hour a mother of nations. In America she had begotten a great people, and her emigrant ships were still to carry on the movement of the Teutonic race from which she herself had sprung. Her work was to be colonisation. Her settlers were to dispute Africa with the Kaffir and the Hottentot, to wrest New Zealand from the Maori, to sow on the shores of Australia the seeds of great nations. And to these nations she was to give not only her blood and her speech, but the freedom which she had won. It is the thought of this which flings its grandeur round the pettiest details of our story in the past... England is only a

small part of the outcome of English history. Its greater issues lie not within the narrow limits of the mother island, but in the destinies of nations yet to be.[106]

Green is supposed to have been a liberal, and indeed the major theme of *A Short History* is highly libertarian: the struggle for freedom of the ordinary English people (hence the book's full title) against kings and tyrants, from the middle ages on. The pride expressed in this rare glance of his into the wider world relates to the 'free' colonies rather than the despotic ones: Australia and even the United States, not India; which emphasis was perfectly consistent with the liberalism of the time. It is not 'imperialistic', therefore, in the full or literal (*imperium*) sense.

Nevertheless it is easy to see how it could become so. Green is not one of those who believes or pretends that Britain's settlement colonies were 'virgin' when the British arrived there, but nor is he shocked by the dispossession of their *indigènes*—the 'Kaffirs', Hottentots, and Maoris—as Hume, for example, had been in the case of the native Americans. Instead he seems to relish the battles with them that the 'sowing' of British freedom required. That is clearly imperialistic in a much more profound sense. Add to this the racism implied in this passage—all that 'Teuton' business, the suggestion that freedom itself is a racial characteristic, peculiar to the British (or 'Teutons'); that there is a 'freedom gene', in other words, which only the latter carry—and we have a very different kind of imperialism from the simple pride in the spread of liberal *ideas* which seemed to be more or less the sum of it before then. This view was new in the 1870s—unless Green was merely voicing existing but unspoken prejudices. It is not a *necessary* mutation from liberalism, and indeed many liberals resisted it, both before and after 1874. It clearly showed, however, that liberalism was no reliable prophylactic against imperialism, and might even, in certain circumstances, aid its birth.

5
Trade, Liberty, and Empire: The Middle Classes to 1880

The relative lack of an imperial education in their schools in the first three-quarters of the nineteenth century did not, of course, leave the middle classes ignorant of the empire all their lives. It is almost inconceivable that they could have been. Some had personal links with it: through the emigration of family, for example, and correspondence with them, or through their work. The newspapers and journals they read carried regular—if not particularly frequent—accounts of events in the colonies. Occasionally more light than usual was shone on a particular part of the empire, usually by a war. There were popular shows and displays featuring it, ranging from cheap circus sideshows of performing 'savages' to the more serious colonial and Indian galleries of the Great Exhibition of 1851. There was a great deal of imperial ephemera around. No middle-class person could escape this. What they made of it all, however, is less clear.

* * *

A survey of the literature and other media available to the middle classes shows how the empire was presented to them. ('High' art and literature are excluded here because they will be covered in a later chapter, but as these rarely featured the empire, this should make little difference.) Their first and most important source of information was the extensive periodical literature of the time, ranging from national and local daily and weekend newspapers, through to the more reflective or entertaining weeklies, monthlies, and quarterlies. Some of these appealed more to the 'higher' levels of the middle classes, which for the purposes of this study have been bracketed with the uppers (in Chapter 3). On the other hand, many will have percolated 'down'. (The boundaries between these classes and subclasses were never watertight.) Those who did have access to the great 'reviews' of the age—the *Fortnightly*, the *Quarterly*, and so on, with average circulations in the mid- to high thousands[1]—could be certain of being able to keep up, if they wished to, with the current imperial debates. (Even so, India was felt to be neglected in the reviews, as we shall see.) Among more popular upper-middle-class journals, *Punch* (circulation around 40,000) sometimes touched on imperial questions satirically, and the *Illustrated London News* (*c*.100,000) featured them whenever there was a suitably picturesque colonial war. *The Times* (50,000–100,000) and other 'establishment' newspapers always carried regular 'Foreign Intelligence' sections, which also kept the local and provincial press supplied, at secondhand.[2]

This was how daily news of the empire trickled down to the middle-middle classes. Usually European reports came first, followed by the remainder of the world, where of course most of Britain's colonies were situated; but it is as likely that this was because it seemed logical to begin with the news that was close at hand, as that it indicates any scale of priorities.[3] It did not stop extra-European events getting extensive coverage when they merited it. The great imperial 'crises' were always fully reported, especially those that could be presented sensationally. The Indian and Jamaican revolts provided ideal journalistic material of this kind, with exactly the kind of 'atrocity' aspects that editors knew their readers thrilled to. (That did not prevent many papers giving the Mutiny a lower billing than some nearer-to-home sensations of the day, including—in the week news of it first arrived—a poisoning in Glasgow and a garrotting in Manchester.)[4] It needed something on this scale to highlight imperial issues; but in between atrocities readers were presented with enough information, in the 'Foreign Intelligence' columns, to keep fairly well abreast of what was going on in their colonies. Even the most provincial of Victorian newspapers were anything but parochial.

Information picked up from newspapers could be supplemented, for the middle classes, from the scores of weekly and monthly 'family' journals that were such a colourful feature of their culture from the 1830s and 1840s on. These ranged from the monthly *Cornhill Magazine*, at the expensive end of the market, but still managing a circulation of around 80,000 in the early 1860s; through Charles Dickens's famous weekly middlebrow *Household Words*, with a circulation of 100,000 at its (early 1850s) peak; to cheap papers like the weekly *Penny Magazine* (circulation 200,000 in the 1830s) and *Chambers's Edinburgh Journal* (60,000–70,000 in the 1840s), which were aimed at the working as well as the lower-middle classes, but in reality never penetrated deeper than the very topmost section of the already respectable skilled working class.[5] Many of these were predominantly literary journals, or vehicles for the serialization of popular (but non-imperial) novels,[6] and all of them avoided what they called 'politics'; but a lot of imperial exposure was still possible within these bounds. *Ainsworth's Magazine,* for example, which was one of the most 'literary' (it was subtitled *A Miscellany of Romance, General Literature, and Art*), and which abjured politics explicitly,[7] still managed to find room in its early volumes for a description of 'A South African Pic-nic' by a Mrs Ward, 'A Bengal Yarn' by Captain [Thomas] Medwin, and lashings of 'orientalism'.[8] Other journals carried much more empire-related material. A single year's subscription to *Chambers's* (1834–5) could teach the attentive reader about Lander's and Thompson's latest travels in Africa; catamarans in the Indian ocean; society and warfare in the West Indies; the anti-slave squadron off West Africa; the aborigines of St George's Sound, Australia; how the Boers lived in South Africa; emigration; a Canadian winter; and a great deal about India, including the 'Mussulmauns' (*sic*), 'Noor Jehan, The Mogul Empress', what to look for in Benares and Delhi, and how to shop in Calcutta.[9] William Chambers's publications[10] were unusual in the extent of their imperial coverage—it may have been because he was Scottish—but there is a lot of such material scattered throughout the others too. Missionary magazines and pamphlets were a prime source of information about—and pre-formed attitudes towards—other 'races' for the disproportionately influential middle-class minority (mainly Nonconformists) they served.[11] For solider reading there were numerous books of travel and exploration, including Sir Charles Dilke's path-breaking *Greater Britain* (1868), which was the first to attempt to describe the empire as a whole. The cost of most of these latter works probably restricted them to the upper part of the middle-class market, though libraries will have spread a few of them lower down, and almost anything written about David Livingstone—an icon for the religious middle classes—was guaranteed a good sale.[12] If any middling Victorian, therefore, was ignorant about Indian religion, Australian frontier life, the great capitals of the empire,[13] African society, the quaint and thrilling customs of the South Sea islanders, the wildlife of Canada, or why the

Indians and Jamaicans had mutinied, then he or she had only him- or herself[14] to blame. The information (of a kind) was there.

❦❦❦

Even if they did not read, or did not read much, there were other ways for them to learn about the empire. Occasionally it was featured in various kinds of 'show'. An example is a performance put on by a 'Mr Batty and his troop of horses and ponies' in Birmingham in 1844, depicting 'the Affghanistan [*sic*] War; or the Revolt of Cabul, and British Triumphs in India'. That formed part of a programme with 'Turpin's Ride to York', 'The Gypsy Heir of Rookwood', 'Mazeppa, or the Wild Horse of Tartary', and the 'Battle of Waterloo'; so the empire was not all that customers came to see.[15] Another form of popular entertainment, in this case likely to have fostered racist attitudes, was travelling exhibitions of African and other 'savages' in traditional costumes, presented as sensationally as possible in order to thrill potential customers. These had originated early in the century, with the celebrated—but also highly controversial—'Hottentot Venus' (Sartje), exhibited in London in 1810: controversial because of the humanitarian outcry against her exploitation that it provoked.[16] But the high point of this phenomenon came in the 1840s and 1850s, which saw eight or nine separate shows of native Africans, Americans (north and south), and Laplanders, exhibited first in London (usually in the Egyptian Hall), then touring the provinces, often brought over (like the 'nigger' minstrels) by American entrepreneurs. One exhibition, of Bushmen (1847), was advertised as 'particularly addressed to those interested in the exciting events now going on in South-Eastern Africa, in the Kaffir War, in the great question of race, and the probable extinction of the Aboriginal races'—this might be people's last opportunity to see them—together with 'the progress of the Anglo-African Empire, and the all-important questions of Christian mission and human civilization in that quarter of the globe'.[17] In other cases the imperial connection was not so blatant; which is not to say that they did not feed imperialistic prejudices. As well as these, there was an almost continuous succession of Chinese exhibitions in London, including a junk moored on the Thames. Richard Altick is right to point out that we cannot possibly know how more 'ordinary beholders' regarded these displays: 'Certainly their motives were mixed and, in some instances, complicated and even contradictory.' But in any case they seemed to lose interest in this genre after the mid-1850s—Altick thinks their appetite for 'primitive races' may have been sated—when the phenomenon virtually came to an end.[18]

Another contemporary medium for empire-related displays was the 'panorama' or moving backdrop, a forerunner of the cinema. (Variants were called 'bioramas', 'cosmoramas', 'pyrodramas', and *tableaux vivants*.)[19] In the 1840s a giant 'moving panorama' depicted the 'Overland Route to India', while London saw a spate of them in 1851, to coincide with—and cash in on—the Great Exhibition. These featured 'trips' up the Nile and the Ganges, and views of the Cape, Natal, New Zealand, Australia, Ceylon, Calcutta, Malta, Africa, the (north) Polar regions, and the Holy Land, which was apparently the most popular of these vicarious venues. Some of the subjects were colonial, but they were clearly chosen because of their exoticism, among scores of others with no imperial connections at all: Mount Etna, Mont Blanc, Versailles, Oregon and California, Southampton Water, Grace Darling, and many more. One 'Diaphanic Panopticon' climaxed with an 'Enormous Transparency, set in a jewelled frame . . . Representing Britannia introducing Peace and the Arts and Sciences to the World', which is easy to read imperially; as is James Wyld's enormously popular 'Great Globe' in Leicester Square, 60 feet in diameter, which customers viewed from the inside. The *Notes* that were sold to accompany it mentioned 'pride' in the empire explicitly.[20] Later, naval and military battles became favourite subjects for panoramas, some of which were bound to have imperial settings, including one picturing exciting incidents from the Indian Mutiny which toured the country in 1858.[21] That was the main way in which imperial*ism* in its narrower sense—of conquering and ruling—was depicted: in the occasional battle scene.

Away from these strictly commercial enterprises, government authorities, societies, and middle-class philanthropists also put on shows for the public. Usually these sought to instruct as well as entertain. There was less overt imperial propaganda here than might be expected from such sources, though there was some. Exactly how much is (as ever) problematical. Attempts have been made to associate all museums and zoos with empire; but in most cases such attempts rest on the presumption that collecting and cataloguing exotic phenomena was an intrinsically imperialistic project, rather than on more direct empirical evidence. Harriet Ritvo, for example, in arguing that 'the discourses of zoo keeping and hunting . . . justified and celebrated Britain's imperial enterprise', short-circuits the awkward lack of evidence for this by suggesting that zoo people were 'reluctant or unable to avow a project of domination directly'; which sounds unlikely (why should they be embarrassed?), and even if it were true might be thought to indicate a dominant *anti*-imperial discourse. Whether zoo visitors took home imperialist messages cannot be known. Ritvo's claim that 'English citizens *of all classes recognised* the fledgling Zoological Society as a more elaborate iteration of a symbol of imperial dominion with which they had long been familiar' (italics added) is just a guess. (Again, surely *someone* would have articulated it if it were true?)[22] Likewise, Thomas Richards's characterization of the collection and ordering of artefacts in museums as an essentially 'imperial' enterprise only works for the early part of the century if one takes 'imperial' to cover the activities of collecting and ordering, by definition.[23] The British Museum, to cite the greatest example, concentrated almost entirely on ancient Rome, Greece, Egypt, and Mesopotamia—in other words, the 'cradles' of (European) 'civilization'. Everything else, including colonial artefacts, was relegated to 'five paltry cases' (for China and Japan); an 'ethnological' section of 'curiosities'; or—worst of all—the cellars, where it was never seen. 'You have also, I imagine, Byzantine, Oriental, Mexican and Peruvian Antiquities stowed away in the basement?', Sir Anthony Panizzi, the Museum's principal librarian, was asked by a Parliamentary Committee in 1860; to which he replied: 'Yes, a few of them; and I may add, that I do not think it is any great loss that they are not better placed than they are.'[24] That indicates a cultural arrogance that can be related to imperialism, but is not necessarily imperialistic in itself. Later in the century museums became more overtly imperialistic, and popular exhibitions were deliberately organised around empire themes. For the early and middle years of the century, however, the only way of interpreting such activities imperially is by extrapolating an imperial consciousness from the surrounding context; which, as we are finding, is by no means unambiguous on this point.

We are on firmer ground with the scientific and cultural institutions which were one of the glories of most large Victorian municipalities: all those 'Literary and Philosophical Societies' (of which Newcastle's is the most remarkable survivor, still with its library intact), which served the same public, probably, that bought the serious monthly periodicals of the day—a small but locally distinguished one. Imperial topics featured very occasionally at these meetings. Between 1856 and 1871, for example, over 400 public lectures were delivered at the Birmingham and Midland Institute, five of which were on India—the only directly imperial ones (four of them in the immediate aftermath of the Mutiny)—plus four on African exploration, and another on the 'Evils and Remedies' of Britain's trade in Central Asia.[25] In 1848 Birmingham's Eclectic Society debated whether colonies were worth having.[26] Issues of 'race', which could be seen as related, were more common. Newcastle's 'Lit and Phil' seems to have been less overtly interested in the empire, but perhaps only because its constitution forbade 'controversial' subjects, like politics and religion. It did, however, mount an exhibition of Maori heads, complete with tattoos, in 1837, which at least one visitor—an enthusiast of the new 'science' of phrenology—thought showed clear proof of racial inferiority, though there was a range of views in the Society over this.[27] Birmingham also hosted lectures by the (national) Ethnological Institute on race differences in the mid-1850s, delivered to 'large, respectable and "influential" audiences'.[28] Missionary lectures added to people's 'knowledge' on these race issues, especially the churchgoers' (mainly Nonconformists) who subsidized the missionaries' efforts. These were enormously enhanced by the use of 'magic lanterns', not always very scrupulously. A middle-class memoirist remembered attending one such lecture in the 1870s, where 'the speaker showed the usual oriental scenery. A friend who was present said to him at the end, "You old fraud. You know there are no palm trees where you come from." "I know," was the reply; "but you see the British missionary audience demands palm trees." '[29] How large the 'British missionary audience' was is difficult to say; we occasionally read of missionary talks being delivered to other than Nonconformist audiences: at more open meetings, for example, and at public schools.[30] What seems to be clear is that race was certainly a hot topic for middle-class Britons in the middle of the nineteenth century, but that the empire *per se* was less so.

Then there were the exhibitions put on by those same missionary societies and other professional bodies to publicize their work. Ray Desmond describes some of the early nineteenth-century London ones in his history of the India Museum:

> Africa, Australasia and Oceania as well as Asia were represented in the Royal Asiatic Society which by the mid-1830s could boast one of the best collections of Oriental arms and armour in the country. The Tower of London also had a notable collection of Indian arms and armour, largely presented by the East India Company; unfortunately much of it was lost in the great fire of 1841. Many of the natural history specimens from South Asia in the museum of the Linnean Society had been presented by the Company. The so-called Indian Museum and

Exhibition at 80½ Pall Mall was actually nothing more than a sale room of models, implements, musical instruments, statuary, paintings and an array of 104 pictures, grandly dubbed 'the Indian Cosmorama', on the life and exploits of Rama. *The Times* for 9 January 1823, not at all impressed, comforted its readers by telling them 'that a very good fire is kept in the room which contains all these wonders ... and ... the admission is not a heavy one.' Clothes, artefacts, weapons and 'especially the idols given up by their former worshippers from a full conviction of the folly and sin of idolatry', all collected by zealous missionaries in India and elsewhere, filled the museum of the London Missionary Society. The general public were occasionally allowed to admire the Oriental arms and relics such as the uniform worn by Tipu Sultan at Seringapatam in the Royal United Services Institution. In 1825 Bullock's Egyptian Hall in Piccadilly acquired the Burmese imperial state carriage, glistening with thousands of gems, which had been captured by the British the year before. Less exotic objects were always being brought home by the crews of East Indiamen and someone in London was usually prepared to display them for the promise of profit; for a shilling the public at the Exeter Hall could marvel at a 24 foot temple full of statues of the Buddha, and about the same time seventy-eight life-size figures representing 'the principal images of Hindu worship' were on display at St Katherine's Dock. None of these motley collections, however, could compete with the more comprehensive display of Asian materials in the [India] Museum in Leadenhall Street.[31]

What they did, however, was provide further opportunities for some early Victorians—how many we shall never know—to experience their empire vicariously. Obviously the view they acquired will not always (ever?) have been an accurate one. Missionary exhibitions, for example, were unlikely to be fair to 'native' value-systems. The LMS's museum will have been part of a strategy to shock people into donating money for its cause. Commercial impressarios needed to go for sensation, as we have seen, in order to attract customers. Nevertheless, such exhibitions would have promoted some kind of empire awareness.

All these were private or voluntary enterprises. At governmental level there was almost no attempt to publicize the empire except—feebly—to encourage the emigration there of the potentially dangerous poor. The government had an opportunity to do more when in the wake of the abolition of the East India Company in 1858 the state assumed responsibility for its 'India Museum' in Leadenhall Street, London; only to neglect it thereafter, however, and eventually (in 1874) to close it down. This was in spite of pleas from imperialists that this could be a prime way of imperializing the working classes, in particular; strong evidence that, had it been easier to get to (in the 1860s visitors had to climb up 140 cramped stairs to reach it), the demand was there; and very respectable attendance figures when it *was* made more accessible in 1870–1, when 42,545 people passed through its turnstiles in eleven months. The main obstacle was the expense, which was born by the Indian taxpayer; no one thought that the British exchequer should pay.[32] Other reasons will have been that governments at this time were not in the business of 'publicity' in any case; a certain nervousness—which we shall return to later—about *over*-educating the working classes; and the fact that governments did not seem to be especially proud of the empire: much less so, for example, than they were of Britain's industrial growth, trade, freedoms, and stability. An example of this is the Great Exhibition of 1851, which shows the official status of the empire at this time exactly.

The Great Exhibition was the first time that Britain (or any country) had ever 'exhibited' itself in quite this way. Other countries had held *national* exhibitions,[33] but none before 1851 had dared to put itself on show by comparison with other countries. Half of the floor space in the new 'Crystal Palace' built specially for the occasion was given over to them. The theme of the Exhibition was 'industry', which was what justified Britain's hogging the other half. The building itself, made of prefabricated sections, also reflected this. The message was designed partly to rub in Britain's superiority in this field, of course; but also to make an internationalist point: that all other nations could become as prosperous as Britain if they followed her examples of peace and free trade. This message was repeated constantly. It was Prince Albert's main rallying cry in appealing for private funding (again, it would have gone against all the principles of the time for the government to pay for the Exhibition), expressed in almost Cobdenite terms at a banquet in 1850 in which he described the coming event as a milestone along the road to the 'great end to which, indeed, all history points—the realization of the unity of mankind'.[34] Queen Victoria called it a 'peace festival'.[35] This was the lesson taught to young people too. Readers of *Little Henry's Holiday at the Great Exhibition*, for example, learned that foreign visitors would be so impressed by the marvellous display of the peaceful applications of human ingenuity in the British section that they would all soon be beating *their* swords into ploughshares: 'Men have learned once for all the proper use of iron and steel. They know now what God sent it for.'[36] It was also what good Prince Albert had aimed at, according to another children's primer:

> The Great Exhibition is intended to receive and exhibit the most beautiful and ingenious things from every country in the world, in order that everybody may become better known to each other than they have been, and be joined together in love and trade, like one great family; so that we may have no more wicked, terrible battles, such as there used to be long ago, when nobody cared who else was miserable, so that they themselves were comfortable.[37]

That was what everyone was told.

It may not have been what everybody heard—least of all the foreign visitors. Other messages will have been more subliminal, including some with imperialist undertones. Jeffrey Auerbach points out that the British colonial displays were located at 'the very centre' of the Exhibition, as indeed some of them were (along the transepts), though they shared that centre with, for example, China, Tunis, and Greece, and were given less floor space overall than France.[38] India had a great display. What people made of the fairly restrained orientalism of this section is not known, though the Koh-i-Noor diamond—a 'present' for the queen from the Punjab when it was annexed in 1849—attracted long queues.[39] Apparently the Indian show was intended by the organizers to encourage British industrialists to utilize Indian materials and designs.[40] The East India Company however, which arranged the unit in collaboration with the organizing committee, may have had another agenda. One of its displays of native craftsmen had a British soldier overseeing them.[41] Other colonial sections implicitly underlined the economic value of the empire, and managed to gloss over what Auerbach calls 'the negative side of imperialism—the oppression, subjugation, and stripping of natural resources'. He quotes the *Art Union* (a journal) as claiming that the effect of all this would be to impress 'every visitor with the importance of such possessions to Great Britain'.[42] So far as India is concerned, it seems to have stimulated some public interest, with visits to the India Museum doubling in 1851 from the previous year.[43] Some may have come away from the Exhibition with impressions of colonial peoples that were racist and stereotypical, though not necessarily through the fault of the Exhibition itself. (The crudest stereotypes were found in low comic books published to coincide with it.)[44] There were certainly contradictions between the internationalist official message and these others. (Another, which was pointed out at the time, was the displays of guns.) This is not surprising, however, in view of the way the Exhibition was organized, with its different sections in effect franchised out, allowing a multiplicity of contemporary discourses—

many of which *were* contradictory—to be reflected there. It certainly does not mean that the official version was hypocritical, as one authority asserts.[45] The 'overarching tenor' of the Exhibition, writes Auerbach, really was 'pacifist internationalism'. If it was trying to define Britain, as in a way it was, then this was in terms of her industry, ingenuity, and 'freedom'. Her colonial achievements hardly came into it. The exhibits that most impressed, by all accounts, were the great engines: 'the crowding masses of men and things, raw materials and manufactured articles, machines and engines that surround you on every side!'[46] The colonial sections—even the Indian—hardly appear in contemporary recollections.[47] They were marginal, both to the intentions of the organisers, and in the perceptions of the Exhibition's roughly 4 million visitors.[48] Indeed, so marginal were they that when the the Exhibition came to an end, and the Crystal Palace was re-erected and restocked as a permanent show at Sydenham in 1854, the Indian and colonial exhibits were not thought worth transferring there. The empire disappeared.[49]

⁂

Context is all. Taking these imperial reports and displays out of context gives a misleading impression of their ubiquity. Most of them are thinly scattered, marginal, trivial, occasional, or temporary. Other places and issues were of far more interest and importance to the early and mid-Victorians: the machinery at the Great Exhibition; the Egyptian mummies in the British Museum; European and American affairs to newspaper readers who took any interest in the 'Foreign Intelligence' columns at all. These, and domestic events, are what dominated the media. The empire came very low on their scale of priorities.

Of course it came somewhere. It would have been extraordinary if, in an expansive society like Britain's, many of its best-educated sector had *not* taken an interest in exotic places and events. Some of those places and events had to do with the empire; but it does not follow from this that the middle classes' interest in them was imperial*ist*. India as an object of curiosity is not the same as the Raj. Nor does it follow that these interests necessarily turned people *into* imperialists; that reading about the exploration of Africa, for example, or shopping in Calcutta, reminded people of the scope of their empire, or made them want to extend it. It may have done so in some instances; especially, perhaps, accounts of 'savage' societies which implied that they might become less savage if Britain took a hand.

But we should not leap to this conclusion. The Victorian middle classes' interest in exotic places, peoples, and customs, even if they happened to feature the empire, could have been quite imperially innocent.

This is what many of the middle-classes claimed. Certainly the empire never loomed large in their literature or any other media *as* an empire: as a structure or vehicle of government in itself. Indeed, the word itself was hardly ever mentioned. The rare general surveys that appeared chose other terms for it: 'Greater Britain', in Dilke's famous phrase; 'Mrs Britannia's children', in a lesser-known one.[50] The obvious explanation for this somewhat contrived nomenclature—that there was a taboo on the 'e' word because of its Napoleonic associations—is not quite sufficient. The mid-Victorian middle classes—most of them—did not call the British empire an empire, because they did not think of it as one. The main reason for this was ideological, the prevalent contemporary belief in 'free trade'.

This is crucial. Free trade was the great new idea of the early and middle years of the nineteenth century, and was supposed to be *anti*-imperial. Richard Cobden, for example, the great parliamentary leader of the free-trade lobby in mid-nineteenth century Britain, claimed that eventually it would do away completely with the 'desire and the motive for large and mighty empires', and also for armies and navies, uniting everyone in the world 'in the bonds of eternal peace'.[51] Imperialism implied conquest, control, and exploitation; free trade explicitly abjured these. The basic idea was that it gave every individual free choice to exchange his or her goods with any other individual, thus taking the 'power' element out of the equation entirely. It was also supposed to maximize production and so spread prosperity everywhere, not only on one (the imperial) side of the arrangement. Imperialism, as the free traders understood it, was not only wrong morally, but also counter-productive, in that it acted as a brake on the generation and spread of wealth; this was why free trade was *intrinsically* incompatible with it. At the very least, therefore, it was difficult for free traders to accept that a British empire was a permanent good.

The doctrine had two other anti-imperial implications. The first was that it was as anti-national as it was specifically anti-imperialist. This also followed from the theory: if the only important and profitable units of society were the individual and the entire world community, *any* formal grouping of people between these two must be an incubus, including nation states and federations as well as empires. This accounts for the mid-Victorians' surprisingly cool attitude towards continental European nationalist movements, at a time when the continentals tended to assume that the two things, liberalism and nationalism, were inseparable. Of course they do not have to be in logic. One can have illiberal nations and liberal federations or empires. The British separation of them can be clearly seen in the foreign policy of Lord Palmerston, Britain's most middle-class and free-trade-friendly foreign minister, who notoriously championed liberalism on the European continent, to the fury of the despots, at the same time as irritating continental liberals by refusing to back their national ambitions.[52] It was also manifested in Britain's continuously (until 1886) anti-national policy towards Ireland; and, possibly, in the virtual absence of a sense of common national identity for Britain herself. It is one of the reasons why Britons were rarely in this period *patriotically* imperialistic. Patriotism was not a respectable or rational sentiment in this new world of individual freedom, global brother- and sisterhood, and collapsing barriers and boundaries. It was regressive, and therefore to be discouraged.

But it only needed to be discouraged; not necessarily *fought*. This was the third way in which free-trade ideology could be seen as intrinsically anti-imperialist: in the assumption that lay behind most of these mid-Victorian expressions of it that free trade and the better world it promised would evolve naturally and inevitably, simply because it was self-evidently beneficial to everyone, whatever some of them might think now, so that it need not be spread by (imperial) force. The word often used for this was 'Providence' (with a capital 'P', aligning it with 'God'). Middle-class writings are full of this message, as in this confident assertion in the inaugural issue of the very free-trade *Howitt's Journal* in 1847: 'the current of true civilisation has set in with a force that no contrary force can overcome.'[53] *Household Words* also referred to a 'current'; in this case, 'the *eternal* current of progress setting across the globe in one unchangeable direction'. There might be backsliders (it was alluding here to China), and stumbles along the way. Generally, however: 'Our present period recognises the progress of humanity, step by step, towards a social condition in which nobler feelings, thoughts, and actions, in concert for the good of all, instead of in general antagonism, producing a more refined and fixed condition of happiness, may be the common inheritance of great and small communities, and of all those nations of the earth who recognise and aspire to fulfil this law of human progression.'[54] This—'Providence'—was a more powerful and a more worthy force than imperialism as the mid-Victorians understood the word. All they had to do was sit back and wait for it to happen. That was not 'imperialism' at all.

Of course the Victorians could have been fooling us, or themselves. Today free trade is often seen as a fig-leaf to cover a more nefarious *de facto* imperialism, both at the time and afterwards. In the nineteenth century some terrible things were certainly done in the *name* of free trade, most notoriously the 'Opium Wars' of the 1840s and 1850s, when Chinese ports were bombarded to allow the free import there of hard drugs. (To be fair, most contemporary British free traders thought this was going too far: 'not the work of Christians, but of demons', as *Howitt's* put it in 1847.)[55] Elsewhere the consequences of incorporation into the Europe-dominated world market could be equally ambivalent, as they still are today: increasing prosperity (for some), but also undermining local craft industries, encouraging monocultures in place of diversity, and throwing whole social structures into disarray. Then again, the idea of 'inevitability' can be deeply problematical. 'Providence' has been an unreliable guide throughout history, with the Marxist version being only the most recent one to let us down. There is an arrogance about the assumption that you know where it is leading, which is not very far away from one of the motors of imperialism. 'Providence' can also be used as a cloak to cover some very *un*providential acts: you can see the direction history is leading, so you help it along. That was exactly how many British colonies came to be first established during the course of the nineteenth century. Still others were established under the *pretence* of it. Thus it was that a supposedly anti-imperial ideology could give rise to its antithesis. You can be an imperialist riding on the back of 'Providence', as well as in any other way. But one can see how, at the time, this possibility might be missed.

This explains a great deal about the treatment of empire in the middle-class periodicals of the early and mid-nineteenth century. It is why there was so little in them about the empire *as* an empire, and almost no positive pride expressed towards it.[56] All the exceptions present the empire as something that will be new to readers, as if they have never considered it before, at least as a whole. This is certainly the implication of Dilke's *Greater Britain* (1868), which has traditionally been regarded as the first book to reveal to the (or some) Victorians that they had an empire at all. This may have been simply a rhetorical technique or convention, but it may also have been a response to a degree of genuine apathy. The same is true of earlier pieces that deal with just parts of the empire, India in particular. Most begin by bemoaning the ignorance of these important matters—not of India itself, but of Britain's governance of it—which they believe *every* class of Briton shares.[57] The 1857 Mutiny gave rise to a spate of such books and articles, all designed to inform the public, tardily, about a possession that was now rudely thrust on their attention after decades of ignoring it. (A common feature is a potted history of British India.)[58]

Similarly, pieces in journals that feature places that happen to be British possessions rarely mention that fact, and certainly do not give them preference over non-colonies. The latter seem to have aroused *more* interest, if anything; which may possibly have been predatory, and hence incipiently imperialist, but there is little sign of this. In middle-class journals India came way behind China (apart from 1857) in the amount of coverage it received, and was usually treated in much the same fashion, with its indigenous history, culture, and artefacts featuring far more often than Britain's stake there.[59] Usually mention of the latter was omitted entirely, which was why so much catching up was necessary after the Mutiny. It is difficult to believe that readers could have been unaware that they were supposed to be ruling India (indirectly), but that is not impossible, and there is certainly little sense given in these middling magazines of any feeling of *identity* with those who were actually ruling it (directly), on the ground. Most references that there were to the British Raj before 1857 were highly critical, especially from the free-trade lobby of the press.[60]

The settlement colonies were entirely different. Middle-class interest in them was warmly empathetic: not with their British rulers (governors) necessarily, but with the emigrants who effectively—because they had more democracy than in Britain—ran them. They were the middle classes' own kind. Long 'letters' from middle-class colonists, occasionally warning their compatriots off certain colonies, but usually recommending colonization generally, appear frequently in many of these journals.[61] Some of these letters were sponsored by emigration societies, most of which were concerned—in good imperialist fashion—to direct emigration *to* the colonies if they could.[62] On the other hand, California features as often as British Columbia in these journals overall as a promising destination for intending migrants.[63] Most columns of 'advice to emigrants' apply to both colonial and non-British destinations. Scarcely ever is Australia, for example, recommended editorially in preference to the United States, on imperialistic, patriotic, or any other grounds. National allegiance was hardly ever an issue, so long as the land in question was one of (individual) opportunity. From all these points of view, the empire qua empire really did not seem to matter much. This may be why it was not typically marked out in red on world maps until comparatively late in the century, though that would seem an obvious thing to do. It was almost as if, for the middle classes (and those beneath them), the empire did not exist.

It was really a question of focus. Countries and peoples—just like individuals—relate to one another on different levels simultaneously, and in all kinds of complex ways. Modern historians and other scholars have focused on the imperial or quasi-imperial relationship as the most significant of these, certainly in the nineteenth and twentieth centuries, and (for some of them) also at the present time. Perhaps it was, although one suspects that fashion and politics may be partly responsible for the emphasis that is placed on this. To see the world as these liberal, middle-class, mid-Victorians saw it, however, we need to soften or even dissolve that particular focus, so revealing the other patterns and details that were more evident and important to them. These will also explain how they could be so genuinely blind to the possible imperial implications of what they thought and did; if those implications *were* imperialistic, which is a matter of judgement and semantics, once again.

❦❦❦

Part of that judgement may rest on their views of other 'races', which modern scholarship tends to relate closely to 'imperialism', although the connection may not be inevitable and is certainly not straightforward. The Victorians' race attitudes have been well worked over by historians, the most discriminating of whom acknowledge the variety of opinions there were on this issue among the middle classes.[64] On the whole those opinions were charitable rather than otherwise, though that word—'charity'—implies a condescension that could be regarded as imperialistic in itself. The charity took two distinct and, indeed, contradictory forms. One was a seemingly genuine respect for other people's customs and cultures. The other was a belief that, despite the savagery or corruption of those cultures, other peoples were reclaimable, improvable, capable of becoming as 'civilized' as Britons, in time. Neither of these approaches is unproblematical. The second comes within our definition of 'culturist', and reveals an arrogance whose putative connection with imperialism has been noticed already. The former could easily become discriminatory or even racist, if the 'worth' of other cultures was presented as a reason why those living by them could or should not be allowed to be 'enlightened' in a Western sense. Many mid-Victorians fell into one or other of these traps. There were also, however, positive aspects to both outlooks.

There were many exceptions to these 'charitable' views throughout our period, including some quite developed racist ideologies, especially in scientific and elite circles (Thomas Carlyle and the ethnologists are examples, though their influence is difficult to trace lower down the social scale), as well as in two particular cases. The first concerned the *most* 'primitive' peoples—American 'Indians', South African Bushmen, and Australian aborigines were usually the three unlucky losers—who were widely reckoned to be doomed. The argument here was that these peoples had dropped too far behind in 'progress' to be able to catch up before the more advanced, but also more wicked, white man (for Europeans, especially colonists, were not presumed to be *better* than other peoples) wiped them out.[65] Whether they were *capable* of progress was a moot point, but also merely an academic one; in all likelihood they would never get the chance to find out. The second major exception was a temporary one. At certain times, and at two in particular, the reported savagery of certain groups of non-Europeans, highlighted and sensationalized by the press for its own purposes, shook the confidence of many of the mid-Victorian middle classes in the ultimate salvation of *all* humankind. The Indian 'mutiny' was the first of these occasions. We have already seen the typical way in which schoolbook authors treated that. The second was the Jamaican rebellion of 1865, which provoked this—again typical—reaction from a provincial newspaper: 'We would not say that the negro is incapable of being civilised; but the ease with which he relapses into a state of barbarism forces upon us the conviction that hitherto his moral and intellectual progress has not been such as to justify his claim to rank equal with his Anglo-Saxon brother. Like the elements fire and water, the negro makes a very good servant, but a very bad master.'[66] That came after a report of wholesale butcheries, burnings, dismemberments, and other atrocities.[67] The New Zealand wars unleashed similar devils of the mind.[68] These may represent the dredging up, in extreme circumstances, of deep-laid racial prejudices. On the other hand, they also mirror fears of the British working-class mob, as we have seen.

Even in these cases, however, there were dissenting voices. Disraeli's famous reaction to the Indian Mutiny—blaming it on the insensitivity of the British towards the Indians' natural (and admirable) conservatism—was unusual in the immediate aftermath of the event, and maybe more characteristic of the conservative upper classes than of the liberal middles, but it was picked up by some schoolbooks.[69] Others placed the onus on misgovernment by the East India Company, an obvious target for free traders.[70] In the Jamaican case much of the horror felt against the rebels there was trumped by revulsion against Governor Eyre's equally savage suppression of the revolt, which was the main focus of the controversy in Britain that followed, in which Eyre was both defended and denounced, with Carlyle and Kingsley on the former side, but J. S. Mill and Darwin among those who entered the lists against Eyre.[71] The black rebels had a number of more positive defenders too. Certain traders and missionaries, who *needed* to believe still in their 'improveability', found other ways to explain the horror than in terms of negro depravity: too fast a transition to freedom after 1833, for example; or a lack of missionary influence in certain areas.[72] And later, after the initial shock of these rebellions had receded, people calmed down again.

Apart from these cases, most middle-class Victorians—judging from their popular literature—followed the 'culturist' rather than the 'racist' path, measuring other peoples against themselves in terms of 'civilization', and attributing any differences to cultural environment rather than to some innate superiority or inferiority. South Sea islanders, for example, indulged in cannibalism, Indians in *thuggee,* Chinese in infanticide, Africans in slavery, just about every other race in sexism, and Maoris in—horror of horrors—'communism',[73] because of bad religions and ideologies. Replace these, and the South Sea islanders and the rest would soon be on the right 'progressive' track. All that was required of them was that they open their minds to the new enlightenment. That was what China refused to do, which helps to account for some of the severest attacks upon her.[74] An article in Dickens's *All the Year Round* in 1865 showed what could happen when individual Chinese managed to escape this cultural prison; it describes the transformation that comes over a group of them who emigrate to Australia, whose own culture releases all the natural commercial talents that other commentators, too, have observed in them.[75] Christianity had a similarly 'civilizing' effect on nearly everyone it touched.[76] Former slavery abolitionists, visiting the West Indies after emancipation, professed to see miraculous moral improvements in the black population there, once it was released from—this time a western-imposed—tyranny, and allowed to take its chance as free agents in the marketplace.[77] This inspired hope for probably the majority of the early and mid-Victorian middle classes, who, because they needed to, took this to be the way of the world.

The alternative approach—cultural tolerance or relativism—seems to have been less common at this time by comparison with both earlier and later periods, but could still sometimes be found. It was relatively unproblematical in relation to Europeans. 'Was the British constitution fit for every soil?' asked Henry Bright in 1823, objecting to the Radical Joseph Hume's complaint at the government's allowing Dutch law in South Africa. 'Could the laws of one country be transplanted to another, to the advantage of a people who had been accustomed to a very different system? Certainly not. The best system of law was that which agreed best with the habits and manners of a people.'[78] Similarly with reference to the French Canadians, Lord John Russell in 1838 thought that Britain should adapt to 'the peculiar usages, the peculiar wants, the religious habits, and the peculiar aptitudes of the people over whom they ruled'.[79] But the French and Dutch—whatever their other failings—were at least white. Tolerance of this kind towards non-European cultures is found less often, especially among the culturally confident middle classes. There was some genuine admiration for Indian and Chinese intellectual and cultural achievements, despite their strangeness.[80] Some commentators thought that India and China surpassed Britain in these respects, though that could be a double-edged compliment coming from the philistine middle classes. More 'primitive' cultures also had their champions.[81] Many writers, especially those with intimate, first-hand experience of foreign places, were aware of and warned against the superficial judgements of their cultures that could be made by travellers with no real empathy, and a tendency to use western yardsticks too rigidly. A reviewer in the *Quarterly Review* in 1840 castigated one author for basing his view of the whole of China on only a fleeting visit to Canton, a city that was deeply untypical, having been corrupted by foreign influences.[82] In 1834 the (more downmarket) *Penny Magazine* printed a translation of a poem written by a Chinese visitor to London, the charming misrepresentations in which, it suggested, should serve as 'a warning to English and other travellers' to China, whose ignorance of the local 'language and institutions' often gave rise to similar errors.[83] Even what today is widely vilified as 'orientalism' was distrusted by some (there is a nice satire on it by George Augustus Sala—best known as Dickens's co-writer on *Household Words*—in a short story he published in 1860).[84] The Victorians knew that these were difficult questions, and quarrelled over them endlessly. This is why we cannot generalize about their 'racial' attitudes.

Sometimes the quarrelling could become quite fierce. Dickens, for example, strongly objected to the admiration he saw around him for Chinese civilization and (worse) Bushman culture, represented by the travelling shows that were so fashionable at this time (the 1850s), and which provoked in him several outbursts that read like 'racism', though it was probably not as simple as that. Here he is writing about the 'noble savage', whom he refuses to see in this light at all: 'I call him a savage . . . a howling, whistling, clucking, stamping, jumping, tearing savage . . . cruel, false, thievish, murderous; addicted more or less to grease, entrails, and beastly customs; a wild animal with the questionable gift of boasting; a conceited, tiresome, bloodthirsty, monotonous humbug . . .', and so on. What Dickens objected to here was the reactionism implied in these culturally tolerant views of 'native' cultures, which he believed threatened enlightenment and progress more generally. He compared them to the prejudices of Tories who regretted the passing of the 'good old times' at home.[85] It was dangerous sentimentalism to laud this kind of thing. Drooling over African squalor because it was picturesque would only perpetuate squalor in England. It was also, of course, inherently patronizing. (It is not much of a compliment to be told that you are happy because you have not yet had to cope with the challenges of 'civilized' life.)

Dickens—one of the few nineteenth-century English 'canonical' novelists in touch with a wider circle of society than just the literary elite—typifies a widespread, though not universal, mid-Victorian middle-class attitude on this matter. It was an attitude that stemmed not from the middle classes' experience or awareness of empire, but from much more native ideological roots. It was applied consistently to continental Europeans as well as to non-Europeans; they too were patronized, regarded as being 'behind' Britain in their social and political development but capable of emulating her, and warmly congratulated when they did.[86] It was also applied to Britain's own working class, which was seen as 'improvable' in much the same way: the assumption that lay behind the Gladstonian Liberal party's policy of enfranchising the latter *gradually*, as they showed signs of 'deserving' the vote. Essentially that meant becoming more like the middle classes themselves,[87] which was also the most important difference between the middle-class view of the workers and that of the upper (or ruling) class. The same basic outlook informed their views of other 'races'. Middle-class Britain was seen as being in front, rather than on top; other classes and peoples as being behind rather than beneath: a progressive view, rather than a static, hierarchical one. This is a crucial difference. We have seen the part that middle-class education played in this; especially the history that at least some of them were taught, emphasizing Britain's own rise from barbarism to civilization. But education was probably not at the root of it. The middle classes regarded other peoples as 'improvable' because they needed to, for reasons that were just as 'functional' to them as other ideologies were for their compatriots in the field.

At bottom this came down—again—to free-trade ideology, which was important in this connection in two ways. On a practical level, the need to trade cheaply with other peoples required the existence of other peoples who were *capable* of trading with Britain, without the burden—the cost and the distraction—that ruling them would require. In the settlement colonies these were the European emigrants, who performed this role at almost no expense at all to the metropolitan economy. (It may not be too cynical to suggest that this was partly why the native Americans, Bushmen, and Australian aborigines who shared these colonies with them were—metaphorically and literally—trashed.) Elsewhere, however, and especially in Africa and Asia, it was necessary to believe that the Africans and Asians could sustain this role themselves, otherwise the prospect lay ahead of aeons of burdensome intervention. But that was not all. Free trade was justified on other, more elevated grounds. It was *mutually* profitable, which is what stopped it being merely a self-serving philosophy—though it was that as well. It functioned as a vehicle for spreading 'enlightenment' (or 'civilization') in the world, and furthering there the kind of 'progress' that Britain had achieved for herself over the course of the past 2,000 years. The Victorian middle classes needed to believe that, too. Some of them were aware of the hypocrisy that could be said to be involved in this view. Yes, admitted the *Illustrated London News* in 1842, there *was* terrible suffering and injustice in Britain too, especially among the unemployed; something the 'charity begins at home' brigade (including Dickens) had been urging for years. But 'no amount of domestic wretchedness can banish from the bosom of our country the impulses and sympathies which she would fain shed round in beautiful humanity upon all the world beside.'[88] (Whether that satisfied the charity-at-homers cannot be known.)

On the 'culturist' front, the middle classes tried not to make it seem as if Britain was trying to impose her own peculiar customs on the world. Their version of 'enlightenment' had a plausibly objective look to it. The aspects they usually emphasized were personal liberty, education, openness, respect (not equality) for women, peace, and the absence of tyrannical government and arbitrary law. Put like that—vaguely and theoretically—these had the appearance of universal values. They were also—this was where history came in again—inevitable, and so did not need to be imposed. Lastly, these values were undoubtedly at odds with conditions the Victorians could really see in many less 'enlightened' parts of the world. These were the standards by which the middle classes claimed to judge both themselves and other people, and to which they believed both could aspire. Even if the Victorians were inconsistent (which they probably were), and deluded about the objectivity of these values (which they may have been), the latters' effect on attitudes was substantial, and substantially *different* from what a more extraneously based ideology—one based on literal racism, for example, the belief in ineradicable differences; or genuine imperialism, the desire to dominate—would have had.

This could have been merely a pretence. All these high-sounding 'progressive', 'universalist', and 'culturist' notions may have cloaked an instinctive racism and imperialism beneath. It would not be altogether surprising if this were the attitude of many Britons in the early and middle 1800s: naturally xenophobic, perhaps; ignorant; peppered with negative images of non-Europeans in their cheap magazines, sideshows, and other forms of popular entertainment; and unreceptive to the subtler messages that many of their schoolbooks, for example, were endeavouring to impart. The argument here, however, has been that this did not have to be so. The counter-influences were also powerful. Most Britons did not approach these questions of race and empire out of nowhere, their minds a *tabula rasa,* but came to them carrying significant ideological baggage, derived from their situations ('functions') in British society, which gave them a particular and, as it happened, very un-xenophobic perspective on these matters, and which could have impacted at least as much on their racial attitudes as did the empire or anything connected with it. The empire had surprisingly little influence on the early and mid-Victorian middle classes' views either of other races or even of the empire itself. They were too self-confident as a class, and two expansive as a nation, for that.

❦❦❦

The ways the empire featured on the national political stage in the early and mid-nineteenth century mirror this. The House of Commons—mainly middle class, and increasingly so as the century wore on—debated colonial affairs, of course, as it was bound to do, being ultimately responsible (together with the Lords) for the running of the empire. Big issues like slavery, emigration, the Canadian rebellions, the Maori Wars, and the Indian Mutiny and its aftermath provoked large-scale debates. In between, the Commons spent between 10 and 15 per cent of its time discussing colonial matters.[89] That does not indicate any great neglect. The middle classes' parliamentary representatives, therefore, were kept abreast of what was happening in the empire. But it did not *affect* them greatly. In most respects these debates were notably *un*-imperial. The colonies were discussed from a very British agenda. There was no 'imperialization' of British politics generally; none of what many liberal-minded Britons always feared during the entire lifetime of the empire: that Britain's despotic rule in the dependent colonies would bring (as the elder Pitt put it) 'not only Asiatic luxury, but, I fear, Asiatic principles of government' in its train.[90] For those among the middle classes reared on the classics, there was an unsettling precedent for this: the transition in ancient Rome from *res publica* to *imperium*, which most English commentaries of the eighteenth and early nineteenth centuries associated with civic decline.[91] Some cited more contemporary European examples.[92] There may be a case for saying that civic decline became one of the unwanted legacies of empire much later. But as yet British politics was scarcely touched—and certainly was not changed—by the empire. Domestic 'British' ideals and values ('discourses') proved more powerful.[93]

One reason for this is that parliamentary liberals were on the outlook for this effect of imperialization, and resisted it. Miles Taylor argues that this was the main reason for their taking an interest in the empire at all.[94] They did not want Britain corrupted by this kind of imperialism: what one might call the 'empire strikes back' effect. This formed the basis of their case against some who *had* been imperialized, for the worse, out in 'the field': against Lord Torrington for his cruel and, it was claimed, 'un-British' over-reaction to a minor rebellion in Ceylon in 1848, for example (it had included the execution of a Buddhist priest in full religious garb by firing squad for allegedly communicating with the rebels);[95] and against Governor Eyre for his much more notorious repression of the Jamaican revolt of 1865. The campaign against slavery partook of some of that same spirit: the elevation of 'British' liberties against an essentially alien philosophy of rule. In all of these cases the imperial tyrants (Eyre, Torrington, the slaveowners) gathered champions back in Britain, most of them obvious racists; but they were ultimately powerless *in Britain* (not in the colonies) against the liberals, which was all the latter were bothered about. If the liberals had been more concerned for the empire and its subjects they might have done more to ensure that such atrocities could not be repeated; that the systems of command or the frame of mind[96] that gave rise to them, for example, were modified. But that would have meant taking a constructive interest in the empire *per se*.

On other colonial questions the same British priorities dominated. Emigration was nearly always debated as a domestic issue, a solution to the problem of poverty and the dangers of civil unrest at home, rather than for the way it could build up the settlement colonies. The major argument was about whether 'shovelling out paupers'[97] would really solve Britain's overpopulation problem, or would the poor simply breed more (*à la* Malthus) to fill the gaps? Even those who were genuinely concerned about the colonies focused on this aspect of the issue in an attempt to win the majority over.[98] (They could still pursue the colonies' interests—for example, in not just getting the mother country's 'dregs'—behind the scenes.)[99] The Navigation Acts were abolished purely for British reasons, and against what many colonists perceived to be their own interests. When British North America was debated (aside from the emigration issue) it was usually in the domestic context of saving British taxpayers' money (spent on its defence), opposing 'jobbery', and—again—preventing a despotic form of government there that might be used 'as a fulcrum for the lever of oppression at home'.[100] Occasionally imperial issues were used simply as sticks to beat governments with. There are suggestions of this in the 1848 Ceylon case, and in debates over the Canadas.[101] For the empire itself, however, few liberals and radicals seemed to care a fig.

This is reflected in the debates themselves. Usually only a small and select number of experts, or 'crotchet-mongers',[102] took an active part, most of whom were marginal figures in parliamentary terms. Their numbers actually diminished during the first half of the century; one reason for this was the abolition in 1832 of 'pocket boroughs', which had been one route by which 'colonials' (that is, those with colonial trading interests) could become MPs before.[103] Colonial debates had the reputation of being boring,[104] and were thinly attended as a result. 'The introduction of any subject connected with Indian affairs', wrote one observer in 1840, 'acts as a spell in clearing the benches of either House of Parliament.'[105] Twelve years later little had changed. 'Next to Indian questions,' claimed a contributor to the *Westminster Review* in 1852, 'none are so unwelcome to parliament as those which affect the colonies.' In 1870 the same Review reprinted these words verbatim, on the grounds that they still applied.[106] Often colonial debates had to be 'counted out' because they were inquorate.[107] In 1833 Macaulay complained that even on great issues, like the revision of the East India Company's charter, the attendance in the House of Commons was less than 'on a turnpike-bill'.[108] In April 1849 there was actually a debate on the *lack* of debate in the Commons on colonial issues. It ended inconclusively.[109]

Nor was there much enthusiasm shown for the empire in the debates that did take place. MPs—like most of their compatriots—rarely used the *word*, in connection with Britain's overseas possessions at least. Occasionally they allowed themselves some modest self-congratulation at the growth and spread of their *colonies*, which Sir Robert Peel, for example, believed augmented 'the glory of England' tremendously;[110] but that was rare, and usually intended to refer only to the 'settlement' type of empire. This sort of pride was felt as much by politicians who favoured colonial self-government as by those—like Peel—who wanted to preserve the imperial tie; it was the spread of British 'freedoms', that is, which was the source of it, rather than of British rule. 'There is no more legitimate kind of national pride than that which exults in viewing our country as the parent of many nations', said the Irish nationalist MP William O'Brien in 1840, including the United States in this encomium explicitly.[111] Even Richard Cobden—by reputation the arch anti-imperialist of the day—went along with this: 'He was not opposed to the retention of colonies ... He was as anxious as any one that the English race should spread itself over the earth; and he believed that colonization, under a proper system of management, might be made as conducive to the interests of the mother country as to the emigrants themselves.'[112]

What proportion of MPs actually favoured colonial self-government (or 'separation') is difficult to estimate, because no vote was taken on the issue in parliament, and because many thought the question was academic, as separation would happen in any case.[113] There were certainly some outright separatists: such as Sir Isaac Coffin, MP for Ilchester, who in 1822 considered Canada to be such a drain on Britain's resources that 'it would have been a good thing for this country' if it had been 'sunk to the bottom of the sea'; but fewer, probably, than later pro-imperial Conservative propaganda maintained. (Coffin himself was more American than British).[114] A more common attitude may have been this one, expressed by Lord Derby in a later Canadian debate: 'I am one of those who would deeply regret that separation, although in the course of time I anticipate it, as the natural result of the growth and progress of democratic principles.'[115] Others favoured a halfway house, which in retrospect looks very similar to the twentieth-century ideal of the 'Commonwealth': 'an empire of communities', or 'a union of co-equal states', as the *Edinburgh Review* put it in 1870.[116] Most of the positive support that was expressed for the empire *qua* empire in the early and mid-Victorian years in these high political circles—and there was precious little of it—was for this sort of concept. Other kinds of imperial pride—in British conquests, for example—were more often than not dismissed at this level as 'vainglory'. Thomas Macaulay called them 'childish'.[117]

India is a case in point. As the largest of Britain's possessions in terms of population, largely conquered by British arms, and ruled directly by British men, it should have formed the central focus of any contemporary enthusiasm for 'imperialism' in this sense. India, of course, came up in debates in Parliament, but usually only among a small number of experts. In the reviews that the political elite read it featured less than the settlement colonies, and hardly at all if we exclude articles which are more about India's history, culture, and ethnology than about the British link.[118] In pieces about the empire more generally it is usually treated as an anomaly.[119] No doubt British India's history as a 'private' enterprise before 1858 had something to do with this. From the written record it seems to have impressed foreigners more than Britons: including some (usually Frenchmen) who condemned it,[120] and a Swedish diplomat, Count Magnus Björnstjerna, whose paean to it published in 1840—'one of the most extraordinary phenomena in the history of the world'—contrasts sharply with what appears to be the contemporary British disregard.[121] Even among 'educated Englishmen', noted one reviewer of Björnstjerna's book, 'India is almost a *terra incognita*... the ignorance and indifference which prevail concerning it are well nigh incredible'.[122] According to later commentators this indifference even survived the Mutiny.[123] It was almost as though the rulers of India were frightened of publicity, in a Britain that they could not entirely trust to tolerate their methods of rule if they were brought more directly to its attention. Some Victorians were certainly not impressed, even upper-class ones, by the common ruling argument that some races, like the Indians, had to be governed by others, like the British, for their own good:

'the argument of every despot', as the *Edinburgh Review* put it in 1846.[124] The Indian empire was certainly anomalous in terms of many other Britons' boasted *liberal* values. For both parties there was clearly a lot to be said—in terms both of the Raj's authority and the British people's illusions—for not making the contradiction too plain.

We must not forget the more positive and obvious imperialists: Eyre's defenders, for example; the upper-class paternalists; and the men in parliament with colonial interests.[125] Most of these, however, felt they were on the defensive, out of step with the majority of educated opinion, whether this view was justified or not. This certainly applies to Thomas Carlyle, whom Catherine Hall credits with 'changing the discursive terrain' in Britain in the 1840s by speaking 'the unspeakable', rather like Enoch Powell's 'Rivers of Blood' speech did in 1968,[126] but whose influence was almost certainly far narrower than the latter's. Carlyle in fact would have been surprised—and even possibly irritated—by how seriously he is sometimes taken today as a spokesman for his own age, when he regarded himself as heroically embattled against it. The failure of his highly idiosyncratic imperialism to catch on widely may have been partly due to the emotional and irrational style he chose to express it—'Brave fathers, by valiant blood and sweat, purchased for us, from the bounty of Heaven, rich possessions in all zones; and we, wretched imbeciles, cannot do the function of administering them?'—which did not strike many chords in this self-consciously rational age.[127] Most other proud imperialists expressed their creed more soberly. Usually they also deferred to liberal opinion more than did Carlyle. The British ones (unlike the corrupted Eyres and Torringtons) were far more sympathetic to other 'races', for example.[128] Their excuses for empire were gentler. They also rarely used them to advocate *enlarging* the British empire. Imperialism of this kind was all but dead.

* * *

All this was at the level of 'high' politics. This was one way in which middle-class people could become acquainted with the empire, and even—a few of them—interested in it. It brought them close to the imperialists' world. But this does not mean that the middle classes in general shared this interest. The widespread view at the time, on the contrary, was that MPs' constituents were by and large ignorant of the empire, and unconcerned about its fate.[129] Sir William Molesworth—an imperialist himself—even felt that this was natural. 'The people of a mother country', he said in 1838, 'are necessarily uninterested and unacquainted with the affairs of their remote dependencies.'[130] 'Remote' is the operative word here. It clearly refers not only to geographical distance, but also to most people's lack of any sense of a personal and material stake in the colonies. No one carried out any kind of systematic canvass of opinion on this issue at this time, so we cannot tell how sound this estimate was. In a fictional one, for what it is worth, covering the Marylebone constituency in the later 1860s, Anthony Trollope's young political hero Phineas Finn, in his first ministerial job as colonial under-secretary—chosen because it was considered one of the lowest positions in government—found that '[n]ot one man in a thousand cares whether the Canadians prosper or fail to prosper', though they did care 'that Canada should not go to the States because, though they don't love the Canadians, they do hate the Americans'. Trollope knew his constituency politics—he once stood for parliament as a Liberal—so this may not be entirely a guess.[131] It seems to be borne out by the striking lack of local agitation—political meetings or demonstrations—over any colonial issues apart from slavery and emigration (the latter usually organized by middle-class colonizers in an attempt to persuade the working classes to leave, so not really part of the political process) for the whole of the early and mid-Victorian period. It was almost never an issue in elections.[132] This contrasts with the hundreds of meetings called over other political questions: electoral reform, labour laws, religious tolerance (usually against it), 'freedom' in Europe, slavery in the United States, and so on. (So it was not parochialism that held them back.) The Victorians were not undemonstrative, but they seem never to have demonstrated over the empire until the 1880s, at the very earliest. Catherine Hall's claim that '[i]ssues regarding the empire inflected this public political life directly and indirectly', seems unsupported by any empirical evidence from her own case study (Birmingham, 1830–67), though the use of such an imprecise word ('inflect') obviously leaves room for manoeuvre here.[133] Most indications are more negative.

Of course, this lack of active interest *could* be a sign that the Victorian middle classes were perfectly happy with the way the empire was. There was, after all, no popular agitation against it either. Middle-class imperialism may have been simply sleeping, waiting for a more insightful politician to wake it up. By many accounts that politician was Disraeli, who in the 1860s calculated that here was a seam of potential support for the Conservatives that might trump the Liberals' conventional support among the lower middle classes, and even the (small) working-class constituency enfranchised for the first time by his own Parliamentary Reform Act of 1867. If that was so, then he thought he knew the buttons to press. Pride in the empire was one, so he made some vague references to that.[134] Some Liberals joined in too. In 1867 E. W. Watkin, an 'independent' Liberal MP, reckoned that less than 1 per cent of the British people supported the separatists.[135] Even the working classes, claimed Robert MacFie, another Liberal, who was also a sugar refiner, were deeply concerned about 'the relations between the mother country and her colonies'.[136] (No doubt his own workers were more conscious than most of their connection with the West Indies, in particular.) Either the elite had got it wrong before then, or public opinion had completely veered around. Whichever it was, Disraeli thought it a useful stick to beat Gladstone's Liberals with. The story was that they had been plotting to get rid of the empire for years. 'If you look to the history of this country since the advent of Liberalism—40 years ago,' Disraeli told Conservatives at a famous banquet in the Crystal Palace on 24 June 1872, '—you will find that there has been no effort so continuous, so subtle, supported by so much energy, and carried on with so much ability and acumen, as the attempts of Liberalism to effect the disintegration of the Empire of England.'[137] That is supposed to have touched a patriotic and imperialistic nerve that was either new, a product of the 1860s; or had always been there, but hidden.

In fact nothing certain about this can be inferred from the famous Conservative electoral victory that followed in 1874. The empire was not the only issue on which Disraeli appealed for the people's support. At the Crystal Palace, for example, he also offered them social reform, which may account for any working-class votes he managed to garner more than his stance on colonial questions.[138] There is no way of telling. His colonial policies during the ensuing administration—even including his celebrated 'victory' over the Eastern Question in 1878[139]—could not save the Conservatives when the next election came around. Indeed, insofar as the empire played any part in that (1880) contest, it seems to have been Gladstone's view of it that went down best. His line was that it was the Liberals who had done most for the unity of the empire, by decentralizing it, and so cultivating the colonists' affections; whereas Disraeli was actually endangering it, by seeking to accumulate new possessions which added 'no strength at all' to the whole.[140] At any rate, that was what the people voted for. This could either have been because they went along with this very different kind of imperialism, or because the issue was not all that important to them.

❦❦❦

It is difficult to generalize about the middle classes. It would be surprising if it were otherwise. The term covers a wide range of very different interests, from professional people and great industrialists, through shopkeepers and clerks, to the skilled craftsmen and women who were strictly just out of the middle class's range, but were associated with it through ties of 'respectability'. Individualism was supposed to be their forte. The upper classes had their public schools to encourage *esprit de corps*; the working classes their common sense of exploitation. (Neither attitude was all-embracing, but both bound their respective classes to an extent.) The middles felt less solidarity. They had certain vague aspirations in common, like respectability, and some shared ideals, like 'freedom', but nothing that indicated a clear-cut, class-based position on the issues that are the subject of this book. 'Freedom', as we have seen, certainly did not do it. It led many of the middle classes to believe that they were non- or even anti-imperialist, but that could have been because they misunderstood what imperialism was. That depends in turn on what *we* think imperialism was, or is.

Three important generalizations, however, can be made. The first is that the early and mid-Victorian middle classes were not *demonstrative* imperialists. They rarely mentioned their empire as such, either to laud or to criticize it. The impression that comes through most of their literature is that they did not conceive of it *as* an empire at all. Maybe that is why they did not colour-code it on their maps. They sometimes took an interest in imperial issues, like slavery and the Indian Mutiny; but almost never in the imperial *dimension* to them. Slavery, for example, was discussed in terms of morality and economy alone. When India is featured in magazine articles or other media, except with reference to the Mutiny, it is sometimes difficult to tell from them that she is ruled by Britain at all. There are almost no middle-class expressions of pride in the empire generally from this period: in the fact, that is, that Britain exerted such widespread domination abroad. Perhaps people were just being modest. Obviously this does not indicate that they disapproved of the empire, otherwise there would have been more signs of that, too. The likeliest explanation is that they simply did not think about it. If they *were* imperialists, therefore, it was without knowing it.

The second general point is that the middle classes were selective about which aspects of what *we* call imperialism they did take pride in. The settlement colonies were the main ones: extensions of Britain's free institutions, as they saw them, to the waste places of the world. Often the United States was included here, equally with the colonies that Britain still ruled, which indicates that it was not the ruling aspect of them that people took pride in. Usually it was their rugged, radical independence; which is also why the upper classes were less enamoured of them. What really puffed up the middle-classes' chests, however, was the vast spread of Britain's trade overseas, which is sometimes regarded today as a version of imperialism, but was seen then—because it was 'free', supposedly—as almost its antithesis. Some of the non-settlement colonies could be justified as serving this trade: coaling stations, trading posts, and the like. In these cases, again, their imperial characteristics—their ruling structures, governors, district officers, soldiery—were largely ignored. Other colonies were regarded as unfortunate survivals from a less enlightened past, like the West Indies; or simply with incomprehension, like India. India was a problem to the middle classes. There is little sense in these sources that they felt they 'owned' her, identified with her government, even after 1858. That was the upper classes' province.

Thirdly: middle-class attitudes to the empire, such as they were, arose not *from* the empire—were not essentially imperial ideas, that is—but from more home-grown ideologies, rooted in the middle classes' domestic rather than their imperial functions. We have seen how this applied to their racial thinking in particular: much affected as it was by their reading of their own history, which gave them the idea of 'progress' from savagery to 'civilization'; which was then applied to other cultures to explain the (temporary) differences between them. This again marks them off from the upper classes, whose view of human categories—home-based again, but from a radically different viewpoint—was more static. For the middle classes, their own national past told them all they needed to know about the 'Other', and their present condition about the state to which all those foreign 'Others' (with a few unfortunate exceptions) could aspire and would eventually attain. That could be used to justify imperialism, though this by no means followed; nor did it follow from the rival and more strictly 'racist' view that peoples were essentially different. (There was arguably no need for imperialism if other peoples were bound to 'progress' in any case; and no point in it if they could not.) What it could affect was the *kind* of imperialism that was espoused or excused. In the middle classes' case that tended to be more 'liberal'. That was the only way that many of them could live with the empire. The empire itself had little impact on this. When they looked at it, they saw it through spectacles manufactured, and rose-tinted, almost entirely at home.

There are two lessons to be drawn from this. The first is that imperialist policies do not need to have cultural origins which are distinctively imperiali*stic* in any way. Almost any domestic ideology will do. Racism, fascism, religion, capitalism, and socialism are obvious examples; libertarianism—the Victorian middle classes' dominant dogma—is certainly another. (Even *anti*-imperialism can turn into its opposite.) None of these *has* to mutate into imperialism; but they all have the potential to do so. What determines this is usually material circumstances, rather than cultural; a country's *actual* relations with the outside world, which nearly always come before the rationales that are invented for these. These sorts of 'motives' are always excuses in retrospect. Even when such a mutation occurs—this is the second lesson—there is no need for imperialism to react on the home culture significantly. In the case of early and mid-nineteenth century Britain it is hard to see the empire having any significant impact on the dominant middle-class discourses at all. That will have been a relief to many contemporaries: those who feared the 'empire strikes back' scenario. All the traffic went the other way: the empire, or perceptions of it, may have been affected by middle-class ideas, but not vice versa. The same applies, as we shall see in a later chapter, to their literature and art.

6
Not in Front of the Servants

Whatever else it may have been, the British empire in the early and mid-nineteenth century was not a 'people's' empire. Those who say it was, or that imperialism pervaded British culture and society generally during this period, are simply wrong. Either that, or they are deliberately excluding the 70–80 per cent of people who made up the Victorian *working* classes: much as the Victorian middle classes did, of course—'culture' was generally taken to mean 'high' culture then, and one of the commonest usages of the word 'society' was simply to denote people high up the social scale.[1] There is no direct evidence that this great majority of Britons supported the empire, took an interest in it, or were even aware of it for most of the century; whereas much circumstantial evidence points the other way. That evidence includes their life situations, which left them little time for such awareness; their own testimony, which rarely mentions the empire; their education, which almost never featured it; and the clear lack of interest among the upper—and more imperialist—class in sharing its empire with them.

* * *

If the latter had wanted to instil imperial knowledge and patriotism into the working classes, the schools were the obvious means. That is how national achievements and values are usually disseminated. In extreme cases it is done through ceremonies at the beginning or end of the school day: saluting the flag, singing patriotic anthems, reciting oaths of allegiance, and so on.

Another way is through the teaching of particular versions of history and selections of national literature. According to Edward Said, this is the bane of 'all known systems of education today'.[2] If that is true of the present, however (which seems likely), it was emphatically not so of the large majority of British schools during most of the nineteenth century. Patriotism, in any form, even the most cleverly disguised, was simply not taught there. It follows that a regard for the empire was not either. In fact the topic was deliberately avoided. This may have been a unique feature of the British educational system, by comparison with all other European and American ones at this time.[3]

One reason is the poor standard of education for the working classes generally. Some children did not attend school at all before 1870. When they did, it was usually at voluntary or Sunday schools, probably for two to three years each (intermittently) on average, and not beyond the age of 11.[4] That did not leave much time to get anything valuable (let alone patriotic or imperial) into them. The poor quality of the teaching is notorious from the novels of the period, but is also corroborated in autobiographies.[5] It was provided almost exclusively by people who were just a little ahead of their young pupils in knowledge, and of the same social class.[6] In 1870 education was made compulsory in Britain up to the age of 11, and the first state (or 'board') schools were built; which seemed however to make little difference in this regard. Teachers had the reputation of being incompetent, certainly before 1870: the 'refuse of other callings', according to Thomas Macaulay; 'discarded servants, or ruined tradesmen; who cannot do a sum of three; who would not be able to write a common letter; who do not know whether the earth is a cube or a sphere, and cannot tell whether Jerusalem is in Asia or America.'[7] In County Durham they allegedly included 'the halt, the maimed, the drunken, even the idiotic'.[8] Physical conditions in schools were squalid. Teaching was basic and by rote.[9] Some contemporaries thought education at this level was literally worse than useless. One mid-Victorian school inspector claimed that 'at certain schools he could tell pretty accurately by the pupils' faces how long they had been at school. The longer the period, the more stupid, vacant, and expressionless the face.'[10] Matthew Arnold's famous description of what he found in the schools he inspected in the late 1860s corroborates this: 'a deadness, a sickness, and a discouragement ... If I compare them with the schools of the Continent I find in them a lack of intelligent life.'[11] Perhaps we should be chary of accepting all such contemporary criticisms at face value, and as typical.

There may have been some fine teachers. In Wales and Scotland, where the profession was at least respected, there certainly were. But it is difficult to disregard altogether the remarkable unanimity that exists as to the inadequate standard of at any rate English schooling at this time.[12] That is one reason why we should not expect the Victorians to have been made aware of the empire (or of almost anything else) in their schools; especially if Macaulay's ignoramus (not knowing where Jerusalem was) was wielding the chalk.

There was more to it, however, than simple incompetence. One of the reasons why the workers were not educated more broadly and interestingly was that it was not their 'place' to be. British education in the nineteenth century followed class lines quite rigidly. (Some would say it still does.) That explains why, when the Victorians started to feel serious concern about the state of their education in the 1860s, they set up not one Royal Commission to inquire into it (as most countries would have done) but three: one for the lower classes, one for the middle, and the third for the public schools.[13] As one of these declared quite baldly: 'the different classes of society, the different occupations of life, require different teaching.'[14] Robert Lowe, an ex-vice-president of the Education Department, put it thus: 'The lower classes ought to be educated to discharge the duties cast upon them. They should be educated that they may appreciate and defer to a higher cultivation when they meet it, and the higher classes ought to be educated in a very different manner, in order that they may exhibit to the lower classes that higher education to which, if it were shown to them, they would bow down and defer.'[15]

One of the implications of this view, of course, was that the working classes should be educated *less*. '[A]ny attempt to keep the children of the labouring classes under intellectual culture after the very earliest stage at which they could earn a living', as another education chief declared at around the same time, 'would be as arbitrary and improper as it would be to keep the boys at Eton and Harrow at spade labour.'[16] Nearly fifty years later that was still a respectable opinion to hold. 'Shorthand', wrote the journalist Harold Gorst in 1901, 'is not a very promising preparation for the plough; and French and mathematics are equally valueless accomplishments for the carting of manure. Dairymaids need neither history nor geography; they can even do without grammar.'[17] To be fair, many of the workers themselves agreed. 'Look here, youngster,' Frederick Rogers reported one of his workmates telling him in the 1860s, 'we don't warnt eddication, we warnts work.' That was apparently a common view.[18] There was also a theory doing the rounds that this difference was genetic.[19] Some of these rationales may have been covers for deeper, political fears. One working man, recalling his education in the 1850s and 1860s, thought he detected a 'certain distrust of general literacy' then, on the grounds that it could be 'dangerous'.[20] This is what the agricultural workers' leader Joseph Arch also suspected in 1898: '[t]he less book-learning the labourer's lad got stuffed into him, the better for him and the safer for those above him, was what those in authority believed and acted up to'.[21] 'Is it going to turn the heads of ploughboys,' asked *The Times* of a proposed broadening of the curriculum in 1880, 'and make them look down on their destined walk in life?'[22] That would seem to vindicate Arch. It would set them thinking, warned another educationalist in 1881, and that kind of thing could put a nation 'in an abnormal state'; 'There should be underlying all movement and political activity, a settled respect for law and a feeling that law once made must be obeyed.'[23] To instil that was the main function of schools for the labouring poor, at least as seen by those above them socially. Hence their different education from the other classes, and their different views of empire, as of just about everything else.

This also had obvious implications for citizenship; which was an alien concept in Britain in any case. Britons—unlike contemporary French and Americans, for example—were 'subjects' for a reason. 'Citizen' had alarming undertones of equality, and even revolution: 'aux armes, citoyens!'[24] So the upper classes shied away from it. This situation was clearly not likely to nurture an equal sense of Britishness. In fact, as Brian Simon writes: 'The educational system of England... far from being designed to encourage common experiences and a common culture, has operated to enhance, and even to exacerbate, already existing social differences and experiences. Far from being a solvent, it became a separator...'[25] This is crucial. It explains not only why there were different cultures in Britain, but also why those cultures were unlikely to appeal to the empire, or any other national symbol, to bring them together. The whole strength of the British system relied on its different sections' being complementary but apart. This is easiest to see at the top and the bottom of the social hierarchy, where public schoolboys learned to rule and serve those beneath them, and lower-class children to obey and serve (in another way) the men at the top. None of this required either class to be taught to serve its *country*. It was assumed that the best interests of the country would be best served if each class performed its social role aright. National unity was to be achieved by attaching the classes to each other, not to a greater whole. This obviously devalued citizenship-enhancing subjects like history and literature, and made the empire irrelevant, for this purpose at least.

There were two further reasons to be wary of trying to inculcate 'patriotism' in children of this class. One was idealistic. Nationalism (the obvious prerequisite for patriotism) was felt in certain liberal quarters to be anachronistic. It was also believed to be the prime cause of wars. Another of Richard Cobden's visions for the future had all nations withering away, and people becoming one; then there could be no more war. This may be one reason why patriotism was so rarely recommended in the middle classes' schoolbooks.[26] One or two openly advised against it. 'A love of one's country is certainly a commendable feeling,' conceded *Chambers's Information for the People* in 1841, 'but it should be a love arising from examination and conviction, not from prejudice.' Other countries deserved respect, whatever we might think of their internal arrangements. We might, after all, be wrong. National allegiances were only practical conveniences in any case, scarcely different in kind from a dozen other forms of contractual arrangement: 'The nation is but a composition of many families, knit together by kindred sentiments and mutual wants.'[27] That removed any spiritual or mystical reason for patriotism. That was the *principled* anti-patriotic argument. But there was also a more cynical one.

This was that patriotism could be dangerous. It was regarded in the eighteenth and much of the nineteenth centuries as a profoundly anti-authority ideology (hence the Tory Dr Johnson's famous jibe: 'the last refuge of a scoundrel'). Patriots—'your prating Patriots', as one loyalist propaganda organ called them[28]—were people who believed in the defence of British liberties against British governments which were trampling them underfoot. This bore on the subject of history in particular, because the problem was partly seen in historical terms: the 'liberties' were Anglo-Saxon, the 'trampling' being done by the Normans who had taken over in 1066 and still—in the persons of the aristocracy—ruled.[29] For radical patriots history showed how far Britain had regressed: a further good reason, if one were needed, to steer clear of the subject in schools. Patriotism was problematic, therefore, for those who might want to use it to cement national as against class loyalty; and arguably more so if that national loyalty had an imperial ingredient. For many working people it was the ideal that aroused in them (as one autobiographer put it) 'a sympathy for ... the wronged and oppressed of all countries'.[30] That *might* be squared with imperialism, and was to be later, by other people; but it required a confidence in the British state as a vehicle of that 'sympathy' that no early Victorian proletarian could possibly have. This illustrates a broader point. Educationists were not filling empty vessels; they were confronted by a positive alternative culture (or cultures). Just as the working classes had their own version of history, so they also had their own systems of thought and values in other fields. (Labour and social historians have known this for years, and have even managed to reconstruct them.)[31] That made their resistance to external indoctrination more solid than it might otherwise have been.

In working class ('elementary') schools, therefore, patriotism was *never* taught. The subjects that could have supported it, like history, geography, and English literature, were almost completely absent from the syllabus. (It follows that virtually none of the textbooks discussed in Chapter 4 ever found its way into these schools.) Instruction was restricted almost entirely to reading (often not even writing) and arithmetic, plus Bible morality, the latter designed to make the pupils good and obedient workers.[32] In Sunday schools—where most children in the early nineteenth century may have learned to read and write[33]—the social lesson was sometimes preached quite openly. The radical George Jacob Holyoake remembered the local vicar delivering an address at his school 'in which he counselled young men to be content in the station and with the lot which Providence had assigned them'; Holyoake did not think much of that.[34] After the middle of the century the Bible was largely supplanted in day schools by the new gospel of 'political economy' as the means of inculcating the right sort of morality.[35] (Perhaps the Good Book was thought to be unsound on property.) At a few schools it was bolstered by military drill, designed (initially, at any rate) to inculcate order.[36] This did not prevent a few innovative teachers from introducing other subjects, until that more or less came to an end in 1862 when a new system of funding schools—'payment by results'—only rewarded the 'three Rs'.[37] The direct result was that the schools 'cut off geography, grammar and history lessons', as an official report put it in 1865.[38] Occasionally, wrote one school inspector, these subjects might 'still occupy their places upon the "timetables", and that I fear is all'.[39] Between 1867 and 1900 the utilitarian rigidities of that widely unpopular regime were gradually relaxed, enabling other subjects to qualify for funding also, albeit less generously, but without making very much difference so far as the empire-friendly subjects were concerned. One historian calls it 'window-dressing... It cost nothing to enumerate a long list of "specific subjects" which *might* be studied'.[40] In reality the number of children tested in any of these new optional subjects between 1875 and 1895 never exceeded 4.4 per cent (1883), and declined to 2.4 per cent in 1895.[41] The standard of teaching them was low according to school inspectors, one of whom described it as 'like a hideous dream'.[42] One of the reasons is that there were no specialist historians or geographers in teacher-training colleges before 1905, leaving these subjects to 'general' tutors.[43] The end-results in the classroom were a travesty. Nearly all working-class memoirists who bother to mention them at all agree that history and geography were taught boringly and by rote.[44] For a weary inspector in 1879, most lessons he sat in on seemed to 'combine the respective disadvantages of the multiplication table and the Newgate Calendar; being little better than a list of dates and battles, enlivened by murders and other crimes, with a sprinkling of entertaining stories, most of which are no longer regarded as authentic'.[45] This was obviously far from ideal, even for the 2.4 to 4.4 per cent.

Even if these subjects had been better taught, however, it probably would not have done the empire much good. The latter seems to have been far from the minds of those who championed history-teaching in schools, including the most social-controlling of them, whose particular notion of social control had no—or very little—place for it. History was valuable because it taught individual virtue, not, generally speaking, patriotism. Virtue for the lower orders invariably meant deference, though it was not often put as baldly as that. History's part in this was to furnish examples to be emulated, as illustrated by this government advice from a slightly later period:

> To younger scholars History should be taught orally through a series of biographies of typical heroes or heroines. These should be treated in the main with a view to illustrating in the actions of real persons the principles of conduct and qualities of character which promote the welfare of the individual and of society. The lives of great men and women, carefully selected from all stations of life, will furnish the most impressive examples of obedience, loyalty, courage, strenuous effort, serviceableness, indeed of all the qualities which make for good citizenship.[46]

It followed logically, of course, that these role-models did not need to be British.[47] Before the 1880s very few were British *imperialists*, because—as we have seen—these were not considered to be admirable enough. Scarcely any educationalist suggested that boys and girls might derive pride from a contemplation of Britain's colonial exploits.[48] It does not seem to have occurred to anyone that pupils could identify with them. That would have required a sense of common citizenship. Instead, the workers were to be taught their civic virtues, which were a very different thing.

In much the same way geography, which could also have been used to encourage imperial pride, was almost always deliberately parochialized. 'Readers' compiled for country schools in the early and mid-nineteenth century—in lieu of proper books, which such schools could rarely afford—'felt no need to inform their readers of life beyond the rural scene'. Even London was presented as a place best avoided.[49] Pupils were told to map their schoolyards and learn the distances to the nearest towns.[50] Some schools may have had globes or maps; but we have seen that those great world maps with the empire proudly marked out in red that are supposed to have hung on nearly every classroom wall in Victorian times are a myth.[51] Literature, finally, was generally excluded from curriculums because it was 'imaginative', and schools were there to impart 'facts'. (Dickens's Gradgrind really existed.)[52] That stems from another Victorian fixation, for 'utility'. Utility did not have much of an imperial dimension, either.

All this applies to schools for the working classes over which their betters exerted any kind of control, but these were rare. One of the distinctive effects—possibly an advantage—of the free-market anarchy that dominated British education before 1870 was that it gave its customers the power to choose. There is evidence that this enabled working-class parents to influence school syllabuses, for example, against the preferences of their masters. This seems to have been especially true of the Sunday schools, where competition between churches to attract pupils, together with their reliance on working-class teachers, who were unpaid and so could not be pressured to toe any particular line, forced them into compromises with parents wanting their children to be taught only literacy without too much religion; making them often—according Thomas Laqueur—a 'largely working-class institution' in effect.[53] Workers also set up their own day schools in opposition to 'charity' ones, in order to resist what they regarded as pro-capitalist propaganda from their oppressors.[54] After the new 1870 system came on stream, they occasionally captured local school boards.[55] Within schools, truancy, classroom disorder, school strikes, and even 'dumb insolence' have been interpreted as expressions of resistance.[56] Working-class children were not putty, and it is condescending to think of them as though they were.[57]

Then, if all else failed, there was always the counter-influence of the home. 'It is all too easy to forget', writes J. M. Goldstrom,

> when we are looking at the influence of schools on children, that school was one influence among many in a child's life. The nineteenth-century schoolchild spent only a few hours of each day there, and probably left when he was twelve. He came to school from a working-class home where values were often different from those the schools were so assiduously trying to instil in him. With his schooldays behind him he would encounter ideas through clubs, pubs, the working-class press, Sunday papers, trade union meetings and street corner discussion with his friends. Such ideas would be bound to modify the precepts that had been dinned into him at school, and probably only half understood.[58]

Parents knew this. One Nonconformist father, for example, asked in 1861 why he sent his son to an Anglican school, replied that it was because it was also a 'first-rate' one, adding: 'Do you think that if they put anything into the child's head during the day about religion which I did not approve of, that I could not shove it out at night?'[59] That could apply equally to ideas about country, or empire, if they were ever 'put into children's heads' in elementary schools in the early and middle years of the nineteenth century; which however was unlikely, as we have seen.

***

Entirely unschooled in imperialism, it may have been difficult for the working classes to pick it up afterwards. The struggle and narrowness of their working lives militated against it. Work was hard, long, and tiring, with little spare time left over at the end of the day or the week to think of much beyond where one's next meal was coming from. Most working people lived very parochially, venturing no more than a few miles from their home towns or villages through the whole course of their lifetimes, unless it was to join the steady drain of working families from the depressed rural areas to the thriving but hellish new industrial cites, or to disappear abroad. Their horizons were restricted. Thomas Hughes describes the situation in one fictional village in the 1840s (the context is its people's ignorance of India): 'The yearly village feasts, harvest homes, or a meet of hounds on Englebourn Common, were the most exciting events which in an ordinary way stirred the surface of Eaglebourn life; only faintest and most distant murmurs of the din and strife of the great outer world, of wars, and rumours of wars, the fall of governments and the throes of nations, reached that primitive, out-of-the-way little village.'[60] There must have been many places like that, in a Britain that was still more than 50 per cent rural. If these people or their relatives in the city ever became interested in politics, it *had* to be only in the politics of their own class. There was too much to be settled there—questions of wages, working conditions, combination, unemployment, poor relief, possibly (at a stretch) the very morality of capitalism itself—before they could ever think of looking to the 'great outer world'. We have seen that few of them worked 'for' the empire in ways that they could have known about, or encountered its peoples, except in certain dockland areas. Nor did their 'betters' seem anxious to tell them about it. So how were they expected even to learn of it, let alone become imperial enthusiasts?

Reading was not the way. Many of the working classes never learned to read, or forgot how to after they left school (one woman blamed this on having had 'such a big family').[61] Literacy rates are notoriously difficult to compute for any period; the usual measure—the proportion of marriage partners who could sign their names in church registers—may give too rosy a picture, as some had learned *only* to write their signature. They also varied regionally. For what it is worth, however, 42 per cent of English people outside London signed with 'marks' in 1845, falling to 20 per cent in 1875.[62] Contemporary samples taken in Manchester in the 1840s suggest that at least half of all children there left school illiterate; some put it as high as 75 per cent. That automatically rules out a large—albeit diminishing—proportion of the population from even the possibility that they could have been influenced directly by imperial literature. For others, it would have been difficult. There were few free libraries for the working man, except those set up by his 'superiors' in order to 'improve' him, and apparently widely boycotted for that reason.[63] Besides, as the critic Edward Salmon observed in 1886: 'Between the free library and his home, morally and materially, stands the public-house.'[64] The more charitable blamed those long working hours: '[A]s for reading, sir,' says a gamekeeper in Charles Kingsley's *Yeast* (1850), 'It's all very well for me, who have been a keeper and dawdled about like a gentleman with a gun over my arm; but did you ever do a good day's farm-work in your life? If you had, man or boy, you wouldn't have been game for much reading when you got home,—tumble into bed at eight o'clock, hardly waiting to take your clothes off, knowing that you must turn up again at five o'clock the next morning.'[65] Industrial work was no less demanding: 'The working members of the family . . . were too busy earning bread and butter . . . an aspect of things forgotten by better-off people who reprove the ignorance of the poor.'[66] When the working classes did manage to get any leisure time, other attractions competed for it besides books. This was stony ground for any class of authors to scatter their seed upon, imperial or otherwise.

Few of the working classes read newspapers, the usual medium of colonial intelligence, though 'reading aloud', as Jonathan Rose points out, could make up for this.[67] This was especially true in rural areas, like Thomas Hughes's fictional 'Eaglebourn':

> So far as written periodical instruction is concerned (with the exception of the *Quarterly*, which Dr. Winter had taken in from its commencement, but rarely opened), the supply was limited to at most half a dozen weekly papers. A London journal, sound in Church and State principles, most respectable, but not otherwise than heavy, came every Saturday to the rectory. The Conservative county paper was taken in at the Red Lion; and David the constable, and the blacksmith, clubbed together to purchase the Liberal paper... Besides these, perhaps three or four more papers were taken by the farmers. But, scanty as the food was, it was quite enough for the mouths; indeed, when the papers once passed out of the parlours they had for the most part performed their mission. Few of the farm-servants, male or female, had curiosity or scholarship enough to spell through the dreary columns.[68]

As late as the 1880s one north Devon village apparently had to make do with a single weekly newspaper for the whole of it, passed around the cottages and read aloud by any educated child who could be found: 'Rumours might reach us of a war with the Zulus, or the tragedy of General Gordon: but it was all too distant to disturb our sleep, or excite our fear.'[69] In urban and industrial areas, especially those populous enough to support local papers,[70] news was more accessible; which is not to say that it was necessarily accessed. Few working-class memoirs from this period mention serious newspaper reading. A survey of a working-class parish in London in 1843 revealed that 57 per cent of households read no newspaper at all.[71] Women were almost certainly behind the men in this respect. As a result, recalled one 1870s slum child, 'current public affairs hardly touched us. We could not afford a penny a day for a newspaper.'[72] In the towns and cities, however, you did not need to be able to afford a newspaper in order to read it, with copies shared between houses (as in the countryside) and available in libraries, public houses, and clubs. It is this multiple readership which makes it hopeless to try to work out the extent of these publications' influence from circulation figures, which were often small.[73] On the other hand, the same factors that limited the industrial working classes' reading more generally—poor literacy, and exhaustion after hard days' work—undoubtedly dissuaded a large proportion of them from ploughing through the *Manchester Guardian* say, or the *Leeds Mercury*, both solid and wordy broadsheets; or even their 'own'—that is, expressly directed at the working classes, but no less substantial—*Northern Star* and *Reynolds's Newspaper*. Taking all this into account, it must be a safe guess (though still only a guess) that at least half the adult population of Britain was entirely impervious to whatever political intelligence may have been available to it theoretically, until the 'new journalism' boom of the 1880s and 1890s.

This must be borne in mind when considering the periodical literature that was specifically directed at the working classes, and certainly got through to a large number of them. This came in three broad categories. The first was the working classes' own papers, produced by themselves or (more often) their self-styled champions, and usually radical in their politics. The leading examples are the *Northern Star* and *Reynolds's Newspaper*.[74] The second was journals published for them by their 'betters', in order to lead them to Godliness, and—in particular—away from the radical snares of newspapers like the *Northern Star*. Many of these were connected with the churches and the temperance movement. Some had huge printings, which does not, however, necessarily imply a heavy take-up among their target class.[75] (R. K. Webb surmises that the workers generally used them as firelighters, 'or to serve baser but vital domestic purposes'.)[76] The third was the sensational sheets. These have been a constant feature of British literary life since the eighteenth century: cheap periodicals relying for their popularity on a diet of murder, other violent crime, its retribution (executions), war, disaster, torture, pathos, and sex (some were even semi-pornographic, with titles like *Peeping Tom*, *The Star of Venus*, and *Paul Pry*).[77] At various times governments tried to ban them or tax them off the streets. The liberal Victorian alternative was to try to educate their readers into demanding more exalted fare: a strategy, however, that failed. Each decade of the nineteenth century had its own versions of this enduring genre: *Dibdin's Penny Trumpet* in the 1830s, the *Penny Sunday Times* in the 1840s, the *London Journal* from 1845, the *Illustrated Police News*—all murders and hangings—from the 1860s, *Tit-Bits* from 1881 through to the new century, and many more. These were what the working classes read. But it was still only a minority of them.

Not all of these papers covered politics in any depth. The most political were the radical weeklies. They also kept attentive readers in touch with what was going on in the empire. *Reynolds's* and the *Northern Star*, for example, both carried brief, minutely printed syndicated items of factual news from the colonies. From 1852 the *Northern Star* renamed its regular 'Foreign' column 'Foreign and Colonial Intelligence', but without any effect on its content, which remained—like all of its competitors'—overwhelmingly European.[78] Leading articles—the true measure of the importance editors, at any rate, attached to various questions—almost never featured imperial issues, save at times of major colonial crisis, which meant effectively (before the 1880s) only in 1857 and 1865. Most editors were committed Chartists or socialists, with purely industrial, social, and political agendas.[79] Franchise reform, trade unions, the aristocracy, the fall of ministries, freedom movements abroad, and the evils of capitalism and its various products (accidents at work, train crashes, shipwrecks, crime, and so on) dominated their leader pages. One assumes that these were also the priorities of the politically conscious working-class people who subscribed to these papers: about 50,000 weekly in each of these two cases.[80] Even the internationalists ('fraternalists') among the early and mid-Victorian working-class radical community rarely looked beyond Europe, with an occasional glance at the United States. The coverage of George Julian Harney's short-lived *Democratic Review*, probably the least parochial of all these papers, stopped at Hungary.[81] Edward Salmon complained in the 1880s of how 'rare' it was 'to find a working-man's newspaper pointing out the advantage of the colonies to the people'.[82] There were exceptions. The 1860s weekly *Working Man*, for example—motto: 'All Labour is Sacred'—carried features on colonial emigration, which it attacked; 'Indian Ornamentation', which it hugely admired; and a strikingly sympathetic piece on the Jamaica revolt.[83] But this was unusual, most working-class newspapers contenting themselves with only token references to events in the colonies. How these struck their subscribers is difficult to say. A clue may be given by a later reader of working-class origins: 'these were remote from our little sphere, and only affected us like stories in books'[84] (though that 'only' will not cut much ice with those who believe that 'stories in books' are quite powerful enough on their own to turn people into imperialists).

The second group, the 'improving' papers, almost never referred to the colonies. This seems to bear out the point made earlier in this chapter, that the empire was not seen at this time as a means of inculcating loyalty from above. It certainly was not in *Chambers's Information for the People*, a popular encyclopaedia published in weekly parts in 1841–2, designed for the working classes and probably bought by many of the more 'respectable' of them. That had a section describing the British colonies, as it would need to do in the interests of completeness; but without giving them any particular prominence—certainly not lauding them—and mainly concentrating on the 'white' colonies (along with the United States) as potential fields of emigration for its readers.[85] The major leitmotif running through it, in articles on history, geography, law, and politics, for example, is firmly domestic and social, played *tutti* in one issue called 'Public and Social Duties of Life', which covers its readers' duties as subjects, electors, neighbours, spouses, masters and servants, international citizens ('We have no right to insult the feelings of the people of any nation'), and in the face of 'inequalities of rank and condition', which a little reflection will show to be providential and wise.[86] This shows where its priorities lay.

In the more patronizing sheets (Webb's 'firelighters') imperial patriotism was in equally short supply. That was not how the workers were to be kept in line, but by encouraging the sort of conduct in working men and boys[87] that would enable them to serve their 'betters', rather than to serve their country in any more direct way. Readers were taught the virtues—and the benefits to themselves, of course—of hard work, honesty, sobriety, self-control, loyalty (often illustrated with stories of faithful dogs),[88] and self-improvement in exceptional cases, or otherwise contentment with their lot. The same themes are found in the middle-class propaganda pamphlets that came out at this time targeted at the same readership: typically fairy tales allegorizing the truths of political economy, which may have insulted their readers' intelligence.[89] Examples taken from the monthly *British Workman* in the 1860s include: 'The Secret of Success, or, How a Carpenter Rose in Life' (the secret is temperance); 'A Swearer Reproved'; 'Enemies' (socialist agitators); 'Right Wrongs No Man' (against strikes); 'Industry Rewarded'; 'Evils of the Credit System' ('Addressed to the Working Classes, by Uncle David, Author of "Good Servants, Good Wives, & Happy Homes" ');[90] and a remarkable piece on 'Celebrated Africans' who have worked their way up. (We shall return to this shortly.)[91] When national figures feature, especially royalty, it is as exemplars of such qualities, with stress on their devotion to duty despite the hardships of *their* conditions (poor Queen!), and on their spotless domestic lives.[92] 'Imperialists' hardly ever feature—perhaps because their private lives were more spotted—and even then seldom for their imperial achievements. A missionary from India, featured in the *Band of Hope Review* in 1876, for example, reveals nothing about the East or his work there, only that he 'owed everything to Sunday-schools'.[93] A 'Heathen King' from the Sandwich Islands is featured in the same paper only because he has managed to 'forsake the dreaded habit' of alcohol.[94] The absence of imperial and colonial topics *per se* in this genre of literature, in which the middle classes preached to those at the bottom of the social heap, seems extraordinary. Could it have been partly due to apprehension of the way the workers might react to anything relating to emigration, which many of them resented (certainly early in the century), and the necessity for which could be seen as a mark of the failure of the economic system these papers were championing; or to images of the exploitation of other races which it might occur to them to compare with their own treatment at home? Editors of these improving journals clearly could not be confident that their readers would respond to imperial material imperialistically—the occasional mentions of the empire by their radical competitors suggested not.[95] For this reason if no other, it was probably safest to avoid the topic entirely.

The cheaper papers, our final category, mainly eschewed politics, but did feature the empire in other ways. They were led there in pursuit of the sensational, for which exotic locations seemed an obvious source. The first volume of the *London Journal*,[96] for example (1845), carried amongst its domestic and historical horrors (assassinations, tortures, hangings, madmen, ghosts, wars, and a series on the Spanish Inquisition, a subject certainly not chosen for its historical or theological interest) pieces on 'Indian Barbarity and Heroism' in the Sandwich (Hawaiian) Islands, featuring the burning alive and dismembering of an enemy; cannibalism in Polynesia; Australian aboriginal 'superstitions'; scalping and facial self-mutilation by the North American Indians; a 'Barbarous Murder in New Zealand'; and an African journey, with a picture of a man being attacked by what looks like a cross between a sabre-toothed tiger and a hippopotamus.[97] When the same journal came to cover the Indian and Jamaican insurrections some years later, it did not stint on the terror.[98] This was probably how most working-class men and women learned of the empire, if they learned of it at all. Such coverage could also have hardened 'racist' prejudices, especially through some of the illustrations that accompanied these articles.

A note of caution, however, should be inserted here. The ostensible messages of these pieces were far from straightforward. The *London Journal*'s 'Barbarous Murder in New Zealand', for example, was committed by a European, not a Maori. A later report of 'Torture in India' turns out to be about sufferings inflicted on native criminal suspects by British officials in Madras.[99] In the case of the 1857 Indian uprising, most blame is placed at the door of the English, for their lack of cultural sensitivity in a land where 'it is quite possible that the *odium theologicum* has as bitter a seat in the heart of an Asiatic as in that of a European'.[100] (The same cannot be said of the same journal's coverage of the Jamaica revolt.)[101] Features on 'oriental' societies nearly always counterbalance criticism with what is regarded by their writers, at any rate, as praise; though the problem here, as ever, is that they are often judging by 'western' standards. Rare meetings with non-Europeans aroused only mild interest and puzzlement: 'Bean't two of 'em women, sir?' asks a Midlands collier during a visit to his pit by a Chinese commissioner and his entourage—presumably sporting pigtails—in 1866.[102] There is nonetheless a genuine fascination with China in particular, and admiration for its craftsmanship.[103] Sometimes this is the case even when the illustrations prefacing such articles seem grotesque.[104] 'Savages' are almost never portrayed as incorrigibly so, with the 'barbarity' of the Sandwich Islanders, for example, at least partly compensated by their 'heroism', and later by a highly favourable account of their ex-queen Emma, who 'is really one of the most unaffected, dignified, as well as one of the most prepossessing young ladies whom one is fortunate enough to meet in any society of the civilised world'.[105] A piece based on Livingstone's African travels, published in 1857, stresses that 'The nature of man is the same in all ages, whether it be in savage or in civilised life; in Africa, or in Europe; in a republic, or in an empire. There is always a Nimrod, an Alexander, a Caesar, a Napoleon, a Nicholas, or a Moselekatse, among mankind.'[106] That Africans were as capable of 'civilization' as Europeans was strikingly exemplified by an account in the *London Journal* in 1857 of the career of 'Ira Aldridge, the African "Roscius"', as a Shakespearean actor: 'the only member of the sable human family who has ever been known to make an appearance on a British stage.' The illustration accompanying this shows him, inevitably, as Othello (with Charles Kean as Iago); but the article also stresses his versatility, his astonishing success in America and all over Europe as well as in Britain, and the medal for Latin composition he was said to have won at Glasgow University.[107] This is not a unique case: later articles portray 'negroes' as doctors;[108] large-scale planters and ship's captains (this in explicit response to those who were claiming that they were genetically inferior);[109] and as kings, great military men, and philosophers. 'Enough has been said', concluded the last of these pieces, 'to show that the

African is capable of excelling in any human pursuit.'[110] This was just three years after the Jamaica revolt. These are neither 'racist' images, nor particularly 'imperialistic' ones. There is just a hint of social empathy in them, by oppressed workers in Britain for their similarly exploited brothers and sisters overseas. On the other hand, we should perhaps not infer too much from just a few articles scattered in periodicals which were probably—especially those provided for the working classes by their 'betters'—not very widely read.

As well as this, 'empire-related', which is what most of this material was, is not the same as 'imperial'. Exotic locations do not necessarily imply an interest in British rule there, any more than, they do in boys' adventure stories, as will be argued later. From these working-class periodicals it is often difficult to tell which of the locations featured are 'British' and which not. India, for example, is treated as a foreign country in much the same way as China, the bulk of which was never a formal British colony and which managed to resist even 'informal' imperialism successfully until 1900. It was the exoticism that was important, not the imperialism. There is little pride expressed in Britain's possession of those countries which were colonies, and there is rarely any feeling that readers were being encouraged to identify with them. They seem distant, not only geographically but also psychologically. On the rare occasions when the colonial tie is alluded to, it is often critically, even implicitly anti-imperially. This may be because the working classes associated the empire with their rulers rather than with themselves. This can be no more than a hypothesis, but it would be natural in a country with no idea of a common citizenship embracing all classes. It might explain both the sympathy shown in working-class papers to Indian natives and (sometimes) West Indian blacks, who shared with them a common oppressing class, and also the marked lack of enthusiasm for colonies like Australia and Canada, which were widely regarded at that time less as lands of opportunity than as places of bitter exile.

❦ ❦ ❦

After all this, it is not really surprising to find so few references to the empire in working-class autobiographies from this period.[111] They certainly do not enthuse over it. Most are too parochial for that. When they do look abroad it is usually to the continent of Europe or to America, which clearly appeared far more exciting and possibly (given their nationalist and anti-slavery movements, for example) more sympathetic.[112] Hardly any of them mention any imperial connections, apart from, very occasionally, relatives and neighbours who have either emigrated (and usually vanished without a trace) or suffered in military service abroad. There is almost no mention of imperial events, or of the empire-related 'shows'—dancing Hottentots and the like—that are sometimes assumed to have made such an impression on people. 'O great and glorious empire!' exclaims Tom Barclay in his 'autobiography of a bottle-washer', but only as an ironic comment on the poverty and filth he sees around him in England, which he claims are worse than among the Papuans and Basutos.[113] (Perhaps he learned about these from one of the shows.) Charles Manby Smith, a journeyman printer, has a brief dig at missionaries, who should stay back in Britain to help his sort, he thinks, rather than trying to 'prevent Quackoo from griddling his grandmother'.[114] The casual racism implied in that comment is not uncommon, but is certainly not overtly imperialistic: rather the opposite. Less casual allusions to other races are more often complimentary than otherwise, like George Jacob Holyoake's assertion that it was intelligent Zulus who converted the notorious Bishop Colenso to free thought.[115] Non-Europeans hardly ever feature directly, obviously because there were so few of them around in Britain at this time. All in all, allusions to anything related to the empire or the colonies are extremely rare.

This may have something to do with the intrinsic nature of autobiographical evidence, which is unlikely to be generally representative. This certainly applies to working-class memoirists, who, if they had leisure to write, were able to do so, and thought the effort worth making, were almost bound to be set apart from their fellows. Nearly all nineteenth-century working-class autobiographers were men,[116] and a high proportion were political radicals. Holyoake is an example; no one would take him as typical. Also over-represented in autobiographical accounts were those at the very bottom of the social heap.[117] Among the middle classes, the literati were obviously more likely to write about their lives than practical women and men. It also may be a general rule, covering all classes, that writers are less likely than the normal run of people to be mindless xenophobes. That would put the imperialists at a disadvantage. Most memoirists had particular agendas. The literati were mainly interested in tracing their own individual cultural development, to which far-off imperial events will have seemed irrelevant, whether they really were or not. For most of the working classes their purpose in writing was to show what everyday life was like—in particular, how hard it was—for the working class. That, after all, was where their expertise lay, and was the thing their readers would presumably be most interested in. It follows that if they did have views on imperial or any other broad, extra-labour political matters they might not think it worth mentioning them. In this way the signs of 'imperialism' could very easily be left out of their accounts, and evidence of subconscious imperial attitudes—imperial mentalities they were scarcely aware of, perhaps because they were too deep-seated—would certainly be. This is why the horse's mouth may not be the best guide to what the majority of horses really felt.

Nonetheless, the evidence, such as it is, does suggest a rather low level of imperial commitment—consciously, at any rate—among the working classes in the first three quarters of the nineteenth century. Most of them cannot have known enough about the empire to have had an informed opinion of it at all. That still leaves room for prejudice, of course, which can do perfectly well without knowledge; but would at least require the working classes to be *aware* of the empire, which many seem not to have been, in any significant way. It was certainly far from the main concerns and priorities of most of them, which were likely to revolve around other issues entirely: mainly how to improve their lives, their relations with authority, and so on, *collectively*. It was in order to prevent that kind of dangerous speculation that their 'betters' concentrated, in the education they provided for the working classes both in school and through 'improving' literature, on drumming into them the need for discipline and obedience as a class, rather than for loyalty as citizens. Hence the almost complete lack of any kind of imperialist propaganda, explicit or hidden, directed to the working classes in this period from 'above'. Another good reason for that lack was that, as a class, they were politically irrelevant in any case. The working classes were not part of the political nation. Although they comprised a huge majority of the population, they had no parliamentary vote, at least until Disraeli enfranchised a minority of them in 1867. So it did not matter what they thought about anything, except the issues they might riot about; which *never* included colonial policy, as we have seen. They could be safely left to stew in their imperial ignorance, therefore; until almost the end of the century, when many more of them were given the vote, and as a result needed to be cultivated by imperialists, as well as by others. How their previous imperial disengagement managed to stand up against this new propaganda, we shall discover later on.

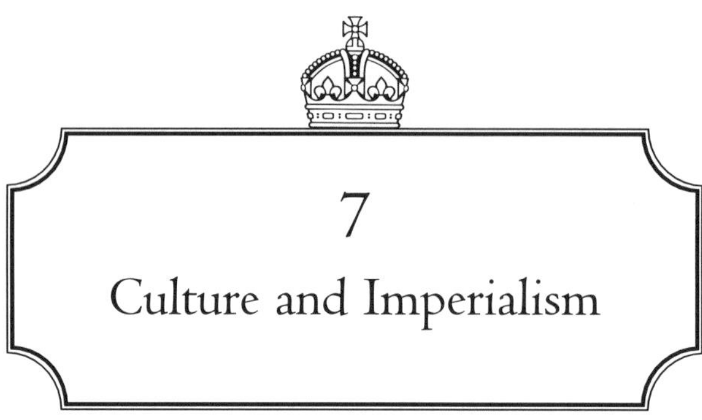

7 Culture and Imperialism

With the empire featuring so little in the concerns of the great majority of early and mid-Victorians, one would not expect it to be reflected prominently in the arts and literature of the time. Of course it left traces. Almost every Victorian novel, for example, carries a reference or two to a colony, or a colonial people, or emigration, or someone who has worked in or for the empire in some way. (We have met with one already: Trollope's *Phineas Finn.*) This is scarcely surprising, considering the sheer length of most contemporary novels; authors would have had to make a deliberate effort to exclude all imperial allusions—and why should they want to do that? Most such references however are marginal, and would not be missed. The same is true in the other arts. There are almost no 'good' books, poems, paintings, sculptures, musical compositions, or great buildings from the early and middle years of the nineteenth century that have a significant imperial component to them: works that one cannot imagine still existing almost identically if the British empire had never been. In this respect at least, art truly reflected the society around it.

That is not something that should be taken for granted. Culture in this 'high' sense may not be a reliable mirror of society in any place or time. This certainly applies to the cultural artefacts that have 'survived' to the present day, in the sense of still being valued. There are rules governing such 'survival'. Most of the Victorian literature that has survived, for example—the 'canon'—has done so not because it was the most popular at the time, or necessarily the most typical, but because it is judged to possess a 'quality' of some sort that transcends its time. That might even make it atypical. This is why it is fundamentally unsound to generalize about British culture in the broader sense, on the basis of these works of culture in its narrower sense: from what in an earlier chapter I (as a historian) called 'mere' literature. Novelists and other artists, even great, timeless ones, certainly cannot be divorced from their surrounding cultures. But they may not reflect the *majority* culture of a place or time. If they did, they might not be so timeless, or so great. So the fact that they so seldom took on imperial or empire-related themes in this period signifies little on its own. There could be special reasons for that.

There were. 'Art' and society were in conflict in nineteenth-century Britain in many ways. Large swathes of British society were essentially philistine, and distrusted 'high' culture *per se,* supposing it to be 'effeminate' and parasitic. In some quarters this prejudice extended to any kind of intellectual pursuit.[1] It was found among all classes: working-class parents resisted schooling for their children, because it was held to be 'useless'; there was a pervasive myth among the middle classes that their nation's industrial supremacy had been built on the practical skills of ignoramuses unfettered by book-learning;[2] and the aristocracy was notorious for its preference for hunting, drinking, and wenching over any intellectual pursuits at all. Such philistinism could even be a matter of pride. The converse of intellectuality was not foolishness, but 'common' sense and practicality; hence Thomas Carlyle's depiction of the English as 'of all the Nations of the world at present ... the stupidest in speech, [and] the wisest in action',[3] which was intended as an unalloyed compliment. On their side, many artists and intellectuals took a far from friendly attitude towards the utilitarian middle classes, which explains why those classes are grossly under-represented in the 'best' literature of the day, or else are caricatured in it (as in Dickens).[4] This is one obvious area in which 'high' culture, if relied on alone, must give a seriously misleading impression of the gamut of British society. And that is without even considering the huge working class, whose lives and concerns were barely reflected—except patronizingly—in this culture at all.

Imperialism could have been excluded for similar reasons. It was a field of action, not of art or thought; of crude physicality rather than sensitive feeling. The true literati spurned it for this reason, out of a kind of snobbery, claims Martin Green.[5] Again, however, the feeling was reciprocated. 'Book-learning is not business', the imperialist Charles Kingsley has Sir Francis Drake say in *Westward Ho!*; 'book-learning didn't get me round the world; book-learning didn't make Captain Hawkins, nor his father neither, the best shipbuilders from Hull to Cadiz; and book-learning, I very much fear, won't plant Newfoundland.'[6] In Carlyle's eyes this entirely explained what he, too, saw as the lack of an imperial culture and literature in Britain: 'thy Epic, unsung in words, is written in huge characters on the face of this Planet—sea-moles, cotton-trades, railways, fleets and cities, Indian Empires, Americas, New Hollands: legible throughout the Solar System.'[7] Empire was its own art. It did not need literature and the rest to celebrate or support it, and might even do better without them. The early twentieth-century musicologist Cecil Forsyth thought there was an innate contradiction between imperialism and (in this case) music. In Britain, empire-building diverted energies that might otherwise be poured into music composition,[8] hence her poor showing as a musical nation. The obverse of this was that the more Haydns you had, the fewer Havelocks. One could not both write—or paint, sculpt, or sing—and be imperial.

So, 'high' culture is an unreliable guide to society at large. It follows from this, of course, that nothing should be inferred from Victorian culture's lack of a significant imperial component: contemporary society could still have been imperialistic in spite of this. In that case, one might still expect the imperialism to surface occasionally and accidentally, perhaps 'between the lines' of the culture of the day. It could even be implied by culture's *silence* on these matters, which Patrick Brantlinger (referring to the novel) claims is testimony to a sense of popular imperial confidence: 'That the early and mid-Victorians did not call themselves imperialists . . . suggests merely that they did not feel self-conscious or anxious about their world domination. They could be imperialists without subscribing to any formal doctrine, so thoroughly were the patterns of expansion and hegemony established at home and abroad.' For Brantlinger, the imperial discourse 'was continuous, informing all aspects of Victorian culture and society.'[9] It did not need to be expressed at all in the culture of the time; indeed, the less it was expressed, the more it could be shown to have been assimilated. This is a disturbing notion for an empirical historian, but it is plausible. Another view is Edward Said's suggestion that the purpose of such cultural neglect was to demean the empire's subjects by marginalizing them: 'regulating and confining the non-European to a secondary racial, cultural, ontological status', for imperial ends.[10] Elsewhere he suggests it was done so as not to *upset* the empire; the 'main purpose' of this 'novelistic process' was 'not to raise more questions, not to disturb or otherwise preoccupy attention, but to keep the empire more or less in place.[11] (But that implies—does it not?—that people might not be so willing to support the empire if it were kept less quiet.) The main point is a fair one. The cultural evidence does not speak for itself, but needs to be interpreted.

If we grant this, which is reasonable, and also—but for the sake of argument only—that nineteenth-century culture *must* have reflected an imperial discourse, there are a number of possible ways of teasing the latter out. One is by looking for the code words and concepts that betray imperial preoccupations, or can be interpreted as being related to imperialism in other ways. Martin Green chooses 'adventure': '[t]o celebrate adventure was to celebrate empire, and vice-versa';[12] and (though this seems more far-fetched) 'jewel' imagery, which is apparently what shows up Shakespeare as an 'imperial writer'.[13] Others have recourse to John MacKenzie's concept of an 'ideological cluster' of concepts which, he claims, surrounded British imperialism later in the century—militarism, monarchism, hero-worship, the cult of personality, and scientific racism[14]—in order to justify branding these phenomena as sure indications of an imperial mentality, wherever and whenever they may be found. (MacKenzie himself gives no sanction for doing this.) Other concepts have been added to the 'cluster' since, including masculinism and chivalry. The purpose is to reveal the hidden imperialism in many apparently innocent nineteenth-century cultural artefacts; like holding a page of invisible writing in front of a fire.

There are problems with this approach. The first is that MacKenzie's 'cluster' is by no means complete. Nineteenth-century imperialism took many forms, some expressions of which bear almost no trace of any of the elements of this particular 'cluster' at all. It would be perfectly possible to compile an entirely different, and far less fascist-sounding, list to suit what later came to be called 'liberal' imperialism, for example; including internationalism, a belief in racial equality, 'culturism' (as opposed to racism), libertarianism, paternalism, altruism, and even pacifism, at a pinch. People holding these beliefs could justifiably call themselves imperialists too. The second problem with Mackenzie's 'cluster' is that each of its elements could exist independently: you could be a militarist, say, without believing in the British empire or its expansion. People could, and usually did, support the Volunteer movement, for example, or military conscription, for entirely defensive reasons (invasion scares were frequent).[15] They could worship peace-loving heroes. Queen Victoria could have been venerated for many of her qualities, quite apart from the fact that she was (as the coinage put it)

'Ind. Imp.'. Later we shall see that there were important *domestic* motives for being racist. Chivalry could be harnessed to all kinds of causes: St George and the dragon later became the logo of the Bradford Independent Labour Party. So MacKenzie's list is by no means an infallible guide to the presence of imperialism in any cultural production. That presence can never be taken for granted, but needs to be demonstrated in every case.

For there to be the presumption (without proof) that these characteristics did indicate an imperial mentality, one of two things would be necessary. The first would be to establish from other sources that the empire was indeed a widespread preoccupation in Britain, which would make it likely to leave significant traces in her culture. We have seen that this cannot be assumed (to put it no more strongly) for the nineteenth century before around 1880. The second approach is semantic: we can define 'imperialism' in such a way as to include these phenomena *by* definition. Imperialism can then be seen to essentially embrace not only physical conquest or control, but also MacKenzie's cluster, plus travel, exploration, mapping, an interest in non-European cultures, and a host of other features which imply (so these broader imperialists say) a wish to imperialize the world *conceptually*.[16] The point has already been made that there is nothing 'wrong' with this: if one chooses to define a bird as anything that flies, then it is entirely permissible—albeit not very practical—to include wasps as well. Short of that, however, it is surely wiser to be cautious when looking for imperial signs in any narrower sense among the cultural remains of nineteenth-century Britain, both 'high' and 'low'. They certainly cannot be taken as read—or seen, or heard.

* * *

The novel is one of those areas of British culture that always used to be thought of as relatively empire-free; until, that is, the cultural theorists cracked the code. 'No Victorian wrote a good novel about the colonial world', wrote Jonah Raskin in 1971.[17] George Watson agreed: the classic English novel was invariably 'metropolitan or regional'. Even if one included the period of Kipling and Conrad, '[t]he intellectual and imaginative impact of British imperialism in its greatest age surprises by its moderation, and one might also say by its triviality'.[18] Mentions of the empire were nearly always incidental and minor. Generally it was pressed into service as a mere literary device, typically as a place to put leading actors in when they needed to be removed from the main action for a while. 'In

Victorian novels,' writes Raskin, 'the colonies are usually places to transfer burned-out characters, or from which to retrieve characters when they were needed. They are especially convenient for the beginnings, turning-points and endings of fiction. The plot began—or flagging interest was revived—when a character returned from abroad, and the action terminated when the characters left for the colonies.'[19] This is hardly an elevated role. The colonial aspect is rarely central in such cases, and might easily be replaced: Magwitch could have been locked up in Wormwood Scrubs rather than sent to Botany Bay;[20] Guy Mannering did not have to have served in India (he seems to have brought very little of it back with him to south-west Scotland, where the bulk of Scott's novel is set);[21] Sir Thomas Bartram did not need to be a West Indian slave-owner (Edward Said's analysis of *Mansfield Park* makes a great deal of this)—indeed, there is no clear indication in Austen's text that he was.[22] If novelists had not had the colonies to banish their ne'er-do-wells to, they could easily have found somewhere else. Occasionally they did. At the end of Trollope's *The Way We Live Now*, for example, Lady Carbury's feckless son Felix is packed off to East Prussia, in preference to Australia, where it is feared he might 'kill himself with drink in the bush'.[23] Other imperial allusions are trifling: a metaphor here, a splash of colour there; most nineteenth-century novels could be stripped of them with very little loss of meaning or effect. (They would be most missed in *Jane Eyre*.)[24] That at any rate is how it looks on the surface, before the code-breakers have started their work.

Whatever may lie hidden beneath this surface, then, it must be significant that these 'serious' novelists were not more explicit about the empire. There are some exceptions. Charles Kingsley's historical *Westward Ho!* (1855), originally intended for adults but essentially a children's book,[25] is one. There is a minor genre of unambiguously adult novels set in India, like Philip Meadows Taylor's fairly celebrated *Confessions of a Thug* (1839); but most of these are by Anglo-Indians, and can be seen as products of that peculiar culture (Kipling was to be another), probably not intended for the same kind of market as *Pride and Prejudice* or *Vanity Fair*. (*Confessions* is very gory.)[26] Most other leading novelists, however, avoided the colonies almost perversely. Even when such allusions might seem entirely natural—difficult, indeed, to avoid—they often were avoided. One example is Anthony Trollope's *The Way We Live Now* (1875), whose anti-hero, Melmotte, is an international financier based in London; one would surely expect him to have *some* colonial stocks in his portfolio, but apparently he does not. The overseas speculation that brings him down is a Mexican, not an African, railway.[27] We cannot blame ignorance for this omission, certainly in Trollope's case: he travelled extensively in the colonies—he had a son who farmed in Australia—and even wrote non-fiction books about them.[28] Dickens too wrote about Canada;[29] and Charles Kingsley visited Trinidad. Little of this knowledge, however, found its way into their novels. This was not due to parochialism: at least one 'serious' novelist made a healthy living from books that are mostly set on the European continent,[31] while Dickens, Thackeray, and others were never chary of sending their characters to France or Germany, and—what is more significant—following them there.[32] Europe and America are far more visible in Victorian fiction than Britain's own possessions abroad. It seems remarkable that colonial allusions were either so absent from the literature of the time, or (if one takes the 'Saidist' view) needed to be so heavily disguised.

Fiction was not the only non-imperial form of literature. Poets cold-shouldered the topic too.[33] So did the 'serious' theatre, none of the secondary works on which—including a book entitled *Acts of Supremacy: The British Empire and the Stage*—is able to cite a single play from this period on an overtly imperial theme.[34] All theatre plays were supposed to be submitted to the Lord Chamberlain for censorship in the nineteenth century; the surviving lists of these suggests that very few related to the empire in any way.[35] Catherine Hall, looking for much imperial references in early and mid-Victorian Birmingham, can come up with nothing apart from *Uncle Tom's Cabin,* which does not count as 'imperial', and a 'Vocal and Pictorial Entertainment' at the Odd Fellows' Hall in 1853 entitled *An Emigrant's Voyage to and Travels in Australia,* which should probably not count as serious theatre.[36] The silence is deafening.

As for the hidden imperial signals claimed by the code-breakers, many of these appear speculative at best. That Heathcliff in *Wuthering Heights* was modelled on a negro ex-slave living in Emily Brontë's Yorkshire is an interesting idea, but is not necessary to explain the character.[37] That Bertha's violence in *Jane Eyre* symbolized the fears of the Jamaican plantocracy of black rebellion is merely conjectural.[38] The idea that Sir Walter Scott really meant India when he wrote about eighteenth-century Scotland seems fanciful.[39] The claim by one of its modern editors that Anthony Trollope's *The Eustace Diamonds* is an essentially imperial novel, mainly on the grounds that its anti-heroine Lizzie's shortcomings are intended as a metaphor for the colonial enterprise, could do with at least a scintilla of evidence.[40] Edward Said's famous 'post-colonial' deconstructions of *Mansfield Park* and *Great Expectations* in *Culture and Imperialism* (1993) surely put more weight on very incidental aspects of their plots than they can bear.[41] Apparently these aspects exemplify the 'hegemony of the imperial ideology' in Britain; the 'massive influence' of India on all aspects of British life; the 'overwhelmingly more powerful and successful pro-imperial culture that took Britain over from the mid-19th century'; and the 'virtual unity of purpose on this score' that came to affect all classes, and both genders, towards the end of the century, from which 'scarcely any dissent, any departure, any demurral, can be found.'[42] But they can only be said to illustrate all of this if one brings these assumptions to them at the beginning; which seems not to be justified by all the other evidence.

What these sources tell us more about are the literati themselves and their readers. These writers were aware of other countries and peoples, and of Britain's relations with them, whether they saw the latter in 'imperial' terms or not. Most of them probably tolerated the empire, though that is not certain, because of the nebulousness of the concept at this time. We know that some writers—Trollope, Dickens, and Kingsley, for example, and beyond them Carlyle and Ruskin for brief moments—were interested in it;[43] but Dickens resented it as a distraction from social issues, and Trollope was a separatist. Other writers will have been totally unconcerned about it, in common, as we have seen, with the majority of their compatriots, who had no pressing need to take much notice of it. There was obviously no great public demand for empire novels, otherwise Trollope, surely—with his acute antennae for the market—would have responded to it.[44] In refined intellectual circles there was clearly a certain prejudice against colonial subjects, deriving from the perception that the colonies were barbaric, certainly by comparison with Europe (including even European foreigners), and so peopled by characters who could not be expected to share the 'cultured' thoughts, feelings, and sentiments that were necessary to sustain great literature and art. These included rough white colonists, of course, and also Americans. (Trollope's novels feature a number of these, but mainly as a foil for European refinement.)[45] The common stereotype of 'colonials' in certain educated British circles has always been culturally disparaging.[46] In this sense the marginalization of the empire in nineteenth-century fiction may well indicate a condescending view of them.

There are condescending views of other 'races' too, but these are too thinly scattered, and varied, to generalize from.

We certainly cannot generalize on the basis of this kind of evidence about British nineteenth-century society and culture as a whole. The English literature that is generally studied today was produced by an elite, for a minority. Far fewer contemporaries read the 'great' Victorian novels than is often assumed: 'Not more than 4 per cent of the people here . . . ever heard of my writings', Thackeray wrote to Dickens when he was campaigning to be elected MP for Oxford in 1857; 'Perhaps as many as 6 per cent know yours, so it will be a great help to me if you will come and speak for me.'[47] It is difficult to believe that he got the figure right for Dickens, but 4 per cent may well be fairly near the mark for other classic novelists. Sales figures—though it is difficult to know how to interpret these, bearing in mind multiple readership, libraries, and pirated editions—bear it out.[48] How this minority of readers and the elite who wrote for them stood in relation to the rest of British society, including the other elites within it, is problematical. We have already shown how unlikely it is—because of class divisions—that they could have represented the majority of people. Their cultures were just too different. On the question of imperialism, this of course can cut both ways. There was no market for empire-related novels among the 'cultured' classes; but this could have been one of the things that cut them off from the majority.

The same could be true in other cultural fields. If the canonical literature of the time is a poor guide to the state of domestic imperialism or empire-awareness, the other fine arts are worse ones. Even more than literature they were minority tastes: art in Britain, wrote a contemporary, 'is little more than a dead corpse, galvanised into spasmodic life by a few selected practitioners, for the amusement and delight of a small section of the specially educated classes'.[49] In fields such as painting, sculpture, theatre, and music, British nineteenth century culture does not bear comparison in breadth and achievement with that of contemporary continental Europe and Asia. Not everyone regretted this; indeed, like the prevalent anti-intellectualism of this period, it was a matter of positive pride to some. Art was regarded as effeminate, by contrast with 'manly' pursuits like building bridges, running factories, or simply making money. One middle-class philistine even saw it as basically primitive: only 'backward' countries, like the least 'progressive' of Britain's neighbours, still bothered with it. It was something a nation grew out of in its capitalist maturity, like toys.[50] Carlyle's remarks about Britain's 'Epic' being written in her world-wide material achievements rather than in works of art express the same point. Though by no means a universal feeling, this was a potentially oppressive one, and meant that artists felt could feel unappreciated and marginalized. Often they responded to that by marginalizing themselves all the more, like the *fin de siècle* aesthetes. Others tried to over-compensate, as we shall see. In neither case can such artists be taken as representative of any other group or ethos in British society, any more than the literati can, irrespective of whether their work can be read as 'imperialistic' or not. This point applies to the 'fine' arts, at this 'higher' level. It may not apply to more popular forms of art; or to the particular case of architecture, which differs from the other arts in being necessarily more practical and public, and is also a field where the Victorian British arguably did excel for a time.

'Serious' ('classical') music can be dismissed almost entirely as an imperial or imperialist medium. There *was* music in Britain in the nineteenth century, despite Oscar Schmitz's famous dismissal of 'das Land ohne Musik' in 1913. Little of it, however, prior to Elgar, has stood the test of time. This may be for deep cultural reasons ('Great musicians are things to be ashamed of', Elgar is said to have told a pupil in the 1890s);[51] or it might have been an accident. What if Thomas Linley had not drowned freakishly in 1778, or Samuel Wesley (the elder) not banged his head in 1787?[52] Musical traditions are not so strong in most countries as to be able to withstand interruptions like these. After a time British music-lovers came to persuade themselves that Britons were almost genetically incapable of writing or even performing 'great' music, which loaded the dice against any of their compatriots who might want to try. (Singers apparently used to Italianize their names in order to be heard.)[53] This may also explain why a disproportionate number of nineteenth-century 'British' composers were Irish.[54] Most serious music heard in Britain was imported from Germany and Italy, and so was highly unlikely to be British-imperial;[55] but native music was no more so. The continental forms that mediocre British composers aped (symphony, concerto, sonata, etc.) were seldom conducive to imperial themes. Even if they had been it would be difficult to be sure that they were intended this way. 'Absolute' music is notoriously difficult to attach to political concepts, even where a composer explicitly mentions one.[56] There are no peculiarly imperialist intervals, keys, or even orchestrations. We need words to be sure: either libretti, or the titles of orchestral works. When we come to late Sullivan and Elgar we do have one or two 'Empire marches' and the like. Before this, however, there is virtually nothing.

This is hardly unexpected in the case of church music, the genre in which most of the best British music between Boyce and Elgar was written. That mostly took the form of settings of religious texts, few of which can be regarded as imperial, even allegorically. It may be more surprising that not one out of 3,000 English operas composed between the seventeenth century and the present day has a colonial setting, in view of the attraction, one would have thought, of India or the South Sea islands for romantic plots and exotic tunes.[57] 'Classical ballet', writes Jeffrey Richards, 'likewise eschewed the Empire.'[58] Of other works with titles—songs, oratorios, named symphonies, descriptive overtures, and the like—a hunt through authorities like *Grove* throws up virtually none before the mid-1880s with any imperial resonance.[59] A very minor composer called John Pridham wrote piano 'divertimenti' and marches describing major events of the day in graphic terms, several of which, by the nature of things, were empire-related: *The Battle March of Delhi* (1857), *The Abyssinian Expedition* (1868), and *The Ashantee March* (1874). (The *Abyssinian Expedition* contains an Ethiopian 'War Dance and Song', the words of which are 'Ya ha yah ha yah ha'.)[60] Otherwise there is nothing.[61] Interestingly, continental composers, especially the French, were not nearly so coy: they took up imperial subjects and oriental styles with enthusiasm.[62] This is where British concert and opera audiences will have got most of their 'orientalism' from. So far as the native scene was concerned, however, music was yet another no-go area for empire.

Again, the possibility arises that British musicians did not so much ignore the empire, as allude to it more subtly. They composed their share of marches, for example, though no more than most other nationalities; and 'militarism'—if that is what marches represent—is not a sure pointer to imperialism. Few British marches before Elgar, though, have imperial themes.[63] Sullivan's stirring 'St Gertrude' (1871), though ostensibly a hymn tune, comes closest to this, with the clear crusading implications of the words it was composed for, 'Onward Christian Soldiers', which could have made it a favourite of missionaries out to culturally colonize the world.[64] Otherwise British nineteenth-century music is noticeably less bombastic than, say, contemporary German or Austrian. There were some patriotic pieces, but again patriotism does not necessarily imply empire-loyalty, as we have seen. Nor, emphatically, does the protestantism that inevitably appears in much English church music of the time, despite Jeffrey Richards's attempt to harness this to MacKenzie's 'imperial cluster', which of course would bring reams of additional music on board.[65] Most 'serious' British music of the time was about love, landscape, or sheer abstract beauty. Possibly one might infer an imperial arrogance—as with literature—from the fact that it did *not* display more interest in other cultures, but remained stubbornly Eurocentric in its musical styles and subject-matter; but on the other hand if it *had* embraced exoticisms it would probably now be regarded as imperially patronizing. Since Edward Said's influential *Orientalism* in 1978, artists have not been able to win on this issue.

Three possible explanations for the neglect remain. Jeffrey Richards's—following Martin Green's line on the literature—is that 'serious' composers were simply too snobbish to want to dirty their hands with what they saw as the crude and plebiean sentiment of imperialism. This is why the most overt imperial allusions appear in more popular forms of music, whose practitioners had more of 'an eye to the market'.[66] We have already met the second explanation: Cecil Forsyth's idea that imperialism drained composing energies away. The third possible solution is that the composers really did reflect their times, and were not interested in the empire because the majority of British people were not. This seems unlikely in view of their peculiar 'elite' situation in British society, but it could still *happen* to be true. Later we shall take a look at one or two more popular forms of music, to see if this may have been so.

❦❦❦

The same neglect of empire is found in the visual arts. Both fashionable and avant-garde painters preferred other subjects. The most celebrated nineteenth-century British 'schools' today are the early romantics, especially Constable and Turner, and the Pre-Raphaelites. The former confined themselves almost exclusively to landscapes. Turner travelled abroad for some of his, but never to a British colony. The Pre-Raphaelites' aim was to return to earlier ideals of 'truth' in art. They also often chose medieval subjects for their narrative paintings, which automatically ruled the British empire out. The subjects of other narrative paintings were usually English-historical, with the middle ages, the classical world, and the Bible providing most of what the Victorians craved by way of the exotic, without needing to look further afield. Sculpture slavishly followed Greek models. A few 'oriental' genre paintings did find their way into the annual exhibitions of the (very fashionable) Royal Academy, but they were far less common there than in French galleries, may not have been as disparagingly 'orientalist' (and hence implicitly imperialist) as the modern use of the term implies, and were almost entirely confined to settings—North Africa and the Middle East—that Britain had no stated intention of colonizing just then.[67] This relative lack of 'orientalism' is noteworthy; some French critics, for example, contrasting it with their own artistic tradition, found it difficult to understand: '[a]lthough this great colonizing race possesses an immense Eastern empire, Orientalism has taken possession of only a few isolated minds.'[68] Other fashionable subjects of the time were portraits, and the (modest) female nude. Some of the portraits were inevitably of soldiers who may have fought in the colonies, but very rarely of colonial governors, though their uniforms were just as gorgeous. 'Battle paintings' were looked down on, possibly—suggests the main authority on this genre—due to the 'pervasive myth of anti-militarism' of the time; the Royal Academy for example seems to have definitely discriminated against battle painters when it came to elections to its coveted membership. Most of what there were took the Napoleonic and Crimean wars as their subjects, rather than colonial battles, which only started to feature later on.[69] Landscapes and other paintings set in places like India did exist, and are appreciated and exhibited today, but were not in their own time, at least in British public galleries: '[M]ost of the artists of the outer possessions,' writes John MacKenzie, 'were (in art-historical terms) lesser figures, and many of them were amateurs.'[70] They stood outside the main artistic establishment. Whether that placed them any nearer to a broader public sentiment must be doubted.

Again—as with music and literature—it is possible that the imperial references may have been in code. Some modern cultural scholars have not been slow to try to break these. In October 2001 an entire television documentary timed to coincide with an exhibition of Victorian nude paintings at the Tate Gallery was predicated on the idea of 'the naked body as a symbol of the British Empire itself'. Apart from the ('subjected') females featured, Frederic Leighton's mould-breaking sculpture *Athlete Wrestling with a Python* (*c.*1874) was supposed to embody 'the very spirit of the empire . . . a very good powerful metaphor of the British empire keeping corrupt forces at bay'. There is, however, no evidence to suggest that this was ever Leighton's intention, or the way the piece was interpreted by its contemporary audience.[71] Similarly, the statue of 'Asia' which stands on one of the four plinths surrounding the Albert Memorial in Hyde Park was presented as depicting Britain's control of India, though there is no need at all to see it in this way. (It features dignified, eastern-garbed figures dominated by a powerful and transgressive Indian woman astride a recumbent elephant, redolent—to this admirer—of Delacroix's *Marianne*.)[72] One art critic has even brought John Constable into the imperial project by claiming that the Thames estuary pictured in the background of his *Hadleigh Castle* (1829) represents Britain's expansion into the world. Again, there is no evidence that this was the artist's intention[73]. Perhaps landscape painting itself expresses a subconscious desire to annex territory. Classical models can also be 'read' as imperial: when sculptors in particular followed Greek and Roman patterns, it could have been because they regarded them as ideal aesthetically, or because the Greeks and Romans had had empires too. Even the Pre-Raphaelites' middle ages might be seen to connect with imperialism through the ideal of 'chivalry', which was sometimes bruited in colonial contexts as well.[74] None of these interpretations is at all obvious, and all require a strong injection of 'context' in order to hold them up. This however is the problem, as we are finding.

One branch of the visual arts was more widely accessible than most, though it may still have originated in an elite. Public sculpture—mainly statues of famous men and (a few) women—could hardly be avoided by anyone walking or riding in most towns and cities, though it may often have been forgotten through over-familiarity. What is notable about this genre is how very thinly imperial heroes were represented during the nineteenth century, with the exception of a handful of military men. Of eighty London statues erected before 1880 and still standing, only five are of obvious 'imperialists', all of them soldiers mainly known for their colonial campaigns.[75] These have to compete with Nelson, of course, thirty-one royals, and a mixed bag of doctors, philanthropists, statesmen, strictly local worthies, admirals, poets, engineers and entrepreneurs (there are more of these than all the colonials put together), prison reformers, painters, artists, and a philosopher (J. S. Mill). Taking account of those that have been removed or destroyed does not alter these proportions greatly.[76] Other cities have even smaller numbers of imperial statues. (Glasgow is an exception; but then Scotland was always keener on the imperial enterprise than her southern neighbour.)[77] Victorian city fathers, therefore, and others responsible for such monuments, clearly did not feel that the empire needed—or perhaps deserved—to be commemorated in this way.

In fact British cities were singularly devoid of imperial imprints generally. All the major ones were, of course, affected by the—mainly commercial—contacts they had with the outside world. The most visible signs of this were the huge dockyards in the coastal and riverine towns, and the buildings that were erected to service these trades: shipping company offices, foreign banks, 'exchanges', and the like. These were where foreigners could be seen in Britain, if they were to be seen at all. Glasgow, Liverpool, Bristol, and London were the most affected by these global links. Not all these links were imperial, however, unless one defines imperialism precisely in *terms* of foreign trade; and few of the physical signs of that trade in British cities were distinctively imperial in any other sense. In the case of London, the imperial metropolis, this was often regretted at the time. A nation commanding the greatest empire known to man ought to have a capital to match it. London was not that capital. To walk its streets, went the constant complaint, you would not know that you were at the hub of an empire at all.[78]

There were ways in which the empire impacted on London before the 1880s: a few bungalows in the outer suburbs, for example; the very occasional statue; exhibitions; billboards advertising transparently colonial produce; and exotic plants found in middle-class shrubberies.[79] But these are trivial by comparison with the ways it did not. First, London did not take on any of the *colour* of the empire by adopting Asian or African conventions or even details in its buildings, for example; unlike in the colonies themselves, where a great deal of cultural interchange, producing exciting fusions of eastern and western architectural styles, did take place.[80] The best known exception (though a little way from London) was the Prince Regent's Royal Pavilion in Brighton, a pastiche of Indian architecture built in 1815–18, at the tail-end of an 'orientalist' craze that swept Europe (and not only the imperial nations of Europe)[81] in the later eighteenth century, but then melted away.[82] Most orientalisms that survived into the nineteenth century, in the form of 'Chinese pavilions' and the like, were to be found in the grandest private houses, cut off from the hoi polloi by long drives and hedges, and so unlikely to impact on them. Most public architecture relied on classical Roman or occasionally Greek patterns, or—for those who craved the exotic—dug back into Britain's own middle ages for inspiration. In the 1860s a celebrated 'battle of the styles' broke out between the classical and the 'gothic', over the design of a new Foreign and India Office building in Whitehall. It is tempting to read this as a clash between imperialism, represented by the imperial Roman style, and something else (pre-imperial insular nationalism?) represented by the gothic; except that such issues were not explicitly raised in the loud and wide-ranging debate that actually took place at the time.[83] In fact they almost never were raised, most of the architectural controversy of the time centring on how 'honest' or 'pure' or 'national' or 'modern' the various styles on offer could be said to be.[84] In any case, very little nineteenth-century classical architecture can be regarded as 'imperious' in this sense; the major public examples—Smirke's British Museum (1823–48), for example, and Wilkins's National Gallery (1832–8)—were far more modest and unpretentious than their counterparts in other countries, notably in supposedly anti-imperialist Washington DC, and were regarded as such at the time.[85] This relates to the other way in which the empire seems not to have impacted on its capital city before the 1880s. The latter was not grand enough. Several efforts were made to remedy this during the nineteenth century: great new roads, buildings, even whole town plans were sketched out, some of which were partially achieved (the eventual Foreign Office building, for example, in its compromise 'Italianate' style, though far less grandiose than the original plans for it, does have a certain dignity). On the whole, though, it was still widely felt that London was 'put to shame by Paris, Berlin, Vienna, Rome, Chicago and New York' as late as 1892.[86] Even Brussels did better.[87] By contrast, London's public buildings were 'feeble', 'totally uninteresting', 'mean', and 'commonplace', according to the editor of the *Builder*, the leading architectural journal of the day, in 1896. They were 'simply a disgrace to the nation'.[88]

The reasons for this were a mixture of parsimony, the confusion of London's management, and a national sense of modesty. Money was always a problem, aggravated by a running row between local London ratepayers and taxpayers over who should foot the bill for buildings that the former saw as having a national significance and so chargeable to the nation as a whole, but which the latter felt were privileging the capital over the provinces. (In the case of the new India Office this problem was solved by charging it to the Indian exchequer.) Ironically, money was tightest—causing the cancellation of great public building plans more than once—at times of colonial crisis.[89] The management problem arose from London's lack of a unitary authority, which stymied almost any great building project that was likely to intrude into more than one of the parishes that constituted the city at that time.[90] Individual property rights in land could also be a block. The Victorians were much enamoured of such rights, of course, and also of the private, commercial, and democratic values that they saw as the real obstacles (and highly desirable ones) to the sort of state intervention that would have been necessary to implement any such great schemes as these. As well as underlining the Briton's independence, these values also ensured social stability. This was the individualist's reply to those who were continually holding up Haussmann's Paris as the example to shame Londoners: 'Paris was rebuilt in at least fifteen years less than it has taken the British nation to build one block of four Public Offices', wrote the *Builder* in 1877. 'But the cost to Paris has been a catastrophe [that is, the uprising of 1871] which no-one believes could happen to London.'[91] Lastly, there was the prejudice against public 'show'. 'Little Belgium', writes David Cannadine, 'might spend more than Great Britain on its metropolitan law courts, but . . . the English regarded such petty one-upmanship with disdain.'[92] 'What do we want with the Hôtel de Ville from Paris on the edge of St James's Park in order that a few hundred clerks may execute their daily tasks?' asked *The Times* in connection with the earlier, more elaborate, and eventually abandoned Foreign Office designs: 'The Colonies may be ruled from a building which is without the Pavillon de Flore at one extremity and the Pavillon Marsan at the other.'[93] 'It was not much in the habit of the British people', said Samuel Wilberforce in 1853, echoing Carlyle and Cecil Forsyth yet again, ' . . . to raise eminent structures as emblems of their power and vocation.' Instead, they preferred to leave their monuments in the shape of deeds.[94] Grand buildings were for nations with inferiority complexes. *Except* that Britain certainly did not eschew 'eminent structures' when it came to her provinces, and especially the great town halls of cities like Leeds and Manchester (the one very grandiose and classical, the other a veritable Hôtel de Ville); which suggests that it may in fact have been a question of priorities, with imperial coming lower than civic pride in the Victorian middle classes' scale.

❦❦❦

It could have been different at other social levels. It is Jeffrey Richards's main argument that the empire was far more popular than elitist—'above all *the people's* empire', he claims for the post-1876 period—which is why it was so much more reflected in 'the ballad, the hymn, the music-hall song, the march' than in symphonies, operas, and art songs,[95] and by extension, academic painting, sculpture, and architecture. Whatever the situation may have been after 1876, however, this does not appear to have been the case for the rest of the century. Popular forms of culture were almost as bereft of imperial associations as elite ones.

Popular songs, for example, were rarely very obviously imperialistic. Before the 1860s they tended to be radical and obscene. That was when they genuinely came from the streets, in the form of broadside ballads and pub songs.[96] A singer called Henry Russell also peddled a line in songs about emigration (usually to California, not the British colonies), with a message that was as sad as it was celebratory:

> I left my love in England,
> In poverty and pain;
> The tears hung heavy in my eyes,
> But hers came down like rain.

Other songs explicitly attacked emigration, like Mrs Benedict Vaughan's 'Oh! Take Me Not To Other Lands'.[97] This whole genre collapsed when the 'music hall' came along in the 1850s, bringing down with it, suggests Laurence Senelick, the last truly democratic form of popular music in England. There is much uncertainty about how genuinely music-hall songs reflected the political and other feelings of the working classes in the second half of the nineteenth century; an uncertainty borne of their generally reactionary tenor, which contrasts sharply with the ballads of just a generation before. The suspicion, of course, is that their content was determined more by the capitalist music-hall proprietors than by their customers, or perhaps by the new professional, middle-class song-writers and working-class (but with social aspirations) performers.[98] Alternatively, the working classes themselves may simply have regressed; a point we shall return to later, in connection with the music-hall 'jingoism' of the 1890s.

Before then patriotism was a fairly common theme in some music halls, especially as belted out by 'the Great Macdermott' (real name George Farrell), a 'man of colossal build and stentorian voice', whose famous Eastern Crisis 'War Song':

> We don't want to fight, but by jingo if we do,
> We've got the ships, we've got the men, we've got the money too.
> We've fought the bear before, and while we're Britons true,
> The Russians will not have Constantinople

added the word 'jingoism' to the English language.[99] The 'Jingo Song', as it is more often known, implies imperialism—it refers to Britain's 'Road unto the East' as a reason for resisting the 'Russian Bear'; as do, for example, Fred Albert's 'We Mean To Keep Our Empire in the East' and Henry Rickards's 'Hats Off To the Empire' from the same period, 1876–8.[100] But such messages only appear at times of diplomatic excitement and crisis, and the 'imperialism' in them is clearly secondary to simple 'John Bull' boastfulness, and Russophobia. 'You can always make pretty sure of a music-hall audience,' wrote a critic later, 'either by attacking the vices of the aristocracy or by abusing Russia.'[101] (Another way to make a song popular, of course, irrespective of the subject, was to give it a rousing melody; 'Historians tend to forget', writes Hugh Cunningham, 'that songs had tunes as well as words.')[102] There were also some *anti*-jingo songs; including a parody of Macdermott's by his gentler, but equally popular, rival Herbert Campbell:

> I don't want to fight, I'll be slaughtered if I do,
> I'll change my togs and sell my kit and pop my rifle too.
> I don't like the war, I ain't no 'Briton true',
> And I'd let the Russians have Constantinople[103]

and a 'comical popular song' performed by Arthur Roberts and J. W. Rowley called 'What Shall We Do With Cyprus?' (Disraeli's prize from the Eastern Crisis), whose theme was that Britain had too many colonies already without adding to them. One of its suggestions for Cyprus is to dump everyone not wanted in Britain there, including the entire aristocracy, 'with lives as black as ink', and 'sev'ral thousand Jingoes, who are lately out of work | But perhaps they wouldn't care for *them* in Cyprus'.[104] The picture for the pre-1880 period, therefore, is very unclear. Audiences cheered both bellicose and anti-bellicose songs. There are very few of these from before the Eastern Crisis, or from after it, until the late 1890s,[105] and the imperial element in all of them is tangental. Most patriotic songs were on other themes entirely: the queen, Britain's liberties, roast beef, and 'The Envy of the World Down at Westminster';[106] and even these were greatly outnumbered by songs on more domestic themes: humour, drink, comradeship, the seaside, ill-fortune, courtship, betrayal, marriage, policemen, mothers, the sufferings (note) of ordinary soldiers, and so on. There was also the occasional 'black-face', 'nigger', or 'Ethiopian' act, a genre imported from America in the 1830s, which in a British setting may have reinforced certain imperial stereotypes.[107] Overall, however, the music hall was not yet a clearly imperialistic medium.

Popular prints, of the kind the working-classes hung on the walls of their hovels, reveal the same thing. Usually their subjects were religious, romantic, or fluffy animals. Sometimes they were of the queen, and occasionally they showed historical events, almost always domestic. There were some popular battle scenes, mostly from the Napoleonic War period. 'On the walls', recounted a working-class memoirist describing a London slum dwelling a little later (*c.*1900), 'are heavily-framed and very chilly engravings of *The Bath of Psyche*, *The Monarch of the Glen*, *The Thin Red Line*, and a real oil-painting in a gilt frame, representing a row of tumbledown cottages.'[108] David Livingstone started to appear on the walls of devout Christians in the 1850s. That was about as near to empire as this genre came.

***

'Lower' forms of literature, too, seem superficially bereft of imperial content, though it may be possible to interpret them otherwise. A survey of titles of popular (but 'respectable') novels published in the first three-quarters of the nineteenth century throws up almost no obviously imperial subjects,[109] and only a few quasi- ('orientalist', for example) ones.[110] Modern studies of Anglo-Indian fiction usually begin towards the end of the century, when this genre starts coming on stream.[111] One that purports to cover the whole Victorian period only manages to dig up three adult examples from before the 1880s, before hurrying on to richer pastures with Henty and Kipling.[112] This seems surprising in view of India's potential for exotic backgrounds to set tales of romance, mystery, and adventure against. It does suggest that the Raj had not yet caught the popular imagination fully. We may not be seeing the whole picture here; middlebrow nineteenth-century fiction is not a common topic for scholarly study, for understandable reasons—much of it is very long and not very rewarding as literature. It is just possible that a popular imperial sub-genre is still lying there, ripe for rediscovery. It is likely, too, that middlebrow novelists made as many tangential references to empire-related phenomena as their betters did, betraying similar attitudes.[113] Most of their main themes, however, were just as incorrigibly domestic as were those of the canonical authors, with love, social relations, crime, and adventure being easy favourites. Almost no popular-fiction writers tackled the empire head-on.

One exception was boys' adventure novels, though even here the imperialism was rarely direct. In one famous case it was: Charles Kingsley's *Westward Ho!*, published in 1855. Set mainly on the galleons of the great Elizabethan voyagers and in the new western lands they discovered, it makes a point of confronting the 'politically correct' view of the day, which was to decry such enterprises.[114] Kingsley also uses the story to propagandize on behalf of the empire of his own time.[115] The book was widely criticized when it appeared for its brutal tone.[116] Whether its young readers took on board the imperial lessons Kingsley intended must be debatable (this is a recurrent problem with juvenile fiction).[117] There could not have been many of those readers initially. *Westward Ho!* had fairly moderate sales on its first publication, and only really caught on after Kingsley's death in 1875, when at last it seemed to strike a chord with its public.[118] Kingsley was ahead of his time here, as he was in his racism, his armchair militarism, and his admiration for the similarly racist and militarist Thomas Carlyle.[119] He is almost *sui generis*.

None of Kingsley's more popular contemporaries among boys' novelists was as consciously imperialistic. Politically, R. M. Ballantyne and Mayne Reid were both liberals; which did not prevent their being imperialists, but did make it less likely that they would be militarist and racist ones. Captain (Fred) Marryat was an imperial defeatist, believing that the British empire would perish as the Roman did;[120] and the American Hermann Melville, whose more exotic tales were also a favourite of British boys, inveighed against the 'pollution' of tropical cultures by the white man.[121] The others clearly believed in the civilising mission of the West, especially among the most barbarous peoples of the world, among whom they liked to pitch their stories if they could. This was obviously because barbarism made for more exciting and bloodthirsty reading, which was what Ballantyne in particular believed his adolescent readers craved for, and which he gave them in spades.[122] Barbarity was not a racial characteristic, however; it could be cured, and quickly, by Christianity. Ballantyne's *Coral Island* features a black missionary hero, for example; an idyllic converted South Sea island village: '[e]verything around this beautiful spot wore an aspect of peace and plenty . . . I could not avoid contrasting it with the wretched village of Emo, where I had witnessed so many frightful scenes'; and some white villains (pirates) who are 'more blameworthy even than the savages'.[123] It also has its narrator falling into savage ways himself at one point, in order to stress the importance of environment rather than race.[124] Savages could and therefore should be 'civilized', but not necessarily imperially. There is no suggestion in *Coral Island*, or in most of these tales, that European power is necessary to impose this 'civilization'; free missionary enterprise will be enough. This may be another reason—aside from the fictional need for barbarism, which ought to be found less in colonies—why these novels are so very seldom set in empire locations, and indeed seem to avoid them almost deliberately. Another is that it was far less fun for a teenage boy to pit himself against savagery knowing that he had the protective power of a colonial government to fall back on if he got into too much of a scrape. The South Seas are a favourite setting; followed by the American West, unexplored and as yet uncolonized Africa, the oceans, and the fairly distant past.[125] Yet again, India is virtually nowhere to be seen.[126] Patrick Dunae finds the 'spirit of empire... subdued' in these adventure stories.[127] In a strict and narrow sense, therefore, this is not an 'imperial' literature at all.

The case for its inclusion in the imperial canon by some critics rests on three things: the overseas settings, in parts of the world which, while not yet colonized, typified those that soon would be; the general sense they display of superiority over other cultures; and the accent they place on 'adventure', which is supposed to have been a driving force behind imperialism. The last is another of those equations that requires some solid historical or theoretical backing to make sense of it. In other contexts adventure can clearly be linked with totally different ideologies and activities; *anti*-colonial guerilla warfare, for example, might be one. In the context of nineteenth-century Britain, for it to necessarily imply the 'celebration' (Martin Green's word) of empire, it would have to be shown that there was nothing else it *could* be celebrating at that place and time. But this cannot be taken for granted. A love of adventure could be *harnessed* to the idea of empire, and was so harnessed, quite deliberately, in later boys' literature; but both then and earlier it could just as easily be harnessed to other things. Crime was one that concerned contemporaries. Overseas settings may well have turned some young, adventurous spirits towards the empire (if it did not inspire them to become pirates), but they were given little explicit advice in this direction; 'no editorials', writes Patrick Dunae, discussing boys' magazines of this period, 'exhorting readers to capitalise upon their imperial heritage'[128]—and there were plenty of other options. One was missionary work, encouraged no doubt by Ballantyne's and others' images of benighted but improvable heathens; others were trade, travel, exploration, scientific research, railway building, diplomacy, emigration, and a dozen other promising opportunities abroad for excitement-seeking young folk, none of which necessarily involved the empire, or imperialism, unless that word is broadened to include all kinds of activity abroad. That is permissible, of course; but in that case it must not be confused with the sort of imperialism that requires domination, possession, or control.

By the same token, if imperialism is held to be the inspiration of this type of literature, then it has to be quite loosely defined. The fact that so little of the genre features the formal empire suggests that it was not this that fired its practitioners. Interest in the wider world certainly did, but that did not need to be colonial. Two of our boys' authors who had first-hand experience of some of the locations they wrote about, Ballantyne and Marryat, gained that in quasi-colonial roles;[129] the rest however—and also Ballantyne for most of his books—relied on travelogues written by others, who usually had nothing to do with the British empire and little interest in it.[130] Fascination with foreign parts was much more likely to be fostered by accounts of traders, explorers, and missionaries. Other European nations, including some that can have had no pretentions to empire, shared this fascination, with similar literary manifestations; for example, Johann Wyss's *The Swiss Family Robinson* (1813). So boys' adventure stories cannot be said to have been an outcome of imperialism especially, unless it was an imperialism in which Switzerland can be said to have shared. This is not as ludicrous as it may sound: in one sense, 'imperialism' can be regarded as a Europe-wide phenomenon, in which even landlocked nations could participate vicariously, or even directly if we characterize it as much in terms of trade, exploration, and proselytism as by formal rule.[131] Boys' adventure books may well have been influenced by 'empire' in this inclusive sense. But it is still noteworthy how tenuous its links were to the more formal and literal kind.

It almost goes without saying that girls' books were even less imperialistic. Most of them were restricted in their scope to the domestic and parochial. The values they promoted were those conceived at the time as womanly ones: 'Remember, maidens,' wrote Charlotte Yonge, one of the most prolific of nineteenth-century girls' authors, 'that you are the hope of England, and her joy: and this you can only be, if you are modest, gentle, brave, truthful and Godly'.[132] The point of this was to fit them to support their menfolk, in part by improving them morally. Yonge, for example, set much store in 'a gentle conscientious girls's power to bring chivalry into the life of a brother'.[133] This could help him to run the empire later on, of course (chivalry was another of those ideas that became harnessed to imperialism), but that was neither a matter of choice for his sister, nor of concern for the authors of these books. As a result many girls found the latter unfulfilling—too 'goody-goody', was one young reader's judgment of Charlotte Yonge[134]—and so read boys' books secretly instead. One contemporary authority even applauded this on the ground that boys' books 'ought to impart vigour and breadth to a girl's nature, and to give sisters a sympathetic knowledge of the scenes wherein their brothers live and work';[135] which may have reassured parents who feared the threat that books like *Mr Midshipman Easy* and *The Gorilla Hunters,* in the hands of their daughters, posed to traditional gender roles. It was not until the very end of the century that girls' novels began to feature strong transgressive heroines, and in imperial settings, in similar ways to the boys'.

❦❦❦

But in any case, these sorts of fiction were not what 80 per cent of the British population actually read. The working classes formed no part of either of these cultural worlds. Those among them who read at all—and we have seen that these were probably a minority—did not generally go for Austen or Trollope, or even to any great extent for Yonge or Ballantyne.[136] If they did, they almost certainly took different messages away from them than the middle classes. One ambitious late nineteenth-century rural reader who was put on to *Sense and Sensibility* reported that he 'could make nothing of it, but this did not keep me from reading it.'[137] Of course he could make nothing of it; it relates to an entirely different world. Dickens resonated with them more, though he was apparently enjoyed more in performance than through reading.[138] Socialist autodidacts read Kingsley, Carlyle, and Ruskin, but for their social radicalism, not their imperialism, which in any case was very obscure in the latter two cases.[139] For these most literate of working-class readers, religion, socialism, and very old fiction were their staples, judging from working-class memoirs.

Lists of favourite titles in these memoirs are remarkably consistent. Religious works abound, together with 'useful' books (non-fiction), and—for the radicals—key revolutionary texts. Top, however, come Defoe's *Robinson Crusoe,* Bunyan's *The Pilgrim's Progress,* and Milton's *Paradise Lost.* Some progressed from there to Burns, Cowper, and James Thomson (their favourite poets), Swift's *Gulliver's Travels, Cook's Voyages,* and occasionally Shakespeare.[140] These were read because they were generally the only books available to working-class children on the little shelves of their hovels; because pious parents believed the religious content of some of them meant they were safer than novels (this was why Shakespeare was less accepted); and because despite this they were still imaginative enough to gratify young minds seeking for vicarious adventure and escape. 'They were all', points out Jonathan Rose, 'thrilling tales of adventure, about amazing journeys and terrific struggles, and memorable heroes who, with the help of God, miraculously prevail.'[141] Even the Bible was read in this way.[142]

None of these books carries any obvious imperial message, unless adventure in exotic locations is regarded as intrinsically imperialist. Attempts have been made to read 'imperialism' into Shakespeare, but these seem anachronistic. In *Paradise Lost* the imperial images are attached to Satan. In *The Pilgrim's Progress* Christian seeks individual salvation by journeying through another's empire. *Crusoe* is perhaps the likeliest soil for empire-diggers,[143] but even that is ambivalent on the question. For any careful reader its main lessons are: that wandering in foreign parts is not at all laudable but a mark of greed and restlessness, which can get you into trouble; that other cultures should not be judged by European standards; that all people are the same under the skin, and only differentiated by environment, culture and the Revelation of Christ, the last of which can make the grossest savage into a civilized person in no time at all; that Europeans can easily lapse into barbarism, and often do; that they should be careful about sailing near the north African coast lest they be captured as ('Turkish') slaves; that in spite of this 'orientals' can be decent, and African negroes kind; and—lastly—that authority, or temporal rule, is justified only by, first, your own labour, which gives you rights over any territory you have tamed, and secondly by the need to the protect others, in which case it needs to be ratified by contract. The potential for imperialism is here, especially in the last point. Contemporaries also could have inferred other morals from *Crusoe*, especially when presented to them in cheap, condensed and sensationalised 'chapbook' forms: the woodcut image of a naked Friday cowering before an imperious Crusoe that appeared on the covers of many of the latter might well have entirely negated any more subtle messages.[144] The point is, however, that imperialist or racist morals did not need to be drawn. *Robinson Crusoe*'s vivid portrayal of an individual's extreme struggles and sufferings is what has attracted generations of readers to it, and not, for example, to its much more empire-related—but largely forgotten—sequel.[145]

In any case these wholesome classics were only part of the picture, and possibly—feared an 1886 observer—a diminishing part as the century wore on.[146] 'It is not easy to indicate precisely what other books they read,' he continued—a good indication of the lack of communication between the classes, this—except to say that '[n]o idea of the reading of the working classes can be arrived at by comparing it with the reading of the upper classes.' Cheap editions of 'good' books and sales figures in the thousands indicated only a shallow penetration, for 'the working men and women of England do not number thousands, but millions'. 'Shakespeare, Scott, Marryat, Dickens, Lytton [and] Eliot' consequently passed them by.[147] Instead they read cheap 'chapbooks' early in the century—tiny pamphlets, often describing scandals, murders, executions, and 'last dying speeches'—and 'penny dreadfuls', short sensational novels for teenagers, usually about crime, the supernatural, and love, later on.[148] A list of titles in the autobiography of a working man born in 1852 gives the flavour: *Alone in the Pirate's Lair*; *Deadwood Dick*; *Hounslow Heath and its Moonlight Riders*; *Starlight Bess, Queen of the Highwaymen*; *Black Rollo the Pirate Chieftain, or the Dark Woman of the Deep*; *The Skeleton Horseman or the Shadow of Death*; *Admiral Tom, Boy King of the Buccaneers*, and *Spring-heeled Jack the Terror of London* . . .[149] There were also crude plagiarisms of Dickens (*Oliver Twiss, Nickelas Nicklebery, Martin Guzzlewit*),[150] and a highly popular ersatz *Crusoe* called *The Adventures of Philip Quarll, the English Hermit*. That replaced Friday with a trained monkey, which may have raised unfortunate associations in the minds of those who had read *Crusoe* too.[151] Possibly the second-most popular British novelist of the entire century—though he has hardly 'lasted', partly because his cheaply produced books tended to literally disintegrate—was G. W. M. Reynolds, the proprietor of *Reynolds's Newspaper*, who attracted hundreds of thousands of readers in the 1850s with a regular menu of blood, guts, sex, and radical politics, but hardly a whiff of anything imperial.[152] Similar lists could be compiled of popular plays. The following comes from a working man's recollections of the London East End productions he saw in the 1860s and 1870s: *The Watercress Girl*; *A Poor Girl's Temptations, or a Voice from the Streets*; *Fifteen Years of a British Seaman's Life*; *Waiting for the Verdict*; *The Guilty Mother*; *Lady Hatton, or the Suicide's Tree*; *The Man with the Iron Heart*; *Jack Sheppard* (a great favourite this, and the one that most unsettled the middle classes, with its raffish criminal-hero); and of course *Sweeney Todd, the Barber Fiend of Fleet Street*.[153] Of these only the *British Seaman's Life* suggests some possible colonial allusions.[154] It is difficult to be certain, of course, without poring over many more of these tedious narratives; but scarcely any of those that are commonly cited had any remotely imperial or even racial reference.[155] Crime was the main topic, usually positively *celebrated* in ways that alarmed the middle classes mightily;[156] closely followed by denigration of the upper classes, which alarmed them even more. 'They thrive', wrote Edward Salmon, 'on the wicked baronet or nobleman and the faithless but handsome peeress', and especially on tales of pure young working-class girls ravished and ruined by 'that incarnation of evil, the sensuous aristocrat, standing six feet with his dark eyes, heavy moustache, pearl-like teeth, and black hair'.[157] Distant India and Canada could never compete with this.

The middle classes felt this literary diet was unwholesome, and tried to counter it, but probably with little success. Their weapons were religious tracts and those moral tales on political economy mentioned already, which also avoided the empire; encyclopaedias published in penny instalments, aiming to instil what was called 'useful knowledge';[158] and cheap magazines with the same aim.[159] Many working men who wished to improve themselves undoubtedly profited greatly from these; others however regarded them as 'intolerable nuisances', coming to 'darken the world, and shed their blighting influence on the opening intellect of the "youthhood" '.[160] For boys (and girls to a lesser extent) some reformers had the better idea of trying to compete on the penny dreadfuls' own ground, by furnishing them with 'wild and wonderful, but *healthy* fiction', some set overseas, mixed in with the 'useful knowledge';[161] but these rarely achieved the kinds of circulations which would suggest they reached far beyond the much more amenable middle classes.[162] When R. M. Ballantyne, whose bloodthirstiness might have been thought to give him a natural advantage in this market, launched a 'Miscellany' of small novelettes designed specifically 'for the poor' in 1864 it failed badly, perhaps because of the piety that made up the other half of his formula; and when it was relaunched five years later it was directed at the middle classes instead.[163]

Who won this war overall is still a contentious—or it may be a meaningless—question; but it does not matter much for our purposes, because neither side made much of the British empire in it. Insofar as the middle classes aimed to use fiction to control the workers socially, it was not by encouraging imperial patriotism, but through the old devices of hammering home their *class* obligations, and the like. The workers themselves,when they did happen to come across colonial references, may not have thought they were true; or no more so than Crusoe's island or the Slough of Despond. They did not relate any more closely to their material experiences. So what few imperial allusions there were could easily have gone over their heads; or into the imaginative parts of them.[164] It is always difficult to know how readers respond to what is written for them; but in this case the obvious imperialism, at any rate, was so very thinly spread it must have passed them by.

❦❦❦

So, to sum up: what does all this—the evidence from literature and the arts at all these levels—tell us about the relationship between the empire (or imperialism) and domestic British life in this period? That is not easy to say. One thing it does seem to tell us, though this partly depends on semantics and interpretation, is that the empire's impact on British *culture* was very slight. Some peripheral allusions in 'serious' novels, a struggling museum, one mediocre building (the Foreign and India Offices), a few shows, the occasional 'orientalist' painting, no musical influences whatsoever, and virtually nothing that touched the huge working-class majority of the population: this is a poor cultural return on the considerable national investment in empire that Britain was making then. If we exclude features that have no intrinsic connection with empire we are left with almost nothing. References to the exotic, for example, did not depend on empire; if we can imagine a hypothetical nineteenth-century Britain which had somehow managed to resist the temptation to subdue and colonise, but still travelled and traded, most of them could still have remained. So—probably—would chauvinistic and race prejudice, which had less to do with Britain's having an empire, either as effect or cause (the most chauvinistic Britons, those who believed that 'inferior races' were incorrigible, used that as an argument to leave well alone), than with human nature (most nations think they are superior to others), religion (a 'one true' religion is bound to encourage disparagement of less true ones), and the fact that, at that particular point in history, Britain *was* objectively superior to most other nations in at least two respects: her material prosperity and her domestic political liberalism. There would also have been enough material in her history to provide her artists with the battle scenes they craved, without requiring colonial wars; for imperialism is not essential to 'militarism' either. 'Empire' involves not only victories, but conquest, rule, domination, control; and there is precious little of that among the literary and other cultural achievements of the pre-Kipling nineteenth century. Slavery is the most extreme form of this type of imperialism, and that is invariably condemned in Victorian literature, including (by implication) the by now notoriously slave-ridden *Mansfield Park*. (It is worth pointing out here, although we are concerned primarily with British culture, that the runaway 'short-term' best-selling book of the entire nineteenth century was the American Harriet Beecher Stowe's anti-slavery *Uncle Tom's Cabin* (1852), which sold one-and-a-half million copies in its first year.)[165] India was the next best example of a 'controlled' colony, and also, as it happens, the least featured in the literature, art, and music of this time. The most exotic literature—boys' adventure stories—avoided the empire deliberately, as we have seen. However, even if we broadened our definition of empire to include these—places like Ballantyne's 'Coral Island', for example—we should find that it made very little overall impression. British culture at all levels in the nineteenth century was surprisingly parochial, for a state with such a huge presence in the world.

Did this accurately reflect British society? It may not have done. Several ways of avoiding this conclusion have been mentioned already. The first is the one that was most favoured by imperialists at the time: that empire and culture generally were incompatible, so that the latter could never be representative of the former, which was nonetheless the *un*cultured majority's ideology. Martin Green's thesis, that an elitist literary establishment deliberately boycotted imperial topics, neatly complements this. Slightly different is Patrick Brantlinger's idea that the lack of almost any mention of the empire in nineteenth-century texts shows how comfortable the early and mid-Victorians were with it. If they had featured it more it could only have been because they had doubts. Then there is Edward Said's argument that the canonical authors, who were subtler than the rest, deliberately soft-pedalled on the empire so as *not* to raise doubts about it. Lastly, it could be argued that the reluctance of the British to allow their cultures to become contaminated with colonial influences shows how arrogant—that is, *essentially* imperialist—they were. All these are plausible readings, and have the advantage of making immediate sense of all the minor references to empire that pepper these texts, without needing to seek any further. These were the half-hidden signs of the real imperial commitment that lay behind even the most seemingly non-imperial work. But it requires the *assumption* of a commitment to be able to interpret them in this way. Without this, they become equally compatible with a much more negative but also complex scenario: one in which most Britons were hardly aware of their empire, and certainly felt no allegiance to it, while those who did know about it responded in widely different and—and this applies to positive 'imperialists' too—even contradictory ways: as we shall shortly see.

This is the most straightforward conclusion to be drawn from the cultural record, and also the one most consistent with both the British people's material involvement in the imperial enterprise, and their education, as previous chapters have shown. There are, in other words, no reasons why the Victorians *should* have been more imperially minded than their literary and artistic achievements, viewed superficially—that is, without seeking for hidden meanings beneath the surface—indicate. In fact if we survey those achievements overall, without imperial cherry-picking, they probably give a pretty good idea of the major concerns and priorities of most British men and women in the greater part of the nineteenth century, before the coming of the 'new' imperialism: personal dramas of course, greed, villainy, love, laughter, and (for boys, and girls secretly) adventure; but in the public sphere chiefly class, religion, and gender, with relations (chiefly through wars) with European neighbours following a little way behind; and the whole informed by one overarching theme: the problems attendant on Britain's *progress*, the unprecedented domestic changes she was undergoing in this period, for ill as well as for good. It is these themes that dominate the Victorians' art and literature at all levels. Empire came very low indeed on this list of priorities, and almost nowhere in its impact on people's thinking. Unless, of course, they talked of little else, unrecorded, in their clubs, at their dinner parties, and down the pub.[166]

8
Peril and Propaganda, *c*.1900

The signs of Britain's empire are there, in her literature, culture, and so on. That shows—if we needed to be told it—that she was an imperial power. What it does not show, however, is that the empire was an important part of their identity for most Britons. The most noteworthy aspect of all this is how minimal the cultural impact of the empire was. This is extraordinary: certainly by contrast with its very real presence outside. That does not *prove* that it was insignificant to Britons, of course; other reasons could be found to account for this cultural neglect. Taken together with other factors, however, this does seem the likeliest explanation. Most classes of Briton had little sympathetic contact with the empire. Their lifestyles and alternative discourses will have alienated them from it. The more imperial classes had no reason to share it with the others. Finally, and probably the clinching reason: the empire itself did not require this kind of interest and commitment from the British people; it could function perfectly well—indeed, probably better—without it. Hence the widespread indifference of most British people towards their empire in the early and mid-19th century. It did not need them, and they did not need it.

From the 1870s and 1880s onwards, however, all that changed. The empire and society began to need each other. The question then was, whether these old obstacles to a more general imperial consciousness and commitment could be overcome. The very fate of the empire may have depended on this, as it had not, by and large, before. That, at any rate, is what many *soi-disants* imperialists came to believe.

❦❦❦

On the external front the main change was the entry of other European nations into competition with Britain over colonies. Foreign countries had, of course, been involved in overseas imperialism before; Spain, Portugal, and the Netherlands had empires that were spread as widely throughout the world as Britain's in the nineteenth century, albeit smaller in territory and more static, while France's empire was both extensive and expanding. Looking outside Europe, and broadening the definition of empire slightly to include contiguous expansion, the United States and Russia were two of the most imperialistic powers throughout the century. Several non-European empires still had to be reckoned with: the Chinese in Asia; the Ottoman in three continents; and the Tongan and Hawaiian in the Pacific. Multiple empires, therefore, were not a new phenomenon; but competition between them, to the degree that is found in the late nineteenth century, was. One reason for this was that the spaces between them were diminishing. For most of the century the expanding empires had broadly enough 'empty' territory to push into—meaning countries occupied only by *indigènes*—to obviate the need for them to expand at the expense of others. There were one or two clashes (between Britain and France in South-East Asia, for example, and between Britain and Russia, often vicariously, on India's North-West Frontier), but nothing serious. Expansionary energies could be diverted into new *terrae incognitae*. By the end of the century, though, these *terrae* were becoming scarcer as expanding empires came up against empires expanding from other directions, forming frontiers between them for the first time. Soon there would be no 'empty' territory left. That could have—though it required a particular mindset to think this way—two worrying implications for Britain. The first was to make it imperative for her to grab as much of the best free land available while it lasted, otherwise France or some other rival would get it. The second was to raise concerns about the defence of Britain's colonies once the surplus territories had been formally distributed. If her rivals remained hungry, their eyes would be bound to fall on other empires, as the only spaces left to expand into. That posed a new potential threat to the largest—and hence meatiest—of all the empires. Securing it in this environment would require far more effort, and consequently more commitment, than before.

These inferences were not inescapable. Gladstone, for example, always refused to accept that Germany's bid for colonies in the 1880s, which effectively kicked off the new game, altered things at all. 'If Germany is to become a colonising power,' he told the House of Commons airily in March 1885, 'then all I say is "God speed her!" She becomes our ally and partner in the execution of the great purposes of Providence for the advantage of mankind.'[1] For Gladstone and many other Liberals at that time this view was easier to stomach than the idea of a direct German colonial challenge to Britain (which was undoubtedly how Bismarck intended it), with its inevitable corollary that the latter should respond in kind. The consequences of that were almost too disturbing to contemplate. First, it would involve a far larger state expenditure, in terms of both money and personnel, than the empire had required heretofore, and than free-market liberals could ever feel ideologically comfortable with. Even from a commercial point of view it made little sense to secure foreign markets for British industry by means, such as more government and higher taxation, which were bound to blunt that industry's edge in those markets. (A solution would have been to monopolize the latter, but that was absolute anathema.) Secondly, the imposition of governments on peoples was against everything nineteenth-century liberalism was supposed to stand for. Classical liberalism was anti-government in any form, believing that, like frontiers, it would wither away naturally under the beneficent influence of free trade. Empires, a black word in the earlier liberal vocabulary, must be the first to go. Hence the contortions that Liberals had gone through to deny, downplay, or ignore the clear imperial implications of much of their foreign and commercial policy in the early and middle parts of the century: they were just opening up markets, spreading enlightenment (Gladstone's 'Providence'), saving people from worse tyrannies, or taking them in hand temporarily. Gladstone continued this line in the 1880s, with a quite restrained response to Bismarck's original bid: the division of West-Central Africa the latter gave rise to is conventionally called the 'Scramble' for Africa, but Britain did not scramble seriously at this stage;[2] always looking for inexpensive ways of running the additional overseas obligations incurred, as 'protectorates' rather than overt colonies, for example, or by farming them out to private companies; insisting that the occupation of Egypt (1882) was merely short-term, and for the international good, not just Britain's; and even *withdrawing* on two occasions: from the Transvaal, after a military defeat at the hands of the Boers in 1881, and from the (formerly Egyptian) Sudan, at the cost of the life of the disobedient but nonetheless hero-worshipped General

Charles Gordon in 1884–5. Gladstone obviously did not see any pressing reason to change tack.

Others did, however. Some simply felt humiliated by Gladstone's appeasements, especially in the Sudan. That gave rise to a vociferous backlash against him—'GOM', for 'Grand old Man', was transposed into 'MOG', 'Murderer of Gordon'—which contributed to his electoral defeat (mainly over Home Rule for Ireland, another concession) in 1886. Some critics had deeper objections. Those on the Right had long derided Gladstone's whole attitude to foreign affairs as 'unrealistic', and consequently unsafe. Lord Salisbury, for example, who was probably the most 'realistic' British statesman of the entire nineteenth century (a Conservative, of course), always preferred to work on the assumption that nations were natural enemies rather than partners, and in 1898 famously predicted a pseudo-Darwinist scenario for the world, clearly based on the current competition among empires for new colonies, in which 'strong' nations would gobble up what he called the 'dying' ones, inevitably.[3] Some even appeared to relish this prospect, like Lord Rosebery (*not* a Conservative), who talked a great deal about fitting Britain domestically 'for the keen race of nations' that lay ahead.[4] Some capitalists felt the same, no longer trusting in free trade alone to save them in this new commercial environment in which other countries threatened to monopolize and so cut off their colonial markets. The so-called trade 'depression' of the 1870s and 1880s compounded these fears, and led some manufacturers to make brazen demands for new colonies.[5] More and more people were *asserting* their imperialism. It was no longer seen as something to be apologized for or covered up.

On the home front things were changing too, in ways which were thought to affect the relationship between British society and the empire fundamentally. One crucial change was the incorporation of many more Britons into the political nation through the Parliamentary Reform Acts of 1867 and 1884, which expanded the electorate from 1.3 million to 5.6 million men, many of them from the working classes.[6] That made it more difficult to enforce the separation between classes which had rendered it unnecessary to involve the lower orders in *any* nationwide enterprise up till then. The workers were gradually getting their hands on the reins. The dangers of this were exacerbated by the new indiscipline of many of them, their unwillingness to accept their 'place' in society that had been crucial to the cohesion of that society in the past, manifested in strikes and riotous demonstrations, and the resurrection of organized socialism in Britain after thirty years of quiescence, with the founding of the Social Democratic Federation in 1880, the Fabian Society in 1884, and the Independent Labour Party in 1893. Socialism was not a force to be reckoned with yet (it was still mainly a middle-class phenomenon), but the underlying disillusionment with traditional economic liberalism, represented by the riots, may have been. This was part of a broader movement—exemplified also by protectionism abroad and that call of a minority of manufacturers for new colonies—of reaction against free-market capitalism generally. So far as these workers and their middle-class sympathizers were concerned, it had not fulfilled its promises: its benefits were not 'trickling down'. There were still grotesque inequality, unemployment, insecurity, poverty, suffering. A stream of books and pamphlets, from Andrew Mearns's shocking *The Bitter Cry of Outcast London* (1883) to Charles Booth's and Joseph Rowntree's statistical studies of poverty in London and York in the 1890s and 1900s,[7] drove the message home. The implications for the traditional form of government in Britain were ominous. The ruling elite could no longer count on the working classes' *complementary* loyalty to the classes above them and the system they upheld. Class war, the ghost of which had been thought to be laid with the failure of Chartism way back in the 1840s, threatened again.

A new social adhesive had to be found. It was against this background that patriotism was brought into the picture, as a possible alternative means of social control. If the workers were no longer happy with their traditional sectional 'place' in British society, perhaps that could be substituted with this new one: a vicarious share in the broader national enterprise that had been previously appropriated by the upper classes alone. Include imperialism in that and you killed two birds with one stone, by strengthening the empire in these new and testing times for it, as well as uniting the country behind the government. Cecil Rhodes famously thought the link might be even closer. 'The Empire', he is alleged to have said in 1895, '... is a bread and butter question. If you want to avoid civil war, you must become imperialists.' He meant that its goods and markets could be used to bribe the workers away from socialism. (The quotation is famous because of its later use by Lenin to prove that imperialism was the final 'stage' of capitalism, a desperate ploy to stave off the inevitable revolution.)[8] The workers' anti-capitalism might actually help here, giving them something in common with those imperialists who also opposed the 'freest' version of that ideology, albeit for different reasons. It was a way of uniting them both against the Liberals. This was not a new idea; for years critics had associated imperialism with hostility to liberal free trade. The maverick Carlyle had espoused both the empire and anti-capitalism, while Disraeli had hinted at a symbiotic connection between them, with his 1870s 'imperialism and social reform' programme, thereby becoming the first leading politician to try to appeal to the working-class electorate on imperial-patriotic grounds. While he was in power Disraeli did little to implement either of these agendas, let alone elucidate the precise relationship between them: possibly because there was no burning need to yet. That need hit Britain in the 1880s, with the German bid for colonies, the near-doubling of the electorate, social unrest, and the undermining of confidence in free-market capitalism generally; all of which together created the conditions in which a broader-based imperialism was much more likely to be encouraged—and even to flourish—than in the past.

⁂

For some imperialists alarm bells had started ringing quite early on. However absent-mindedly the British had accumulated their empire hitherto, wrote an anonymous contributor to the *Westminster Review* in 1870—he did not use this phrase, but the argument uncannily anticipates Sir John Seeley's in his celebrated *The Expansion of England* of thirteen years later—it was in danger now if the people did not rally to its aid.[9] When Seeley used the expression it was not, as is sometimes assumed, because he believed the empire really had been won 'in a fit of absence of mind', but in order to ridicule the history books of his time which, by marginalizing the empire, gave this impression.[10] He believed that this threatened its existence. Others joined in. The historian H. E. Egerton claimed it had been lack of popular imperial knowledge that had 'wrecked our first Colonial Empire'.[11] The Liberal prime minister Lord Rosebery, in the preface he contributed to a new, explicitly imperialist geography book for elementary schools in 1892, warned that if children continued to grow up in ignorance of it, the present empire was also 'doomed'.[12] Several imperialists tied this in with the extension of the franchise: like it or not, wrote C. P. Lucas in 1911, the empire was now in 'the people's' hands; 'If the democracy of the United Kingdom is not given sound, sober, thoughtful teaching about the Empire, how can it be expected to form sound, sober, thoughtful views on imperial questions?'[13] It had been different before, as Lord Meath pointed out:

In former years the burdens of Empire or of the State fell on the shoulders of a few, now the humblest child found on the benches of a primary school will in a few years' time be called upon to influence the destinies of not only fifty four millions of white, but also three hundred and fifty millions of coloured men and women, his fellow subjects scattered throughout five continents of the world. Such overwhelming responsibilities have never before in the history of the world fallen upon any people.[14]

'No prudent guardians', he told the House of Lords in 1893, using an analogy that he clearly thought would resonate with his aristocratic audience, 'would bring up the heir to a large estate without telling him all about its extent and capabilities of development.'[15] Walter Frewen Lord believed that 'Imperial education—the teaching of the history of the British Empire from the patriotic point of view'—was crucial if the 'vermin of anti-imperialism' was not to 'devour the body politic'.[16] This mood of alarm was new. No imperialist had ever liked the way that all Britain's hard work in the colonies had gone unnoticed and unappreciated at home in former years—it had been irritating, even hurtful. Now, however, it was coming to seem positively dangerous.

We should not take these views necessarily at face value. The situation may not have been as bad, from their point of view, as the Cassandras claimed. (Imperialists often tended to be pessimists.) Even if they were right about the imperial ignorance and apathy of previous times, a number of new trends might be thought to favour the growth of imperial awareness now. People were more concentrated in towns and cities: around 70 per cent of the population in 1900;[17] which left fewer of them effectively isolated in sleepy villages from great events. People also travelled more, thanks to cheap rail fares; travel is supposed to be mind-broadening. Then again, Britain was a far more literate country than it had been thirty or fifty years previously, with 97% being able to read by 1900;[18] which meant that more people could discover the empire in this way. Governments had greater control over school curricula, which could be useful for imperial propagandists. The press was undergoing a revolution, especially in the provision of cheap weekly and daily newspapers for the lower middle and skilled working classes. A new factor here was the entry into the field of great capitalists ('press barons') with different agendas from the old proprietors: mainly bulk sales, and therefore high profits; which they thought to achieve by appealing to base instincts like sensation and scandal. The two main barons were Lord Northcliffe, who founded the *Daily Mail* in 1896, and

Sir Cyril Pearson, who acquired and transformed the *Daily Express* in 1900. Both were rabid imperialists: 'Our policy is patriotic; our faith is the British empire', declared Pearson at the launch of his new paper.[19] More important, however, was the fact that imperial events could provide, if presented in a certain light, just the kind of sensational copy the new 'yellow press' throve on.[20] The 1880s and 1890s saw a succession of happenings in the colonies which were genuinely dramatic, beginning (before the *Daily Mail* was born) with the 'Gordon affair' in the Sudan in 1884–5, whose tragic climax—the 'murder' of the Christian hero Gordon by Muslim 'fanatics' on the steps of the British residence in Khartoum, represented in a hundred paintings, drawings, and engravings—became iconic.[21] Not many contemporary Britons can have been unaware of that.

Direct participation in the empire also undoubtedly increased towards the end of the century. The number of British administrators was still quite small at this time: about 2,000 ruling India and 2,700 running the other colonies; but other opportunities had expanded greatly. Trade took hundreds of people to the colonies, missionary work several thousand,[22] and soldiering accounted for around a quarter of a million.[23] Whether this was also reflected in a greater colonial presence in Britain is debatable. Census reports counted 111,627 colonials living in England and Wales in 1891, compared with 51,572 in 1861. How many of these were black—and so more likely to be true colonial 'subjects'—the censuses do not make clear.[24] 'England is so shut off from the rest of the world by being an island,' wrote the author of a guide to 'citizenship' in 1886, 'that very many English people never see foreign countries at all, and very seldom see the people who live in them.'[25] 'You would never see a coloured person in the streets then at all,' wrote one London East Ender, referring to the turn of the century; 'The only dark-skinned person you would see then was the Indian Toffee Man. You would look upon him as some sort of mystic or curio.'[26] Yet we know that there was a sizeable community of Indian students, professionals, and seamen domiciled in London in around 1900: Jonathan Schneer guesses there were about a thousand of these all told.[27] One or two other memoirists began to notice them. 'One sees all nationalities', wrote Margaret Harkness about East London in the later 1880s: 'A grinning Hottentot elbows his way through a crowd of long-eyed Jewesses. An Algerian merchant walks arm-in-arm with a native of Calcutta. A little Italian plays pitch-and-toss with a small Russian. A Polish Jew enjoys sauerkraut with a German Gentile. And among the foreigners lounges the East

End loafer, monarch of all he surveys, lord of the premises.'[28] As this quotation indicates, European immigrants were still more visible than colonials—and no less exotic; but the latter were there, in little pockets like Whitechapel and London's dockland, for those native British who lived or worked there, or were drawn there by curiosity.

* * *

All this probably constituted a richer soil for the growth of domestic imperial sentiment than had existed before. Most imperialists however, could not see it: all they noticed were the obstacles. Walter Frewen Lord's 'vermin of anti-imperialism' was one (how much he may have exaggerated this, we shall see), although that mainly affected the more educated classes. It was its potential impact on the classes 'beneath' them, though, that was mainly feared. 'The simple-minded working man or farm labourer', wrote an anonymous propagandist in 1901, 'cannot, of course, picture to himself the complex and delicate organisation and the solidarity of a world-wide Empire', or the benefits that accrued from it. It was on 'the narrowness of that man's horizon', he went on, that 'the Little Englander sets to work... with oily, benevolent voice, and with soft and well-gloved hands'.[29] Some seemed to think there was little one could do about this. It was an inherent problem with 'the democracy', claimed the right-wing *National Review* in 1907, that it was so 'easily misled'.[30] (A year later it would characterize the entire working class electorate as 'unpatriotic... scum'.)[31] Imperialists who felt this way often rejected democracy altogether, either openly, or thinly disguised as 'party politics'.[32] On the other hand they were not bound to, since if the workers were so easily misled, surely it followed that they could be led in the right direction just as easily. Their lack of patriotism was a matter of upbringing. This, incidentally, had been J. R. Seeley's major concern as early as the 1860s, long before he hit on his imperial idea: 'Now that the Americans, the Germans, the Italians, are almost drunk with the sense of their national greatness,' he wrote in an 1868 essay on national education, 'it would surely be well if our own population could be brought to think of England otherwise than as a country where wages are low, manners very cold, the struggle for life intolerably severe.'[33] Seventeen years later, and two years after the publication of *The Expansion of England,* Seeley was still hoping to see the day—which he obviously did not feel had arrived yet—'when one may mention the name of England [in secondary schools] without raising a laugh'.[34] This was in fact a common contemporary perception of the English: that they were almost temperamentally—even proudly—*un*patriotic.[35]

At the bottom of this were apparently three factors: decades of indoctrination by woolly internationalist liberals; a shorter period of socialist propaganda, teaching the workers to put class before country; and what was called 'national deterioration', an umbrella term for a variety of enervating ills that were supposed to be afflicting Britain at this time (among them, physical weakness, feeble-mindedness, alcoholism, gambling, crime, sexual deviation, laziness, and professional sport).[36] For these ills a number of solutions were mooted, ranging from the disciplinarian, like compulsory military service, to the reformist, like free school meals in deprived areas to fatten children up. The latter approach, it was thought, might also address the 'socialist' obstacle in the way of a broader patriotism by winning back the workers' allegiance to imperialistic governments. This was Disraeli's old agenda, writ much larger now. In the early 1900s the term for it was 'social imperialism'.[37] In much the same way, old-fashioned liberalism might also be countered by appealing to the workers' self-interest, this time by promising to 'protect' their jobs from the foreign competition that the liberal shibboleth of free trade had left them vulnerable to. Most 'protectionists' were also in favour of an empire trading area (or 'Zollverein'), which made the connection with imperialism more explicit.[38] These were all possible ways of winning over hearts and minds.

It was not, however, going to be easy. Old allegiances ran deep: liberalism, for example, had solid religious (largely Nonconformist) roots as well as material ones. The class divisions that made working-class loyalty problematical were not just the fault of socialist agitators, as we have seen. The upper classes were complicit in this. For years they had quite deliberately excluded the 'lower' orders from any sense of identity with themselves or their imperial achievements. The reason for that was structural: it was the way British society worked. This was bound to leave a lasting mark. Denied one allegiance, the working classes had constructed others: to their class, for example, or local nationalities, or regions, or religions; and to cultures and value systems entirely of their own. This applied to the middle classes too. These alternative cultures were not necessarily incompatible with empire loyalty, but they might be difficult to reconcile with some aspects of it, and certainly with the more committed forms of imperialism demanded by the zealots. The empire certainly featured less prominently in them than in upper- and upper-middle-class culture, and very differently. The gulfs between these cultures would be difficult to bridge; not least because it would require the upper classes themselves to change the habits of a lifetime, in order to genuinely accept the middle and working classes as co-citizens, and hence co-imperialists.

Few of them did grasp this nettle. It involved too great an upheaval of the imperial class's worldview. To admit the working classes as equal citizens with themselves would undermine their claim to be uniquely fitted to govern them, and hence to govern anybody else. A handful of upper-middle-class educationalists seem to have flirted with the idea: they have appeared already in this account, believing that the workers could become 'gentlemen' under public-school influence—the word 'gentleman' being almost interchangeable with 'Englishman' among this set—but with little success.[39] Most imperialists rejected this route, and sought instead to inculcate a different sort of imperialism in the working classes, one that was still compatible with the latter's subordinate role. It is expressed perfectly in an elementary school textbook published in 1901, on 'Famous Englishmen', which uses this analogy: 'In every age we may call the great man the statue, and the people who supported him the pedestal. Few people in our time will become statues, but we can all take our share in forming a firm pedestal in support of a great leader and a great cause ... Remember, then, that men and women who wisely obey wise laws, who greatly support great men and great aims, are just as necessary as the famous leader himself.'[40] So working-class imperialists could take the same pride in the empire as, for example, a bricklayer might take in his humble contribution to the building of a great house. It was a serving rather than a participatory kind of imperialism. Hopefully, that might avoid the more dangerous implications of the latter sort.

Propaganda along these lines began effectively only in the 1880s, and took a number of forms. Propaganda organizations—societies, leagues, associations, movements—were started up. Schools were particularly targeted, together with the activities of children outside school hours. Literature (at all levels) was a favourite vehicle, together with the other arts, albeit to a lesser extent. Social reform was another medium; the idea being that fitter and happier subjects would be more patriotic ones. The amount of imperial propaganda in Britain in the late nineteenth and early twentieth centuries was prodigious, and is now the subject of a considerable research industry, inaugurated by John MacKenzie's pioneering work and continued by the 'school' of imperialism studies which that inspired.[41] There can be no disputing the fact that the imperialists were propagandizing. The only questions have to do with how effective their propaganda was.

These questions will be addressed in the following chapter; but first the propaganda scene itself needs to be briefly surveyed. The various imperialist associations that mushroomed at this time are the most obvious manifestations, though not necessarily the most influential. Some of these pre-dated 1880, notably the Royal Colonial Society, founded in 1868 mainly as a meeting place for those already involved with the empire, but which took on a propaganda function later on.[42] It was followed by the Imperial Federation League (1884), the British Empire League (1896), the League of the Empire (1901), the Empire Day Movement (1903), the Royal Colonial Institute (1909), the Round Table Group (1909), the Overseas Club (1910), and for the 'ladies', the Daughters of the Empire (1901)—though this was mainly a colonial body (it still flourishes in the United States)—and the important Victoria League (1899).[43] Supplementing these were quasi-imperialist organizations: that is, bodies campaigning on behalf of other causes, but with plainly imperialist agendas. These included the Fair Trade League (1881) and the Tariff Reform League (1903): from the 1880s protectionism was usually linked with imperial federation; a cluster of new emigration societies founded from the 1880s, all recommending the colonies now in preference to the United States;[44] pressure groups devoted to strengthening Britain's imperial defences, like the Navy League (1894) and the National Service League (1906);[45] and a number of organizations directed towards turning boys (and later girls) into better imperial citizens.

Propaganda methods varied. The public meeting was an obvious one, but probably the least effective in most cases: people usually only attend meetings about causes they support anyway, or at least on subjects they are interested in. Another ploy was to seek to make the empire attractive, or even fun. Exhibitions were a part of this.[46] The first official exhibition with a specific imperial theme was the 'Colonial and Indian' held in South Kensington in 1886, with the express object of enabling 'all classes of Her Majesty's subjects...to realise the greatness of the British empire'.[47] Working men and schoolchildren were especially targeted.[48] It also, incidentally, inspired—if that is the right word for what is not one of Sir Arthur Sullivan's best works—the first piece of overtly imperial 'serious' British music, in the form of an 'Ode' for its opening with words by Tennyson. (The refrain is 'Britons, hold your own!')[49] This was the last occasion before the great 1924 Empire Exhibition at Wembley that the government got involved in such a project. Most later imperial exhibitions were the commercial brainchildren of Imre Kiralfy, a Hungarian-born and Barnum-trained impresario, and were frankly sensationalist.[50] His 'Empire of India' Exhibition of 1895 also gave rise to a musical work: 'An Operatic-Historical Production in Two Acts' called *India*, with words by Kiralfy himself and music by one Angelo Venanzi, which starts with 'A Hindu Suttee', and ends with the 'Glorification of Victoria, the Empress Queen'.[51] Imperial exhibitions were held in provincial cities too.[52] These were just the tip of the iceberg: there were scores of other, smaller empire-related shows. Museums too became more empire-friendly.[53] The permanent exhibition at the Crystal Palace, which had forsaken its imperial side when it moved from Hyde Park to Sydenham in 1855, started taking it all back in the 1890s.[54] Perhaps Queen Victoria's 'jubilee' processions of 1887 and 1897 should be included in this category, as great public displays of the glories of the empire in effect.[55] Clearly these were attractive ways of getting the imperial message across.

❦❦❦

The arts played their part in this. For the first time books, poems, paintings, statues, cantatas, and the like were produced that were explicitly imperial, in the sense of either portraying the empire or lauding it. (So there was no need now for the code-breakers.) Kipling and Conrad are the leading examples in the field of the novel, while poetry boasted Kipling again, Sir Henry Newbolt, Alfred Austin, and Alfred Noyes.[56] Painting had Lady Elizabeth Butler,[57] Byam Shaw,[58] George W Joy,[59] and the 'orientalist' Frank Brangwyn.[60] G. F. Watts sculpted an equine statue called *Physical Energy*, now in London's Kensington Gardens, which is supposed to represent imperialism's essence. (It appears to be a gelding.)[61] Less ambiguously, more statues of imperial heroes appeared in the streets.[62] In music there is Edward Elgar's 'Imperial March' (1897), 'Land of Hope and Glory' (1901), and the 'Crown of India' (1912);[63] but also the even more imperialist Arthur Sullivan,[64] Alexander MacKenzie,[65] and on a lighter note, Edward German.[66] One movement of Stanford's Fourth Irish Rhapsody (1914) is entitled 'The Death of General Wolfe'. Music also threw up some 'orientalists' in the 1890s and 1900s: Samuel Coleridge-Taylor (himself of African descent), Gustav Holst (inspired after a visit to Algeria), Granville Bantock, and Amy Woodforde-Finden ('Pale hands I loved beside the Shalimar').[67]

By contrast, imperial architecture still generally eschewed 'orientalisms'. This of course makes it more 'imperial*ist*' in the mainstream sense of the word. Eastern styles were simply inferior to Western; 'wonderful made picturesqueness but no intellect', as Sir Edwin Lutyens wrote. (Yet he was the man commissioned to design the Raj's great new capital in New Delhi.[68]) Unsurprisingly, none of his fine British buildings (mainly houses) reveals any obvious colonial features. There are one or two 'Cape Dutch' houses in England, dating from the 1900s.[69] The real imperial style of the time, however, was different: Roman-classical still, but more severe and overbearing than previously. The main front of Buckingham Palace, the old War Office, the British Museum's Edward VII Galleries, and Selfridges store, all in London, are probably the best—certainly the biggest—examples.[70] In 1913 a genuine imperial architect, Herbert Baker, arrived in London from South Africa to ruin Nash's Bank of England with a disastrous upwards (classical) extension, and to spoil Trafalgar Square with the large but soulless South Africa House.[71]

There was plenty of imperialism at 'lower' cultural levels too. The most notorious purveyors of it were the music halls, which were the despair of imperial critics like J. A. Hobson during the Boer War. Examples of clearly imperialistic songs were Winifred Hare's 'Britannia's Sons shall Rule the World' (1897):

> So join with me, all of you, while I sing Britannia's praise,
> The empire on whose shores the sun has cast no setting rays ...[72]

and Roddick Anderson's 'Another Little Patch of Red':

> For he meant to have a pull, did young John Bull,
> He found it wouldn't do to lie a-bed;
> And this plucky little chap
> Soon began to paint the map
> With an ever-growing patch of red.[73]

Others celebrated the help the Dominions and India gave to Britain in her colonial wars:

> The other nations fret, and envy us, you bet,
> Because we know the way to colonise.[74]

In popular theatres there was a little spate of plays and shows around 1900 with imperial themes and settings, something which was almost unprecedented.[75] The new medium of cinema joined in, coming just in time to bring events of the Boer War home to people in the form of moving photographic images, though few of the clips shown were of actual military action (they were usually of parades and army camps), unless they were fakes: one film of the 'bombardment of Mafeking' shown in Kinemas all over the country in 1900 was actually staged on a Home Counties golf course.[76] China also furnished some terrific themes for early films, as the following dramatization of a supposed incident during the Boxer Rising (1900) suggests:

A little girl is sitting in the fields, and the nurse is seen walking towards her with the baby in her arms... The nurse places the baby by her side and begins to sew a garment, the baby meanwhile playing about. Whilst the nurse is intent on her work a Boxer, concealed in the vegetation, crawls stealthily up, and, snatching the baby, raises it above his head, and flings it crash on the ground at the nurse's feet, who starts up in terror, and reaches for the child, only to be roughly dragged to the ground by the Boxer, who at this moment is reinforced by a number of other Chinese... The screams of the nurse, however, have caught the ear of [a] British officer... He fires his revolver to give alarm, and a party of British soldiers are quickly on the scene, upon which the Boxers drop their captives and fly, the soldiers pursuing them... The officer has fortunately observed the Boxer who is making off with the child, and, giving chase, manages to capture him, and saves the child, which is restored to the arms of the nurse, who passionately clasps it to her breast.[77]

That has everything: alien savagery, female vulnerability, imperial rescue. It must have made an impression.

Then there were prints, usually of imperial heroes, battlescenes, or the death of General Gordon, which could be bought relatively cheaply now—some were given away with magazines—and hung on the walls at home. The most famous of the Gordon pictures, George W. Joy's *Gordon's Last Stand,* was so popular that the scene was reproduced in wax at Madame Tussaud's.[78] The empire was also celebrated in the more popular forms of music, like the scores of marches and 'descriptive fantasias' for the piano that appeared on Sudan and Boer War themes, usually with battle scenes depicted on the covers,[79] and musical monologues like Kipling's notorious 'Gunga Din'. 'Treasuries of suitable works for recitation continued to come from the presses,' writes Ronald Pearsall, 'almost every one of them featuring "The Relief of Lucknow"; and seasoned hands at musical evenings winced when a gentleman—it was more often a gentleman than a lady—got out his grubby piece of paper.'[80] These pieces were probably targeted at the middle-class market; at 1s. 6d. a time, the sheet music would have been beyond the pocket of the workers, even those with pianos. More trivially, but maybe as effectively, the empire appeared in advertisements: 'Britain's Might is (W)right', for example, for a popular brand of soap, picturing a lion in front of a Union Jack; on biscuit-tin lids; and on 'cigarette cards', inserted into packets to encourage boys to smoke.[81] Most of these forms of propaganda were new: certainly the incidence and intensity of them were.

The intensity was no less in the field of popular books and magazines. The proportion of empire-related subject-matter in mainstream magazines during this period—leaving aside the Boer War years, which were exceptional—was between 5 and 10 per cent, most of it celebrating Britain's imperial role, at least implicitly.[82] The amount of coverage was probably about the same in newspapers, which were far more widely read at this time than they had been earlier. Younger readers were particularly well served: the amount of imperialist and empire-related material directed to them in this period is phenomenal. The stars here were G. A. Henty and Gordon Stables, each of whom published more than a hundred full-length novels between 1880 and 1905, many of them with overtly imperial settings and themes, some right up to date: both men, for example, published Boer War novels while the war was still going on.[83] These were supplemented by children's magazines, ranging from the respectable *Boys' Own Paper*, launched in 1879, through *Boys of England*, *Boys of the Empire*, and the *Union Jack* (owned by Henty), down to the comic books *Pluck*, *Marvel*, *Grip*, and *Chums*. The *BOP* was a leader here, with empire-related features still accounting for nearly 20 per cent of its contents in the early 1910s.[84] Other boys' papers pushed the empire less, but never ignored it entirely.[85] Unlike earlier in the century, by this period there can be no doubt about the message they sought to purvey. A brochure advertising three of these papers commended above all their imperial content, and their 'stories of England's prowess on land and sea, and of her great naval and military heroes'.[86] Henty was similarly open about his imperial agenda: the 'courage of our forefathers', he wrote in his preface to *St George for England* (1885), 'has created the greatest Empire in the world ... if this empire is ever lost, it will be by the cowardice of their descendants.'[87] On the other hand, warned Manville Fenn, another story-writer, boys 'don't like being preached at';[88] which is why the imperialist lessons were dressed up in tales of action and adventure. Girls had their 'female Henty', Bessie Marchant, who also wrote more than a hundred novels, this time usually featuring young heroines in what earlier would have been regarded as very transgressive roles, 'riding, the wilds, shooting, and dominating ferocious tribesmen or backwood desperadoes', with the trappings of empire—consuls, governors, soldiers (often needed to rescue the brave girls at the end)—all around. Unlike Henty and Stables, Marchant had no first-hand experience of the empire, being, as her *Times Literary Supplement* obituary charmingly puts it, 'a traveller only on the enchanted carpet of imagination'.[89] Girls also had their own magazines, with less imperial content, but still some.[90] All of these children's books and magazines are full of disparaging stereotypes of other races, which it is difficult to see as other than rankly rac*ist,* unlike earlier examples.[91] Even plucky English girls were portrayed as inherently superior to savage African tribesmen and amoral Chinese. The 'culturist' model simply does not fit here.

❦❦❦

This was a very 'scatter-gun' kind of imperialization, however: no one could be sure where or how it would impact. Much of it seemed merely visceral: the music-hall 'jingoism', for example, which many of the most zealous imperialists distrusted, realizing that it was not quite the same as imperialism, even when it took an imperial event (the Boer War) for its object. 'The Imperialism which squeaks through the penny trumpets and swaggers in the music halls', wrote an anonymous contributor to the *Fortnightly Review* in 1902, 'is of all the sentiments masquerading in the name of patriotism anywhere in the world, the most vulgar, blatant and inept.'[92] Something more solid and responsible was required. The key to this was education. That had failed the empire before, as the zealots saw things, and—indeed—as we have found. This was where the serious work needed to be done if the British were to be nurtured into—as imperialists at this time sometimes put it, using the 'r' word characteristically loosely—a truly 'imperial race'.

The way seemed clear. The opportunities for imperial teaching or propaganda in state schools, for the problematical lower classes, mushroomed from the 1880s onwards, helped by the general expansion of elementary education that took place in this period, with the extension of the minimum leaving age, for example, from 10 to 11 in 1893, and then to 12 in 1899,[93] and the broadening of syllabuses to include geography and history in most schools, this time genuinely.[94] It also helped that the state began to take a more positive role in prescribing school curricula. History as a subject took off in the 1890s, rising from a very low base in 1890, when only 414 elementary schools out of a possible 23,000 taught it, to 3,597 schools in 1895 and 5,659 in 1898.[95] Its great turning-point came in 1900–2, when history was officially designated a subject to be studied 'as a rule' (or *almost* compulsorily) in state secondary and elementary schools, pushing the proportion of schools offering the subject up to nearly 100 per cent.[96] This was also when teacher-training colleges began engaging history and geography specialists for the first time.[97]

One of the reasons behind this change was almost certainly a new recognition of the potential value of history, in particular, for inculcating a sense of national identity and therefore loyalty. That was at any rate one school inspector's interpretation soon after the event: 'it is on the grounds of patriotism', he wrote in 1903, 'that history [has now] been given prominence in the schools.'[98] Geography was promoted for the same reason. 'Let our teaching be from the British standpoint,' Halford Mackinder urged a conference on 'Imperial Education' in 1911, 'so that finally we see the world as a theatre for British activity.'[99] There was also a little spate of school-books specifically on patriotism—though more often called 'citizenship'—which was new.[100] The empire featured in this, in two ways. First, readers were taught to feel proud of their imperial past; secondly, they were enjoined to be good citizens in order to ensure an imperial future. 'Be true to your imperial forebears', was a common refrain, combining both approaches: 'Let every British boy and girl resolve never to do anything unworthy of their brave ancestors, and try to hand on unimpaired to future ages the traditions of Liberty, Justice, and Mercy, which have raised our empire to the position she now holds in the world.'[101] This approach was also very new.

Imperial propagandists strained to maximize the empire's profile in education. Shortly after Seeley's complaint about empire-free history teaching in 1883, the Royal Colonial Institute (RCI) responded by writing to public- and grammar-school heads urging colonial studies on them, and by instituting a prize imperial essay competition of its own for schools and colleges. Later other imperialist organizations, especially the League of the Empire and the Victoria League, joined in.[102] The League of the Empire set up a 'History section' for this purpose, run by prominent empire historians, in 1904, and held a 'Federal Conference on Education' (the 'federal' referred to the idea of imperial unity) in 1907.[103] It also directly commissioned and sometimes even subsidized empire-friendly textbooks for schools.[104] The RCI pushed for imperial studies in universities too.[105] In parliament the movement was spearheaded by Lord Meath, the leading imperial propagandist of the day, who asked the government in 1893, and repeatedly afterwards, to 'lay greater stress' on the 'history and geography of the British empire' in its next revision of the Education Code: 'especially' (for some reason, which he did not spell out) 'in the case of girls.'[106] 'All hopes of a sound Imperialism for the future', claimed one imperialist in 1908, rested 'on the spread of education in Imperial matters'; only in this way could one ensure the development of what he called a 'sane' (as opposed to 'jingo') sense of imperial duty among the democracy. The alternative was 'utter ruin'.[107]

On the surface the campaign appears to have been a success. The empire featured in just about every new history book published after 1880, and far more prominently than before. A good way of measuring this is to compare successive editions of *Little Arthur's History of England* (revised by other hands after Callcott's death in 1842), where one can see the colonies creeping in incrementally. (The first mention of the *word* empire comes in 1880.)[108] The 1888 edition of S. R. Gardiner's short *Outline of English History* devoted eighteen pages to India, four to the Afghan wars, twelve to the colonization and loss of America, and three to the 1881 Egyptian campaign and the death of Gordon, out of a total of 236;[109] considerably more than previous British histories. Other texts carried whole chapters on India.[110] There were also books devoted entirely to the empire, a spate of which appeared in the 1890s and 1900s, most of them written by zealots and clearly designed for the 'higher' end of the school market.[111] But at the 'lower' end too, in elementary and secondary school 'readers', the empire is scarcely less visible.[112]

These books were generally less critical of the empire also, with none of the carping that had so disfigured many of the mid-Victorian texts. The greatest beneficiaries of this were probably the Elizabethan voyagers, generally painted earlier as disreputable privateers and slavers, but now suddenly rehabilitated as loveable 'sea-dogs' (even the slaver Hawkins), exemplifying typical 'Anglo-Saxon' qualities of courage and enterprise.[113] Similarly, nothing could be said against Clive now, and even the controversial Warren Hastings escaped censure: he was the 'greatest' of all the governors-general of India, according to Charles and Mary Oman.[114] The Indian, Chinese, and Afghan wars, over which mid-Victorian textbook opinion had been sharply divided, now became almost universally justified, usually on the grounds of aggression, 'treachery', or insufferable anarchy on the other side. As well as this, the American Revolution was coming to be retailed as a tragedy, rather than a triumph of 'English freedom', which shows perhaps how the emphasis of many of these books was changing, from the spread of liberty to the growth of empire.[115] Some of these books were highly partisan, C. R. L. Fletcher and Rudyard Kipling's rabidly imperialistic *A School History of England* (1911) being the most notorious example;[116] but even the calmer Omans finished their *Junior History* (1904) by recommending the idea of imperial federation, which was controversial at the time, in order that 'the future of the world would lie in the hands of the Anglo-Saxon race'.[117] There are exceptions. Not all history textbook writers were conscious propagandists, and some strove so scrupulously for fairness and objectivity that they avoided any judgements at all, apart from those that were implied by their choice of arid 'facts' to retail.[118] Others retained their critical faculties. Slavery was usually condemned if it ever featured;[119] the Chinese and Afghan wars occasionally;[120] and the 'wild and piratical' Jameson Raid almost universally in the later books.[121] Valerie Chancellor, referring to the turn of the century, finds it 'remarkable that at such a time so many authors of children's textbooks succeeded in maintaining a critical attitude to the conduct of their own nation abroad'.[122] But always this criticism was for falling short of the highest imperial ideals. The imperial project itself was scarcely ever questioned.[123] Usually it was represented as, despite the occasional lapse, a force for good in the world; which marked a significant shift.

Geography followed the same path. A new official 'code' for the subject in 1882 recommended that Canada and Australia be brought into syllabuses at Standard IV (for 9-year-olds), and 'the British Colonies and Dependencies' at Standard VI, mainly to encourage emigration.[124] Textbooks geared to this agenda propagandized British imperialism enthusiastically. As with history, there was a flood of books specializing in the empire.[125] But even the more general ones puffed it. 'The gaining of so extensive a territory by Britain', boasted one of *Chambers's Geographical Readers* in 1901, 'is "one of the greatest miracles of history".' The result was 'a system of rule that has spread the blessings of peace, security, and justice'.[126] 'The position of Britain in India', wrote Halford Mackinder in an 'elementary' geography text of 1911, 'is one of the most wonderful things in the world.'[127] 'When we consider the relative areas and populations of the governing British Isles and the subject land of India,' averred a *Nelson* Reader in 1902, 'we are struck with amazement.'[128] A few texts also emphasized the colonies' value to Britain in a way that had been rare, and would have been regarded as partisan, before.[129] 'The national pride of England is proverbial,' wrote a commentator in 1903 (probably mistakenly); 'History and geography are so taught that children cannot fail to be impressed with the greatness of the British empire.'[130] That must have warmed the imperialists' hearts.

Most of this writing probably did not set out deliberately to be propagandist, in the narrow sense of cynical or deceitful. There is at least one exception: Halford Mackinder, the leading geographer among the imperial zealots, and later to become famous as the inventor of 'geo-politics', who was quite blatant about *his* propagandist purpose in the 1911 lecture quoted already, in which he urged that geography be taught in schools 'from the British standpoint'. He went on: 'This, no doubt, is to deviate from the cold and impartial ways of science. When we teach the millions, however, we are not training scientific investigators, but the practical striving citizens of an empire which has to hold its place according to the universal law of survival through efficiency and effort.'[131] This agenda may explain the bias of his own textbooks. Few other pedagogues, however, were quite as shameless as this. Stephen Heathorn credits them with being just as 'immersed' in the discourse they were peddling as they wished their readers to become. This means that their work should be taken as reflecting some of the assumptions and values of the section of society they came from—all were middle class, generally academics, teachers, and educational administrators, and male, claims Heathorn[132]—whatever their impact on their young consumers may have been.

The same may have been true of these books' portrayals of other races and cultures. Here again the emphasis had changed quite radically from that of the mid-nineteenth century. The change can be traced in the successive editions of a staple classroom text of the nineteenth century, the Revd Alexander Stewart's *Compendium of Modern Geography*, whose favourable references to Indian crafts and manufactures in its first version (1828), noted above, had by the time of the thirty-fifth edition (1889) been replaced by this: 'The civilisation of the Caucasian race in Asia has been lop-sided, the ornamental arts, as those of the goldsmith and jeweller, which minister to luxury, being far in advance of the useful arts, which minister to daily and universal wants; and Mongolian civilisation, represented by that of China, is chargeable with stationariness.'[133] Utility was a common contemporary measure of Britain's superiority over more 'artistic' peoples. In case the moral of this is lost, Stewart (or his reviser: it is difficult to credit that the original author could have penned versions sixty-one years apart) also openly justifies British rule in India in this new edition in terms of 'the inability of the inhabitants to govern themselves', and the material and moral benefits it has brought.[134] Others also sought to denigrate eastern culture:

Seen at a distance, glittering in the rays of the sun, their effect upon the beholder [the domes of Moslem mosques] is imposing. He imagines he is about to enter upon some enchanted scene. On a nearer approach, however, he is frequently disabused of this impression, as he finds himself in the midst of narrow, crooked and dirty streets...

[N]owhere in the world is anything to be seen to compare with [Indian temples and mausoleums, like the Taj Mahal], either in elegance of design, or costliness of materials. In fact, it might be supposed that they had originally been erected to commemorate the virtues of some great benefactor of our species, instead of being the whim of some prince who dawdled away his years in indolence or pleasure.[135]

That rubbed some of the gloss off.

The trend now in geography books was to emphasize the *differences* between cultures and races. This was new. Earlier texts—especially from before the 1850s—had generally dwelt on the common humanity of other peoples. These ones highlight the 'otherness'. Sometimes it is done quite sensationally: 'A real Chinese will eat mice, rats, kittens, or puppies, when they are cooked.' That was for very young children. 'As a rule, the men wear a sort of petticoat; the women, on the other hand, wear trousers or pantaloons...' 'On the whole, the Australian natives are an ugly, unprepossessing people, with degrading and filthy habits.' 'Like the beasts of prey... the Malays are always on the watch, to assuage their thirst of blood and plunder.' 'The tribes [of Nigeria]... are extremely savage, practising horrible forms of religion, accompanied by human sacrifices...' Treatment of women was, as ever, a way of making a telling contrast. In China, for example, 'the women indulge freely in smoking'; among the aborigines, 'the women, or "gins", are considered by their husbands mere beasts of burden. They are so badly treated that a native woman is usually a mass of scars, and seldom lives beyond the age of thirty.'[136] Peoples—'races'—were *defined* by their differences, which, it was implied, were static. Kathryn Castle, in her fine study of these 'stereotypes', not only in textbooks but also in children's fiction, calls this 'the creation of a cast of "imperial subjects"'.[137] It looks very much like that.

The stress on 'difference' was certainly a deliberate part of Mackinder's imperialist agenda. 'In these days,' he said in his 1911 lecture, 'when international affairs have become worldwide, it is necessary that the great human contrasts which are the outcome of universal history should be generally known, and that—to take only one category, by way of illustration—the distinction of Christian, Mohammedan, Hindu and Buddhist should be generally realised.'[138] His own works in the textbook genre exemplify this. 'My aim has been', he wrote in the preface to one of them, 'to equip the young citizen of a free country, which is also one of the Great Powers of the globe, with a knowledge of the chief *contrasts* of the political and commercial world. We must think of the *competing* nations of today in their geographical setting.'[139] D. R. Stoddart sees this as a typical characteristic of what he calls the 'imperialist', as opposed to the 'liberal', tradition of geographical writing in Europe generally in the nineteenth and twentieth centuries.[140] It was fairly strong in Britain at this time.

It was not quite ubiquitous. A trawl through the geography texts of the period throws up some contrary indications. 'Civilization' (defined Eurocentrically) was often acknowledged, where it was found: the Chinese were still complimented for their great learning, for example; the Persians for their scientific expertise; Brahmins for their sobriety.[141] A *Nelson* Reader was impressed by an Indian's having become Senior Wrangler at Cambridge in 1899.[142] Africans were less often complimented, but in 1901 we find a *Chambers Reader* averring that 'the Negroes are a great world race—a race that has yet a great history before it'.[143] Others still took pains to avoid obvious racism (as opposed to 'culturism'): like A. J. Herbertson (later Professor of Geography at Oxford), whose *Man and His Work* (1902) stressed the impact of climate on human behaviour, in a way that curiously anticipates Arnold Toynbee's famous *Study of History*, and which he used to defend the Australian aborigines, usually the most despised of 'races', against 'the many shocking charges brought against them by early colonists'. They were the same as us, but forced to live as they did by 'the nature of their country'.[144] Others continued with the old nineteenth-century idea of 'progress', pointing out—as a *Manual of Moral Instruction* of 1908 put it—that 'Every nation develops from what was at first a barbarous race', which meant that there was no essential difference between any of them, save chronology.[145] None of this ruled out imperialism, however, which was regarded as no less justified as a means of 'raising' backward people than of protecting inferior ones. Even *Chambers*'s 'great Negro race' needed

European tutelage to enable it to achieve the place in history that lay ahead of it.[146]

❦❦❦

That seems quite an onslaught. In fact it looks slightly less impressive when set against the broader educational context of the time, as we shall be doing in the next chapter. It was certainly less reassuring to imperialists than one might expect. This was why the latter did not rely solely on the school curriculum to get their ideas across to young people, but gathered other strings to their bows as well. These were directed at the extra-curricular sides of schoolboy and schoolgirl life, and may for that reason have been more effective from a propaganda point of view.

There were dozens of these initiatives. One was the 'Empire Day' movement, one of Lord Meath's pet causes, though it was not his idea originally.[147] This was supposed to attract children to the empire by giving them a half-holiday (24 May) to mark it. They would spend this 'in exercises of a patriotic character, and in pleasant instruction in matters pertaining to the Empire and its responsibilities'. The 'pleasant' was crucial. That would drive its importance home to them.[148] It took off in the mid-1900s, despite the Liberal government's lukewarmness towards it. Only a minority of local education authorities resisted.[149] Already by 1907 12,544 out of 20,541 elementary schools in England and Wales were celebrating Empire Day in some form or other, according to the movement's own propaganda (which may not be reliable).[150] An Empire Day parade in London in 1911 was attended by 10,000 children, performing 'a series of flag movements symbolising imperial unity';[151] not a bad crowd, though smaller than at this time turned out to watch West Ham United Football Club's home games on most Saturday afternoons. (West Ham's education authority, incidentally, was one of the last to hold out against Empire Day.)[152] The movement was strongest initially in the Home Counties, south coast resorts, and cathedral cities.[153] In the participating schools children were made to act out little tableaux on imperial and patriotic themes.[154] Some were visited on the great day by imperial bigwigs, usually military men, or even by Lord Meath himself.[155] Later Meath claimed it was his Empire Day movement that had inspired the 'rush to the colours' of August 1914.[156] That could be regarded as a pretty good return on all his hard work.

Among other efforts, the League of the Empire and the Victoria League both organized pen-pal and 'twinning' schemes between British and colonial schools, which caught on in a small minority of the former.[157] There was a plan to send older British students to colonial universities, a kind of Rhodes Scholarship scheme in reverse.[158] The various leagues also distributed cheap imperial wall-maps to schools, which may partly explain the sudden flowering of them in classrooms at this time.[159] Another wheeze was to get elementary schools to fly the Union Jack daily, perhaps with a little morning ceremony—modelled on the American one—with 'the best boy in the school carrying the flag round, the whole school saluting it and singing patriotic songs meanwhile'.[160] The 'Duty and Discipline Movement' (1912) was another of Meath's imperial ideas; its object was to combat 'softness and slackness' in the young and 'give reasonable support to all legitimate authority' over them.[161] This raises the question of the degree to which such boys' movements were really designed for imperial ends, rather than for purely reactionary, domestic ones. Most had elements of both. An early version of Baden-Powell's Boy Scout oath, for example, called for loyalty to employers as well as to 'God' and 'the King'.[162] There was plenty of imperial content here too, however.[163] The 'Scouts' were the most phenomenally successful of these empire-inspired movements of the 1900s, attracting 128,397 boys to its ranks in 1912, and 184,393 (including 'cub' scouts) by 1918.[164] It could also be argued that it was the most radical in many ways, especially in its efforts (despite the 'loyalty' oath) to cut across the social classes. Baden-Powell's *Scouting for Boys* explicitly preaches class tolerance: 'If you despise other boys because they belong to a poorer class than yourself you are a snob; if you hate other boys because they happen to be born richer and belong to higher class schools than yourself you are a fool.'[165] While this could be seen as merely a means of countering socialist 'jealousy', he also believed that public-school values could be passed down directly to the workers.[166] *Scouting for Boys* is full of this theme, even reproducing Henry Newbolt's famous public-school poem 'Play the Game!'[167] It may be one of the reasons why scouting caught on so; though there were limits to its appeal among the working-class lads that Baden-Powell was particularly targeting—'the vast hordes of slum boys in the great industrial centres'—as we shall see.[168]

The other main way of attracting those slum boys, and their parents, was through 'social reform'. That meant improving the material conditions of the working classes. The imperial rationale for this was simple: because the empire was so much under threat, it now needed every last Briton to be as fit and loyal as possible to keep it from harm. Unfitness and disloyalty were by no means novel phenomena in Britain, but this was the first time they were thought of in quite this imperial way. In earlier times the connection had been quite different; the colonies' role was to act as a safety-valve for social discontent. The discontented could *go* there, thus relieving the pressures at home. Now they were wanted *at* home, to add to the strength of 'the heart of the empire', as the title of a contemporary book on this question put it;[169] but obviously in a shape that made them assets, not liabilities. The urgency of this was highlighted by the revelation just after the Boer War that between 25 and 90 per cent of volunteers from the big cities (the precise figure depended on which alarmist report one read) had had to be rejected by the army on grounds of poor health or physical disability.[170] That made the connection pikestaff-plain. 'The Empire', wrote the imperial propagandist Arnold White (who was also much exercised over Jewish immigration, regarding it as diluting the indigenous British 'stock'), 'will not be maintained by a nation of outpatients.'[171] One of the obvious solutions was government intervention to toughen the people up. This would also make the working classes more likely to accept the *upper* classes' imperial agenda. That was equally important.

This was not the lesson that all imperialists drew. Lord Meath thought on the contrary that the main problem was too much state coddling, not too little. 'No other nation', he claimed in 1908, 'maintains an army of paupers out of the enforced taxation of the industrious. No other State provides hotel accommodation gratis'—he meant the dreaded workhouse—'for those of its citizens who dislike work.'[172] This was the cause of what was widely perceived as the 'degeneration' of the British 'race'.[173] The Egyptologist Sir Flinders Petrie agreed, warning that the country was 'drifting... into State Communism, where ability will be held back, and equal wages for unequal powers will destroy the stronger breeds to encourage feeble mediocrities'. 'When our Empire makes of unworth its cornerstone,' he went on, 'and lays its foundation in an alms-fed proletariat, the day of some conquering Attila will not be far distant.' Not that Petrie was against state intervention altogether—if, for example, it could be used to dissuade or prevent the 'unfit' from breeding, which was his preferred answer to the problem.[174] This view was based on the contemporary 'science' of eugenics, which some upper-class worthies flirted with at this time, including Winston Churchill, but which never caught on in Britain as it did later in Germany, Sweden, and the southern states of America. (Compulsory sterilization, the logical conclusion of this way of thinking, never stood a chance.)[175] Others preferred the more laissez-faire (and British) way of simply leaving the unfit to starve.[176] Meath took yet another route: discipline and 'Swedish' drill. (The advantage of the latter over the rather more popular 'military' drill, he told parliament in 1889, could be measured in chest-size: a recent experiment showed that military drill put an average of half an inch on to lads' chests in six months, whereas the same period of Swedish puffed them out by a good two inches.)[177] That way the general social stock could be strengthened without culling it. These policies also had the advantage over the 'social reform' solution of avoiding the social*ism* that many right-wing imperialists espied lurking in the latter, and reacted against viscerally. The drawback, however, was their lack of electoral appeal, especially the 'let the runts die' platform, which seemed unlikely to catch on widely in an age when so many of the runts now had the vote.[178]

These then were dead ends. Social imperialism, as it came to be called, was the more promising path. The unfitness of the working classes was not genetic, but was caused by their environment. This is what most imperial propagandists preferred to believe, and focused on. 'Look', wrote one of them in 1901,

> at the unhealthy aspects and dwarfish forms of the thousands of weary workers, artisans, mechanics, labourers, who swarm in the smoke-begrimed factories, mills, and evil-smelling workshops, the hive bees who make the honey for others to enjoy: whose miserable lives are an unceasing round of daily toil from year's end to year's end; who pass a joyless existence in the endeavour to earn a wage barely sufficient to keep themselves and their families from starvation; in many cases, too, employed in 'industries that kill' or are fatal to health; where such deleterious substances as phosphorous, arsenic, lead, and various poisonous chemicals and drugs are handled...

That was where the trouble lay.[179] 'Brought up in the dingy slums of joyless cities, without air or sanitation, often without accommodation, inured from early years to long hours of monotonous labour, unrefreshed by the healing influences of the country', wrote Cuthbert Medd two years later, it was 'hardly to be expected' that the urban working classes could 'support the burden or solve the problems of a world-wide Empire'. Hence the latter's decline and fall (Medd was posing as a historian looking back from the year 2031).[180] 'It is this degeneracy in the large masses in our cities which is the real danger to the British Empire...', wrote Walter Meakin; 'If everything that makes life worth living is sacrificed to the spirit of money-grubbing, the end is only a question of time.'[181] The remedy was radical, but simple:

Thomas Macnamara, a Canadian-born Liberal MP for an inner London constituency, suggested—among other things—providing the working classes with cheap municipal housing and free transport, making drill compulsory, and abolishing poverty, no less. 'All this sounds terribly like rank Socialism', he admitted. 'I'm afraid it is; but I am not in the least dismayed. Because I know it also to be first-class Imperialism. Because I know Empire cannot be built on rickety and flat-chested citizens.'[182] The word, 'socialism', held no terrors for him.

Even many less radical imperialists found that they could live with some of the features of socialism. They had a common enemy, after all. Many imperialists' descriptions of the horrors of conditions in the industrial cities are tinged with that anti-capitalist sentiment which had been inculcated in them in their public schools. It was the free market, not the upper classes, that was responsible for the slums (Meakin is quite explicit about this). Some imperialists blamed the 'commercial spirit', as it was more often called, for every other aspect of 'deterioration' in contemporary British life too: selfishness, greed, conspicuous consumption, public corruption, amorality, superficiality, philistinism, crime, pornography, the yellow press, jingoism, professional football...[183] They were also not particularly uneasy about state intervention to put some of these things right. The more old-fashioned among them were used to thinking in terms of looking after those who could not look after themselves, which had been the basis, after all, on which feudalism was supposed to have been built. It would be better if it could be done from the Hall and the vicarage, but that was hardly possible in inner-city areas, where gentry and parsons were thin on the ground; so it would have to be the state's role. The other advantage, besides toughening muscles, was that it might cement the people's imperial loyalty, something that would never happen, claimed the journalist J. L. Garvin in 1907, 'unless we are prepared to raise their lives... He who would rule the people must appear to love the people.' He went on: 'Social policy and Imperial policy are parallel, and, indeed, inseparable.'[184]

Of course this was not really socialism, in the sense that most *soi-disant* socialists would recognize. Its aims were suspect, for a start; not just the imperialism, but also the 'controlling' function clearly implied by Garvin's 'He who would rule the people must appear...' The word 'appear' also raises doubts as to his own good faith. For most social imperialists, such as Macnamara, reforms that were shared with more left-wing radicals were mixed in with others, like compulsory drill and military conscription, that no self-respecting 'real' socialist would touch with a bargepole. That made the whole package something of a curate's egg. Though it had 'the democracy' in its sights—in the common meaning at this time of the ordinary masses—it was not democratic in any other sense. Indeed, one of its chief objects was to serve as an *alternative* to democracy, steering people away from dema*gogues* who might fill them with wrong notions about the empire. It also obviated the need to grant them full citizenship. The same applied to women, for whom the imperialists' version of social reform merely meant making them better mothers, or helpmeets for their imperial husbands.[185] This agenda left a lot to be desired, from most reformists' point of view. 'Socialism' was a misnomer: socialism used for a nationalistic purpose, most political theorists would contend, is socialism distracted and distorted. (German *Nationalsozialismus* had much the same broad aim, though the parallel should not be pursued much further than this.) This raises again the question of ulterior motivation: was it really the empire the social imperialists were concerned about, or their own status, property, and privileges? Even if the imperialism was genuine, some contemporaries protested against using that as a reason for advocating policies that ought really to be accepted for their own sake. 'One day', wrote the Countess of Warwick—an unlikely convert to real socialism—'there may arise a new kind of statesman who will regard a healthy nation as a thing good in itself even though no food for cannon be needed.' In the meantime, however, she was 'thankful for almost any motive' that might further the cause of social reform.[186] She was willing to touch it, therefore; but *only* with a bargepole.

These unprecendented efforts of imperialists to bring their compatriots on board from the 1880s on indicate two things: first, the magnitude of the empire's new crisis, as the imperialists saw it; and second, the unsatisfactory state—again from their point of view—of British public opinion towards the empire up until then. Beyond that it is impossible to infer anything definite. The flood of imperial propaganda in Britain at this period suggests two further conclusions: but unfortunately they are mutually incompatible. The first is that people must have been convinced by it, simply because it was so ubiquitous. That is certainly the impression given by taking just one side of the picture, as we have done in this chapter, and piling up all the evidence. The other possible inference, however, is that it *cannot* have been as effective as this, or imperialists would not have felt the need to continue propagandizing as they did. (If anything, overt imperial propaganda increased progressively over the following decades.) This seems to be borne out by the imperialists' constant complaints that, despite all their efforts, their message was not getting through. But we cannot rely on this either. Imperial zealots, like many right-wingers, tended to be constitutionally pessimistic, and also extreme in their conception of what constituted an adequate degree of imperial commitment in society. To say that Britain was not imperialist enough by their standards is not to say that she was not imperialist at all; she could have been so in other or lesser, but still significant, ways. To find out if this was the case, we need to look at the broader picture: at the context (again) of this great imperial onslaught of the turn of the century, and the likely effect of this context on the way the propaganda was received, especially—to revert to John Finnemore's metaphor—among the bricks that made up the social 'pedestal'.

9
What About the Workers?

There can be no doubt that Britain became a more imperialistic society from the later years of the nineteenth century on. Contemporaries noticed this, and coined the phrase 'the new imperialism' to describe it. That may have exaggerated the novelty of it: certainly if it was meant to refer to Britain's policy or conduct in the world, and to imply that she only became an imperial or imperialistic *power* then. In fact Britain was no more imperialistic in effect in 1900 than she had been in, say, 1850; the only difference was that now she was more open about it. Something like this could also have been true of the empire's impact at home. Formerly it had been pervasive but hidden; now it was simply more obvious. For reasons given in previous chapters, however, this is probably wrong; there is no convincing evidence to show that the mass of the British population was silently imperialistic in the first eighty years of the nineteenth century, or that the nature and situation of the empire required it to be. Britain's imperial policy did not need an imperial culture to support it, save among a small elite; nor was it bound to impact significantly on the culture (or cultures) of the non-elite majority. What happened after 1880, then, does not simply represent the surfacing of feelings that had been there all along. It *was* something new.

Because it was new, however, some people also exaggerated the extent of it. Around the turn of the century it was natural for anti-imperialists to fear the rise of popular imperialism, signs of which were appearing in their streets, in the form of the demonstrations that celebrated the 'reliefs' of Mafeking and Ladysmith during Britain's most imperial war, the violent break-up of their own meetings, and the pro-war bricks that came hurtling through their windows. It looked as though the propagandists, aided by events, had done their work well. But this impression was misleading. Many imperialists perceived this more clearly than their opponents. Though no more reliable than the latter as objective witnesses—the imperialists tended to exaggerate the extent of socialism, for example—they were right to doubt whether such occasional outbursts of popular bellicosity ('jingoism') really signified a serious and enduring imperial commitment. That such a commitment became more widespread at this period seems clear; but it had its limits, as this chapter will try to show.

❦❦❦

The 'jingo' demonstrations, after all, only happened once or twice, and within a very narrow period of time. The Mafeking and Ladysmith celebrations took place in February and May 1900, while the famous pro-war riots in Margate and Scarborough (which had to be put down by the military) happened in March of the same year. 'There has been nothing like it since', pointed out Frederick Willis, a contemporary working-class Londoner, in 1948,[1] and there had been nothing like it earlier. The old queen's jubilees (in 1887 and 1897) and the new kings' coronations (in 1902 and 1911) cannot be counted, because they also celebrated other things. One historian doubts whether the latter were even patriotic, let alone imperialist: '[t]he ceremonies were a form of street theatre and the London crowds had, through the growing importance of music halls and theatres, a sophisticated taste for theatrical effects.'[2] This is corroborated by one account of a Jubilee fête held for 30,000 schoolchildren in Hyde Park in 1887, which the queen attended, only to be completely upstaged, apparently, by 'Herr Winkelmeier, the 8ft. 9ins. Austrian giant, who was engaged for the occasion'.[3] Turnouts for other patriotic celebrations in peacetime—Trafalgar Day, for example (21 October)—tended to be disappointing.[4] The 'mafficking' of February–May 1900 seems to have been a brief aberration. Not too much should be read into that, of course. It might just have been because the British did not go in for this sort of thing. 'It was like discovering that nine-tenths of the people of England were foreigners', was the fictional Soames Forsyte's reactions on being caught up in the City of London crowd on Mafeking Night.[5] Englishmen tended to be, as Stephen Neill puts it, 'torpid and placid' on these issues.[6] 'Perhaps', suggested Edward Elgar in 1916, 'we are a little too much afraid of that awkward self-conscious feeling, that so readily attacks the Briton, to let ourselves go in the matter of patriotic expression.'[7] On the other hand the British did 'let themselves go' on other issues. Demonstrations, sometimes violent, are a common feature of the late Victorian and Edwardian public debate: over pay and conditions, for example, trade-union rights, foreign (as distinct from imperial) policy, religion, temperance, and votes for women; which suggests that they may have felt more strongly about these issues than about the empire, either way.

As for the Boer War demonstrations themselves, there are doubts over both their composition, with clerks, medical students, and public schoolboys featuring more prominently in the detailed accounts we have than the working classes (though this may be simply because the working-classes' presence was less well recorded);[8] and over the feelings of those who participated in them, whoever they were. It seems reasonable to suppose that these were usually relief at the deliverance of British soldiers, or patriotic pride, or simple high spirits, rather than anything especially associated with the empire. Soames Forsyte took no imperial comfort from these shenanigans at all: 'The crowd was cheerful, but some day they would come in different mood!' 'I say,' his cousin George says to him; 'one of these days we shall have to fight these chaps, they're getting so damned cheeky—all radicals and socialists. They want our goods.'[9] Jingoism was fickle, at best. It seems not even to have lasted the length of the war. When Britain finally won it, in May 1902, there were scarcely any celebrations at all, perhaps because the British victory took so long to come about. 'We have always felt', said the *Fortnightly Review* in July 1902, possibly speaking for many, 'that the Boer was a preposterously little fellow, and the work of crushing him ... was not in itself an essentially pleasant or heroic thing to carry through.'[10] That may have helped dampen the exceptional 'jingo' ardour of the earlier, more febrile stages of the conflict.

The other spectacular manifestation of popular imperialism in the 1890s and 1900s, supposedly, was the culture of the city music hall. Many anti-imperialists regarded this as the major villain of the piece. J. A. Hobson, for example, reckoned the music hall was 'a more potent educator' of certain sections of the working and lower middle classes than 'the church, the school, the political meeting, or even the press', and was largely responsible for the jingoism of the Boer War years.[11] The music hall and popular, excessive imperialism became inseparably associated, especially in the minds of respectable middle-class critics (who included the more sober imperialists as well as the antis), most of whom probably never went to a music hall in their lives. If they had done, they might have revised their view.

To begin with, there must be doubts about the pure working-class credentials of the music halls. They were not owned by the workers, but by impressarios, often fairly big businessmen running 'chains' of halls, whose commercial interests were likely to incline them to the political Right. One factor encouraging this was the Liberals' perceived hostility to 'vulgar' entertainment of all kinds, and especially any involving the sale of alcohol. Many of the halls' clientele will have resented this too.[12] Furthermore, the latter were certainly not exclusively working class; there were some quite up-market halls in the West End and suburbs of London, for example, and many others with mixed audiences of workers (in the cheap galleries) and well-off young 'blades' (in the stalls).[13] Songs like Vesta Tilley's 'Burlington Bertie', performed in male evening dress, were directed at both classes at the same time: with one class identifying with the 'masher' (or upper-class fop), and the other jeering at him.[14] In much the same way, political songs were often performed in order to set one part of an audience against another. Most lyrics were biased towards the Conservatives, with Liberals, socialists, and suffragettes common targets for mockery. This does not mean they were uncontroversial, however. Frederick Willis recalls political acts being greeted with 'howls of execration' as well as with 'cheers'. We sometimes forget the howls. That was all part of the fun.[15]

It is unlikely that 'jingo' songs were also meant to be provocative, though they too may have had more of an imperial resonance with some parts of their audiences than with others. It is true that most of them were patriotic. There were very few pro-Boer songs during the South African War, for example.[16] A few were overtly imperial, but these were relatively rare. Most offerings had a narrower compass: they were war songs rather than empire songs, supporting Britain simply because she was fighting, or 'standing up' for herself, or repelling imagined 'slights', rather than because she was defending or expanding her territory.[17] They would have been little different if Britain had been fighting, for example, the French or Russians over the balance of power in Europe. Most of the patriotic references are to 'Old England' rather than to the empire. As for the rest of these songs, the dominant themes are very different indeed from the celebratory jingoism they are usually associated with.

Satire was one. It was hardly trenchant, and certainly did not imply any disillusion with Britain's colonial wars; but it could be read as in a way distancing the singers and their audiences from them. Favourites were Gus Ellen's 'The Bore o' Bef'nal Green':

> I finks a cove sh'd fink afore 'e talks abaht th'woar,
> There's blokes wot talks as dunno wot they mean . . . [18]

J. P. Dane's 'Khaki all over the Shop':

> Khaki's getting all the rage, we meet it ev'ry-where,
> Men are wearing khaki ties, and women khaki hair;
> It's bound to be the fashion, so you'd better all prepare,
> For a universal breaking out of khaki[19]

and Charles Bignell's immensely popular 'The Baby's Name', about a mother who insists on christening her new son with a string of names of Boer War generals and place-names:

> The war, the war, the blooming war, Has turned my wife insane,
> From Kruger to Majuba, she's The Transvaal on the brain.
> And when to christen our first child, Last Sunday week we tried,
> The parson said, 'What's this child's name?' And my old girl replied—
>
> 'The baby's name is Kitchener, Carrington, Methuen, Kekewich, White,
> Cronje, Plummer, Powell, Majuba, Gatacre, Warren, Collenso,
> Kruger, Capetown, Mafeking, French, Kimberley, Ladysmith, 'Bobs',
> Union Jack and Fighting Mac, Lyddite, Pretoria, Blobbs!'[20]

Another genre was the maudlin-sentimental: songs like 'Some Mothers Will Lose a Son'; 'Goodbye Dolly Gray', which came from America, and was probably the most popular of all these pieces; 'The Girl You Leave Behind You'; 'Don't We Like to Hear of Victory' (but remember the slain); 'Sweet Marguerite' and 'The Wearers of the Little Grey Cloak' (both about Red Cross nurses); 'God Bless Daddy at the War'; 'The Boers Have Got My Daddy'; 'Break the news to Mother', another American import, written originally for the Spanish-American War; and ''Tis Not Only Bullets that Kill' (but a sweetheart's faithlessness while her boy is at the front).[21] That gives the flavour. Thirdly, there was the clearly implied class-consciousness of the songs that lauded the ordinary squaddie at the expense of the officer class: 'Only a Trooper', 'Private Tommy Atkins', and 'To Him of the Absent Mind'.[22] Lastly, there are the many songs that enjoin the nation not to forget the wives (or widows) and families of the poor troopers: Kipling's 'The Absent-Minded Beggar' (with a tune by Sir Arthur Sullivan); 'Ordered South'; 'The Un-Commercial Traveller'; 'Tommy, Don't You Worry!',

'Who'll Care For the Children', 'Thank You Kindly'; and 'Oh Mr Kipling': the last of these directly attacking the politicians whose blunders are putting their soldiers' lives at risk.[23] These are typical of most of the 'Boer War' music-hall songs. They outnumber the tub-thumpers by about ten to one; while songs that have nothing at all to do with the war or the empire outnumber these by about the same proportion.[24] These *may* have been the ones that went down best in the gallery. It is impossible to tell.[25]

The patriotism was there; but it was only tenuously linked to the empire, and was overlaid, even in the patriotic songs, by other, more personal and intimate or class-specific concerns. If the late Victorian and Edwardian music hall did *not* accurately reflect contemporary working-class opinion, which seems to be the modern consensus,[26] it at least had to bend to it, otherwise it would not get an audience. If the hall owners did not know how to do this, the artistes (usually from the working classes themselves) and songwriters did. Jingoism went down well, because it was exciting and an excuse for celebration. But it was, as the true imperialists of the time always feared, very superficial. It can hardly ever have led to a thoughtful or joined-up imperialism on the part of the jingoes: partly because the music hall was not conducive to joined-up thought in any case. It resembled the modern right-wing British tabloid press in this regard: more politically effective in a negative way, making its customers cynical about all politics, for example, and everyone in authority, with the sole exception at this time of the queen,[27] than in engendering a constructive ideology of an imperial or any other kind. British colonial wars were an excuse for a party, or a riot. Beyond that the singers and songwriters, who knew their public, simply used them as hooks on which to hang the perennial, favourite themes: humour, gentle mockery, poverty, class, anti-authority, boy and girl, mothers, sentimentality. These themes outlasted the Boer War; but the imperialism did not. The halls returned to other hooks. The wartime songs, except the sentimental ones ('Dolly Gray'), did not remain in their audiences' minds for very long thereafter; very few working-class memoirs, for example, recall them.[28] This may have been simply because their melodies were so unmemorable, which would be understandable, after all: songsmiths would not want to waste their best tunes on what were bound to be mere topical ephemera.[29]

* * *

Two of the most commonly cited indicators of turn-of-the-century popular imperialism, therefore, may be less reliable than they have sometimes been taken to be. We shall need to dig deeper in order to determine just how effective the imperial propaganda of these years was. One promising field, as with our account of the earlier period, is education. We have already noted the increased imperial—and imperialistic—content of many of the textbooks that came out of this period. Given that propaganda is harder to resist at a young age than later, this seems a powerful reason to think that imperialism must have taken a stronger root among the working classes than it had in the bad old days, when it had been deliberately kept from them.

It certainly did with some. Robert Roberts, a Salford slum boy in the 1900s who published two volumes of his childhood reminiscences in the 1970s,[30] remembered the impact of his imperial schooling vividly.

> Teachers, fed on Seeley's imperialistic work *The Expansion of England*, and often great readers of Kipling, spelled out patriotism among us with a fervour that with some edged on the religious. Empire day of course had special significance. We drew union jacks, hung classrooms with flags of the dominions and gazed with pride as they pointed out those massed areas of red on the world map. 'This, and this, and this,' they said, 'belong to us'.[31]

This account has been much quoted in recent studies, and there is no reason to doubt the truth of most of it. (We can perhaps enter a caveat about the 'Seeley' connection, which Roberts is unlikely to have been aware of at the time.) Roberts insisted that most of the lumpenproletariat remained enmired in this reactionary nonsense for the rest of their lives, though he—being more intelligent—escaped.[32] Some other working-class memoirs (not many, however, by the lumpen) corroborate this.[33] The schools seemed to be bringing the working-class imperial bacon home.

But this is not quite the whole picture. It takes no account of the resistance there certainly was to the more overt kinds of imperial propaganda, at least, in these lower-class schools. Roberts may have been unlucky; he seems to be almost alone among working-class memoirists in attesting to this degree of imperialization, which perhaps explains why he is almost the only one ever quoted on this. Others remembered things differently. Few of them ever mention the contents of the courses they took at school, preferring to concentrate on how badly they were delivered (still), and on the canings: 'Fear was at the back of all education of my generation.'[34] The implication is that very little of whatever they *were* taught got through. 'It was all exceedingly elementary,' wrote Frederick Willis of his London schooling around 1900, 'and attention was concentrated on Reading,

Writing and Arithmetic.'[35] If they recalled history and geography lessons at all it was as dull litanies, in the one case of kings and queens with their dates; in the other of capital cities and major rivers.[36] Willis claimed his history lessons never got beyond the Tudors:

> 'History', as taught by the board school, left us with a vague impression that up to the time of Elizabeth this country had been occupied exclusively by kings and queens, good, bad and indifferent, and from Queen Elizabeth onwards were the Dark Ages, since we never heard of anything happening in that period. The American War of Independence, indeed the existence of the United States of America, was hushed up. So far as history was concerned the board school boys started out in the world very oddly equipped.

Any imperial knowledge they emerged with will have been derived from their geography lessons, which centred on the colonies and their products. 'The only reference to people that I remember was "The Indian can live on a handful of rice a day" '.[37] (That may have reinforced a powerful imperial stereotype, however.) 'With reference to Geography or History,' wrote one poor girl of her elementary education a little later, '. . . I had only the haziest idea.'[38] Accounts of specifically imperial lessons taught in the schools are rare, and inconsistent. 'It didn't make much of an impression on me, though', wrote Jim Flowers; 'It went into my brain and I stored the facts because you had to, but patriotism never struck me as being very clever. See, I'd read Tom Paine.'[39] That would explain it. Fred Mattock recalls learning history from a socialist teacher who deliberately avoided 'the books', and gave them his own version of 'India and places like that', bringing home to him 'what a load of rubbish we've been taught in the past'. Bristol schoolgirl Edna Rich did not need this kind of mediation to turn her into an anti-imperialist; 'somehow or other' the patriotism that was forced down her throat 'stirred a bit of rebellion in me' on its own.[40] These are unlikely to be typical cases (all of them grew up to be radicals). But they do suggest that classroom imperial education at this time (*c*.1900–14) may have been neither universal, nor universally effective among those it targeted.

One problem (from an imperialist point of view) was the teachers. They may not have been particularly knowledgeable about the empire themselves. Before 1902 their historical training generally left much to be desired.[41] Afterwards, with the first appointments of history specialists in the training colleges, it improved, but could still leave them ignorant of British empire history, unless they took one particular option out of the five that were recommended after 1906 (the others covered mainly constitutional, labour, and social history, reflecting some of the other pressing priorities of this time).[42] It is possible, of course, as Heathorn suggests, that this made them more dependent on their propagandist textbooks;[43] but the main problem was—or was believed to be—political. Teachers were considered unreliable. 'Ninety per cent of our Elementary teachers have themselves been brought up in Elementary schools,' wrote a critic in 1908; 'They are the children of working people, and bring to their work all the prejudices and limitations of their class.'[44] They were also supposed to be vocationally left-wing.[45] That subjected them to other pressures than the patriotic one: from those who believed school history should be more critical and questioning, for example, which was a potential blow to propagandists of all kinds;[46] and from those who thought it should relate more closely to 'everyday life'.[47] This could be frustrating for imperialists. Walter Frewen Lord warned anyone seeking to persuade 'a schoolmaster of his acquaintance' to take the empire on board to prepare for a battle: 'He will have to fight his way through being told (1) to mind his own business, (2) that teachers have 'their own academic way' of treating history, (3) that patriotism is politics, (4) that 'there are two sides to the question', and (5) finally, that there is not room in the curriculum for a new subject.'[48] Teachers simply could not be trusted: they were too independent, out of control. This suspicion of the teaching profession's un-imperialism persisted on the Right of British politics well into the inter-war period, as we shall see. Indeed, in a slightly different form it lasted much longer, being one of the main motivations behind Margaret Thatcher's efforts to impose a 'sounder' national history curriculum on teachers in the 1980s.[49]

That would have been impossible in the 1900s. Even if it had wanted to, the state could not have imposed any kind of imperial or even patriotic education on schools. This is an unusual phenomenon, and worth emphasizing. 'It is well known', wrote W. E. Forster (of 1870 Education Act fame), 'that our English educational system is almost alone in the refusal of the Government either to prescribe or to authorise school books.'[50] Teachers, whatever their politics, valued their professional integrity too much to be told what to teach, except in the broadest terms. Governments did not dare to prescribe the *content* of syllabuses, or particular books. That would have been regarded as authoritarian. '[I]t would be with great hesitation and reluctance,' the president of the Board of Education told the House of Lords in 1902, on being asked by Lord Meath to make colonial subjects compulsory, 'that I would propose at the present moment to add to [the] Code by insisting on the teaching of certain *details* of history and geography in the elementary schools.'[51] The Board of Education could advise, but no more. It did advise: on teaching methods, for example, and on the objectives of elementary education, one of which was to train good 'citizens'. (The word 'citizen' was invariably preferred to 'patriot' in this context, probably because it sounded more politically neutral.) Occasionally it suggested suitable areas of study, including the (settlement) colonies,[52] but always tentatively, and with the clear proviso that, as a set of *Suggestions for the Consideration of Teachers* issued by the Board in 1905 put it, teachers 'should have the greatest liberty' to frame syllabuses, and to choose 'on which events'—this was for history teachers—'they wish to lay particular stress'.[53] Beyond that, government carefully avoided risking stepping on teachers' toes; and possibly on parents', who could also feel strongly about these things.

Whether or not this was in fact the reason, many imperialists remained far from satisfied with the job the schools were doing. Lord Meath, predictably, was in the van of the grousers. In 1902 he described a visit he had recently paid to a group of school-leavers, only one of whom responded when he asked 'if those lads who had heard of a war in India, or of a Sepoy war, or of an Indian mutiny would hold up their hands'. That, he was told, was because their history stopped at the Tudors.[54] Apparently this ignorance of post-Tudor history was common,[55] prompting some educationalists to advocate starting history teaching at the present and moving backwards. That way the empire could not be missed (it was called the 'regressive method').[56] In 1915 C. P. Lucas, ex-Colonial Office, now a writer of imperial textbooks himself, claimed that 'nine out of ten workingmen' knew and cared very little about the empire, because 'they have never been systematically taught to know or care'. This, he believed, was 'positively dangerous'.[57] Others complained that there were no suitably imperial school texts, despite what we have seen of the change that came over most history books and readers in this period.[58] They must have meant that these were not imperial *enough*.

The imperial classes, however, were not entirely blameless in this regard. Their own commitment to imperial education for the working classes could sometimes seem in doubt. At the root of this lay their own class prejudices, and particularly the one against sharing the empire on any kind of equal terms with others. Such sharing involved the concept of 'citizenship'. Some 'progressives' at this time (including imperialists) did indeed believe in this, and saw the elementary schools as possible vehicles for its promotion. The school, wrote one very forward-looking inspector in 1899, referring specifically to rural areas, 'has it seems to me a high function to fulfil... Its work is national, not to say imperial, rather than parochial. Its business is to turn out youthful citizens rather than hedgers and ditchers'—which of course had been the main object before.[59] The 'progressive' party on the London School Board also wanted to use schools to teach 'the self-respect of citizens' as well as useful skills.[60] The liberal philosopher T. H. Green went so far as to advocate, at least by implication, *comprehensive* schooling as the best way of 'levelling' people into a common sense of identity.[61] Most educationalists stopped far short of that; but something similar was implied in various turn-of-the-century suggestions designed to bridge the gap between the public schools and elementary schools, for example, and in the 'classless' aspects of Baden-Powell's philosophy. Any of these measures could have brought everyone into the national community, ironing out—at least in theory—all those harmful social divisions, and broadening the base of ownership of the empire. But it was a lot for Britain's ruling (and imperialist) classes to stomach. 'No one seems to have seriously suggested... that schools should be used for social levelling', writes David Wardle, unsurprisingly.[62] For them the whole idea of true 'citizenship' was fraught with peril. In the hands of the wrong people it could be dangerous. 'There are those who say', said the socialist Stuart Headlam in a London School Board election speech in 1888, 'that we are educating your children above their station. That is true; and if you return me I shall do my utmost to get them such knowledge and such discipline as will make them thoroughly discontented' with their social lot.[63] A humanist writing in 1915 saw elementary-school children being raised to a *higher* form of citizenship altogether, a more international one, expressly eschewing 'jingoism'.[64] That would not do at all.

In any case many imperialists, especially Conservatives, remained resistant to the idea of working-class children being given *any* kind of broader education, on the old familiar ground that it could give them ideas above their station, and so be socially destabilizing. When C. P. Lucas became principal of the London Working Men's College in 1912—a highly unsuitable choice, one would think—he stated explicitly that its 'purpose... ought not to be to enable the workers to climb the social ladder, but merely to make the poor man happier with his lot'.[65] That is why drill still easily outstripped games as the preferred mode of physical education for elementary schools in the 1900s, instilling as it did—this is Meath again—'Habits of discipline, obedience, [and] quickness to hear and obey'.[66] One of the most imperialistic school textbooks of the period, the anonymous *The Citizen Reader*, actually defined 'patriotism' for the lower orders in terms of 'kindness, truth, honour, and *obedience*'.[67] So far as 'knowledge' was concerned, Lord Kimberley (a former colonial secretary) frankly thought that the lower orders would be better off 'given practical lessons in the geography of their own localities' than 'being shown maps [of the empire] they are not well versed in; and which do not convey much to their minds'.[68] There was a strident view going the rounds that Britain's chief problem was that she had too *much* education, of all kinds, rather than too little, and that all this book-learning had to be drastically cut down 'if the Anglo-Saxon race is to survive in the struggle of nations'.[69] 'A store of undigested knowledge robs us of an open mind', was how one critic rationalized this in 1901.[70] To be fair, this was not an argument that was only applied to the workers, but was also eagerly seized on by the proudly philistine public schools. 'Compared to foreign boys the average Eton boy, of my time at any rate, could only be described as ignorant,' wrote an imperialist in 1890. 'What is it then that sets the ignorant above the learned and gives them a repose and a dignity, which all the knowledge contained in the Encyclopaedia Britannica fails to do?'[71] (The answer was the Etonian's respect for his mother.) Ignorance was not a bad prophylactic against social unrest, and was not necessarily harmful to the empire either, so long as everyone knew his or her place in that too.

The important thing was that everyone knew what to *do*. At the higher social level that meant how to rule. Some educationalists also felt it meant more technical training than British schools could offer at that time: 'To the nation which is supreme in the scientific spirit the twentieth century must belong', wrote one author in 1901; 'and if England is to remain the international ignoramus ... then the wavering balance in which the future of the country hangs must drop downwards'. (He suggested that public schoolboys give up their games to make room for science lessons.)[72] For the workers the equivalent was classes in laundry work, digging, and so on—few educationalists thought *they* could be made into scientists. This was Lord Meath's view also, despite his support for basic imperial studies in schools. Otherwise he too despised 'book learning'. At present, he complained, children left school having 'learnt no trade, the girls can neither cook, wash, nor make their own garments unless the materials are cut out for them. They cannot even scrub properly ... Undisciplined, untrained, with their heads filled with notions of their own importance, and unable and unwilling to work with their hands, is it astonishing that our streets are filled with armies of incapables who call themselves unemployed?' 'And this is the way', he concluded, rising to his main imperial theme, 'we are content to raise an imperial race destined to rule, save the mark! one-fifth of the human race!'[73] Girls were a particular worry. 'What girl on leaving school has the faintest idea of how to manage a house or a husband?' asked Madge Barry, in an essay on 'Women and Patriotism' in the right-wing *National Review* in 1909.[74] Until they became skilled in these basic functions, they could be of no use to the empire. (They were certainly no use agitating for political rights, claimed Barry: 'Patriotism is what we need in women, not suffragism.' And—even more bluntly—'woman's true place is in the background'.)[75]

The question, then, was how this system of social statification could be reconciled with loyalty to the empire. What most imperialists hoped was that the workers could be made proud to *serve* it. Everyone, wrote A. J. Berry in a senior geography textbook he published in 1913, was involved with it. 'It is concerned with all sorts and conditions of men ... The result has been that gentleman and sea-robber, private trader and chartered company, statesman and soldier, miner and farmer, missionary and merchant, have more or less unconsciously co-operated to make the British Empire the grandest the world has ever seen.'[76] That emphasized the empire's social inclusiveness (of men, at any rate). The workers would surely respond to that; but the imperialists had to be careful. Identity could not be allowed to slide into equality. Instead, boys and girls—and later men and women—had to be made proud of their *subordinate* roles in the imperial enterprise. This was the point of Finnemore's 'statue/pedestal' analogy. That would avoid the perils of 'citizenship': indeed, imperial patriotism might even prove an effective prophylactic against it. C. P. Lucas, for example, recommended the empire as 'the most wholesome and effective antidote' to democracy[77] (demonstrating the strong anti-democratic and anti-socialist threads bias that was common to much of the imperialist writing of this time; and again raising the question of which—imperialism or anti-democracy—was being used to serve which). The antidote might work, but only so long as the workers did not have any higher aspirations.

For those uncomfortable with the concept of citizenship, another possible means of forging a sense of national or imperial identity was the idea of race. Race could bind society without reforming it. If people could be made to feel that they had *this* in common with their rulers, they would not need to share economic wealth, social status, or political power with them. The advantage of this for those who wielded the wealth, status, and power is obvious. And there was something to build on here. 'Anglo-Saxonness'—the racial identity usually claimed by the English—had a long, if interrupted, pedigree in British thought.[78] It had been constructed originally to distinguish the English from other Europeans, rather than from a colonial 'other' (and so cannot be said to be an effect of imperialism). It was widely associated with 'liberty', as if this were an ethnic characteristic; a connection which worked the trick—a difficult one, one would think—of linking liberalism with racism, so enabling Britons to embrace both. Later on their Anglo-Saxon origins were also widely credited with the independence, courage, and enterprise that had made the English so much more successful colonists than other racial groups (we have seen how this was anticipated by J. R. Green). As 'Anglo-Saxons', therefore, English men and women should automatically feel an affinity with their empire, whatever their class.[79]

There were problems, however, with this too. Britain contained other ethnicities besides the 'Anglo-Saxons': Celts, for example, Scandinavians, later immigrants, and the Norman-French. The main difficulty was with the Normans, who were still identifiable in British society, at least in radical mythology, as its ruling caste, descended from the wicked barons whom William I had forced on England in 1066. In the earlier nineteenth century it had been mainly working-class left-wingers who had talked of 'Anglo-Saxon liberties', as a stick to beat their 'Norman' oppressors with. That had made race a divisive rather than a nationally unifying concept. On the issue of empire, it was difficult to see it forging a common imperial ethos. Even if 'Anglo-Saxonness' did lie behind imperialism, it could only be credited with one face of it: the commercial and colonial (settlement) kind of empire, represented by countries like America. The situation in India looked much more 'Norman'. Race thinking only served to accentuate these differences.

If race was to be used to unite the classes in a common imperial loyalty, then some work was going to have to be done on this. Stephen Heathorn has shown how the history 'Readers' of the 1890s and 1900s set about it by claiming that the Normans (together with the Celts) had been assimilated into Anglo-Saxondom, for example; by tracing a common origin for both 'races' in the forests of Scandinavia—'It was easy for them to mix, for English and Norman were really brothers in blood'; by commending the combination of the two sets of racial characteristics, usually Saxon 'solidity' with French 'spirit'; and even by inventing an entirely spurious new lineage for Britain's Hanoverian queen—'the descendant of the Saxon chiefs who settled in Wessex', as one school history Reader asserted quite brazenly in 1895.[80] The contrived nature of these expedients indicates both the importance that was attached to the issue, and the inherent difficulties it presented. Whether any of this worked is impossible to say. It depends on whether the working-class 'Anglo-Saxons' were convinced by it, and could be persuaded to put 'blood' before class; on whether the Celts took umbrage; and on whether they were all content to be 'pedestals'.

❦❦❦

In fact 'race' does not appear to have attracted the workers to imperialism, particularly. For them the empire continued to be marginal. This cannot be known for certain, even as a generalization, but the evidence—and particularly, the *lack* of evidence to the contrary—is compelling. Even when the working classes behaved in an imperialistic way it was invariably for unimperialistic reasons. 'Mafficking', singing jingo songs, celebrating Empire Day, scouting, visiting empire exhibitions, reading the yarns of G. A. Henty or Bessie Marchant, were all usually done for what *else* could be got out of these activities, rather than for the imperialism: for the sugar, that is, not the pill. What attracted working-class children to Empire Day was the half-holiday; to scouting, the outdoor activities; to the empire exhibitions, the funfairs; to Henty and Marchant, the derring-do. It is possible that they swallowed some of the imperialism down along with these pleasures, this being the point of the exercise as far as the imperialists were concerned; but that certainly cannot be assumed, and it is not what the imperialists themselves thought. It also does not seem inherently likely, in view of where these working-class children (and adults) came from, socially and culturally; their particular situation, which was bound to affect the way they received and responded to the imperial propaganda that was fed to them.

Empire Day is a good example. When it was first floated in parliament it was in conjunction with another scheme—also Lord Meath's—to have a flag-raising ceremony at the beginning of each day in all state schools, to remind children of their empire and their patriotic duties.[81] That got nowhere, partly because of fierce opposition from school boards, local councils, and—in London in 1902—the Gasworkers' Union, who protested against its 'undemocratic spirit', 'the worship of a national fetish,' and its 'jingoism'.[82] Meath thought it was simply because Britons did not go in for ceremonial in the way the Americans did. When the Liberal government turned down a similar proposal in 1906, Lord Crewe, its spokesman, put on the best face he could by suggesting that it might be unwise even from a patriotic point of view 'to associate the national emblem in [children's] minds with school'.[83] That, incidentally, does not say much for the effectiveness of the elementary school generally as a medium for propaganda.

Empire Day itself, however, did better, at least in the country at large, although it was criticized on much the same grounds as the flag-raising idea, and for that reason was never officially sanctioned by the government in this period.[84] In the Commons it was a very minority cause, pursued by a few fanatics. Predictably, the Irish objected to it: could its advocates say what the empire had ever done for Ireland, asked one Nationalist MP in 1908, 'that her people should take off their hats and shout on Empire day?'[85] Some Liberals affected not to know that it existed;[86] asked for the date of Empire Day in 1913, Prime Minister Asquith replied: 'It is the twenty fourth of May *I think*'. (He was right.)[87] The Liberal government even declined to allow flags to be flown from government buildings on Empire Day, despite repeated taunts from the other benches: 'Has the right hon. Gentleman become a Little Englander?'[88] In 1907 Sir Henry Campbell-Bannerman claimed there was not 'sufficient interest' to justify Empire Day's being made official.[89] 'We do not attach the same importance to Empire Day as some hon. Members opposite', admitted R. B. Haldane, the war minister, in 1909.[90] In 1910 a Commons motion to introduce an 'Empire Day Bill' was defeated by 242 votes to 150.[91] The Day had to wait until 1916, and the heat of war, before it was officially recognized; fifteen and eleven years after Canada and Australia respectively.

It is important not to jump to the wrong conclusion from all this. You did not need to be anti-empire to be anti-Empire *Day*. 'We do not think the Empire is held together', said Haldane, 'by the flying of flags.'[92] Sir Charles Dilke worried that setting aside a special day might, 'in some parts of the Empire', be 'a source of division and peril among people equally patriotic'. In any case, people had the present king's birthday on which to celebrate the empire if they wanted to.[93] Then there was the perennial problem: that schools, compelled to glorify the empire, might see this as interfering with their autonomy and political neutrality. It was a 'delicate' matter.[94] The main reason for resisting Empire Day, however, was that many parents,[95] teachers, and local-education authorities[96] objected to it on political grounds. Even one or two children did. Ethel Mannin, for example, claimed she was threatened with expulsion for refusing to salute the flag on Empire Day: 'My Flag was the Red Flag, according to the creed set forth by my father.' In the end she was made to kneel in a corner while all the other children saluted, boosting her 'terrific sense of martyrdom for a splendid cause'.[97] But she was braver than most, especially in the company of her schoolfellows, for whom losing Empire Day would have meant missing a half-holiday.

It is clear from contemporary reminiscences that this was the main reason for its popularity.[98] It was what gave it an advantage over the flag-raising project. Children may not have taken Empire Day's imperial content seriously (though Robert Roberts did);[99] and indeed that content sometimes seems to have been very mild. One contemporary described how at some schools, usually in towns where the Labour party was influential, Empire Day was actually used (Meath would have said, misused) to preach international peace.[100] That could be considered subversive. Other accounts describe quite tame or jolly affairs, many of them apparently bereft of imperial content entirely: with English folk-dancing, children dressing up as Elizabethans, acting out scenes from *English* history, forming the shapes of British national emblems (English rose, Irish clover, the Union Jack), re-enacting 'Merrie England', and so on.[101] This may have given the word 'empire' gentler associations, but it did little for the children's imperial education, properly so called. Even when the imperialism was plainer, Stephen Humphries thinks that children were discriminating, enjoying the activities of Empire Day while rejecting its 'ideological trappings'.[102] Such rejection did not have to be conscious: Londoner Harry Burton, for example, admitted he enjoyed singing patriotic songs on Empire Day, 'but it did us no harm because it never went very far', and in any case 'no-one knew where the empire was'.[103] (That was because of the poor geography teaching.) Children could enthuse over the trappings of such events without being deeply persuaded. 'It seems', writes James Greenlee, reflecting on the contrast between these displays and the working classes' reluctance to lend their support to more constructive imperial projects in the 1900s and 1910s, 'as though it was difficult to translate ephemeral enthusiasms into a day-to-day acceptance of imperial burdens and obligations.'[104] That was the rub.

The situation with scouting was similar. Again, its main attraction was extraneous to its propagandist function, which in any case was toned down considerably in order to attract the working classes (Baden-Powell's 'slum boys'). The 'Scout Law', for example, emphasized loyalty, discipline, and obedience to rightful authority, but carried no explicit reference to the empire or the military. On the other hand, it enjoined Scouts to be courteous to women, children, old people, and invalids; to be kind to other social classes; to be 'a friend to animals', never killing them 'unnecessarily, even a fly'; and to be thrifty, clean-living, and cheerful. 'Whistling' was particularly recommended[105] (though not for Girl Guides—Baden-Powell's sister Agnes thought it would cause them to grow moustaches).[106] Whether the imperial message still crept in must be questionable. It is clear that most scouts and guides joined because they liked the outdoor activities, especially camping, rather than for patriotic reasons. This was what persuaded the working-class Edward Ezard, for example, to enrol:

> Mr Wills-Hope outlined the aims of the movement and the kind of activities we should engage in. 'We shall route march to our own band,' he promised. 'Learn all about scoutcraft and woodcraft: play scouting games with other troops: camp out in the country: box, swim and generally learn to take care of ourselves and other people when they need us. Scouts toughen themselves to endure hardship and are trained in developing resource to overcome difficulties.'

It was only later that the imperial indoctrination crept in: with war games against 'a savage tribe (represented by a Putney troop)'; Wills-Hope 'yarn[ing] away about some of his adventures in desert or upon veldt'; and reminders of past colonial wars at church parade. Wills-Hope obviously had the knack; his successor, however, Mr Crocker, soon depleted the troop by talking down to them and making them do PT.[107] This kind of behaviour may be one of the reasons why scouting, according to all the evidence, caught on less among the working classes than among the middles;[108] together with parental opposition in some cases—William Tucker's father 'saw "army" written all over' it, for example,[109] difficulties in affording the uniforms, and the 'ribald jeers, derisive songs and occasional stone-throwing' scouts were subjected to by many of their peers.[110] Baden-Powell himself, with undisciplined working-class youths clearly in his sights from the start, will have been disappointed.

Everywhere we look we see the same phenomenon: the working classes sucking the sugar, then *probably* spitting the pill of imperial propaganda out.

Many of them read Henty as children; socialists even recommended him, as giving children the historical and geographical knowledge they would have lacked from their schooling.[111] There is a view that they must have soaked Henty's imperialism in with this: 'It provides a sediment in the mind,' writes Jeffrey Richards, 'which it requires a conscious intellectual effort to erase. Since the majority of people are not intellectuals, it follows that only a minority will for a variety of reasons make this effort.' That is one view. The fact that it sounds patronizing does not make it necessarily wrong.[112] But some contemporaries disputed it. A. J. P. Taylor, for example (not working class, admittedly), claimed that as a boy he loved the adventure in these books, but found their political message 'very great nonsense'.[113] J. S. Bratton surmises that 'The reader's deep satisfaction in the fantasy Henty offered was probably much more primitive, and less admirable, than the doctrines he professed to teach... [T]he nature and direction of the influence may not have been any more closely channelled towards inspiring imperialism than Gothic melodramas inspired banditry and a belief in ghosts.'[114] In other words, it was possible to enjoy the swashbuckling in Henty without ingesting the imperialism, just as it is eminently possible to be unaware of the imperialistic message of 'Land of Hope and Glory'—'Wider still and wider, May thy bounds be set'—while belting out its terrific tune.[115] 'There is', points out Victor Kiernan, in this context, '... a problem of psychology as to what hold ideas put into heads artificially can have over them.'[116] Such a hold partly depends on where the heads come from; on this, more than on whether they are 'intellectual' or not.

In fact the empire played a very minor role in general popular reading during this period; almost as minor as it had ever done. Surveys of schoolchildren's reading preferences in 1888 and 1908 show novels on colonial subjects (including shipwreck narratives like *Robinson Crusoe*) always in a minority, with school and detective stories easily in the lead.[117] In middle-class boys' story papers, similarly, imperial adventure is only one of a number of themes, even in Henty's *Union Jack*, where empire topics were 'relatively few in the paper's early years', according to John Springhall, and were almost entirely elbowed out by Sexton Blake detective yarns after 1904.[118] In 'family' magazines the favourite topics were certainly not colonial ones, but romance, crime and detection, history, 'smart' society and high finance, domestic politics (especially socialism), art, English country towns, new scientific inventions, the sea, fashion, children, cuddly animals, and life and events in continental Europe.[119] Lower down the social scale the imperial content becomes even thinner. Most of the cheapest literature of the period, certainly outside the Boer War years, hardly bore at all on imperial matters: humorous comics, for example;[120] penny dreadfuls, covering much the same kinds of theme that had dominated this genre for decades;[121] the new 'police' broadsheets, mainly reporting—and illustrating in grisly detail—notorious murders, executions, and mortal disasters;[122] sporting prints; and, for more serious autodidacts, the old familiar classics (Shakespeare, Defoe, Dickens), other 'improving' literature, and radical or socialist texts.[123] According to working-class autobiographies, taste in fiction at this level seems hardly to have moved on at all since the 1860s, with *The Girl who Took the Wrong Turning* and *A Girl's Cross Roads* being typical of the novelettes that were most widely read, and plays like *In the Shadow of Night, Woman and Wine, Sporting Life, A Woman of Pleasure, The Face at the Window,* and *The Lights of London* packing them in in the cheap theatres.[124] In the slightly more respectable, but still popular, theatres and concert halls the situation is same.[125] One strangely popular literary genre among working-class boys was public-school stories, which probably appeared exotic to them, and from which they may have picked up some values—'we learned to admire guts, integrity, tradition; we derided the glutton, the American, and the French'—but not, infers Jonathan Rose from the published recollections of a dozen working-class 'Greyfriars' fans, the imperialism.[126] Most of the overt imperialism is closely bunched around the Boer War years, falling off sharply afterwards. It was also gendered, with women and girls being subjected to far less of it. It was certainly not overwhelming.

Even Imre Kiralfy's specifically and spectacularly 'imperial' exhibitions are likely to have overwhelmed in other than imperial ways. Frederick Willis, a working-class Londoner who enjoyed them hugely, called them 'Cities of Make-Believe'.[127] The 1909 'Imperial International Exhibition', for example, held at the White City, included 'Alpine and Submarine Railways', 'Arctic and Tropical Sensations', a 'Messina Earthquake', palmistry and astrology tents, a 'Spider's Web', a 'Spiral and Canadian Toboggan', a 'Water Whirl', 'Witching Wares' (?), 'The Flip-Flap' (which threw people up and down in the air), and a 'Wiggle-Woggle', described in the official guide as 'a decidedly laughter-provoking adaptation of the popular chute'.[128] Apart from anything else, what did the Alps and Messina have to do with the empire? Willis also remembered 'sideshows, fortune telling, distorting mirrors, haunted castles, switchbacks, Electrophone (forerunner of the wireless)...and instantaneous photography'. Did the paying public have time for the genuinely colonial exhibits hidden among all this? If so, could they take them seriously? Willis thought not: 'The majority of visitors were more interested in the lighter side, which was extensive and hilarious.' It was an excuse to dress up, go out, and have fun.[129] The more serious shows—the 'anthropological' ones that flourished in these late Victorian and Edwardian years, for example, many of them implicitly racist—may have been even less effective. In the first place there is the problem of relating racism to imperialism, which we have discussed before (and shall again). Quite apart from this, however, such exhibitions may not have been patronized much by the workers (their best historian is at pains to downplay their 'popularity' in this sense).[130] There is no way of knowing for certain; but contemporary working-class autobiographies hardly ever mention them.

On their own such accounts prove nothing, of course. We have mentioned the difficulties with working-class memoirs before: those who were clever enough to write them may not have been representative of the rest of their class; that is, of Jeffrey Richards's non-'intellectuals', whose very non-intellectualism might have been what made them especially prone to the sorts of prejudice—xenophobia, racism, and the like—that a certain kind of imperialism fed off. It is commonly believed that uneducated workers, especially men, are instinctively tribal, xenophobic, and violent; which could be a reason for not giving them the benefit of the doubt over this issue. It may not be too patronizing to assume that most working-class people did value their own kind and country above all others, and that there could have been a strong element of racism in this. (That is to make no judgement about whether such a feeling was 'instinctive' or not.) But this is surely true of most people everywhere, even liberals. It takes more than that, as this book has consistently argued, to make someone an imperialist. This is where the propaganda came in, designed to direct those 'natural' prejudices into empire-friendly channels. It could have worked, at some levels; the fact that our witnesses later recalled only the sugar on the pill is immaterial. It may be equally irrelevant that this particular medicine was so thinly distributed among the people as we have seen it was, and seems so insignificant when viewed against the general cultural context of the time. A pill does not have to be swallowed repeatedly and for long periods for it to do its work. If the relatively small doses were well dispensed, they could have struck home. So more evidence is needed to show that imperialism was not, in most senses, a 'popular' ideology, even in this highly imperially charged period. To do this, it is necessary to look at the working classes' material and social situation; and then at what the propagandists themselves thought they had achieved.

***

In the memoirs, chronicling lives or former lives *as* working people, the empire scarcely figures in any guise. Many of the writers do not allude to it at all.[131] That may mean that they were not conscious of it as such, or that they did not think it was their place to mention it in this kind of account, written to enlighten the other classes about how workers *lived*. Obviously the empire was not felt to be part of this; as neither were political questions more generally. There are many references in such memoirs to a lack of interest in all national politics, except in a very superficial way. Arthur Newton remembers his mother, for example, being wholly ignorant of politics: 'her whole world was Hackney, Bethnal Green and her family circle.'[132] 'Current public affairs hardly touched us', remembers another working man.[133] There could be great excitement at elections, but no more—and of no different a kind—than at a football match. 'Thus this good sport would end,' writes Frederick Willis, 'and in about a week the average man in the street had forgotten which party was in power.' Working-class Conservatism was a well-known phenomenon, but it was rooted in some strange ideas. 'Briefly, a youth regarded the Conservative Party as the owners of the Union Jack, the patrons of festivals and providers of cakes and ale. The Liberal Party were looked upon as kill-joys, sour misanthropes who were in a secret conspiracy to close all the pubs and erase for ever that joyous spirit that was known as "Merrie England" '.[134] (Hence the right-wing bias of the music halls.) There was little to hook a serious discussion of the empire on there. Nine-tenths of the imperial allusions that do occur in these memoirs relate to the Boer War, or rather to its cultural offshoots. 'I was vaguely aware of the war,' wrote the Walworth-born Charles Chaplin, who was 10 in 1899, 'through patriotic songs, vaudeville sketches and cigarette cards of the generals.'[135] W. H. Davies remembered a friend wearing a 'slouched hat' like a Boer's.[136] The 15-year-old Ruth Slate's only mention of the war in her diary is: 'they say the price of everything will go up'.[137] These are detached memories, at best, of the major imperial event of the age. After the war explicit references to imperial events dry up almost entirely. There are none in Robert Tressell's famous autobiographical novel *The Ragged-Trousered Philanthropists* (1914), despite the fact that 'Tressell' had been to South Africa himself.[138] Most imperial allusions are peripheral: to emigration, for example, though this is still rare; to 'coloured' men seen in dockland areas;[139] and in the empire-related names that were often given to urban buildings and streets in the 1900s: Imperial Road, Mafeking Avenue, General Gordon Place, and so on.[140] A very few working-class memoirists, as we have seen, recall being taught about their empire at school. Otherwise these books appear to be surprisingly reticent on imperial matters.

Other sources are scarcely more helpful. Elections are no guide to popular feeling on the issue: only 6–8 per cent of voters chose Labour in the 1906 and 1910 general elections, but then 90 per cent of parliamentary constituencies had no Labour or socialist candidates for people to vote for if they had wanted to, and in any case only a minority of the working classes—and none of their women—had the vote.[141] There were no other polls of opinion taken at this time. The mixed motives behind Mafeking Night and other 'patriotic' demonstrations have been looked at earlier. Volunteering for imperial wars also cannot be taken as a measure of imperial patriotism, the motives for this being similarly confused.[142] One trooper—albeit possibly an atypical one—averred that 'there was only one patriot' in his Boer War battalion, 'and he was generally regarded as peculiar'. The others had joined to escape from domestic problems, or dead-end careers, or because of 'the promise of a new start in South Africa' after the war was over.[143] One very severe critic from the imperialist side maintained that this lack of real imperial commitment was evidenced by what he claimed was the men's all-too-frequent cowardice in the field.[144] But speculation about motives can only be guesswork. What evidence we have of people discussing imperial issues outside the normal political bodies (where they could be suspected of being unrepresentative activists, a matter discussed in the next chapter) points to a range of views, a general spirit of tolerance, and—even at the height of the Boer War—scarcely any 'jingoism' at all. This is what comes out of Richard Price's celebrated analysis of the Working Men's Club movement, for example; or at least of those clubs that did not deliberately avoid all political issues on the grounds that their members did not want to be 'bothered' with them 'after a hard day's work'.[145] The clubs, however, mainly catered for the 'respectable' working classes; the less respectable may have been different. Robert Roberts claimed that it was they—he called them 'the undermass'—who were the most instinctively imperialistic of all.[146] Others thought so too, especially among the middle and upper classes. The 'undermass' had a reputation at the time for stupidity and violence, which may well say more about the other classes' phobias than about the reality, but which made it an obvious suspect for the mindless jingoism that both critics and supporters of the empire deplored at the turn of the century. Few of the 'undermass', unfortunately, have left memoirs.[147] So the fact has to be faced: we shall never know how empire-aware or imperialistic the working classes were as a whole, or how solid and useful that imperialism was, if it existed. This makes it tempting to fall back on broader prejudices: that the workers were 'naturally' sheeplike, for example, easily manipulated by any plausible 'agitator', but by the same token also open to persuasion by subtle propaganda; or were natural *Sun* readers (or the early twentieth-century equivalent), stupidly (or solidly) tribal (or patriotic), and easily impressed by circuses, with or without the bread; or—on the other side—that they were ever the clear-eyed international idealists of socialist myth.

Evidence from the organized Labour and socialist movements, the best-recorded sections of the working classes, is suggestive, though not conclusive, since political activists could have been more radical than their fellows.[148] Socialism, in most of its contemporary guises, was almost unequivocally critical of imperialism. This comes out in papers like *Reynolds's*, in trade-union deliberations, and in the contributions to colonial debates of the small band of Labour MPs in the House of Commons in the 1900s.[149] In all of these areas we can find exceptions, workers who had been bitten by the imperialist bug: the *Clarion* newspaper, for example, edited by the ex-army sergeant Robert Blatchford, whose consistent anti-imperialism before 1898 withered in the heat of the build-up to the Boer War;[150] the politician John Burns, another ex-soldier, who could turn a jingo phrase with the best of them;[151] and the occasional handfuls of votes that were cast in opposition to anti-Boer war motions in the working-men's clubs.[152] Later, the Social Democratic Federation's ex-leader H. M. Hyndman had an imperialistic wobble, but he was middle class. (He may be the only Marxist leader in history who has played county cricket as a 'Gentleman'.)[153] But these were all unusual cases, and were regarded as anomalous in mainstream socialist circles at the time.

Generally the organized Labour movement's response to imperial issues took one of two forms. The first was to try to ignore it. That was the early strategy in parliament, for example, where Labour MPs very rarely involved themselves in debates about day-to-day imperial issues. This could be taken as an indication of their lack of any fundamental objection to the empire, but was mainly a sign that they saw it as someone else's—the ruling classes'—affair. They were also anxious not to be distracted by such questions from their main concerns, the reasons for their being in parliament at all, which were the economic and social conditions of their class. It must be remembered that the Labour parties at this time, right through to 1914, saw themselves rather as a special-interest group than as a putative government, whatever their enemies may have forecast.[154] The danger of imperialism to them was that concern over it might cause those special interests to be sidelined. (Some Labour activists even suspected, resurrecting a venerable radical argument, that raising colonial issues was a deliberate play on the part of the imperialists to divert the workers from attending to their just claims.)[155] They should not be fooled into taking that road, whatever they might think of the empire per se—if they thought about it at all.

After 1899 this attitude gave way to more active opposition, as was almost inevitable in light of the impact the empire was perceived to be having on the working classes. It was then that the famous 'anti-capitalist' line on imperialism, which the more philosophical socialists and J. A. Hobson had been working on for some time, came into its own. Sometimes this was tinged with anti-Semitism, fastening on the suspicion that many of the 'stock-jobbers' blamed for the Boer War were Jews.[156] That may have been a low attempt to exploit current working-class fears and prejudices about foreign Jews, arising from a sudden influx of them into the poorer areas of London at around the turn of the century;[157] but anti-Semitism, or any other kind of racism, does not appear to have been at the root of it. The attraction of the Hobsonian line for the Labour movement—as against, say, the ethical one preferred by Liberal pro-Boers—was the way it dovetailed into preconceived notions about those who were doing labour down. Yet again we find reactions to the empire being affected—even determined—by class-related domestic concerns. The 'capitalist exploitation' argument became Labour's special contribution to the Edwardian public debate about empire. It also influenced which particular colonial issues its MPs decided to concentrate their fire on. In South African debates, for example, they homed in on the 'labour' question, like working conditions for black Africans, 'a subject', as Keir Hardie put it when kicking off a discussion of this subject in December 1900, 'in which naturally he had a more direct interest'.[158] Later on, Labour was in the forefront of the parliamentary attack on the system of indentured Chinese labour ('Chinese slavery') in the Transvaal.[159] It also took an interest in similar issues in other colonies.[160] These were always treated *as* labour issues, never as racial ones; in 1912 the Sheffield MP Joe Pointer, for example, expressed his 'perfect abhorrence' of the idea that Africans and the like might be 'of a different kind of human clay, as it were, from the European, and especially from the Englishman'.[161] It was the colonial workers' relationship to the means of production that was the crucial consideration, not their ethnicity. That was the public stance of Labour's leaders, at any rate. But they might have been out of touch with working-class attitudes as a whole.

❦❦❦

A look at the broader context of their lives might take us a little further towards answering the question of the their more general response to the empire. The 1890s and 1900s were a time of great material hardship for most of the British working classes, with real wages generally stagnant or declining, and several periods of serious unemployment.[162] Hence the growth of socialism at this time, however far 'down' it may or may not have penetrated; and the huge industrial disruptions, culminating in the 'Great Labour Unrest'—massive, nationwide strikes, often accompanied by violence—of the early 1910s. These, rather than feelings about the empire, were the occasions for the biggest popular demonstrations of this period, and the inspiration for the best slogans and songs.[163] This was another good reason for propertied imperialists to be nervous of organized Labour, quite apart from its effect on the empire. Sometimes it is difficult to know which fear was uppermost in their minds: in 1913 Sir Basil Thomson, head of the Metropolitan Police 'Special' (or political) Branch, who should have been in a position to know, predicted that the country was headed for bloody revolution, no less, 'unless there was a European war to divert the current'.[164] He will have felt relieved on 4 August 1914, when the diversion came; but others did not, with contingency plans being prepared to combat any socialists who tried to use a future war as a *cover* for revolution, including martial law and shooting on sight.[165] Paranoid though these reactions may have been, they do accurately indicate the working classes' main concerns. The only external issue that could compete with these industrial questions was the ever-increasing threat of war with Germany, fed in the 1900s by stories of the Kaiser's provocative naval building, German spies and saboteurs spotted in Britain, and so on. Needless to say, it was the German menace to Britain herself that was feared, rather than to her empire, though the latter was under threat too.[166] The empire came a poor third at best behind these much more urgent priorities for most working people: anxiety about where their next meal was coming from, and then about whether they were about to be bayoneted by the Hun.

One way out of this situation was emigration, which in fact peaked during this period, and began for the first time (in 1904) to favour the British colonies over the United States.[167] That could have been a plus in terms of increasing empire-awareness. In an age of universal literacy it is likely that more emigrants kept in touch with 'home' than previously; at any rate more émigré letters from this period survive. A few even made the voyage back to Britain to visit.[168] Some knowledge of the colonies will have seeped back in this way (there are very occasional references to émigré friends and relatives in the memoirs).[169] The question remains, however, how enthusiastic for the empire this made the stay-at-homes. The few observations that are recorded by working people paint emigration mainly as a 'tragedy' for the families involved. 'It do seem 'ard. 'Course, she'll do better out there; 'er young man is doin' well, but it do seem 'ard to 'ave to go so far. That's 'er poor father, there, look. Don't 'e feel it?'[170] It could be argued that anyone who had been really enthusiastic about the empire would have gone there; from which it might seem to follow—though this is a pretty tenuous rider—that non-emigrants were also likely to be non-imperialists.[171]

A similar difficulty attaches to returning soldiers; soldiering being of course the other main way in which working-class men could experience the empire at first-hand. Their material situation was clearly a factor here too, with many joining up simply to escape the unemployment of the time. About 200,000 men served in the Boer War, a record for a colonial conflict, most of whom returned home.[172] One would expect that to have had an impact domestically, but evidence of this is scanty. Military experience does not appear to have made these men particularly imperially aware, let alone supportive; nor to have turned them into likely disseminators of imperial knowledge and patriotism back home. Most first-hand accounts dwell on their material privations and constant friction with their officers, rather than on the glories of the empire. Non-military memoirs, writes Jonathan Rose, 'sometimes discuss family members who fought in South Africa, but with no apparent awareness of what they were fighting for. "It was so far away it didn't seem real somehow," remembered one charwoman. "It was a story-book sort of war." '[173] In such accounts returning soldiers usually feature as 'characters', seemingly alienated from civilian society; very much so in the case of poor 'Chelsea', a Battersea celebrity in the 1900s, clad (according to Edward Ezard), 'in kind of stage make-believe army clothes: slouch hat turned up at one side, Boer war fashion: worn soldier's khaki tunic and obviously discarded officer's breeches: puttees and heavy regulation boots. Brandishing a stick he tore around the field bawling out words of command, in imitation of a military engagement.' Ezard also describes a conversation he had as a child with another Boer War veteran:

> I asked him about those Boers, whom I thought sounded like queer creatures... 'Oh, them', he replied. 'They was just farmers and the like in their ordinary clothes, carryin' rifles and slung around with bandoliers, nearly every one with 'is own fast pony. That's why sloggin' along on foot we couldn't ever catch 'em. They'd pot at you from be'ind a rock and be away like the wind... I'll get out my medals to shew you sometimes, along with the chocolate box Queen Victoria sent each one of us, bless 'er.'[174]

This was all very fascinating, and probably true, but hardly likely to heighten young Edward's appreciation of Britain's role in the world. How these veterans' war stories were received in working-class pubs is anyone's guess (there are almost no accounts of this). One recollection describes a soldier being stabbed in the chest in a brawl *outside* a pub, but we are not told what it was about.[175] Arthur Harding, a famous London East End criminal, tells of a neighbour who 'joined a Scotch regiment and got transferred to India' but then deserted, a second who 'went to the South African War and... never came home no more', and a third who 'lost her husband in the South African war; she had a pension; she was a cunning old cow she was'.[176] That too hardly sounds inspirational. Soldiers in fact do not seem to have been regarded very highly by working-class civilians, if Robert Roberts's testimony (from early twentieth-century Salford) is anything to go by: 'One eldest son, I remember, who after a row at home walked out and joined the Fusiliers[,] was considered by his father (a joiner) to have brought "shame and disgrace on all the family." '[177] A music-hall song of 1895 seems to corroborate this.

> When they found I was a soldier,
>   Sister Mary went right off her head;
> Father he got drunk—Mother done a 'bunk',
>   And the tom-cat fell down dead, oh, glory!
> Down came the lodgers with a rush,
>   But they didn't stop there long;

> When they saw my sword they exclaim'd,
> 'Oh, Lord! There's another man gone wrong!'[178]

That may have had something to do with the military's occasional role in smashing working-class strikes and demonstrations, which put soldiers on the other side of the all-important class line. This is likely to have made them poor ambassadors for imperialism, but we cannot be sure.

* * *

Whatever the real state of popular opinion, imperial zealots remained pessimistic over it. The working classes were not to be relied upon. Perhaps in rural areas they could be. Francis Younghusband—who knew a thing or two about the frustrations of being an imperialist in these post-1902 years, having just returned from winning Tibet for the British empire, only to be told to give it back again—thought he detected 'a far worthier spirit—the spirit of a great people in the greatest age the world has seen'—among the British peasantry. That was probably because the land-based ruling classes still had them under their feudal eye. But it was different in 'the slums' where, Younghusband claimed in 1910, folk 'would ask of what use India or the Colonies was to them, what harm there would be if Ireland did separate from England, or even if Germany conquered England'.[179] The newspaper editor J. L. Garvin espied exactly the same attitude, in what he described, in a telling phrase, as 'the deeper and darker strata of the masses'.[180] Here skulked monsters: chiefly socialists, the imperialists' especial *bêtes noires,* who were able to sink to these levels and poison the minds of all around them; people who 'care not for our commercial supremacy, sneer at our glorious history, and spell Empire with a small "e"'.[181] All imperialists sensed an 'unfounded animus' towards the empire from the new Labour party.[182] That would become even more ominous when Labour supplanted the Liberals on the left of politics, as many were predicting as early as the first decade of the 1900s.[183] A number of imperialists thought Labour's influence could be counteracted, for example, by offering the workers the same material improvements, in return for their imperial loyalty, that the socialists were tempting them with.[184] Others professed to believe that the working man (and by extension, one assumes, the working-class woman) was 'solid' underneath.[185] Even these acknowledged, however, that the solidity needed to be teased out. This was the general right-wing perception at this time: that the working classes were still dangerously bereft of imperial knowledge and commitment, and might even be—if only superficially—hostile to the whole enterprise. It was from this 'threatened breach between Democracy and Empire', as a contributor to the *National Review* warned in 1908, that 'we have most to fear'.[186]

These fears were compounded by the imperialists' own perceived failures when they tried to propagandize the people overtly—that is, without sugar-coating the pill. The reason, of course, was class, as everyone recognized. Meriel Talbot, secretary of the Victoria League, laboured womanfully to try to 'get rid of the silly idea that the VL is a classy sort of thing',[187] but without much success, partly because its members' upper-class slips kept showing. Their own relations with colonials are revealing: Talbot described how on a visit to Tasmania in 1910 'the dear dim little people almost curtsied' to her, which must have been for a reason; probably because she could not hide her opinion of Australia as a 'gigantic servant's hall', as she confided to her diary.[188] Talbot and her fellow members had no better idea of how to relate to working- or even middle-class people back home. 'Audience gave the impression of suspicion, of hostility to the subject and of considerable indifference to the conditions prevailing in the colonies', was the Victoria League executive committee's note on one awkward attempt to reach a 'lower' audience, through the Workers' Educational Association, in 1911. Violet Markham thought that 'trying to persuade the working man in the North of England' was a 'forlorn hope'.[189] According to Will Thorne, the working classes did not take kindly to being lectured to by 'highbrows' in any case.[190] Other imperial propaganda organizations seem to have been equally ineffective at this level. The imperial *Zollverein* idea was thought to stand a better chance than most, appealing as it supposedly did to the workers' material interest: the argument being that the tariff wall that would enclose the empire would also protect British workers from European competition; but efforts to sow the seeds of that idea on Labour soil, for example, through a 'Trade Union Tariff Reform Association', met with only limited success.[191] (The free traders' response to this—a highly effective one—was to raise the spectre among the poor of dearer food.)

It is easy to understand the upper-class imperialists' frustrations. They seemed constitutionally unable to hit the mark with the 'people'. A contributor to the right-wing *National Review* in 1908 thought the underlying problem was that 'the Imperial party ... is associated in the working man's mind with the landlord and the capitalist'.[192] It was resentment of the 'Norman' again, fed by the suspicion that there was a hidden agenda to all this propaganda, and that the real motive behind these upper-class calls to put imperial before sectional interests and so on was to keep the workers (or women) down rather than the empire up. There may have been something in this. Obviously 'the subordination of selfish or class interests to those of the State... and the inculcation on the minds of all British subjects of the honourable obligation which rests upon them of preparing themselves, each in his or her own sphere, for the due fulfilment of the[ir] duties and responsibilities', as Meath put it in 1921, would be of benefit to the established order in Britain as well as to the empire.[193] We can see this in Baden-Powell's philosophy too. This was one of the drawbacks of the 'pedestal' kind of patriotism that was the furthest Meath and his ilk were prepared to go to incorporate the lower orders in the imperial nation—that it was likely to make the pedestal distrustful of the great weight that was standing on it.

However 'imperialistic' we may think the working classes were, therefore (and that depends largely on semantics), it was nowhere near enough for the imperial zealots. They were difficult to please, of course. Give them an official Empire Day, and they would probably have demanded an Empire Week. They may also have been paranoid, about the threat from socialism and the rest in general. Nonetheless the standard they set at least gives us a 'maximum' to measure the 'imperialism' of the working classes against. In the zealots' view, this did not reach the bell at the top of the pole. One of the reasons was undoubtedly the failings of the propaganda agencies that sought to push it there, most of which—with the partial exception of Baden-Powell's brainwave—simply failed to penetrate the crucial class barrier. They did not speak the same language. The other main reason was the complement of this. The working classes lived different lives from the imperialist classes. Their houses, work, education, reading, thinking, feelings, ways of socializing and organizing—their whole life experience, in other words—made them in effect a separate country, with almost nothing in common with the higher classes. Out of that separation arose a very different political culture (or cultures), with priorities and values of its own, which the imperialists were very unlikely to be able to penetrate.

Anyone who has really immersed him- or herself in the surviving archaeology of this culture, rather than merely poked about in it for the occasional imperial shard, real or imagined, will be aware of this: of the strength of Edwardian working-class culture, its singularity, and the unlikelihood that it could take on board a full- or even a half-blown imperialism easily. James Greenlee rightly castigates those 'imperial propaganda' historians who leave the impression 'that the labouring classes constituted a *tabula rasa* upon which clever bourgeois propagandists could write as they pleased. Surveying the literature one is hard pressed to find references to Taff Vale, the Osborne Judgement, and the wave of industrial strife which swept England in the last years before the Great War'.[194] For the working classes—as well as many others of their contemporaries—these latter were the really great issues of the day. Everything else was marginal. Nothing should be allowed to distract from them, let alone alter their views of these questions, as the imperialists, and also the 'anti'-imperialist J. A. Hobson (though for other reasons), sought to do. (The imperialists wanted the working classes to sink their dispute with capital in the interests of patriotic unity; Hobson was trying to persuade them that imperialism was one of the ways capital was using to exploit them.) This is why their political representatives ignored the empire in the House of Commons, apart from its 'labour' aspects, because these did relate to this separate culture of theirs. It also explains why, whenever the empire is mentioned in working-class memoirs, it is typically through its more trivial by-products: 'mafficking', Boer War cigarette cards, slouch hats, a mad old veteran, the alcoholic Canadian soldier who went with Louie Stride's prostitute mother,[195] Union Castle ships,[196] India Pale Ale.[197] Overall it appears distantly, through a haze, on the edges of the working classes' perceptions; as someone else's business, not theirs. In view of this marginalization it scarcely seems particularly relevant, or important, to know whether the working classes 'supported' the empire or not. It is the quality of their imperialism we should be looking at, not the width. They did not think much about it. They seem generally not to have identified with it. This is what the imperial propagandists felt, and feared.

For this the latter really only had themselves—or the class from which they mainly came—to blame. For most of the nineteenth century they had not much cared whether the working classes identified with the empire or not, for reasons that have been spelled out already. On the whole they preferred not to share the empire with them, if it meant sharing other things, like 'citizenship' or 'national identity', as well. In view of this it is scarcely surprising that the workers developed their own indigenous loyalties and cultures, almost totally apart from those of their rulers. By the time some of those rulers had come to suspect that this separation might be dangerous, in view of the growth of democracy and the external threats mounting against Britain and her empire, it had already had years—indeed, centuries—to bed down in. Cultures that are planted in such rich *material* soil cannot be so easily uprooted. Grafting is also difficult. The task of 'imperializing' the working classes in this sense, therefore, was always going to be problematical.

But in any case it is clear that most upper-class imperialists did not wish to go as far as this. There was some talk about breaking down class barriers, in order to persuade the workers of their stake in the empire—Morant's idea of extending the public-school games ethic to elementary schools, for example; Baden-Powell's vision of upper- and working-class lads mingling together at scout camp; and various imperial 'League' initiatives to broaden their membership—but little was achieved. Educational apartheid, probably the single factor most responsible for sustaining England's class divisions, remained.[198] British society, at least in the cities, remained segregated in almost every way: housing, work, diet, language, reading, culture. Politics became, if anything, more class-confrontational in the 1890s and 1900s than it had been before, which—in combination with the perceived anti-imperialism of the working classes' own political leaders—may have scared the imperialists off the idea of welcoming them on to the ship of empire's bridge more than anything else. (Once up there, they might not like what they saw.) Besides, most of the upper classes felt far more comfortable with the workers in their old place, the engine room. This is why so much imperialist propaganda in the early twentieth century was directed towards making the working man simply 'happier with his lot', and in particular a more disciplined and obedient employee, resistant to the allure of socialist 'agitators'. Imperialists claimed that this was in order to give the empire a secure base (or 'pedestal'), but it also raises the possibility that they had their own class interests more in mind; a point that did not escape contemporary Labour leaders. Such a propagandist effort was never likely to succeed in the working-class culture of that time; which could be the main reason why imperialism probably never really caught on among that class, except for the occasional jingoistic flutter, and maybe as a general feeling of support for and even mild pride in—we shall never know—this entity which was nonetheless not very *important* to them.

10 Imperialists, Other Imperialists, and Others

The workers may have been the least—or the least seriously—imperialistic of all the social classes in late nineteenth- and early twentieth-century Britain. Even 'above' them, however, and in this period of more heightened imperial awareness and enthusiasm than before, not everyone was equally imperialistic, or imperialistic in the same way. Of course they could all be said to be imperialists in a sense. Every one of them was complicit in the empire (as indeed were the workers). They tolerated it. There were no significant movements of protest at this time against imperialism generally. Even so-called 'anti'-imperialists, as we shall see, did not believe that colonies should be freed entirely, and at once. Most other people seemed comfortable with the idea that their country ruled hundreds of millions of people beyond the oceans, and even proud of it to a greater or lesser extent. Some were fanatical about it. But this shared imperialism—defining the word very loosely—is not the significant thing. It masked wide and important differences between sorts and degrees of imperialists. It also gives a totally wrong impression of the place of the empire in British society. For a few people, like the fanatics, it was central; most others, however, still saw it as merely tangental to their lives. For this reason it was not allowed to change their lives, or their philosophies and value-systems, which were still mainly rooted in domestic considerations that had nothing to do with the empire at all. Conversely, it was these domestic value-systems that governed peoples's perceptions *of* their empire; in other words, their imperial*ism*. They saw it through British-tinted spectacles. This was another thing that frustrated the pro-imperial fanatics (or zealots), as much as the apathy or hostility—as they saw it—of the working classes; and probably rightly, from their point of view.

* * *

The zealots came from two broad groups in British society: the upper classes (including the upper middles), and outsiders. The upper classes, of course, had provided Britain's traditional 'ruling' type of imperialist for years. The milieu that bore and nurtured them was described in Chapter 3. Little about it changed during these 'high' imperial years. The upper classes still ruled Britain, formally.[1] They also furnished most of the personnel who ran the empire, both at home and 'in the field'. Their peculiar training, or indoctrination, did not change much either, despite calls to make the public-school curriculum more 'modern or 'relevant', which were generally ignored. The schools stuck firmly to the classics in the classroom, and team games outside (for 'character-building'), because the formula was still felt to work. It produced the goods: a stream of high-minded, confident, and dedicated young imperialists to shoulder the 'white man's burden' of ruling people who could not rule themselves. They were sustained by a very special ideology of imperialism which spread into domestic British society too, but not very far. These were probably the most imperialistic Britons; certainly the most imperialistic in the most imperialistic ('ruling') sense of the term.

Ruling-class imperialism was based mainly on the idea that this class had the right to rule others, and the duty to rule them benevolently. It involved, therefore, both arrogance and altruism. The single word to describe this approach was 'paternalism'. Put simply, this meant 'looking after' their wards—both British working class and 'native'—as though they were children. Such a role was always problematical. First, individuals did not always live up to its high (that is, paternalistic) ideals: colonial officers could 'go bad'. Secondly, the schools could transmit certain unfortunate characteristics to their pupils as well the worthy ones: discouragement of originality and initiative, for example; lack of empathy; arrested emotional development; and all the semi-masonic mysticism that surrounded such institutions.[2] Thirdly, even their 'best' values were steeped in condescension. Colonial servants could behave with genuine altruism, benevolence, and compassion towards those they ruled, just as their gentry friends and relatives were supposed to towards their peasants back home; but it was always from a highly patronizing point of view—father (*pater*) knew best. He was also there to punish, if his wards did not 'behave properly'; which could mean hanging, flogging, incarceration in appalling conditions (just as in England), or having his troops fire bullets into them (which only happened in England occasionally).[3] Fourthly, paternalism could easily turn into racism. This is where the 'children' analogy falls down. When whole peoples were regarded as childlike, it was difficult not to think that there must be some genetic, unchangeable basis for this. Public-school headmasters occasionally inveighed against racism,[4] but it saturates the boys' own school magazines and literature.[5] Even those who believed that other races were capable of 'rising' to the European level eventually usually assumed that this would take decades, or even centuries. So they were, at the very least, 'slow'.

The other side of this philosophy was a tolerance of other cultures which could be a positive asset. This derived from the rulers' conservatism: they did not like change. In particular, they distrusted many of the changes they saw going on around them in the Western world just then, like the march of materialism (capitalism) and of democracy. Occasionally they paid lip service to the latter. Edmond Warre, for example, headmaster of Eton from 1884 to 1905, once praised 'liberty' as 'a high and holy thing, only to be enjoyed by such countries . . . as are fit for it'.[6] That was a clever way of reconciling it with—and subordinating it to—imperialism. Otherwise, however, most imperialists saw no reason why these evils should be visited on other peoples too. Because they had no burning liberal agendas, they tended to regard indigenous societies and cultures more favourably than those who were always measuring them by their own 'civilized' standards. Many even developed a respect for them. David Cannadine has shown how some of them took to aristocratic and 'tribal' structures that reminded them of home, especially the simple, 'lord–peasant' relationship.[7] They often befriended both sides (though on different terms), treated them well, and sometimes even envied aspects of their cultures, especially the 'feudal' parts. Very occasionally they fell for these indigenous cultures in a big way, usually romantically: adopting patterns of 'native' life when they retired, for example (particularly in India), and even professing the superiority of these cultures in some respects. This, for example, was roughly the position taken by the great traveller-philosopher Mary Kingsley, niece of the imperialist novelist Charles Kingsley, and an early influence on the ideology of 'indirect rule' ('rule the native on native lines'), who championed the

African as a more spiritual and also a more 'feminine' people than the European.[8] But she was a racist too, holding that this difference was genetic. That is sometimes the reverse side of a 'respect' for other cultures. Racism of this kind is by no means incompatible with racial tolerance in one's personal relations: you can like, cultivate as friends, be protective of, even envy beings that are considered 'inferior' to yourself. This sort of imperialist felt exactly the same way towards the 'lower' classes back home.

The major drawback of this 'relativistic' cultural approach was that it did not satisfy those who stood for 'progress' in the colonies, including many of the *indigènes* themselves, who aspired to freedom and nationhood along Western lines, and so regarded 'indirect rule', for example, as merely a means of holding them back. There may have been something in this: 'ruling the natives on native lines', the new imperial method of the early twentieth century, was not adopted simply out of respect for indigenous cultures and institutions, but also because it was cheaper than the alternatives, and would prevent the natives from getting their hands on certain aspects of Western culture, like liberalism, that might be imperially dangerous. That was quite apart from the racist implications of it, one of the commonest manifestations of which in this period was the stereotype of the 'westernized native', the African or Indian with a veneer of British culture—Hurree Jamset Ram Singh in the 'Greyfriars' novels is a relatively affectionate example of this[9]—who was sometimes cruelly ridiculed, much more than those 'natives' who were content to remain in their 'place'. Westernized natives transgressed the natural cultural order of things. They were similar to uppity workers, or women who demanded the vote—both of whom came in for the same sort of satirical treatment—in this respect.

But it was not only these 'natives' whom this particular imperial philosophy offended. It also conflicted with other sorts of imperialism. We have seen the role that anti-capitalism played in the education of young imperial rulers in their public schools in the nineteenth century, which could lead to problems when they came to deal with capitalists in the field. European planters in India, for example, were forever complaining of what they saw as ICS obstruction of them, on sentimental grounds that had no place in the modern, capitalist world.[10] Perhaps the best example of this is the battle the British Colonial Office waged with industrial developers in Nigeria in the 1900s, in defence of traditional African ways against large-scale palm-oil production, which the modernizers (in the person of Sir William Lever of the famous soap firm) eventually lost.[11] It also flared up in a different way during the Boer War. The capitalist components of that war were obvious, even blatant (irrespective of whether they lay at the root of it or not).[12] Many of the British officer class who served in it were deeply unhappy about fighting for 'stock-jobbers' against people who, when they got to know them, seemed to have a great deal in common with themselves: old-fashioned landowners whose peasants just happened to be black, and who only wished to be allowed to live in their traditional ways. '[I]t is a great pity', wrote Captain Ballard of the Norfolk Regiment from the front in 1901, 'that good English soldiers and good yeoman Boers should be killed in order that a lot of German Jews may wax more fat and oily.'[13] (There may be doubts about the upper class's anti-black racism; there can be none at all about its anti-Semitism, which was rife.) Some of them also cavilled at the methods that were used to defeat the Boers in the later stages of the war, what the Liberal leader Sir Henry Campbell-Bannerman famously (and bravely) described in June 1901 as 'methods of barbarism': the wholesale farm burnings and the 'concentration camps'. That offended against their upper-class sense of 'chivalry' (the concentration camps were for women and children).[14] 'All you soldiers are what we call pro-Boer', said colonial secretary Joseph Chamberlain once, in clear exasperation at these sorts of complaints.[15] At the very least their 'gentlemanly' backgrounds and up-bringing gave them a particular perspective on the empire, which other classes by and large did not share.

Even the second of our two groups of 'imperial zealots' around the turn of the twentieth century did not share it entirely. These were the 'outsiders', people who stood apart from all the main social classes in Britain, although in different ways (so they do not really comprise a 'group'). They tended to be harder-nosed, for one thing, than the chivalric gentlemen. Joseph Chamberlain himself could possibly be included as one of these: co-opted into the governing classes but originally a capitalist and a radical, who would have been distrusted by the *echt* upper classes for that reason alone, even if he had never, in his social radical days, once threatened to demand a 'ransom' from them in return for their right to keep their ill-gotten landed property.[16] Sir Alfred (Lord) Milner, probably the hardest-nosed of them all, and personally responsible to a great extent for the outbreak of the Boer War, was born and received his early education in Germany, whose contemporary brand of aggressive nationalism seems to have rubbed off on him.[17] Other prominent imperialists also had foreign backgrounds. Lord

Meath and R. B. Haldane had both attended German universities. (Meath's title was Anglo-Irish, which could also be thought to edge him outside the pale.) The prolific imperial propagandist J. Ellis Barker hailed from Cologne, né 'J. Eltzbacher' before he immigrated and changed his name. Leopold Amery, a later colonial secretary very much in the Chamberlain mould, had been born in India, and largely indoctrinated in South Africa under the apparently magnetic influence of Milner, in common with several other members of what was known as 'Milner's kindergarten'.[18] The grammar-school boy Cecil Rhodes moved to South Africa at the age of 17. India and South Africa of course were British, but were not unlike foreign countries in view of the 'un-English' values that service there inevitably spawned. This was what made the Indian-bred Rudyard Kipling seem so alien in the British environment, not least to himself: Britain never lived up to his ideal of what he felt it should be.[19] Other 'cultural' imperialists also had 'foreign' origins: like the three greatest imperial showmen of the early twentieth century, Imre Kiralfy and the Korda brothers, film-makers, all Hungarian; Joseph Conrad, one of the few 'canonical' English writers to use imperial settings and situations in his novels, who was Polish; and the rare imperialist painter Byam Shaw, born in Madras. How significant is this? These examples are probably too few in number to justify any kind of broad generalization, such as that the more extreme or showy forms of imperialism in Britain were a foreign incubus. But there was something ill-fitting about such people in the mainstream British society (or societies) of their time, indicated perhaps by the depth of loathing that Chamberlain, Milner, Rhodes, and Kipling in particular attracted, as well as passionate support.

This alienation, more than anything else, must explain the deep pessimism that gripped many of these 'zealots', wherever they came from, about the prospects for imperialism in Britain. For their kind of imperialism to have prevailed, the country would have had to be totally transformed. Most imperial zealots, for example, believed that 'tariff reform'—coupled with 'imperial preference', to unite the empire commercially (the word often used to describe it was a German one, *Zollverein*)—was a necessity; but free trade had been embedded in the British national psyche for nearly a century. Leopold Amery once denounced the latter, extraordinarily, as 'the negation of the whole meaning and essence of human society, the denial of law and morality';[20] which, whatever might be thought of the merits of the argument, shows how divorced he was ideologically from the society around him. Other favourite ultra-imperialist nostrums—military conscription, for example; massive rearmament; the abolition of political parties or even parliament; and patriotism in the sense demanded by the imperialists—seemed equally alien.[21] Even 'ornamentalism', the taste for flummery that many imperialists developed overseas, was not to the taste of most stay-at-home Britons, except on great state occasions, when it was presented as theatre.[22] These zealots were a race—using that word as loosely as contemporaries often did—apart.

Not all the upper classes, of course—or even 'outsiders'—were 'zealots'. There were a few mavericks among them; many apathists, such as the country house hunting-and-shooting set; and probably more simple ignoramuses. In 1894 a South African speaking to the Royal Colonial Institute quoted a member of the Convocation of the Church of England as saying that there was no need to appoint a new chaplain for King William's Town in the Eastern Cape, 'because we had one at Grahamstown and another at Natal, and surely the two could arrange between themselves to ride over on alternative Sundays and take the services required'. He thought such ignorance in so unexpected a quarter was ominous.[23] There were also rebels against imperial indoctrination in the public schools, as we have seen. But one should not make too much of such exceptions. The upper classes were riddled with imperialism, of a peculiar kind. It grew out of the same social origins and functions that cut them off from their compatriots in other ways too. '[T]he distinction between gentlefolk and the rest of Victorian Society', writes Mary Peterson, 'is the largest rift in the Victorian social structure.'[24] Obviously Germans and Hungarians were even more cut off. The rift continued into Edwardian times; some gentlefolk, as we saw in the last chapter, were well aware of it. Others were not, but carried blithely on with their attempts to win the other classes over to their particular brand of imperialism; 'little realising', in James Greenlee's words, 'how widely [their] vision of the "Brave New World" differed from that of most Britons'.[25]

⁂

It could have differed from the middling classes' vision too. (By 'middling' here is meant those beneath the public-school-educated elite, from professional people and medium-sized capitalists down to small shopkeepers, schoolteachers, and clerks.) In their case there is more evidence than there is for the working classes of widespread imperial enthusiasm; but it was of a different kind from the that of the uppers. This was probably the sector of society that was most receptive to the imperial propaganda of the time. Any imperial schooling that was available came their way; they read the imperialist *Daily Mail*; many of them visited the museums and shows that exhibited and classified their colonial conquests;[26] and they flocked to Imre Kiralfy's spectaculars, and to the much more serious Colonial and Indian Exhibition of 1886, which attracted a record attendance of 5,550,745 visitors.[27] A school textbook put the awakening of public interest in the empire directly down to this event: 'for the first time people at home ... realised how far the power of England extends.'[28] The middle classes may also have made up the bulk of the 'maffickers' of 18 May 1900.[29] They were the ones who were most aware of and moved by the reports from the colonies of exciting events that flooded in almost continuously from the middle of the 1880s to the early 1900s: the Gordon Affair, the war in the Sudan, more 'little' wars in Africa and China, climaxing in the big one—Britain's major imperial war of this period—in South Africa in 1899–1902. There can be little doubt about the popularity of imperialism in this quarter during this fifteen to twenty-year period. It shouts from the middle classes' literature, their music (Elgar's crudest imperial offerings date from this time),[30] their celebrations, their politics. Resisters were mocked, branded as 'Little Englanders' (or worse: a 'murderer', in Gladstone's case), and were even subjected to physical violence at the height of the Boer War. 'Back in London: Imperialism in the air,' recorded Beatrice Webb in her diary for 25 June 1897; 'all classes drunk with ... hysterical loyalty.'[31] The middle classes generally were fascinated by their empire, proud of it, and committed to it at this time: up to a point.

It was that point that worried the zealots. In spite of all these cheering signs, they were never quite confident of the middle classes' reliability on this issue. They suspected that their imperialism might be superficial, and feared its abating after the Boer War was over, with no similar dramatic events to keep the fire stoked up. Even before the war started they were voicing doubts over whether voters (who were still mainly middle class) would support the conflict when it came. 'You cannot realise', wrote the colonial under-secretary to Milner in South Africa on 7 October 1899, 'the enormous difficulty we have had with public opinion at home.'[32] Luckily Kruger then issued his ultimatum, which made the war for Britain technically a defensive one. After it, however, the zealots' insecurities returned. Several commentators were sure they could detect a waning of interest in imperial questions: the understandable desire to revert to domestic concerns

(a)

(b)

1. Two emigration pictures from the mid-nineteenth century: (a) 'News from Australia' by George Baxter, 1854; and (b) Ford Madox Ford's famous—and sorrowful—'The Last of England', 1860.

(a)

(b)

2. Imperial art: (a) Byam Shaw's 'The Boer War', 1901, whose title presumably refers to the thoughts in the head of its subject—perhaps of a husband or lover away at the front; and (b) G. F. Watts's 'Physical Energy', completed in 1905, which Watts decided after meeting Cecil Rhodes should personify the spirit of empire. This version is in Kensington Gardens in London; a copy stands in front of Rhodes's memorial near Cape Town.

3. Imperial architecture: J. P. Seddon and E. B. Lamb's abortive 'Imperial Monumental Halls and Tower', 1904, symbolically dwarfing both church and (nation) state.

(a)

(b)

4. Images of 'the savage': (a) A surprising view of the Australian aborigine, from the Rev J. Goldsmith, *A Grammar of General Geography*, 1823 edn.; and (b) an Ancient Briton from a school history textbook of 1861.

(a)

(b)

5. Positive images of the 'Orient': (a) A proud 'Asia' flanking the Albert Memorial, 1863–72; and (b) Walter C. Horsley's 'Arbitration', exhibited at the Royal Academy in 1899.

(a)

(b)

(c)

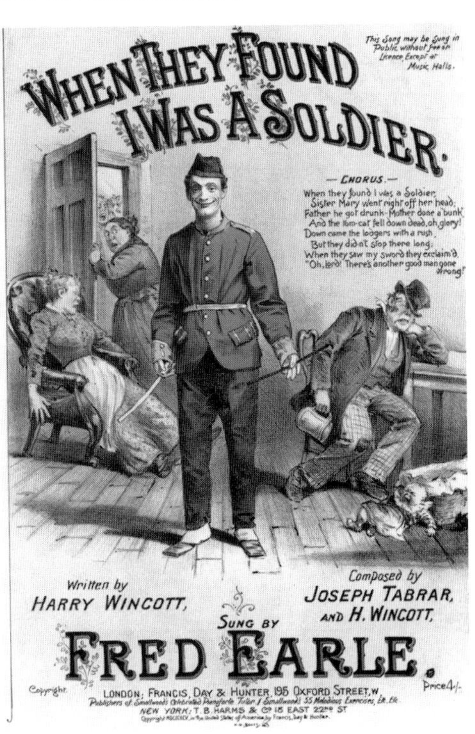

(d)

6. Empire and the music hall, 1895–1900: (a) the patriotic 'Another Little Patch of Red', sung by Reddick Anderson; (b) and (c) two maudlin songs by Charles Harris: 'Break the News to Mother', and ''Tis not Always Bullets that Kill' (about a sweetheart who is unfaithful while her man is away at the front) and (d) Fred Earle's anti-militaristic 'When they found I was a Solder'.

AN ALMOST EXTINCT SPECIES!

7. The short-lived belief that 'anti-imperialism' was defunct is illustrated in this *Punch* cartoon, from the height of the Boer war.

(a)

(b)

8. Visitors to Empire exhibitions could easily be distracted by the funfair aspects of them. These postcards illustrate (a) the popular 'Flip-Flap', at the 1909 'Imperial International Exhibition' at the White City; and (b) the boating lake and Australian building at the Wembley Empire Exhibition of 1924.

'after years of heroic flag-waving', as one put it in 1902;[33] a 'visible tendency to sink back into the slough of inertia', as another saw it, less sympathetically;[34] 'all the familiar signs of [an] anti-imperial reaction', according to a third.[35] It was, in truth, difficult to engender quite so much excitement over post-war issues like tariff reform, peasant proprietorship, and South African confederation. Following their rejection by the electorate in 1906, partly over an imperial question (Chamberlain's 'Imperial *Zollverein*' policy), many Conservatives talked and wrote as though the imperial game was up right then; harping, for example, on the number of old 'pro-Boers' who had been recruited to the new government, and regarding the Liberal Imperialists who sat alongside them as 'broken reeds'.[36] Trying to explain issues like imperial federation to men like these, wrote a commentator in 1907, was 'like talking to mud'.[37] One alarmist in 1909 spotted 'Anti-Imperialists of all shades' looming all around him, '... working their hardest to bring about an appalling catastrophe to the human race—the downfall of the Empire'.[38] This, in fact, was why most of the new imperial 'leagues' and other propagandist organizations of the early 1900s were founded in the first place: to combat, as James Greenlee puts it, 'the moral challenge to imperialism raised during the South African war'.[39]

The challenge was certainly there. During the war itself its strength tended to be hidden by the noise and commotion that came from the other side: by the 'mafficking', for example, or by the bias of the London press, which was 100 per cent pro-war, which certainly did not reflect the general spread of opinion, nor even the views of many of its reporters, who were rigidly censored, and could even be sacked if they strayed from the loyalist line.[40] This led to caution among many of imperialism's opponents. They also felt it would look like treachery to criticize their own side while their brave soldiers were under fire. So they kept their heads down: 'For the moment', said the *Westminster Gazette*, a Liberal-leaning paper, 'the Boer ultimatum has salved uneasy consciences ... The momentary duty is to support the Government.'[41] The Opposition leader in parliament deliberately kept his own instinctive anti-war feelings quiet for the first twenty months of the fighting, to avoid accusations of 'treachery' and keep his fissiparous party intact. 'I am very much in harmony with your views,' Campbell-Bannerman wrote to the pro-Boer Francis Channing in November 1899, 'although I am not at liberty to speak out quite so freely.'[42] His judgement seemed justified in the face of the serious divisions that opened up in the Liberal party during the course of the conflict, which threatened at one time to cause a repeat of the disastrous Liberal split (mainly over Ireland, but imperial issues were involved here too) of 1886.[43] In October 1900 the Liberals lost an election called and fought over the war issue specifically. For the first year of the war, therefore, the dissenters were scarcely heard.

But they were there. The 1900 'khaki' election was not, in fact, an unambiguous endorsement of the war (many 'pro-Boer' MPs, for example, survived it);[44] and support for the conflict seems to have waned rapidly from then on, even while it still continued. What turned the tide appears to have been the incompetence of the army in prosecuting the war, and some of the desperate methods, such as the 'scorched earth', policy and the 'concentration camps', it resorted to as a result.[45] The fact that Campbell-Bannerman felt it safe to raise his head above the parapet on this issue in June 1901, with his famous 'methods of barbarism' speech, indicates that opinion had shifted quite far by then. The resolution of the war—the final Boer surrender of May 1902—was greeted more with embarrassed relief than as an imperial triumph, as we have seen. Interestingly enough, few contemporary middle-class autobiographers admit to having been enthusiastic themselves over the Boer War, though this may be because it had become so unfashionable by the time they wrote.[46]

What this tells us about middle-class attitudes to the empire more generally, however, is hard to say. On the one side, there could be motives other than imperial enthusiasm for wishing the British army in South Africa well. Victories in the field, such as there were, could be celebrated merely *as* victories, and not with any implication of support for the wider cause. Richard Price suggests that this may have lain behind much of the 'mafficking' of May 1900.[47] It may also account for the astounding response to appeals made for charity for the men fighting in the war and their families (or 'Widers and Orfins', as a collecting-box described them), far exceeding in real terms Bob Geldof's 'Live Aid' appeal of 1985, as Andrew Thompson points out; most of which came from the middle classes, because they had the money to give.[48] On the other side, criticism of the government's conduct in the war certainly cannot be assumed to indicate a broader anti-imperialism. Much of it targeted military inefficiency, and came from people who wished the war to be prosecuted more vigorously, not less so. Even those who were entirely against the war could still be imperialists, the argument here being that wars weakened the fabric of the empire, as this one may well have done.[49] So the Boer War cannot be used as a litmus test of opinion on *imperialism* at this time, important an imperial war as it undoubtedly was.

There was, however, plenty of opposition to imperialism generally, certainly among middle-class authors. John Atkinson Hobson's *Imperialism, a Study* (1902) was only one work, albeit the most influential later,[50] in a substantial genre of anti-imperialist writings at this time. Hobson's book attributed imperialism to systemic capitalist over-production, and/or (Hobson is confusing over this) a capitalist 'conspiracy'.[51] Other critics—usually Christians or 'old' liberals—saw it as simply unethical:

The Brotherhood of Man is a long way off; it may never be reached; but as an ideal it is better worth having than that of half-a-dozen sullen Empires, trading only within their boundaries, shut up behind high tariff walls over which they peer suspiciously, scanning one another's exports and imports with jealous eyes, and making from time to time fawning alliances with one rival, while cultivating enmity with another, maintaining millions of men under arms and spending billions of pounds in armaments, and all the time waiting, waiting, waiting for an affrighted sun to rise upon the day of Armageddon.

If this were to be the destiny of the human race, far better would it be if the planet could be spun off its axis and allowed to disappear into the 'illimitable inane'.[52]

One bible scholar thought he recognized the British empire as the Beast of the Apocalypse, no less:

We have also in the Book of Revelation a description of a vision in which the Apostle saw a woman sit upon a scarlet coloured beast, full of names of blasphemy, having several heads and ten horns. Here we have trade sitting upon the back of war—that is, Great Britain sitting on the back of Europe. The woman was arrayed in purple and scarlet colour, and we who have lately heard so much about an imperial policy and painting the map of the world red must be struck with the fidelity of the portrait. The woman is decked with the emblems of her riches, gold and precious stones and pearls, having a golden cup in her hand ful of abominations and filthiness of her fornication. There can be no doubt as to the significance of the word fornication, as it is almost a perfect synonym for commerce . . .[53]

This is strong stuff. It is scarcely surprising that pro-imperialists should have taken it seriously. One was so cowed by the onslaught as to suggest that his fellow 'imperialists' shed the *name* entirely, so tarnished had it become by its association by hostile critics with negativities. 'There is about the word a suggestion of orders given and obeyed, of agreement forced down people's throats at the sword's point, which is repellent', and which in his view did not fairly represent the empire, which was really just a big happy family.[54] However widespread or not anti-imperialism may have been in Britain—some modern historians present it as no more than an indulgence of the 'chattering classes' of the day[55]—it certainly managed to get under the imperialists' skin.

* * *

The 'chattering classes' claim is difficult to gainsay. It is a common argument in favour of the idea of Victorian and Edwardian popular imperialism: that critical middle-class authors were atypical because they were 'intellectuals' (Jeffrey Richards); that working-class memoirists were different because they wrote books; that by becoming a Labour MP or even a socialist a man immediately cut himself off from his working-class roots; and that the literati and other artists represented no one but their own snobbish set. Anyone who put pen to paper, it seems, or brush to canvas, was immediately disqualified from speaking for any large group of people; which, in an age before opinion polls, makes it difficult for historians who want to find out what the others thought. The main burden of this criticism is sound: intellectuals may not reflect accurately the society around them. The inference that is sometimes drawn from it, however, that they *cannot* represent that society, is obvious nonsense. They might mirror aspects of it, even accidentally. In this case the inference seems to be compounded by the assumption that one needed a degree of intellectuality to be able to resist or avoid the seductive blandishments of the imperial programme in the late nineteenth and early twentieth centuries, appealing to 'lower' instincts which uncultured or 'lower' people possessed to a greater extent than the rest.

In this book we have generally dealt with this 'silent majority' problem by looking at people's situation in society, and their early education, in order to see how they were positioned to receive these blandishments. In the case of the turn-of-the-century middle classes their school textbooks give a number of clues. We have seen how much more empire-friendly the new history and geography books became. We can assume that any child now who managed to get beyond the Tudors in history learned something about the American settlements and Clive in India, for example, as well as the Glorious Revolution and the Great Reform Act. That was progress. But it may not have been enough. The empire was scarcely ever *central* in such texts; which is undoubtedly what was meant by those who were still claiming as late as 1907 that there were no suitable imperial texts for schools. In 1911 such a text was produced, Fletcher and Kipling's famous *A School History of England* (1911),[56] which is sometimes taken as representative of its time, probably because of Kipling's fame. In fact it was highly atypical, particularly in its emphasis on the empire, which few other contemporary texts shared.

It was also highly controversial. Some of the original reviews were scathing: 'as nearly worthless as a book can be' (the *Manchester Guardian*); 'a perversion of spirit from first to last' (the *Daily Chronicle*); 'almost too bad to be true' (the *Star*); 'It is a long time since we have read a book which combines so much impertinence with so much stupidity' (the *Daily News*); 'crude . . . uncontrollable and irresponsible' (the *Educational Times*); and 'we should be loth to place the book in the hands of a child' (*Outlook*).[57] It managed to offend both Catholics (something the authors probably did not mind) and Irish Protestants—the latter for its use of the term 'Catholic' instead of 'Roman Catholic';[58] and even offended many colonials themselves, especially those of Irish and Scots origin, who resented the gratuitous slights on them that the book contained.[59] There were some favourable reviews, mainly in the upper-class periodicals, and one even called it 'scrupulously fair';[60] but teachers will have been fully aware that this was a book to be recommended only if they wanted to propagandize, not enlighten. In any case it was too expensive for an elementary or secondary school text (at 2*s.* 6*d.* it would have eaten up most schools' per capita book budget for an entire year).[61] Though it sold well, it never rivalled the really big historical blockbusters of the day,[62] and was probably mainly bought by 'prep' schools and parents, perhaps for Kipling's embedded poems (his main contribution),[63] or the colourful illustrations. There is no evidence, therefore, that this was ever a significant vehicle of indoctrination for those classes that required to be indoctrinated in imperial ways.

The more typical school texts were different. They included the empire now, but did not spotlight it. Imperial topics and values still had to compete with others, in particular those associated with 'liberty'. J. R. Seeley had wanted 'empire' to oust 'liberty' as the main theme of British history since the seventeenth century, but that never came about; nearly every one of even the most 'patriotic' history and civics texts of the time still dwells mainly on the latter, citing it as the main reason why children should be proud of their country, and consequently loyal to its government. That did not rule out a pride in the empire (though perhaps it should have done), but did relegate it to a lower place. James Reid's *Manual of Moral Instruction* (1908), for example, gives 'freedom' as the chief reason why children should obey the laws of their country. A chapter on 'patriotism' lists the 'duties' associated with it as the 'preservation of liberties' first, followed by the 'abolition of evils' at home, then the 'care of the weak and the poor', with the 'preservation of [Britain's] position among other nations' only bringing up the rear. When we look that up ('Britain's position'), we find it defined elsewhere in terms of shipping, commerce, science, and invention, with 'power' getting no mention at all ('National prestige *used* to depend mainly upon a nation's fighting strength'—but no longer). The empire scarcely figures,[64] and is certainly not crucial. This is normal in such texts.[65] 'Liberty'—not imperialism—lay at the core of British history.

One reason for this will have been that 'liberty' was too valuable a tool for controlling the 'people'—the main purpose of popular education, still, in the early 1900s—to risk ditching it for Seeley's preferred emphasis. Persuade people they are 'free' and they will be content with almost anything—as the Americans, for example, have found throughout their history. Pride in their nation's imperial 'greatness' might fulfil the same function, but that was probably not so dependable. Britons had grown used to the first idea, in any case, through generations of an entirely different kind of education and propaganda; which made it potentially perilous to switch. At the very least they would need to be persuaded of both; which is what was attempted in this period. The British were told to take pride in both their liberties and their empire. The fit, however, was not always a very comfortable one. There were obvious inconsistencies. Consequently there were bound to be adjustments in the conceptualization of one or other of these ideals, where they were seen to clash. Usually, because of the historical strength of the liberal ideal among Britain's working and middle classes, it was the 'imperialism' that was adjusted, to conform to the latter ideal. Hence the zealots' unease. Halford Mackinder, for example, did not like this emphasis at all: the British spirit of freedom was all very well, he wrote in one of his geography texts, but it 'has also its great defects. We at times think so much of the individual and his rights that we thing too little of the safety of the State and of the common good . . . But none the less,' he rather churlishly conceded, 'the British tradition is worth preserving.'[66] That indicates how powerful it was.

Almost every history text of the time exemplifies this. They may have incorporated more empire, and been kinder to it, but they still hardly ever—except in the empire-specific histories—gave it the starring role.

The growth of liberty remained the central theme, to which the empire was grafted on: the latter presented as a means of *extending* liberty, through the spread of freedom and enlightenment, beyond Britain's domestic boundaries, either through settlement or by conquest (always provoked) and rule. It could even be seen as the inevitable *corollary* of liberty, as S. R. Gardiner hinted in 1888: 'Freedom is good because it sets us at liberty to make the best of ourselves for the sake of others.'[67] That was one way of connecting the ideals. It was also what distinguished the British empire from others (the Spanish was still the usual comparison), and so, in a way, made it less imperial*ist*. This may have been a travesty of the real, practical British imperialism that was actually going on at this time. It was clearly, at least in part, a construction designed to reconcile squeamish Britons—those who did not have the stomach for sheer conquest and exploitation—to their empire. Nonetheless it is significant that it was felt necessary to present the empire to pupils in this way. It indicates that the domestic 'liberal' discourse in the field of middle-class education was still more powerful than any new imperial or imperially derived one. Confronted by the contradictions represented by the dependent empire, the textbook writers stuck broadly to their Whiggish principles, merely bending them at the edges to make room for the new phenomenon as well.

This process had two consequences. The first was to exert a certain liberal restraint on imperialism, which was only to be tolerated if it remained true to its liberal ideals.[68] The practical effect of this may be difficult to discern in much British colonial policy of the time, but it was not insignificant, manifesting itself in the protests that the most illiberal excesses of that policy provoked in Britain—the 'scorched earth' strategy during the Boer War, for example, and the Amritsar Massacre—and possibly, though more silently, in the care that governments and colonial officials took not to arouse such antagonism too often. It meant that however deeply imperialism may have permeated late nineteenth- and early twentieth-century society, it was never—for the majority of people in that society—allowed to be the final arbiter of national conduct.

It also, however, had another effect. If imperial policy had to be justified by liberal (rather than strictly imperial)[69] criteria, imperialists could be tempted to distort the real facts of those policies in order to fit this bill. For a start, imperialism had to be presented in entirely philanthropic terms. It is notable how little was made in most school textbooks of the economic value of the empire as a reason for supporting it;[70] it continued to be presented as a burden that Britain was assuming for the sake of 'civilization', and not for her own selfish ends. This is reflected in the reasons that were now given for most of Britain's imperial interventions: provocation, and so on. Imperialism was still as 'reluctant' as ever, but with the difference now that it was something to take pride in—Kipling's 'Take up the white man's burden'. Its victims had to be presented as beneficiaries (liberalism, after all, was supposed to have no victims). Those who resisted it were demonized as incorrigibly *il*liberal: usually primitive, treacherous, or cruel—Kipling's 'fluttered folk, and wild'. This too was necessary to sustain the 'liberal' myth. The Afghans especially came under this kind of fire in the 1880s, probably because it was difficult to justify Britain's repeated invasions of their country in any other way.[71] That was the other side of the liberal–imperial nexus. On the one hand it may have helped keep imperial policy relatively liberal; but on the other it encouraged imperialists to pretend it was more liberal than it was, to the detriment of its victims/beneficiaries. That was certainly the impression given in most of the schoolbooks of the time. It was a kind of subversion of imperialism; the corruption of the Fletcher and Kipling message to fit the much more dominant domestic discourses of the time.

❦❦❦

Most of the middle-class imperialism of this period seems to stick pretty closely to this agenda. The moralism of it is sometimes cloying, and can arouse suspicions of hypocrisy, but it was probably this that enabled the middle classes to stomach the empire at all. This was certainly so in Elgar's case, as is made clear in words such as these (by Shapcott Wensley), from his oratorio *Banner of St George* of 1897:

> O ne'er may the flag belovèd,
> Unfurl in a strife unblest,
> But ever give strength to the righteous arm,
> And hope to the hearts oppressed![72]

Elgar's support for the empire was contingent on its being used for good (he made much use of the 'St George' image).[73] This may be why he appears to have cooled in his own attitude towards the empire after 'methods of barbarism', although we have no direct evidence on this.[74] It is reasonable to suppose that much of the rest of the perceived weakening of the imperial spirit in the 1900s came about for similar reasons. In middle-class eyes the empire was never its own justification. At its best it could exemplify Britain's more highly prized home-grown values. If it seemed to offend against those values, or even rubbed against them a little, people would be less keen on it.

Within these parameters, middle-class attitudes to the empire took a variety of forms. In a sense—though a rather exacting one—they could all be described as 'imperialist'. Everyone connived in the empire, albeit to varying degrees, and for reasons, sometimes, which may not have been imperial per se. One such reason was the belief (largely true) that really there was no *non*-imperial choice for Britain; that the alternative to her ruling India, for example, or parts of Africa, was not those countries' independence as nations, but their reconquest by (in these cases) Russia and France respectively. Either that, or they would revert to chaos. A more radical version of this view was that British conquest and rule had disrupted these societies so much that they were now *less* likely to survive on their own than before. The eggs had been broken; there was no immediate hope of scooping the contents back into their shells. Even the empire's most dedicated opponents were unwilling to countenance this outcome, unless they had no regard at all (as some did not) for their colonies' peoples. This 'chaos' hypotheses may have been influenced by a racist presumption: that 'primitive' societies were innately incapable of looking after themselves. On the other hand, it was also reasonable to doubt that they *could* look after themselves in a world of powerful and in many cases quite unscrupulous predators—not only European but also American and later Japanese, and not only nations but also capitalist companies—without some kind of external 'protection', which could only be an imperialism of an alternative kind; at least until some supranational authority could be created to bring law to this international jungle, which did not look likely to happen yet. This was one of Hobson's reasons for not recommending immediate decolonization, and for pressing for a 'League of Nations' later on.[75] Such a view could also be used as an excuse for imperialism, of course, and was so used quite frequently throughout the nineteenth century and for a long while afterwards, which rather sullies its credibility. It would be wrong to infer from this, though, that everybody who employed this argument was really a willing imperialist. Some may not have been.

There are two other considerations that made it unlikely that many British people at that time would be anti-imperialists *pur*. The first is the status of the idea of nationalism in Britain, which we saw in Chapter 5 to have been less developed than in other countries. That made Britons less immediately sympathetic to the idea of *colonial* nationalism—usually seen as the antithesis and antidote to colonialism—than anti-imperialists usually are. This was why Hobson's suggested alternative to empire, for example, was not national independence, but international control. Socialists had their own brand of internationalism, based on class solidarity across national boundaries, which was meant to represent a higher stage of political organization than the old nation states. This is another reason why we must not expect early twentieth-century British anti-imperialists to be colonial freedom fighters too.

The second consideration is more problematical. Very few turn-of-the-century Britons who called themselves anti- or non-imperialists opposed the spread of 'western enlightenment' in the world. Those who did were either racists, believing that some peoples were inherently incapable of enlightenment; 'indirect rulers'; or members of a tiny minority of people who seem genuinely to have preferred *un*enlightenment. The title of one of Edward Carpenter's most idiosyncratic works, *Civilisation: Its Cause and Cure* (1889), expresses this last attitude neatly.[76] Generally, though, left-leaning people in Britain believed that other world races deserved the blessings of 'civilization' and 'progress' as much as they did. That could be said to be 'imperialistic' in itself, though nearly all contemporaries made a distinction between the 'free' spread of enlightenment, and the forcing of it on people through imperial conquest and rule. Imperialism generally (as such critics understood it) distorted the 'enlightenment' process in any case, through the villainy or incompetence of its agents, the corrupting influence of power and greed, and its lack of sensitivity towards cultural differences that might have nothing to do with a people's state of enlightenment. That is why *soi-disant* anti-imperialists were against the empire. But they were not against 'civilizing' the world in ways that stopped short of this.

If this is counted as imperialism, then there was no *anti*-imperialism in Britain at this period at all. Scarcely anyone believed that colonies could be 'liberated' immediately, or that what today we call 'cultural imperialism', if it was not forced on people, was necessarily wrong. Almost every argument that appeared about imperial issues at the time, on any side of what was a wide-ranging and vigorous debate, accepted these two points, at least implicitly. It was a kind of residue, found in otherwise imperially empty bottles as well as the full ones.[77] Whether this was for imperialist *reasons* can be debated; it did not have to be. Unless 'enlightenment' and 'internationalism' are seen as essentially imperialistic, included in the definition of the word, it is possible to square them both with what otherwise would appear to be a perfectly genuine hostility to (for example) overt imperial conquest, rule, and exploitation. Neither of these two ideals appears to have had an imperial genesis; both, as we saw in earlier chapters, are entirely explicable in terms of the liberal discourse of nineteenth-century Britain alone. Of course they may have been shams, convenient excuses hiding more clear-cut imperialist ambitions beneath. That is a matter for judgement in each instance: not, however, a priori and overall. But whatever position we want to take on this issue, the fact remains: that this was as anti-imperialist as anyone in Britain got at the time.

That was one end of the spectrum. Further along, the imperial residue grew thicker. In Hobson's case it was considerably thicker, surprisingly, perhaps, for the author of the leading 'anti'-imperialist text of the time. For Hobson believed that intervention in the affairs of 'primitive' countries in order to make them more efficient economically was justified in certain circumstances; that 'unprogressive' peoples had no right to resist 'progress' if it was to the detriment of the world as a whole.[78] That conceded half of the imperialist argument at a stroke.[79] Hobson justified this in terms of what he called 'human utility': a higher desideratum, in his view, than the claims of simple individual or national occupancy, and incidentally just as applicable to unproductive English landowners, who he said should also be dispossessed if they were holding back development. Maybe that takes away some of the imperialist sting. He tried to suck the rest out by insisting that any such 'utilization' of unproductive colonial territories by advanced countries had to be overseen by an international body higher than the nation-states and capitalist corporations that were only too likely to abuse the process; but it can be argued that imperialism is no less imperialistic for being under international control, especially if the rules the latter is enforcing can be regarded as essentially 'western' ones. (This in fact was one of the complaints made later against the League of Nations 'mandates' system, which owed something to Hobson's thinking.)

There is not much light to be glimpsed between this view and the more overt imperialism of Hobson's fellow radical George Bernard Shaw, who shared his view of 'efficiency'—'the state which obstructs international civilisation will have to go, be it big or little'—and also his preference for some kind of international oversight, but believed that in the meantime, until the desired 'world federation' was achieved, there was no choice but to use existing empires to carry out the job.[80] Shaw's blueprint for empire reform, in a book he wrote under the auspices of the Fabian Society in 1900, was one of the more bizarre manifestations of the ferment of creative imperial thinking that gripped the British (and Irish) intelligentsia in these post-Boer War years: in effect, a kind of super-welfare state, or socialism practised on an empire-wide scale. Again, the argument was that this was the best—even the only—way of preventing the exploitation and oppression of colonial peoples that current imperialism brought in its train. 'Freeing' them would not do it. Native races 'must be protected despotically by the Empire or abandoned to slavery and extermination'.[81] Another way of putting this is that only imperialism can prevent the excesses associated *with* imperialism. The crucial distinction between these two kinds of imperialism for both Hobson and Shaw was that one was informed by internationalist ideals, the other by national and capitalist greed. That distinction may not seem quite so crucial to modern-day critics as it did to them.

One of Shaw's purposes in coming out imperially in this way was to enable the Fabians to ride what he saw as an irresistible tide for entirely other ends. The Fabians were a tiny body; they needed to work through others. The Labour party was too small as yet to fulfil this function (though they were affiliated to it). Imperialism seemed the driving political force of the time. Another Fabian, Hubert Bland, warned that they would be 'entirely crippled if we throw ourselves dead athwart the Imperialist, or any other, strong stream or tendency'.[82] So Shaw, Bland, and some of the other Fabians (the society split over this) gambled on Lord Rosebery's 'Liberal Imperialist' faction's winning control of the equally split Liberal party, which would then enable them to 'permeate' it—and so, hopefully, the next government—in a way they would not have been able to do if they had alienated the party on this issue. Then they could smuggle through social reforms. This was a common strategy at the time. Others spotted a similar opportunity when the panic over the physiques of army volunteers broke out during the Boer War, turning many imperialists' heads towards social reform, which people who had long been social reformers for other reasons, entirely unconnected with the empire, could exploit. George Newman for example, chief medical officer for the Board of Education, and a Quaker (so unlikely to be a rabid imperialist), bade imperialists remember that their empire depended 'not upon dominions and territory alone, but upon men, not upon markets alone, but upon homes': clearly as a way of catching any imperialist wind that might be blowing his way.[83] There was a lot of this bandwaggoning, especially at the very cusp of the century, when the imperialist train for a while looked unstoppable, and a lot of people who were not really imperialists climbed aboard. This demonstrates two things: first the strength of the imperialist propaganda at this time, since it persuaded so many people that it was so dominant; but secondly, that imperialism took on board some very unreliable fellow-travellers. These were the people who dropped away (many of them) after the middle of the Boer War, when the tide of popular enthusiam suddenly showed that, as tides invariably do, it could also recede. The Fabians published no more books or pamphlets on the empire after 1900. Like the majority of the population, apart from the zealots, they returned to their regular and much more basic priorities.

Thereafter middle-class imperialism seems to have continued at a rather low key. There was no more 'jingoism', obviously. There were also no demonstrations against the empire, for reasons we have seen. Everyone was aware of the empire, which had possibly not been the case earlier, though there was still much ignorance—people being unable to name a single colony, for example; horror-stories from the classroom; one account of Australia in which a youth stood 'twining his tame young kangaroo with flowers'—which was much ridiculed, and thought by the zealots to bode no good.[84] Opinions seem to have varied, between the parameters already stated: from those who simply accepted the empire as a fait accompli, to those who thought of it as a power for 'good' in the world. Some of those who accepted it, and so must be included as 'imperialists' for this reason, were nonetheless highly critical of Britain's version of imperialism, and could even be deeply ashamed of it (this includes Hobson and Shaw). They were almost certainly outnumbered by those who felt pride in it; ranging from the fuzzy warm feeling it occasionally gave those whose material situations and more urgent priorities prevented their taking any real interest in it, through to the quasi-religious ecstasy that took hold of men like Milner, Curzon, Rhodes, Chamberlain, Kipling, and Rosebery—though these are all from the 'zealot' class—when they beheld 'the greatest secular agency for good that the world has ever seen'. (This is Rosebery, but all the others made similar noises.)[85] *What* they took pride in, however, could vary enormously, as it always had. William D. Hamilton, writing in the *Westminster Review* in July 1901, made this distinction:

> The people have in their minds one empire, the rulers have another in theirs. The people's empire is one in which every noble impulse will have scope to grow. The ruler's empire is but an extension of the conditions which prevail here—a huge scheme of class aggrandisement, where the many are called to toil and sacrifice continually that a few may obtain exclusive possession of the opportunities of life and labour—the earth. We have no objection to a people's empire, that is, an empire where all men shall have equal rights to life, liberty, and the pursuit of happiness... Lord Rosebery's empire, [however,] no matter how he seeks to conceal it, is an empire based on force, an empire of military dominion... [and of] race superiority.[86]

It is unnatural to elide these two versions of empire together. This is where the utility of the very word 'imperialism', to define an ideology or an attitude, breaks down.

❦❦❦

Art reflects society rather erratically in respect of *fin-de-siècle* imperialism, but that is what we have grown to expect by now. We ran through the main contributors in Chapter 8. As usual, clustering them together can make them appear more significant than they really were. Put in context, the positive imperial contribution to British literature and art in this period was quite thin, and also attracted hostility. In every field we find other topics and influences hugely overshadowing imperialism: aestheticism in the arts, for example; Wagner and Verlaine in music and poetry; and 'Arts and Crafts' in architecture and design. Most of the best-known artists and writers of the period, such as Wilde, Pinero, Beardsley, Hardy, Leighton, Stanford, Parry, and Delius, never addressed empire questions directly. Only two pictures at the Royal Academy exhibition of 1899 had imperial themes; most of the rest were rural landscapes, portraits, historical paintings (usually on medieval themes), sentimental genre-pieces featuring children or small animals, chaste female nudes, and pictures celebrating peace.[87] There is almost no significant imperial poetry apart from Kipling. There were even some *anti*-imperialist poets:

> They talk of the white man's burden. Trash!
> The white man's burden, Lord, is the burden of his cash.

That was the Egyptophile and racehorse breeder Wilfred Scawen Blunt.[88] The imperial influence on architecture was slight overall; even Selfridges could not make London into a *truly* imperial metropolis. In some areas of the arts it is difficult to find any imperial influences at all. Jeffrey Richards, who is not usually shy about detecting imperial resonances in works of art, admits this of almost the entire symphonic, operatic, balletic, and 'art song' output of the time.[89] The 'serious' theatre seems to have snubbed the empire completely, apart from some of Shaw's plays, where most of the allusions to it in *Arms and the Man* (1894), *Captain Brassbound's Conversion* (1906), and the Preface to *John Bull's Other Island* (1904) are hostile, despite the fact that Shaw was, as we have just seen, an imperialist of sorts himself.[90] Sculpture generally avoided the empire, unless one wants to read it into representations of imperial 'masculinity', for example, or conversely the female body (as an object of colonial desire). These are huge gaps.

Those who bucked the trend were often abused for it. Battle paintings in particular (imperial or otherwise) struggled for acceptance in both the artistic and fashionable worlds, being widely regarded 'as a genre for militarists totally deficient in taste'.[91] Kipling was subjected to some savage criticism, and not only for his awful history book; he was a 'hooligan' in the eyes of one reviewer, a 'Barbarian Sentimentalist' according to another.[92] Even Elgar came in for some knocks along these lines:

> Now it is quite possible that the immortal 'Land of Hope and Glory' tune may at some time or other have aroused such patriotic enthusiasm in the breast of a rubber planter in the tropics as to have led him to kick his negro servant slightly harder than he would have done if he had never heard it, and served to strengthen his already profound conviction of belonging to the chosen race; but however admirable and praiseworthy such a result may be from the point of view of empire building, it has no meaning whatever from the point of view of art.

That was the music critic Cecil Gray in 1924. His stated reason for objecting to *Pomp and Circumstance March No. 1* was that art should be 'dedicated *ad majorem Dei gloriam*, and not to the greater glory of John Bull or any similar tribal fetish'.[93] 'Orientalism' was also not widely approved of, though for other reasons. In 1884, for example, John Ruskin feared that the English 'school' of painting might lose its 'national character' if it tried to be (among other things) too 'decoratively Asiatic'.[94] It smacked of 'going native', that unpleasant phrase ubiquitous among colonialists to describe Europeans who embraced African or Asian cultures. Even architects may have suffered from the hostility of fashion. A design by the architects J. P. Seddon and E. B. Lamb for a group of 'Imperial Monumental Halls and Tower' in Westminster in 1904, which would have symbolically dwarfed both the Houses of Parliament and Westminster Abbey, was criticized by *The Builder* for having 'a little too much of the megalomania about it.' It was, of course, never built.[95]

A host of contemporary prejudices came into play here. Artistic snobbery was one, compounded perhaps by jealousy of the popularity of artists like Kipling and Elgar. That made them popul*ist*: never a good thing for a serious artist to be. Elgar even wrote for the music hall, or something very like it, when he conducted his *Crown of India* music at the new Coliseum Theatre in London in 1911 as part of a bill that also included an 'Eccentric Comedian', some 'Gymnastic Equilibrists', a 'Ventriloquial Novelty', and a whole pantomime.[96] That could be considered 'going native' too. Tradition was another problem. 'Neither as an imperial nor a commercial Power has Britain [ever] stirred the imagination of our great writers', wrote the author Gilbert Thomas, looking back on this period. 'It is always to the green fields or the sea that we return in English literature.'[97] English dislike of 'show' (the Westminster project) was another prejudice; cultural chauvinism (Ruskin) one more. None of these obstacles necessarily reflects or implies a lack of imperial interest or feeling in the country at large. Indeed, some may even suggest the opposite. Much of the bile that was directed at Kipling and Elgar, for example, could have been a tacit acknowledgement of imperialism's popularity. And the Ruskin line—resisting imperial influences—is entirely consistent in with imperial arrogance.

The prejudice however was not entirely one-sided. It was not as though imperialists craved to be celebrated in art. Most of them felt they could do pretty well without it; or, if they were art lovers, did not necessarily want it to remind them of their day jobs.[98] Art and imperialism were not thought to be particularly natural bed-fellows, or even compatible. 'Art proper', wrote Dr Emil Reich in 1905, 'is impossible in countries of excessive Imperialism.' So far as he was concerned that was no great loss.[99] Art could pose a positive danger to the imperial enterprise, even when it did not (like Shaw and Blunt) directly target it. Imperialists were particularly nervous of the 'aesthetic' movement, because of the 'effeteness' and 'decadence' it was associated with. It was difficult to see Oscar Wilde keeping the empire up. This could well have been one of the factors behind his persecution in the 1890s: fear of the effect the example of his lifestyle might have on the young manhood that Britain depended on to defend her place in the sun. (Presumably his persecutors were unaware of the homosexual propensities of some of their imperial heroes.)[100] All the mavericks who went along with imperialism were alive to this fear, and some went to great lengths to reassure the imperialists. Elgar's country-gentleman affectations (his garb, country sports, etc.), his moustache (to stiffen the upper lip), the theory he liked to put forward that English music was more 'out-door' and 'bracing' than continental music, and the extraordinary impression he liked to give that he was really a philistine at heart, were probably part of this effort.[101] So was the painter and illustrator Byam Shaw's deliberate avoidance of the fashionable 'Bohemian' dress while he was at art college, standing out from all the other students 'in a suit of loud checks, looking more like a bookie'.[102] It was all an attempt to persuade the men of action they so much admired that they were 'real men' too, despite their artistic bents. Which was slightly ironical in view of the fact that both Elgar and Byam Shaw were physical weaklings, Kipling did not cut the most 'masculine' of figures, and the leading imperial battle-painter of the day, Lady Elizabeth Butler was a woman. All of them were more sensitive creatures than they liked it to be known.

It may be this sensitivity that partly explains the slight ambivalence of their views on imperialism as expressed in their art, when the latter is looked at closely. Kipling's poem 'Recessional' (1900) is well known for its gloomy tone and warning against imperial triumphalism. There is evidence that the *Pomp and Circumstance March No. 1*, which after all is not an intrinsically triumphalist tune (it depends how it is played), originated in a setting of Kipling's poem that Elgar sketched but then abandoned.[103] One of his later themes was the transience of all earthly empires, compared to the enduring nature of art.[104] Elgar was never a 'natural' imperialist, not coming from that class of people, and taking it on mainly in deference to his—very imperial—wife.[105] Elgar and Kipling are often bracketed together as the twin laureates of Edwardian imperialism, when in fact they could hardly be more different; which may be why Elgar set so little Kipling, and in private found much of his work repugnant.[106] According to Tim Barringer, Byam Shaw's paintings, too, are shot through with images hinting at imperial frailty, including his *Boer War, 1900*, which in fact portrays a grieving war widow in an English rural setting.[107] J. W. M. Hichberger has detected an anti-war and anti-imperial subtext in Lady Butler's great canvases, especially the later ones.[108] Butler, incidentally, was another who was born into a non-imperial family and took her imperialism from her spouse, which may account for its lack of deep roots.[109] Joseph Conrad's complex stance on the issue of European empires is well known. Even the most imperialistic art, therefore, posed disturbing questions; as of course the best art should.

In Britain, 'high' culture does not often reflect society very accurately. In these instances the artists would have felt insulted if it had been suggested that they did. Their whole purpose in life, after all, was to transcend ordinary day-to-day concerns, especially the 'vulgar' sort. Nonetheless they were typical in one way: they did not all agree, about anything. In this they mirrored the wider society they stood apart from so deliberately. The popular image of late Victorian and Edwardian Britain as staid and complacent before the catastrophe of the First World War intervened is a travesty. Beneath and beyond the social and artistic elites the period saw a greater flowering and clash of ideas, more cultural dissent, and more social and other kinds of conflict than had occurred for many decades. Imperialism was an element in this, but only one among several. Other trends and influences in British society and culture could affect it, or people's perception of it, as much as it affected them. Hence the range of different kinds and degrees of imperialism that the 1890s and 1900s manifest. Though the artistic culture of this period may not adequately reflect the sheer volume of imperial interest and feeling in Britain in this period, it does mirror this complexity; which includes the uncertainties that so many 'ordinary' people, as well as artists, felt about the empire at the time.

❦❦❦

William Hamilton accounted for the complexity in terms of class. This is what we have also found. Social class and function were the two main factors determining, not only how imperialist different kinds of Britons were, but—more importantly—how they regarded the empire, both in the sense of how they constructed or interpreted it in their own minds, and in the sense of what they thought should be done with it: defend it, extend it, reform it, or let it go. There was no nationwide consensus over these questions. The upper and middle classes saw the empire mainly as an extension of their functions as rulers. 'I believe', said Joseph Chamberlain in 1895, 'that the British race'—he must have meant the Normans—'is the greatest of governing races that the world has ever seen.'[110] 'Governing' was the key concept there. For the middle classes it was the spread of liberal enlightenment. That too stemmed from their historical class function, and the culture that had arisen from that. They needed to believe that this was the empire's mission, otherwise they could not bring themselves to support it. Some, as we have seen, turned against it for this very reason: because they found it difficult to recognize 'enlightenment' in the activities of those greedy capitalists in the Transvaal. Others allowed themselves to be persuaded of the beneficence of British rule in other parts of Africa, Asia, and elsewhere, which was not difficult in view of the sort of intelligence from the colonies that was fed back to them. (The missionaries came in useful here.) It was this that enabled the empire's rulers to get away with some fairly illiberal practices, so long as they were not blatant enough to be noticed back home, and did not involve too much expence. That may have helped to keep the empire relatively respectable—less cruel, that is, than if there had not been these liberal scruples in Britain—and also cheap to run. The working classes were an unknown quantity: many imperialists suspected that their imperialism, such as it was, was too superficial to be relied on when the next imperial crisis came along. From the sketchy evidence we have on this, it appears they may have been right.

When it came to thinking about the empire, most people were less affected by it than by their other, domestically rooted, concerns. Perceptions of the empire were twisted in order to fit in with these, rather than the other way around. Indeed, the fact of having an empire affected hardly anyone's fundamental view of anything. This is what so bothered the zealots, who thought that the empire *should* change people's outlooks; should be promoted to the forefront of their thinking, in fact, and lead the rest. This was the point of J. R. Seeley's new reading of British history in the 1880s, which put the empire at the core of it, but with only minimal effect on school and college syllabuses thereafter, where the other J. R.—the liberal Green—continued to dominate. It is what tariff reformers, too, required in the realm of fiscal policy, that it be redrawn to meet the priority of imperial union; again ineffectively, when tariff 'reform' was decisively rejected by the electorate in 1906. People accepted the empire as an appendage, and only so long as it did not challenge—or could be represented as not challenging—what they from their different sectional viewpoints saw as Britain's core values, which were entirely extraneous to it. This meant, in effect, that the empire existed on sufferance. That was a weakness, as the zealots well knew.

The zealots themselves were a small minority, though they sometimes made more noise than that would suggest. They did not represent any of the mainstreams of British life and culture. A few of them had foreign origins or educational backgrounds, especially German, which may have been what put them at odds with those mainstreams initially. Others were returnees from the colonies, whose original, more homespun values—if they had ever embraced them in the first place—had been squeezed out or overlaid by the culture they had absorbed in their new roles as rulers or members of a ruling 'race'. This is why so many of them felt uncomfortable when they did return, usually to ghettos of their own, like Cheltenham. Rudyard Kipling is a prime example: a *sahib* to his fingertips, who as a result found himself deeply alienated from the British society he eventually came to live amongst; hence his notorious grumpiness in later years.[111] Other leading imperialists were marginal to the mainstreams in other ways. Many were not at all firmly rooted class-wise, but came from the interstices of British society: Irish (and so not really kosher) aristocrats; younger sons; middle-class men with social pretensions; aspirant working classes (who often became missionaries);[112] women frustrated by their traditional roles in Britain; the men (and a few women) with sexual habits that could not be so easily indulged in Britain whom Ronald Hyam has discovered, in surprising numbers, throughout the empire;[113] weaklings who admired the strength that the empire represented (Kipling again?); rogues; ruffians; Scots. Add to these the public schoolboys—representing a more mainstream culture, but one that was peculiar by most standards, and very cut off from the rest—and these may well have accounted for 90 per cent of this period's most dedicated imperialists. Is this what imperialists had in common: social or moral displacement? We must be careful here. It may not be too difficult to find displacement if one is looking for it. It could be that most zealots or achievers in late nineteenth- and early twentieth-century British society, in every field, came from its interstices; needed that background, perhaps, to spur them on. The fact remains, however, that imperialists who put the empire first (our definition of a zealot, and one possible definition, perhaps, of an imperialist) were peculiar in many ways, and detached from other parts of British society, including the broad masses of the middle and working classes, who tended to put it further back.

11

Empire on Condition, 1914–1940

Throughout the 1900s the zealots had been warning that if the country as a whole did not become more imperially committed, the empire itself could be at risk. Their own zeal, combined with only the tepid support of the majority of people, would no longer be enough to hold it up. They were being alarmist, as always; yet the 1914–18 war proved them right to an extent. Despite promising early signs, the long-term effect of the war was to weaken Britain and shift the balance of power in the wider world detrimentally to her imperial role. The people *had* to pull together for it now. So the imperial propaganda was resumed; but with a different emphasis. People were appealed to on other grounds than their putative pride in their empire's glory or strength or power. Instead they were asked to admire it—reverting to a mid-nineteenth-century perception—for its *non*-imperial qualities. That seemed more in tune with the more dominant middle- and working-class discourses of the day, whose part in obstructing or diverting popular imperialism before the war have been noticed already. That this adjustment was felt to be necessary can also be taken as an implicit acknowledgement of those discourses' dominance. It largely worked; but at a price. Lauding the empire for its liberalism made it difficult to defend by other than liberal means. When those less-than liberal means became necessary, support drained away, and the fundamentally non-imperial nature of that support for decades was exposed.

Initially the war was the occasion of both hopes and fears for imperialists. The biggest fears were that Britain might be defeated, and so have her empire taken from her; or that she might win, but at the cost of the empire, which would buckle under the strain. Another fear was that the conflict might test the imperial patriotism of Britons themselves, which was thought to be fragile and incapable of weathering a prolonged war on the empire's behalf. On the other hand, if it were a short war it might boost that patriotism, both in Britain herself and in her colonies. War also offered an opportunity to extend the empire at the expense of Britain's enemies, in particular Germany and Turkey, who had overseas possessions that some British imperialists coveted. That, of course, depended on her winning it.

In the end she did win it (or was on the winning side), but after a much longer struggle than she—or anyone—had wanted. As a result, the impact of the war on the empire was mixed. On the one hand the latter did not collapse under the strain, and indeed appeared to pull together quite gratifyingly, especially most of the settler colonies. On the domestic political front it provided an opportunity for a number of imperial zealots to resume careers that had been interrupted by the Liberal victory of 1906, including Lords Curzon and Milner, who both made it into Lloyd George's five-man inner war cabinet. It was partly their influence—Milner as colonial secretary, Curzon as foreign secretary—that ensured that the imperialists' bold ambitions for an enhanced empire were actually achieved post-war, with most of the defeated powers' ex-colonies coming to Britain as spoils.[1] That—for the imperialists—was the plus side. On the other were the facts that the war did cause stresses and necessitate concessions in certain colonies, notably India; that it stimulated national feelings even in the most 'loyal' ones, like Australia; and that many of the territorial acquisitions Britain made after the war very quickly turned out to be more trouble than they were worth, especially Mesopotamia (Iraq) and Palestine. In addition, Britain was greatly impoverished by the war, to America's benefit. Luckily America chose not to take advantage of this shift in the real balance of resources and power to challenge Britain yet, and Russia—her other potential rival—was riven by civil war; so the British empire was granted some breathing space.[2]

So far as popular support for the empire was concerned—our main concern here—the war gave out confusing signals. People remained generally loyal, which was a relief to those imperialists who had feared much worse. We have seen how Lord Meath credited his 'Empire Day' movement with that. Through it, a generation of lads had imbibed the imperial patriotism that then, he claimed, translated into the mass volunteering for the army of August 1914. But that seems nonsense. Few ordinary soldiers appear to have seen themselves as fighting *for* the empire in this conflict. That was hardly ever mentioned in the war propaganda that was produced at the time for domestic consumption, most of which limited its appeal to the narrower patriotism of 'king and country', or else to those other, more liberal and humanitarian values that we have seen were far more rife before the war: freedom, fairness, anti-(Prussian) militarism, defence of the underdog ('plucky little Belgium'), and so on.[3] This must indicate that the propagandists, at least, thought that imperialism might not strike a chord. Ordinary soldiers in their letters focused on 'hearth and home'—especially wives and children—rather than their nation more generally; or on simple loyalty to their 'comrades', the men in the trenches with them, as reasons for soldiering on.[4] A few of them—a minority, but a significant one, and worrying to the authorities, who used draconian measures to discipline them—showed themselves disloyal to the war effort altogether, by rejecting the draft, deserting, mutinying, striking, or campaigning for a negotiated peace.[5] When asked to serve on in theatres like the Middle East after the war in Europe had ended, conscripts hugely resented it, as we shall see. For most of those who served in it, the 'Great' war was first and last a European one, and strictly defensive to boot. This is reflected too in the thousands of memorials that were raised later to commemorate the sacrifice of those who died. Some of these allude to 'King and Country'; others commemorated the fight for 'Liberty'; some public-school ones mentioned cricket;[6] most were simply for 'the Fallen'. Virtually none of them refers to the empire as one of the causes they had Fallen for.[7] That is because it was not.

On the other hand the war could not help but make people—both servicemen and those who stayed at home—more aware of it. For some it gave them first-hand experience of the empire for the first time: those who served as soldiers in Egypt, for example, or in the soon-to-be-colonized Middle East. On the western (European) front they fought alongside divisions from New Zealand, Canada, Australia, South Africa, and India (the Indians are often forgotten),[8] in many cases meeting men from those countries for the first time. Usually the dominions troops were noticeably healthier, better paid, and also more democratic than the British, the effect of which could have been to instil imperial pride in the breasts of the latter, or alternatively jealousy and resentment against their own imperial government for allowing them to fall so far behind. White colonial troops also appeared in British streets in fairly large numbers, or billeted in British homes, in which guise they feature quite frequently in working-class memoirs of the time, nearly always as a novelty.[9] (The Indians were less visible, generally taking their leave behind the lines in France.)[10] Most people were aware of the assistance that all these 'daughters' of Britain were giving her. That was made a great deal of in the contemporary propaganda, partly in order to prove how right her cause must be if her children supported her so willingly.[11] How long those memories and feelings would last into the post-war period remained to be seen.

* * *

Many of the signs looked promising. Over the course of the war the empire had become more materially important to Britons. This had little to do with its new additions (the 'mandated' territories), but was a result of the increasing share that her older colonies were taking of her commercial activities overseas. In the later 1930s they accounted for 41 per cent of Britain's trade and 86 per cent of her new foreign investment, as against 31 per cent and 46 per cent respectively in the early 1910s.[12] This gave her people a real practical interest in their empire they had not had to the same degree before. Britain's abandonment of free trade in the early 1930s gave her the opportunity to build on this by granting tariff preferences to the colonies, as a step towards the imperial economic 'union' that imperialists had been hankering after for years. This was also a way, the zealots hoped, of bringing the working classes on board, if the empire could be presented as a way of protecting jobs. (Unemployment was the big social issue of the 1920s and '30s.) If that did not work, the empire was still there as a safety-valve, with emigration resuming in the 1920s—around 870,000 people left from Britain for the colonies during the decade as a whole[13]—which created another tie; one closer in this century, probably, than in the previous one, when émigrés had tended to disappear from their friends' and families' ken.

More colonials came to visit Britain, too. The 1931 Census registered 225,684 people from the colonies and dominions living in Britain on the day it was taken, which was more than ever before. (This compared with 307,570 'foreigners'.)[14] Improved communications helped here; (the first 'Imperial Airways' passenger flight between Britain and Australia was inaugurated in 1934, though the trip still took twelve days.[15] The colonial presence became more visible. Most visible of all, despite their small numbers, were the squads of cricketers that visited Britain from the colonies almost every year from 1919 to 1939, with England (or 'MCC') teams returning the compliment in the winters. Cricket at this time, unlike football, was an almost exclusively imperial game. Australia and South Africa had sent teams before the war; afterwards the West Indies (1928), New Zealand (1929), and India (1932) were added to the roster.[16] The games were followed avidly (this was a time when cricket was still a major sport in England). The impact of cricket should not be underestimated. It may well have been the most constant reminder of the existence of at least *these* parts of their empire to the majority of Britons (or Englishmen) between the wars. It also, of course, gave out very good messages about it: 'playing the game', and all that. (When, that is, English fast bowlers bowled at batsmen's wickets rather than at their bodies. The infamous 'bodyline' tour of Australia in 1932–33 did no good to imperial relations at all.)[17]

This increased colonial presence was something for the zealots to build on. It helped at the start that their men still held the reins of power. Milner remained in government until 1921, Curzon until 1924. When they left, the torch for the 'zealous' brand of imperialism was carried on by Leopold Amery, a disciple of Joseph Chamberlain and protégé of Milner, as colonial and/or dominions secretary from 1924 to 1929. There were plenty of other imperial enthusiasts in the upper reaches of society and government. They also had a potent new tool at their disposal: government propaganda, which was effectively a product of the war.[18] An example is the Empire Marketing Board, set up in 1926 to help sell empire products, but with a clear broader agenda too: persuading the public of the importance of the empire to them.[19] One of its 'cutest' inspirations (Sir Keith Hancock's word) was a recipe for an 'Empire Christmas Pudding' it published in 1929, 'cooked according to the recipe supplied by the King's chef Mr Cedard with Their Majesties' Gracious Consent', and utilizing the widest possible range of colonial produce in order to rub home the imperial message.[20] Then there was the new British Broadcasting Corporation (originally Company), founded in 1922, which was supposed to have an arms-length relationship with the government but was usually co-operative over imperial matters.[21] No pre-war government ever had means like this of spreading the word.

There was more. Most of the pre-war non-governmental imperial pressure groups—the Royal Colonial Institute, Empire Day Movement, Victoria League, Round Table[22] and so on—were still active. They were supported by a generally pro-empire press, especially Lord Beaverbrook's revamped *Daily Express* (slogan: 'For King and Empire'). Imperial history and geography had become embedded in school syllabuses at last, with one High School Certificate Board offering a discrete history option in 'the Expansion of the British Empire', for example;[23] and a wide range of new and explicitly imperial history and geography textbooks for sympathetic teachers to use.[24] J. R. Seeley would have been delighted with some of these. 'For the next two centuries', wrote one Arthur D. Innes in a new 1923 text, '. . . British history is the history not of the British Isles but of the British Empire':[25] which was exactly the line Seeley had urged. The controversial 'Fletcher and Kipling' will have really begun kicking in now, too, with who knows how many middle-class schoolchildren leafing through their dog-eared copies of the 55,000 it sold in its first ten years. Maps of the empire adorned most classroom walls. Empire Day was a fixture, officially recognized in Britain (at last) in 1916, and celebrated in nearly all schools on every subsequent 24 May.[26] Supplementing all of this was a stream of empire magazines, novels, 'Annuals' for boys and girls, and songs; stirring imperial films, both British (many by the Korda brothers) and, perhaps surprisingly, from Hollywood;[27] 'Empire Day' broadcasts on the BBC;[28] and a host of other highly popular imperialist vehicles, described and analysed in the well-known books by John MacKenzie, Jeffrey Richards, and others.[29] Then there were the statues. Quite suddenly figures, busts, and medallions of imperialists began appearing all over the country: eleven in London alone in the inter-war period, for example, including some of men one would have expected to have been statued much earlier, like Clive (1917) and Wolfe (1930); more recent luminaries like Curzon (1931) and Milner (1931, but only a medallion, and probably in recognition of his social work); and even Lord Meath (another medallion, in Lancaster Gate, 1934).[30]

The most spectacular example of this propaganda—quite literally—was the great British Empire Exhibition held at Wembley in 1924–5, as a joint public-private enterprise, 'to demonstrate to the people of Britain the almost illimitable possibilities of the Dominions, Colonies and Dependencies overseas'. A visitor would learn more about the empire from a day spent there, it was claimed, 'than a year of hard study would teach him.'[31] The impact was immediate. 'As the visitor alights from the train at the Exhibition station,' wrote Donald Maxwell, an artist commissioned to record it, 'he feels himself in the heart of Asia. On the left are the slender pinnacled towers of Burma. In front rise the white domes and minarets of the Indian

Palace...' and so on. There was also a 'British Government Building', where Britons could see 'the whole romance of history unfolded—the most wonderful history of any nation on earth.' It was magnificent. (Maxwell's own pictures capture—and probably embellish—much of this.)[32] The 67-year-old Elgar was commissioned to compose a new 'Empire March' for the opening, though in the event it was not performed through lack of rehearsal time. Instead he conducted his earlier (1897) 'Imperial March', which the *Morning Post* thought breathed 'the very spirit of that broad and tolerant Imperialism, to which the King had referred in his speech'.[33] As he mounted the podium Sir Edward felt 'something wet roll[ing] down my cheek—& I am not ashamed of it'.[34] It was all a great show, and undoubtedly the imperialists' greatest propaganda coup. (It was repeated in Glasgow in 1938.)[35]

The propaganda did not let up, therefore, after World War I. If anything it was probably more intrusive and ubiquitous now than before. No one could have been unaware of the empire: but that had been the case now for many years. The question is, as always, just how this propaganda impacted. There are a number of alternatives, or rather varieties of response: for different groups of people will obviously have taken it in different ways. One was to feel enthusiasm for the empire; another, of course, was hostility; a third was indifference; a fourth was pride in one sort of empire, but not in another, as we saw had been typical in the mid-nineteenth century; a fifth was passive acceptance of it, as a 'fact of life'; a sixth was acceptance of it as a kind of *imagined* identity, or myth. These differing responses had a bearing on the extent or depth of people's interest in the empire, too—where they placed it on their scale of priorities. The enthusiasts obviously put it at the top, others pushed it much further down. Fairly low on the scale, in fact, seems to have been the commonest place for it. As for the other alternatives, the imagined or mythic one was certainly important, for reasons that reach a long way back, as we shall see.

❦❦❦

One glaring gap in the impact of all this propaganda will not be unexpected by now. 'Fine' artists still tended to shy away from the empire. None of the new cultural trends of the time was conducive to the expression of 'imperialism' in almost any sense. One possible exception is the 'orientalist' element in (for example) 'art deco', but the relationship of this with empire, especially in this period, is complex to say the least. Abstract art, functionalist architecture, surrealism, post-impressionism, vorticism, realism, serialism . . . ; it is difficult to read imperial subtexts into any of these styles. Neither the new 'modern' architecture nor the restrained Georgian classicism of its opponents could ever have expressed 'imperialism' adequately, even if their practitioners had wanted to. (Nazi and Stalinist brutalism might have done it better, but that never caught on in Britain.) Picture galleries virtually never hung imperial scenes. The most celebrated British musical composers of the day avoided the subject almost perversely, including Arthur Bliss (later Sir Arthur), though he looked the part, and Ethel Smyth, despite being made a 'Dame' of the British Empire in 1922. The main exceptions are old Elgar's 1924 Empire Exhibition music, and the young William Walton's brilliant Elgar pastiche, *Crown Imperial* (a march), written for the coronation of 1937. Arnold Bax, by preferring Irish themes and flirting with Irish nationalism for a time, could even be counted an *anti*-imperialist composer. (The neglected John Foulds may be another.)[36] The same is true of the genre called 'light' music: Coates, Ketelby, and the rest. There *are* some imperial pieces. In 1919, for example, Margaret Meredith trod where Elgar had not dared to, and set Kipling's 'Recessional' 'for Chorus of Mixed Voices, Organ and Brass Instruments'; but who has ever heard of it, or, for that matter, of her?[37] In the novels of this period the empire is, as it nearly always had been in the past, good for just a few marginal references at best, or otherwise—in the three most celebrated examples of 'colonial' literature from this period: E. M. Forster's *A Passage to India* (1924), George Orwell's *Burmese Days* (1934), and Joyce Cary's *Mister Johnson* (1939)—treated highly critically.[38] Otherwise 'modern' artists in all genres concentrated on other themes.

This came about as a conscious reaction against the pre-war generation, which did, in truth, have a lot to answer for: the war especially. Those who seemed to represent that generation, but who survived into the new era, bore the brunt of this. Elgar for example, reeling (one imagines) from that cruel attack on him by Cecil Gray in 1924 (the charge that *Pomp and Circumstance March No. 1* could inspire Malayan planters to kick their 'negroes'), certainly felt unfashionable and neglected, and lost the will to write substantial works after 1919 (though not for this reason alone).[39] Kipling too felt the world had turned against him, and relapsed into a life of 'venomous' reactionism after the war.[40] Rider Haggard—to descend a little on the cultural scale—stopped writing altogether. Henry Newbolt wrote far less poetry of any kind after 1914, and the best of that on countryside rather than patriotic themes. If John Masefield wrote any imperial *pièces d'occasion* in his role as Poet Laureate (1934–67), he did not think them good enough to be anthologized.[41] Alfred Noyes wrote a long poem 'To the Empire' for the 1924 celebrations; which makes the familiar point, however, that it was deeds that upheld the empire, and *not* poetry:

> Through steadfast minds that are not fooled by lies;
> Through men that serve mankind, and are not heard,
> Through inarticulate lips and honest eyes,
> The living Power still speaks the living word . . . [42]

which could be said to prove the point. Empire was for the inarticulate. The very articulate, in whatever cultural or artistic media they worked, avoided it.

So did others. The artistic elite was not alone in its seeming immunity to the imperial propaganda of the time. Others positively contested it. They included educationalists, who had come to feel uneasy over the way history, geography, and the new-fangled 'civics' had been used to inculcate imperial patriotism in the recent past, and were now pressing for these subjects to take on a more 'social' or internationalist or 'relativist' slant.[43] 'In the past,' wrote a critic in 1933, 'geography has been too much concerned in the schools with bringing out the *differences* between peoples rather than the vastly greater number of *likenesses* which exist between them. The schools have been more apt to point out that a negro is black than that he is a man. This emphasis on differences is undoubtedly the main factor in the general failure of geography teaching to produce a world mind.' (That seems a direct swipe at Mackinder.) Things were changing, however. The war—claimed this author—was the cause of this. It had 'redirected the conscience and the consciousness of the world towards the problem of conciliation and co-operation. In this work it is perhaps the historians who have been most to the fore. The conception of history as a school subject has, within the last ten years or so, been slowly developing from a purely national to a world conception'.[44] There are at least as many inter-war textbooks, in fact, taking this line as the imperial-patriotic one.[45] This surely accounts for the markedly defensive tone of several of the latter, warning their readers against those who, for example, 'will tell you that we gained our Empire by fraud and violence, and have no moral right to our possessions', or who denounce 'empire history as a story of aggression, domination and glory', or who 'would belittle the Empire simply because it is British': approaches that were clearly thought insidious enough to need confronting head on.[46] There seemed to be, wrote a Scottish history professor, looking back over the inter-war period from 1940:

> a school of thought which attributes our every action to low motives—usually economic—and takes no account of the valour by which an empire has been won... Who is to blame if the youth of today, including some foreigners in our midst who listened avidly, came to believe that our empire, founded on force and maintained with incompetence, was not worth defending, and proposed to give away, with the generosity of youth, things which had been won by the courage and blood of our ancestors... ?[47]

One imperialist, frustrated by such attitudes, suggested that the very effort to push for more imperial teaching in the schools might have been counter-productive, as it merely stiffened the resistance of the 'vast legion of rebels among the teachers'; and, besides, could provide a dangerous precedent if (for example) the communists ever came to power and wanted to impose *their* ideology through the syllabus.[48] Educationalists also resisted the imperializing of schools broadcasts by the BBC, and the great fuss the latter made over Empire Day, where they had the backing of some within the Corporation too. 'None of us like [*sic*] the Empire Day programme', wrote one employee in 1931. Another regarded it as boring, 'a dead letter day'.[49] In 1937 many education authorities banned Empire Day.[50] In the universities the continued neglect of imperial topics in nearly every area was alleged to be because dons and students alike also found them 'boring'.[51] At the very best, wrote the historian Philip Guedalla in 1924, it held no more than 'a dim interest for research students'.[52] So it was educationally unfashionable too.

* * *

Unfashionable, however, does not necessarily mean unpopular. Such reactions, from artists and pedagogues, represented 'largely intellectual views, which are a poor guide to popular imperialism in the inter-war period'. This argument has been met before.[53] It is certainly true that they are no *necessary* guide to 'public' opinion. Indeed, in the case of 'high culture' they may have not even reflected the opinions of its practitioners themselves, who cannot be assumed to have been indifferent to the empire simply because they did not think it was a proper subject for art. At 'lower' levels there are signs that imperial culture was better received. The environment of the time may have been unfavourable to the creation of brand-new 'imperialist' works, but the old ones were still around and, by all accounts, popular still. Elgar, for example, despite his feelings of rejection, was frequently recorded between the wars; and often played on the new 'wireless', with his *Imperial March* getting sixty-five airings on the BBC between 1922 and 1934, and *Pomp and Circumstance March No. 1* too many to be counted.[54] The pre-war Kipling also remained very much in print, with a 'Complete Works' published in 1926–30, and poetry selections in 1919, 1927, 1919, 1933, and 1940.[55] So did Henty, with steady reprintings through to the 1950s.[56] Newbolt's famous *Vitae Lampada,* with its clear imperial message (the 'Play up and play the game' one), was so popular that he came to regard it as his 'Frankenstein's monster', 'falling on my neck at every street corner!'[57] Elgar felt much the same about *Land of Hope and Glory*.[58] This suggests quite a gap between the 'high' and popular culture of the time, with the latter—Noyes's 'inarticulate'—probably less sniffy about imperialism than the snobs.

The question here, however, as ever, is how serious and committed this popular imperialism was. Other indications suggest that it may not have run very deep. People could obviously love Elgar and Kipling—still can—for other than imperialistic reasons. The same applies to the Wembley exhibition of 1924, where the sugar coating, as with Kiralfy's pre-war shows, could well have obscured the more serious message underneath. This was a common observation at the time. 'I've brought you here to see the wonders of the Empire,' says one of Noël Coward's characters, 'and all you want to do is go on the dodgems.'[59] The exhibition was a financial failure.[60] Whether its educational impact compensated for this is hard to tell. Leopold Amery recalled travelling back from the exhibition by train one day in 1925 and overhearing 'two well-dressed ladies' who still, after it all, were under the impression that Japan was a British colony, and that California tinned fruit counted as an empire product.[61] It should perhaps also be pointed out that Elgar's tears at the inauguration ceremony were stimulated not by the pomp and circumstance of it all, but by the sight of a daisy on the Wembley turf: he found the rest of it 'all mechanicil [*sic*] & horrible—no soul & no romance'.[62] (This may account for the subversive note that is hidden in another of his contributions to the occasion, a *Pageant of Empire* song cycle, one verse of which—by Noyes—points out the fragility of all earthly empires compared to the enduring quality of great art.)[63] This is not to deny that many—perhaps most—visitors may have been more impressed than he was, and came away from it better educated in imperial geography than Amery's 'well-dressed ladies'. In any case one can be impressed without being educated. It is entirely possible that Amery's ladies were much more susceptible to the charms of an empire that included Japan and California than they would have been if they had gleaned a more accurate knowledge of it. (It is interesting that Amery made no attempt to correct them.) Many of the sneers at the expense of the Exhibition may have been motivated by high-cultural snobbery, as John MacKenzie suggests. All of this 'evidence' is selective, hearsay, and anecdotal. What it serves to iterate, however, is the obvious point: that propaganda does not always have its intended effect.

The imperial classes were very pessimistic about this situation (but then, had they not always been?). One zealot wrote to the Colonial Office in 1921 complaining of the 'neglect of the Crown Colonies by the British public', which he attributed to the latter's 'amazing ignorance in regard to them—an ignorance common to nearly every class including the most educated'.[64] Sir Harry Johnston, the last of the great British African explorers, agreed that 'the general public is apathetic about Africa . . . this is painfully obvious to anyone who is trying to work on behalf of the continent'. As so often in the past, lack of education was to blame: 'The ignorance on African matters of even the most educated and thoughtful sections of the community is really appalling; even their ideas of geography are absurd ("Oh, you live in Rhodesia. I wonder if you have met my cousin; he's out there in Nairobi." Such sentences are of common occurrence) . . . '[65] In 1923 a Colonial Office official minuted that, so far as 'our masters, the public' were concerned, ' . . . I frankly despair of making the great heart of England take any really intelligent interest in any Colony'.[66] Ralph Furse, the director of Colonial Office recruitment, was also 'appalled' by this ignorance, which he thought did not 'beseem a great imperial power'.[67] A 1927 Colonial Office Conference recorded its unease at 'the prevailing ignorance' of colonial matters in the country at large.[68] Humanitarians felt similarly frustrated. 'When you get into a job like this,' wrote the missionary J. H. Oldham to Lionel Curtis in 1929, 'you discover how comparatively few people really care about the overseas Empire.'[69] The chairman of the Empire Day Committee noted in 1931 how many 'dark corners in Great Britain' there were, 'especially in the industrial areas, where the rays of our Empire have not yet been able to penetrate'; and this 'in spite of unremitting efforts [at propaganda] for a number of years'.[70] Apparently this ignorance even extended to MPs. 'I am afraid,' said Drummond Shiels, 'there are very few members of the House of Commons who could pass an examination in regard to the names of the constituent parts of the British Empire, and as to where they are situated.'[71] So Amery's 'well-dressed ladies' may have been in good company.

This is compelling evidence—the sheer number of statements of this kind—but it is not conclusive. Imperialists had reasons of their own for emphasizing popular ignorance. They were also not in a position really to know how the 'lower' orders felt. Nor are we. It would be good to have some quantitative data on this, but we do not for this period; scientific public-opinion polling did not begin in Britain until 1937, and in any case did not start putting questions to people about the empire until much later on. That may be significant in itself. The only pre-war exception was a 1938 question on whether people would be willing to hand the former German colonies back: 85 per cent replied no, but probably more on anti-German than on pro-imperial grounds.[72] When Germany was not involved, respondents revealed themselves to be rather more liberal; 77 per cent of Gallup's sample in November 1939, for example, thought that India should be granted independence soon.[73] The first proper survey of attitudes to the empire came in 1948. It was carried out on behalf of the Colonial Office, from a sample of 1,921 people from all classes. Its findings *may* be applicable to the pre-1939 period too. They do seem to back up the imperialists' contention that most people were both ignorant of the empire, and not particularly enamoured of it. The survey found, for example, that 75 per cent of people were unaware of the distinction between a colony and a dominion, that 49 per cent could not name a single colony, and that 3 per cent (fifty-seven people) believed that the United States still was one. (One respondent named 'Lincolnshire' as a colony.) The report ended: 'In fact the general conclusion to be drawn ... is that people's knowledge of the Colonies, and our relations with them, is sketchy and inadequate in the extreme', including among 'the most highly educated sections of the population'. Ironically, the knowledgeable were marginally more likely to be critical of the empire than the ignorant. As well as this, the survey found that 'Nearly half the sample evinced little or no interest in the colonies', only 22 per cent were rated 'as showing a *high* degree of interest in the topic of the survey', and a mere 4 per cent reckoned they had any kind of 'connection' with them.[74] On the other hand, the project did only cover the 'colonies', a word that at this time excluded the self-governing dominions and India (hence the question on the difference between the terms). It is a fair assumption that far more respondents would have displayed an interest in, and knowledge of—say—Australia, if asked (Bradman's great cricket team was touring England at just the time the survey was carried out). That was the people's empire, as opposed to the patricians'. So we are still essentially in the dark.

❦❦❦

There are other reasons, however, for thinking that the majority of people were unlikely to have been greatly concerned about the empire in this period. One is that there were so many other matters that must have concerned them more. Here it is important to see these imperial questions in a much broader context. World War I was part of this. Its specific influence on the way Britons may have regarded their colonies pales into insignificance by the side of some of its other repercussions, whose *indirect* impact on their imperial awareness must have been far greater. For example, the war made militarism less respectable than it had been, for obvious reasons, thus chipping away at one of the pillars that had supported one version of imperialism before the war. Hence the new 'internationalism' that was being pressed now in some of the schools. Secondly, it had an impact on social discipline at home, in ways that at the very least acted as a distraction from the empire, and might even be thought to threaten it. The war was unsettling for nearly everyone who survived it, and for the relations between the different groups and classes of them. The British establishment was ever aware of this, and even frightened by it, especially when they looked abroad: at the great Russian Revolution, for example, which had been triggered by the war, and by the series of smaller (and less successful) communist uprisings that afflicted Germany and other European nations in its wake. Many people feared—or hoped—that revolution might happen in Britain too, which was after all far riper for it according to strict Marxist theory. At the end of the war there were Secret Service reports of the Bolshevik 'virus' infecting the British armed forces in Germany, and of secret, Russian-style 'soviets' being set up in several English towns, including Tunbridge Wells.[75] How could anyone concentrate on the empire while this was going on?

Tunbridge Wells must always have been an unlikely seedbed for the class war, and the Secret Services' fears more generally were certainly (and typically) misplaced; but there is no doubt that a revolution of sorts was stirring at this time. The biggest event was the rise of labour. The Labour party was well on its way to ousting the Liberals by the end of the war, amassing 2,385,472 votes in the general election of 1918, as against 505,657—its previous record—in January 1910.[76] In 1924 it formed its first government—albeit a minority one. Trade-union membership nearly doubled during the course of the war. The first post-war year saw nearly 35 million days lost in strikes, which was the second highest figure ever recorded; followed by 85,870,000 in 1921—a clear record—and 162 million in the famous 'General Strike' year of 1926.[77] In January 1919 the hammer-and-sickle flag was hoisted over Glasgow Town Hall in the course of a strike there, and the army had to be sent in with tanks. In some places even the police 'came out'. Things calmed down on the industrial front after 1926; but labour (and Labour) questions continued to dominate the political scene for years after that. The Great Depression, of course helped here. In the 1930s foreign affairs came into the public gaze again; but almost always continental foreign affairs—European security, the broader struggle against communism, the rise of the dictators—rather than imperial ones. The latter were a minority, tangental concern to most folk. Even imperialists felt that these other questions took priority, or ought to, in view of the threats they—especially communism—posed to the very vitals of the empire.[78] Others did not even make that connection. These domestic issues were separate, and of far more significance to most people on every level than almost any concerning the empire. It was they that defined the terms of most of the major contemporary political debates of the time, with the empire hardly getting a look in. As Jan Morris puts it:

> Thick and fast came rival historical movements . . . which seemed to make the existence of the Empire more than ever peripheral to English life. The rise of the Labour Movement to power had nothing whatever to do with Empire. Communism was passionately opposed to it. Empire did not save the British people from the Great Depression or the General Strike. Empire contributed nothing to the new functional architecture, the new abstract art, the social experiments that were gradually changing the form of English society. So immediate and so vivid in the 1890s, Empire now seemed dimmer and more distant, and was becoming, like the British institutional architecture of the day, pompously retrospective.[79]

It was, in other words, crowded out of the public debate.

This is demonstrably true on the political front, where imperial questions were dwarfed by these other ones. Apart from the problem of what was to be done with India, which excited a number of Conservatives (called 'diehards') in the 1930s, colonial parliamentary debates commonly took place in near-empty Houses, even when substantial issues were at stake. 'I can only express regret that a much larger number of Members were not present to listen to what has been laid before us', said a Liberal MP in the first full-scale colonial debate after the war: the one in which Amery told the Commons what his government thought of the revolutionary new League of Nations 'mandates' system for Britain's new acquisitions.[80] Reasons offered for low attendance included poor scheduling: colonial debates were often held on Friday afternoons, or in one case in the middle of the Eton–Harrow cricket match,[81] though they would surely have been given more popular slots if Members had wanted it; the fact that colonial business seemed unexciting, though that was in the eye of the beholder; and its uncontentious nature. 'When an uncontroversial subject comes up the House is practically empty,' said one MP in 1928; 'Hon. Members cannot have a fight, and therefore they do not come to the House.'[82] This may indicate that everyone was happy with the broad direction of British colonial policy, and hence—by implication—with the empire; but others blamed simple apathy on the part of MPs. It was usually the same faces that turned up to debates: only about fifteen or twenty of them, according to the imperialist MP Charles Ponsonby, who reckoned that this was the maximum number of those who were actively interested in colonial questions in the 1930s.[83] 'The ordinary Member... cares little about Africa', wrote one commentator.[84] This apparently extended even to ministers. Sir Alfred Milner—not the most disinterested witness, admittedly—considered that he and Amery stood 'rather alone' in Lloyd George's post-war government, 'among people who have very little sympathy with the things which we both care about'.[85] John Ramsden attests that Stanley Baldwin, prime minister for much of the 1920s and '30s, took little or no interest in empire issues.[86] He and his fellow politicians had more important matters on their plates.

At the other end of the political spectrum the labour movement seemed similarly unconcerned. Few of its leaders were enthusiastic imperialists. There were of course exceptions, chief among them the much ridiculed J. H. ('Jimmy') Thomas—'We love our Empire. We are proud of the greatness of our Empire'—who was thrilled to become Labour's first colonial secretary in 1924; but he was something of a maverick.[87] Socialists by and large did not buy the imperialist argument for an imperial tariff union, seeing it as a Conservative ploy to ensnare them (as it largely was).[88] Nor, on the other hand, were they as anti-imperialist as one might expect. There was a left-wing anti-imperialist movement in Britain between the wars—'anti-imperialist' in this context taken to mean working for the dismantling of the empire, not just its reform—but it was fragmented and weak.[89] Imperialism was a natural target for those who believed it represented the last desperate gasp of the propertied classes to keep a self-destructing capitalist system going; but not many British socialists were as Marxist (or Leninist) as that. Hobson's *Imperialism,* which also related imperialism to domestic economic and social issues, was not much read until its virtual rediscovery (and republication) in 1938, according to Peter Cain.[90] The British Communist Party was anti-imperialist, of course; as was the Independent Labour Party, much influenced by the lifelong anti-colonial campaigner Fenner Brockway. The (main) Labour Party Conference passed a general anti-imperial resolution in 1921, sponsored by the ILP, on very Hobson–Leninist lines, as it happens; but that was a one-off.[91] Otherwise there were occasional calls for quicker progress towards Indian (rarely anyone else's) self-government.[92] The Labour Party's other main concerns were with 'native labour' in the colonies, where it felt it had a special expertise, and race equality. Neither of these issues implied a wish to get rid of the empire; indeed, it would have made it more difficult for the party to press for labour rights and racial justice there if these places had been 'free'. Only when Britain's imperial rule seemed not to be delivering these advantages did Labour consider alternatives. An example is Walter Citrine, the famous trade-union leader, who when he visited the West Indies as a member of a Royal Commission to report on working conditions there in 1938 reacted thus: 'I had seen so many glaring injustices in the West Indies that I could scarcely contain myself. I felt that if Britain could do no better for these poor, simple, and patient folk than we were doing then I for one would not wish to keep them in the British Empire. Let them have complete self-government, or go to some other country which might be able to do better for them.'[93] Even there that last sentence, suggesting that another empire might take over the British West Indies, indicates how unimportant the question of imperial principle was for him. This is neither imperialist nor anti-imperialist; or—by another way of looking at it—it is both. It accepts the necessity for empires (plural) implicitly; but it holds no brief for the British empire in particular. Like most Labour activists, Citrine was simply unconcerned about that.

This is likely to have reflected apathy towards the empire in the country more broadly. MPs and trade unionists were not fools. They were sensitive to public opinion, and felt that it was cold on this matter. Although the colonial question was a 'very big' one, said one delegate to Labour's Annual Conference in 1933, it was 'not one that [would] fire the enthusiasm of the electors at a general election' or 'win for us a majority'.[94] 'I do not think', wrote one of those electors in 1930, 'we sent a man to Parliament to spend all his time troubling about people who are many thousands of miles away... [I]f Mr Buxton wants to continue to represent us he should get down to brass tacks and let the natives of Rhodesia and Nyasaland look after themselves for a while.'[95] When sitting MPs were defeated in elections they sometimes attributed this to their being too tied up with colonial affairs.[96] In the absence of public-opinion polls, and also incidentally of almost any mention of the empire in contemporary working-class autobiographies, this view might be taken as a rough-and-ready indication of people's feelings; although no one could know for certain what made them vote in various ways.

If this *was* the situation in the inter-war years, then—it has to be said—the Colonial Office partly had itself to blame. It was a poor educator. For most of the inter-war period it made no effort of its own to enlighten the general public about the empire, and indeed obstructed such enlightenment purposely. Suggestions for schemes of education to be sponsored by the department, for example, were turned down.[97] 'Puffing'—propaganda—was rejected through fear of appearing too 'political', and because such 'puffs' might be exploited by shady characters to attract imperial investment fraudulently.[98] Even innocent requests for information were turned away; it was 'no part of the duty of officers or members of this department', wrote one official in 1929, 'to satisfy the idle curiosity of members of the public'.[99] When information was put out by the Colonial Office, it was in ways that had 'the *advantage*', as another official put it, 'of not being immediately accessible to the man in the street'.[100] There was one overriding reason for this. The more Britain's colonial activities were advertised, the more material it might give for malcontents to attack them. 'Critics may fasten on this', was a frequent excuse for keeping things back.[101] From the Colonial Office's point of view, public apathy had a lot to be said for it; it meant that not too many questions would be asked (this fits in with the 1948 survey's findings, as we have seen). That left the office free to serve its colonial subjects benevolently (no one there doubted the benevolence), without damaging interference from pseudo-'experts' from outside.

This suggests two things. The first is that practical imperialists—those who actually ran the empire—agreed with nearly everyone else about the lack of support for and even interest in the empire of the majority of their compatriots. This was why colonial policy had to be conducted at so low a key. (It helped that in most areas this policy was very conservative in this period, not much inclined to change.) The second implication—really only an impression—is that they were quite happy with this. It was the *im*practical imperialists—the 'zealots' and propagandists—who wanted imperial feeling to become more widely diffused. Colonial officials were almost as dismissive of these people, incidentally, as they were of the outright antis.[102] The officials seemed quite content to keep colonial policy a mystery, which only a small priesthood, selected from a restricted class of society, could understand. They did not want the hoi polloi sharing it with them.

It is partly for this reason that the colonial (and Indian) services remained so astonishingly narrow in their recruitment bases in the inter-war years, selecting their officials usually from existing colonial and Indian 'families', nearly always from the public schools, and from certain types *within* the public schools—not usually the brightest or most imaginative. This was entirely deliberate, as we have seen. The man responsible for this policy at the Colonial Office was Major Furse, the head of recruitment, whose preference for public-school products we have noted already. He was also one of those quoted above as being 'appalled' by the lack of imperial interest he found in Britain at this time. But he did not mean among the 'people'; it was these elite circles he was referring to. His solution therefore was to start propagandizing—but only through the pages of *The Times*, and in the public schools.[103] Furse and people like him did not regard imperialism as a democratic enterprise, but as a patrician one. They *wanted* to keep the empire to themselves.

❦ ❦ ❦

Popular ignorance of and apathy towards the empire can be pretty well established for these inter-war years, therefore; but that does not get to the bottom of the British people's relationship with it at this time. The empire was there; they knew it, unlike for long periods in the nineteenth century; they benefited from it materially, at least on the surface (for there were always people who argued that it damaged the British economy long-term); and they seem—judging by the lack of any great, openly expressed objection—to have tolerated it, albeit apathetically. But what was it they tolerated? Was it the empire as it actually existed? If they were as ignorant about it as it appears they were, that seems unlikely. So it must have been some other construction, or constructions, of their own.

It is hard to be sure—the apathy makes this difficult, as it means that they did not often record their opinions—but it is likely that the empire as they saw it was rather different from the empire that had been presented to people before the war. Then it had been associated with conquest, glory, and exploitation: a legacy of the Boer War and the atmosphere that had surrounded it. Now it was settling into a far more gentle, conservative, and caring mode. This must have been what George V meant when he referred to the 'broad and tolerant' imperialism of the time at the opening of the Wembley Exhibition in 1924; a theme that was taken up explicitly in one of the Elgar–Noyes songs for that occasion:

> 'Twas love that linked our realms in one
> And love in joy that bound them.
> Then Freedom took her throne,
> And peace was breathed on ev'ry sea,
> And music swelled around them;
> No more the dreams of war shall sound
> When hearts and realms in love are bound,
> For love binds all our hearts in one...

and so on. That seems an age away from the bravado of 'Wider still and wider, May thy bounds be set'.[104] It is at about this time that the word 'Commonwealth' came into general use as an alternative title for at least the self-governing parts of the empire, a highly significant development, not least for the impression that the *sound* of the word gave out.[105] Labour took to it especially.[106] At the same time the dependent empire—the directly ruled colonies—was pushed into the background. None of the 1924 songs, for example, refers to it.[107] Africa and India did not fit easily with the warm, familial kind of imperial entity that Noyes and probably millions of his compatriots felt most comfortable with: an empire (or Commonwealth) rejoicing in its freedom and its cricket, and setting an example to the rest of the world.

School textbooks reflect this shift clearly. There is a huge change in this department, from the almost ludicrously crude imperialism of Fletcher and Kipling's *School History*—to take the most extreme pre-war example—to a far gentler approach. 'Fletcher and Kipling' itself hit rough critical seas in the 1920s, being banned in at least two British colonies for its 'gross libels on the King's coloured subjects',[108] and with Oxford University Press, its publisher, clearly feeling uncomfortable about the way it gave 'offence' not only to them but also to the Irish.[109] The new textbook authors were different. Progressive geographers made the point that 'the citizen of to-day is more than a citizen of a country, or even of an empire. He is these, but he is also a citizen of the world . . . It is vital, therefore, for the intellectual and moral enlightenment of our future citizens and for the peaceful progress of the world that our pupils, as they progress to maturity, should come to an intelligent and *sympathetic understanding* of other world-communities'.[110] Following this, human geography texts were noticeably kinder to other 'races' than before the war, if not significantly less stereotypical: with happy grinning picanninies, for example, replacing snarling savages.[111] Empathy ran through many of them, in line with the new internationalist spirit of the time. Even the more imperialistic of textbooks took to the word 'commonwealth' early on. (Kipling never did.) 'Empire', wrote Sir Charles Lucas in a empire history for senior schools commissioned from him by the organizers of the Wembley Exhibition, 'is very commonly held to be a misnomer, as indicating military power, domination and dependence', which was not what the modern British empire was about at all.[112] The real 'end, or object, of its existence', agreed another author, was far better 'indicated by its official title—to promote the Common "Weal", or "Good", of all the Nations within its compass'.[113] This view had a huge impact on the kind of imperial history that was now being taught. G. W. Morris and L. S. Wood announced that the central theme of their *The English-Speaking Nations* (1924) was not to be 'the military achievements of our ancestors', but rather 'the development of the Commonwealth ideal and the gift to the world of the sense of imperial trusteeship', which was a big change from most pre-war texts.[114] Wars, and indeed any kind of conflict, were marginalized. Most histories that included India skated over the 'Mutiny' and its suppression with almost embarrassed haste; two late (1939) works even missed it out entirely.[115] Tropical Africa also dropped out of many of these accounts, as if the self-governing dominions were the only kind of empire now that counted.[116]

Some went further. The big revolution in empire historiography in the inter-war years was an almost entirely new reading of Britain's imperial past, that admitted no place in it for violence at all. This, apparently, was what differentiated British from all other imperialisms, and made the word 'empire' so incongruous in the former case. 'They . . . sought not for realms to conquer,' claimed Lucas of *all* Britain's empire builders, 'but for footholds for trade and for regions wherein to grow.'[117] 'It [the empire] grew not by warfare and conquest, but by peaceful emigrants working with axe and spade'.[118] '[F]ighting against nature has been more common than fighting against man'.[119] One author argued that it was the historical absence of a militaristic strain in British society that made her upper classes so much better colonial governors—more flexible ones, especially—than those of other nations.[120] It was also claimed that the humanitarian strain in British imperialism could be traced back to the earliest days. Morris and Wood detected it in Drake's and Raleigh's treatment of the American *indigènes*, which 'set an example for Englishmen of all time', so that it was 'not extravagent to trace the first consciousness of the "white man's burden", which forms a large part of the Imperial conscience, to the great example of these two knights'. (The slaver Hawkins was quietly ignored in this account.)[121] The Commonwealth's other allegedly distinctive characteristic, the combination of unity with national freedom, had its seeds in the very same period—in the unions of Scotland, Wales, and England, for example[122]—or even earlier: 'All the long centuries before these [last] three hundred years had been spent in making ready for these new events'.[123] In this way was a new tradition, or myth, constructed: of a uniquely gentle kind of British imperialism, utterly undeserving of the associations that usually accrued to the 'i'-word, and stretching right back to its beginnings.

The language used to describe and discuss the empire changed accordingly. Out with the military events went the military and related words: fighting (used metaphorically), winning, expanding, controlling, dominating, glorying, and anything at all boastful ('Maficky'), except perhaps for a sense of modest pride in being part of so altruistic and liberty-loving a 'race'. The words that replaced these came from a different vocabulary entirely: community, co-operation, tolerance, freedom, even love;[124] expressed most often in the metaphor of the 'family', which made a big comeback (it had been used in the nineteenth century too) at this time. '[I]t is no mere figure of speech to call Great Britain and her colonies a family circle', insisted several authors.[125] A. P. Norton and J. Ewing (1929) explained:

> To recognize a young family is easy because the children are all beneath the control of their parents... For a family of adults the old unity of dwelling has gone, the interests of its members are wider and more varied, but their spirit and love of the family remain. In much the same way, the unity of the Empire has ceased to be an easily described unity that can be fitted into a logical system on paper, but it persists in a subtler form, and the comparison with a growing family is more than a mere metaphor.[126]

Just as families could live alongside other families in broader societies, so the British empire/commonwealth need not be in conflict with other nations or federations. It was particularly compatible with the League of Nations, believed most of these new textbook authors, some of whom even presented it as a kind of precursor of that organization.[127] 'Just as the League of Nations stands for peace in the world,' proclaimed a junior-school history book in 1929, 'so also this smaller League of British Nations stands for peace and good fellowship within the Empire, and for peace and good will towards all the nations of the world.'[128] A 1936 text set as an essay title, '"The British Commonwealth is a second League of Nations." Say what this means.' (Not even 'Discuss'!)[129] Others saw the League's 'Mandates' system as essentially based on British colonial practice:[130] another way in which the British empire was presented as simply anticipating internationalism, rather than being set against it. This will have surprised those internationalists who had originally conceived of the League of Nations as essentially an anti-imperial device. But it had its precedents in earlier British imperial ideology, as we have seen, and it was a clever way of bringing British internationalists on board.

A similar change can be traced in the development of scouting and guiding in this period. However imperialistic in a militaristic sort of way their Edwardian origins may have been (and we have seen that the picture is more complex than this), by the 1930s—after an earlier struggle between imperialists and internationalists, leading to some defections[131]—they had largely grown out of this. This probably owed much to the movement's huge international spread at this time, which was bound to bring a certain degree of international*ism* in its train. The new tone first asserted itself among the girl guides (possibly because of their gender), whose ideology metamorphosed, as Allen Warren puts it, from 'a defensive imperialism through which efficient mothers at home became the Empire's first line of defence', into 'an emerging multi-nationalism within a widening imperial framework' during the 1920s.[132] For a time the two trends jostled for supremacy; the first post-war volume of the *Girl Guide's Gazette,* for example, carried 'messages' both from Earl Meath, centred on the empire still and even the need to fight to defend it, and from the chief guide (Lady Baden-Powell), enthusiastically lauding the new League of Nations and peace.[133] A great Guide 'Peace Celebration' held at the Albert Hall in November 1919 similarly havered between imperialism ('God save the King and our Empire of Liberty!') and pacifism, but with the empire element fairly well tamed. Among the songs sung on that occasion was Elgar–Benson's 'Land of Hope and Glory', but with one possibly significant change: 'Wider still and wider | May thy bounds be set' becomes 'Greater still and greater | Shall thy glory be'.[134] In 1926 Guide Headquarters forbade companies to affiliate with any imperialist organizations; the following year it moved the day when guides renewed their 'Promise' from Empire Day to the founder's birthday (22 February).[135] By then the new spirit was also passing to the boys. It appears, for example, in Baden-Powell's address to the movement's coming-of-age 'Jamboree', representing scouts from forty-two nations, in Birkenhead on 1929: 'Let us set about teaching that the highest virtues are friendliness and good-will. And there will be no more war.'[136] This reads like genuine internationalism. The metamorphosis was never unambivalent, or complete. Left-wingers continued to distrust scouting, both for what they took to be its militarism, and for its anti-socialism—which it certainly retained. It was challenged by more socialist and pacifist rivals—the Kibbo Kift Kindred, the Woodcraft Folk, and others—throughout this period.[137] Nonetheless, it had softened in many respects, and as a result not only weathered the new circumstances of the time, but even managed to increase and socially broaden its appeal.[138]

Commonwealthism helped to make the empire more widely palatable domestically. Of course people knew that they (or their agents) also ruled other peoples more despotically; but they seem to have pushed that to the backs of their minds. Hence the inability of so many of them actually to name any colony where this kind of rule was going on. Presumably they believed that Britain was ruling her colonial peoples benevolently: that her purpose was, as the Labour MP J. R. Clynes put it in 1918, 'to civilise, not to exploit'.[139] They were able to do this because they assumed that colonial subjects needed 'civilizing', and that the process would take a long time yet; which is why there were so few calls for African progress towards self-government in this period, for example, by contrast with Indian. That clearly indicates a number of widespread prejudices: 'culturist'—the identification of 'civilization' with European values; developmental—the idea that all peoples 'progressed' in the same way; and, at the root of them all in many cases, racist—the notion that Africans were somehow genetically programmed to be slower than other people in achieving this 'civilized' end. That last prejudice would have been difficult to avoid in a culture that habitually stereotyped black people in the most patronizing and often disparaging ways: in children's books and comics, for example, where the 'Little Black Sambo' image was almost ubiquitous.[140] It also did not help that the Colonial Office made no moves in the direction of self-government in this period for the territories under its control, being content simply to administer them; which gave the impression that 'progress' could be left to some future time.

As for the principle of colonial government—of a 'civilized' or 'advanced' power ruling a 'backward' one—that appears to have been largely accepted as a fact of life, which is why there was so little outright anti-imperialism in the 1920s and '30s. This was a period, we should remember, when most of the world was controlled by empires of one kind or another, not all of them European, and not all the European ones what we would call 'formal'; and when small states—Abyssinia, Czechoslovakia, Korea—were highly vulnerable to the more predatory of these. To many the choice seemed to be not between imperial rule and national independence, which might have been the ideal, but between different kinds of imperial control: predatory and not predatory, bad and good. If Britain let any of her colonies go, a worse colonial regime—Germany, say, or Japan—would be bound to step in, or failing that, international capitalism, against which small, weak countries would have no defence, and which many socialists believed was the worst of all forms of imperialism. This was the Independent Labour Party's line, for example: that simple decolonization for most countries (apart from India) could not be considered before '[t]he creation of a world economic organisation, with the object of establishing a progressive international standard of labour conditions, the protection of native peoples from Capitalist exploitation, the rationing of the world's supplies according to need, and the regulation of world credit'. This was why the ILP did not advocate immediate liberation for Africa, though it did for India.[141] It was a perfectly rational stance, and arguably more essentially 'anti-imperialist' than the more obvious one. One means towards this for the vulnerable territories that was much touted by radicals and socialists was the League of Nations mandates system. Short of that, however, and bearing in mind the League's obvious weaknesses, a kindly British empire was the next best bet, and preferable to, say, Nazi or Meiji or international capitalist rule. This could have been a mere excuse; but the humanitarian argument for it was plausible. Together with the softening of the image of British imperialism through the idea of the 'Commonwealth', and the low profile that was accorded to the non-Commonwealth empire, it explains why so many Britons were able to accept the empire in the inter-war years, without being enthusiastic about it at all.

❦❦❦

It hardly needs saying that the empire they accepted did not exactly mirror the empire as it really was. The latter was nowhere near as happy a place as Noyes's warm verses implied, especially around 1920–1—just three or four years before he penned them—which probably witnessed a greater concentration of 'atrocities' there, by any objective criteria, than any other comparable period in the history of the empire, for sixty years at least. The worst was undoubtedly the Amritsar massacre of April 1919, when an Indian Army general, Reginald Dyer, killed nearly 400 unarmed Indians by firing into the backs of them, in order—as he saw it—to prevent a repeat of the Mutiny. Others were the aerial bombing of Iraqi, Kurdish, and Palestinian villages to keep them in order in 1920–1; and the notorious excesses of the semi-disciplined 'Black-and-Tans', a detachment of special police sent in to Ireland to keep down the natives there in 1921.[142] Thereafter there was almost continuous trouble in the empire: rebellions in Sarawak, the Sudan, and Hong Kong in the 1920s, for example; huge civil unrest in India (1920s and '30s), Palestine (1936–9), and the West Indies (late 1930s); constant friction between races—European, African, and Indian—in east-central Africa; and problems of exploitation, repression, abuse, and racism (especially by white settlers) almost everywhere. Even happy Australia saw two late massacres of aborigines in 1926 and 1928.[143] Between 3 and 4 million Indians died in the Great Bengal Famine of 1943–4, comparable to the numbers of those who perished in the Nazi holocaust (few British histories of the empire even mention this).[144] There were intermittent rows between Britain and her dominions, many of which were feeling their national feet for the first time, and were proving particularly stubborn over the question of tariff preferences; it was this more than anything that stymied the zealots' dreams of a great imperial economic union. Elsewhere the British colonial record in this period is characterized by conservatism and inaction; colonies were simply administered, with hardly any attempt to reform or 'improve' or move them forward.[145] One reason for this was that the British government was unwilling to spend money on them. The empire, then, was not exactly a utopia in the inter-war period.

It was not all like this, of course. There was enough good practice—dedicated colonial officials, governmental probity, real justice, racial tolerance, economic progress,

Peaks of snow, and happy valleys
Where eternal summer lies;
Flocks that drift like clouds in heaven;
Lakes that gleam like fallen skies

(this is Noyes on New Zealand)[146]—to keep the myth going. The myth itself may have had an impact. The reality could not be seen to conflict with it too starkly: there was only so much covering up of bad behaviour that could be done. It was easy enough for the Colonial Office to cover up in the territories it controlled, perhaps, because they were so little in the public eye; one of the advantages of aerial bombing in the Middle East, writes Anthony Clayton, was that that 'its effects could often be concealed from critics, both metropolitan and local'.[147] Even so, it still stimulated some public and much private unease, especially in the army and among some of the pilots, one or two of whom resigned because they considered bombing innocents from the safety of airplanes to be basically cowardly,[148] and in the 1920s it was scaled down.[149] The widespread outrage that the Amritsar massacre provoked in Britain meant that that sort of tactic could not be tried again.[150] Thereafter colonial policing aimed to be subtler, modelled on British or (more often) Irish—but not Black-and-Tan—precedents.[151] When the high commissioner for Palestine found his police were using what he called 'Turkish methods' there in 1936, for example, he put a stop to it.[152] Secret intelligence was boosted, as a way of forestalling the need to employ repression in more clumsy ways.[153] Atrocities focused attention on the empire, which scarcely any imperialists (except the 'zealots') wanted. So did expense. One of the reasons for the resort to aerial bombing in Iraq was that it was cheaper than policing with soldiers, enabling the army garrison stationed there to be reduced from twenty-three battalions to just two between 1921 and 1928.[154] That took care both of the protests of the conscripts, who objected to being kept in uniform after the war in order to hold down this new empire, and of the considerable middle-class backlash that suddenly sprang up in 1921 against the cost—or 'waste', as it was called—of ruling Iraq in this way.[155] By being cautious on these two fronts, governments found they could sustain the ignorance and apathy on which the broad public's acceptance of the empire partly depended, and consequently the latter's very continuance. But it did tie the imperialists' hands somewhat. They could neither control the empire as they may have wanted, nor do as much for it as they would have liked.

Did this situation contribute to the empire's fall, very shortly after this? Post-World War II Conservative diehards thought so. One of their explanations for Britain's humiliating (as they saw it) imperial climbdown from the 1940s to the 1960s was a lack of national 'will' to hold on. As ever, they mainly blamed 'socialism' for this. If the people had been more resolutely imperialist, Britain would have her empire still. It is difficult to take this view very seriously, in view of the huge material damage that Britain suffered in World War II, and the indigenous (nationalist) and outside (diplomatic) pressures on her that followed, which made her continued imperial status in the post-war world seem increasingly anomalous. Churchill was one of the few people to believe that he was fighting that war *for* the empire: or at least, as he famously put it in November 1942, that he had not become Britain's war leader in order to 'preside' over its 'liquidation';[156] but he had a notably romantic—rather Noyesian—view of the colonies' essential loyalty to the 'mother' country. Later on, in 1951, when a keen new Conservative MP called Enoch Powell reportedly burst into his office offering to reconquer India for him if he would only give him ten army divisions, Churchill had long come to the realization that the game was up.[157] 'Will' would probably not have prevented this, but only prolonged the process of decolonization, and made it nastier, as it was for France. Imperial apathy was not responsible for the demise of the empire, though it may have made it easier to bear when it came about; that, and some of the myths that had been established in these inter-war years, especially about the Commonwealth being essentially a family whose whole purpose was to enable its youngest members to fly the nest eventually—which made decolonization seem more of a culmination than a reverse.

None of this was new. The lack of imperial commitment that characterized the majority of the British people from the 1940s onwards was simply a continuation of what had gone before. Even at the empire's greatest extent (around 1920) or most exciting times (the 1850s, '80s, and '90s) Britain had never been a convincing imperial society. That is what has been argued in the earlier chapters of this book. We shall be recapitulating those arguments, and exploring some of their implications, in the concluding chapter. Before then, however, we must digress, briefly, to a different but allied matter; which is the *impact* of the empire on Britain. That could have been greater than its influence. The two are not the same, though they are sometimes confused.

12
Repercussions

To say that Britons did not particularly take to their empire in the nineteenth and early twentieth centuries—or took to it less enthusiastically, at any rate, than is often assumed—is not the same as saying that they were unaffected by it. Indeed, it could have affected them more *because* of their relative uninterest in it, which might have allowed the empire to—so to speak—creep up on them unawares. This is all the more probable in a country like Britain, which for most of this period was not a full democracy, and where, even when she became one, those who were more imperially minded than the average exerted disproportionate influence and power. Quite apart from this, however, the very fact of having an empire was bound to impact on Britain's broader society in ways that none of these people, even the imperialists, planned or desired. That is the way of empires. So much is incontestable, even obvious.

This is no place to discuss these wider repercussions, which would require far too much sheer speculation to be of any value historically. There is always an element of science fiction about this kind of exercise: imagining 'alternate' universes, 'what would have happened if' some factor or other were altered or taken out of the actual equation—in this case it would be the British empire, whatever that is thought to have consisted of (do we include its 'informal' side, for example?)—and then trying to predict the knock-on effects, which are bound to be complex and unpredictable. Take the empire away, and *something* would have replaced it. Some pretty drastic alternatives might be imagined. Economically, for example, Britain could have been much worse off without her empire, or much better off, according largely to one's ideological preconceptions. (Avner Offer *has* speculated along these lines.)[1] Diplomatically one can imagine her staying out of World War I, or even World War I's not happening at all, if colonial rivalries were one of the causes of that conflict; or her still becoming involved in it but on the other side, if they were not. The possible impact of any of these scenarios on her society and people is incalculable. So we shall not even attempt to calculate it here.

This chapter will be less ambitious, restricted to exploring—tentatively only, and incidentally—some of the empire's more direct possible repercussions. One of its objects will be to show that it could have had such repercussions, without necessarily affecting Britons' ways of thinking, which have been the main concern of this book until now. Another will be to show how difficult it is to isolate these repercussions from the effects of other factors at the time. If there was an imperial reason for doing something, it does not automatically follow that this was why it was done. More importantly, for my general argument here: you could have a widespread imperial legacy which did not embrace a widespread imperial*ism,* in any sense. This was Britain's situation both while she possessed her empire, and afterwards.

⁂

There are many areas of British social and political life in which the empire clearly had an impact, but not necessarily a decisive one. The most obvious are those concerned with 'strengthening' the nation in various ways, like army reform, and social policy. The imperial input is clear in both these cases, especially in those nervous years for the empire during and after the Boer War. The empire may have affected certain related social discourses of that time, particularly those to do with gender (fears for masculinity, reflected in anti-homosexual and anti-women's movement tendencies), patriotism, and race. It is tempting to explain these entirely in terms of the demands of the empire: imperialism required a fitter, 'manlier', and more loyal 'race' to sustain it. In this way the empire can be seen to have impacted on British domestic life immensely. But this kind of interpretation is too easy, and too reductionist.

We have seen this already in the case of the celebrated social reforms of the 1905–14 Liberal governments, where the imperial input is easily exaggerated. These reforms included free school meals for poor children, enabled by an Act of 1906; compulsory school medical services, enacted in 1907; and state pensions and unemployment and sickness insurance, introduced in 1909 and 1911. That last measure also included maternity benefits for nursing mothers, paid to them directly, rather than through their husbands, in 1913. Less familiar is a new Mental Health Act of 1913 which allowed for the involuntary segregation of 'mental defectives' in institutions;[2] and a plethora at around the same time of municipal and voluntary initiatives to combat poverty, slum housing, bad sanitation, and in particular poor 'mothering', which was widely blamed for the supposed degeneration of the 'race'. (For many of the middle classes that was a more comfortable explanation than looking for deeper social and economic factors.)[3] Some of these reforms pre-dated the 'new imperialism';[4] but this cluster of them in the 1900s—seen by many historians as an important stage in the evolution of what later came to be known as the 'welfare state'[5]—inevitably suggests that the scare over Britain's imperial deficiencies that came in the wake of the Boer War played a part. A tangible link can be traced back via the 'Committee on Physical Deterioration' that had been set up in the wake of the war to find out why so many volunteers had to be rejected, and one of whose key recommendations was free school meals.[6] That should help provide a few more fit and loyal riflemen, in the course of time, to safeguard the empire's frontiers.

That however is nowhere near the whole picture. *Post hoc* does not always indicate *propter hoc*; and in any case there were many other *hocs*, quite apart from the Boer War, to account for most of these measures. The persistence of poverty, new ideas and approaches in medicine and the social sciences, the growth of democracy, the surge in socialist activity and propaganda at around the turn of the century, the waves of strikes that broke out in the 1890s and 1910s, and the fundamental reassessment of its social values that was going on in the Liberal Party in this period, spearheaded by the so-called 'New' Liberals—nothing at all to do with imperialism, this—are surely enough to explain the 1906–11 legislation (and other measures) on their own, whether they do so in fact or not. Socialists had been demanding free school meals for twenty years before 1906,[7] but had had no parliamentary influence to help get the measure enacted before winning thirty seats in the general election of that year. 'Poor mothering' had been a concern as early as the 1860s,[8] and infant mortality—one of the reasons for the growth of interest in this problem in the early 1900s—was brought to people's attention less by the Boer War than by the epidemics of infant diarrhoea that were a feature of the abnormally hot British summers of 1898–1900.[9] Many of the leading advocates of social reform in the 1900s do not seem to have been influenced by imperial considerations at all, though they sometimes referred to them incidentally in order to glean some additional imperialist support. Few if any of these reforms had an imperial *genesis*, while the extent to which imperialism helped them along is debatable. Many imperialists were against such reforms, while others—the Liberal and 'Progressive' Lord Rosebery, for example—could have been social reformers quite independently of their own imperial ideology. Contemporary anti-imperialists believed that imperialism was far more likely to act as a distraction from social reform. This is a serious possibility, even if the distracting effect of imperialism among the workers was—as we have argued—only marginal: margins can be crucial.[10] It is difficult to make a convincing case for the opposite contention: that imperialism was responsible for reform.[11] The best that can probably be said is that concern for the health and loyalty of the people at the 'heart of the empire' may have brought some people who would not normally have been associated with such 'progressive' causes on board. That may have been important later on for other, political reasons, as we shall see.

When extraneous considerations did come into the picture—extraneous, that is, to the simple welfare of the poor—they may not have been strictly imperial ones. There was undoubtedly a 'national' dimension to the debates about social policy in the late nineteenth and early twentieth centuries that was new. This in fact was a Europe- and America-wide phenomenon, and so probably had a broader underlying cause. 'If efficiency was a response to imperial decline,' writes Jonathan Rose, then 'why did it also obsess turn-of-the-century Americans', whose empire seemed to be in the ascendant in this period, but who also had a vigorous 'national efficiency' movement running there?[12] Similar ideas were prevalent in France and Germany, where imperial fears *might* have been a factor (they both had empires), but also, for example, in Sweden, which neither had nor (presumably) hankered after any sort of overseas empire at this time.[13] In Britain the new emphasis can be seen in the language that was used to describe the issue of poverty and its associated evils at around the turn of the century: as a question of '*national* deterioration' now, rather than 'the social problem', the more common phrase in the 1870s and 1880s; or simply 'the problem of the poor', which is what more humanitarian and individualistic mid-Victorians had generally called it. 'National' has different connotations from 'social'. A society is commonly conceived of in terms of its internal relationships; a nation only has meaning and significance in apposition to other nations. The new use of that term in this connection in Britain and elsewhere in this period indicates a subtly different way of looking at social problems, one that now took into consideration—in a way that would have disturbed mid-Victorian liberals—questions of national strength.

National strength is not the same as imperial sway, however. The two are sometimes conflated by historians of this period, during which Britain's national power was often conceived of in imperial terms; but it was not so conceived by everyone. In the debates over social policy of the 1890s and early 1900s, the strength of Britain as an empire featured far less than her competitive position as a trading nation, and her resilience simply as a nation state: especially in relation to Germany, whose main threat to Britain was seen in European rather than colonial terms. This applies to the military reforms of the 1900s too.[14] 'National deterioration' was a concern because it laid Britain open to the risk of defeat in Europe. The Boer War was significant as a pointer to that, rather than to Britain's imperial weakness per se. The argument was generally: 'if we are not fit enough as a nation to repel an invasion by a rabble of peasants in Africa without making a pig's ear of it, how are we going to cope when Germany invades *us*?'[15] In the years leading up to Britain's eventual clash with what one 1907 commentator called the 'manlier Teutons',[16] this was far and away the major 'national' concern of those who embraced social and other reforms in order to make Britons 'manlier' too. The empire hardly came into it, except as furnishing salutary warnings of this much greater danger ahead.

⁂

Related to this are questions of gender. (The 'manlier Teuton' reference hints at that.) The empire's influence in this area is confused. We should expect it to be reactionary. Much of the 'deterioration' literature of the 1890s and 1900s targeted 'effeminate' men, by which was meant homosexuals, and the 'feminization' of the public sphere by allowing women into it. There were two specifically imperial reasons for fearing that. One was that empire-building was necessarily a 'virile' activity, which women's 'softer' qualities might undermine. Female legislators would shy away from sanctioning necessary colonial wars, for example, out of maternal concern for their soldier sons. The second was that many millions of Britain's colonial subjects, being even more sexist than the British (Muslims were the group that was usually singled out here), would not respect any authority in which women had an active role. Both of these arguments were widely deployed in the 1900s. It was imperative, said the *Anti-Suffrage Review* in 1911, to save the British empire from this 'most hazardous experiment', which, whatever else its effects might be, 'would undoubtedly cause a weakness at the heart'.[17] Prominent imperialists were at the forefront of the anti-suffrage movement in the 1900s, including Lord Cromer, ex-ruler of Egypt, who was president of the National League for Opposing Woman Suffrage, Lord Curzon, his chairman, and Lady Jersey of the Victoria League, a deputy president.[18] Probably about half of the organized imperialist women's movement were against votes for women.[19] It is suggestive that this 'anti' tendency took off so strongly in this period. Before then the suffragist cause had been progressing fairly well.[20] Then, in the 1890s, it quite suddenly ground to a halt. It is easy to believe that 'new imperialist' opposition could have tipped the balance against women's suffrage before the World War I, if only because that cause was lost quite narrowly.[21] On the other hand, there were undoubtedly other contributing factors: our familiar problem; and in any case the setback did not last long—the principle of votes for women was conceded in 1918. So imperialism can only have caused a short delay, at worst.

Besides this, the impact of the empire on women may not have been entirely negative. In one way it could be said to have aided them by raising the profile and therefore the status of 'women's work'. This might be regarded as the positive side of the contemporary 'separate spheres' doctrine, that assigned different 'natural' roles to men and women. We can see this in the new emphasis that was placed on the importance of 'mothering' in the 1900s, partly at the behest of the imperial 'physical deterioration' lobby, which itself was fuelled by imperialist fears. This could be said to be a way of getting society to value women more. The counter-argument, though, is that this was a valuation based on their roles as mothers (even wombs) only, rather than as people, especially as most maternalists believed that one way of making women better mothers was to stop them taking jobs or even being educated.[22] More important and beneficial, probably—certainly more 'progressive'—were some of the other ways the empire boosted women. One was through their various supportive organizations, like the Victoria League. These greatly expanded the area of women's public activity in the early twentieth century, albeit within certain bounds. The Victoria League, for example, concentrated very much on 'women's sphere' subjects: imperial education for the young, providing hospitality—the comforts of a home—for colonials visiting Britain, and 'imperial health' (or social reform).[23] Beyond that they rarely ventured, with imperial policy, for example, being mainly left to the men.[24] Nonetheless, these causes gave women a platform, and so opportunities of excelling in areas they were supposed by the 'antis' not to be equipped for, like organization and public speaking.[25] (The same is true of certain anti-imperialist women, like Emily Hobhouse, who uncovered and publicized the horrors of the South African concentration camps almost alone.) Some found this contradictory, as though anti-suffrage Victoria Leaguers were undermining their own case by speaking so manfully—as they often did—against it.[26] For Violet Markham, however, one of their most effective speakers, it only went to prove what she saw as a very pro-woman point: that the main (natural) gender difference was not between strong men and weak women, but between different kinds of—and therefore different appropriate spheres for the exercise of—strength.[27]

This situation relates to metropolitan women: those based in Britain, that is, for at least part of their lives and careers. For those living in the colonies—as wives of administrators, missionaries, nurses, and so on—the empire was bound to have changed their lives and attitudes more, just as it did with their menfolk. There may also have been an impact in the opposite direction, with the presence of women in the colonies subtly impacting on the empire: 'feminizing' it, as 'femininity' was conventionally regarded then. Many contemporary femin*ists* believed that the empire needed exactly this: an injection of care and compassion—women's particular virtues—in order to make it more moral and less brittle than an empire based simply on power and control. They desired 'to remould imperial power by moving from a reliance on masculine physical force to feminine moral influence'.[28] (This 'masculine–feminine' dichotomy may be problematical; we shall return to it in a moment.) Feminists were active in trying to help or 'raise' Indian women, for example; an enterprise that required them to collaborate with imperialism in order to be *able* to raise them.[29] The impact of this 'feminization' on the empire is uncertain. One possibility is that it did indeed soften the empire's hard edges. Janice Brownfoot believes that in Malaya it helped 'bring about the end of that Empire', presumably by softening its edges too much.[30] In other cases, however, the effect of the empire on women imperialists appears to have been the reverse: to have 'unsexed' them—again, as gender roles were conceived at that time. The famous 'memsahibs', consorts of the (always male) British imperial officials in India, are an example. They were apparently almost never feminists, but nor did they conform very closely to the 'separate spheres' pattern that was established for non-feminists back home. This was because of the complicating factors of race and authority, which overrode this pattern. By the side of their menfolk they were women; in relation to the native Indians, however, they were members of the imperial 'masculine' race. Recent studies show them to have been essentially 'masculinized' by this experience. They shied away from the 'good works' that would have been expected of them in Britain, for example, like 'raising' their Indian sisters. Instead they took up hunting and shooting; wrote Indian Mutiny novels in their spare time, with women as heroines (rather than the victims of mid-Victorian myth); and developed ideologies of imperial rule, and of Indian racial inferiority, that were frequently 'harder' than those of their husbands. Nearly all of them sent their children to boarding schools in England, which could be seen in itself as a suppression of their maternal and so 'naturally' feminine instincts. (The Indians thought so.)[31] They too have been charged with bringing the empire down, this time because of their haughtiness.[32] But that might have been a function of their upper-middle classness rather than their Indian experience; the native English upper-middles, after all, sent *their* children to boarding schools too.

That issue, however, is outside our present remit, only bearing on it if the imperial experience—either direct, as in the case of the memsahibs, or vicarious—impacted on the situation of women at home. Antoinette Burton claims it must have done in the case of suffragism: '[t]he fact of empire shaped the lives and identities of those who participated in the women's movement, making it a constituent part of modern British feminist identities.'[33] But it is difficult to put one's finger on exactly how this might have worked. So far as the memsahibs were concerned, they could only have influenced the metropole when they returned to it; and we have already seen that 'colonials' generally tended to keep themselves apart from other Britons when they retired. Most memsahibs were the daughters of memsahibs themselves, which confirmed them as a caste apart.[34] They tended to be ridiculed outside their own circle. It is difficult to imagine their being taken as role models by anyone else.

Perhaps some of their 'Mutiny heroine' novels percolated a little way beyond the caste, especially Flora Annie Steel's *On the Face of the Waters*, which we are told was 'an instant bestseller' when it came out in 1896.[35] These novels were not alone in projecting more feisty role models for girls and women in the early twentieth century. We have already come across Bessie Marchant, who also favoured brave, hardy, and adventurous heroines in colonial settings. John Buchan regularly featured athletic, spirited, and intelligent 'gals' in his highly popular adventure stories, even those with no colonial references at all. ('She'd have made a dashed good soldier,' remarks a male admirer in one.)[36] After 1909 real-live girls got their chance to be fairly soldierly, when the Girl Guide movement was formed. Initially Baden-Powell and his sister Agnes had been anxious to keep it ladylike, with domestic skills emphasized and patrols (platoons) given flower instead of animal names: 'Daisy' rather than 'Lion', for example; but the girls demanded to go camping and learn self-defence like their brothers, and so Guiding too became more 'masculine'.[37] An imperial genesis can be traced in most of these influences: Flora Steel was the wife of an ICS officer; Buchan had experience in South Africa, and was later to become governor-general of Canada; and Baden-Powell . . . well, we know about him. (Only Marchant made it all up.) This does not make the empire responsible on its own for liberating middle-class women from the trammels of domesticity and gentleness, of course. At the same time that all this was going on the famous 'new woman' of the *fin de siècle* was pushing in the same direction, albeit from a very different—more radical—base. This has been a familiar difficulty throughout this book: to separate imperial influences out from other contemporary trends. But the empire may have helped to bring about such change. At the very least this can be seen as a positive influence, to set against the anti-suffrage one.

This 'gender' idea can be taken further. Implied in much of what has been said already is that the empire was a distinctively male construct—'It was a masculine world of power, authority and control', writes Janice Brownfoot[38]—which required the influence of the women to soften and 'purify' it.[39] One rider to this view, suggested by Ashis Nandy, is that it reacted back on British metropolitan society by 'masculinizing' *it* as well; making it 'harder' and more aggressive than it would have been otherwise.[40] It may be that turn-of-the-century Britain did become tougher in this sense, though it is difficult to think of a reliable way of measuring this; and there were countervailing trends. She—or should it now be 'he'?—certainly became more bellicose at times, more mean-spirited in certain circles,[41] and more reactionary in the field of sexual morality (the case of Oscar Wilde, for example).[42] There are difficulties, however, with tying these changes in with 'imperial masculinity'. In the first place, the 'masculinization' of the country was far from completed in this period, with strong resistance to its militarization, for example—compulsory military service and rifle training—despite vigorous men's campaigns on its behalf. Secondly, calls for 'harder' measures did not need to be primarily motivated by imperial considerations at this time, as we have seen; concerns about *national* security were enough. Beyond this, however, there are problems with this whole 'masculine' characterization of British imperialism. It obviously begs some theoretical questions. (For example, are gender differences anything more than social constructs?) But it also may not be empirically sound. In that case, any 'masculinizing' effect of the empire on British society may not be entirely clear-cut either.

For one thing: just because the empire was ruled by men, it does not necessarily follow that the way it was ruled can be linked with this. That could have been far more influenced by the situations the rulers found themselves in, and their ruling functions, which would have been the same even if they had been women. That may in fact be the lesson to be drawn from our memsahibs' behaviour: not that their femininity had been subverted by the maleness of their menfolk, but that as human beings placed in roughly the same situations as the men, they reacted in the same ways. Furthermore, nineteenth- and early twentieth-century British imperialism was not only 'masculine' in character, but also included some conventionally 'feminine' traits. This was without any input at all from the women, so far as we can judge, and derived again from the men's functions, together with a public-school training which did not only stress the 'harder' virtues like strength, control, bravery, and so on, but also softer ones like gentleness (in the 'gentle-*man*'), and service to the less fortunate, usually called 'paternalism', though many features of it were more gender-neutral—'parental' perhaps—than that word implies. For this reason it may be misleading to regard the empire as *needing* a woman's touch to make it kinder and more caring, and wrong to go on from this to assume that its only likely impact on British society was a 'macho' one. In fact, as we saw at the beginning of this chapter, one of its most important possible repercussions, social reform, was anything but 'macho' in its essence.[43]

Most of the social repercussions so far mentioned worked through the upper or upper-middle classes: memsahibs, Victoria Leaguers, top anti-suffragists, paternalistic social reformers. This is how the empire usually impacted on British society. The same is true in politics, where the effect of empire was most powerful among the upper classes, affecting the way they governed. They were the ones who picked up colonial *ways* of governing, either directly or at their public schools; other Britons were then subjected, literally, to those. Yet again it is difficult to isolate this factor. We have seen already that much of the 'governing' traffic went the other way: the upper classes ruled the colonies as they had been bred or taught to rule their peasants at home. But there was also a kick-back. The empire probably increased their authoritarian tendencies. And it certainly taught them a few techniques they might not have thought up on their own.

Some of these were in the field of policing. Britain's very first official police system was tested out in the semi-colony of Ireland (1822) before being unleashed on Britain in 1829, albeit with modifications to satisfy mainland Britons' more liberal sensibilities.[44] Fingerprinting was first developed in India, mainly as a means of disciplining the natives there, before being brought to Britain, again with a modified aim: to detect crimes, not to control.[45] These are instructive examples, illustrating the impact of the empire, but also—because of the way these colonial methods then had to be adapted—the strength of the counter-colonial discourse in the metropole. In a third case there was less need for adaptation, because the transfer was kept secret. In 1883 the Special Branch of the London Metropolitan Police was set up, to cope with what today would be called Irish terrorism. It offended against all the liberal principles of the existing police forces in Britain, in its 'political' function and its widespread use of spies and informers. This is why it was kept secret, and also why it was officered almost exclusively in its early years by men with experience in Ireland or India, which was where its methods were first perfected.[46] This pattern, of developing policing techniques in the colonies before bringing them to Britain, and of taking people with colonial backgrounds to run Britain's secret services, continued almost right through the twentieth century. (Malaya and Kenya in the 1940s and '50s were testing-grounds for counter-subversion techniques that were then shipped to Northern Ireland and Britain; and Stella Rimington, head of MI5 between 1991 and 1996, was first spotted as a likely recruit in the British High Commission in New Delhi.) It is one clear example of what we might call the 'empire strikes back' effect: imperial methods and mentalities coming home to roost. Whether it is a significant one, however, may be questionable. There are broadly three different ways of regarding the British security services' contribution to British history in the twentieth century: as effective and benevolent (preventing plots); effective and malevolent (undermining democratically elected governments: e.g. the Zinoviev letter); or useless (because stupid). This is no place to arbitrate between these alternatives. But whatever the truth, the empire had a hidden hand in it.

This is probably exactly the sort of case our eighteenth-century Cassandras had in mind when they warned of imperialism's bringing 'Asiatic principles of government' to Britain. At the turn of the twentieth century J. A. Hobson revived this old bogey, confidently predicting that the inevitable casualties of imperialism abroad would be 'peace, economy, reform, and popular self-government' at home.[47] We have seen that this pessimism was by and large not borne out with regard to the ordinary government of Britain in the nineteenth and early twentieth centuries. The country did not become another India. Despite the efforts of a number of leading imperialists to undermine Britain's ancient constitutional practices in order to make her more 'efficient' imperially—abolishing political parties, bringing colonials into parliament, introducing military conscription, protecting colonial trade, outlawing strikes, and so on—the way Britain was governed did not change very significantly. Hence the even greater pessimism of the imperial 'zealots' in this period, and much of the alienation from metropolitan society felt by imperialists in the field when they retired back home. The reason for these failures is that other ethoses were too solidly rooted in British society to be subverted in this way. The only ways in which imperialist programmes could be implemented in the domestic political field, therefore, were on the very edges of society; secretly (as with the Special Branch); or in collaboration with other groups and forces that had different main agendas from the imperialists, but happened to be aiming in the same directions on certain fronts. This was the commonest way. Imperialists were most successful—perhaps were only successful—when they were in harness with alien beasts.

Their pulling together with socialists and radicals over 'social reform' is the best example of this, and may mark the imperialists' most significant material impact on the British political scene overall. In the Liberal 1900s their help may not have been strictly necessary, as we have seen. Later on, however, it could well have been important for the cause of social reform that it had friends in the Conservative Party too, some of whom may have been friends for imperialistic reasons. That party did, after all, dominate British politics for most of the twentieth century. Before the 1900s it had looked like evolving into a free marketist party *pur*. This was one of the repercussions of the Liberals'—the traditional party of the market—also turning more and more to collectivism, for other reasons, from the 1880s on. Many of the upheavals the Liberals experienced then—the defections and splits, including 1886—can be at least partly explained by this. The row was over creeping 'socialism'. Many Liberal Unionists, the defectors on the 'Home Rule' issue, felt quite strongly over that too.[48] As they grew closer to the Conservative Party, the latter hardened its economic ideology to welcome them in. It might have become the unequivocally 'hard' party soon after that, had it not been for the imperialist section of it, which kept the older 'paternalism' alive. Paternalists abroad were likely to be paternalists at home too; which was why the Conservative Party played its part in sustaining social reform in Britain, and in particular the post-1951 'welfare state'; so long as the empire—which was what propped up this tendency in the party—remained.

This analysis is difficult to back up with empirical evidence. Imperialism certainly had an important anti-capitalist element, which is likely to have had a domestic impact generally. We have touched on this before, but it is worth recapitulating here and taking on further, into the twentieth century. The empire's beginnings were steeped in capitalism: in the trade and exploitation that first brought most of Britain's colonies to her attention in the first place, and in defence of which—either directly or indirectly—they were usually formally colonised. That last step, however, was, in strict free-market terms, a retrograde one. Free trade, which was the flag Britain sailed under, was not supposed to be compatible with imperialism of this sort. It is this that accounts for the reluctance that we have already noticed on the part of so many mid-Victorians to acknowledge, against all the evidence, that they *were* an imperial people. It also created a practical problem. Nineteenth-century free marketeers were not only (theoretically) against colonial government; they were broadly unsympathetic to governing of any kind. It was seen as an unproductive distraction from the real, 'manly', and important business of life, which was facilitating the production and exchange of products, so creating wealth for others and also, naturally, for themselves. The empire had been accumulated thanks to their capitalist enterprise, but that very quality fitted them badly for ruling it, even if they had wanted to. Other attributes—indeed, another mindset—were needed for that. 'Gentry' values furnished at least a basis for this. The older upper classes of Britain were used to the idea (even if they were not always true to it) of service to others, especially to the less fortunate, like their peasants (the Saxons), who could be regarded as a kind of paradigm for 'natives' everywhere. It was these classes that still shouldered most of the burdens of government within Britain throughout the nineteenth century: not the capitalist middle classes who drove her economy. They were the obvious ones to call on when the empire needed governing. As the latter expanded, boosting the demand for governors, their stock—and that of the value system that motivated them—rose. Hence their survival, in the teeth of the new capitalist trend, and even, perhaps, of the flow of history.

The public schools had a clear role here: sustaining that value system, and injecting it into the young men (men only, of course) they turned out to paternalize over the peasantry both at home and abroad. The obverse of this was that the demand for these people and this ethic also helped sustain the public schools in this form well into the twentieth century; until, perhaps, the headmaster of Westminster School's famous call to them in 1980 to turn out fewer 'proconsuls' and more 'pirates', in response to the revival of free marketism ('piracy') at that time.[49] Exactly how important the empire was to this process is difficult to say. We have seen that only a relatively small number of public-school boys went on to become colonial rulers, missionaries, army officers, and so on. This suggests that it was not this particular employment opportunity—the 'demand' for practical imperialists—that kept the schools going, on its own. But it could have had a disproportionate effect on their peculiar ethos, which it is difficult to imagine surviving long if there had not been an empire out there for some of their Old Boys to rule. It was the empire above all that justified—made sense of—their clinging on to their old notions of *noblesse oblige* and the rest, when in almost every other way, with the progress of capitalism and democracy, the *noblesse* appeared to have had its day. Without the empire the schools could well have found themselves teaching the 'piratical' virtues much sooner than they did. Whether or not this is so—and it seems impossible to prove either way—there can be no doubting the extent to which these schools took to imperialism in the late nineteenth and early twentieth centuries; far more than did any other sector (or class) of education. This was bound to affect not only those Old Boys who went on to serve the empire directly, but also the majority that did not. Wherever they went and worked they took the same ethos with them: the imperialism usually, but even if not that—if they turned against it, as a small number did—then the social values that informed the public schools' particular version of imperialism. A revealing example of this is the future Labour prime minister Clement Attlee, often credited with creating the British welfare state, who was a student at Haileybury from 1896 to 1901, and indeed one of those whom headmaster Edward Lyttelton flogged for their over-imperialism in March 1900, but who retained an affection for the place,[50] and whose later conversion to socialism may not be as remarkable as appears at first sight, if we bear in mind the paternalist and anti-capitalist base that will have been erected for it there. A case like this could not have occurred if the pirates had taken over earlier than they did.

Yet again, the empire's part cannot be taken as read. There are other reasons for the failure of free-enterprise dogma and its associated values to take as tight a hold on Britain in the nineteenth and twentieth centuries as they did on contemporary America, for example. Having an aristocracy was one. The persistence of widespread social deprivation was another, fertilizing the soil for the revival of socialism that came in the 1880s, and sowing doubts—either from fear of this, or for more humanitarian motives—in the minds of many middle-class people, whose original faith in the free-market system had rested on the belief that its benefits must more than 'trickle' down. They included that doyen of mid-Victorian liberals John Stuart Mill, who as early as the 1870s had come to the conclusion that socialism must be preferable to an *inegalitarian* capitalism.[51] That may be enough on its own to account for the reaction against capitalism on this side of the political fence. On the other side we have Disraeli ('imperialism and social reform') and the later social imperialists to confirm the link. But even the Conservative Party had its 'paternalistic' traditions before imperialism came on to the scene. The argument here is that it was the empire that helped to keep them alive after that; so long, of course, as it still remained.

This came to an end in the 1970s. It was then, under Margaret Thatcher, that the free marketeers in the Conservative Party finally prevailed over the paternalists (or, as she called them, the 'wets'). It can hardly be entirely coincidental that this happened at the very moment that the empire finally fell—it was Thatcher, in fact, who gave away the last two substantial bits of it[52]—thus removing the 'wets'' essential prop. The free marketeers rose as the empire collapsed. By this reading, the phenomenon called 'Thatcherism' was one of the repercussions of the fall of the British empire. Conversely, it was the empire that had delayed Britain's evolution before this into a fully capitalist state. That was how she had been evolving for most of the nineteenth century, and would probably have gone on evolving, in one of our 'alternate' universes. But then along came the empire and, through the effect it had on the imperial classes, led her down a different road, which at the time seemed to be the path of progress, but turned out to be only a cul-de-sac. In this way the empire can be said to have held Britain 'back' developmentally—which is not to imply any judgement about whether 'backwards' was a bad or a good way to go.[53] Such a reading is not easy to establish empirically, and so may never rank as any better than a large hypothesis. Much of the evidence is of the *post hoc* kind: Thatcher coming *after* decolonization, for example. But it does seem to 'fit'. If so, then its significance as one of the domestic repercussions of the empire can hardly be overplayed.

Nonetheless, if these were the sum total of the empire's domestic repercussions, it may be felt that Britain got off lightly. An extra hand to the plough of social reform; one of several spanners in the works of women's emancipation, temporarily; a half-holiday for every school to celebrate the empire (or something) eventually; a secret but not very intrusive or effective political police; some golden cricket; more and more empire products; and then some vaguer possible consequences which are difficult to verify: masculinism, more respect for the monarchy, an extended lease of life for the paternalistic upper classes, and so on: really this was very little, measured against the hopes of the imperial zealots of the day and the fears of the antis. On the other side of the balance sheet stood the great growth of socialism and trade unionism in this period; strike waves that came close to civil war; votes for women; Labour governments; and, most galling of all, the loss of one whole part of the United Kingdom, Ireland—in reality Britain's first colony—in 1920. Overall things looked to be going quite badly for those who felt that the British people needed to be reformed out of all recognition in order to keep the empire afloat. Or, looking at it from another perspective: to be going surprisingly well for those who—like Hobson—had feared a much more serious backlash at home. Imperial Britain was very far from being, yet, Hobson's 'imperialist state'.[54]

Impacting as little as this domestically in its lifetime, it is probably not to be expected that the empire would have left much of a residue when it died.[55] Many people, however, believed it had. Foreigners especially could not credit that a nation that for more than a hundred years had mainly been presented to them *as* an empire was not clinging on to some of her moth-eaten imperial ermine still. The empire was held responsible for a number of ills, especially, that were perceived as afflicting Britain in the post-imperial years: racism; anti-Europeanism; pro-Americanism (seen as snuggling up to her imperial successor); British arrogance generally; the Falklands and Iraq wars (reprises of late nineteenth-century imperialism); managerial failures in industry; hooliganism at international football matches; and writing books or presenting television series about the British empire that were not outrightly critical. Britons, especially those anxious to 'modernize' the country, also seized on the empire as a scapegoat. For a time hardly anyone admitted to loving or missing it, but there were plenty around to attack those few who did. This in fact may well be the empire's major domestic legacy to post-imperial Britain, overshadowing all others: the reaction against it, the resultant constant apologizing for it, and the blaming it for everything; which also served the convenient function of morally distancing modern British critics from all of its evils, both genuine and imagined.

Aside from this, the search for post-imperial legacies at home can be problematical. The obvious ones—the most visible detritus of the empire—seem trivial. Feature films about the empire were still occasionally produced,[56] together with nostalgic television series, both fictional and documentary; some, incidentally, not so nostalgic as to obscure the seamier side of empire completely.[57] At least two museums were founded to commemorate the empire, and temporary exhibitions put on, again with a critical angle to most of them.[58] Indian restaurants and 'takeaways' sprang up all over the country; definitely a postcolonial rather than a colonial phenomenon, this. (Why was that? The end of imperial arrogance?)[59] The Indian subcontinent also bequeathed polo to the British class that was closest to it; the leg glance in cricket (Prince Ranjitsinhji); corner shops; yoga; Sikh regiments; thousands of doctors; scores of distinguished academics; and a handful of words to the English language: chutney, mulligatawny, bangle, bungalow, dinghy, khaki, punch, pyjamas, shawl, swastika, thug, verandah ... and so on.[60] A few old statues of imperial heroes remained, and some new ones were even erected in the 1950s and '60s, though you had to look hard for them;[61] and of course the old buildings: the Royal Pavilion at Brighton, the India Office (now part of the Foreign Office), Baker's awful South Africa House, and so on. To these could be added the Commonwealth Institute's bright new headquarters in Kensington High Street in West London, built in 1962. There was a continuing fascination in Britain for Australia especially (there was less for the other 'old' dominions), through cricket (though interest in that was declining in England), soap operas, a visiting comic genius from Melbourne ('Edna Everage'), and some fine wines and films: though the regard hardly seems to have been reciprocated, if the favourite Australian pastime of 'pom-bashing' is anything to go by. Then there were the 'e' and 'i' words, which survived in, for example, the 'Empire Way' leading to the old England football stadium at Wembley, built originally for the 1924 Empire Exhibition, but demolished in 2002; 'India Pale Ale'; 'Indian Tonic Water' (with quinine, for the malaria); the Honours list ('OBE' and so on); and the names of several hotels.[62] Occasionally these words might cause offence, for historical reasons. In November 2003, for example, the British black poet Benjamin Zephaniah publicly rejected the offer of an OBE—'Up yours, I thought'—because it reminded him of slavery.[63] Otherwise they meant nothing; a much lesser material mark on the fabric of Britain and her society than one would expect, from such a massive undertaking. But we have seen the reasons for that.

Any deeper lasting influences are difficult to pin down to the empire or imperialism specifically. The best we have come up with already are welfare socialism and its post-imperial demise (the 'social-imperial' factor), and the Secret Services. It is unlikely, however, that the empire was a crucial influence on either of these. On the issue of Europe, where residual imperial pretensions are often blamed for Britain's semi-detached stance towards the 'Common Market' and its successors, there are a dozen other possible explanations too. There were not many people whose commitment to the empire was deep enough to make this their major consideration when it came to deciding whether or not they wished Britain to join 'Europe'. For many of those who did feel this way it could have been their 'Commonwealthism', and the multiracial internationalism it was supposed to embody, that made them chary of transferring to what could easily be presented as a rich white man's club, rather than a hankering after their lost imperial 'greatness'. And even for those who did so hanker, it cannot have been obvious that withdrawing into a little-England isolationism—which was the only realistic alternative to Europe[64]—was a better way of regaining it than joining something that at least had the potential to be great, and that Britain might come to lead. So there is no logical reason why ex-imperialists *had* to be anti-European.

There are also other reasons, entirely unrelated to the empire, why others might become so. Simple xenophobia was one. That pre-dated the empire, of course; blatantly exists in non-imperial as well as imperial countries; and has even less necessary connection with imperialism than isolationism does. Britain's simple island situation was another. Nostalgic reactionism (pounds, ounces, and smacking children) is a third. Anti-bureaucracy is a fourth (Britain had always considered herself different from an overregulated Europe in this regard).[65] Democracy is a fifth—a perfectly respectable motive for wanting to keep political and economic decisions as locally accountable as possible. Underlying all of these non-imperial reasons for Britain's caution towards the EEC, certainly in the years immediately preceding her entry in 1973, was the material fact that her trading patterns were substantially out of alignment with Europe's at that time, with a majority of her trade going beyond Europe while the EEC countries' trade was predominantly with their new partners; which meant that entry was bound to cause more dislocation to Britain's economy than to theirs. Whether the empire can be blamed for *this* is controversial. Here we hit the old problem once again, of disentangling nineteenth- and twentieth-century 'imperialism' from other contemporary trends, like, in this case, the worldwide expansion of British trade. The mid-Victorians denied any such connection. By stretching our definition of imperialism, on the other hand, it is possible to take all of trade on board. Between these two extremes it is difficult—probably impossible—to say exactly how much of Britain's extra-European commerce and investment depended for their establishment and growth on her imperial authority. By the 1960s, however, trade and empire had clearly separated, and trade patterns on their own had become a sufficient reason for doubting the wisdom of joining a narrower European trading bloc.

For the truth was that Britain was very much more than an ex-imperial power in this period, just as she had been much more than an empire before then. Most of the national attitudes and policies that distinguished her from other nations, including European ones, had other roots entirely: the peculiarities of her class structure; the residual paternalism of her upper classes; the powerful individualist libertarianism of her middle classes; and—obviously informing the latter to a great extent, if not wholly determining it—her free-enterprise capitalist economic system: the core—more than the empire—of her national being, whose relationship with imperialism was, as we have seen, by no means easy or straightforward. It is this economic factor that may best explain Britain's differences with the European continent, which never embraced the logic of the market to the same extent, and also her sense of affinity with the United States, which did. Imperialistically as America undoubtedly behaved in the post-World War II period, this is unlikely to have been Britain's main reason for wishing to cling on to her coat-tails. The two countries were infrastructurally similar, especially from Thatcher's time on, when both the formal-imperial and the socialist obstacles to their 'special relationship' were swept away, and Britain caught up again with—or reverted back to—the point on the road of capitalist evolution where America now stood. That seems a sufficient explanation, without bringing the imperial ermine into it.

The same difficulties of disentangling post-imperial from other influences follow us everywhere. With 'attitudes' it is particularly hard. Imperialism is often blamed for the periodic racism that manifested itself in Britain from the 1958 Notting Hill riots onwards, for example; but of course the beginnings of that racism coincided with the new phenomenon of (relatively) mass immigration from the West Indies, which on the surface would seem to offer an adequate explanation for 'poor white' resentment on its own. Of course, the reason why they migrated to Britain rather than anywhere else *was* a legacy of empire. Did the memory of the empire make Britons arrogant? Well, first of all it could be argued that other peoples are more arrogant (the French and Americans are the usual candidates); and secondly, that having *lost* an empire should have had the opposite effect. Tabloid and hooligan chauvinism seems to be mainly based, rather, on the belief that Britain had won World War II. (Or beaten the Argentines in the Falklands: the Falklands themselves—a sad remnant of Britain's former imperial glories—are nothing to be proud about.) Did residual imperialist attitudes undermine British business management in the post-colonial years? Again, this is essentially unknowable. Ex-colonial civil servants, if they were young enough, sometimes did transfer into management jobs in Britain when their work overseas was done (some of them became university administrators; those of us who came across them in that role thought we could spot the signs). What impact their imperial experiences had cannot be measured. Those who retired in England, with their imperial attitudes intact, typically writing periodically to the *Daily Telegraph* about how the country had gone to the dogs, became a national joke. (The political cartoonist David Low had already immortalized them in the 1930s, in the person of 'Colonel Blimp'; *The Goon Show*, a popular radio comedy of the 1950s, also had one: 'Major Bloodnok'.) But they may not have deserved this prominence. In context this factor—returning imperialists—appears a marginal one; as the empire, it has been argued here, always had been.

Even Britain's post-imperial wars are problematical. One of those was fought over a colony: the Falklands campaign of 1982. Two others saw Britain returning (on America's coat-tails) to old colonial haunts to repel and then to remove a nationalist leader: the Gulf War of 1991 and the Iraq War of 2003. There must be an 'imperialist' dimension here. Margaret Thatcher was a self-confessed admirer of the empire, despite the fact that it was she who gave Britain's two last substantial colonies away,[66] while Tony Blair's stance on foreign policy generally—not only in Iraq but also most notably in Africa—was redolent of the more idealistic kind of late nineteenth-century imperialism, as many commentators have pointed out. On America's side the imperialism is even plainer, with the old 'capitalist imperialist' motive (oil) also allegedly coming into the picture in Iraq, and many powerful US policy advisers in the early 2000s espousing a form of it quite openly. Yet again, however, we meet difficulties when we try to trace this through to the common British cultures of the time. It is difficult to see a connection on that level between past imperialism and Britain's modern wars. The mass of the British people did not support these wars for reasons that should really be called 'imperial'. That is why Britain's leaders presented them—disguised them, perhaps—as something else.

In the Iraq case, as with the much earlier Suez crisis, a majority of people appears to have been opposed to the wars in any case: certainly before and immediately afterwards. (While 'our boys' were actually fighting it was different.) With the two other wars the enemy's aggression was blatant and so a military response could be justified defensively, without imperial *casūs* needing to be invoked. In the Iraq case, too, 'defence' was the main propaganda reason given for the war, though that began to look somewhat threadbare soon afterwards. The other stated pretext for all these wars was to rescue innocents (Suez Canal shareholders, Falkland Islanders, Kuwaitis, 'ordinary' Iraqis) from aggressive tyrants (Nasser, Galtieri, Saddam Hussein). This is interesting in a British perspective, because it invoked quite another historical tradition from the 'imperial' one. No one appealed to the memory of the British empire. Protecting innocents from tyrants struck a much deeper national chord: going back to the Armada, at least (it could have gone back to the Norman invaders if Harold Godwineson had won), through Napoleon and the Kaiser, to Hitler. Eden's direct comparison of Nasser with Hitler in 1956 is often derided. What may be more significant, however, is the reason why he felt he had to make it, which was that the old imperial excuses for adventures like this would no longer do. Suez needed to be a re-run of World War II, not the Boer War. Hitler's name was involved frequently in the run-up to the Iraq invasion too. This was a respectable precedent, in the way imperialism was not. British governments may still go to war for imperialistic reasons. The British people, however—the main focus of this study—generally do not.

⁂

Tangible imperial legacies, then, are difficult to trace. Another way of going about it would be to speculate on how things on the home front might have turned out if the British empire had never been; but that gets us into the realm of science fiction again. Obviously Britain would not have had to defend the Falklands, which could have prevented Thatcher's second election victory (where the 'khaki' factor was important), which might then have changed Britain's subsequent domestic history significantly. But then so many other things in British society would have already been so different as to make Thatcher's political dominance unlikely in any case. That might have been because there was no need for her, if one of the 'alternate universes' that was hypothesized earlier in this chapter had really happened: with the 'natural' development of capitalism in Britain *not* being temporarily diverted by imperialism into a more 'socialist' direction, and following instead the American path earlier. There are other possibilities. The upper and upper-middle classes, without an empire to feed their appetites for controlling and dominating, might have atrophed, leading to greater democracy in Britain. Or they might have turned to fascism in the 1920s and '30s—it can be argued that imperialism was Britain's (gentler) substitute for this—so that one effect of the empire on Britain may have been to save her from that. A fascist Britain allied to a fascist Germany would have made the present-day world vastly different. (But then, would the result of World War I, which was largely responsible for feeding fascism in Germany, have been the same?) If not having an empire meant being without colonies like Australia and New Zealand to soak up Britain's surplus population—if the Chinese had colonized them instead, for example—there could have been even more poverty and unrest in Britain than there was.[67] (On the other hand, there was still California; unless that was still in the hands of the native Americans.) If Lenin was right about imperialism being the 'last stage of capitalism' before socialism, then if Britain had skipped this stage to become the first country to experience a communist revolution, as by far the most 'advanced' capitalist economy in the nineteenth century, she might have managed it better than Russia; so that communism still survived. The possibilities are endless.

All this is fanciful; hardly more, really, than a diverting historical game. It makes the point, however, that the empire's long-term legacy for Britain could well have been considerable. Her empire may have transformed her in crucial ways. But—and this is the vital point for our purpose here—it did not need to do that by imperializing her too. The two processes are entirely separate. However much Britain was affected by her empire, it was not by making her people into imperia*lists*. In this more direct sense—in their fundamental ideas and values—most Britons were relatively *un*affected by it. The previous chapters of this book have shown how this could have been.

13 Recapitulation and Conclusion

It is annoying, to say the least, that the empire used to be so neglected in British history books until recently. This distorted Britons' view of their past, and even their present, grotesquely. Foreign observers could not understand it. For them, Britain was *defined* by her empire, and by the power, arrogance, and sometimes atrocious behaviour they associated with it. This was because the face Britain usually presented to them, *as* foreigners, was her imperial one. All the while, however, she was presenting an entirely different self-image to most of her own people: of a free, moderate, and peaceful nation, marked off from other nations by those qualities, and by the domestic 'progress' that had formed the main motif of her history for 400 years. The almost exactly contemporary empire (most historians placed its origins around 1600) played almost no part in this; certainly not a central one. It was marginalized. This was J. R. Seeley's great complaint, expressed in the text from which the title of this book is taken. There may be a parallel here with the contrast between the way Americans are regarded today by foreigners, based on their governments' and corporations' external policies, and the way they regard themselves: all that 'shining city on the hill' stuff. Each is a half-truth. A proper picture of the United States today, and of imperial Britain in the nineteenth and early twentieth centuries, must take both perspectives on board. Otherwise people might confuse the two: assume that their imperialism was (or is) not really imperialism, for example, but merely 'liberation' (or some such virtue); or that America's and Britain's vaunted libertarianism is no more than a fig-leaf, covering a much more potent imperial culture underneath.

Both of these are common positions today. There are plenty of people, however, who dispute the first, certainly in the case of the British empire, the conventional wisdom on which is now to dismiss totally its—frankly questionable—liberal pretensions. From the latter view, the fig-leaf one, there are fewer dissenters. The ubiquity of the 'cultural imperialist' reading of modern British history in present-day academia and the media was mentioned in the preface to this book. The subsequent chapters have been devoted to examining this reading critically. In fact, as I have argued, the relationship between Britain's external imperialism and her domestic society and culture was far more ambivalent than such a reading implies. This may seem surprising in view of the apparent enormity of the imperial enterprise. One would assume that the latter *must* have been either rooted in a widespread imperial discourse, or have given rise to one. Both the empirical evidence, however, and the context surrounding it suggest that this was not so.

❦❦❦

We have seen how this ambivalence was possible. To recapitulate: the empire, huge and significant as it was, did not require the involvement of any large section of British society for it to live and even grow. So long as a minority of men (and their female helpmeets) was committed enough to actually ruling it, the rest of the population could be left to concentrate on other things. The empire made no great material demands on most people, at least none that they were aware of, and did not need their support or even interest. All that was required was a minimum of apathy. It would not do for too many people to oppose imperialism on principle. This was easily secured, at a time (early on) when the idea of one people ruling another was not quite the anathema it became later—it was happening in Britain after all (one *class* ruling others); when the 'national' alternative did not seem to be so clear-cut—there were no true nations, for example, in many of the parts of the world that Britain colonized; and when people realized anyway that you could have tyrannical nations as well as liberal ones, just as with empires. Two other factors dampened potential anti-imperialism: the reluctance of many of the early Victorian middle classes to admit that Britain *was* an imperial power; and the presentation of the empire in the twentieth century, however falsely, as a means *towards* national self-determination. This was why there was so little root-and-branch domestic British opposition to the empire per se before, say, the 1930s. (Even J. A. Hobson was not an anti-imperialist in this sense.) The empire needed nothing more positive in the way of commitment from the British people, at least until the 1940s and '50s; and there must be considerable doubt over whether a deeper and more widespread imperial enthusiasm even then could have stopped the rot. Before then, the empire could get along perfectly well without it.

Many imperialists themselves clearly thought so. This was why they were so relaxed about the almost total lack of imperial education in schools for most of the nineteenth century. It was as though they did not want to share their empire with the people, for which they had good reason, as has been shown. Sharing implied a common citizenship, the idea of which ran right against the whole structure of British society, which was built on the principle that each class only needed to know its obligations towards the other classes, thus providing the adhesive for attaching them together complementarily. So, the working classes were taught to work hard, obey, and so on, and the upper classes to rule and serve. This is why the working classes, before the end of the century (when it may have been too late), were not encouraged to be patriotic. Later on we found a similar reluctance on the part of professional imperialists to let the people in on the mysteries of their calling, albeit for a different reason: the fear that the more they knew, the less they might approve. This was one of the things that the imperial propagandists who came on to the scene in a big way around the turn of the twentieth century—when new external threats to the empire suggested that it might not be able to carry on very much longer without a deeper and wider public commitment—had to battle against: the empire being seen as the exclusive bailiwick of just one class.

To digress for a moment: this has implications for imperialism—the word—that may be important. Often it is used as a way of categorizing *countries*, when in fact it fits classes or other groups *within* countries better. Throughout the nineteenth century, for example, when the 'British' are conventionally regarded as the imperialists and Australians, say—all of them—as colonial subjects, each of those populations in reality comprised mixes of both categories: the ruling classes in Britain lording it over their own lower classes in almost exactly the same way as they lorded it over their colonial peoples, and a large part of the immigrant population of Australia standing in relation to the *indigènes* there as much greater imperialists (certainly more powerful and brutal ones) than the distant British ruling classes stood in relation to them. Though it may suit modern Australians (and even Americans) to present themselves as ex-colonial victims and anti-imperialists collectively, because of the bad odour that came to attach to the 'i'-word in the twentieth century, the historical reality is far more complex. There is even an argument for saying that the *most* imperialistic people, in most senses of the word, were many of those who actually went to the colonies, leaving the metropole relatively bereft of them, and with a *less* imperialistic society and culture, therefore, than if the imperialists had stayed at home. That might explain why 'Empire Day' caught on so much more in places like Canada and Australia than it did in Britain, which initially resisted it officially. However that may be (and the subject of colonial imperialism is beyond the scope of this book), broad-brushing all nineteenth- and early twentieth-century Britons as necessarily on the same side of the colonial master–subject divide is clearly misleading. Only the imperial ruling class can be unequivocally located there.

Obviously this did not prevent other people from getting to know about the empire if they wanted to. It was, after all, a rather impressive and exciting phenomenon, however much the middle classes tried to play it down, and an natural focus for national pride for those who, despite the discouragement, wished to feel that way. The empirical evidence, however, throws some doubt on the extent of this. Most of the signs of imperial interest, in the nineteenth century especially, are patchy: concentrated in certain areas but scattered much more thinly elsewhere. That is, if we restrict our search to unequivocally imperial references. The imperialization of British society and culture can be made to look greater than it was by, firstly, ignoring the bare patches and bunching the imperial 'finds' together; and, secondly, including items that do not refer directly to the empire but can be argued to derive from or contribute to an imperial mentality. Race attitudes are the commonest example; others are an interest in maps, manufacturing and selling anything that might be destined for abroad, attending missionary lectures, visiting zoos, reading adventure stories, and drinking tea. There is no way of proving that such phenomena were not all manifestations of a deeper-rooted imperial mentality. That is possible. What this book has sought to show, however, is that they were not *necessarily* so, but could have been related to other common discourses in Victorian and later British society, which were much more pervasive than the imperial ones, but which many more empire-centred researchers ignore.

This leads on to a larger point. Even people's unequivocal attitudes towards the empire, where they had any, were not necessarily imperially *derived.* That is to say, they owed little or nothing to people's awareness (however distorted) *of* the empire, or to any factors that could be said to arise essentially from the imperial relationship. Rather, they were home-grown constructions, based on domestic values and prejudices, which might have been exactly the same if the empire had not existed; and which were then imposed on the empire, regardless. An example is the idea of 'progress', which informed much British popular thinking about other countries in the early and mid-nineteenth century, and appears to have originated entirely in the way the history of Britain, regarded quite parochially, was presented in schools. Britain had progressed; other peoples would too, and by the same route. There is an arrogance about this that is almost breathtaking, though also understandable in view of Britain's real achievements at this time; the best modern comparison is probably with the present-day United States. In neither case is this attitude incompatible with imperialism; rather the reverse, with the idea of bringing progress to the 'backward' a useful justification for it. But there are two points that need to be emphasized here. The first is that 'progress' was not intrinsically or necessarily an imperialistic idea; it did not derive from the empire, and could have been restricted to the domestic scene. The second is that this meant there was less likely to be any imperial recoil on Britain. If the ways she conceived her empire were based on home-grown discourses in any case, it meant that they could not return to distort those discourses in any way. The social, political, and cultural impact on her of the empire, qua empire, was likely to be minimal. That, in fact, is what we have found.

This may be a peculiarity of the British empire; or it may reflect a more general 'law'. Empires do not require imperial 'cultures' to sustain them, but only the right material infrastructure. (It is about time that material factors made a comeback in discussions of this kind.) Nations turn to empire-building when they are large and powerful ('Alle Grossmächte sind imperialistisch', said Finland's President Paasikivi in 1940, adding that Finland would undoubtedly be so too if she were bigger);[1] when their economies overproduce; when they require foreign national resources; to curb internal tensions; and to pre-empt external threats. In all these cases the way any such process is perceived may be influenced by 'culture', but not by any cultural discourse that can be said to be peculiarly or specifically 'imperialist'. Likewise, 'imperialist' discourses are not necessary to keep empires going; almost any discourse will do. We have seen how the middle-class doctrine of 'progress' was used to support British imperialism in the nineteenth century. Others can do the same job. Paternalism is one such discourse; racial arrogance is another, but so is racial tolerance; racism, but also egalitarianism; obscurantist reactionism (Schumpeter), but also rational enlightenment (Napoleon); conservatism, but also liberalism (the latter often); evil intentions (Nazi Germany), but also good ones (the present-day United States?). Usually these discourses are indigenously, not externally, derived. They do not cause or even enable imperialism (the material factors do that), but they may influence the public perception of it. That was certainly one of their functions—possibly the only one—in Britain's case.

So far as Britain was concerned, most people's attitudes towards the empire were derived from discourses related to their social *class*. In the nineteenth century the classes lived in different worlds, unable sometimes even to communicate, except at the level of giving and taking orders. This affected their 'cultures' (plural) greatly, with peoples' views and values on virtually every matter, not only the empire, being far more influenced by their class situation—in particular, their class *functions*—than by any more general, 'national' discourse. The latter in fact did not really exist for most of the nineteenth century, and was still being contested at the end of the twentieth. It is for this reason that general attitudes towards the empire or empire-related matters cannot be inferred from, for example, the writings of the literati of the time, who had their own peculiar agenda, as we have seen. It has been argued in this book that class was by far the most important factor influencing people's attitudes to the empire in this whole period: not only the simple degree of their imperial commitment, but also the conceptions of the empire they were supposed to be committed to. So: the most committed classes were the uppers and upper middles, for reasons to do more with their social origins and education than with the empire itself, together with some enthusiastic foreigners; the middle classes might also be committed, but to a very different kind of empire from the uppers', and for basically non-imperialistic reasons; and the working classes were either apathetic towards the empire or superficial in their attitude to it, for structural, 'class' reasons, again. These are over-generalizations, naturally, but are not nearly so misleading as interpretations of the British 'imperial discourse' which take less account of the social divisions and indigenous domestic influences of the time.

The way perceptions of the empire were distorted in order to harmonize with home-grown and class-based discourses explains one other thing: how the British could so often have got their empire so wrong. Insofar as they supported or (more often) tolerated the empire, it was an empire that bore only a rough approximation to the reality. It was a construction of their own. This was one of the main problems with popular imperialism, according to the imperial 'zealots' (as we have called them): that it did not embrace the full imperial*ness* of the empire, with all the obligations on people that this would imply, but was merely a sugar-coated version, designed to be palatable to them. The culmination came with that extraordinary inter-war propaganda line on the Commonwealth that painted it as a kind of happy family or a proto-League of Nations, born in peace and maintained in perfect amity; but something like this had been regularly peddled to the British from the nineteenth century on. It was a travesty (though not a total one: the present author is not one of those who subscribes to an entirely negative view of the British empire); but the significance of it lies elsewhere. To be widely accepted, the empire had to be presented as conforming to other British values, like liberty, tolerance, and progress. This shows how much more pervasive and deep-rooted than any imperially-derived ones these other discourses were.

They could even have had a moderating influence on the practical implementation of imperialism. 'Commonwealthism', for example, may have contributed towards decolonization as well as easing the pain of it. Before then, governors, district commissioners, army officers and others in 'the field' knew that home opinion would not brook too much expense, or atrocity. Consequently they had either to hold back on these, or to hide them—which could weaken their hand. It is impossible to know how effective this was. But it emphasizes the point that, so far as stay-at-home Britons were concerned, theirs was always a *contingent* imperialism; contingent, that is, on these other indigenous discourses, that had very little to do with the empire and its needs per se.

* * *

This interpretation, of course, rests on a particular definition of the word 'empire'—and its derivatives—which many may find over-restrictive; especially in its insistence on 'domination' as an essential component. In fact that may not be as problematical as it appears. If it is only a question of semantics, then it is not important. The point was made near the beginning of this book that there is no 'correct' way of defining the 'e' and 'i' words. My own usage is merely a preference, chosen not only for pedantic reasons (their Latin roots), but also on grounds of utility: broaden their reference too much, and they lose their cutting edge. If others wish to use the words to cover foreign travel, for example, or map-making, trade, zoo-keeping, or tea-drinking they are entitled to do so. The only thing I would ask is that they accept that there may have been *differences* between these sorts of 'imperialism' and my 'dominating' kind. In that case one of my arguments could be restated thus: that 'dominating' imperialism had little influence on, and less influence than, these other kinds. This gets us over the semantic difficulties, if that is all they are.

The problem comes when the inclusion of these two different phenomena in a single category, 'imperialism', is taken to imply that the one phenomenon—travel, map-making, or whatever it might be—is necessarily tarred with the same 'dominating' brush as the other. For those who do assume this, the argument of the present book will seem inadequate, and probably superficial, resting as it does mainly on the more overt expressions of dominating-imperialism, and largely passing over its more subtle, latent, perhaps subconscious signs. I have little to say in reply to these critics except, first, that even subtle signs require evidence to show that they are signs of what the critics believe them to be signs of; and secondly, that my treatment of the broader social and cultural contexts of these phenomena suggests that these particular ones did not *need* to be signs of them. Logically it is possible to conceive of contacts between Britons and the wider world in this period which did not have 'imperial' undertones in the 'dominating' sense. The only reason for thinking that they *must* have done, therefore, if the 'dominating' implication was not stated explicitly or at least clearly hinted at, is that British society generally was so saturated with the ethos of dominating imperialism that no aspect of its people's extra-national interests and activities could possibly have escaped it. This book has tried to show how implausible that assumption of 'saturation' is; which—if it is right in this—destroys the only reason for believing that trade, tea-drinking, and the like were necessarily manifestations of dominating-imperialism.

This is not to say that the two kinds of imperialism could not have been linked in certain cases. Explorers *did* blaze trails for imperial armies, missionaries for colonial administrators, and racists for the excuses that would follow for keeping 'inferior' peoples in thrall. These are the subtler forms of 'dominating' imperialism, whose effect on the British public should also be considered, as well as that of the more overt and conscious sort. But it was not invariably so. Britain related to the wider world in many ways that did not appear to be dominant-imperialist, and may not have been so in fact. As a nation she was more 'outward-looking' in the nineteenth century than any nation anywhere before that time: more widely engaged, that is, with the world. That situation clearly arose not from any 'imperial' propensities before this time, but from her material situation as the world's first great industrial capitalist economy, with a huge surplus of goods and capital avidly seeking markets further and further afield. The rest followed; including dominant-imperialism (often, to secure those markets), but also these other forms of expansion, activity, interest, and so on, in the outside world. Not all of this expansion was related to a wish to rule or control, certainly not consciously; and there is no reason to suppose it was subconsciously either, from what we know about the broader context of Britain's society and culture (or cultures) then. To 'look' is not necessarily to covet. To simply elide these two phenomena, imperialism and 'outward-lookingness'—or, if you like, 'dominating' imperialism and the other kind—without proof in each case of the connection, is at the very least unhelpful. It is like eliding all male sex, or sexual desire, with rape. (That analogy has been chosen because it is just about arguable, though I personally would not want to argue it.) It muddies a vital distinction. Which is why we have not generally admitted these other manifestations of 'outward-lookingness' under the rubric of 'imperialism' in this book.

⁂

The main area of difficulty here, and the one where it may be felt that this book has underestimated the impact of empire most seriously, is probably 'race'. British racial attitudes are so often attributed to or connected in other ways with imperialism as to almost identify them together in some people's minds.[2] It would be lazy, though, to take this as read. It should go without saying that you do not need to be an imperialist to be a racist; unless the definition of imperialism is stretched to cover any feeling of superiority by one group of people over another, which could be said to imply, perhaps, a subliminal or repressed urge to dominate. Some of the most blatant examples of wholesale and even deadly ethnic prejudice, especially in recent times, have been found in small and manifestly non-expansionary countries (unless they learned it from their former imperial masters).

In Britain's case the link between imperialism and racism appears more plausible: first, because she did in fact rule an empire; and secondly because empires require—do they not?—an assumption of superiority by the imperial nations over those they colonize. It is just about possible to claim that this lies at the very root of imperial expansion: one people takes over another *because* it regards it as inferior; though I do not know of anyone who has ever argued that in a joined-up way. A more sophisticated version of this is that racism provides a justification for conquering peoples on other grounds. Thus, while you might want a territory for its land, gold, oil, or strategic situation, you can square this with your conscience by persuading yourself that the territory's current population is unfit to live, or needs to be forced to labour, or requires superior people to look after it, or deserves to be 'raised' from its present position of cultural inferiority by those same people. Thus, it will undoubtedly help the imperial enterprise if there is a pre-existing domestic racist opinion consistent with it; which is what some scholars have detected in Shakespeare's time, just before the empire really started up, and enabling it to do so. In this way the racism implied in the Prospero–Caliban relationship in *The Tempest,* for example, can be regarded as *proto*-imperialist. Thirdly, racism can *result* from empire. The very fact of ruling other races makes people look down on them: if they have to submit to you—and, it could be added, to so very few of you—they must be inferior. Domination creates its own discourse of relative human rankings. When imperialism did have an impact on racial attitudes (which is much more likely than vice-versa), it was probably through a combination of this and the 'justification' factor.

Because Britain did have an empire, it is difficult to imagine how she would have viewed other peoples if she had not. It seems unlikely that it would have saved her from the scourge of racism, if the experience of other non-imperial nations—including non-European ones—is anything to go by. The question is, then, what difference her empire made to the *nature* of her racism; for racism is not a monolith, but comes in a bewildering variety of forms. It has been argued here that one set of attitudes that is commonly included under 'racism' should not be, because it expressly repudiates the link between human ranking and race (or genetic make-up), preferring instead to emphasize the importance of 'culture': so that, for example, a black person could achieve equality with white people by adopting their 'civilization'. This betrays a huge prejudice in favour of European institutions, but not a 'racist' one. I have called it 'culturism'. It is possible that I have made too much of this, and that 'culturism' was in fact a thin disguise for what were in fact deeper-seated racist attitudes; or anyway was just as wounding, because equally patronizing. But it still illustrates two important points. The first is that racial attitudes could vary greatly in Britain, and change over time, partly as a reflection or a result of the different kinds of imperialism Britons indulged in. An example of this is the controversy over West Indian slavery at the beginning of the nineteenth century, reflected (very marginally) in Jane Austen's *Mansfield Park*, where two very different kinds of imperialism came into conflict: the definitely racist sort of the slave-owners, justifying slavery in terms of African inferiority, and the more liberal sort of *Mansfield Park*'s heroine, wishing to use Britain's imperial authority to impose more humane, and in some cases egalitarian, standards on the world. The second point is that not all racial attitudes had imperialistic (or, at any rate, imperial) origins. 'Culturism' did not. It derived from British views of their own 'progress' as a people and a nation from pre-Roman times onwards, which were then imposed, without any effort to adapt to local cultural or 'racial' circumstances, on everyone else. The paternalist view of 'natives' that regarded them as like the British working classes is another example of the same phenomenon: a racial attitude based on the assumption of sameness, rather than on observation of 'the other'. The empire had very little effect on opinions like these. Which is not to say, of course, that we cannot regard such paternalism as essentially 'imperialistic' in yet another sense; if, that is, imperialism is associated with national arrogance.

It can be shown, then, that different kinds of imperialism gave rise to different sorts of racial attitude, not all of them rac*ist*, and that even the racist ones varied in the degree of their disparagement and in their implications. It was possible, for example, for people to positively admire the special peculiarities of some other peoples; though there are few examples of this where there is not a strong whiff of condescension about it too: as in the case of the so-called 'martial races' of northern India. It is arguable in fact that one of the effects on Britain of her very variegated empire was to ensure that British views of other peoples were not as generalized, simplistic, and stereotypical as in countries that only had their ignorant prejudices to guide them. Imperialism could have had a marginally anti-racist effect, therefore. But this only applies to those who took an active interest in these questions, who we have seen were a minority at most times. (The period of anti-slavery agitation is the chief exception.) These were the people who had significant views about other races; significant, because they could actually affect the lives of the latter. But what of the rest?

The way the majority of the stay-at-home population formed their views of other races was very different. This is the sphere of influence of cheap magazines and comics, boys' adventure books steeped in racial stereotypes, 'savage Africa' sideshows and 'nigger minstrel' performances, and highly sensationalized accounts of British wars with 'natives' in popular newspapers. These do not appear to have been particularly pervasive early in our period, when we have found that the images of non-Europeans filtering down to the middle and working classes were fairly sparse, and by no means unrelievedly racist in any sense. From the last quarter of the nineteenth century onwards, however, the situation gets—from an anti-racist viewpoint—worse. That coincides, of course, with the advent of the 'new' imperialism in Britain, and is likely to have been connected with it. Much of this popular racist discourse undoubtedly derived from the presentation of certain colonial events in the contemporary media: the Cawnpore 'massacre' and Jamaican rebel 'atrocities' early on; Afghan 'treachery'; the Muslim 'fanaticism' responsible for the 'murder' of General Gordon; Arab and Zionist 'terrorism' in Palestine; Mau Mau 'atrocities' after World War II, and so on.[3] On the other hand there were other sources for these images too. The United States was one: the original home of the 'nigger minstrel' phenomenon, for example, and the medium through which Helen Bannerman's entirely innocent *Little Black Sambo* (1899) was, according to Elizabeth Hay, transformed into a racist text. There are also questions over how these accounts were received. One imagines it must have been fairly passively, because of the scarcity of countervailing images at this level in this later part of our period; but we cannot be sure, because there is no way of testing the working and middle classes' racial opinions at this time. One reason for this is that there were so very few black people living in Britain for them to vent their feelings on until the late 1950s, when immigration from the West Indies began. So, whatever views the working and middle classes had before then are likely to have been superficial, and unimportant in any practical way. The whole issue did not matter to them. That—the *depth* as well as the breadth of these prejudices—is something else that needs to be borne in mind.

The race question illustrates some of the more general difficulties of relating these kinds of phenomena to imperialism, and the dangers of assuming that they must have been *propter* just because they were *post* (or in some cases *ante*) *hoc*. Even where one might expect the connection to be closest—this is why 'race' has been highlighted here—there must be doubts. The same applies with probably more force to all the other British domestic social and cultural phenomena of the period that are sometimes taken to have an 'imperial' provenance: monarchism, militarism, masculinism, mapping, museums ... and several others that do not begin with the letter 'm'. These are where the subtler effects of imperialism are supposed to have operated. In many cases they did, but very unevenly, and certainly not exclusively, which is why they need to be empirically established in every case. Simple assertions about the imperial significance of this or that cultural trait simply will not do. The objection to this is not only that such assertions are unproven, but that they do violence to the enormous and fascinating complexity of British society in this period, and ignore all the other and very different social trends and cultural 'discourses' that were going on. For most British people these latter were far more powerful. The empire was marginal. Even subtly, it was unlikely to have made much of an impact. There should certainly be no presumption that it did.

* * *

If the empire made so uneven and generally superficial an impression on British society and culture while it was a going concern, it follows that its dissolution did not need to have much of an impact either. This is borne out by the equanimity with which most Britons appeared to accept this fate in the post-World War II period, with only a small minority of Conservative zealots actively seeking to halt the process—in one instance by becoming technical *anti*-imperialists, in order to defend white supremacy in Rhodesia against an imperial government that seemed set on a more liberal solution—and with the single body dedicated to actually reversing it, the 'League of Empire Loyalists' (1954–67), being rightly regarded as very much a 'fringe' movement.[4] The majority of Britons seemed uninterested. We saw that most of them had agreed that India should be given self-government as early as 1939; so they accepted that when it eventually happened in 1947. Enoch Powell, walking the streets that night trying to come to terms with it, cannot have bumped into many others as traumatized as he was. The Suez adventure caused only a political ripple; most Britons were against that in any case. When the fifth Earl of Salisbury resigned from the Cabinet in March 1957 over the issue of Cyprus—another colony about to be liberated—scarcely anyone even noticed the event. It certainly had no further repercussions.[5] Few anticipated then that the remainder of the colonies would follow so soon afterwards—especially the African ones, which were regarded as particularly 'backward' (whose fault was that?)—but people swallowed that easily also. The official Conservative line, even, in the 1960s was that decolonization was going forward perhaps a little too rapidly for comfort, but was right in principle.[6] Granted, the blow may have been softened for many people by the fact that most of the ex-colonies decided to remain within the Commonwealth, which for a time looked as though it might furnish a more significant successor to the empire than it turned out to be.[7] That was important for the minority of the population that had any strong feeling for such matters. For the rest, however, decolonization—like the original empire it was dismantling—was just another of those marginal issues of politics, which might interest their politicians, but not themselves.

Hence its probable lack of impact in other ways. We discussed these in chapter 12. The end of the empire had some important material implications, but few repercussions on the feelings or thoughts of the mass of people that are easy to demonstrate. The biggest practical effect *may* have been—this is no more than a hypothesis as yet—to bring Britain closer to America in her economic ideology, the empire having previously diverted her from the extreme capitalist path she might have gone down otherwise. This may be a better explanation for Britain's reluctance to fully commit herself to the more traditionally statist 'European' way of doing things than the one that attributes this to a hankering after old imperial glories. Two more practical effects were immigration and post-colonial curries. Other features that are sometimes attributed to the loss of empire may not be its 'fault' at all: anti-Europeanism is one, racism another. There are perfectly credible explanations for both these (deplorable) traits in modern British society, without requiring us to resort to the 'imperial hankering' one. They are not, after all, peculiar to Britain. The only reason for the wide currency of the post-imperial explanation may be the common misunderstanding about Britain's degree of imperialization earlier on.

The same even applies to Britain's early twenty-first century 'new imperialist' adventures in Afghanistan, Iraq, and elsewhere. Martin Jacques was one of those who thought he saw a reversion to nineteenth-century type here. 'Once an imperial nation' he wrote in October 2002, 'always an imperial nation, even when the substance of power has long since disappeared. It is a mentality, a way of being and thinking.'[8] Well, it may have been, for some. Tony Blair, who was responsible for this policy almost on his own—it is difficult to imagine any alternative Labour leader leaning quite so far towards George W. Bush over Iraq in particular—was certainly aware of Britain's imperial past, and seemed not too ashamed of it.[9] Several commentators detected a touch of Gladstone in him.[10] One similarity was their attitudes towards the 'i' word itself; Gladstone never liked it applied to him, over his 1882 invasion of Egypt, for example, because, he said, he wanted no territory, and aimed to get out as soon as possible. These are precisely the arguments that Britons and Americans who deny their own imperialism today deploy.[11] They could both have been fooling themselves. (As always, this is largely a matter of semantics.) If they *were* imperialists, however, it was not necessarily because of the existence of a widespread imperialistic 'culture' at the time. In modern Britain's case there was certainly no such culture. Firstly, around 50% of the British people – the exact figure fluctuated – did not support Blair's Iraq policy anyway. Secondly, insofar as they did, it was not usually for 'imperialist' reasons, as we have seen.[12] The same might be said of most modern Americans. Thirdly, even the few 'real' imperialists could not have inherited their imperialism from a previous general imperial culture, because there never was such a thing. This is what the present book has sought to show. Only a small number of 'zealots' had ever been committed imperialists. (The equivalents in modern America are probably the 'neo-conservatives'.)[13] There was no widepread imperial 'mentality', therefore. Imperial culture was neither a cause nor a significant effect of imperial*ism*. That is not the way these things work.

This is because neither needed (or needs) the other. Empires arise for mainly material reasons. Once they have arisen, almost any cultural trait or ideology can be harnessed to support or excuse them: even anti-imperialism and anti-racism, as we have seen. In Britain's case in the 19th century, as probably in America's today, those traits and ideologies were home-grown, arising out of domestic discourses, and owing almost nothing to the fact of Britain's expansion into the world. Even her imperial rulers' mind-set grew out of their traditional functions within British society, rather than from anything particularly related to their governance of other peoples. This is clear from the way they were taught, in their public schools. For the rest, most people's 'mentalities' were forged by domestic concerns, usually related to class, and the ideals they gave rise to; which then had far more influence on their ways of looking at the empire than the empire itself did, and may also have had more of an effect on imperial policies than those policies reacted back on society at home. (That would have been a relief to eighteenth century Whigs, who had feared otherwise.) This is the way 'culture' *can* impact on imperialism: not by giving rise to it, but – occasionally – by influencing its character. Thus, to take the recent case of Iraq: the way

American imperialism was implemented there in 2003–4 may well have had something to do with aspects of indigenous American culture: its idealism, for one thing; but also a certain roughness – to put it quite mildly – in its approach to many things (like criminals). But these are not signs of an 'imperialist culture', properly so called. They would exist without imperialism, and do not need to give rise to it. Nor is there much evidence, so far, that their experience of imperialism is greatly affecting Americans' culture back home. The same is true of Britain in the nineteenth and early twentieth centuries. There can be no assumption that she was 'steeped' in imperialism, by any useful definition. Efforts to discover this in the fabric of her society are fundamentally misconceived. The traffic, such as there was of it, mainly went the other way.

Endnotes

PREFACE

1. Examples include Sarah Curtis's film *Mansfield Park* (1999)—the most extreme one, enormously extending Said's famous 'postcolonial' interpretation of the novel: see below, p. 139; and a TV adaptation of Trollope's *The Way We Live Now* broadcast in 2001: below, p. 369, n. 27. In 2003 a BBC2 documentary about the building of Brunel's *Great Eastern* implied that the ship was designed to be 'a fitting symbol for the mightiest empire the world has ever known'; which its producer, Simon Winchcombe, has subsequently admitted to me was an anachronistic interpolation (e-mail to author, 24 Oct. 2003).
2. In his *Orientalism: History, Theory and the Arts* (Manchester, 1995), 5.
3. Derived, of course, from J. R. Seeley's famous *The Expansion of England* (1883), the text of which also furnishes the title of the present book.
4. See R. E. Robinson, 'Non-European Foundations of European Imperialism: Sketch for a Theory of Collaboration', in E. R. J. Owen and R. B. Sutcliffe (eds.), *Studies in the Theory of Imperialism* (1972) [place of publication is London, unless otherwise shown].
5. See John MacKenzie, 'Scotland and the Empire', in *International History Review*, 14 (1993); and, on Ireland, David Fitzpatrick, 'Ireland and the Empire', in Andrew Porter (ed.), *The Oxford History of the British Empire*, Vol. 3: *The Nineteenth Century* (Oxford, 1999).
6. For an overview on the churches, see Andrew Porter, 'Religion, Missionary Enthusiasm, and Empire', in Porter (ed.), *Oxford History of the British Empire: The Nineteenth Century*; and on gender, Rosalind O'Hanlon, 'Gender in the British Empire', in Judith Brown and Wm. Roger Louis (eds.), *The Oxford History of the British Empire, Vol. 4: The Twentieth Century* (Oxford, 1999), and below, Ch. 12.
7. Only some. Apparently I am not alone here. For a recent critical approach to this ideology, see Erin O'Connor, 'Preface for a Post-Colonial Criticism', in *Victorian Studies*, 45 (2003).

CHAPTER I

1. Edward Said, 'Always on Top' (review of Catherine Hall's *Civilising Subjects*), *London Review of Books*, 20 Mar. 2003, p. 3. The *Dizionario Italiano Sabatini Coletti* (1997) defines *senso comune* as 'modo di interdue edi sentive proprio della maggior parte degli romini' ('way of understanding and feeling proper to the greater part of mankind').
2. See e.g. Miles Kahler, *Decolonisation in Britain and France: The Domestic Consequences of International Relations* (1984); John Darwin, 'The Fear of Falling: British Politics and Imperial Decline Since 1900', *Transactions of the Royal Historical Society*, 5th ser., 36 (1986); and Peter Marshall, 'Imperial Britain', *Journal of Imperial and Commonwealth History*, 23: 3 (1995), 380.

3. Peter Marshall, 'Imperial Britain', in Peter Marshall (ed.), *The Cambridge Illustrated History of the British Empire* (1992), 232.
4. Frederick Madden with David Fieldhouse (eds.), *The Dependent Empire and Ireland . . . Select Documents* (1991), p. xix.
5. Ged Martin, 'Was There a British Empire?' (review article), *Historical Journal,* 15: 3 (1972), 562. See also Thomas Richards, *The Imperial Archive: Knowledge and the Fantasy of Empire* (1993), Introduction.
6. Andrew Roth, *Enoch Powell: Tory Tribune* (1970), 46.
7. Ibid. 51.
8. J. Enoch Powell, speech to Royal Society of St George, 22 Apr. 1961, in Powell, *Freedom and Reality,* ed. John Wood (1969), 338.
9. J. Enoch Powell, speech at Trinity College, Dublin, 13 Nov. 1964, in ibid. 324–35.
10. Ibid. 325.
11. e.g. Susan Thorne, *Congregational Missions and the Making of an Imperial Culture in 19th-Century England* (Stanford, Cal., 1999), 4; and Catherine Hall, *Civilising Subjects: Metropole and Colony in the English Imagination 1830–1867* (2002), 5.
12. See Shula Marks, 'History, the Nation and Empire: Sniping from the Periphery', *History Workshop,* 29 (1990), 112; and Antoinette Burton, 'Rules of Thumb: British History and "Imperial Culture" in Nineteenth- and Twentieth-Century Britain', *Women's History Review,* 3 (1994), 483–5.
13. Jeffrey Richards, *Imperialism and Music: Britain 1876–1953* (Manchester, 2001), pp. 211, 525.
14. Catherine Hall, *Civilising Subjects: Metropole and Colony in the English Imagination 1830–1867* (2002).
15. Burton, 'Rules of Thumb', 486.
16. See e.g. Hugh Cunningham, 'The Language of Patriotism', in Raphael Samuel (ed.), *Patriotism* (1989), i. 69–89; and other contributions to this three-volume collection.
17. James Greenlee, *Education and Imperial Unity, 1901–1929* (New York, 1987), p. ix.
18. Gayatri Spivak, 'Three Women's Texts and a Critique of Imperialism', in Robyn Warhol and Diane Price Herndl (eds.), *Feminisms: An Anthology of Literary Theory and Criticism* (New Brunswick, NJ, 1991), 798.
19. e.g. Jonah Raskin, *The Mythology of Imperialism: Rudyard Kipling, Joseph Conrad, E. M. Forster, D. H. Lawrence and Joyce Cary* (New York, 1971).
20. An example may be Edward Said, whose background before he wrote *Culture and Imperialism* was exclusively Middle Eastern and American, and whose earliest encounters with the British were as officious occupying soldiers and slightly mad teachers in an English school in Egypt which aped 'public' school ways. See his *Out of Place: A Memoir* (1999).
21. Said's *Culture and Imperialism,* for example, for all its great qualities, is singularly bereft of 'theory' in the normally understood sense. It gives no arguments, for example, for its assertions of the importance of 'culture' by his definition of it (pp. xii–xiii): reasons, that is, why that *should* be so; or, in the British case, of 'imperialism' as an important factor within that culture. An idea is not a theory.
22. See Richard Koebner, *Empire* (Cambridge, 1961); and id. and H. D. Schmidt, *Imperialism: The Story and Significance of a Political Word, 1840–1960* (Cambridge, 1964).
23. Koebner and Schmidt, *Imperialism,* ch. 1.
24. Quoted in W. D. McIntyre, *The Imperial Frontier in the Tropics 1865–75* (1967), 11.

25. J. A. Gallagher and R. E. Robinson, 'The Imperialism of Free Trade', *Economic History Review*, 6 (1953).
26. T. C. McCaskie uses the word 'inculturation' to describe this: 'Cultural Encounters: Britain and Africa in the Nineteenth Century', in A. Porter (ed.), *Oxford History of the British Empire*, Vol. 3: *The Nineteenth Century* (1999), 665.
27. Jack Goody, *The East in the West* (1996).
28. Below, p. 66, and n. 13.
29. Peter Marshall, 'No Fatal Impact? The Elusive History of Imperial Britain', *Times Literary Supplement*, 12 Mar. 1993, p. 8.
30. On British architecture in the empire, see Jan Morris, *Stones of Empire: The Buildings of the Raj* (1983); Robert Fermor-Hesketh (general ed.), *Architecture of the British Empire* (1986); Thomas R Metcalf, *An Imperial Vision: Indian Architecture and Britain's Raj* (1989); and Mark Crinson, *Empire Building. Orientalism and Victorian Architecture* (1996).
31. Martin, 'Was There a British Empire?', 565.
32. See Fred Anderson, *Crucible of War: The Seven Years War and the Fate of the Empire in British North America, 1754–1766* (2000), p. xviii.
33. For a discussion of this see Stephen Howe, *Ireland and Empire: Colonial Legacies in Irish History and Culture* (Oxford, 2000).
34. On the contribution of the latter, see Joseph E. Inikori, *Africans and the Industrial Revolution in England: A Study in International Trade and Economic Development* (Cambridge, 2002).
35. William Woodruff calculates that in 1860 the United Kingdom had 25% of the world's trade, France 11%. *Impact of Western Man: A Study of Europe's Role in the World Economy 1750–1960* (1966), 313.
36. On the Opium Wars, see Gerald S Graham, *The China Station: War and Diplomacy 1830–1860* (Oxford, 1978); J. Y. Wong, *Deadly Dreams: Opium and the Arrow War (1856–60) in China* (Cambridge, 1998); Glenn Melancon, *Britain's China Policy and the Opium Crisis* (Aldershot, 2003).
37. See C. J. Lowe, *The Reluctant Imperialists: British Foreign Policy 1878–1902* (1967).
38. J. R. Seeley, *The Expansion of England: Two Courses of Lectures* (1883; 2nd edn. 1895), 10. The full quotation is given below, p. 380, n. 10.
39. Ann Laura Soler, 'Rethinking Colonial Categories: European Communities and the Boundaries of Rule', in Nicholas B. Dirks (ed.), *Colonialism and Culture* (1992), 321. See also Dirks's own Introduction to this; T. O. Beidelman, *Colonial Evangelism: A Socio-Historical Study of an East African Mission at Grassroots* (1982); John and Jean Comaroff, *Ethnography and the Historical Imagination* (1992); and Ann Stoler's and Frederick Cooper's introductory chapter, 'Between Metropole and Colony', to their (edited) *Tensions of Empire: Colonial Cultures in a Bourgeois World* (1997). These comments mainly occur in relation to the differences in the agendas and outlooks of colonial representatives in 'the field'; but there is also the recognition—implied especially in Beidelman's interesting analysis of the class and educational origins of his east African missionaries (ch. 3), later taken up by the Comaroffs (ch. 7)—that this could be pursued back to the metropole. Some recent historians have also referred to this tendency, sometimes dubbed (reversing Said's charge against Western 'Orientalists') 'Occidentalism'; e.g. D. A. Washbrook, 'Orients and Occidents: Colonial Discourse Theory and the

Historiography of the British Empire', in Robin W. Winks (ed.), *Oxford History of the British Empire, Vol. 5: Historiography* (Oxford, 1999), 596–611.

40. This, it seems to me, is Said's position, in his *Culture and Imperialism*. The only kind of culture he seems interested in is a 'national' one (e.g. p.12). He is not rigid over this, allowing for a weaker national cultural hold in some places, for example, and for the possibility of individual dissent *against* the national culture; but not for the possible existence of a *variety* of cultures (or discourses), let alone conflicting cultures, within a single 'nation'. Or, to put it another way, he acknowledges the hybridity, but not the plurality, of the British discourse. John MacKenzie's critique of Said's view of 'culture' in *Orientalism: History, Theory and the Arts* (1995), Preface and ch. 1, is very pertinent in this context.
41. The Nationality Act of 1983 was the first to describe Britons as 'citizens'.
42. Natalie M. Houston, Introduction to Mary Elizabeth Braddon, *Lady Audley's Secret* (1862; new edn., Toronto, 2003), 21. Italics added.
43. Benjamin Disraeli, *Sybil, or The Two Nations* (1845). The title and subject-matter of Mary Gaskell's *North and South* (1855) address the same divide.
44. See Correlli Barnett, *The Collapse of British Power* (1972); and Martin J. Wiener, *English Culture and the Decline of the Industrial Spirit 1850–1980* (1981).
45. Several were domiciled on the European continent. One such community is described in Pierre Tucoo-Chala, *Pau, Ville Anglaise* (Pau, 1979). Their culture was certainly regarded as distinct (usually more reprobate) by critical stay-at-home Britons; an example is [Felix McDonagh], *The Hermit Abroad*, 4 vols. (1823).
46. This describes certain tendencies, and not a consistent picture. The favourable impression of small traders is derived from Mary Kingsley's influential books on Africa: see below, p. 406, n. 8.
47. See Peter Godwin and Ian Hancock, *'Rhodesians Never Die': The Impact of War and Political Change on White Rhodesia c.1970–1980* (Oxford, 1993).
48. The concept of 'culture change' comes from Bronislav Malinowski, and is used by him to describe the impact of colonialism on native cultures. For its application to the cultures of the colonizers, see the Comaroffs, *Ethnology and the Historical Imagination*.

CHAPTER 2

1. These figures are extrapolated from the *Colonial Office Lists* for 1862 and 1898, and the *India Office Lists* for 1860 and 1886. They include everyone working at the Colonial and India Offices down to porters, together with closely allied occupations like emigration officers and colonial land commissioners, who did not actually work at the Colonial or India Offices, and every British employee 'in the field'. Lance E. Davis and Robert A. Huttenback, *Mammon and the Pursuit of Empire: The Political Economy of British Imperialism* (Cambridge: 1986), 14, have slightly different figures, but this can be can be easily explained: it depends whom you count. The *1861 Census* (vol. 3, p. 213), registers 2,561 government employees in India in that year; again, the discrepancy is not significant. The important point is that British colonial administrators numbered *only* in the low thousands.

2. These figures are taken from Andrew Porter (ed.), *Atlas of British Overseas Expansion* (1991), 118–22 (this section by Peter Burroughs); Chris Cook and Brendan Keith, *British Historical Facts 1830–1900* (1975), 185; David Omissi, *The Sepoy and the Raj: The Indian Army, 1860–1940* (1994), 133; and Saul David, *The Indian Mutiny* (2002), 346 (for Indian reinforcements). The army figures are for European troops (e.g. not Indian sepoys), and include *only* troops on colonial stations; besides these there were around 25,000 stationed in Ireland, and usually another 30,000–50,000 in mainland Britain itself. The *1861 Census* (vol. 3, p. 88) gives the following figures for men in the army, navy and merchant service combined stationed abroad in the middle years of the 19th century: 1831—76,221; 1841—121,050; 1851—126,561; 1861—162,273.

   Miles Taylor gives the following figures for other countries' armed forces *c.*1848: Russia 900,000; Austria-Hungary 400,000; France 324,000; Prussia 127,000. 'The 1848 Revolutions and the British Empire', *Past and Present*, 169 (2000), 150.
3. An Appendix to the *1861 Census Report* (vol. 3, pp. 177–213) gives figures for the 'white' residents of various colonies, but these are neither dependable nor necessarily useful for my purpose. Most of the 61,375 whites living in the West Indies, for example, as well as the 28,000 in South Africa, will have been domiciled there. The same may not apply to the 511 recorded for the West African colonies, who were probably there temporarily; or to most of the 40,371 British-born men and women (excluding the armed forces) living in India, of whom 26,882 were clearly the families of the men with jobs there ('engaged in domestic offices or duties of Wives, Mothers, Mistresses of families, Children . . . ' etc.), 5,504 engaged in business, 1,591 in the 'learned professions', 803 mechanics, 679 Army pensioners, 495 farmers or planters, and 68 labourers.
4. This is only a guess. For more reliable later figures, see below, p. 171 and n. 22.
5. William Woodruff, *Impact of Western Man* (1966), 106; B. R. Mitchell and Phyllis Deane, *Abstract of British Historical Statistics* (Cambridge, 1962), 50–1; Porter, *Atlas*, 85.
6. H. J. M. Johnston, *British Emigration Policy 1815–1830* (Oxford, 1972), 25–6, 88, 94.
7. One contemporary working-class autobiography, *The Life of Snowden Dunhill, Written by Himself* (1834), repr. with an Introduction by David Neave (Howden, 1987), ends with his transportation to Botany Bay, and a brief but doleful narrative of his experiences on that 'accursed soil' (p. 23).
8. See e.g. David Fitzpatrick, *Oceans of Consolation: Personal Accounts of Irish Emigration to Australia* (Melbourne, 1995).
9. The *Potters' Examiner*, 8 June 1844, quoted in Helen I. Cowan, *British Emigration to British North America: The First Hundred Years* (Toronto, 1961), 174.
10. Ibid. 93, 130.
11. *The Working Man: A Weekly Record of Social and Industrial Progress*, 2 (1866), 296.
12. Joseph Arch, *Joseph Arch, the Story of His Life, Told by Himself* (1898), 366.
13. Haines, *Emigration and the Labouring Poor*, 256, raises the question of why this was so, as 'an important field for future research'. One of his suggestions is that these were simply the least adventurous and enterprising; which is good to think if you are an Australian or a Canadian.
14. See Charlotte Erickson, *Invisible Immigrants: The Adaptation of English and Scottish Immigrants in Nineteenth Century America* (1972), 5; Fitzpatrick, *Oceans of Consolation*, 24. Some exceptions—usually emigrants pleading with their families to come—are to be found, however, in the latter.

15. Quoted in K. D. M. Snell, *Annals of the Labouring Poor: Social Change and Agrarian England, 1660–1900* (Cambridge, 1985), 13.
16. There are examples in Haines, *Emigration and the Labouring Poor*, 257–9.
17. 'Irish immigrants came from a country in which primary loyalties had been to family, then clan, then town, region, or at its widest county': Patrick O'Farrell, *The Irish in America* (Kensington, NSW, 1987), 197. On British 'patriotism', see below, ch. 6, *passim.*
18. This refers to the African west coast in the 1830s. Peter Burroughs, 'The Human Cost of Imperial Defence in the Early Victorian Age', *Victorian Studies*, 24 (1980), 15; Philip D. Curtin, *The Image of Africa* (1965), 71.
19. [James Dawson Burn], *Autobiography of a Beggar Boy* (1855), 133–4.
20. There is a useful list of such memoirs in Carolyn Steadman (ed.), *The Radical Soldier's Tale* (1988), 297–8.
21. Quoted in C. A. Bodelsen, *Studies in Mid-Victorian Imperialism* (1924; new edn. 1960), 42. Andrew Hassam, *Through Australian Eyes: Colonial Perceptions of Imperial Britain* (Melbourne, 2000), is based on the diaries of nine Australians (out of 70 he has found) who paid temporary visits to Britain in the last third of the 19th century.
22. George Baxter, *News from Australia*; reproduced in Fitzpatrick, *Oceans of Consolation.*
23. The most celebrated collections of these are Erickson, *Invisible Immigrants*; and Fitzpatrick, *Oceans of Consolation*. There are lists of the others in Robert F. Haines, *Emigration and the Labouring Poor: Australian Recruitment in Britain and Ireland, 1831–60* (1997), 291–2; and in Snell, *Annals of the Labouring Poor*, 10, n. 20. According to Fitzpatrick, 'a thousand or so' letters between Ireland and Australia survive, 'out of the millions exchanged... in the nineteenth century'. The reasons for their survival are largely accidental. How representative the thousand are of the 'millions' is of course impossible to say. Fitzpatrick thinks it is unlikely that they are typical. Fitzpatrick, *Oceans of Consolation*, pp. vii, 28. The 'millions' figure is, of course, a guess, albeit a likely one.
24. Walter Southgate, *That's the Way it Was: A Working-Class Autobiography 1890–1950* (1982), 13. On Irish emigrants' letters, see Fitzpatrick, *Oceans of Consolation* Patrick O'Farrell, *Letters from Irish Australia* (Sydney, 1984).
25. Thomas Hughes, *Tom Brown at Oxford* (1861; new edn. 1929), 442.
26. Some of their propaganda journals are listed in Cowan, *British Emigration*, 178. Carefully selected pro-emigration letters also appear frequently in Charles Dickens's *Household Words*, which gave strong backing to Mrs Chisholm's 'Family Colonisation Society' in the early 1850s: e.g. 1 (1850), 19–21, 514–15; 3 (1851), 228; and 4 (1852), 529–34. Could some of them have been commissioned, or made up? Charlotte Erickson and David Fitzpatrick note how atypical they were, and particularly in this respect: 'private letters rarely encouraged migration.' Charlotte Erickson, *Invisible Immigrants: The Adaptation of English and Scottish Immigrants in Nineteenth Century America* (1972), 5; Fitzpatrick, *Oceans of Consolation*, 24.
27. Burroughs, 'Human Cost of Imperial Defence', 11.
28. See Peter Burroughs, 'Crime and Punishment in the British Army, 1815–1870', *English Historical Review*, 100 (1985), 549–50.
29. Catherine Hall gives the example of Mary and William Swainson of Birmingham, who emigrated to New Zealand in 1841 (after some of their investments had crashed), and kept up a regular correspondence with their immediate families and friends. *Civilising Subjects: Metropole and Colony in the English Imagination 1830–1867* (2002), 285–9. Most of the

emigrants' letters published in *Household Words* (see above), are by middle-class rather than working-class settlers.

30. Anthony Trollope, *An Autobiography* (1883; new edn. 1950), 341. The book was *Australia and New Zealand*, 2 vols. (1873).
31. Compulsory retirement from the Colonial Service around 1900 was at age 55, but officers could retire at 45 if they wanted. In the Sudan Political Service retirement was compulsory at 48 or 50. Furlough entitlements varied from colony to colony, according to the climate, but were usually between one month in four and one month in seven, accrued and taken after 'tours' of one to four years. Anthony Kirk-Greene, *Britain's Imperial Administrators 1858–1966* (2000), 143–4, 184. Army officers had no pensions before 1871, but could cash in their (purchased) commissions, and live on the proceeds of that. (Information supplied by Peter Burroughs.)
32. Based on tables in Michael Barratt Brown, *After Imperialism* (revised edn. 1970), 110–11.
33. Davis and Huttenback, *Mammon and the Pursuit of Empire*, 42. See also Phyllis Deane and W. A. Cole, *British Economic Growth 1688–1959* (Cambridge, 2nd edn. 1967), 187; and *Annual Abstract of Statistics* for various years, for the proportion going to the empire.
34. The *Census of Great Britain, 1851* (1854), vol. 1, p. ccxx, records 750,849 employed in the flax and cotton industries. By the time of the *1911 Census* (vol. 10, p. 4) this had fallen to 609,317. For the destination of exports, J. R. McCulloch, *A Statistical Abstract of the British Empire* (1837), ii. 74, has 17.25% of Britain's cotton exports (by value) going to the colonies in 1833.
35. e.g. Anon., 'Shall We Retain Our Colonies', *Edinburgh Review*, 93 (1851), 480–1 (quoting Sir William Molesworth).
36. e.g. an anonymous review article on 'Canada' in *Westminster Review*, 8 (1827), 1–30; G Cornewall Lewis, *An Essay on the Government of Dependencies* (1841); and the review of Lewis in *Edinburgh Review*, 83 (1846), 547.
37. See Davis and Huttenback, *Mammon and the Pursuit of Empire*; Patrick O'Brien, 'The Costs and Benefits of British Imperialism 1846–1914', *Past and Present*, 120 (1988); and Avner Offer, 'Costs and Benefits, Prosperity and Security, 1870–1914', in Porter (ed.), *The Oxford History of the British Empire*, vol. 3: *The Nineteenth Century* Oxford, (1999), 690–711.
38. Walter Citrine, *Men and Work. An Autobiography* (1964), 30. Socialism of course was not a sure-fire prophylactic against imperialism, as the rest of Citrine's autobiography clearly shows.
39. Hall, *Civilising Subjects*, 272.
40. For British working-class hostility to Irish and Jewish immigrant labour, see R. Swift and Sheridan Gillet, *The Irish in Britain 1815–1939* (1898); Graham Davis, *The Irish in Britain 1815–1914* (*c*.1991); and Bernard Gainer, *The Alien Invasion: The Origins of the Aliens Act of 1905* (1972); among several others.
41. 'Foreigners' numbered 50,289 in 1851, and 247,758 in 1901. These figures are summarized in the *1931 Census Report, General Tables*, 240.
42. Germans, Austrians, and Prussians combined, from *1861 Census Report*, vol. 2, p. lxxv.
43. See e.g. Rosemary Ashton, *Little Germany: Exile and Asylum on Victorian England* (Oxford, 1986); Panikos Panayi, *German Immigrants in Britain during the 19th Century, 1815–1914* (Oxford, 1995); Lucio Sponza, *Italian Immigrants in Nineteenth Century Britain: Realities and*

Images (Leicester, 1988); and (for the 'dangers'), Bernard Porter, *The Refugee Question in Mid-Victorian Politics* (Cambridge, 1979).

44. *Foreign* sub-Saharan Africans living in Britain in 1861 numbered 396, and Chinese 146. *1861 Census Report*, vol. 2, p. lxxv.

45. 15,000–20,000 'negroes' were estimated to be living in London in the 1770s. That may have been an exaggeration. James Walvin, *The Black Presence: A Documentary History of the Negro in England, 1555–1860* (1971), 12, 15.

46. Anon. ('Authorship Unacknowledged'), *Narrow Waters, The First Volume of the Life and Thoughts of a Common Man* (1935), 110. See also Robert Roberts, *A Ragged Schooling: Growing up in the Classic Slum* (Manchester, 1971), 110–13.

47. [James Dawson Burn], *Autobiography of a Beggar Boy* (1855), 67–70. Another exception is Helen Corke's recollection of meeting the half-African composer Samuel Coleridge-Taylor, who lived round the corner from her. He had 'a soft step, and a soft, husky voice. He is not tall, but has a large head, with a thick black mop of curls.' Helen Corke, *In Our Infancy: An Autobiography. Part I, 1882–1912* (Cambridge, 1975), 102.

48. Hall, *Civilising Subjects*, 284–5, 289.

49. 100% of Britain's tea came from China in 1831, and 87% in 1875. Indian tea began overtaking it around 1900. William Woodruff, *Impact of Western Man: A Study of Europe's Role in the World Economy 1750–1960* (1966), facing p. 302.

50. 'Man is what he eats.' Ludwig Feuerbach in *Blatter für Literarische Unterhaltung*, 12 Nov. 1850; according to *Quotez*, at www.digiserve.co.uk.

51. 76% of Britain's sugar came from the British West Indies in 1831; but after the abolition of slavery the decline was sharp, the figures being 37% in 1850, 22% in 1875, and 4% in 1900. Brazil, Cuba, and Europe were the main suppliers from the 1870s, with Europe supplying 80% in 1900. Woodruff, *Impact of Western Man*, facing p. 302.

52. Sidney W. Mintz, *Sweetness and Power: The Place of Sugar in Modern History* (New York: 1985), 119.

53. Quoted from *The Rambler* in Revd. Richard Dawes, *Suggestive Hints towards Improved Secular Instruction* (1857), 47.

54. *Guardian*, 3 May 2002. Low as geographical education may be esteemed in Britain today, it was certainly far worse in the 19th century (see below, ch. 4). Making this point at a research seminar in London in 2002, and being met with objections that the Victorians '*must* have known' where their food originated, I asked who in that sophisticated audience could tell me where their red peppers came from. No one knew.

55. David Burton, *The Raj at the Table: A Culinary History of the British in India* (1993), 72–3.

56. The other exception is mulligatawny (*milakutanni*) soup. See Jane Grigson, *English Food* (1974; new edn. 1992), 22, 119–20.

57. See Nupur Chaudhuri, 'Shawls, Jewelry, Curry, and Rice in Victorian Britain', in Chaudhuri and Margaret Strobel (eds.), *Western Women and Imperialism: Complicity and Resistance* (Bloomington, Ind., 1992), 238–41. Though I have taken my evidence from this fascinating paper, my reading of it is different from that of the author, who believes it demonstrates a much deeper imperialisation of British society. For example: 'Since the latter half of the nineteenth century, the imperial ethos was so strongly grafted on to most people *irrespective of their class* and gender that the English families embraced curry

and rice in their diets' (p. 241: emphasis added). (The context makes clear that she means 'since 1850' rather than 'since 1900', which is what 'since the latter half of the 19th century' strictly means.) As all Chaudhuri's sources are either upper-middle-class magazines like the *Ladies Own Paper* and the *Queen*, or cookery books directed to the same constituency; as 'curries' feature so sparcely even in these texts; and as—by her own account—the only places one could buy the ingredients for them were fashionable stores like Fortnum & Mason, I cannot accept the social generalization implied here.

58. 'Curry powder' is another essentially English mutation, according to David Burton, *The Raj at the Table*, 73: 'the idea that a single ready-made spice mixture can be added to fish, chicken, eggs or whatever to produce real Indian "curry" is preposterous, to say the least.'
59. See the list of imported spices in Chaudhuri, 'Shawls, Jewelry, Curry, and Rice', 238.
60. 'Bush and Beach', in *Household Words*, vol. XIX (1859), 365.
61. Chaudhuri, 'Shawls, Jewelry, Curry, and Rice', 238.
62. Samuel Laing, *Notes of a Traveller, on the Social and Political State of France, Prussia, Switzerland, Italy, and other parts of Europe, During the Present Century* (1842), 367–8. His argument was that England's 'greater simplicity and frugality of diet', because it was quicker and cheaper to prepare than continental delicacies, left her people more time and energy for the important things in life, like industry and trade.
63. Chaudhuri, 'Shawls, Jewelry, Curry, and Rice', 232–5. Again, my general interpretation of Chaudhuri's evidence differs from hers. One of her sources for the popularity of cashmere shawls is the 'Sales and Exchange' columns of gentlewomen's magazines; especially advertisements placed by ladies recently returned from India who wished to get rid of their cashmeres, and who seem—significantly?—to have outnumbered those wanting to acquire them.
64. *Brewer's Dictionary of Phrase and Fable*, 'Classic Edition' (1894; repr. New York, 1978), 188.
65. Robert Anderson, *Elgar and Chivalry* (Rickmansworth, 2002), 313.

CHAPTER 3

1. David Cannadine, *The Decline and Fall of the British Aristocracy* (New Haven, Comm., 1990), 420.
2. Ibid. 425.
3. See Patrick Dunae, *Gentlemen Emigrants: From the British Public Schools to the Canadian Frontier* (Vancouver, 1981).
4. 'Cape Sketches', in *Household Words*, vol. I (1850), 608.
5. These are conveniently listed in Chris Cook and Brendan Keith, *British Historical Facts 1830–1900* (1975), 50–1, 272–3; and David Butler and Jennie Freeman, *British Political Facts 1900–1960* (1963), 47–8, 167–8.
6. For army officers see Cannadine, *Decline and Fall*, 264–80, and for bishops, ibid. 427–8.
7. Lance E. Davis and Robert A. Huttenback, *Mammon and the Pursuit of Empire: The Political Economy of British Imperialism* (Cambridge: 1986), ch. 7; P. J. Cain and A. G. Hopkins, *British Imperialism: Innovation and Expansion 1688–1914* (1993), ch. 2.
8. The classic early statement of the theory that the financial classes benefited from imperialism at the expense of the rest of society is J. A. Hobson, *Imperialism: A Study*

(1902), esp. ch. 6. Subsequent scholarship has greatly refined but not essentially supplanted this: e.g. Davis and Huttenback, *Mammon and the Pursuit of Empire*; and Cain and Hopkins, *Innovation and Expansion*, and *British Imperialism: Crisis and Deconstruction 1914–1990* (1993).

9. Anthony Kirk-Greene, *Britain's Imperial Administrators 1858–1966* (2000), 98–9. Most came from army, clerical, old ICS, legal, medical, and business backgrounds.

10. Ibid. 135–7; Robert Heussler, *Yesterday's Rulers: The Making of the British Colonial Service* (Syracuse, NY, 1963), 122.

11. Kirk-Greene, *Britain's Imperial Administrators*, 9–22. This seems to me convincing; but not his argument for an 'unusual spread of the educational catchment area' for imperial administrators, by which he means that they came from *more* public schools than is often assumed (p. 19). That still seems quite narrow to me.

12. Kirk-Greene, *Britain's Imperial Administrators*, 180, tells a nice story about how one applicant for the Sudan Civil Service (this was not Furse's department) was rejected after it was found that he had 'ostentatiously left his copy of *The Times* open so as to reveal the crossword completed'. Finlay Murray, 'The Making of British Policy on Tropical Africa: Approaches to and Influences on Policy-making', Ph.D. thesis, University of Newcastle upon Tyne (2001), 99, suggests that Furse's low regard for academic qualifications may have something to do with the fact that his own Oxford degree was a third.

13. Ralph Furse, *Aucuparius: Recollections of a Recruiting Officer* (1962), 17, 223, 230.

14. Heussler, *Yesterday's Rulers*, 24.

15. He destroyed the Kipling not necessarily on account of its message, however (at that stage in his life), but because it made him look 'pi' (pious) in front of his school chums, which was 'bad form'. Alaric Jacob, *Scenes from a Bourgeois Life* (1949), 26, 69.

16. Kirk-Greene, *Britain's Imperial Administrators*, 100.

17. Percy Young, *Alice Elgar: Enigma of a Victorian Lady* (1978), 20–7, 95.

18. Field-Marshall Lord Birdwood, *Khaki and Gown: An Autobiography* (1941), 25–6, 29, 237, 309–10, 375, 411, 434. The brothers and sons, incidentally, are given names, but the women generally referred to only as 'my sister' or 'my eldest daughter'.

19. This is one B. R. Armstrong, opposing the 'partition of Africa' in a debate at Wellington College in February 1891, reported in the *Wellingtonian*, 12: 1 (Mar. 1891), 10.

20. See David Gilmour, *The Long Recessional: The Imperial Life of Rudyard Kipling* (2002), *passim*.

21. Dennis Kincaid, *British Social Life in India, 1608–1937* (1938; 2nd edn. 1973), 313.

22. Virginia Woolf, *The Years* (1937; new edn. 1968), 302.

23. Ibid. 162. The date is 1911.

24. On this whole question see Elizabeth Buettner, 'From Somebodies to Nobodies: Britons Returning Home from India', in Martin Daunton and Bernhard Rieger (eds.), *Meanings of Modernity: Britain from the Late-Victorian Era to World War II* (2001), 221–40. The 'Norbiton' reference is on p. 231.

25. This comes from the *Cornhill Magazine*, and must be from the late 1890s, for the full article is about Kipling, and Ann Elgar, whose scrapbooks it is taken from, died in 1900. Quoted in Robert Anderson, *Elgar and Chivalry* (2002), 34.

26. Earl Grey, *The Colonial Policy of Lord John Russell's Administration* (1853), i. 4–15.

27. Anna Gambles, *Protection and Politics: Conservative Economic Discourse, 1815–1852* (1999), 150.

28. *Hansard*, 3rd ser., 169 (5 Feb. 1863), col. 96.

29. *Westminster Review*, N.S., 38 (July 1870), 55, 61. The 'back foot' expression is sometimes thought to imply defensive play. Anyone with a knowledge of cricket knows that the most basic 'defensive' shot is in fact a 'forward' one, and that runs can be scored as easily off the back as off the front foot. That suits my use of the metaphor here, however, which is meant to imply aggression against some fast or clever bowling by the other side.
30. Grey, *Colonial Policy*, 12; and cf. E. G. Wakefield, quoted in *Edinburgh Review*, 93 (1851), 882; and *Westminster Review*, N.S., 37 (1870), 65, 73–4.
31. *Edinburgh Review*, 91 (1850), 61 (italics added). Is this the first application of the 'sun never sets' phrase to the British empire? Long before this, it was used in the 16th and 17th centuries to describe the Spanish and Dutch empires: see *Brewer's Dictionary of Phrase and Fable*, Millenium Edition (2001), 391.
32. *Cornhill Magazine*, 2 (1860), 121. The author was J. W. Kaye, an Indian Civil Servant and noted military historian (*Wellesley Index of Victorian Periodicals*).
33. The free-trade imperialist argument was that it was only Britain's rule over her colonies that kept them true to free trade: e.g. *Westminster Review*, 2: 2 (Oct. 1852), 19. This argument was weakened when colonies imposed their own tariffs regardless, as the *Edinburgh Review* pointed out in January 1870 (131: 287, p. 107). The *Westminster*'s retort (N.S., 38 (July 1870), 61–2) that those tariffs would have been even higher without the colonial connection seems weak.
34. Carnarvon in the House of Lords, 14 Feb. 1870 (*Hansard*, 3rd ser., vol. 199, col. 212). The *Westminster Review* fairly summarized the two sides of this argument thus: 'Strict economists, reasoning from tangible interests alone, say that we should be as well without it [the empire]; others, professing to take a wider view of the subject, affirm that it brings us many advantages besides those which can be computed': N.S., 2: 2 (Oct. 1852), 8. The latter tack is also taken by the *Edinburgh Review*, 93 (1851), 477; by Arthur Mills, in *Colonial Constitutions* (1856), quoted in C. A. Bodelsen, *Studies in Mid-Victorian Imperialism* (Copenhagen, 1924, reissued London, 1990), 40; and by Thomas Carlyle with his attack on 'the Gospel of M'Croudy', quoted in ibid. 25.
35. *Westminster Review*, N.S., 38 (July 1870), 48.
36. e.g. Earl Grey, *Colonial Policy*, i. 15, and ii. 121; *Edinburgh Review*, 98: 199 (July 1853), 71.
37. *Edinburgh Review*, 93 (Apr. 1851), 490.
38. *Hansard*, 3rd ser., 41 (6 Mar. 1838), col. 483. This does not necessarily follow. America's presence in the empire would have strengthened the anti-abolition lobby.
39. Charles Ellis in House of Commons, 18 Mar. 1825, in *Hansard*, 2nd ser., 23, col. 1085.
40. Earl Grey, for example, warned of the Maoris' total extermination if Britain did not use her imperial authority to curb the settlers there, in *Colonial Policy*, 15.
41. *Hansard*, 3rd ser., 29 (14 July 1835), col. 552.
42. *Edinburgh Review*, 131: 287 (Jan. 1870), 104. Gladstone believed that 'despotism' was 'monstrous' for 'free-born Englishmen' but quite allowable for 'primitive' peoples: *Hansard*, 3rd ser. 121 (21 May 1852), col. 955.
43. This was (the Liberal) Sir Charles Dilke's—slightly unusual—position, in his famous *Greater Britain* (1868).
44. This is one of the themes of my *Britannia's Burden: The Political Evolution of Modern Britain 1851–1990* (1994), 22–3 *et passim*.

45. See e.g. *Chambers's Information for the People*, 1 (1840), 379; and *Good Words*, 1 (1860), 251.
46. *Edinburgh Review*, 129 (1869), 480.
47. Bernard Semmel, *Democracy versus Empire: The Jamaica Riots of 1865 and the Governor Eyre Controversy* (1962; New York edn. 1969), 87.
48. See Malcolm I. Thomis and Peter Holt, *Threats of Revolution in Britain 1789–1848* (1977); and, for the subsequent period, Donald Richter, *Riotous Victorians* (1981).
49. *Working Man*, 2 (1866), 199.
50. David Cannadine, *Ornamentalism: How the British Saw Their Empire* (2001), e.g. p. 8.
51. Imogen Thomas, *Haileybury 1806–1987* (Haileybury, 1987), 6–7. It boasted none other than Thomas Malthus as its first 'Professor of History and Political Economy'.
52. Ibid. 43.
53. W. E. Bowen, *Edward Bowen, a Memoir* (1902), 115.
54. J. G. Cotton Minchin, *Old Harrow Days* (1898), 114. It was Montague Butler, head of Harrow 1860–85, who instituted a modern history prize (the Bourchier) in 1866, mindful that history was 'not as powerful at Harrow as it ought to be'. Edward Graham, *The Harrow Life of Henry Montague Butler* (1920), 188.
55. Bowen, *Edward Bowen*, 108.
56. Minchin, *Old Harrow Days*, 115.
57. H. A. L. Fisher, *An Unfinished Autobiography* (1940), 40.
58. M. V. Hughes, *A London Family 1870–1900: A Trilogy* (1981), 55, 126.
59. Ronald Hyam, 'The Study of Imperial and Commonwealth History at Cambridge, 1881–1981', *Journal of Imperial and Commonwealth History*, 29 (2001), 76.
60. J. R. Seeley, *The Expansion of England* (1883), 7–10; Gustav Adolf Rein (trans. J. L. Herkless), *Sir John Robert Seeley: A Study of the Historian* (1987; original edn. 1912), 28; and see Peter Burroughs, 'John Robert Seeley and British Imperial History', *Journal of Imperial and Commonwealth History*, 1 (1973); James G. Greenlee, '"A Succession of Seeleys": The "Old School" Re-examined', *Journal of Imperial and Commonwealth History*, 4 (1976); Deborah Wormell, *Sir John Seeley and the Uses of History* (Cambridge, 1980); Christopher Parker, *The English Historical Tradition Since 1850* (1990), 67; and P. B. M. Blaas, *Continuity and Anachronism: Parliamentary and Constitutional Development in Whig Historiography and in the Anti-Whig Reaction Between 1890 and 1930* (1978), 36–40.
61. Hyam, 'Imperial and Commonwealth History at Cambridge', 76, 79; and my own recollections of the Cambridge History Tripos in the 1960s in the Preface.
62. Frederick Madden, 'The Commonwealth, Commonwealth History, and Oxford, 1905–1971', in Madden and D. K. Fieldhouse (eds.), *Oxford and the Idea of Commonwealth* (1982), 8–9; and Ronald Robinson, 'Oxford in Imperial Historiography', in ibid.
63. Quoted in James G. Greenlee, *Education and Imperial Unity, 1901–26* (1987), 29.
64. Madden, 'Commonwealth History and Oxford', 9.
65. Greenlee, *Education and Imperial Unity*, 115; Madden, 'Commonwealth History and Oxford', 15. Egerton in his Inaugural Lecture also regretted that the main Oxford history syllabus stopped in 1837, the very 'starting-point of the self-governing British Empire of today'. Quoted in Richard Aldrich, 'Imperialism in the Study and Teaching of History', in J. A. Mangan, *Benefits Bestowed? Education and British Imperialism* (Manchester, 1988), 29. Against this it should be pointed out that Oxford had long been a distinguished centre for the study of Indian history; and that both universities housed

some dons who wrote about the subject, even if they did not teach it. Madden, 'Commonwealth History and Oxford', 8, 14.

66. See Walter Frewen Lord, 'The Lost Empire of England', *Nineteenth Century*, 65 (1909), 238.
67. P. E. Lewin, 'The Co-ordination of Colonial Studies', *United Empire*, 4 (1913), 487–97.
68. Rein, *Seeley*, 71; and Wormell, *Sir John Seeley*, 67, which suggests that he was influenced by the German nationalist school.
69. The proportion varied from school to school. Those most patronized by imperial and military families were probably Haileybury, which when it was refounded deliberately exploited its colonial links by advertising in Indian newspapers: Thomas, *Haileybury*, 32; the United Services College at Westward Ho! in Devon, which was a kind of poor Service-man's equivalent; and Wellington College in Berkshire, founded in 1856 in memory of the great Duke.
70. I have consulted a sample of these only, from the 1860s, when the genre properly starts up, to the 1900s. This comprises: the *Brentwoodian* (only because it was my own school); the *Cliftonian*; the *Etonian* (very early); the *Haileyburian*; the *Harrovian*; the *Malvernian*; the *Marlburian*; the *Radleian*; the *New Rugbeian*; the *Wellingtonian*; and the *Wykehamist*.
71. *Wellingtonian*, section on 'Wellington Abroad', in most issues after 1889.
72. The *Cliftonian* for example printed regular dispatches in 1879–81 from an OC calling himself 'One of the "Bengal Tigers"' fighting in the Afghan wars: e.g. vol. 5 (1877–9), 398–402; vol. 6 (1879–81), 1–6, 41–4, 86–90, 376–79. Other examples taken at random are 'Through Africa to Lake Nyassa', *Haileyburian*, 180 (1889) 253–7; 'My Experience with the Mandalay Man-Eater', *Malvernian*, 174 (1890), 3–4; 'Half a Day in the Queensland Bush', *Wellingtonian*, 12: 12 (1892), 181–3; reports of visiting lectures on 'Melanesia', *Radleian*, 146 (1884), 611, and 'Canada', *Haileyburian*, 307 (1901) 328. By the 1890s most issues carry *something* imperial, with the possible exception of the *Marlburian*, where sport hogs more of the space than in the other magazines. Most of the reports from the colonies describe 'adventures' of one kind or another.
73. e.g. *Marlburian* (13 Oct. 1890), 142; *Wellingtonian* (July 1892), 184; *Wykehamist* (19 Dec. 1893), 453; *Harrovian* (26 Feb. 1898), 3; *Marlburian* (10 Oct. 1900), 319.
74. See Patrick A. Dunae, 'Education, Emigration and Empire: The Colonial College, 1887–1905', in Mangan, *'Benefits Bestowed'*.
75. *Wellingtonian*, 11: 9 (9 Dec. 1889), 138–9.
76. e.g. *Radleian*, 169 (Dec. 1886).
77. Out of 125 substantial articles or reports featuring separate colonies in my sample, before October 1899 when South Africa came to dominate, 37% were about India, 19% about Egypt, the Middle East and North Africa, 12% about tropical Africa, 9% about South Africa, 9% about Australia and New Zealand, and 5% about Canada. One of the rare pieces on Australasia, in the *Wellingtonian* (Sept. 1885), 98–101, is subtitled 'A tale hitherto untold'.
78. John Roach, *A History of Secondary Education in England 1800–1870* (1986), 129. Where public schools also had 'day boys', it is arguable that the gulf between them and the boarders was greater than between them and non-public school boys. See Bernard Porter, 'Boarder or Day Boy?', *London Review of Books* (15 July 1999), 13–15.
79. Welldon, 'The Imperial Aspects of Education', *Proceedings of the Royal Colonial Institute 1894–95* (1895), 333. According to Welldon, Harrow was supposed to have a particular

affinity with the empire; it was no coincidence, he claimed in that same lecture, that they both originated in Elizabeth's reign. The key year was 1572, when Harrow was founded, and Drake started out on his first circumnavigation (p. 325). He returned to this theme often; in an 1899 essay on 'Schoolmasters', quoted in Rupert Wilkinson, *The Prefects: British Leadership and the Public School Tradition* (1964), 101, for example: 'An English Headmaster, as he looks to the future of his pupils, will not forget that they are destined to be the citizens of the greatest empire under heaven... He will inspire them with faith in the divinely ordered mission of their country and their race'; and in his two sets of memoirs, *Recollections and Reflections* (1915), 137–41, and *Forty Years On: Lights and Shadows* (1935), 119–20. Winston Churchill was at Harrow in Welldon's time, and famously unhappy there, which does not mean that the latter may not have worked his magic on him.

80. John Roach in *Secondary Education in England*, 133–43 *passim*, nominates Warre of Eton, Thring of Uppingham, Moss of Shrewsbury, Johnson of Eton, and Butler of Harrow, as well as Welldon.

81. Examples are given in J. A. Mangan, 'Images of Empire in the Late Victorian Public School', in *Journal of Educational Administration History*, 12: 1 (1980), 34. F. W. Farrar, '*In the Days of Thy Youth': Sermons on Practical Subjects, preached at Marlborough College from 1871 to 1876* (1876), carries some good examples, especially Sermons 2 and 34.

82. The three named ones come from the *Haileyburian* (7 Mar. 1889), 194–5, (27 June 1891), 164–5, and the *Malvernian* (Nov. 1876), 396.

83. e.g. a lecture by H. F. Wilson on Imperial Federation, reported in the *Wykehamist*, 225 (1887), 189 ('great applause'); George Parkin on 'War and the Empire', reported in the *Marlburian*, 542 (1900), 271–3 ('immense cheers'); and a lecture by Lieut H. T. C. Knox on the Navy League, which received 'tumultous applause' at Marlborough in 1899: *Marlburian*, 531 (1899), 128–9, and then 'vociferous applause' at Winchester in 1902: *Wykehamist*, 397 (1902), 461. Geoffrey Drage's *Eton and the Empire*, delivered at the college on 15 November 1890, was separately published shortly afterwards.

84. See e.g. *Wellingtonian* (Apr. 1870), 133; *Haileyburian* (17 Oct. 1889) 367–8.

85. *Brentwoodian* (Oct. 1891), 9.

86. Published in 1857. The main imperial reference is Tom East's going off to soldier in India after leaving Rugby, but then—as recounted in *Tom Brown at Oxford* (1861)—becoming disillusioned with the work there, resigning, and emigrating to New Zealand. None of Tom's other schoolmates land up in the colonies. There are also proud references to Browns (meant to be a typical 'yeoman' family) and Old Rugbeians 'leaving their marks in American forests and Australian uplands' (p. 2) and living 'under the Indian sun and in Australian towns and clearings' (p. 219); a veiled criticism of the way the empire is run (p. 355); and some very tangental references to 'the great lake in Central Africa' (p. 18), 'Hottentot kraals' (p. 19), 'Border-ruffians' (p. 283), and 'a South-sea island, with the Cherokees or Patagonians, or some such wild niggers': this to comically illustrate Arthur's geographical ignorance (p. 310). (Page references are to the OUP 'World's Classics' edn., 1989.) Frederic W. Farrar's sanctimonious and cloying *Eric, or Little by Little* (1858) has fewer imperial references, apart from Eric's parents, who are serving in India, which he remembers only as 'a distant golden haze'; and a school friend, Horace, who lands an Indian cadetship.

87. See Geoffrey Best, 'Militarism and the Victorian Public School', in Brian Simon and Ian Bradley (eds.), *The Victorian Public School* (1975), 136–8; Archibald Fox, *Public School Life: Harrow* (1911), 59. Queen Victoria was so delighted with Warre of Eton's efforts in this area that she gave him the VD (Volunteer [Officers'] Decoration): C. R. L. Fletcher, *Edmond Warre* (1922), 156.
88. e.g. 'Our Colonial Policy' by 'an Old Harrovian', *Harrovian* (11 Dec. 1869), 62–3; Anon., 'Our Austral Empire', *Wellingtonian* (Sept. 1885), 98–101; and a review of Drage's *Eton and the Empire*, in *Wykehamist* (22 Dec. 1890), 106.
89. Examples: motions to pull out of India were lost 11 : 4 at Radley in 1867: *Radleian* (Dec. 1867), 2; and 10 : 5 at Winchester in 1877: *Wykehamist* (Dec. 1877), 123. At Malvern a motion to give up the entire empire was lost 20 : 8 in 1876: *Malvernian* (Nov. 1876), 400–1. Wellington voted by 32 : 14 for *immediate* war with Russia to preserve the Indian empire in 1885: *Wellingtonian*, 9: 5 (1885); Winchester approved Britain's *permanent* occupation of Egypt in 1893 by 20 votes to 4: *Wykehamist*, 286 (1893), 327; Wellington carried Imperial Federation in 1890 'by a large majority': *Wellingtonian*, 12: 3 (1891), 41–2; and the Boer War was approved by Harrow 41 : 12, and by Winchester 56 : 16, both in 1900: *Harrovian*, 13: 2 (1900), 29, and *Wykehamist*, 366 (1900) 145–7. It is interesting in this connection that there were large votes for 'fair' as opposed to 'free' trade at Wellington in 1885 ('by acclamation'): *Wellingtonian*, 9: 8 (1885), 119–20; and Winchester in 1902 (34 : 19): *Wykehamist*, 389 (1902), 376.
90. *Wykehamist*, 369 (May 1900), 172–3. There is a photograph of the Harrow celebrations in the *Harrovian*, 13: 5 (July 1900), 64.
91. *Rugbeian*, 6 (1860), 231–6; *Haileyburian* (10 Oct. 1882), 446–7.
92. Gordon is commemorated in Greek in the *Harrovian* (10 July 1884), 77; in Latin in the *Radleian* (Dec. 1885), 728; and in English in the *Haileyburian* (8 Apr. 1884), 205 and the *Harrovian* (6 July 1899), 55. There are also poems to Bartle Frere in the *Haileyburian* (25 June 1884), 268–9; to Wolfe in the *Wellingtonian* (Mar. 1889), 21; and 'In Memory of an Officer Killed at the Battle of Abu Klea' (Colonel Fred Burnaby?), in the *Haileyburian* (8 Apr. 1885), 438.
93. *Marlburian* (22 May 1866), 129–31.
94. Quoted in John MacKenzie, *Propaganda and Empire* (Manchester, 1984), 194. Attlee was an Old Haileyburian.
95. See. A. L. Rowse, *A Cornish Childhood* (1942), 184; E. C. Mack, *Public Schools and British Opinion Since 1860* (New York, 1941), 124; Brian Simon's Introduction to Simon and Bradley (eds.), *The Victorian Public School*, 15; T. W. Bamford, 'Thomas Arnold and the Victorian Idea of a Public School', in ibid. 64.
96. *Radleian* (Dec. 1873), 1.
97. *Brentwoodian* (Apr. 1900), 1.
98. *Marlburian*, 537 (7 Mar. 1900), 205–6. It is in a group of five *comic* war poems, and begins: 'There was an old fellow called Cronje.'
99. *Haileyburian* (8 Mar. 1883), 521–2; (Nov. 1883), 96–7.
100. *Brentwoodian* (Dec. 1900), 6; and see R. R. Lewis, *The History of Brentwood School* (Brentwood, 1981), 235. An earlier Volunteer Rifle Corps had been set up in 1861, but collapsed in 1870. At that time the school had only 87 pupils. Ibid. 147–8.
101. Duff Cooper, *Old Men Forget* (1953), 20.
102. *Radleian* (Feb. 1884), 611.

103. In my sample they quadrupled, on average, around the time of the Boer War.
104. J. E. C. Welldon, *Forty Years On: Lights and Shadows* (1935), 121; *Radleian* (Mar. 1869), 1; *Haileyburian* (14 Mar. 1885), 421; and *Harrovian* (12 Feb. 1880), 129: which, however, also suggested that boys became wiser and so more Liberal as they moved up the school.
105. Bowen, *Edward Bowen*, 120.
106. See the *Haileyburian*, 13: 294 (Mar. 1900), 106–7. Attlee claimed that 72 of them were punished in this way: Attlee, *As it Happened* [n.d.], 19. The boys had demanded a half-holiday, and when the head refused this had broken bounds by marching to Hertford to express their patriotism, noisily. Lyttelton protested that he had beaten them only very lightly—'four of the gentlest possible strokes' (but that makes 288 strokes altogether). Nonetheless he was castigated in the press over this as a 'pro-Boer'.
107. Christopher Hollis, *Eton: A History* (1960), 295–6.
108. *Harrovian* (14 Dec. 1878), 11.
109. e.g. a pacifist poem in the *Haileyburian* (5 June 1872), 81; and a pro-Home Rule piece in the *Malvernian* (Apr. 1892), 209–11.
110. See e.g. the 1867 Radley, 1876 Malvern, and 1877 Winchester votes recorded above, n. 89.
111. *Haileyburian* (18 Mar. 1885), 420–2. There were also near-unanimous anti-government votes recorded in the *Harrovian* (3 Mar. 1885), 20; and the *Wellingtonian* (Apr. 1885).
112. *Wellingtonian* (Mar. 1991), 10.
113. *Radleian* (Dec. 1867), 2; *Malvernian* (Dec. 1873), 101; *Haileyburian* (12 Dec. 1883), 157–8; ibid. (17 Oct. 1890), 40–1 (the opponent here was one L. G. Curtis, soon to become a leading imperialist ideologue); *Wellingtonian* (Mar. 1891), 9–11.
114. *Wykehamist*, 367 (Mar. 1900), 152–3 (Federation); 296 (Dec. 1893), 443 (Rhodes); 379 (Mar. 1901), 267 (Chamberlain, though in this case the majority voted for him); 364 (Nov. 1899), 126 (Boer War); and 391 (Apr. 1902), 396–8 (unpopularity).
115. Quoted in Simon and Bradley (eds.), *The Victorian Public School*, 16. Clifton has a particular reputation for bone-headed imperialism, due in part to Henry Newbolt's famous mystical-imperialist poem about its chapel; but it also tolerated independence of mind, according to Arthur Quiller-Couch, *Memories and Opinions* (1944), 62.
116. Orwell, *Such, Such were the Joys* (1957), first essay, on his experiences at St Cyprian's: 'It is not easy for me to think of my schooldays without seeming to breathe in a whiff of something cold and evil-smelling . . .' (p. 35); and Alaric Jacob, *Scenes from a Bourgeois Life* (1949), 55–69 *passim*. Of the 'Cambridge Four', Burgess was at Eton, Maclean at Gresham's, Philby at Westminster, and Blunt at Marlborough.
117. *Wellingtonian* (June 1889), 65.
118. 'The Palladium of this country, whatever cynics and philosophers may say to the contrary, is its respect for its womankind': Drage, *Eton and the Empire* (Eton, 1890), 17.
119. Welldon, *Recollections and Reflections*, 80–1. At Eton new headmasters were solemnly presented by the captain of the school with a birch tied up with blue ribbons. C. R. L. Fletcher, *Edmond Warre*, 179, calls it 'the most sacred symbol of office'.
120. Drage, *Eton and Empire*, 11.
121. Mack, *Public Schools . . . since 1860*, 107.
122. J. G. Fitch, *Lectures on Teaching* (1881), 50–1.
123. e.g. Drage, *Eton and the Empire*, 17.

124. Quoted in Kirk-Greene, *Britain's Imperial Administrators*, 96. In some cases it is clear that scholarship and intelligence were distrusted per se; the somewhat unscholarly Welldon of Harrow, for example, puzzled and irritated by Edward Bowen's radicalism, comforted himself by attributing it to the latter's cleverness: Welldon, *Recollections and Reflections*, 129.
125. J. R. de S. Honey, *Tom Brown's Universe: The Development of the Victorian Public School* (1977), 114.
126. Examples are given in Mack, *Public Schools and British Opinion Since 1860*, 219–21; including a fierce debate in the correspondence columns of *The Times* in January 1903.
127. Welldon, 'The Imperial Aspects of Education', 329.
128. Quoted in J. A. Mangan, 'Athleticism: A Case Study of the Evolution of an Educational Ideology', in Simon and Bradley (eds.), *The Victorian Public School*, 158.
129. Quoted in Richard Holt, *Sport and the British* (1989), 92; and cf. Welldon, *Recollections and Reflections* (1915), 98: do not 'forget that boys, if they are not playing games, may be doing worse things'.
130. On this topic generally, see J. A. Mangan: *Athleticism and the Victorian and Edwardian Public School* (1981), *The Games Ethic and Imperialism* (1986), and (ed.), *The Cultural Bond: Sport, Empire, Society* (1992).
131. Rudyard Kipling, *Stalky and Co.* (1899; this edn., St Martin's Library, 1962), 180, 184. This is a Conservative MP who comes to lecture them on 'the Flag'. He also offends them because of the assumption that they *need* to be lectured on patriotism; and because his talk interferes with their clandestine brewing activities.
132. 'I'll sing you a good old song / Made by a good old pate, / Of a fine old English gentleman, / Who kept an old estate'—in the old feudal manner; 'For while he feasted all the great, / He ne'er forget the small . . . ' etc. Then comes the moral: 'Now surely this is better far / Than all the new parade / Of theatres and fancy balls, / "At Home", and masquerade . . . ' This is neither an inclusive nor an aggressive patriotism. For its popularity, see e.g. G. K. Chesterton, *Autobiography* (1936), 11; and an article on 'Songs' in the *New Rugbeian* (Dec. 1861), 290. It is the latter that characterizes it as a 'patriotic song'.
133. Bowen, *Edward Bowen*, 176; which also reproduces most of his songs, only one of which, 'The Khalifa, 1898', is on an empire-related topic.
134. *Wellingtonian* (Nov. 1891), 97–8.
135. Quoted in Honey, *Tom Brown's Universe*, 55.
136. Paraphrased in ibid. 149; which also quotes Canon Bell of Marlborough: 'parents are the last people who ought to be allowed to have children.'
137. Rowse, *A Cornish Childhood*, 185–6 (italics added). See also Honey, *Tom Brown's Universe*, 123.
138. See also Quiller-Couch, *Memories and Opinions*, 63, which recalls intelligence and free thinking being cultivated well at Clifton in the 1870s, despite its 'cult of Roman stoicism and service', from which he observed other pupils suffering more.
139. Honey, *Tom Brown's Universe*, 41. Even after this there were some fairly serious rebellions, including a gunpowder plot at Eton in 1879: ibid. 106–8.
140. Honey, *Tom Brown's Universe*, 225; and cf. T. W. Bamford, *The Rise of the Public Schools* (1967), 64.
141. Harold E. Gorst, *The Curse of Education* (1901), 50.

142. See Brian Simon and Ian Bradley (eds.), *The Victorian Public School*, 15.
143. Quoted in Fletcher, *Warre*, 162.
144. Robert Cecil, *A Great Experiment: An Autobiography* (1941), 14.
145. G. B. Grundy, *Fifty-five Years at Oxford: An Unconventional Autobiography* (1945), 63.
146. Fletcher, *Warre*, 232.
147. Anon., 'Our Colonial Policy', *Harrovian* (11 Dec. 1869), 62.
148. M. S. Ware, *Haileyburian* (17 Oct. 1898), 41.
149. One example of many is Thomas Hodgkin, 'The Fall of the Roman Empire and its Lessons For Us': an address delivered to the Social and Political Education League in 1897, and published in *Contemporary Review*, 73 (1898). Anti-imperialists also used the Roman analogy as a warning: e.g. a Mr Bowden in a school debate at Malvern, reported in the *Malvernian* (Nov. 1876), 401; and a Mr Domenichetti at Haileybury, reported in the *Haileyburian* (15 Mar. 1881), 70. See also Raymond Betts, 'The Allusion to Rome in British Imperialist Thought of the Late Nineteenth and Early Twentieth Centuries', *Victorian Studies*, 15: 2 (1971), 149–59.
150. Some schools were more empire orientated than others; but it has been calculated that e.g. just 2.3% of Cheltenham College leavers joined the various colonial services between 1841 and 1910; between 2.2 and 5% of Wykehamists over roughly the same period; and a similar proportion of Rugbeians in certain sample years: 7% of the class of 1840; 1.5% in 1860; 0.65% in 1875, and 2% in 1885. See Bamford, *Rise of the Public Schools*, 219 (for Cheltenham); T. J. H. Bishop, *Winchester and the Public School Élite* (1967), 64–8; and calculations based on *Rugby School Registers*, vols. 1–3 (Rugby, 1886, 1891). The most aristocratic schools tended to spurn colonial service, except at the very highest level, like Viceroy of India. Eton provided 9 out of 22 of these between 1798 and 1898, but scarcely any colonial middle management. See Bamford, *Rise of the Public Schools*, 216, 239.

    The inclusion of imperial soldiering would boost these figures considerably—adding about 10% to all of them—and there is no way of telling how many who went into the Church ended up as missionaries or colonial bishops; or if they chose business careers, became Malayan rubber planters or West African factors. One account claims that a third of boys from some public schools were finding their way to the colonies by one route or another by the 1880s, which could be true in a small number of cases: Avril Maddrell, 'Empire, Emigration and School Geography: Changing Discourses of Imperial Citizenship, 1880–1925', *Journal of Historical Geography*, 22: 4 (1996), 378; although no source or rationale for this figure is provided here. A safer overall estimate—administrators plus military plus church- and businessmen, together with a few emigrants, and sundry others—might be about 20%.
151. On 'crammers', see Kirk-Greene, *Britain's Imperial Administrators*, 97–8. Oxford taught Indian history to ICS probationers from the 1880s; Cambridge first put on an extension course in imperial history in 1893. Madden, 'Commonwealth History and Oxford', 8, 10, 14.
152. e.g. J. H. Stocqueler, *A Familiar History of British India, from the Earliest Period to the Transfer of the Government of India to the British Crown in 1858* [n.d.], which is advertised 'for the use of schools and colleges', but was probably only read by those preparing for service in India. Its whole ethos is totally different from—e.g. much more racist than—that of genuine school textbooks, which are treated in the following chapter. In 1843

Stocqueler (1800–85) returned from India to establish an East Indian Institute of his own in London (*DNB*). His other books—all for the Anglo-Indian market—are *The Handbook of India, A Guide to the Stranger and Traveller, and a Companion to the Resident* (1845); *The Oriental Interpreter and Treasury of East India Knowledge* (1848); *The Overland Companion: being a Guide for the Traveller to India via Egypt* (1850); and *India: Its History, Climate, Productions, and Field Sports; with Notices of European Life and Manners, and of the various Travelling Routes* (1853).

153. Hughes, *Tom Brown's Schooldays* 255, 283. On the question of class and race generally, see D. A. Lorimer, *Colour, Class and the Victorians: English Attitudes to the Negro in the Mid-19th Century* (Leicester, 1978).

154. As described in David Cannadine, *Ornamentalism: How the British Saw Their Empire* (2001); whose subtitle however is misleading, if it is meant to imply that this was a widespread view.

155. T. W. Bamford, 'Thomas Arnold and the Victorian Idea of a Public School', 63; and see Hollis, *Eton*, 288.

156. See Archibald Fox, *Public School Life: Harrow* (1911), 76; and the episodes in Hughes's *Tom Brown's Schooldays* where the college boys come into contact with plebs: pp. 86, 255, 275.

157. J. E. C. Welldon, *Recollections and Reflections* (1915), 90.

158. Fletcher, *Warre*, 225. Apparently in MI5 in the 1940s the snobs employed the same means to discomfit an unpopular—because merely grammar-school-educated—director general. Christopher Andrew, *Secret Service: The Making of the British Intelligence Community* (1985), 489.

159. Graham, *Harrow Life of... Butler*, 319.

160. Basil Maine, *The Best of Me: A Study in Autobiography* (1937), 124. According to the *Dictionary of National Biography, 1931–40* (Oxford, 1949), 896, he was once 'severely jostled by a party of miners and very nearly rolled into the river'. There were some exceptions: e.g. Frederick Temple, head of Rugby 1858–69, who had worked as a farm labourer as a boy; there was a story about him that when a young Rugbeian objected to mucking out a pigsty he took the shovel and did it himself: Alicia Percival, *Very Superior Men: Some Early Public School Headmasters and their Achievements* (1973), 168; and (when he was not talking Latin) Edmond Warre, according to the *Dictionary of National Biography, 1912–21* (Oxford, 1927), 555.

161. See e.g. Martin J. Wiener, *English Culture and the Decline of the Industrial Spirit 1850–1980* (Cambridge, 1981), 16–24; Corelli Barnett, *The Audit of War* (1986), 214–23.

162. Vachel, *The Hill*, e.g. p. 152. His name is Beaumont-Greene.

163. e.g. Farrar, '*In the Days of thy Youth*', 241; Drage, *Eton and the Empire*, 8, and the attack on Cobdenism on pp. 11–12. On the other hand Drage also inveighs against the 'snobbery... of being ashamed of trade' (p. 28); and J. G. Cotton Minchin, *Old Harrow Days* (1898), 47, represents it as 'one of the few *drawbacks* of a public school that you do not meet with boys who can ever claim to be self-made' (italics added); until, that is, the likes of Beaumont-Greene came along.

164. Drage, *Eton and the Empire*, 8–9.

165. John Huntley Skrine, 'The Romance of School', *Contemporary Review*, 73 (1898), 438. The 'chivalry' image is ubiquitous. See e.g. Lionel Cust's description, in *A History of Eton College* (1899), 294, of the ideal Etonian as 'A verray perfait gentil knight'.

166. See T. W. Bamford, 'Thomas Arnold and the Victorian Idea of a Public School', in Simon and Bradley (eds.), *The Victorian Public School*; and the early chapters of Hughes's *Tom Brown's Schooldays*.
167. See Kathleen Woodroofe, *From Charity to Social Work in England and the United States* (1962), ch. 3.
168. e.g. the account of a visit to the 'Wellington College Working Men's Club' in Walworth Road, London, in the *Wellingtonian* (June 1886), 209–11. Eton's 'mission' in Hackney Wick was a failure according to C. R. L. Fletcher: 'it must be confessed that they have done little to bring rich and poor as a whole on to a common level, and little to leaven the mass of unthrift [*note*] and squalor which pullulates in the East End... Let us be frank, and say such things are not "natural" subjects of interest even to the most high-minded boys': *Warre*, 137–8.
169. Drage, *Eton and the Empire*, 25; and cf. W. R. Lawson, *John Bull and His Schools* (Edinburgh, 1908), 218.
170. P. McIntosh, *Physical Education in England Since 1800* (1952), 145–8; R. J. W. Selleck, *The New Education 1870–1914* (1968), 172.
171. Skrine, 'The Romance of School', 437.
172. Honey, *Tom Brown's Universe*, 152.
173. W. D. Rubinstein, 'Education and the Social Origins of British Elites, 1880–1970', *Past and Present*, 112 (1986), 203. This is Rubinstein's *maximum* figure for the 'candidate group' for elite recruitment.
174. Geoffrey Best, 'Militarism and the Victorian Public School', in Simon and Bradley (eds.), *The Victorian Public School*, 130 (emphasis added). Best gives three examples: the adoption of the 'house' system in the new 'Borstals' of the 1900s; the popularity of public-school stories; and the working classes' acceptance of the public-school-educated officer class in World War I.
175. There is no mention of any specifically imperialistic propaganda in the famous (and critical) accounts of their preparatory schools by George Orwell, *Such, Such were the Joys*, and Alaric Jacob, *Scenes from a Bourgeois Life*; although R. D. Pearce, 'The Prep School and Imperialism: The Example of Orwell's St Cyprian's', *Journal of Educational Administration and History*, 23 (1991), argues persuasively that it was implied there. This of course relates to the early 20th century. For the earlier period, Donald Leinster-Murray analyses the 'imperialism' taught in 'prep' schools in 'The Nineteenth-Century English Preparatory School: Cradle and Crèche of Empire', in Mangan, *Benefits Bestowed?* His evidence for it, however, is somewhat thin, boiling down in effect to (1) some sermons given by the head of Elstree School which 'obliquely'—Leinster-Murray's word—bear on empire; (2) stories written by the head of Eagle House School for the *Boy's Own Paper* extolling 'adventure, fair play, and sportsmanship' (only); and (3) the assertion that Fletcher and Kipling's notoriously imperialistic *School History of England* (1911) was 'probably' (*sic*) a main text. One would have expected there to be more overtly imperialist content than that.
176. e.g. the *Brentwoodian*, 1891–1903, where the only articles about India are from a letter from an ex-tea planter about 'sport' there (Dec. 1891), 3–4; and an interview with 'The Last Survivor of Cawnpore' (July 1895), 7–8. All other empire-related features are about South Africa of course: (1899), 2 *et passim*; Australia and Canada (e.g. Dec. 1898), 5; (Dec. 1900), 2; or else general encomiums on the empire, generally arising from a

royal event, like the Jubilees, or Victoria's death (Oct. 1896), 1; (Mar. 1901), 1. Brentwood was effectively a new creation in the 1890s, though it claimed continuity from a grammar school founded in 1557. Lewis, *History of Brentwood School*, 186–7.

177. Joseph Schumpeter, *The Sociology of Imperialism* (first German edn. 1919; this edn., New York, 1955), 22. Schumpeter's main target was the Hobson–Lenin 'capitalist' theory of imperialism.
178. Quoted in Peter Fleming, *Invasion 1940* (1957), 192.

CHAPTER 4

1. They are listed in in J. A. Gallagher and R. E. Robinson, 'The Imperialism of Free Trade', *Economic History Review*, 6 (1953), 2–3.
2. One was to be for the upper middle and professional classes; another for boys destined for the army and 'lower' branches of the legal and medical professions; and the third for the children of tenant farmers and small tradesmen. Brian Simon, *The State and Educational Change: Essays in the History of Education and Pedagogy* (1994), 37.
3. Quoted in Richard Altick, *The English Common Reader: A Social History of the Mass Reading Public 1800–1900* (Chicago, 1957), 148.
4. Nathaniel Woodard, 1850s, quoted in David Wardle, *The Rise of the Schooled Society: The History of Formal Schooling in England* (1974), 13–14.
5. *Schools Enquiry Commission*, vol. 1, *Report of the Commissioners* (1867–8), 25.
6. John Roach, *Secondary Education in England 1870–1902: Public Activity and Private Enterprise* (1991), 34–6, and *A History of Secondary Education in England 1800–1870* (1986), ch. 5; Brian Simon, *The State and Educational Change: Essays in the History of Education and Pedagogy* (1994), 38; Olive Banks, *Parity and Prestige in English Secondary Education: A Study in Educational Sociology* (1955), 31.
7. Roach, *History of Secondary Education*, 25, 71, 74.
8. e.g. the Orcadian Samuel Laing, who wrote to to the governors of his local grammar school in Kirkwall in 1823 advising them to limit its curriculum to 'reading Caesar and Virgil in Latin and the first five chapters of St Matthew in Greek; the extraction of the Square Root with the elementary branches of Arithmetic such as Decimals; and . . . basic Trigonometry'. This, he maintained, was 'the basis of everything useful'. Quoted in Bernard Porter, '"Monstrous Vandalism": Capitalism and Philistinism in the Works of Samuel Laing', *Albion*, 23: 2 (1991), 264.
9. See e.g. M. V. Hughes, *A London Family 1870–1900* (1981), 42; Lord Meath in House of Lords, 1 Dec. 1902: *Hansard*, 4th ser., vol. 115, col. 816.
10. Arnold Bennett *Sketches for Autobiography*, ed. James Hepburn (1979), 11.
11. Altick, *English Common Reader*, 183–4.
12. Bennett, *Sketches*, 12.
13. According to Jeremy Black, *Maps and History: Constructing Images of the Past* (New Haven, Conn., 1997), colour maps did not come into general use 'until after 1850 with the development of chromo-lithography . . . and thematic mapping' (p. 50). Even then the colours were more often used to demarcate continents. An example of this is the fold-out map of the world that appears in an 1850s edition of Revd J. Goldsmith, *A Grammar of General Geography* (revised by Edward Hughes), facing p. 161. Megan

Norcia tells me that the same is true of the cartographic jigsaw puzzles that (rich) children played with in this period (far more of which, incidentally, featured British counties or European nations than 'the world'). Some wall maps from the 1840s and '50s use pink, probably hand-painted, for British colonies, but for other countries too: J. & C. Walker's *Map of the World* (1840); G. F. Cruchley's *Map of the World* (1855): both in the Cambridge University Library Map Collection; *Wyld's Wall-Map of the World* (1842): in the British Library. The earliest I have come across which has *only* British possessions in red is John Dower's *A New Chart of the World* of 1845, followed closely by Gilbert's *New Map of the World*, 1848 (loc. cit.). Thereafter this became a fairly common convention, including (Zoe Laidlaw tells me) for missionary maps. All of these maps, however, were far too expensive for middle-class (let alone elementary) schools. The first I have found that looks as though it could be a schoolroom map is *Lett's Map of the World on Mercator's Projection* of 1884 (in Cambridge University Library); but there were probably others around that time. (It was not as though cartographers did not know about colour-coding. Fragmented European states (like Prussia), and even English counties (Flintshire) and episcopal sees (Durham), had been indicated by this method for years.)

14. There are no examples in Iona and Peter Opie, *The Lore and Language of Schoolchildren* (Oxford, 1959). For later ones, see below, p. 399, n. 98.
15. See the working-class Robert Roberts, *A Ragged Schooling: Growing up in the Classic Slum* (Manchester, 1976), 156: 'In our mock-war singing game, "English and Romans", elderly people noted with amusement how over two decades the "Roman" enemy had been successfully replaced by Russians, French, Boers and finally, after 1907 and 1908, by Germans, all following on national feeling and policy.' So the 'Boer' game (which does of course have an imperial resonance) seems to have been very transitory, if it needed 'elderly people' to remind Roberts and his friends of it in the early 1910s, the period he is specifically recalling. If this single report is reliable, 'English and Romans' appears to have been the fall-back version. It would be interesting to know which of these camps—imperialist or patriotic—was generally preferred by the boys.
16. H. G. Wells, *Experiment in Autobiography* (1934; new edn., 1984), 85, 91–2. Radicalism does not preclude opinions that can be interpreted as 'imperialistic', and Wells indeed managed to combine both later on, when he became one of the minority of Fabian socialists who embraced pro-empire views in the 1900s. See below, p. 246.
17. My trawl of books for this chapter is certainly not complete. I have made every effort to trace history texts which sources like Valerie Chancellor's excellent *History for their Masters: Opinion in the English History Textbook, 1800–1914* (Bath, 1970) suggest were the most popular ones. From the 150-odd titles listed in that book, plus the handlist of Gordon Batho's collection at the Durham University Institute of Education, and a few chance discoveries in libraries, I have read about 70. In addition, I have examined 40 geography texts. Two collections of essays that bear on the relationship between geography and empire are not particularly helpful for this early period: Anne Godlewska and Neil Smith (eds.), *Geography and Empire* (Oxford, 1994); and Morag Bell, Robin A. Butlin, and Michael Hefferman (eds.), *Geography and Imperialism, 1820–1940* (Manchester, 1995).
18. David Hume, *History of England from the Invasion of Julius Caesar to the Revolution in 1688* (1754–61; followed by several editions and abridgements ['Student's Humes'] until

1891). It seems mainly to have been read by the upper classes. The 'Continuation' by Tobias Smollett, *The History of England from the Revolution to the Death of George the Second*, 5 vols. (1763), has much more on the colonial side. This could be explained by Smollett's own colonial experiences as a young man: see *DNB*, xviii. 583.

19. This was written expressly for students entering the new Civil Service exams. 'Empire' in this context usually indicated that Scotland, Ireland, and Wales were to be covered as well as England, but not the colonies. Cf. *Chambers's Educational Course*, no. 21, *History and Present State of the British Empire* (1837).
20. e.g. in Thomas (Lord) Macaulay, *The History of England* (1858 edn.), i. 95.
21. e.g. Charles Selby, *Events to be Remembered in the History of England* (1852), which omits India entirely; 'Mrs Markham' [Elizabeth Penrose], *A History of England ... for the Use of Young Persons* (1823; new edn. 1851), whose sole reference to its conquest is the following: 'Lord Clive was very successful in the East Indies' (p. 457); and Henry Ince, *An Outline of English History ... Designed for the Use of Schools* (1832), which vaguely mentions a war with India (p. 104), but no more.
22. Review of John Malcolm's *Life of Robert Lord Clive*, in *Edinburgh Review* (Jan. 1840), repr. in *Lord Macaulay's Essays and Lays of Ancient Rome*, Popular Edition (1897), 502.
23. [(Sir) John Robinson], 'The Future of the British Empire', *Westminster Review*, 38 (1870), 49. Robinson (1839–1903) was the first prime minister of Natal.
24. Chancellor, *History for their Masters*, 112.
25. The relevant section follows a passage on the cruelties of the Spaniards and Portuguese. I am assuming it is meant ironically: 'The more scrupulous protestants ... established the first discovery as the foundation of *their* title; and if a pirate or sea-adventurer of their nation had but erected a stick or a stone on the coast, as a memorial of his taking possession, they concluded the whole continent to belong to them, and thought themselves entitled to expel or exterminate, as usurpers, the ancient possessors and inhabitants.' Hume, *History of England* (1802 edn.), vi. 95. The criticisms of the Elizabethan voyagers come in v. 262, 377, and vi. 93.
26. e.g. Lady (Maria) Callcott, *Little Arthur's History of England* (1835), 178; Anon. [A. T. Drane], *A History of England for Family Use* (1873; new edn. 1881), 432.
27. e.g. Thomas Keightley, *The History of England*, 2 vols. (1837/9), i. 527; Revd G. R. Gleig, *First Book of History: England* (1850), 130; Revd D. Morris, *History of England ... Adapted to Standards VI and VII* (1883), 277–8.
28. See Chancellor, *History for their Masters*, 133. The only books I have found that could be said to criticize the rebels in any way are Gleig, *First Book*, 250–1, which ascribes to them dangerous 'levelling' tendencies, but still blames the British government for the split; and an anonymous *History of England*, reprinted from the *Cottager's Monthly Visitor* (*c*.1852), 249, which, while expressing the conventional admiration for Washington, believes that 'we are quite as well without' America: for what reason is not made clear. One or two point out that the colonists only won because the perfidious French supported them: e.g. Thomas and Francis Bullock, *The Illustrated History of England* (1861), 213.
29. [Drane], *A History of England for Family Use*, 682.
30. *Chambers's Information for the People*, 2 vols. (Edinburgh, 1841–2), i. 371–2.
31. Revd J. M. Neale, *English History for Children* (1845), 266.
32. Keightley, *History of England*, ii. 562.

33. e.g. Ross (1873), quoted in Chancellor, *History for their Masters.* 123; Anon., *Royal School Series: The Reign of Queen Victoria* (1881), 88–9, 98–9; Revd D. Morris, *History of England . . . Adapted to Standard V* (1883), 88.
34. Caroline Bray, *The British Empire: A Sketch of the Geography, Growth, Natural and Political Features of the United Kingdom, its Colonies and Dependencies* (1863), 34.
35. e.g. Revd J. Goldsmith, *A Grammar of General Geography for the Use of Schools and Young Persons* (new edn. 1823), 71.
36. Ibid. 75.
37. See Favell Lee Bevan, *Far Off; or Asia and Australia Described* (1852), 99, referring to India: 'What a sad thing that Christians should set a bad example to heathens!'; and 239, describing how the *indigènes* of Kamchatka have been 'corrupted by the Russian soldiers'.
38. e.g. J. C. Curtis, *A School and College History of England* (1860), 500. See also Anon. [A. T. Drane], *History of England,* 767; J. Roscoe Mongan, *The Oxford and Cambridge British History for School Use* (1882), 168; *Gill's Imperial History of England, for School and College Use* (1883), 369; Morris, *History of England . . . Standards VI and VII,* 256.
39. i.e. the *Arrow* incident.
40. J. Roscoe Mongan, *The Oxford and Cambridge British History,* 198; Arabella B. Buckley [Mrs Fisher], *History of England for Beginners* (1887), 342.
41. Charles Knight, *The Popular History of England,* vol. 8 (1858), 461.
42. Neale, *English History for Children,* 262. Cf. Keightley, *History of England,* ii. 522, deploring the way these same wars 'almost turned the head of the nation'; and, for more general expressions of pacifist feeling, Knight, *Popular History,* i. p., iv: 'however powerful may be authority and arms however triumphant, there is "something rotten in the state" '; and *Chambers's Information,* i. 636–7, maintaining that no one could be a genuine patriot 'who would countenance such an idiotic process of settling quarrels'.
43. There were exceptions; including Thomas Macaulay's Introduction to his *History of England* (1848; Penguin Classics abridged edn. 1986), 51–2.
44. Charles Knight, *Passages of a Working Life During Half a Century,* vol. 3 (1864), 279; referring to his 8-volume *The Popular History of England,* originally published in monthly parts, 1856–62.
45. A. Buckland, *Our National Institutions* (1886), quoted in S. J. Y. Colledge, 'The Study of History in the Teacher Training College', *History of Education Society Bulletin* (Autumn 1985), 49.
46. e.g. Hume's *History* (1802 edn.), v. 459, compares Elizabeth's government to 'that of Turkey at present'; Charles Dickens, *A Child's History of England* (1853), vol. 2, describes Henry VIII as 'one of the most detestable villains that ever drew breath (p. 86), gives a particularly gory history of Elizabeth's reign, though he is also aware of its glories (p. 186), and calls James I 'his Sowship' all through (pp. 187–8); J. R. Green, *A Short History of the English People* (1874), paints Henry as a despot (pp. 316–19), attacks Elizabeth for her 'usurpations on English liberty' (pp. 393–4), and loathes James I, especially for his 'divine right' nonsense: see the wicked description of him on p. 464. Macaulay's hostility towards Elizabeth's 'persecution' and the Stuarts' 'fixed hatred of liberty' appears in his review of Hallam's *Constitutional History* (1828), reprinted in *Lord Macaulay's Essays* (Popular edn. 1897), 51–99. Among less distinguished historians with similar views of the Tudors and Stuarts, see Mrs [Sarah] Trimmer, *A Concise*

History of England, Comprised in a Set of Easy Lessons...(1816), 250; and Edward Farr, continued by Miss Corner, *Rodwell's Child's First Step to the History of England* (n.d. [1844]), 109.

47. Hume, *History of England,* vi. 186. Cf. Knight, *Popular History,* vi. 270: the American colonies were essentially 'founded upon principles of freedom and toleration, by a race nurtured in those principles' in England, but at a time when those principles had been 'temporarily suspended' (under the Stuarts).
48. Hume, *History of England,* vi. 186; 'Edward Baldwin' [William Godwin], *The History of England, for the Use of Schools and Young Persons* (new edn. 1826), 136; *Chambers's Information,* i. 355, 357.
49. Bray, *The British Empire,* 1.
50. e.g. the Revd Alexander Stewart, *A Compendium of Modern Geography* (1828), 23–4.
51. 'Baldwin', *History of England,* 138–9.
52. S. R. Gardiner, *Outline of English History: Second Period, 1603–1919* (new edn. 1920), 491.
53. *Royal School Series*...*Reign of Queen Victoria,* 99–100. Farr, *Rodwell's Child's First Step,* 142, claims that America had 'no people, or only a few savages'.
54. Knight, *Popular History,* iii. 345. The Revd G. R. Gleig, *First Book of History* (1850), 241, has the tribes just 'giving way'.
55. Francis Fukuyama, *The End of History and the Last Man* (1992).
56. *None,* in fact, of my sample; but that is not complete.
57. *Rodwell's Child's First Step,* 164–5. Mamma goes on: 'A few of them have come to England since then; and as they had no idea there was any country in the world so grand as their own, they were very much surprised at all they saw here.' She then describes foot-binding. 'But it is to be hoped that, when the Chinese come to see more of other nations, they will leave off such foolish customs.'
58. William F. Collier, *History of the Nineteenth Century for Schools* (1869), 150. This did not reconcile every author to the original wrong; e.g. Curtis, *School and College History,* 500: 'Much has been said as to the advantages that have accrued to commerce and religion from these [Chinese] hostilities; but we must not disguise the fact, that the war was undertaken on pretexts which were largely, if not entirely, unjustifiable.'
59. Green, *Short History,* 759, 818. See also Chancellor, *History for their Masters,* 123.
60. *Royal School Series*... *Queen Victoria,* 80–1, 98.
61. Bray, *The British Empire,* 34.
62. A slightly earlier exception is 'J.H.' [James Hewitt], *Geography of the British Colonies and Dependencies* (1860), book I, pp. 14–15: 'It is to the immense population of the Colonial Empire of Great Britain, that a considerable share of her commerce and wealth, and no mean portion of her power and prosperity, are due'. This is a tiny 32-page pamphlet, designed for 'pupil-teachers and the upper classes in National and Trade Schools'.
63. *Chambers's Information,* i. 637 (italics added).
64. e.g. Gleig, *First Book of History,* 244; Dorothea Beale, *The Student's Text-Book of English and General History, from B.C. 100 to the Present Time* (1858), 141; Collier, *History of the Nineteenth Century,* 151–2; Callcott, *Little Arthur's History,* 280; J. Roscoe Mongan, *The Oxford and Cambridge British History for School Use* (1882; new edn. 1928), 198–9.
65. e.g. Mongan, *Oxford and Cambridge British History,* 195.
66. Revd D. Morris, *The History of England from the Accession of George III to the Present Time, Adapted to Standards VI and VII* (1883), 280 (italics added).

67. Callcott [continued by James Rowley], *Little Arthur's History of England* (1971 edn.), 280 (italics added). This first appears in the 1880 edn.
68. Mrs Cyril Ransome, *A First History of England* (1903), 386, 384, 396 (italics added).
69. *Royal School Series . . . Queen Victoria*, 83.
70. Gardiner, *Outline of English History*, 234.
71. The reference is to Kipling's poem with that title, written in 1899 and directed to the American people, urging them to share this 'civilizing' burden with the British (specifically, in the Philippines).
72. Bevan, *Far Off*, 118; and see also p. 276, making a similar feminist point about Japan, and the same author's *Near Home; or, The Countries of Europe Described* (1850), 361, on 'Mahommedan' Turkey.
73. e.g. Farr, *Rodwell's Child's First Step*, 164–5; *Chambers's Information*, i. 398.
74. *Wesleyan Juvenile Offering*, 22 (1865), 106.
75. Green, *Short History*, 734. He devotes 14 lines to it. Smollett made much of it in his continuation of Hume's *History of England* (1804 edn.), 539–43. Knight's *Popular History*, 734, refers its readers to the *Annual Register* for a full account of 'horrors without a parallel in history or fiction' (which they were not). Minor works typically devote three or four lines of greater or lesser outrage to it.
76. *Royal School Series . . . Queen Victoria*, 91. Others that highlight the Cawnpore massacre are Revd Collingwood Bruce, *The Handbook of English History* (4th edn. 1861), 172; Bullock, *Illustrated History*, 255; [Drane], *History of England for Family Use*, 770; Thomas Birkby, *The History of England from the Roman Period to the Present Time* [1871?], 225; Collier, *History of the Nineteenth Century*, 149. The most bloodthirsty accounts I have found of these events come in J. H. Stocqueler, *A Familiar History of British India* [n.d.], 56–7 and 182–3, but this was mainly intended for young men preparing for service in India. A different ethos runs through it. See above, p. 339, n. 152.
77. Green, *Short History*, 732–4.
78. The Jamaica revolt itself came too late for most pre-1880 history texts to be able to include it; but even several that do include the relevant period fail to mention it. Examples are Collier, *History of the Nineteenth Century* (1869); the 1874 edition of Callcott's *Little Arthur*; Anon., *Royal School Series . . . Queen Victoria* (1881); Gardiner, *Outline of English History* (1881); Mongan, *Oxford and Cambridge British History* (1882); and Morris, *History of England* (1883).
79. Keightley, *History of England*, 548.
80. e.g. J. S. Laurie (ed.), *Manual of English History Simplified; or, our Country's Story, told by a Lady* (1866), 264; Anon., *Royal School Series . . . Queen Victoria*, 98–9; and see Chancellor, *History for their Masters*, 123.
81. Charles Dickens, *A Child's History of England* (Leipzig edn. 1853); which e.g. characterises James II's reign (ii. 325) as one of wholesale 'hanging, beheading, burning, boiling, mutilation, exposing, robbing, transporting and selling into slavery'.
82. Chepmell's *Short Course*, 315, relegates the Black Hole to a footnote. Among those who omit all mention of it, in otherwise fairly full coverages of Indian events, are *Chambers's Information*—in 32 closely-printed columns devoted to India (i. no. 24), Neale's *English History*, and Dickens's *Child's History*.
83. *Chambers's Information*, i. 370–84.
84. Goldsmith, *Grammar of General Geography*, 49, 55, 96.

85. e.g. ibid. 49; Revd Alexander Stewart, *A Compendium of Modern Geography* (1828), 173, 180, 213 (this was obviously a highly popular text, passing through 35 editions over the next 60 years); Bevan, *Far Off*, 82–6; and *Chambers's Geographical Reader, Standard VI* (1885), 37. This view of China was by no means universal, as we shall see later.
86. *The Wesleyan Juvenile Offering: A Miscellany of Missionary Information for Young Persons*, 1 (1844), 10–11.
87. Edward Farr, *The Manual of Geography, Physical and Political* (1861), 231.
88. Goldsmith, *Grammar of General Geography*, 92 (original italics). 'The Revd J. Goldsmith' did not in fact exist. The author (or at least the editor) of this text was a publishing entrepreneur called Sir Richard Phillips, who churned out scores of similar books over a variety of *noms de plume*; as well as founding several journals, including the *Monthly Magazine*. Far from being a clergyman—that *nom* was clearly chosen to reassure teachers and parents—he was imprisoned for his wild republican opinions in 1793: Christopher North called him 'a dirty little Jacobin'; had strange views on science (he did not believe in gravity); and was an early vegetarian. See *DNB*. The *Grammar of General Geography* however was clearly influential, going through scores of editions in the early and middle 1800s, usually updated by others; and was, for example, the Brontë siblings' heavily annotated textbook as children: Christine Alexander, *The Early Writings of Charlotte Brontë* (1983), 19.
89. *Juvenile Missionary Magazine*, NS 1 (1866), 141.
90. See e.g. Luis Agagán-Lester, *'De Andra'. Afrikaner i svenska pedagigiska texter (1768–1965)* (doctoral thesis, Stockholm, 2000), 241–5 (English abstract). Sweden did have one overseas colony at this time: the island of Saint Barthélemy in the West Indies, acquired in 1784 and sold to France in 1878 for 320,000 francs.
91. Trimmer, *A Concise History*, i. 6. Very similar descriptions appear in Callcott, *Little Arthur's History*, 35; Neale, *English History*, 2; and Gleig, *First Book*, 1; and survive into a later period: e.g. *Chambers's Preparatory History of England* (1901), 7; *The Jack Historical Readers*, 1 (*c.*1905), 8; and *The History of England Mostly in Words of One Syllable* (*c.*1909), 1 ('Once on a time in this land of ours called Brit-ain there dwelt tribes of men fierce and wild . . . ').
92. Keightley, *History of England*, 1; and cf. Macaulay, *History of England* (popular edn., 1889), i. 2, comparing the ancient Britons to the Sandwich Islanders of his day. One or two writers described the Ancient Britons as a cut above other primitives, which might be thought to distance them genetically. *Pinnock's Catechism of the History of England, from its Earliest Period to the Present Time. Written in Easy Language* (1822), 3, for example, claims they were 'particularly remarked for their honesty and sincerity'. More seriously, the Revd George Bartle, *A Synopsis of English History* (1865), 5, seems more concerned to allay the impression that the Ancient Britons were as low as present-day primitives, holding that they 'were more enlightened, and held a higher position among the nations of the earth, than we have been led to believe'. The idea that they were 'savages' (ever?) originates in a mistranslation of Caesar's *barbari*.
93. Goldsmith, *A Grammar of General Geography*, facing 62. They are naked, but apparently white, with square and solid-looking wooden houses. And see *Chambers's Geographical Readers of the Continents*, the volume on *Australasia* (1902), which begins its description of the Australian aborigines (p. 50): '*Like the ancient Britons*, they usually clothe themselves in skins, or paint their bodies . . . ' (italics added).

94. Many radicals regarded the USA as being at least one step ahead of Britain. See Henry Pelling, *America and the British Left from Bright to Bevan* (1956), chs. 1–3. Rather more quirkily, the early 19th-century travel writer Samuel Laing put Norway in front. See my 'Virtue and Vice in the North: The Scandinavian Writings of Samuel Laing', *Scandinavian Journal of History*, 23 (1999), 153–72.
95. The classic text on this is Herbert Butterfield, *The Whig Interpretation of History* (1931).
96. e.g. *Chambers's Information*, i. 399; Farr, *Rodwell's Child's First Step*, 163, 173; Collier, *History of the Nineteenth Century*, 97, 150, 153; and *Chambers's Geographical Reader, Standard VI*, 37.
97. Morris, *History of England . . . Standard V*, 291–2.
98. Buckley, *History of England for Beginners*, 354.
99. Keightley, *History of England*, 563, describing how the English conquerors of Ireland sank 'nearly to a level with the original natives'.
100. Stuart Hall quoted in Catherine Hall, *Civilising Subjects: Metropole and Colony in the English Imagination 1830–1867* (2002), 17.
101. H. le M. Chepmell, *A Short Course of History* (2nd edn. 1849), 340.
102. 'I have striven throughout that it should never sink into a "drum and trumpet history". It is the reproach of historians that they have too often turned history into a mere record of the butchery of men by their fellow-men.' *Short History*, p. v.
103. Quoted in Anthony Brundage, *The People's Historian: John Richard Green and the Writing of History in Victorian England* (Westport, Conn. 1994), 105.
104. Anon., *History of England* (1852), repr. from the *Cottager's Monthly Visitor*, 251.
105. Gardiner, *Outline of English History*, 62; and cf. (though this is not strictly a school book: see above, p. 339, n. 152) Stocqueler, *Familiar History of British India*, 62.
106. Green, *Short History*, 762. This was probably the most influential general history of its time and for many years afterwards, at several levels, including secondary schools. It sold 32,000 copies in its first year, half-a-million 'during the ensuing decades', and remained in print until the 1960s. See Brundage, *The People's Historian*, 1. On colonial history, only five of its 820 pages are devoted to India, two to Canada, and an occasional passing reference to Africa and the West Indies; with none of the 'e' or 'i' words appearing in the Index.

CHAPTER 5

1. My source for circulation figures for all classes of journals, both here and in the following pages, is Richard Altick, *English Common Reader: A Social History of the Mass Reading Public 1800–1900* (1957), 392–6, which emphasizes, however, the unreliability of many of them.
2. One example which will serve for all is the (very provincial) weekly *Hull Times*, which during the first half of 1857—before the Indian Mutiny—carried reports from China (the war), Persia ('British Expedition to . . . '), Sarawak (the rebellion), the west coast of Africa ('A Captured Slaver and her Cargo'), Australia (a murder), and America ('Mormon wickedness'); together an 'Interesting Speech of Dr Livingstone' about central Africa. Most of these were copied from *The* (London) *Times*, or foreign papers.

3. See e.g. the *Hull and North Lincolnshire Times* for 18 November 1865, whose 'Foreign News' column deals with countries in the following order: France, Italy, Spain, Portugal, Germany, Austria, Greece, Palestine, America, Canada, India, Australia, New Zealand, and lastly—and strictly out of sequence—Mexico.
4. The *Hull Times* of 4 July 1857, for example, leads with 'The Murder of Mr Little' and 'The Glasgow Poisoning Case', with 'Mutiny in Bengal. Delhi Taken by the Mutineers. Massacre of Europeans. A Native King Proclaimed' relegated to two columns on p. 4. By 1 August, 'Breach of Promise in Lincolnshire', 'Garotte Murder and Robbery at Manchester', 'A Countess Convicted of Slandering a Clergyman', 'Anti-Mormon Riot in Birmingham', and 'Brutal Murder of a Wife by her Husband in Birmingham' have taken precedence.
5. By William Chambers's own admission, that the *Journal* only reached 'the *élite* of the labouring community; those who think, conduct themselves respectably, and are anxious to improve their circumstances . . . below this worthy order of men, our work, except in a few particular cases, does not go': quoted in Altick, *English Common Reader*, 336.
6. One exception is the anonymous 'The Settlers of Long Arrow. A Canadian Romance in Thirty-one Chapters', which came out in *Once a Week* in 1861. There are probably others; I have only sampled this genre.
7. *Ainsworth's Magazine*, 1 (1842), p. iii.
8. Ibid. 10 (1846), 173–4; 2 (1842), 57–63; and (for the orientalism), vols. 1 and 10 *passim*.
9. These are all taken from vol. 3 of *Chambers's*.
10. His others include *Chambers's Information for the People*, cited already; *The Youth's Companion and Counsellor* (1857); *Chambers's Social Science Tracts* (1860–3); *Tales for Home Reading* (1865); *Chambers's Historical Questions, with Answers* (1865); *Chambers's Miscellaneous Questions, with Answers* (1866); and *Chambers's System of Book-Keeping* (1871).
11. The Birmingham Baptists, numbering 1,428 in 1837 and over 4,000 in 1851, are the main focus of Catherine Halls's *Civilising Subjects: Metropole and Colony in the English Imagination 1830–1867* (2002); the figures are on p. 290. See also Susan Thorne, *Congregational Missions and the Making of an Imperial Culture in 19th-Century England* (1999). The main Nonconformist denominations numbered around 3,965,000 all told in England and Wales in 1851: 1 million Congregationalists, 705,000 Baptists, 2,260,000 Methodists. Figures calculated from *Census of Great Britain 1851: Religious Worship in England and Wales* (1854), 106 (from column marked 'sittings').
12. His own *Travels* (1857) had sold 30,000 of its guinea edition, and 10,000 of its 6 shilling edition (1861), by 1863, according to Altick, *English Common Reader*, 388. See John MacKenzie, 'Heroic Myths of Empire', in MacKenzie (ed.), *Popular Imperialism and the Military 1850–1950* (Manchester, 1992), 121–5.
13. See e.g. the series on colonial capitals, starting with Melbourne, in *Cassell's Illustrated Family Paper*, 1 (1854), 115–6 *et passim*.
14. Perhaps not women so much. Women-only journals—e.g. Mrs Beeton's *Englishwoman's Domestic Magazine* and *Eliza Cook's Journal*—troubled their readers much less with this, obviously masculine, sphere.
15. John Alfred Langford, *Modern Birmingham and its Institutions: A Chronicle of Local Events, from 1841 to 1871* (1873), i. 149.
16. See Richard Altick, *The Shows of London* (Cambridge, Mass., 1978), 268–72.

17. Ibid. 280. (Strictly this advertisement was for a course of lectures that accompanied the exhibition.)
18. Ibid. 287; and see Jan Pieterse, *White on Black: Images of Africa and Blacks in Western Popular Culture* (New Haven, Conn., 1992), 94–7.
19. For an explanation of these forms, see Michael R. Booth, *Victorian Spectacular Theatre 1850–1910* (1981), 5–6, 18; and David Mayer, 'The World on Fire . . . Pyrodramas at Belle Vue Gardens, Manchester, *c.*1850–1950', in John MacKenzie (ed.), *Popular Imperialism and the Military* (Manchester, 1992). See also 'Some Account of an Extraordinary Traveller', in Charles Dickens's *Household Words*, 1: 4 (20 Apr. 1850), 73–7, which describes the vicarious travels of a 'Mr Booley' via the various Panoramas being staged in London at that time, through the United States, up the Nile, across Australia and New Zealand, overland to India, and finally to the Arctic Regions in the company of Sir James Ross. The main point of the satire is the superficiality of Mr Booley's impressions.
20. James Wyld, *Notes to Accompany Mr Wyld's Model of the Earth, Leicester Square* (1851), p. xi, where that 'pride' is contrasted with people's geographical ignorance, which Wyld's exhibition is designed to redress.
21. I have a poster for one such performance, given in Hull (undated, but from the context 1859), coupling the 'Seige of Lucknow' with 'Garibaldi's March on Rome'. For all this, see Booth, *Spectacular Theatre*, 6–7, 19–22, 62; Ralph Hyde, *Panoramania! The Art and Entertainment of the 'All-Embracing' View* (1988); and Altick, *Shows of London*, 460–7.
22. Harriet Ritvo, *The Animal Estate. The English and other Creatures in the Victorian Age* (Cambridge, Mass., 1987; this edn. 1990), 5–6, 213 (italics added).
23. Thomas Richards, *The Imperial Archive: Knowledge and the Fantasy of Empire* (1993).
24. Edward Miller, *That Noble Cabinet: A History of the British Museum* (1973), 221–2. Panizzi's attitude may have been influenced by his Italian background: he had come to England from Italy in 1822 as a political refugee.
25. Langford, *Modern Birmingham*, i. 293–304.
26. Hall, *Civilising Subjects*, 277.
27. Diary of Richard Lowry, in the Tyne and Wear Record Office; edited version provided for me by Professor Norman McCord: entries for 29 June 1837 and 23 August 1867, the latter describing an altercation at the Lit and Phil over Lowry's racist views.
28. Hall, *Civilising Subjects*, 277.
29. Clara E. Grant, *Farthing Bundles* (n.d. [1931]), 40.
30. A contributor to the *Wykehamist*, 90 (21 Dec. 1875), 6, remarked that 'Winchester, as a school, stood alone in having no part or interest in any missionary work'. Most other public schools, however, had regular visits from missionaries, and letters from them (usually appealing for funds) in their school magazines; e.g. *Haileyburian*, throughout the 1870s (from India); *Marlburian*, 24 (1889–90) (on behalf of the UMCA in Central Africa); *Malvernian*, 30 (June 1874), recounting a lecture by a missionary from Australia (unusually); and, eventually, the *Wykehamist*, 138 (Nov. 1879), which prints a letter from a missionary in Madagascar. On the general question of missionaries stimulating imperial interest in Britain, see Thorne, *Congregational Missions*, and Hall, *Civilising Subjects* (on the Baptists).

31. Ray Desmond, *The India Museum, 1801–1879* (1982), 35.
32. Ibid., *passim*. Under the East India Company the India Museum was housed in the Company's headquarters in Leadenhall Street, London. Even then restrictions had to be placed on visiting to keep away the 'immense crowds' that threatened to overwhelm the staff (p. 27). In the 1840s the average annual attendance was around 16,000 (pp. 36–8), a figure that was boosted by the Great Exhibition in 1851 to 37,490 (p. 41). In the 1860s it was moved to Fife House in Whitehall, then to the top of the India Office building (pp. 91, 93). Plans for a new, purpose-built venue foundered in 1874, when the Museum was closed and its collections sent to become the 'Eastern Galleries' of the South Kensington museums (pp. 140, 143); in 1879, however, these too were closed to make way for an extension to the National Portrait Gallery, and the collections dispersed (pp. 168 ff.).
33. France held ten national exhibitions between 1797 and 1849. Paul Greenhalgh, *Ephemeral Vistas: Expositions Universelles, Great Exhibitions and World's Fairs, 1851–1939* (Manchester, 1988), 6.
34. Quoted in *Official Descriptive and Illustrated Catalogue of the Great Exhibition of the Works of Industry of all Nations, 1851* [1851], col. 1, 3–4.
35. Quoted in C. R. Fay, *Palace of Industry 1851: A Study of the Great Exhibition and its Fruits* (Cambridge, 1951), 47.
36. [Samuel Prout Newcombe], *Little Henry's Holiday at the Great Exhibition* (1851), 119.
37. Anon., *The World's Fair; or Children's Prize Book of the Great Exhibition of 1851* (1851), 3–4.
38. Jeffrey Auerbach, *The Great Exhibition of 1851: A Nation on Display* (New Haven, Conn., 1999), 100, and the floor plan of the Exhibition reproduced on p. 95. The *Official Descriptive and Illustrated Catalogue of the Great Exhibition* (1851), i. 16–17, reveals that India had 30,000 square feet of floor space, and the remainder of the colonies 21,025 between them; which was less in total than France's 65,000 square feet. Other big exhibitors were the USA (40,000 square feet), Germany (35,000 square feet), and Austria (21,750 square feet). The largest colonial exhibitor apart from India was Canada, with 4,000 square feet.
39. Desmond, *India Museum*, 72. Auerbach, *Great Exhibition*, 103 has a fine illustration of the Indian Court, which however seems to have been not noticeably more flamboyant than Pugin's 'Mediaeval' one, illustrated on p. 116.
40. Auerbach, *Great Exhibition*, 100.
41. Ibid. 101. See also Lara Kriegel, 'Narrating the Subcontinent in 1851: India at the Crystal Palace', in Louise Purbrick (ed.), *The Great Exhibition of 1851: New Interdisciplinary Essays* (Manchester, 2001).
42. Auerbach, *Great Exhibition*, 101–4.
43. Above, n. 32; and Altick, *The Shows of London*, 467.
44. Quoted with illustrations in Auerbach, *Great Exhibition*, 173–9.
45. Greenhalgh, *Ephemeral Vistas*, 18: 'On the whole ... it is difficult to see the "peace-mongering" of exhibition speech-makers as anything other than empty banter.' He also claims (same page) that Britain only lauded peace because it made the empire safe.
46. 'The Great Exhibition and the Little One', in *Household Words*, 3: 67 (1851), 357. See also Auerbach, *Great Exhibition*, 161, 104–7.
47. Greenhalgh claims—without citing evidence, but it accords with my own unsystematic reading of the contemporary popular literature—that of the colonial sections 'only the East Indies appear to have left lingering memories in the minds of visitors'.

He also assumes that this will have been a disappointment for the organizers, but that is unlikely. *Ephemeral Vistas*, 54.

48. This is C. R. Fay's estimate, in *Palace of Industry*, 73, based on the official attendance figure of 6,060,986, and allowing for repeat visits.
49. See *Routledge One Shilling Guide to the Crystal Palace and Park at Sydenham* (1854), which also prints the speech of the chairman of its directors (Samuel Laing the younger) at the girder-laying ceremony in 1852, which is certainly non-, and could even be read as anti-, imperialist (pp. 15–30). M. Digby Wyatt, *Views of the Crystal Palace and Park, Sydenham* (1854), confirms the absence of British colonial 'courts' and artefacts. Even Sydenham's 'Historical Portrait Gallery' contains not a single empire-related picture, apart from one of George Washington. *Routledge One Shilling Guide*, 153–4.
50. 'Our Colonies', in *All the Year Round*, 14 (1865–6), 150.
51. Speech at Manchester, 15 Jan. 1846; reproduced in John Bright and Thorold Rogers (eds.), *Speeches on Questions of Public Policy by Richard Cobden* (1870), 362–3.
52. The best example is probably Hungary, on which British policy in the 1850s was to press Austria to liberalize rule there, while keeping it within the Hapsburg empire. Palmerston feared that Magyar independence would weaken Austria in the 'balance of power' which was keeping the peace just then in Europe. Peace was a much higher—more liberal—priority than national self-rule. Britain later backed the *risorgimento* in Italy, but only because it was liberally led (by Cavour, a free trader); because there seemed no chance of reform under its pettier tyrants; and because in this case an Italian nation could strengthen the balance, by amputating Austria's weakest—and weakening—limb, and creating a buffer (Palmerston first favoured a *north*-Italian-only state) between her and France.
53. *Howitt's Journal*, 1 (1847), 2.
54. *Household Words*, 1 (1850), 74; and 3 (1851), 356 (italics added). Cf. 'The World Growing Better', in *Eliza Cook's Journal*, 1 (1849), 209–12.
55. *Howitt's Journal*, 3 (1847), 325–31: and cf. *Household Words*, 3 (1851), 325–31.
56. There are occasional expressions of pride in Britain's imperial—or whatever—role in the world: e.g. in *Household Words*, 1 (1850), 360, stung by Alexandre Ledru-Rollin's attack on British India in *La Décadence d'Angleterre*, translated as *The Decline of England* (1850); and 2 (1850), 590–5, cautioning readers not to be misled by any 'feelings of national pride and self-gratulation' over the conquest of India into neglecting Britain's failures there; which suggests that such feelings may have been more common in ordinary conversation than their few appearances in print imply.
57. See below, p. 108.
58. See e.g. the series of articles in *Cassell's Illustrated Weekly Paper*, 4 (1857), 268 *et passim*; and *London Journal*, 25 (1857–8), 53 *et passim*.
59. A few examples (to indicate the range) are: 'The Cave of Elephanta', *Penny Magazine*, 1 (1832), 121–2; 'of Ancient India', ibid. 1 (1832), 354–5; 'A Fair in Hindoostan', *Chambers's Edinburgh Journal*, 3 (1834), 335; 'Runjeet Sing [*sic*], Late Ruler of the Punjaub', *London Journal*, 1 (1845), 385–6; 'The City of Benares', *Penny Magazine*, 14 (1845), 401–3; 'A Fuqueer's Curse', *Household Words*, 3 (1851), 310–12; 'Pearls from the East', ibid. 4 (1852), 388–9; 'Prawn Curry' ('delicious'), *Once a Week*, 1 (1859), 358–9; and 'Something like a Conjuror' (on snake-charming), *All the Year Round*, 13 (1865), 57–60.

60. See e.g. the series of articles in the strongly free-trade *Howitt's Journal*, 1 (1847), 228–9, 274–6, 329–33, and 338; *Chambers's Information for the People*, 1 (1840), 371–2 *et passim*; 'Indian Railroads and British Commerce', in *Household Words*, 2 (1851), 590–5; much of the newspaper press comment in the immediate aftermath of the Mutiny, for which the leading article in the *Hull Advertiser*, 4 July 1857, p. 5, strongly criticizing the Company, will serve as an example; and 'Aspects of Indian Life during the Rebellion', in *Good Words*, 1 (1860), 250–3.
61. The following are 'Letters' chosen at random from literally hundreds: 'An Emigrant's Struggles' (in Tasmania), serialized in *Penny Magazine*, 1 (1832), 39, 51–2, 58–60; 'Letter from a Canadian Emigrant', *Chambers's Edinburgh Journal*, 11 (1842), 63–4; 'Notes of a Residence in the [Australian] Bush. By a Lady', ibid. 173–5; 'Letter from South Africa', *Howitt's Journal*, 1 (1847), 74; 'A Bundle of Emigrants' Letters', *Household Words*, 1 (1850), 19–21; 'Two Letters from Australia', ibid. 475–80; 'Cape Sketches', ibid. 588–91, 607–10 (and continued in vol. 2) 'Land Ho! Port Jackson', in ibid., 2 (1851), 276–7; and dozens more in this journal in particular. These are all enthusiastic to some extent. There were also scores of articles advocating emigration, and reviewing the various 'Emigrant's Guides' (pamphlets) issued by Colonial and American authorities. *Chambers's Information for the People* (1841–2) had complete (16-page) issues on 'Emigration to' British American Possessions (no. 17), the USA (no. 18), Australia (no. 19), and Van Diemen's Land and New Zealand (no. 20). On the more negative side, 'News of Natal', *Household Words*, 3 (1851), 83–5, gives a very off-putting picture of that colony; and 'Letter from a Convict in Australia', *Cornhill Magazine*, 13 (1866), 489–512, is predictably unkeen.
62. e.g. *Household Words* openly plugged Mrs Chisholm's 'Family Colonisation Loan Society': see 1 (1850), 514–15; 3 (1851), 228; and 4 (1852), 529–34. On efforts to attract emigrants away from the USA and towards the colonies, see H. J. M. Johnston, *British Emigration Policy 1815–1830: 'Shovelling out Paupers'* (Oxford, 1972), 8, 13, 23 *et passim*; Fred H. Hitchens, *The Colonial Land and Emigration Commission* (Philadelphia, 1931), pp. xiv–v; Robin F. Haines, *Emigration and the Labouring Poor: Australian Recruitment in Britain and Ireland, 1831–60* (1997), 2.
63. e.g. *Chambers's Edinburgh Journal*, 3 (1834), 51–3 and 151–2 (both articles recommending emigration to the USA); and *Howitt's Journal*, 1 (1847), reviewing two 'Emigrant's Guides' to the USA.
64. See e.g. Victor Kiernan, *The Lords of Human Kind: European Attitudes to the Outside World in the Imperial Age* (1969); Christine Bolt, *Victorian Attitudes to Race* (Oxford, 1971); Douglas Lorimer, *Colour, Class and the Victorians: English Attitudes to the Negro in the Mid-19th Century* (Leicester, 1978).
65. e.g. *Chambers's Information*, 1 (1840), 52; *Household Words*, 19 (1859), 548–9.
66. *Eastern Counties Herald*, 16 Nov. 1865, p. 3.
67. One widespread report pictured rioters scooping out the brains of one of their European victims, mixing them with rum, and then drinking them: e.g. ibid.
68. e.g. this from Viscount Bury in the House of Commons, 22 July 1869: 'They heard of infants eviscerated, and thrown palpitating and bleeding into their mothers' laps; they heard of men being slain before the eyes of their wives, of their eyes being torn out and eaten; of women only reserved to pass through a period of horrible outrage, and then suffering death by torture': 22 July 1869, in *Hansard*, 3rd ser., vol. 198, col. 456.

69. Disraeli in the House of Commons, 27 July 1857, in *Hansard*, 3rd ser., vol. 147, cols. 440–80; and see above, p. 69. Disraeli's 'alienness' (as an ethnic Jew) may also have contributed towards this cultural tolerance.
70. See e.g. the *Hull Advertiser*, 4 July 1857, p. 5; *London Journal*, 25 (1857), 349, and 26 (1857–8), 53.
71. See Bernard Semmel, *Democracy versus Empire* (New York, 1969); originally published in Britain as *The Governor Eyre Controversy* (1962).
72. See e.g. J. M. Ludlow, 'The "Cornwall Agricultural and Commercial Association of Jamaica"', *Good Words*, 7 (1866), 672–80, which blames the revolt on the *suddenness* of the transition from slavery to freedom, and explicitly reasserts the negro's 'improve-ability', i.e. his capacity to function as an economic man, if he is nursed into the free-market system, by means of 'Associations' such as the one featured; and (among missionary magazines), *The Juvenile Missionary Magazine of the United Presbyterian Church*, N.S., 1 (1866–7), 5: 'The district where the rebellion has broken out is notoriously the worst provided with missionaries, schools, and religious and educational appliances in the whole island.'
73. See 'An Army Chaplain', 'Two Years' Experience of the Maories', *Good Words*, 7 (1866), 699–701. He thought this would eventually lead to the eradication of the Maori: 'Where the distinction between *meum* and *tuum* is practically set at nought, there can be no property, no progress, no civilisation.' (Also to blame, however, was the white man's VD.) See also *Chambers's Information*, 40 (1841), 635, where social equality is directly associated with barbarism.
74. Two of the most extreme anti-Chinese tirades are to be found in vol. 1, no. 25 of *Chambers's Information for the People* (1840), an issue specially devoted to the country, which denies all the Chinese people's supposed good points: their inventions are 'useless', their arts 'grotesque', their 'whole stock of knowledge... a combination of quackery and empiricism', their language 'primitive', and their literature merely 'fanciful'; and in 'The Great Exhibition and the Little One', an attack on China's 'stagnation', in Dickens's *Household Words*, 3 (1851), 356–60. (To be fair to *Household Words*, it also published articles which contradicted those cited here.)
75. 'New China', *All the Year Round*, 14 (1865), 471–4. For Chinese commercial acumen, see above, p. 76, and below, n. 80.
76. See e.g. 'The World's Debt to Christianity', *Good Words*, 1 (1860), 204 ff.; and the contrast between Christian Mango Island and heathen Emo village in R. M. Ballantyne's *Coral Island* (1857).
77. e.g. 'Condition of the Negro Population' (of the West Indies), in *Chambers's Information* 1 (1840), 367–68.
78. Henry Bright in the House of Commons, 25 Feb. 1823, in *Hansard*, 2nd ser., vol. 8, col. 253.
79. Lord John Russell in House of Commons, 23 Jan. 1838, *Hansard*, 3rd ser., vol. 40, col. 468; quoted in G. Bennett, *The Concept of Empire* (1953), 123. Cf. William Huskisson in House of Commons, 21 Mar. 1825: 'all general theories, however incontrovertible in the abstract, require to be weighed with a calm circumspection... and to be adapted to all the existing relations of society': *Hansard*, 2nd ser., vol. 12, col. 1098.
80. For generally complimentary accounts of China, see e.g. 'The Chinese Collection at the Crystal Palace', *London Journal*, 41 (1865), 253, full of admiration for Chinese works of art;

and 'Our Chinese Cousins', *Temple Bar*, 29 (1870), 385, which also congratulates the Chinese on their business acumen: 'The Chinese are born traders and manufacturers'.

81. e.g. the generous entry on the 'Condition of the Negro Population' of the West Indies in *Chambers's Information for the People*, 1 (1840), 367–8, based on an account by the Quaker Joseph Gurney; Mrs Ward's attempt to 'redeem' the 'good-natured, ready-witted, keen-eyed, patient, merry hearted Hottentot' from 'false imputations' in 'A South African Pic-nic', *Ainsworth's Magazine*, 10 (1846), 173; 'From a Settler's Wife', in *Household Words*, 4 (1852), 588, defending the Maoris; and the favourable account of Australian aborigines quoted above.
82. See *Quarterly Review*, 65 (1840), 541. I have to thank Mr Peter Lokken—a senior essay student of mine at Yale University in 1999–2000—for this and the following reference.
83. *Penny Magazine*, 3 (1834), 358–8.
84. G. A. Sala, 'The Secret of Muley Mogrebbin Beg', *Welcome Guest*, 1 (1860), 523–9.
85. 'The Noble Savage', *Household Words*, 168 (11 June 1853), 337–9. There is more where this comes from; e.g., on 'the horrid little leader . . . in his festering bundle of hides, with his filth and his antipathy to water and his straddled legs, and his odious eyes shaded by his brutal hand, and his cry of "Qu-u-u-aaa!" (Bosjesmann for something desperately insulting I have no doubt)'. See also ibid. 1: 25 (1850), 590; and, for Dickens's similarly dismissive views of Chinese culture, above n.74. Dickens was on the 'wrong' side in the Governor Eyre controversy.
86. See my '"Bureau and Barrack": Early Victorian Attitudes Towards the Continent', *Victorian Studies*, 27 (1984), 407–33.
87. See e.g. the pivotal speech by the Liberal MP Edward Baines in 1861, quoted in Trygve F. Tholfsen, *Working-Class Radicalism in Mid-Victorian England* (1976), 317, explaining to a Reform conference of working men why it was right that they should have been denied the vote in 1832, but not now, because of the increase in their education and 'good conduct' in the meantime; and Gladstone making much the same point three years later, quoted in F. B. Smith, *The Making of the Second Reform* Bill (Cambridge, 1966), 2.
88. *Illustrated London News*, 1 (6 Aug. 1842), 193. The context is the movement for the abolition of (American) slavery.
89. Measured—very crudely—in *Hansard* column inches. Of course the figure will depend on where the line is to be drawn between colonial affairs proper and such concerns as e.g. keeping sea-lanes open, stopping Russia grabbing the Balkans, or—on another front—emigration. But in 1840, to take one example—just after the Canadian insurrection, and at the beginning of a Chinese war—out of a total of 6,943 *Hansard* columns: 412 are on Canada; 387 on China; 156 on Australia, including 139 on the transportation of convicts; 71 (only) on India; 52 on the West Indies, mainly the Colonial Passengers Bill; 22 on Africa; 22 on New Zealand; and 62 on emigration generally. That comes to 17% altogether. In 1860, after the government's takeover of India, out of a total of 10,746 columns: 763 are on India, mostly the Indian Army; 238 on the (new) Chinese wars; 29 on colonies generally (who should pay for their defence); 30 on the New Zealand wars and their aftermath; 8 on Africa, mainly the slave trade; 15 on Australia and Tasmania; 6 on Canada and Newfoundland; 5 on Britain's Caribbean and South American colonies; and 3 on Ceylon. That comes to 10%. In both cases I may have missed brief mentions in Queen's Speech and Estimates

debates; and I have not counted foreign-affairs debates on, for example, the 'Near' (today Middle) East, which had an imperial dimension.

90. Quoted in Stanley Ayling, *The Elder Pitt* (1976), 367.
91. See Frank M. Turner, 'British Politics and the Demise of the Roman Republic: 1700–1939', in *Contesting Cultural Authority* (1993).
92. Like Spain and France. See Miles Taylor, 'Imperium et Libertas? Rethinking the Radical Critique of Imperialism During the Nineteenth Century', *Journal of Imperial and Commonwealth History*, 19 (1991), 9.
93. See Peter Marshall, 'Imperial Britain', *Journal of Imperial and Commonwealth History*, 23: 3 (1995), 382.
94. See Taylor, 'Imperium et Libertas?', *passim*.
95. See R. W. Kostal, 'A Jurisprudence of Power: Martial Law and the Ceylon Controversy of 1848–51', *Journal of Imperial and Commonwealth History*, 28 (2000), 16–21.
96. On this latter, see Derek Sayer, 'British Reaction to the Amritsar Massacre 1919–1920', *Past and Present*, 131 (1991), 133, 147.
97. Charles Buller's phrase, quoted in Fred H. Hitchins, *The Colonial Land and Emigration Commission* (Philadelphia, 1931), 96.
98. e.g. Horton, quoted in ibid. 98.
99. Once the principle of state support for emigrants had been established, they could concentrate on vetting the applicants for it, e.g. through the Colonial Land and Emigration Commission.
100. This is the *Leeds Times*, 30 Dec. 1837, quoted in Peter Burroughs, 'The Canadian Rebellions in British Politics', in J. E. Flint and G. Williams (eds.), *Perspectives of Empire* (1973), 59; whence this entire argument (about the Canadas) is taken. On the cost-cutting aspect, see also Burroughs, 'Parliamentary Radicals and the Reduction of Imperial Expenditure in British North America, 1827–1834', *Historical Journal*, 11 (1968).
101. Kostal, 'A Jurisprudence of Power', 10; Helen Taft Manning, 'Colonial Crises before the Cabinet, 1829–1835', *Bulletin of the Institute for Historical Research*, 30 (1957), 43.
102. Anthony Trollope uses this expression in *Phineas Finn* (1869). It is in the *Shorter Oxford English Dictionary* (1973 edn.), which defines 'crotchet' (in this sense) as 'a whimsical fancy; a perverse conceit; a peculiar notion on some (unimportant) point'.
103. Miles Taylor, 'Colonial Representation at Westminster, *c*.1800–65', in Julian Hoppit (ed.), *Parliament, Nations and Identities in Britain and Ireland, 1660–1850* (Manchester, 2003), 210–11.
104. See e.g. C. A. Bodelsen, *Studies in Mid-Victorian Imperialism* (Copenhagen, 1924; reissued London, 1990), 41–2; and Trollope, *Phineas Finn* (Panther Books edn. 1968), 611.
105. *Edinburgh Review*, 71: 144 (July 1840), 330–1.
106. J. Chapman, 'Our Colonial Empire', *Westminster Review*, N.S., 2: 2 (1852), 422–3; repr. in ibid. 37 (1870), 25.
107. Examples are the Newfoundland Fisheries Bill, 26 May 1835: *Hansard*, 3rd ser., vol. 28, col. 168; a discussion of Mauritius, 1 Mar. 1836: ibid., vol. 31, col. 1132; and a debate on New South Wales, 25 Mar. 1841: ibid., vol. 57, col. 608. A quorum was 40 MPs.
108. Ibid., vol. 19, col. 515 (10 July 1833).
109. House of Commons, 16 Apr. 1849: ibid., vol. 104, cols. 313–76. Other complaints at parliament's neglect of the colonies can be found in ibid., vol. 185 (1867), col. 1180, and

vol. 199 (1870), col. 193. See also Frederick Madden with David Fieldhouse (eds.), *Imperial Reconstruction, 1763–1840 . . . Select Documents* (1987), 56–7, where Reginald Buller is quoted using the same comparison as Macaulay between an imperial issue and a 'turnpike bill'; and p. 255, quoting Canning to the same effect.

110. Peel in House of Commons, 16 Jan. 1838, in *Hansard*, 3rd ser., vol. 40, col. 70.
111. Ibid., vol. 54, col. 833 (2 June 1844).
112. Ibid., vol. 70, col. 205 (22 June 1843).
113. C. A. Bodelsen, *Mid-Victorian Imperialism*, 36.
114. Coffin in House of Commons, 13 Mar. 1822, in *Hansard*, 2nd ser., vol. 6, col. 1076; quoted in Bodelsen, *Mid-Victorian Imperialism*, 16. He mainly lived in the United States.
115. Derby in House of Lords, 29 June 1854, in *Hansard*, 3rd ser., vol. 134, col. 844; quoted in G. Bennett, *The Concept of Empire* (1953), 191. This was also the political novelist Anthony Trollope's view: 'that colonial separation must come, not . . . because of men's faults but from their virtues. A large body of *intelligent* men numbering millions will never consent to be even partially dependent in politics, or in any way inferior to another body of men.' Trollope to G. W. Rushden (in Melbourne), 23 July 1873, in N. John Hall (ed.), *The Letters of Anthony Trollope* (Stanford, col., 1983), ii. 594; and see Richard Mullen (ed.), *The Penguin Companion to Trollope* (1996), under 'English World' (pp. 149–50), which summarizes Trollope's attitude to the empire well.
116. *Edinburgh Review*, 131: 287 (Jan. 1870), 101, 120. A similar scheme, involving an 'Imperial Council', is outlined in the *Westminister Review*, 38 (July 1870), 47–74. In 1873 the Liberal MP Robert MacFie proposed an Imperial Council to the House of Commons: *Hansard*, 3rd ser., vol. 214, col. 1105 (28 Feb.).
117. *Hansard*, 3rd ser., vol. 19 (10 July 1833), col. 434; and cf. *Edinburgh Review*, 83: 168 (Apr. 1846), 546–9 and 552, and 131: 287 (Jan. 1870), 105; J. S. Mill, quoted in *Westminster Review*, N.S., 37 (Jan. 1870), 16 n.; and George Cornewall Lewis quoted in Bodelsen, *Mid-Victorian Imperialism*, 39.
118. This is based on a sample of the contents of journals listed in Walter E Houghton (ed.), *The Wellesley Index of Victorian Periodicals* (1966–89).
119. e.g. *Edinburgh Review*, 131: 287 (Jan. 1970), 102.
120. e.g. Edouard de Warren, *L'Inde Anglaise en 1843–44*, 2 vols. (1844); and Alexandre Ledru-Rollin, *La Décadence d'Angleterre*, trans. as *The Decline of England* (1850), 86–103.
121. Count Björnstjerna, *The British Empire in the East*, trans. from the Swedish by H. Evans Lloyd (1840), 1.
122. *Edinburgh Review*, 71: 144 (July 1840), 330–1.
123. e.g. ibid. 129: 263 (Jan. 1869), 200, commenting on how difficult it still was to find *books* about India.
124. Ibid. 83: 168 (Apr. 1846), 546.
125. On these, see Miles Taylor, 'Colonial Representation at Westminster, *c.*1800–1860'.
126. Catherine Hall, *Civilising Subjects: Metropole and Colony in the English Imagination 1830–1867* (2002), 378–9.
127. Bodelsen, *Mid-Victorian Imperialism*, 22–32. The quotation is taken from *Latter Day Pamphlets* (1850). Bodelsen thought as early as 1924 that Carlyle's influence on imperialist thinking in Britain had been exaggerated (p. 24). I myself have found scarcely any references to it in any later 19th-century writings about empire.

128. Grey's *Colonial Policy*, ii., letter 10 (on New Zealand), reproducing a dispatch from Sir George Grey, seems to me an example. 'Sympathy' of course does not imply a belief in their equality.
129. See Bodelsen, *Mid-Victorian Imperialism*, 41–2.
130. *Hansard*, 3rd ser., vol. 40 (23 Jan. 1838), cols. 384–5. Cf. the *Westminster Review*, N.S., 38 (July 1870), 49: 'When it is remembered how few families there are throughout the United Kingdom unrepresented by some member or connection in one or other of the colonies'—by 'families' it probably meant upper and middle-class ones—the 'ignorance concerning colonial matters is somewhat strange.'
131. Trollope, *Phineas Finn*, 464. He stood (and lost) for the Beverley constituency in 1868.
132. Neither Trollope nor any of the other candidates in the 1868 Beverley contest referred to India or the colonies in their election literature, for example. An exception has already been made in the case of slavery, which featured in a minor way in the Northumberland County elections of 1826, albeit uncontroversially (everyone was against it). Peter Burroughs, 'The Northumberland County Elections of 1826', *Parliamentary History*, 10 (1991), 90.
133. Hall, *Civilising Subjects*, 282. (Inflect: 'to bend inwards, to bend into a curve or angle': *Shorter OED*.)
134. The working classes 'are proud of belonging to an imperial country, and are resolved to maintain, if they can, their empire ...'. Crystal Palace speech of 1872, quoted in Robert Blake, *Disraeli* (1966), 523.
135. *Hansard*, 3rd ser., vol. 185 (19 Feb. 1867), col. 1190.
136. Ibid., vol. 206 (12 May 1871), col. 750.
137. Quoted in G. E. Buckle, *The Life of Benjamin Disraeli*, vol. 5 (1920), 194. Did he really believe this? The doubt arises from his famous description of the 'wretched Colonies' as 'a millstone around our necks', in a letter to Lord Malmesbury, 13 Aug. 1852, quoted in W. F. Monypenny and G. E. Buckle, *The Life of Benjamin Disraeli*, vol. 3 (1914), 385; which could be read to imply that he was complicit in the Liberal 'plot'.
138. On this see Paul Smith, *Disraelian Conservatism and Social Reform* (1967).
139. Technically, of course, not a 'colonial' achievement; but it netted Cyprus for Britain, and was intended indirectly to make India more secure. The other major colonial or pseudo-colonial achievements of this government were the purchase of the Suez Canal shares in 1875, the dubbing of Queen Victoria as 'Empress of India' in 1876, the annexation of the Transvaal in 1877, the Afghan Wars of 1878–80, and the Zulu War of 1879. On an earlier imperial adventure of his, the Abyssinian expedition of 1868 (which did not, however, lead to annexation), see Freda Harcourt, 'Disraeli's Imperialism, 1866–68: A Question of Timing', *Historical Journal*, 23 (1980).
140. W. E. Gladstone, second Midlothian speech, Dalkieth, 26 Nov. 1879, in *Political Speeches in Scotland* (Edinburgh, 1879), 64–5; Paul Knaplund, *Gladstone and Britain's Imperial Policy* (London, 1927), 145.

CHAPTER 6

1. 'The aggregate of leisured, cultured, or fashionable persons regarded as forming a distinct class or body in a community': *Shorter OED*.

2. Edward Said, *The Importance of Education for Democracy*, lecture given in Gothenberg in 1997 to mark the 50th anniversary of the Universal Declaration of Human Rights (Stockholm, 1998), 8.
3. Andy Green's comparative study of *Education and State Formation: The Rise of Education Systems in England, France and the USA* (1990), points this particular difference between Britain and his comparators very clearly; quoting Edward Reiner to the effect that 'England'—unlike all the others—'seems to have used schools hardly at all as a means of nationalistic propaganda' (p. 242). Green however attributes this to Britain's 'taken-for-granted national superiority', which is different from the explanation offered here.
4. Attendance and literacy figures for working-class schools are a difficult and disputed area. There is a good discussion of both, relating to day schools, in W. B. Stephens, *Education, Literacy and Society* (Manchester, 1987), *passim*; and another of Sunday school attendance in Thomas Walter Laqueur, *Religion and Respectability: Sunday Schools and Working-Class Culture 1780–1850* (New Haven, Conn., 1976).
5. e.g. Charles Dickens in *David Copperfield* (1849), and Charlotte Brontë in *Jane Eyre*. Richard Altick points out vis-à-vis contemporary memoirs that 'There are few records of a child's having had a pleasurable time in a nineteenth-century English school for the laboring or the lower-middle class': *The English Common Reader: A Social History of the Mass Reading Public 1800–1900* (Chicago, 1957), 149–50. For examples in working-class autobiographies from this period see Joseph Arch, *The Story of His Life* (1898), 25; James Hawker, *A Victorian Poacher* (1961), 11; George Jacob Holyoake, *Sixty Years of an Agitator's Life* (1900), i. 4–5 and 33; [Charles Manby Smith], *The Working-Man's Way in the World, being the Autobiography of a Journeyman Printer* [1857], 3; and David Vincent, *Bread, Knowledge and Freedom* (1981), 97.
6. Martin Lawn, *Servants of the State: The Contested Control of Teaching 1900–1930* (1987), 10.
7. 1847, quoted in Altick, *English Common Reader*, 150.
8. *Report of the Assistant Commissioners Appointed to inquire into the State of Popular Education in England* (*'Newcastle Commission'*) (1861), ii. 335 (report of A. F. Foster); and see a similar characterization of the proprietors of 'Dame' schools in the same report, quoted in Frank Smith, *A History of English Elementary Education* (1931), 247: 'Domestic servants out of place, discharged barmaids, vendors of toys or lollipops, keepers of small eating-houses, of mangles, or of small lodging houses, needlewomen, who take in plain or slop work; milliners; consumptive patients in an advanced stage; cripples almost bedridden; persons of at least doubtful temperance; outdoor paupers; men and women of seventy or even eighty years; persons who spell badly (mostly women, I grieve to say), who can scarcely write, and who cannot cipher at all.' And see Stephens, *Education, Literacy and Society*, 267: 'Over 700 teachers...were said to have signed the 1851 education returns with marks'.
9. See Smith, *A History of English Elementary Education*, 230 *et passim*; R. W. Selleck, *The New Education 1870–1914* (1968), 40–3; Pamela Horn, *Education in Rural England 1800–1914* (1978), 127.
10. Quoted in Altick, *English Common Reader*, 165.
11. Quoted in Smith, *A History of English Elementary Education*, 266.
12. See also Jonathan Rose, *The Intellectual Life of the British Working Classes* (New Haven, Conn., 2001), ch. 5. Horn, *Education in Rural England*, managed to find a handful of exceptions: p. 123.

13. 'Newcastle' 1861; 'Taunton' 1868; 'Clarendon' 1864.
14. Quoted in Simon, *The State and Educational Change*, 28. For the class basis of education see also Brian Simon, *Two Nations and the Educational Structure, 1780–1870* (1960), and *Education and the Labour Movement 1870–1920* (1965); Smith, *A History of English Elementary Education*, 246; David Rubinstein, 'The London School Board 1870–1904', in Phillip McCann (ed), *Popular Education and Socialisation in the Nineteenth Century* (1985); and S. Humphries, '"Hurrah for England": Schooling and the Working Class in Bristol, 1870–1914', *Southern History*, 1 (1979).
15. Robert Lowe, *Primary and Classical Education* (1867), quoted in Smith, *History of English Elementary Education*, 253.
16. Sir Charles Adderley, 1858, quoted in Simon, *Education and the Labour Movement*, 120.
17. Harold E. Gorst, *The Curse of Education* (1901), 36–7.
18. Frederick Rogers, *Labour, Life and Literature* (1913), 52. See also J. S. Hurt, *Elementary Schooling and the Working Classes 1860–1918* (1979), ch. 2; and Stephens, *Education, Literacy and Society*, 123–4; though Stephens also points to working-class enthusiasm for schooling in some areas: pp. 43–52.
19. 'It must take several generations of evolutionary progress in the development of the cerebral organism to produce brains which can be safely as well as successfully crammed as the empiricists of the Education Department would have the brains of millions crammed': *Lancet* (1884), quoted in Hurt, *Elementary Schooling*, 107. That however was extreme (19th-century medics are well known for this sort of nonsense).
20. Thomas Okey, *A Basketful of Memories: An Autobiographical Sketch* (1930), 21.
21. Arch, *The Story of His Life*, 25. See also Selleck, *The New Education*, 14–16; Laqueur, *Religion and Respectability*, 32; Rubinstein, 'The London School Board 1870–1904', 239–40.
22. Quoted in Selleck, *The New Education*, 68; and cf. Rose, *Intellectual Life*, 23–4.
23. J. Fitch, quoted in Selleck, *The New Education*, 60. The idea was not new. Wardle, *Rise of the Schooled Society*, 88, quotes this from the *Gentleman's Magazine* of 1797: 'A little learning makes a man ambitious to rise, if he can't by fair means he uses foul... His ignorance is a balm which soothes his mind into stupidity and repose, and excludes every emotion of discontent, pride and ambition. A man of no literature will seldom attempt to form insurrections or form an idle scheme for the reformation of the State.'
24. Apologists maintained that this severe word—'subject'—did not necessarily imply any restraint on Britons' *liberties*, which may have been true. 'In the United States of America,' said *Chambers's Information for the People*, an early Victorian improving encyclopaedia for the lower middle classes, '... the people call themselves citizens, not subjects; and what we mean by loyalty to the sovereign, they term duty to the commonwealth. It is obvious that there is extremely little essential difference, *practically*, between these phrases, whatever there may be in *feeling*. The subjects of Great Britain are as free as any people in the civilized world.' 1: 40 (1840), 626. What it did, however, was to deprive them of some of the more positive aspects of a sense of citizenship..
25. Simon, *The State and Educational Change*, 76.
26. One of the exceptions was Lady (Maria) Callcott, author of *Little Arthur's History of England* (1835), whose Preface (p. iii) maintained that 'To teach the love of our country is almost a religious duty... Let no one fear', she went on, clearly feeling the need to defend herself on this, 'that to cultivate patriotism, is to make men illiberal in feeling

towards mankind in general. Is any man the worse citizen for being a good son, or brother, or father, or husband?'

27. *Chambers's Information*, 1 (1840), 626, 636–7.
28. *The Good Old Times! A New Light for the People of England*, 28 (13 Sept. 1817), 252.
29. Christopher Hill, 'The Norman Yoke', in *Puritanism and Revolution* (1958).
30. George Elson, *The Last of the Climbing Boys* (1900), 209. Cf. Anon., *Narrow Waters: The First Volume of the Life and Thoughts of a Common Man* (1935), 34, which tells how *his* (private) study of history taught him 'a detached view of home politics'; as of course the study of history always should.
31. e.g. E. P. Thompson, *The Making of the English Working Class* (1963); and E. J. Hobsbawm, *Primitive Rebels* (1959), *Labouring Men* (1964), and several others.
32. See Horn, *Education in Rural England*, 123–7; Selleck, *The New Education*, ch. 1; Humphries, '"Hurrah for England!"', 180–2; and (for the Sunday schools) Laqueur, *Religion and Respectability*, ch. 4.
33. Laqueur, *Religion and Respectability*, ch. 2.
34. Holyoake, *Sixty Years*, i. 33.
35. J. M. Goldstrom, 'The Content of Education and the Socialization of the Working-Class Child 1830–1860', in McCann (ed.), *Popular Education and Socialisation*, 93, 101–2; and Andy Green, *Education and State Formation*, 313.
36. P. McIntosh, *Physical Education in England Since 1800* (1952), 11–12, 109; J. S. Hurt, 'Drill, Discipline and the Elementary School Ethos', in McCann (ed.), *Popular Education and Socialisation*, 169–70.
37. Smith, *History of English Elementary Education*, 255–68; Simon, *Education and the Labour Movement*, 115–6; Gillian Sutherland, *Policy-Making in Elementary Education 1870–1895* (Oxford, 1973), 192–8; Horn, *Education in Rural England*, 125–6; Hurt, *Elementary Schooling*, 179–80.
38. *Report of the Committee of Council on Education* (1865–6), 23, quoted in Peter Yeandle, 'Lessons in Englishness and Empire, *c.*1880–1914: Further Thoughts on the English/British Conundrum', in R. Phillips and H. Brocklehurst (eds.), *History, Nationhood and the Question of Britain* (2004).
39. Mr Birley's 'General Report for the Year 1864', in *Report of the Committee of Council on Education* (1865), 42, quoted in ibid.
40. Sutherland, *Policy-Making*, 193, 195.
41. Hurt, *Elementary Schooling*, 180. Selleck, *The New Education*, 38, gives even lower figures. See also S. J. Colledge, 'The Study of History in the Teacher Training College 1888–1914', in *History of Education Society Bulletin*, 36 (Autumn 1985), 45, and Horn, *Education in Rural England*, 126.
42. Quoted in Smith, *History of English Elementary Education*, 310; and see Colledge, 'The Study of History in the Teacher Training College', 46, for some 1890s howlers.
43. Colledge, 'The Study of History in the Teacher Training College', 46.
44. There are examples in Vincent, *Bread, Knowledge and Freedom*, 96–7.
45. Quoted in Selleck, *The New Education*, 44.
46. Board of Education, *Suggestions for the Consideration of Teachers and Others concerned in the Work of Public Elementary Schools* (1905), 7, 9.
47. See e.g. *The Citizen Reader* (in *Cassell's Modern School Series*, 1886), 28 ff., which uses Columbus; Lady (Maria) Callcott, *Little Arthur's History of England* (1835), 257 and 259,

which suggests children should emulate Washington and even Napoleon; and Anon. [A. T. Drane], *A History of England for Family Use* (1873; new edn. 1881), 705, another admirer of Washington.

48. Bill Marsden claims to have found an educationalist advocating history teaching as a means of inculcating imperial patriotism in 1867, in 'Politicization, Pedagogy, and the Educational Experience of English Children: 1850–1870', in Petter Aasen (ed.), *Proceedings of the Conference of Historical Perspectives on Childhood* (Trondheim, 1990), 40–2. The source he cites, however, Simon Laurie, *On Primary Instruction in Relation to Education* (1867), 144, does not mention the empire, and actually recommends against the teaching of history at this level.
49. J. M. Goldstrom, *The Social Content of Education 1808–1870: A Study of the Working Class School Reader in England and Ireland* (Shannon, 1972), 26–8, 78–80.
50. Hurt, *Elementary Schooling*, 182–3. This example comes from 1896/7.
51. Above, p. 66.
52. See *Report of the Committee of Council on Education* (1865–6), 208, quoted in Goldstrom, *Social Content of Education*, 168; and F. H. Hayward, *An Educational Failure: A School Inspector's Story* (1938), 72. The Gradgrind reference is, of course, to Dickens's *Hard Times* (1851). See Robert Gilmour, 'The Gradgrind School: Political Economy in the Classroom', *Victorian Studies*, 11 (1967), 207–24.
53. Laqueur, *Religion and Respectability*, ch. 3.
54. Humphries, '"Hurrah for England"', 196–7.
55. Ibid. 198; and see (for a later period) Thomas Gautrey, *'Laus Mihi Laus': School Board Memories* (1937), 101.
56. Humphries, '"Hurrah for England"', 185–96.
57. See W. B. Stephens, *Education in Britain 1750–1918* (1998), 15.
58. Goldstrom, 'The Content of Education', 106.
59. *Report of the Royal Commission on Popular Education* (1861), pt. III, 30–1; quoted in Stephens, *Education, Literacy and Society*, 224.
60. Thomas Hughes, *Tom Brown at Oxford* (1861; new edn. 1929), 442.
61. Quoted in Altick, *English Common Reader*, 168–71.
62. W. B. Stephens, *Education, Literacy and Society 1830–1970* (1987), 322–3. These figures are for England and Wales only, excluding London.
63. See e.g. the *Reports of the Assistant Commissioners appointed to inquire into the State of Popular Education in England* (1861), ii. 354–5, reporting on the mining areas of Durham; and Altick, *English Common Reader*, ch. 10.
64. Edward Salmon, 'What the Working Classes Read', *Nineteenth Century*, 20 (1886), 117.
65. Charles Kingsley, *Yeast* (1850), ch. 13.
66. Anon., *Narrow Waters*, 33. He is writing of the 1880s.
67. Rose, *Intellectual Life*, 84.
68. Hughes, *Tom Brown at Oxford*, 441.
69. See Richard Pyke, *Men and Memories* (1948), 17–18, quoted in Rose, *Intellectual Life*, 344. Pyke (1873–1965) rose to become president of the Methodist Conference.
70. A list of provincial dailies between 1855 and 1870 appears in Alan J. Lee, *The Origins of the Popular Press 1855–1914* (1976), 274–8. There were many more weeklies; usually two or three published concurrently in any sizeable town.
71. Altick, *English Common Reader*, 342.

72. Anon., *Narrow Waters*, 33; and for more examples of what Rose calls the 'remarkable . . . lack of knowledge of current affairs' at this time and indeed much later, see his *Intellectual Life*, 220–1.
73. See Stephen Koss, *The Rise and Fall of the Political Press in Britain*, vol. 1, *The Nineteenth Century* (1981), 60.
74. The *Northern Star* ran from 1832 to 1852; *Reynolds's Newspaper* from 1850 to 1962 (shortened to *Reynolds' News*).
75. e.g. the *Band of Hope Review* and the *British Workman* claimed circulations of 250,000 each in 1862 (which is why I have selected them for my examples of this genre). They were mainly bought up, however, by middle-class churchgoers for free distribution among the proles. Altick, *English Common Reader*, 395.
76. R. K. Webb, *The British Working Class Reader 1790–1848: Literary and Social Tension* (1955), 27, referring to the cheap improving pamphlets which were part and parcel of the same propaganda drive.
77. Altick, *English Common Reader*, 346.
78. At this point it was calling itself *The Star of Freedom.*
79. Catherine Hall, *Civilising Subjects: Metropole and Colony in the English Imagination 1830–1867* (2002), 282, claims that 'Chartism had its own implicit maps of empire', but without elaborating this (or explaining what 'maps' means in this context). It may refer to Chartism's *spread to* the colonies, or to the Chartists' opposition to colonial emigration.
80. Altick, *English Common Reader*, 393–4.
81. The *Democratic Review*, a small-scale monthly magazine, came out in 1849 and 1850. See also Henry Weisser, *British Working-Class Movements and Europe 1815–48* (1975).
82. Salmon, 'What the Working Classes Read', 115.
83. *The Working Man. A Weekly Record of Social and Industrial Progress*, 1 (Jan.–June 1866), 401–2, 321, 261; and 2 (July–Dec. 1866), 174, 199, 296. The *Working Man* finished its run after these two volumes. On its Jamaica coverage, see above, p. 48.
84. Allen Clarke, 'A Romance that Staggered the Nation', *Liverpool Weekly Post* (27 Oct. 1934), 2; quoted in Rose, *Intellectual Life*, 344.
85. e.g. *Chambers's Information for the People* 2: 17–24 (1842).
86. Ibid. 1: 40 (1841). The quotations are on pp. 637 and 635.
87. The journals I am covering here seem to be directed to males exclusively. I have not looked at equivalents for women and girls; if there were any, the morality they tried to purvey was probably even narrower.
88. e.g. 'Soldiers and their Dogs', 1 Aug. 1868. The explicit moral of this was to 'impress upon us all the duty of faithfulness in every station of life'.
89. The main early 19th-century purveyors were Jane Marcet, Hannah More, and Harriet Martineau. An example is *Village Politics, Addressed to All the Mechanics, Journeymen, and Labourers, in Great Britain, by Will Chip, a Country Carpenter,* which in fact is by Hannah More (1817). At the request of the discontented Will, a fairy creates an egalitarian society, the result of which, however, is to put poor craftsmen like Will Chip out of work, because they have no rich people's wants to satisfy any more; so he gets the fairy to change everything back again. Later in the century the Religious Tract Society weighed in with a series of slightly more substantial novels with similar, if less childish, themes. Many were written by 'Hesba Stretton' (real name Sarah Smith). Some of these conclude in the colonies, with the long-suffering protagonists ending their days happily

in e.g. 'a log-house of their own, within sound of the lapping of the waves of Lake Huron': *Lost Gip* (1873 edn.), 141. Deborah Morse—who put me on to this author—tells me that *Brought Home* similarly ends in New Zealand, and *Bede's Charity* in South Africa.

90. *British Workman* 1 Jan., 1 Mar., 1 Apr., 1 June 1867; 1 May 1868.
91. Ibid., 1 June 1868; and see below,
92. e.g. 'The Inner Life of Royalty', in ibid., 1 Aug. 1868; and 'Victoria the Beloved', in *Band of Hope Review* (1872), 58.
93. *Band of Hope Review*, 17 (1876–7).
94. Ibid., 58 (1872).
95. See above, the case of the *Working Man*.
96. The *London Journal's* content was mixed. Its subtitle was: *Weekly Record of Literature, Science and Art*, and it did carry serious articles on e.g. (in this first volume), Mozart, US presidents Johnson and Polk, Disraeli's latest novel, the death of Earl Grey, new inventions, and women. These were probably intended to place it in direct competition with 'improving' journals like the *Penny Magazine and Chambers's Journal*. It grew more like them—more 'respectable'—later on, which possibly marked a small victory for the 'improvers'; but in its early years sensation predominated.
97. *London Journal*, 1 (1845), 12–13, 55, 76–7, 93–4, 190, 329, 357–8.
98. Ibid. 25 (1857), 347, 361–2, 405–6; and vol. 26 (1857–8), *passim*; and (on the Jamaica revolt), 42 (1865), 397–8. Cf. the *London Journal's* report on the 1857 rising against Rajah Brooke in Sarawak: 21 (1855), 217–18.
99. Ibid. 21 (1855), 247. The 'tortures' described here are as horrific as anything ever attributed to non-Europeans.
100. Ibid. 25 (1857), 349.
101. This is frankly racist and pro-Eyre; ibid 42 (1865), 397–8.
102. *Working Man*, 1 (1866), 395.
103. See e.g. 'China and its Capital', in ibid. 25 (1857), 9; 'The Population of China—Life on the Waters', in ibid. 149; 'Shang-Hae and the Chinese', in ibid. 41 (1865), 173–4; and 'The Chinese Collection at the Crystal Palace', in ibid. 253.
104. e.g. an article on the Middle East taken from a book by a Spanish traveller, illustrated by a woodcut showing skeletons hanging from what presumably are a kind of gallows somewhere in Arabia, in ibid. 1 (1845), 49; G. M. W. Reynolds's article on 'Runjeet Singh, Late Ruler of the Punjaub', to which is attached a typically 'orientalist' picture of ceremonial elephants: ibid. 385; and 'The Chinese Giant, and his Curious Party', illustrated with the giant standing with a dwarf, both in mandarin costumes, in ibid. 42 (1865), 301.
105. Ibid. 42 (1865), 212–13. The picture illustrating this article has her dressed as a European, which may have helped. The description of her more 'semi-civilized' former subjects which follows, however, is full of praise for everything about them, save their 'recourse to human sacrifices'.
106. Ibid. 25 (1857), 58.
107. Ibid. 137. This seems to be taken from a little contemporary popular chapbook, *A Brief Memoir and Theatrical Career of Ira Aldridge, The African Tragedian* (n.d., but probably 1850s). More modern accounts are Herbert Marshall and Mildred Stock, *Ira Aldridge: The Negro Tragedian* (1958); Folarin Shyllon, *Black People in Britain 1555–1933* (1977), 204–10; and Peter Fryer, *Staying Power: The History of Black People in Britain* (1984), 252–6. From all

these it is clear that Aldridge suffered both prejudice and admiration in Britain on account of his colour.

108. e.g. *Once a Week*, 1 (1859), 435–7.

109. This is Jacob Omnium, a Guinea planter and seaman, in a piece objecting to the racism of Sir Samuel Baker and the new *Pall Mall Gazette*, in *Working Man*, 2 (1866), 174.

110. R.A.B., 'Celebrated Africans', *British Workman*, 162 (1868), 166. The examples given here are—the list is long but will emphasize the extraordinary nature of this article—Sebituane, Chief of the Makololo (recently 'discovered' by Livingstone, and compared here to Caesar and Napoleon); two Hannibals (the lesser-known one a lieutenant-general in the Russian army); Geoffrey L'Islet; Toussaint L'Ouverture and his successors in Haiti; Benjamin Roberts, president of Liberia; Edward Jordan and Peter Moncrief, both senators in Jamaica; King Theodore of Abyssinia; Euclid; Anthony William Amo and Benjamin Banneker, two 18th-century scientists; Capitien, Thomas Fuller, Thomas Jenkins, James Derham, Dr James McClure Smith, and Bishop Payne, all successful scholars in Europe and America; Caesar (of North Carolina), Suana (a 'Kaffir'), Ignatius Sancho, Francis Williams and Phillis Wheatley, all black poets; Origen, Tertullian, Clemens Alexandrinus, Cyril, and Augustine, early Christian divines; and Bishops Crowther and Burns among the moderns.

111. I have not read every 19th-century working-class autobiography, only a sample of about 50. These were chosen carefully, and I have no reason to believe they are unrepresentative, but there is always the possibility that the ones I have not read paint an entirely different picture. David Vincent's much more thorough *Bread, Knowledge and Freedom: A Study of Nineteenth-Century Working Class Autobiography* (1981), however, suggests that my selection is fairly typical.

112. This may also reflect the greater visibility of Europeans and Americans in Britain's major cities. For Europeans, see above, p. 33. American abolitionism was a popular movement in Britain in the 1850s and '60s, fed by a succession of famous visiting orators.

113. Tom Barclay, *Memoirs and Medleys: The Autobiography of a Bottle-Washer* (1934), 7. Barclay (1852–1933) was of Irish and Catholic origin, but he turned socialist in his twenties.

114. [Charles Manby Smith], *The Working-Man's Way in the World, being the Autobiography of a Journeyman Printer* (1857), 318.

115. G. J. Holyoake, *Sixty Years of an Agitator's Life* (1900), ii. 86–7. John Colenso was bishop of Natal from 1853 until he was excommunicated for heresy in 1866. He also championed the Zulus against the British both before then and until his death in 1883. Holyoake also strongly defended the West Indian 'negro' against the likes of Thomas Carlyle: ibid. i. 191.

116. Vincent, *Bread, Knowledge and Freedom*, 8; and *passim*, on these questions generally.

117. e.g. [James Dawson Burn], *The Autobiography of a Beggar Boy* (1855); George Elson, *The Last of the Climbing Boys* (1900); Garth Christian (ed.), *James Hawker's Journal: A Victorian Poacher* (1961); Snowden Dunhill, *The Life of Snowden Dunhill, Written by Himself* (1834), repr. with an Introduction by David Neave (Howden, 1987).

CHAPTER 7

1. See J. Wellens, 'The Anti-Intellectual Tradition in the West', in P. W. Musgrave (ed.), *Society, History and Education* (1970), 58–60.

2. See my '"Monstrous Vandalism": Capitalism and Philistinism in the Works of Samuel Laing', *Albion*, 23 (1991), 253–68.
3. Thomas Carlyle, *Past and Present* (1843), book 3, ch. 5; (1895 edn.), 195.
4. See Martin Wiener, *English Culture and the Decline of the Industrial Spirit 1850–1980* (Cambridge, 1981).
5. Martin Green, *Dreams of Adventure, Deeds of Empire* (New York, 1979), 38, 96.
6. Charles Kingsley, *Westward Ho!* (1855; this edn. 1893), 230; and compare him in 1863, quoted in Altick, *The English Common Reader: A Social History of the Mass Reading Public 1800–1900* (Chicago, 1957), 164: 'Many a man is learned in books, and has read for years and years, and yet he is useless. He knows *about* all sorts of things, but he can't *do* them.' By contrast, in R. M. Ballantyne's *The Coral Island* (1857), Jack's wide reading, initially mocked by the other boys (could Ballantyne have been having a dig at Kingsley here?) proves enormously useful to the young castaways: p. 28.
7. Carlyle, *Past and Present*, 196.
8. Cecil Forsyth, *Music and Nationalism* (1911), quoted in Jeffrey Richards, *Imperialism and Music: Britain 1876–1953* (Manchester, 2001), 249. Of course this is ridiculous. Richards points out that France was able to do both.
9. Patrick Brantlinger, *Rule of Darkness: British Literature and Imperialism, 1830–1914* (Ithaca, NY, 1988), pp. x, 23.
10. Edward Said, *Culture and Imperialism* (1993), 78.
11. Ibid. 88. Said also suggests that the very *form* of the novel was a product of imperialism: '[w]ithout empire, I would go so far as saying, there is no European novel as we know it'; in which case, of course, it will hardly matter what these novels were *about*: ibid. 82. The point is developed *passim*; it involves connecting the novelistic concern for 'moral space' with geography, and hence empire. Obviously this raises larger issues, and involves a broader and looser definition of 'empire', than can be taken on board here. One problem with it may be that it leaves out of account other possible and unrelated influences; one of which—the idea of 'progress', which may also be necessary to narrative—plays a part in *my* argument: above, pp. 77–8.
12. Green, *Dreams of Adventure*, 37. Cf. Brantlinger, *Rule of Darkness*, 11; and Jeffrey Richards, 'Introduction' to Richards (ed.), *Imperialism and Juvenile Literature* (Manchester, 1989), 8.
13. Green, *Dreams of Adventure*, 49. This is an analysis John of Gaunt's famous patriotic speech in *Richard II*, II. i: 'This royal throne of kings, this scepter'd isle . . . This precious stone set in a silver sea, / Which serves it in the office of a wall . . . ', which Green claims reveals Shakespeare as 'an imperial writer' through its 'precious metal and precious stone images . . . combined with the stress on defensiveness'. Well, maybe. But it could also be read as an expression of what later would be called 'Little England' patriotism, present in England (or Britain) from well before Shakespeare's time. It embodies a love of England, but not a hatred of foreigners; an appreciation of her 'happiness', not of her strength; the need to defend, but not to attack; and the virtues of peace rather than war. In the context of its time this seems a far more likely interpretation.
14. John MacKenzie, *Propaganda and Empire: The Manipulation of British Public Opinion 1880–1960* (Manchester, 1984), 2.
15. Catherine Hall connects the Volunteer movement with imperialism via 'masculinism', in *Civilising Subjects: Metropole and Colony in the English Imagination 1830–1867* (2002), 387–8.

16. On travel and imperialism, see Mary Louise Pratt, *Imperial Eyes: Travel Writing and Transculturation* (1992); S. Mills, *Discourses of Difference: An Analysis of Women's Travel Writing and Colonialism* (1991); Inderpal Grewal, *Home and Harem: Nation, Gender, Empire and the Cultures of Travel* (Leicester, 1996).
17. Jonah Raskin, *The Mythology of Imperialism: Rudyard Kipling, Joseph Conrad, E. M. Forster, D. H. Lawrence and Joyce Cary* (New York, 1971), 17.
18. George Watson, *The English Ideology* (1973), 214.
19. Raskin, *Mythology of Imperialism*, 17. Cf. Patrick Brantlinger: 'In the middle of the most serious domestic concerns, often in the most unlikely texts, the Empire may intrude as a shadowy realm of escape, renewal, banishment, or return for characters who for one reason or another need to enter or exit from scenes of domestic conflict'. *Rule of Darkness: British Literature and Imperialism, 1830–1914* (1988), 12.
20. In Dickens's *Great Expectations* (1861).
21. Sir Walter Scott, *Guy Mannering* (1815). Jane Millgate's Introduction to the Penguin Classics edition (2003), p. xvii, points out how Scott distances Mannering from the more typical 'nabobs' who lived in Scotland at that time. There are a few references to Indian melodies, myths, and so on, but nothing crucial or irreplaceable.
22. Jane Austen, *Mansfield Park* (1814); Edward Said, *Culture and Imperialism* (1993),100–16. For doubts about Sir Thomas's slave-owning credentials, see John Sutherland, *Is Heathcliff a Murderer? Puzzles in Nineteenth-Century Fiction* (Oxford, 1996), 1–9. The only overt reference to slavery in *Mansfield Park* (in ch. 21) implies that the topic is an embarrassing one, at the very least. Fanny recounts how the previous evening she had raised the question of the slave trade with Sir Thomas, recently returned from the West Indies, only to be met with 'such a dead silence!' Sarah Curtis's film version (1999), in which slavery plays a much more central role, is a travesty in this respect.
23. Anthony Trollope, *The Way We Live Now* (1875; 'Wordsworth Classics' edn. 2001), 551, 574, 749.
24. Charlotte Brontë, *Jane Eyre* (1847; Penguin Popular Classics edn. 1994). The main themes of this are love, gender, class, social conditions, and morality. But there is a powerful West Indian connection in the person of the dour but masterful hero, Rochester, who has lived in the West Indies—though probably not as a planter or slave-owner—where he picked up his Creole wife, who is revealed in the course of the book as the 'mad woman in the attic', and the reason why Rochester cannot marry Jane. There are plenty of racial referents here: the association of 'darkness' with menace and sensuality, for example; references to 'savagery' and 'superstition', though associated with an older Europe as well as in the tropics; some casual 'orientalism' (pp. 182–83); and metaphors based on the (imagined) Caribbean climate: heat, storms and so on. There are no references to 'empire' as such, except one oblique and implicitly unfavourable one (p. 171); several implicit criticisms of slavery (pp. 16, 309); and the usual Victorian confusion when it comes to 'race', which is used in several different ways here: to mean family (pp. 18, 107), class (p. 370), and humanity as a whole (p. 350), but *never* to denote ethnic differences. This is not an imperial novel; but it would certainly be very different—much blander—without its tropical imagery.
25. Susan Chitty, *The Beast and the Monk: A Life of Charles Kingsley* (1974), 170.
26. Taylor lived in India between 1824 and 1860, working as an administrator, and married the daughter of an Indian prince. *Confessions* is meant to be a 'true-life' novel, being

based on interviews with ex-Thugs (bands of ritual murderers). Although, as Patrick Brantlinger's Introduction to the 'Oxford World's Classics' edition (1998) points out, this subject matter could hardly fail to 'confirm the stereotype of India... as a retrograde, anarchic society', Taylor also 'writes with both a sympathy for and a thorough knowledge of Indian beliefs, customs and languages that even Kipling does not rival' (pp. viii, xii). He wrote five other novels set in India, one of them (*Seeta*, 1873) written from the 1857 Indian mutineers' viewpoint, but none attained the popularity of *Confessions*. Other pre-Kipling 'Indian' novels—all of them early—include James Morier, *The Adventures of Hajji Baba of Hispahan* (1824), Walter Scott's *The Surgeon's Daughter* (1827), and W. B. Hockley, *Tales of the Zenana* (1827).

27. A BBC dramatization in 2001 featured some 'imperialist' content (in a speech at a dinner in honour of the Chinese emperor), which however, had been inserted entirely spuriously. The dinner is in the novel, but not the imperial references. No doubt the adaptor or producer, under the influence of the literary theorists, felt that imperialism must have been implied in the original even if not explicitly stated there, and so needed to be drawn out for the modern TV viewer.

28. Anthony Trollope, *The West Indies and the Spanish Main* (1859), *Australia and New Zealand* (1873), and *South Africa* (1877); and see Asa Briggs, 'Trollope the Traveller', in John Halperin (ed.), *Trollope Centenary Essays* (1982), and Catherine Hall, 'Going a-Trolloping: Imperial Man Travels the Empire', in Midgley (ed.), *Gender and Imperialism* (1998). Two of Trollope's political novels place leading characters in imperial ministries: Phineas Finn as under-secretary at the Colonial Office (*Phineas Finn*, 1869), and Lord Fawn at the India Office (*The Eustace Diamonds*, 1875). In both cases the positions are presented as quite lowly ones, and we are told scarcely anything of what Finn and Fawn are doing there. The father of the heroine of *He Knew He was Right* (1868) is a colonial governor. None of Trollope's *Tales of All Countries*, 2 vols. (1861 and 1863), based, he says in his *Autobiography* (p. 125), on his travels abroad, is set in the colonies. For his attitude to the empire generally, see Richard Mullen, *The Penguin Companion to Trollope* (Harmondsworth, 1996), under 'English World'; and J. H. Davidson, 'Anthony Trollope and the Colonies', *Victorian Studies*, 12 (1969).

29. Charles Dickens, *American Notes* (1842), ch. 15.

30. Kingsley's brother Henry was a gold-rusher to Australia in 1853–8, writing a novel based on his experiences: *The Recollections of Geoffrey Hamlyn* (Leipzig edn. 1864).

31. Charles Lever; whose *The Dodd Family Abroad* (1853–4), for example, sets a Pickwick-like character travelling on the continent. Lever was an Anglo-Irishman who began his career as a physician serving the diplomatic community in Brussels. His other favourite setting is Ireland.

32. The best-known examples are Thackeray's *Vanity Fair* (1847–8), and Dickens's *A Tale of Two Cities* (1859).

33. Victor Kiernan makes a case for considering Tennyson an imperial poet, in 'Tennyson, King Arthur, and Imperialism', in Raphael Samuel and Gareth Stedman Jones (eds.), *Culture, Ideology and Politics* (1982), 126–47; but even 'his verses dealing directly with episodes of this [imperial] kind were not to be very numerous, for so prolific a writer, and not very good' (p. 131). The most overtly imperial (and the least good) were those he produced for various public imperial events in the 1880s: see below, p. 175. In his public life he was a dedicated imperial federationist. Otherwise most of

what Kiernan takes to be his imperial allusions in his major poems were 'disguised' and 'mythic'.

34. J. S. Bratton *et al.*, *Acts of Supremacy: The British Empire and the Stage, 1790–1930* (Manchester, 1991); and see also David Bradby *et al.*, *Performance and Politics in Popular Drama . . . 1800–1976* (Cambridge, 1980).
35. Catalogue of 'Plays Submitted to the Lord Chamberlain' in the British Library (Manuscript Room). This list should include every theatrical performance—plays, opera, operetta, other entertainments—staged in Britain, though it clearly does not (see below, n. 154). I have only sampled this, for the early 1830s, the 1850s, and the late 1890s. All the plays and shows listed there appear to be on domestic or occasionally European political themes, with the exceptions (before the 1890s) of a couple of Indian Mutiny-related pieces in 1858 (below, loc. cit.), and a very few featuring the lives of emigrants in the 1850s, the latter probably staged by colonization societies in order to encourage the poor to emigrate. None of these is likely to qualify as 'serious' theatre.
36. Catherine Hall, *Civilising Subjects: Metropole and Colony in the English Imagination 1830–1867* (2002), 281. Her main source is John Alfred Langford, *Modern Birmingham and its Institutions: A Chronicle of Local Events, from 1841 to 1871*, 2 vols. (1873), i. 136–72 and 495–511, and ii. 421–45, which lists *all* plays performed in the city over this period, not one of which appears—from their titles—to have an imperial or imperial-related theme.
37. Christopher Heywood, 'Yorkshire Slavery in *Wuthering Heights*', *Review of English Studies*, N.S. 38: 150 (1987), 184–98.
38. Susan Meyer, 'Colonialism and the Figurative Strategy of *Jane Eyre*', in J. Arac and H. Ritvo (eds.), *Macropolitics of 19th Century Literature* (1991), 166.
39. Green, *Dreams of Adventure*, 119.
40. W. J. McCormack's Introduction to the 'Oxford World's Classics' edition (1982), p. xxx.
41. Said, *Culture and Imperialism*, pp. xv–xvii, 100–16.
42. Ibid. 9, 160, 201, 62. Said acknowledges that there were exceptions: 'No vision, any more than any social system, has total hegemony over its domain.' However, he holds that what he calls 'resistances' to the imperial ethos were always either 'ineffective' (p. 225), or (and this is based on my own early *Critics of Empire*) compromized by imperialist assumptions: wishing merely, that is, to reform imperialism, rather than to abolish it. 'Still,' he goes on, 'people like Froude, Dilke, and Seeley represented the overwhelmingly more powerful and successful pro-imperial culture' (p. 201). And he singles out 'the women's as well as the working-class movement' in particular as being 'pro-empire' (p. 62).
43. Apart from his travel books, Dickens's fortnightly *Household Words* carried a number of sometimes highly opinionated articles on both the settlement and the dependent colonies: see above, p. 102. Carlyle's interest in colonial matters was mainly confined to his notorious article on the 'Nigger Question' of 1849 in *Fraser's Magazine*, vol. 40; Ruskin's to his brief and incongruous encomium of British imperialism in his inaugural lecture for the Slade Art Chair at Oxford in 1870, republished in E. T. Cook and Alexander Wedderburn (eds.), *The Works of John Ruskin* (1905), xx. 41, which is famous now but was not much noticed at the time. Imperial connections can be found for many other prominent authors. Thackeray was even born in India, the son of a collector, and lived there until he was 6. George Eliot owned colonial stocks:

review by Antoinette Burton of Nancy Henry, *George Eliot and the British Empire* (2002), in *Victorian Studies*, 45: 2 (2003). This makes it the more remarkable that they did not feature the empire more explicitly or significantly in their novels.

44. See his *An Autobiography* (1883), which makes clear that he always tailored his subject-matter to what he felt his readers wanted. His antennae may of course have been faulty; he confesses to have been surprised when his Australian travelogue sold so well (pp. 248–9).
45. The best examples are Hamilton K. Fisker and Mrs Hurtle in *The Way We Live Now*; but there are over 30 American characters in all in his books, according to Richard Mullen with James Minson, *The Penguin Companion to Trollope* (1996), 7–8.
46. F. G. Clarke, *The Land of Contrarieties: British Attitudes to the Australian Colonies 1828–1855* (Melbourne, 1977). And see Said, *Culture and Imperialism*, 127: 'Australians [he means the white colonists] remained an inferior race well into the twentieth century.' In many ex-settlement colonies the descendants of immigrants still smart under this.
47. Quoted in John Halperin, *Trollope and Politics: A Study of the Pallisers and Others* (1977), 115. Halperin conjectures that Trollope too was 'almost totally unknown' in the Beverley contituency he contested in 1868. One presumes Thackeray was referring to the whole population of Oxford, not just the minority who had the vote. Otherwise the 4% would need to be scaled down even more.
48. Richard Altick estimates that Dickens's *Pickwick Papers* sold 800,000 copies in book (as opposed to periodical) form between 1836 and 1863. That was his best-seller. Other 'popular' books usually had print-runs in the thousands or tens of thousands. *The English Common Reader* (1957), 383–6.
49. James Fergusson (1862), quoted in M. H. Port, *Imperial London: Civil Government Building in London 1850–1915* (New Haven, Conn., 1995), 199.
50. See my ' "Monstrous Vandalism" ', 261–3; and K. Theodore Hoppen, *The Mid-Victorian Generation 1846–1886* (Oxford, 1998), 373–4.
51. Reminiscences by Mary Beatrice Alder quoted in Jemold Northrop Moore, *Edward Elgar: A Creative Life* (1984), 172; and cf. a letter of his to his German friend Jaeger in 1902, complaining of 'the horrible musical atmosphere . . . in this benighted country': quoted in Michael Kennedy, *Portrait of Elgar* (1968), 99. Jaeger of course agreed: 'England *Ruins* all *artists*' (original italics and capitalization), quoted in Moore, *Edward Elgar*, 452.
52. Linley, lauded by Mozart as a great prospect, was drowned in a boating accident on a normally placid lake in Lincolnshire at the age of 23; Wesley's compositions fell off after he stumbled into a hole in the road and knocked himself out at 21.
53. 'Mr Brady may sing to empty benches, while il Signor Bradini would "bring down the house" ': Charles Lever, *A Day's Ride* (1863), ch. 42.
54. e.g. (from *Greene's Biographical Encyclopedia, passim*), Michael Kelly (1762–1826), Thomas Moore (1779–1852), John Field (1782–1837), Samuel Lover (1797–1868), Michael Balfe (1808–70), William Wallace (1812–65), Arthur Sullivan (1842–1900), and Charles Villiers Stanford (1852–1924).
55. Wagner wrote a 'Rule Britannia' overture in 1836, hoping for a lucrative invitation from the Royal Philharmonic Society in London to play it, but apparently it was never taken up: Keith Anderson, sleevenote to *Richard Wagner: Marches and Overtures*, Naxos CD 8.555386 (1986). Other settings by famous European composers of British words are usually of Shakespeare (e.g. Berlioz), or of folk song (Haydn, Beethoven).

56. The best example of this is the way Solomon Volkov's book *Testimony* (1979) stood our interpretation of Shostakovich's symphonies on its head.
57. Jeffrey Richards, *Imperialism and Music: Britain 1876–1953* (Manchester, 2001), 248, citing Eric Walter White, *A History of English Opera* (1983). The only exception he has found is Henry Bishop's comic opera *English Men in India* of 1827 (p. 249). Stanford wrote an early opera called *The Veiled Prophet of Khorassan* (1881), which was performed in Hanover and at Covent Garden, which sounds like an 'orientalist' subject. Among operettas there are some colonial allusions in the Gilbert and Sullivan repertoire, but mainly in the later ones (ibid. 34–6). Sullivan's earlier cantata *On Sea and Shore* (1871) apparently has a 'Moresque' interlude (ibid. 25), though if it is anything like Elgar's *Intermezzo Moresque* (1883) the 'Moorish' influence there will be very slight. On Sullivan's overtly imperial later works, see below, p. 385, n. 64.
58. Richards, *Imperialism and Music*, 251.
59. Stanley Sadie (ed.), *The New Grove Dictionary of Music and Musicians*, 2nd edn., 29 vols. (2001).
60. They are eminently collectible for their glorious pictorial covers alone. See Richards, *Imperialism and Music*, 441–2.
61. Henry Russell (1812–1900) might possibly be counted as an *anti*-imperialist composer, writing protest songs against slavery and the ill-treatment of the American Indians, but only while he was living in the USA. Back in England he was involved in colonial emigration schemes for the poor: David Mason Greene, *Greene's Biographical Encyclopedia of Composers* (1985), 615.
62. e.g. Bizet's *The Pearl-Fishers*, Meyerbeer's *L'Africaine*, Saint-Saëns' *Suite Algérienne*, 'Egyptian' Piano Concerto, and *Africa*, for piano and orchestra; and, if we extend the category to cover 'orientalism', Saint-Saëns' *Sampson and Delilah*, Verdi's *Aida*, and much of the oeuvre of Russian romantics like Rimsky-Korsakov. See MacKenzie, *Orientalism*, ch. 6.
63. Henry G. Farmer, *The Rise and Development of Military Music* (n.d. [1912]), suggests that 19th-century British bandmasters—the most prominent of whom he lists on pp. 143–50—overwhelmingly played foreign marches; and preferred other forms when they came to composition themselves: overtures, waltzes, even symphonies and operas. Not a single 'imperial' theme features in the book. See also Richards, *Imperialism and Music*, ch. 12, focusing mainly on the very end of the 19th and beginning of the 20th centuries.
64. The words are by the Revd Sabine Baring-Gould (1834–1924).
65. Richards, *Imperialism and Music*, 13 and ch. 11. Richards's view of this whole question of imperialism in music is diametrically opposed to mine. He claims that British music was 'steeped' in imperialism, certainly during the period covered by his book (1876–1953), but also, as he hints at various points (e.g. p. 3), much earlier. I think this is untenable. See my review in *Journal of Imperial and Commonwealth History*, 30 (2002), 138–42.
66. Richards, *Imperialism and Music*, 525.
67. See MacKenzie, *Orientalism*, ch. 3.
68. Léonce Bénédite, in W. Shaw Sparrow (ed.), *The Spirit of the Age: The Work of Frank Brangwyn ARA* (1905), 19–20.
69. J. W. M. Hichberger, *Images of the Army: The Military in British Art, 1815–1914* (Manchester, 1988), 2, 81, 92.

70. MacKenzie, *Orientalism*, 52.
71. Alison Smith, in 'Empire of the Nude', BBC2, broadcast 27 Oct. 2001. A trawl through the biographies of Leighton throws up no mention of an imperial meaning for *Athlete*. When I contacted Ms Smith at the Tate Gallery she referred me to a source which relates the statue to contemporary views of *masculinism*, but not imperialism. It is slightly puzzling that Leighton did not use oriental subjects for his major paintings and sculptures in view of his first-hand knowledge of the eastern Mediterranean, which he sketched extensively, and from which he impressively furnished at least one large room of his home. Stephen Jones *et al.*, *Frederic Leighton 1830–1896* (1996), 152, 154–5, 172, 239; Leonée and Richard Ormond, *Lord Leighton* (1975), pl. 139 (his 'Arab Hall').
72. See Stephen Bayley, *The Albert Memorial: The Monument in its Social and Architectural Context* (1981); Chris Brooks, *The Albert Memorial* (1995).
73. I heard this in a seminar paper given at Yale University in 1999. In subsequent correspondence with him the author has recanted, and so I promised not to mention his name.
74. I am not aware that any of these ideas has been seriously mooted yet.
75. The Duke of Kent (1827), Napier (1855), Havelock (1861), Sir Colin Campbell (1867), and Sir James Outram (1871). My source is Arthur Byron, *London Statues* (1981). To this list could also be added the statues and busts that decorate the new Foreign and India Offices, but mostly *inside*. I assume that these date from the building's erection in the 1860s. They include Drake, Franklin, and Cook; representations of Africa, America, and Australasia; eight Indian governors-general and viceroys; eight 'of our leading native allies during the Mutiny'; and several representations of 'different Indian races'. Lord Edward Gleichen, *London's Open-Air Statuary* (1928), 30–3. Other monuments that could have reminded Londoners of their empire included a red granite obelisk commemorating the African explorer John Hanning Speke erected in Kensington Gardens in 1866; a drinking fountain dedicated to the Abolitionists erected in Westminster in 1863; and two imperial war memorials: one commemorating the Chillianwallah War, erected in the grounds of Chelsea Hospital in 1853, the other dedicated to sailors who fell in the New Zealand Wars, erected outside Greenwich Hospital in 1874. See the London County Council's *Return of Outdoor Memorials in London* (1910), and C. S. Cooper, *The Outdoor Monuments of London, Statues, Memorial Buildings, Tablets and War Memorials* (1928).
76. The above two lists (both housed in the London Metropolitan Archive) will include any statues that lasted through to 1910, but were then destroyed in the World Wars. Comparing them with Byron's list throws up no new additional imperialist statues, busts, or medallions.
77. See John MacKenzie, '"The Second City of the Empire": Glasgow—Imperial Municipality', in Felix Driver and David Gilbert (eds.), *Imperial Cities: Landscape, Display and Identity* (Manchester, 1999), 226.
78. See Port, *Imperial London*, ch. 2 *passim*.
79. See Rebecca Preston, '"The Scenery of the Torrid Zone": Imagined Travels and the Culture of Exotics in Nineteenth-Century British Gardens', in Driver and Gilbert (eds.), *Imperial Cities*.
80. See e.g. Jan Morris *et al.*, *Architecture of the British Empire* (1986).

81. e.g. Stockholm boasts a 'Chinese Pavilion' (1763) in the grounds of Drottningholm Palace, and a 'Turkish Pavilion' (1788) and 'Saracen tent' (1790), in Haga Parken.
82. Two other major examples are Sezincote House in Gloucestershire, built *c.*1805 in what was called the 'hindoo' style, complete with 'Brahmin bulls' and a 'Surya temple'; and the Royal College of Organists in South Kensington (1875–6), looking like a contemporary Cairo town house: 'quite unlike any other public building of its date', comment Bridget Cherry and Nicolaus Pevsner, *The Buildings of England. London 3: North West* (1991), 495. On this subject generally, see John Summerson, *Architecture in Britain 1530 to 1830* (1953; new edn. 1970), 479–81, and Henry-Russell Hitchcock, *Architecture: Nineteenth and Twentieith Centuries* (1958; new edn. 1971), 26, which put the 'Indian revival' in context; and MacKenzie, *Orientalism*, ch. 4, and the other works cited there.
83. Port, *Imperial London*, 198–9.
84. See e.g. Nicholas Pevsner, *Some Architectural Writers of the Nineteenth Century* (Oxford, 1972). 'Nationalists' usually espoused gothic as being a style more indigenous to England than the classical; some of them preferred late gothic (or Tudor) as being more *distinctly* indigenous. This was the main reason for favouring Tudor; so far as I can discover, no one associated it with (say) overseas expansion. Palmerston (who was the leader of the pack baying for a classical Foreign Office) thought all this was nonsense: 'the real aboriginal architecture of this country was mud huts and wicker wigwams' (quoted in Port, *Imperial London*, 209).
85. Port, *Imperial London*, 14.
86. Frederic Harrison, quoted in Felix Driver and David Gilbert's Introductory chapter to *Imperial Cities*, 9.
87. Port, *Imperial London*, 16.
88. Quoted in ibid. 16. And cf. Anon., *Narrow Waters: The First Volume of the Life and Thoughts of a Common Man* (1935), 55: 'London is perhaps the worst mistake Englishmen have made.'
89. Port, *Imperial London*, 14, 16.
90. In 1855 the creation of a 'Metropolitan Board of Works', formed mainly to co-ordinate the cleansing of the Thames, helped a little; but the problem was not finally resolved until that was replaced by the new 'London County Council' in 1889. Ibid. 10, 18.
91. Ibid. 16.
92. Cannadine, 'The Context, Performance and Meaning of Ritual: The British Monarchy and the "Invention of Tradition", *c.* 1820–1977', in Eric Hobsbawm and Terence Ranger (eds.), *The Invention of Tradition* (1983), 112–13.
93. Quoted in Port, *Imperial London*, 202.
94. Wilberforce quoted in David Newsome, *The Victorian World Picture: Perceptions and Introspections in an Age of Change* (1997), 134.
95. Richards, *Imperialism and Music*, 525 (original italics).
96. Laurence Senelick, 'Politics as Entertainment: Victorian Music-hall Songs', *Victorian Studies*, 19 (1975–6), 151–3.
97. Maurice Willson Disher, *Victorian Song: From Dive to Drawing Room* (1955), 105. The Russell song is called 'Sunshine After Rain'; it was written by Charles Mackay.
98. Senelick, 'Politics as Entertainment', *passim*; and see Peter Bailey, 'Custom, Capital and Culture in the Victorian Music Hall', in R. D. Storch (ed.), *Popular Culture and Class in Victorian England* (1982), 198.

99. Senelick, 'Politics as Entertainment', 168–9; Dave Russell, *Popular Music in England, 1840–1914: A Social History* (1987; second edn. 1997), 147–8. The writer/composer was G. W. Hunt.
100. Cited in Russell, *Popular Music*, 147–8. Albert's song was written by the singer himself; I have been unable to trace 'Hats Off To the Empire'.
101. Anon., 'The Music-Hall', *Cornhill Magazine*, 60 (1889), 74, quoted in Senelick, 'Politics as Entertainment', 169.
102. Hugh Cunningham, 'The Language of Patriotism', in Raphael Samuel (ed.), *Patriotism: The Making and Unmaking of British National Identity*, vol. 1, *History and Politics* (1989), 80.
103. Senelick, 'Politics as Entertainment', 172. Jeffrey Richards sees this as an example of the 'typically English . . . tendency to laugh at the things they love'. *Imperialism and Music*, 326
104. The words were by Edwin V. Page; music by Vincent Davies. The copy I have seen is in the collection of Max Tyler, Historian of the British Music Hall Society; whose help to me in this area has been invaluable.
105. Exceptions are a handful of songs about the Gordon Affair, including 'Too Late!', written and composed by N. G. Travers, and 'sung', we are told on the cover of the sheet-music, by the Great Macdermott, 'amidst the most enthusiastic applause'; and 'Gordon (The Hero of Khartoum)', by Harry Windley: 'Gordon, Gordon, hear his pleading cry; Far o'er the pathless waste, where he was left to die . . . '; and a pathetic song of 1889, 'The Last Bullet' (words H. A. Duffy, music George le Brunn), referring back to the seige of Lucknow during the Indian Mutiny (Max Tyler collection).
106. This is another in Max Tyler's collection; sung by Macdermott (again), written and composed by Arthur Lloyd. It is about parliament. Internal evidence suggests a date in the 1880s.
107. The first 'nigger minstrel', a solo act by T. D. Rice ('Jumping Jim Crow'), crossed the Atlantic in 1836. The first troupe (the 'Virginia Minstrels') arrived in 1843. Information kindly provided by Kathy Castle. Such a show, in Newcastle upon Tyne on 30 November 1847, is described in the MS diary of the middle-class Richard Lowry, in the Tyne and Wear Record Office.
108. Frederick Willis, *101 Jubilee Road: A Book of London Yesterdays* (1948), 103.
109. My sample is far from exhaustive. I have looked through a number of publishers' booklists for selected years, and review articles in scattered popular journals.
110. On this see Gavin Hambly, 'Muslims in English-language Fiction', in R. W. Winks and J. R. Rush (eds.), *Asia in Western Fiction* (1990). It is clear from this that 19th-century fictional portrayals of the Middle East were by no means as stereotypical and adverse as is suggested by Said's *Orientalism* (1978), or even by Hambly's own opening sentence: 'I begin with the assumption that there exists in both Western Europe and the USA a set of luridly coloured, highly distorted, yet widely held impressions of the Middle East and Muslims in general . . . Obviously, there are exceptions, but these are not my concern here' (p. 35). Another essay in the same volume, Donald F. Lach and Theodore Foss, 'Images of Asia in European Fiction, 1500–1800', suggests that the 'East' may have figured larger in European literature in the 17th and 18th centuries than in the 19th.
111. e.g. Alan Sandison, *The Wheel of Empire: A Study of the Imperial Idea in Some Late Nineteenth and Early Twentieth Century Fiction* (1967); and Allen J, Greenberger, *The British Image of India: A Study in the Literature of Imperialism* (1969).

112. Robin Jared Lewis, 'The literature of the Raj', in Winks and Rush, *Asia in Western Fiction*, 53. The three examples are Walter Scott's *The Surgeon's Daughter* (1827), W. B. Hockley's *Tales of the Zenana* (1827), and Meadows Taylor's *Tipoo Sultaun: A Tale of the Mysore War* (1840). In addition Mary Sherwood's *Little Henry and his Bearer* (1814) appears in his bibliography (p. 70).
113. To give just one example: Mary Elizabeth Braddon's popular and 'sensational' *Lady Audley's Secret* (1862) uses Australia as the usual place for characters to appear from and disappear to, and has a few superficial mentions of India and things 'Arabian'; but otherwise nothing. This is despite the fact that Mrs Braddon had a brother in the ICS.
114. Charles Kingsley, *Westward Ho!* (1893 edn.), 8, 389, 525.
115. Ibid. 10, 320, 591.
116. e.g. by W. R. Greg, quoted in Chitty, *The Beast and the Monk*, 171.
117. See J. S. Bratton, *The Impact of Victorian Children's Fiction* (1981).
118. Brenda Colloms, *Charles Kingsley: The Lion of Eversley* (1975), 194. The first edition sold 1,250 copies, the second around 3,000, and a one-volume 1857 edition 6,000. These were respectable figures, but do not begin to compare with e.g. *Little Dorrit*, which sold '35,000 or more' in the year *Westward Ho!* came out, the 100,000 copies of GWM Reynolds's *The Bronze Soldier* which were sold (in ½ *d.* instalments) in 1854; or *Uncle Tom's Cabin*, the British and colonial sales of which reached 1½ million in its first year (1852–3). These statistics are taken from Richard Altick, *The English Common Reader* (1957), 384. 'The really big sales of the book,' continues Colloms, '... came with Macmillan's cheap reprints after Kingsley's death.'
119. He took the pro-Eyre side during the notorious Jamaica revolt controversy of 1865 (Bernard Semmel, *The Governor Eyre Controversy* (1962), 29–30); regarded blacks as racially inferior (Colloms, *Charles Kingsley*, 284); compared Irishmen to 'chimpanzees' (ibid. 242–3); and believed God had sanctioned the genocide of 'inferior' races (ibid. 122–3). These views lost him several friends (ibid. 122, 294–6). It has been suggested that they may have been influenced by his slave-owning ancestry on his mother's side (ibid. 15, 38–9). He had little first-hand knowledge of other races, until 1870 when he holidayed in Trinidad as the guest of its progressive Governor, Arthur Gordon, who may have softened his views (ibid. 317–18). His militarism—curious, but by no means unique, in someone as weak and continually unhealthy as he was—comes out in a tract he wrote on the occasion of the Crimean War, *Brave Words for Brave Soldiers and Sailors* (1854), which was meant to assure them that they were fighting on God's side (ibid. 189; Chitty, *The Beast and the Monk*, 169). He was more celebrated, however, as a socialist (of sorts) and reformer.
120. Stuart Hannabuss, 'Ballantyne's Message of Empire', in Jeffrey Richards (ed.), *Imperialism and Juvenile Literature* (Manchester, 1989), 57–8; Green, *Dreams of Adventure*, 216, 223.
121. Hermann Melville, *Typee: A Peep at Polynesian Life* (1846; Wordsworth Classics edn. 1994), 12.
122. e.g. from Ballantyne's *The Coral Island* (1857; Collins 'School and Adventure Library' edn., n.d.), 207 (ch. 26): 'I saw that these inhuman monsters were actually launching their canoe over the living bodies of their victims ... high above their voices rang the dying shrieks of those wretched creatures, as, one after another, the ponderous canoe

passed over them, burst the eyeballs from their sockets, and sent their life's blood gushing from their mouths ...'

123. Ibid. 241 (ch. 30), 204 (ch. 26).
124. If he could become so hardened to horror, 'how little wonder that these poor ignorant savages, who were born and bred in familiarity therewith, should think nothing of them at all, and should hold human life in so very slight esteem': ibid. 204 (ch. 25).
125. Ballantyne started off with northern Canada in *The Young Fur Traders* (1856), after a period working there as a clerk; before moving on (in his books) to the Pacific (*The Coral Island*; and *The Lonely Island*, on the Bounty mutineers, 1880); Eskimo country (*Ungava*, 1857; *The World of Ice*, 1859; and *The Giant of the North, or Poking Round the Pole*, 1881); the American West (*Twice Bought, a Tale of the Oregon Goldfields*, 1885); South America (*Martin Rattler*, 1858; and *The Rover of the Andes*, 1885), Africa (*The Gorilla Hunters*, 1861; *Black Ivory—A Tale of Adventure among the Slavers of East Africa*, 1873; *The Pirate City*, set in Algiers, 1874; *The Fugitives, or The Tyrant Queen of Madagascar*, 1887; and *Blue Lights or Hot Work in the Sudan*, 1888: this is the only one of his post-Canadian books set in a (quasi-) British colony); the sea (*Red Eric; or the Whaler's Last Cruise*, 1861; *The Lifeboat*, 1864; *Under the Waves, or, Diving in Deep Waters*, 1876; *The Young Trawler*, 1884; and *The Crew of the Water Wagtail*, 1889); and the ancient Viking voyagers (*Erling the* Bold, 1870; and *The Norsemen in the West*, 1872). See Eric Quayle, *Ballantyne the Brave. A Victorian Writter and his Family* (1967); and Stuart Hannabuss, 'Ballantyne's Message of Empire', in Richards (ed.), *Imperialism and Juvenile Literature* (1989).

    Marryat and W. H. G. Kingston wrote mainly about the navy. Marryat also, however, produced a Canadian and a South African adventure: *The Settlers in Canada* (1844), and *The Mission* (1845), to go with his more famous *Mr Midshipman Easy* (1836); and Kingston *On the Banks of the Amazon* (1872). Mayne Reid concentrated on the American frontier: e.g. *The Rifle Rangers* (1850). The American Melville published two more South Sea island adventures as well as *Typee*, called *Omoo* (1846) and *Mardi* (1849); in addition of course to *Moby Dick* (1851).
126. Ballantyne had knowledge of India through his brother James, who was principal of the East India Company's Sanscrit College at Benares, 1845–61. However, when he produced a non-fiction work on *The Overland Route to India* based partly on his brother's experiences, Nelsons declined to publish it. Quayle, *Ballantyne the Brave*, 136.
127. Patrick Dunae, 'Boys' Literature and the Idea of Empire, 1870–1914', *Victorian Studies*, 24: 4 (1980), 107.
128. Dunae, 'Boys' Literature and the Idea of Empire', 107.
129. Ballantyne working for the Hudson's Bay Company; Marryat as a naval officer.
130. Ballantyne was an indefatigable researcher in libraries, as evidenced by the wealth of geological and botanical description found in his books. His sources did not have to be British; one of his most popular tales, *The Gorilla Hunters* (1861), was based on du Chaillu's famous *Exploration and Adventures of Tropical Africa* (English translation published 1861). See Quayle, *Ballantyne the Brave, passim*; which also reveals (pp. 114–15) that *Coral Island* was inspired by—almost to the point of plagiarism—an obscure novel by an American.
131. Tropical explorers are mainly limited to Britain, Germany, France, Italy, Belgium and the Netherlands; but every western European nation had its overseas traders, and none was without its intrepid missionaries, including Switzerland.

132. Quoted in Mary Cadogan and Patricia Craig, *You're a Brick, Angela! A New Look at Girl's Fiction from 1839 to 1975* (1976), 29. That concentrates mainly on post-1880. Less has been written about girls' novels before that period than about boys' after 1880. My own impression of their mainly domestic content is mainly based on stories in girls' magazines. I have not scoured the novels (for this period) for imperial content, so I may be wrong here.
133. Ibid. 27.
134. Edward Salmon, *Juvenile Literature As It Is* (1888), 28.
135. Ibid. 28–29.
136. On working-class reading generally, see Jonathan Rose, *The Intellectual Life of the British Working Classes* (New Haven, Conn., 2001); which, however, stresses the difficulty of assessing the 'cultural literacy' of the working classes before World War I, when we begin to have e.g. library surveys (p. 190).
137. Edwin Muir, quoted in ibid. 376.
138. Ibid. 85, 111–14.
139. Ibid. 44, 49.
140. Altick, *English Common Reader,* 95, 220, 244–58; David Vincent, *Bread, Knowledge and Freedom: A Study of Nineteenth-Century Working Class Autobiography* (1981), pt. 3, ch. 6; Rose, *Intellectual Life,* ch. 3.
141. Rose, *Intellectual Life.* 94.
142. Ibid. 95–6.
143. An 'imperialist' reading of *Robinson Crusoe* features in Martin Green, *Dreams of Adventure,* ch. 3, and is elaborated in the same author's 'The Robinson Crusoe Story', in Jeffrey Richards (ed.), *Imperialism and Juvenile Literature* (Manchester, 1989).
144. I have looked at two chapbook versions, one from the 1840s or '50s (British Library reference CUP 408.m.57 (3)), 8 pages long, half of which are taken up by woodcuts; the other from 1861, published by J. Bysh, 12 pages long. The surprise with both of them is that they devote only a minority of their alloted space to the island. Their treatment of Friday is sympathetic. Another kind of abridgement, *Robinson Crusoe in Words of One Syllable* by Mary Godolphin (1868), intended for children, also reproduces the story pretty faithfully, including the early parts which bear on Africans and Turks, but calls Friday Crusoe's 'slave' (p. 81), presumably because 'servant' has too many syllables. Its frontispiece shows Friday kneeling before Crusoe; as does the frontispiece, by George Cruikshank, of an 1831 edition of the original novel.
145. *The Further Adventures of Robinson Crusoe* (1720), which takes us to (among other exotic locations) the East Indies.
146. 'Years ago, had one walked into almost any poor but respectable man's room in the kingdom, one would probably have found two books at least—the Bible and the *Pilgrim's Progress*... Now it is to be feared that very few working men and women read the *Pilgrim's Progress,* and the Bible is far from being what it was—*the* book of the home.' Edward Salmon, 'What the Working Classes Read', *Nineteenth Century,* 20 (1886), 115.
147. Ibid. 116.
148. See R. K. Webb, *The British Working-Class Reader 1790–1848* (1955), 29–30; and Stephens, *Education in Britain,* 149–54.

149. Tom Barclay, *Memories and Medleys: The Autobiography of a Bottle-Washer* (1934), 16, 20. A similar list appears in Thomas Okey, *A Basketful of Memories: An Autobiographical Sketch* (1930), 20.
150. Altick, *English Common Reader,* 290. Altick lists some other popular titles on pp. 287–9.
151. [Peter Longueville], *The Adventures of Philip Quarll, the English Hermit; who was discovered by Mr. Dorrington on an Uninhabited Island where he had lived upwards of fifty years.* The copy I have seen is a 24-page 'chapbook' edition in the British Library.
152. For Reynolds' readership see Altick, *English Common Reader,* 384. Dickens probably outsold him. I have skimmed three of his novels: *The Soldier's Wife* (1853), *The Bronze Statue* (1854), and *The Loves of the Harem: A Tale of Constantinople* (1855). The first includes a particularly gory flogging, and an execution by firing-squad, but none of this takes place outside the British Isles; the last has some conventional orientalisms (beautiful women, murder, slavery, treachery), but ends with a new, 'liberal' and 'enlightened', Moslem government. That of course *could* be regarded as (informally) imperialist, though it is presented here as an indigenous development.
153. Frederick Rogers, *Labour, Life and Literature: Some Memories of Sixty Years* (1913), 7–9.
154. I have been unable to find the book of this. Plays with this title—or very likely the same one—were premiered in 1830 and 1859, according to Allardyce Nicoll, *A History of English Drama 1660–1900,* vol. 6 (1955), 461, and vol. 5 (1959), 677. In each case the author is 'unknown'. It is not listed, however, in 'Plays Submitted to the Lord Chamberlain' for either of these years, which would have given me access to the text. The Lord Chamberlain's list throws up two titles for 1858 which were probably empire-related: *The Fugitives, or a Tale of India,* by G. Conquest; and *Revolt in the East or the Fugitives and their Faithful Steed* (no author). This is a minute proportion of the hundreds of plays licensed during the Indian Mutiny years.
155. An exception is [Anon.], *The Time and Affecting History of Henrietta Belgrave, a Woman born only for Calamities: being an Unhappy Daughter, a Wretched Wife, and an Unfortunate Mother. Containing a series of the most uncommon adventures that ever befel one person by Sea and Land; particularly the Shipwreck of Herself and her Parents, her falling into the Power of a Brutal Villain, her timely rescue by a Party of Indian Hunters, and her further sufferings, to her Death. Written by Herself, and addressed to her Daughter Zoa* (n.d.), which is partly set in the East Indies, whose natives, as can be seen from the title, are almost the only non-villains she meets.
156. See Patrick Dunae, 'Penny Dreadfuls: Late Nineteenth-Century Boys' Literature and Crime', *Victorian Studies,* 22 (1979), 133–50; also Webb, *British Working Class Reader;* Richard Altick, *English Common Reader;* Stephens, *Education in Britain,* 154–9; Rose, *Intellectual Life,* 367–71.
157. Salmon, 'What the Working Classes Read', 112.
158. e.g. *Chambers Information for the People,* published in 99 weekly issues in 1841–2; Charles Knight's *Penny Cyclopaedia* (1833–46).
159. Like the *Penny Magazine; Chambers Journal;* the *Saturday Magazine.* Webb, *British Working Class Reader,* ch. 3; Altick, *English Common Reader,* 77–80.
160. Hugh Miller, *My Schools and Schoolmasters; or, the Story of My Education* (Boston, Mass., 1855), 27.
161. *Boys of England,* ed. Charles Stevens, 1:1 (24 Nov. 1866), 16 (italics added).
162. See Dunae, 'Penny Dreadfuls', 146, on the failure of W. H. G. Kingston and G. A. Henty's *Union Jack* in the early 1880s.

163. Quayle, *Ballantyne the Brave*, 162–4.
164. On this see Rose, *Intellectual Life*, ch. 3.
165. Altick, *English Common Reader*, 384. The figure is for sales of the British edition in Britain and the colonies.
166. There is a rare account of pub talk (*c*.1900) in Frederick Willis, *101 Jubilee Road: A Book of London Yesterdays* (1948), 57. 'We met simply to be ourselves for a short time; to throw off the trappings that we necessarily had to wear in civilized society, to discuss affairs of the day, sometimes to be very rude to one another, and for a time we all glowed in the fascinating light of human individuality.' That does not help much.

CHAPTER 8

1. Quoted in W. L. Langer, *European Alliances and Alignments* (New York, 1931), 308.
2. See my *The Lion's Share: A Short History of British Imperialism 1850–1995* (3rd. edn. 1996), 101–8 for this.
3. Speech of 4 May 1898, printed in A. L. Kennedy, *Salisbury 1830–1903: Portrait of a Statesman* (1953), 277.
4. *c*.1905, quoted in Marquis of Crewe, *Lord Rosebery* (1931), ii. 575.
5. William G. Hynes, *The Economics of Empire: Britain, Africa and the New Imperialism 1870–95* (1979); and the *Report of the Royal Commission appointed to Inquire into the Depression of Trade and Industry* (1886).
6. Chris Cook and John Stevenson, *The Longman Handbook of Modern British History* (1983), 62.
7. Charles Booth, *Life and Labour of the People of London*, (1st ser., 5 vols. (1892–1903); Seebohm Rowntree, *Poverty: A Study of Town Life* (1901).
8. V. I. Lenin, *Imperialism: The Highest Stage of Capitalism* (new English edn. 1933), 97. The quotation may not be altogether reliable. Lenin's stated source is an interview given by Rhodes to the famous journalist W. T. Stead, then quoted (presumably in German) in *Die Neue Zeit*, 1898. The following passage in Stead's *The History of the Mystery; or, The Story of the Jameson Raid* (1896), which may be the original source, is subtly different. It is not clear from the context here whether this is a genuine interview with Rhodes, or a fictional one. 'My great idea is the solution of the social problem, which, being interpreted, means that in order to keep your forty millions here from eating each other for lack of other victuals, we beyond the seas must open as much of the surface of this planet as we can for the overflow of your population to inhabit, and to create markets where you can dispose of the produce of your factories, and of your mines. The Empire, I am always telling you, is a bread-and-butter question. If you have not to be cannibals, you have got to be imperialists.' That is all very close to the Lenin version, except that Lenin—or *Die Neue Zeit*—has replaced 'cannibalism' by 'civil war'; which may of course be what Rhodes (if he really said this) meant.
9. Anon., 'The Future of the British Empire', *Westminster Review*, N.S., 38 (July 1870), 47–74. The *Wellesley Index of Victorian Periodicals* attributes this article to (Sir) John Robinson (1839–1903), who later became the first prime minister of Natal (*DNB*).
10. J. R. Seeley, *The Expansion of England: Two Courses of Lectures* (1883; 2nd edn. 1895), 10. The full quotation runs: 'We seem, as it were, to have conquered and peopled half the world in a fit of absence of mind... This fixed way of thinking has influenced our historians. It causes them, I think, to miss the true point of view in describing the

eighteenth century.' He was referring to the neglect of imperial history in schools and universities in his own time.

11. 1905, quoted in James G. Greenlee, 'The ABC's of Imperial Unity', *Canadian Journal of History*, 14 (1979), 52.
12. George R. Parkin, *Round the Empire* (1892), p. v.
13. Quoted in James G. Greenlee, *Education and Imperial Unity, 1901–26* (1987), 102–3.
14. Lord Meath, *Essays on Duty and Discipline* (1911), 59; quoted in Kathryn Castle, *Britannia's Children: Reading Colonialism Through Children's Books and Magazines* (Manchester, 1966), 4–5.
15. Meath in House of Lords, 1 Aug. 1893, *Hansard*, 4th ser., vol. 15, col. 985.
16. Lord, 'The Creed of Imperialism', *Nineteenth Century*, 66 (July 1909), 33.
17. E. J. Hobsbawm, *Industry and Empire: An Economic History of Britain Since 1750* (1968), 287.
18. Richard D. Altick, *The English Common Reader* (Chicago, 1957), 171.
19. Quoted in Zara Steiner, *Britain and the Origins of the First World War* (1977), 16.
20. See Alan J. Lee, *The Origins of the Popular Press 1855–1914* (1976); Stephen Koss, *The Rise and Fall of the Political Press in Britain*, vol. 1, *The Nineteenth Century* (1981).
21. This is the way it was seen in Britain. For a fairer view, using Arab sources, see D. H. Johnson, 'The Death of Gordon: A Victorian Myth', *Journal of Imperial and Commonwealth History*, 10 (1982), 285–310.
22. The two major surveys from this period, both edited by the Revd James S. Dennis, give different numbers, probably because they are counting slightly different things. From the *Centennial Survey of Foreign Missions* (1902), which categorizes them by missionary society, I have extrapolated a figure of 10,423; from the *World Atlas of Christian Missions* (1911), arranged by country, 6,126. By no means all of these worked in the empire: 1,065, for example, were in China, 242 in South and Central America (excluding British Guiana), and even two in the USA. Both these totals exclude missions to Jews and to seamen.
23. The strength of the army in 1898 was around 225,000; during the Boer War these were supplemented by several thousand Volunteers. Denis Judd and Keith Surridge, *The Boer War* (2002), 60.
24. *Census of England and Wales, 1891*, vol. 3, p. xxxii.
25. *The Citizen Reader* (*Cassell's Modern School Series*, 1886), 149.
26. Ron Barnes, *Coronation Cups and Jam Jars: A Portrait of an East End Family Through Three Generations* (1976), 61. Barnes is writing here not from personal experience, but from what he was told by the generation previous to his.
27. Jonathan Schneer, *London 1900: The Imperial Metropolis* (New Haven, Conn., 1999), 184, and 294, n. 1. By contrast there were many fewer Africans, though those who were there were important, organizing the first ever Pan-African Conference in 1900: ibid. 203. See also Antoinette Burton, *At the Heart of the Empire: Indians and the Colonial Encounter in Late-Victorian Britain* (1998).
28. 'John Law' [Margaret Harkness], *In Darkest London: A New and Popular Edition of Captain Lobe. A Story of the Salvation Army* (this edn. 1891), 3.
29. [A. O. Eltzbacher], *Drifting* (1901), 39. Eltzbacher was German-born, but later became a naturalized Briton under the new pen-name of 'J. Ellis Barker'.
30. *National Review*, 50 (1907), 523.
31. Ibid. 52 (1908), 3.

32. A few examples (of many) are Eltzbacher, *Drifting*, 13–26; J. A. Murray MacDonald, 'The Imperial Problem', supporting Rosebery's call for an imperialist coalition, *Contemporary Review*, 80 (1901), 483; W. S. Lilly, 'Collapse of England', *Fortnightly Review*, 77 (1902), 782–84; and A. Cuthbert Medd, 'The Judgement of Posterity', *National Review*, 41 (1903), 994. The leading imperialist anti-democrat at this time was probably Sir Alfred (later Lord) Milner. See Hans-Christoph Schröder, *Imperialismus und Antidemokratisches Denken* (Wiesbaden, 1978), *passim*.
33. J. R. Seeley, 'English in Schools' (1868), repr. in *Lectures and Essays* (1895), 262.
34. Seeley, 'Our Insular Ignorance', *Nineteenth Century* (1885), quoted in Deborah Wormell, *Sir John Seeley and the Uses of History* (Cambridge, 1980), 55.
35. See e.g. Alice Roberts (later Elgar), *Marchmont Manor* (1882): 'English people, as a rule, are given to disparage their own country.' Quoted in Robert Anderson, *Elgar and Chivalry* (2002), 50.
36. See my 'The Edwardians and their Empire', in Donald Read (ed.), *Edwardian England* (1982), and the contemporary sources cited there.
37. See Bernard Semmel, *Imperialism and Social Reform: English Social-Imperial Thought 1895–1914* (1960); and G. R. Searle, *The Quest for National Efficiency: A Study in British Politics and British Political Thought 1899–1914* (1971).
38. On this see J. E. Tyler, *The Struggle for Imperial Unity 1868–1895* (1938); B. H. Brown, *The Tariff Reform Movement in Great Britain 1881–1895* (Oxford, 1943); Semmel, *Imperialism and Social Reform*, chs. 4–5; Alfred Gollin, *Balfour's Burden: Arthur Balfour and Imperial Preference* (1965); S. H. Zebel, 'Joseph Chamberlain and the Genesis of Tariff Reform', *Journal of British Studies*, 7 (1967); Peter Cain, 'Political Economy and Edwardian England: The Tariff-Reform Controversy', in Alan O'Day (ed.), *The Edwardian Age: Conflict and Stability* (1979); and Andrew Thompson, 'Tariff Reform: An Imperial Strategy', *Historical Journal*, 40 (1997).
39. Above p. 62.
40. John Finnemore, *Famous Englishmen* (1901), 3, 5; quoted in Stephen Heathorn, '"Let us remember that we, too, are English": Constructions of Citizenship and National Identity in English Elementary School Reading Books, 1880–1914', *Victorian Studies*, 38 (1995), 417. Finnemore adds that 'a really great man' will always look after 'the people who support him' (p. 4), which may have helped.
41. John MacKenzie, *Propaganda and Empire: The Manipulation of British Public Opinion 1880–1960* (Manchester, 1984); which was then followed by the Manchester University Press 'Studies in Imperialism' series edited by him.
42. Trevor R. Reese, *The History of the Royal Commonwealth Society 1868–1968* (Oxford: 1968). Its original object was 'to provide a place of meeting for all gentlemen connected with the colonies and British India, and others taking an interest in colonial and India affairs' (*Proceedings of the Royal Colonial Institute* (1870), quoted p. 17), and not to proselytize at all. It began that in the 1880s, with the institution of an essay competition designed to foster imperial knowledge in schools (pp. 84–5).
43. See MacKenzie, *Propaganda and Empire*, ch. 6, for a general overview of these; Greenlee, *Education and Imperial Unity*, on the League of Empire and the the Royal Colonial Institute; John Kendle, *The Round Table Movement and Imperial Union* (Toronto, 1975); Alexander C. May, 'The Round Table, 1910–66', Ph.D. thesis, Oxford University (1995); J. O. Springhall, 'Lord Meath, Youth, and Empire', *Journal of Contemporary*

History, 5 (1970), on the Empire Day movement; Andrew S. Thompson, *Imperial Britain: The Empire and British Politics c.1880–1932* (2000), on the Royal Colonial Institute; Julia Bush, *Edwardian Ladies and Imperial Power* (Leicester: 2000); and Eliza Riedi, 'Imperialist Women in Edwardian Britain: The Victoria League 1899–1914', Ph.D. thesis, St Andrews University (1997).

44. e.g. the British Women's Emigration Association (1884); the South African Colonisation Society (1902); the Colonial Intelligence League (1910).
45. Thompson, *Imperial Britain*, 44–6, on the Navy League; R. J. Q. Adams, 'The National Service League and Mandatory Service in Edwardian England', *Armed Forces and Society*, 12 (1985).
46. See MacKenzie, *Propaganda and Empire*, ch. 4; and Paul Greenhalgh, *Ephemeral Vistas: Expositions Universelles, Great Exhibitions and World's Fairs, 1851–1939* (Manchester, 1988), ch. 3.
47. *Report of the Royal Commission for the Colonial and Indian Exhibition* (1887), p. xlvii. See also MacKenzie, *Propaganda and Empire*, 101–2.
48. e.g. the organizers wrote to mayors and school boards in industrial towns, suggesting that they raise subscriptions to enable workers 'with their wives' and schoolchildren to come to the exhibition, and offering them reduced entry charges in the off-season: ibid., p. xlviii. The headmaster of Brighton Grammar School helpfully published a set of educational notes to the exhibits, in two versions: one for schoolchildren, and the other for working-men's clubs. *Notes of Lectures given in the Conference Room of the Colonial and Indian Exhibition* (1886).
49. Sir Arthur Sullivan, *Ode on the Opening of the Colonial and Indian Exhibition*. The next year Sullivan also provided an *Ode for the Occasion of Laying the Foundation Stone of the Imperial Institute*, to words by Lewis Morris, which is rather better. See Jeffrey Richards, *Imperialism and Music: Britain 1876–1953* (2001), 26–9.
50. There are good accounts in MacKenzie, *Propaganda and Empire*, 102–5, and Greenhalgh, *Ephemeral Vistas*, 90–5. Kiralfy staged an 'Empire of India' exhibition in 1895, an 'India and Ceylon' Exhibition the following year, a 'Greater Britain' Exhibition in 1899, all at Earl's Court; and an annual series of exhibitions at the White City between 1908 and 1914, some of which had imperial themes. See *The Empire of India Exhibition 1895 . . . The Conception, Design and Production of Imre Kiralfy* (1895).
51. The book is in the British Library, but not, sadly, the music. I have not been able to trace Venanzi in any of the normal musical reference works.
52. MacKenzie, *Propaganda and Empire*, ch. 4, and Greenhalgh, *Ephemeral Vistas*, 58, cite Edinburgh (1886), Glasgow (1888), Bradford (1904), Wolverhampton (1907), and Dublin (1907).
53. See Edward Miller, *That Noble Cabinet: A History of the British Museum* (1973), 318 *et passim*; Annie E. Coombes, *Reinventing Africa: Museums, Material Culture and Popular Imagination in Late Victorian and Edwardian England* (New Haven, Conn., 1994); and Tim Barringer and Tom Flynn (eds.), *Colonialism and the Object: Empire, Material Culture and the Museum* (1998), esp. the chapters by Barringer and Deborah Swallow.
54. MacKenzie, *Propaganda and Empire*, 102.
55. Described vividly in Jan Morris, *Pax Britannica: The Climax of an Empire* (1968), ch. 1.
56. A good selection of imperial (including anti-imperial) poetry from this period is Chris Brooks and Peter Faulkner (eds.), *The White Man's Burdens: An Anthology of British Poetry of*

the Empire (Exeter, 1996). On imperial literature generally, see Patrick Brantlinger, *Rule of Darkness: British Literature and Imperialism 1830–1914* (1988); Allen J. Greenberger, *The British Image of India: A Study in the 'Literature of Imperialism* (1969); Robert H. MacDonald, *The Language of Empire: Myths and Metaphors of Popular Imperialism* (Manchester, 1994); Jeffrey Meyers, *Fiction and the Colonial Experience* (Ipswich, 1973); Thomas Richards, *The Imperial Archive: Knowledge and the Fantasy of Empire* (1993); and A. Sandison, *The Wheel of Empire: A Study of the Imperial Idea in Some Late 19th and early 20th century fiction* (1967).

57. See Tim Barringer, ' "Not a 'modern' as the word is now understood"? Byam Shaw and the Poetics of Professional Society', in David Peters Corbett and Lara Perry (eds.), *English Art 1860–1914* (Manchester, 2000).

58. See J. W. M. Hichberger, *Images of the Army: The Military in British Art, 1815–1914* (Manchester, 1988), chs. 5–7.

59. See George W. Joy, *The Work of George W. Joy, with an Autobiographical Sketch* (1904). Joy—an Old Harrovian—had originally wanted to be a soldier, but could not because of an injury. His most famous painting, was *Gordon's Last Stand,* completed in 1893. His other works include *Dreams on the Veldt* (1900)—an angel hovering over a dying soldier; and *Britannia* (1900)—'Erect but not defiant, leaning on her naked sword, stands Britannia, mother of nations . . . ' (p. 53).

60. See W. Shaw Sparrow (ed.), *The Spirit of the Age: The Work of Frank Brangwyn ARA* (1905), a large folio volume with some beautiful illustrations, including *The Rajah's Birthday* (1908); the same author's *Frank Brangwyn and His Work* (1910); and Brangwyn's contributions to Martin Hardie (ed.), *The Pageant of Empire: Souvenir Volume* (1924).

61. It depicts a naked man, rough-hewn, on the back of a rearing horse, the muscles of both straining. A cast of it was erected in front of the Rhodes Memorial in Cape Town. Watts started work on it in 1886, and completed it shortly before his death in 1904. Originally he had wanted to 'write the names of great names on the pedestal: Genghis Khan, Timon the Tartar, Attila, and Mahomet'. Then he met Rhodes, who said he would have liked it 'to commemorate the completion of the Cape to Cairo railway', with the names of the first subscribers on the pedestal, and the words: 'These people believed that this scheme was possible.' In the event the Cape Town copy is carved with the words: 'The work of G. F. Watts and by him given to the genius of Cecil Rhodes.' In my book that makes it an imperialist sculpture. See M. S. Watts, *George Frederic Watts* (1912), ii. 171, 236, 268–72; iii. 270.

62. The following nine—mainly soldiers—are still extant in London, dating from 1880–1914: Lord Lawrence (1882), Sir Herbert Stewart (medallion, 1886), Bartle Frere (1888), Lords Roberts and Kitchener (busts, 1902), the 2nd Duke of Cambridge (1907), Wernher and Beit (busts, outside the Imperial College of Science, presumably because they donated money to it), and Captain Cook (recognized at last, at the east end of the Mall, in 1914). These are out of 89 surviving public statues in total from this period. Arthur Byron, *London Statues* (1981). To these should be added the original statue of General Gordon in Trafalgar Square (1888); another of Baron Napier of Magdala in Kensington Road (1891), and a bronze tablet (only) to Warren Hastings in Park Lane (1910), all of which appear to have been destroyed since. (Gordon was replaced in 1951.) Other empire-related monuments (not statues) include a memorial to those who fell in the Afghan and Zulu wars at Woolwich (1882); others commemorating the Boer War, including one in St James's Park (1910); and a cattle trough

dedicated to the horses that fell in the same war, in St Peter's Square, Hammersmith (1904). See London County Council, *Return of Outdoor Memorials in London* (1910), in the London Metropolitan Archive; C. S. Cooper, *The Outdoor Monuments of London: Statues, Memorial Buildings, Tablets and War Memorials* (1928); and Tori Smith, '"A grand work of noble conception": The Victoria Memorial and Imperial London', in Felix Driver and David Gilbert (eds.), *Imperial Cities* (1999).

63. See Bernard Porter, 'Edward Elgar and Empire', *Journal of Imperial and Commonwealth History*, 29 (2001).

64. Sullivan was really the imperial composer laureate of the time, furnishing most of the ceremonial music required for great imperial occasions, such as his *Ode for the Opening of the Colonial and Indian Exhibition* (1886), *Ode for the Laying of the Foundation Stone for the Imperial Institute* (1887), *Imperial March for the Opening of the Imperial Institute* (1893), and a 'Boer War' *Te Deum* (1900)—his last work before his death—which incorporates his own 'Onward Christian Soldiers' tune. Sir Hubert Parry was also commissioned to compose a 'Thanksgiving Te Deum' for the 1900 Hereford Festival, which turned out very 'stringy', according to Elgar: 'Fiddles sawing all the time!!!!! *DEAR* old Parry!!!!!!' Robert Anderson, *Elgar and Chivalry* (2002), 210.

65. MacKenzie's overtly imperial works include an *Ode on the Golden Jubilee* (1887); *The Empire Flag*, for soloists, choir, and orchestra (1887); a *Canadian Rhapsody* for orchestra (1905); and *Four Canadian Songs* (1907)—here we have the Scottish-imperial connection; and *An Empire Song* (1908). For the first performance of the *Jubilee Ode* we are told that 'the conductor had electric buttons beside the score to detonate cannon in the grounds, though not all came in on cue': Brian Rees, *A Musical Peacemaker: The Life and Work of Sir Edward German* (1986), 207.

66. German's imperialist credentials are thinner, and mainly rest on his patriotic operetta *Merrie England* (1902). He also wrote 'Coronation' pieces, and set some Kipling poems to music.

67. Coleridge-Taylor is best known for his setting of Longfellow, the cantata *Hiawatha's Wedding Feast* (1898); but he also wrote *Four African Dances* for violin and piano (1904), which do not sound at all African (unless he meant African-American): the music it immediately brings to mind is Dvořák's; a 'rhapsody' called *Kubla Khan*, and *Symphonic Variations on an African Air* (both 1906). Holst's oriental-influenced works include the opera *Sàvitri* (1908), four groups of *Choral Hymns from the Rig-Veda* (1908–12), and *The Cloud Messenger* (1910). Bantock's are the ballet *Aegypt* (1892), and a cantata, *Omar Khayyam* (1906).

    Amy Woodforde-Finden (née Ward), 1860–1919, the daughter of American parents, and a composer from an early age, married an Indian Army officer in 1894 and was inspired in India to write her very popular *Four Indian Love Lyrics* (1902), including the *Kashmiri Song* ('Pale hands . . . '). More 'oriental' songs followed; 'notable', says Andrew Lamb in the *New Grove*, 'for their fluent, sentimental melody'. I am grateful to Peter Burroughs for bringing her to my attention. Albert Ketèlby's orientalisms—*In a Persian Market* (1920), *In a Chinese Temple Garden* (1925), etc.—are just too late to include here.

    On the subject of imperial music generally, see Jeffrey Richards, *Imperialism and Music: Britain 1876–1953* (2001). This is an invaluable work, which, however, in my view exaggerates the imperial content and character of the music of the time. See above, p. 372 n. 65.

68. Jane Ridley, *The Architect and His Wife: A Life of Edwin Lutyens* (2002), esp. 223; and see the same author's 'Edwin Lutyens, New Delhi, and the Architecture of Imperialism', *Journal of Imperial and Commonwealth History*, 26 (1998). Lutyens's rabid antipathy to 'Indo-Saracenic' architecture, and his racism more generally, may come as a surprise to those who see traces of indigenous influence and 'spirit' in his New Delhi buildings.
69. e.g. Shorne Hill, Netley Marsh; Port Lympne (by Sir Herbert Baker); and Good Hope in Wimbledon. (Information kindly provided by Francis Plowden.)
70. See H. R. Hitchcock, *Architecture, 19th and 20th Centuries* (1958); M. H. Port, *Imperial London: Civil Government Building in London 1850–1915* (New Haven, Comm., 1995), *passim*; John MacKenzie, '"The Second City of the Empire": Glasgow—Imperial Municipality', in Felix Driver and David Gilbert (eds.), *Imperial Cities: Landscape, Display and Identity* (Manchester, 1999).
71. Baker was quite clear that one *could* express imperialism architecturally. Writing to Lutyens about his New Delhi commission, he wrote: 'It must not be *Indian, not English, nor Roman, but it must be Imperial*' (quoted Anderson, *Elgar and Chivalry*, 297; original italics). Later he helped Lutyens with the new Indian capital. He had been born in Kent, but emigrated to South Africa in 1892, where he admired and befriended Cecil Rhodes, whose pretentious 'Memorial' on the side of Table Mountain ('The immense and brooding spirit still shall quicken and control. Living he was the Land and dead his Soul shall be her Soul') he designed; as well as many other finer buildings. The *Dictionary of South African Biography*, vol. 1 (Cape Town, 1976), 46, admits that his work in England 'never achieved the same strength as that done in South Africa'. Rhodes House, Oxford (opened in 1929), is pleasant.
72. 'Britannia's Sons Shall Rule the World' (sung by Winifred Hare; words by Rourke, music by Maude Hare). From Max Tyler's collection.
73. 'Another Little Patch of Red' (Roddick Anderson; Lytton/Harrison.) Max Tyler's collection.
74. 'A Pattern to the World' (words and music by Harry Dacre). This is the theme also of 'India's Reply' and 'How India kept her Word' (1895/7, both sung by Leo Dryden dressed up as a sepoy; words by J. P. Harrington, music by George le Brunn); and, from the Boer War, 'Song of our Empire' (Leo Stormont; Ramsay/Bradford), 'For England! The Colonies' Message' (written and sung by Fred W. Mills), 'Brothers, or the Colonies will Fight at England's Side' (Wynne/Wynne), and 'That Was the Soldier's Song' (Marie Loftus; McGlennon/McGlennon). Other songs lauded the contributions of the often despised Irish; e.g.: 'What Paddy Gave the Drum' (Michael Nolan; Connor/Connor); 'Bravo! Dublin Fusiliers' (Leo Dryden and Marie Tyler; Wheeler/ Wheeler); and 'Play Us an Old "Come All Ye"' (Nolan; Hall/Le Brunn). Max Tyler's collection.
75. The list of 'Plays Submitted to the Lord Chamberlain' carries the titles of three clearly Boer War-related popular plays staged in 1899–1900: *The Briton and the Boer* (anon.); *Boer Meisje*, by H. Johnson, and *Fight for Africa*, by L. Mortimer. See also Breandan Gregory, 'Staging British India', in J. S. Bratton *et al.*, *Acts of Supremacy: The British Empire and the Stage, 1790–1930* (1991), describing a spate of 'Indian' plays in the 1890s; Michael R. Booth, *Victorian Spectacular Theatre 1850–1910* (1981), e.g. 70–1; and Ronald Pearsall, *Edwardian Popular Music* (1975), 21, 32, and 34, which mentions some musical comedies with oriental themes.

76. John Barnes, *Filming the Boer War* (1992), 21. Descriptive lists of all Boer War films shown in Britain appear in the same author's *The Beginnings of the Cinema in England*, vols. 4–6 (1976), covering the years 1899–1901.
77. This is a film called 'Attempted Capture of an English Nurse and Children', as described in *The Era*, 14 July 1900, and quoted in Barnes, *Beginnings of the Cinema*, v. 256.
78. I think. A photograph appears in John Finnemore, *Famous Englishmen*, book II (1902), 208. It could be of the painting itself, bought by Tussaud's.
79. Max Tyler has over 60 of these, with titles like 'The Nile Expedition, a musical panorama (composer W. F. Taylor), 'For Freedom and the Flag: Lord Roberts Grand March' (Ezra Read); 'Our Favourite (Bobs) March' (Daniel Smith) 'Going to Table Bay, Patriotic Descriptive Fantasia' (Alan Macey); 'The Night Attack: A Military Scene' (F. Scott) 'Seige of Ladysmith, Grand Divertimento' (Theo Bonheur); 'Return of the Troops, Polka March' (Agnes M. Chambers), etc.
80. Pearsall, *Edwardian Popular Music*, 130.
81. MacKenzie, *Propaganda and Empire*, covers a lot of these trivia.
82. This is based on an analyses of the contents of the following magazines: *Windsor Magazine*, *Harmsworth Magazine*, and *Strand Magazine*, from 1902, 1906, and 1910. The *Windsor Magazine* in 1901–2 (vol. 15), to give just one example, carried eight empire-related items out of 85: two of Kipling's Indian stories, 'A Veldt Love Story', a tale set in Queensland, 'An Incident in the Indian Mutiny', and reports on life among the Boers, the Anglo-Egyptian army, and the Egyptian pyramids. The incidence of imperial items tends to drop slightly after then; although the *Strand Magazine* has a regular short-story writer using North-West Frontier settings in the person of Frank Savile, and, by 1910, a regular 8-page 'Overseas Empire Supplement' (of items from the 'settler' colonies) at the end of each issue. An example of racism, picked entirely at random, is Cutliffe Hynes's story 'The Cholera Ship', printed in the first volume of the *Harmsworth Magazine* (1898–99), with African deckhands portrayed as 'those sullen animal blacks' (p. 164).
83. Stables, *On War's Red Tide* (1900); Henty, *With Roberts to Pretoria* (1902); and see Guy Arnold, *Hold Fast for England: G. A. Henty, Imperialist Boys' Writer* (1980).
84. Vol. 36 (1913–14) e.g. has 32 substantial items featuring colonies out of a total of 190, including a 'Tale of the Malay States', and several other fictional 'adventures' in Africa (usually featuring 'witch-doctors') and the South Seas (with savages); a number of accounts of 'Red Indians' in Canada; an item on 'Pioneer Days in Queensland'; just two (significantly?) related to India; an account of an English cricket tour to South Africa; advice on lacrosse 'by an Australian international'; and tips on 'How to throw a Boomerang'. See also Patrick Dunae, 'Boy's Own Paper: Origins and Editorial Policy', *The Private Library*, 2nd ser., 9 (1976).
85. On this general area see Jeffrey Richards (ed.), *Imperialism and Juvenile Literature* (Manchester, 1989), esp. ch. 6: John Springhall, 'Healthy Papers For Manly Boys: Imperialism and Race in the Harmsworths' Halfpenny Boys' Papers of the 1890s and 1900s'; Patrick Dunae, 'Boys' Literature and the Idea of Empire, 1870–1914', *Victorian Studies*, 24 (1980), 105–21; Joseph Bristow, *Empire Boys: Adventures in a Man's World* (1991); Kathryn Castle, *Britannia's Children: Reading Colonialism through Children's Books and Magazines* (Manchester, 1996).
86. Quoted in Springhall, 'Healthy Papers', 113.

87. Quoted in Jeffrey Richards, 'With Henty to Africa', in Richards (ed.), *Imperialism and Juvenile Literature*, 73.
88. Quoted in Jeffrey Richards, 'Popular Imperialism and the Image of the Army in Juvenile Literature', in John MacKenzie (ed.), *Popular Imperialism and the Military* (Manchester, 1992), 84.
89. Very little seems to have been written about Bessie Marchant. There are tiny biographies of her in *The Canadian Men and Women of the Time* (2nd edn. 1912), *Who's Who in Methodism* (1933), and *Who's Who in Oxfordshire* (1936). She was born in Kent in 1862, was married to a Methodist minister, the Revd Jabez Comfort, and died in Oxfordshire in 1941. I have looked through (not thoroughly read) a handful of her stories: *The Rajah's Daughter: or, The Half-Moon Girl* (1899)—very transgressive; *Held at Ransom: A Story of Colonial Life* (1901), set in South Africa; *The Captives of the Kaid* (1904), whose implied feminism is rather spoiled at the end when the young heroine (Lalla) promises to marry her boyfriend and settle down after her adventures: 'then you can be master' (p. 208); *The Girl Captives: A Story of the Indian Frontier* (1906), in which the women merely endure suffering, and have to be rescued by the men; *The Deputy Boss: A Tale of British Honduras* (1910)—this one has a boy hero; and *Lesbia's Little Blunder* (1934), with a young girl set down among rough Canadian goldminers. Both the quotations come from her (short) obituary in the *Times Literary Supplement*, 15 Nov. 1941, p. 569.
90. A spot check in the *Girl's Own Paper* for 1890–1 and 1907–8 (i.e. deliberately avoiding the main 'jingo' period) turns up an account of the abolition crusade, featuring 'Black and White Heroes'; a piece on 'the Berbers of Kabylia'; a short item on the Church Emigration Society; half a page on 'Life in the Colonies' by Adelaide Ross, recommending emigration (but for the working classes, *not* for the readers of the *GOP*); a medical item on 'Health For Tropical Travellers'; and a couple of reports from female missionaries, in vol. 12 (1890–1); and an account of 'Camping in the New Zealand Bush'; a description of Egypt 'From a Desert Diary'; a piece (illustrated) on 'Indian Gems and Jewelry'; a story from an Assam village with a District Commissioner given a walk-on role; an account of 'Women's Life in the Celestial Kingdom' (China); advice on 'Starting a Missionary Study Band'; a recipe for 'Arabian Stew'; and—the only substantial imperial item—a highly partisan account of the contemporary 'Unrest in India' by Sir Andrew Wingate, in vols. 29 and 30 (1907–8). This was probably enough to keep the empire in its readers' minds. See also J. S. Bratton, 'British Imperialism and the Reproduction of Femininity in Girls' Fiction, 1900–1930', in Richards (ed.), *Imperialism and Juvenile Literature*; and Wendy Forester, *Great Grandmama's Weekly: A Celebration of the Girls's Own Paper 1880–1901* (1980).
91. On the subject of 'race' in children's books, see Castle, *Britannia's Children*; and Patrick Dunae, 'Boys' Literature and the Idea of Race: 1870–1900', *Wascana Review*, 12 (1977), 84–107.
92. Anon., 'England after War', *Fortnightly Review*, 78 (1902), 2; and cf. J. G. Rogers, 'Anxiety of the Hour', *Nineteenth Century*, 50 (1901), 861; Lord Curzon, 'The True Imperialism', ibid. 63 (1908), 159–60; and F. S. Oliver, 'From Empire to Union', *National Review*, 53 (1909), 32.
93. Frank Smith, *A History of English Elementary Education 1760–1902* (1931), 335.
94. David Wardle, *The Rise of the Schooled Society* (1974), 21.

95. These figures are taken from Gordon Batho, 'Sources For the History of History Teaching in Elementary Schools 1833–1914', in T. G. Cook (ed.), *Local Studies and the History of Education* (1972), 139–40; and Heathorn, '"Let us remember that we, too, are English"', 424. They square with S. J. Colledge's figure of 25% of London Board schoolchildren who took history in 1899: 'The Study of History in the Teacher Training College', *History of Education Society Bulletin*, 36 (1985), 45.
96. R. Aldrich and D. Dean, 'The Historical Dimension', in Aldrich (ed.), *History in the National Curriculum* (1991), 96, 98; Pamela Horn, 'English Elementary Education and the Growth of the Imperial Ideal, 1880–1914', in J. A. Mangan, *Benefits Bestowed? Education and British Imperialism* (Manchester, 1988), 42; David Rubinstein, 'The London School Board 1870–1904', in Phillip McCann (ed.), *Popular Education and Socialization in the 19th Century* (1977), 253.
97. Colledge, 'History in the Teacher Training College', 46.
98. Quoted by Peter Yeandle, 'Lessons in Englishness and Empire, c. 1880–1914: Further Thoughts on the English/British Conundrum', in R. Phillips and H. Brocklehurst (eds.), *History, Nationhood and the Question of Britain* (2004), from a Board of Education Report of 1903. Cf. Harold Johnson in 1915: 'patriotism became in fact the dominant purpose of school instruction in history.' *The Teaching of History in Elementary and Secondary Schools* (1915), 98, quoted in ibid.
99. Halford Mackinder, 'The Teaching of Geography From an Imperial Point of View, and the Use Which Could and Should Be Made of Visual Instruction'; a paper read to the Imperial Education Conference under the auspices of the Board of Education in 1911, and printed in *The Geographical Teacher*, 6 (1911), 83.
100. e.g. H. O. Arnold-Forster, *The Citizen Reader* (*Cassell's Modern School Series*, [1886]); James Reid, *Manual of Moral Instruction: A Graded Course of Lessons on Conduct Worked Out on the Concentric Plan* (1908); Lord Meath *et al.*, *Essays on Duty and Discipline* (1910); M. L. V. Hughes, *Citizens to Be: A Social Study of Health, Wisdom and Goodness with Special Reference to Elementary Schools* (1915).
101. Mrs Cyril Ransome, *A First History of England* (1903), 399; and cf. A. J. Berry, *Britannia's Growth and Greatness: A Historical Geography of the British Empire* (1913), 304.
102. Greenlee, *Education and Imperial Unity*, ch. 1 *passim*; Bush, *Imperial Ladies*, 133–41; Eliza Riedi, 'Imperialist Women', ch. 4. Most of the entries for the essay competition were dire, according to Professor Egerton, who was one of the judges. Frederick Madden, 'The Commonwealth, Commonwealth History, and Oxford, 1905–1971', in Madden and D. K. Fieldhouse (eds.), *Oxford and the Idea of Commonwealth* (1982), 11.
103. Greenlee, *Education and Imperial Unity*, 21–2, and 'The ABC's of Imperial Unity', *Canadian Journal of History*, 14 (1979), 57–62. Members of the 'History section' included H. E. Egerton, A. F. Pollard, and J. B. Bury.
104. Reese, *History of the Royal Commonwealth Society*, 84–6; Greenlee, *Education and Imperial Unity*, 90.
105. J. G. Greenlee, 'Imperial Studies and the Unity of the Empire', *Journal of Imperial and Commonwealth History*, 7 (1979), 326–30.
106. House of Lords, 1 Aug. 1893, *Hansard*, 4th ser., vol 15, col. 983; and cf. House of Lords, 1 Dec. 1902, ibid., vol. 115, col. 813.
107. Norman Chamberlain, 'The New Imperialism and the Old Parties', *National Review*, 51 (1908), 650.

108. The first edition came out in 1835; Maria Calcutt died in 1842. There were frequent new editions after then, however (I have compared 1842, 1844, 1866, 1874, 1879, 1880, and 1971), usually bringing the story up to the (then) present day, but also often significantly revising the original text. The editor/reviser of the 1879 edition was James Rowley. See C. E. Lawrence's 1936 'memoir', 'Lady Callcott and Her Book', prefaced to the 1971 edn.
109. S. R. Gardiner, *Outline of English History* (1881; 1888 edn.).
110. Examples include *The Royal School Series: The Reign of Queen Victoria* (1881); J. Roscoe Mongan, *The Oxford and Cambridge British History for School Use* (1882); *Chambers's Historical Readers*, Book 4 (1883); D. Morris, *Third Historical Reader* (1883); Cyril Ransome, *A Short History of England* (1887); A. W. Dakers, vol. 5 of the *Jack Historical Readers* series (1905); Charles and Mary Oman, *A Junior History of England* (1904), where America and India are well covered in the main text and the rest of the empire in a free-standing but substantial chapter at the end; *Chambers's Preparatory History of England* (1901); and John Finnemore, *Famous Englishmen*, Book 2 (1902), where imperial and military heroes figure largely: 11 out of 21 altogether, including 'The British Private Soldier' (at Inkerman).
111. e.g. J. M. D. Meiklejohn, *The British Empire* (1891); George R. Parkin, *Round the Empire* (1892); A. Hassell, *The Making of the British Empire, 1714–1832* (1896); W. H. Woodward, *A Short History of the Expansion of the British Empire 1500–1902* (1899); Lord Meath (Intro.), *Our Empire Past and Present* (1901); C. S. Dawe, *King Edward's Realm: The Story of the Making of the Empire* (1902); Edward Salmon, *The Story of the Empire* (1902); H. E. Egerton, *The Origin and Growth of the British Colonies* (1904); A. W. H. Forbes, *A History of the British Dominions Beyond the Seas* (1910); P. H. and A. C. Kerr, *The Growth of the British Empire* (1911); Eleanor Richardson, *The Building of the British Empire: A Reading Book for Schools* (1913) (this may have had a 'lower' target audience); and A. D. Innes, *A History of England and the British Empire in Four Volumes* (1913–14).
112. On 'readers', which made up most of the market in state-school textbooks in this period, see Stephen Heathorn, *For Home, Country and Race: Constructing Gender, Class, and Englishness in the Elementary School, 1880–1914* (Toronto, 2000), 8, 14–17.
113. e.g. in John Finnemore, *Famous Englishmen*, Book 1 (1902); *Jack's Historical Readers* vol. 3, by A. R. Tilley (*c.*1905), 180–90. And see Heathorn, '"Let us remember that we, too, are English"', 410–12.
114. Omans, *Junior History*, 179.
115. e.g. *The Jack Historical Readers*, Book 5, by A. W. Dakers (1905), 71; *Chambers's Preparatory History*, 139–43; and the Omans, *Junior History*, 172–3. See also MacKenzie, *Propaganda and Empire*, 177.
116. Below, p. 239.
117. Omans, *Junior History*, 249–50. The Omans, incidentally, were both born into Indian and military backgrounds.
118. e.g. James Rowley, *The Settlement of the Constitution 1679–1784* (1903 edn.); *Gill's Imperial History of England, for School and College Use* (1883); and Ransome, *Short History*, whose author's aim is to keep clear of 'party questions ... by confining myself to simple statements of facts'.
119. Mongan, *Oxford and Cambridge British History*, 168; *Gill's Imperial History*, 369; Morris, *Third Historical Reader*, 256; Arabella B. Buckley, *History of England for Beginners* (1887; 1896

reprint), 342; Book 3 of *The Jack Historical Readers*, by A. R. Tilley (*c*.1905), 182: though the last makes it seem just a minor blot.

120. Mongan, *Oxford and Cambridge British History*, 198; Buckley, *History of England*, 342.
121. Omans, *Junior History*, 234.
122. Valerie Chancellor, *History for Their Masters* (1970), 137–8.
123. There may be some anti-imperial textbooks out there, but I have failed to find one.
124. The Code is tabulated in H. Major, *Standard Teaching Helps, Illustrated by Model Lessons ... for Boys', Girls', and Mixed Schools* (1889), 5–6. See also Avril M. C. Maddrell, 'Empire, Emigration and School Geography: Changing Discourses of Imperial Citizenship, 1880–1925', *Journal of Historical Geography*, 22 (1996), 378–9.
125. e.g. C. P. Lucas, *Introduction to a Historical Geography of the British Empire* (1887), *Historical Geography of the British Colonies*, 4 vols. (1897), and (ed.), *An Historical Geography of the British Colonies*, 7 vols. (1888–1923); James Hewitt, *Geography of the British Colonies and Dependencies* (new edn. 1887); E. Protheroe, *Commercial Geography of the British Empire* (1902); Anon. [G Philip], *The British Empire* (n.d.; *c*.1910); H. E. Egerton, *Historical Geography of the British Colonies* (1907–8); F. D. Herbertson, *The British Empire* (1910); and A. J. Berry, *Britannia's Growth and Greatness: A Historical Geography of the British Empire* (1913).
126. *Chambers's Geographical Readers of the Continents: Africa* (1901), 47–8.
127. H. J. Mackinder, *The Nations of the Modern World: An Elementary Study in Geography* (n.d. [1911]), iv. 272.
128. *The World and its People: A New Series of Geography Readers* (Nelson, 1902), 119.
129. e.g. *Chambers's Geographical Readers*, Standard 4 (1884), 98–9.
130. James C. Greenough, *The Evolution of the Elementary Schools of Great Britain* (1903), quoted in Heathorn, *For Home, Country, and Race*, 115.
131. Mackinder, 'Teaching of Geography, 83.
132. Heathorn, *For Home, Country, and Race*, 16–18.
133. Revd Alexander Stewart, *A Compendium of Modern Geography* (35th edn. 1889), 249.
134. Stewart, *Compendium* (1889), 278.
135. *Chambers's Geographical Readers*, Standard 6 (1885), 21, 69.
136. In order: *Chambers's Geographical Readers*, Standard 1 (1883), 64, and Standard 6 (1885), 47; *Chambers's Geographical Readers of the Continents: Australasia* (1902), 48; Maria Hack, *Travels in Hot and Cold Lands* (1877), 95; A. J. Herbertson, *The Junior Geography* (1905), 227; *Chambers's Geographical Readers*, Standard 6, p. 46; and *The World and its People: Australasia* (Nelson, 1903), 100.
137. Castle, *Britannia's Children*, 6. One of the most pervasive African images was disseminated via Helen Bannerman's very popular *The Story of Little Black Sambo* (1899); which Elizabeth Hay, however, argues was relatively free of derogatory racist stereotyping, until American publishers got hold of it, transplanted it to the American South, and replaced the original illustrations with more offensive ones. Hay, *Sambo Sahib: The Story of Little Black Sambo and Helen Bannerman* (1981).
138. Mackinder, 'Teaching of Geography', 82.
139. *Nations of the Modern World*, iv. 1 (italics added).
140. D. R. Stoddart, *On Geography and its History* (1986), 128–9.
141. e.g. *Chambers's Geographical Readers*, Standard 6, pp. 47, 64, 81.
142. *The World and its People: Asia*, 144.
143. *Chambers's Geographical Readers of the Continents: Africa* (1901), 27–8.

144. A. J. and F. D. Herbertson, *Man and his Work: An Introduction to Human Geography* (1902; this edn. 1940), 1–2.
145. Reid, *A Manual of Moral Instruction*, 197.
146. *Chambers's Geographical Readers of the Continents: Africa*, 28.
147. It originated in Canada in the 1890s. See Springhall, 'Meath, Youth, and Empire', *Journal of Contemporary History*, 5 (1970), 105–11; and the parliamentary debates, usually inaugurated by Meath, of 1 Dec. 1902, *Hansard* (Lords), 4th ser., vol. 115, col. 819; 19 May 1908, ibid., vol. 189, cols. 87–9 and 2–3–4; 19 Apr. 1910, ibid. (Commons), 5th ser., vol. 16, cols. 1895–8.
148. Meath in House of Lords, 1 Dec. 1902, *Hansard*, 4th ser., vol. 115, col. 813.
149. See below, p. 399 n. 96.
150. Horn, 'English Elementary Education', 48.
151. Greenlee, *Education and Imperial Unity*, 61. A similar march in 1909 was attended by 5,000 children. Again, figures are the movement's own estimates.
152. Horn, 'English Elementary Education', 48.
153. Springhall, 'Meath, Youth, and Empire', 109, and Horn, 'English Elementary Education', 48.
154. Some are described in Horn, 'English Elementary Education', 48–9, and in Greenlee, *Education and Imperial Unity*, 61.
155. Anne Bloomfield, 'Drill and Dance as Symbols of Imperialism', in J. A. Mangan (ed.), *Making Imperial Mentalities* (Manchester, 1990), 78–9.
156. Quoted in Horn, 'English Elementary Education', 50.
157. By 1913 26,000 children were participating in the League of Empire's 'Comrades Correspondence Club', according to its own figures, cited in James Greenlee, 'The ABCs of Imperial unity', *Canadian Journal of History*, 14 (1979), 54. That was out of 3½ million 5-to-14-year olds altogether: *1911 Census, General Tables*. The Victoria League's scheme was rather different, encouraging exchanges between schools at a number of levels. About 100 British schools (out of about 25,000) were part of it in 1910. Eliza Riedi, 'Imperialist Women in Edwardian Britain: The Victoria League 1899–1914', Ph.D. thesis, St Andrews University (1997), 82–3.
158. P. A. Vaile, 'A New Scheme for Imperial Scholarships', *Fortnightly Review*, 92 (1909), 718.
159. The League of Empire and the Navy League were especially active here. See Greenlee, *Education and Imperial Unity*, 31; and Thompson, *Imperial Britain*, 46.
160. Stanley in House of Lords, 21 Nov. 1906, *Hansard*, 4th ser., vol. 165, col. 762.
161. Springhall, 'Meath, Youth, and Empire', 103–5.
162. Tim Jeal, *Baden-Powell* (1989), 392.
163. e.g. in *Scouting for Boys* (1908; 4th edn. 1911), ch. 9; and in the whole aura that Baden-Powell, one of the greatest imperial heroes, brought with him to it.
164. John Springhall, *Youth, Empire and Society: British Youth Movements, 1883–1940* (1977), 134.
165. Baden-Powell, *Scouting for Boys* (1911 edn.), 272.
166. This is Springhall's point, in *Youth, Empire and Society*, ch. 3.
167. Baden-Powell, *Scouting for Boys* (1911 edn.), 278–9; and see Springhall, *Youth, Empire and Society*, ch. 3.

168. Quoted in Springhall, 'Boy Scouts, Class and Militarism in Relation to British Youth Movements 1908–1930', *International Review of Social History*, 16 (1971), 138–40. There is an extensive literature (apart from Springhall's book and articles) on the Boy Scouts. It includes Tammy M. Proctor, '(Uni)Forming Youth: Girl Guides and Boy Scouts in Britain, 1908–39', *History Workshop Journal*, 45 (1998); Sam Pryke, 'The Popularity of Nationalism in the Early British Boy Scout Movement', *Social History*, 23 (1998); Michael Rosenthal, 'Knights and Retainers: The Earliest Version of Baden-Powell's Boy Scout Scheme', *Journal of Contemporary History*, 15 (1980); Allen Warren, 'Sir Robert Baden-Powell, the Scout Movement and Citizen Training in Great Britain, 1900–1920', *English Historical Review*, 101 (1986), and 'Citizens of the Empire: Baden-Powell, Scouts and Guides, and an "Imperial Ideal"', in Mackenzie (ed.), *Imperialism and Popular Culture* (1986); and M. D. Blanch, 'Imperialism, Nationalism and Organized youth', in John Clarke *et al.* (eds.), *Working-Class Culture: Studies in History and Theory* (1979). Two contrasting biographies of 'B-P' himself are Michael Rosenthal, *The Character Factory: Baden-Powell and the Origin of the Boy Scout Movement* (1986); and Jeal, *Baden-Powell*.
169. C. F. G. Masterman *et al.*, *The Heart of the Empire* (1901).
170. Different statistics from different cities are cited in Bentley B. Gilbert, *The Evolution of National Insurance in Great Britain: The Origins of the Welfare State* (1966), 83; and G. R. Searle, *The Quest for National Efficiency: A Study in British Politics and British Political Thought 1899–1914* (1971), 60. It was not the first time this was noticed. In 1884, according to Lord Meath, 43% of army volunteers were rejected on similar grounds. House of Lords, 12 May 1890, *Hansard*, 3rd ser., vol. 344, col. 648.
171. Quoted in Robert J. Sturdee, 'The Ethics of Football', *Westminster Review*, 159 (1903), 181.
172. Lord Meath, 'Have We the "Grit" of our Forefathers?', *Nineteenth Century*, 64 (1908), 425.
173. See R. Soloway, 'Counting the Degenerates: The Statistics of Race Deterioration in Edwardian England', *Journal of Contemporary History*, 17 (1982), 137–64.
174. W. M. Flinders Petrie, *Janus in Modern Life* (1907), ch. 2, précised (pretty accurately) in a review by William Barry, 'Forecasts of Tomorrow', *Quarterly Review*, 209 (1908), 11–13. Samuel Dill, *Roman Society in the Last Century of the Western Empire* (1898), 231, drew exactly the same conclusion from the fall of the Roman empire, which had been caused, in his view, by the Emperor Martian's efforts 'to provide for the welfare of the human race'.
175. See Mathew Thomson, *The Problem of Mental Deficiency: Eugenics, Democracy, and Social Policy in Britain, c.1870–1959* (Oxford, 1998). That 'eugenics' was a minority, rather cranky movement in Britain also comes out of the evidence offered in Ian Brown, 'Who Were the Eugenicists? A Study of the Formation of an Early Twentieth-Century Pressure Group', *History of Education*, 17 (1988), 295–305, though Brown's own conclusions make it out to be more significant. On Churchill's brush with eugenics, see Paul Addison, *Churchill On the Home Front* (1992), 123–6.
176. This is implied in e.g. W. C. D. Whetham, 'Inheritance and Sociology', *Nineteenth Century*, 65 (1909), 78–9; E. B. Iwas-Müller, 'The Cult of the Unfit', *Fortnightly Review*, O.S., 92 (1909), 219.
177. Meath in House of Lords, 13 May 1889, *Hansard*, 3rd ser., vol. 335, col. 1820. Generally 'Swedish' drill—a more gymnastic sort—was regarded as more 'progressive' than

'military' drill, which involved lots of rather stiff exercises done in rows. See P. McIntosh, *Physical Education in England Since 1800* (1952), 109–21, 148–54.

178. This, for example, is what stymied the eugenicists when they tried to get *voluntary* sterilization through the House of Commons in 1931. Thomas, *Mental Deficiency*, 60–72.
179. W. J. Corbet, 'What Should England Do To Be Saved', *Westminster Review*, 155 (1901), 607.
180. A. Cuthbert Medd, 'The Judgment of Posterity', *National Review*, 41 (1903), 1003.
181. This is a reviewer's summary of the argument of Walter Meakin, *The Life of an Empire* (1907), *Westminster Review*, 167 (1907), 593
182. T. J. Macnamara, 'In Corpore Sano', *Contemporary Review*, 87 (1905), 248. Thomas James Macnamara was born in Montreal into a military family in 1861, but then trained and worked as a teacher in England, before serving as Radical (Lloyd-Georgian) MP for North Camberwell in 1900, and as a minister in successive Liberal governments between 1908 and 1922.
183. e.g. George Trobridge, 'The Reign of Commerce', *Westminster Review*, 158 (1902), 487–8, and 'The Decline of Morals', in ibid. 163 (1905), 608–9; Medd (again), 'The Judgment of Posterity', 1002–5; and Meakin, cited above.
184. J. L. Garvin, 'The Falsehood of Extremes', *National Review*, 50 (1907), 556, and 'The Compulsion of Empire', in ibid. 47 (1906), 505.
185. See Anna Davin, 'Imperialism and Motherhood', *History Workshop*, 5 (1978), 9–65; and below, p. 288.
186. Frances Evelyn Warwick, 'Physical Deterioration', *Fortnightly Review*, o.s., 85 (1906), 504.

CHAPTER 9

1. Frederick Willis, *101 Jubilee Road: A Book of London Yesterdays* (1948), 12.
2. Luke Trainor, *British Imperialism and Australian Nationalism* (Cambridge, 1994), 69; and see James Greenlee, *Education and Imperial Unity, 1901–1926* (1987), 62, referring to the voters' rejection of Joseph Chamberlain's imperial schemes in 1906: 'Head-counting at jubilees turned out to be a poor guage of public support for the empire.'
3. Thomas Gautrey, *'Lux Mihi Laus': School Board Memories* (1937), 96–7.
4. James G. Greenlee, *Education and Imperial Unity, 1901–26* (1987), 290.
5. John Galsworthy, *In Chancery* (1920; Penguin edn. 1962), 217–18.
6. Stephen Neill, *Colonialism and Christian Missions* (1966), 14.
7. Quoted in Christopher Redwood (ed.), *An Elgar Companion* (1982), 144.
8. On this see Richard Price, *An Imperial War and the British Working Class: Working-Class Attitudes and Reactions to the Boer War 1899–1902* (1972), ch. 4; and accounts of public school 'mafficking' above, p. 52.
9. Galsworthy, *In Chancery*, 216–18.
10. *Fortnightly Review*, o.s., 78 (1902), 3.
11. J. A. Hobson, *The Psychology of Jingoism* (1901), 3.
12. Laurence Senelick, 'Politics As Entertainment: Victorian Music-Hall Songs', *Victorian Studies*, 19 (1975–6), 164.

13. Gareth Stedman-Jones, 'Working Class Culture and Working Class Politics in London, 1870–1900', *Journal of Social History*, 7 (1974), 495; and information from Max Tyler. Knowing this sheds new light on the popular song 'The Boy I Love is Up in the Gallery' (1881; sung by Nellie Power, written by George Ware), which may well be meant as a snub to the upper-class lotharios in the stalls.
14. Peter Bailey, 'Custom, Capital and Culture in the Victorian Music Hall', in R. D. Storch (ed.), *Popular Culture and Class in Victorian England* (1982), 200.
15. Willis, *101 Jubilee Road,* 80–1. The specific example he cites is Mrs Brown-Potter's rendition of a pro-tariff reform—and consequently empire-related—song (refrain: 'Those were the words of Mister Joseph Chamberlain!'): 'Imagine, if you can, a beautiful woman, clad in diaphanous draperies, declaiming all that nonsense with all the exaggerated gesture and intonation of a ham actress, and the audience (75 per cent of whom probably had no vote) working itself into a frenzy.'
16. Possibly none. The nearest I have found is 'The Penge Poet's War Song' (words by Joseph Gwyer, music by J. E. Peilgen), which is pacifist in sentiment, but not known to have been popular on the boards. From Max Tyler's collection.
17. This is explicit in 'Why Did You Go To War?' (sung by Paul Perham and Tom Costello; words/music by Pelham/Pether). Other similar patriotic war songs are 'Three Cheers For the Red, White and Blue' (words and music by Felix McGlennon), 'The Boys Are Marching' (Bingham/Bonheur), 'We've Still Got the Lads in Red' (J. G. Forde; Scott/Coates), 'Oh! Mr Kruger' (Jenny Lloyd; Delmar/Parry), and 'A Hot Time in the Transvaal Tonight' (Gus Hindello; Dalton/Willard). All from Max Tyler's collection.
18. 'The Bore o' Bef'nal Green' (Gus Ellen; Imeson/Eplett).
19. 'Khaki All Over the Shop' (J. P. Dane; Leigh/Leigh).
20. 'The Baby's Name' (Charles Bignell; Hall/Murphy).
21. 'Some Mothers Will Lose a Son' (Will Godwin; Godwin/Conran); 'Goodbye Dolly Gray' (many singers; Cobb/Barnes); 'The Girl You Leave Behind You' (Bella Lloyd and others; Harrington/Le Brun); 'Don't We Like To Hear of Victory' (Marie Kendall; Castling/Leigh); 'Sweet Marguerite' (Dacre/Dacre); 'The Wearers of the Little Grey Cloak' (Milly Linden; Baxter/Scott); 'The Boers Have Got my Daddy' (Tom Costello; Mills/Castling); 'God Bless Daddy at the War' (Lottie Lennox; Godwin/Godwin); 'Break the News to Mother' (Alfred Hurley and others; Harris/Harris); ''Tis Not Only Bullets That Kill' (Harris/Harris). Max Tyler's collection.
22. 'Only a Trooper' (Fred Tryon; Atkins/Atkins) 'Private Tommy Atkins' (C. Hayden Coffin; Hamilton/Potter), 'To Him of the Absent Mind' (George Leyton; Graham/Casanova). Max Tyler's collection.
23. 'The Absent-Minded Beggar' (many singers; Kipling/Sullivan); 'Ordered South' ('G. D'Albert and Tom White's Arabs'; Scott/Cotes); 'The Un-Commercial Traveller' (Frost/Frost); 'Tommy, Don't You Worry!' (Ida René; Morris/Tilbury), 'Who'll care for the Children' (Arthur Lennard; Osborne/Baker), 'Thank You Kindly' (Clara Wieland; Thorn/Tennyson); 'Oh Mr Kipling' (Atkins/Atkins). All from Max Tyler's collection.
24. If only for this reason, Paul Greenhalgh's contention that 'nationhood and empire formed the core of subject-matter for [music-hall] singers and comedians' in this

period is clearly nonsense. *Ephemeral Vistas: Expositions Universelles, Great Exhibitions and World's Fairs, 1815–1939* (Manchester, 1988), 113.

25. On this, see Laurence Senelick's interesting distinction between the 'chanson guerrière' and the 'chanson militaire', in 'Politics As Entertainment', 172–3.
26. Ibid. 150, 180; Dagmar Kift, *The Victorian Music Hall: Culture, Class and Conflict* (Cambridge, 1996), ch. 2.
27. Senelick, 'Politics As Entertainment', 159–60, 165–6.
28. For lists of remembered music-hall songs from this period, see Edward Ezard, *Battersea Boy* (1979), 103; John Blake, *Memories of Old Poplar* (1977), 31; Louie Stride, *Memoirs of a Street Urchin* (Bath, n.d.), 15, 31; Archie Hill, *A Cage of Shadows* (1973), 58; A. S. Jasper, *A Hoxton Childhood* (1969), 31; Frank Vernon, *Pride and Poverty: Memories of a Mexborough Miner* (Doncaster, 1984), 9; and *Friday Night Was Brasso Night*, published by the WEA, South-East Scotland District (1987), *passim*.
29. This idea came from Max Tyler.
30. Robert Roberts, *The Classic Slum: Salford Life in the First Quarter of the Century* (Manchester, 1971), and *A Ragged Schooling: Growing Up in the Classic Slum* (Manchester, 1976).
31. Roberts, *Classic Slum*, 112.
32. Ibid. 113.
33. e.g. Arthur Newton, *Years of Change: Autobiography of a Hackney Shoemaker* (1974), 47: 'The population of the country had been schooled in the glories of the British Empire and the deeds of her victorious armies'—which is why, he goes on to say, they expected World War I to be very short. Pamela Horn, 'English Elementary Education and the Growth of the Imperial Ideal, 1880–1914', in J. A. Mangan, *Benefits Bestowed? Education and British Imperialism* (Manchester, 1988), 44, claims that 'Teachers ... often embraced imperialist sentiments with enthusiasm'; which may be true, but is supported here from no other sources than Roberts.
34. Anon., *Narrow Waters: The First Volume of the Life and Thoughts of a Common Man* (1935), 11.
35. Willis, *101 Jubilee Road*, 74. Cf. Ethel Mannin, *Confessions and Impressions* (1930), 37; Anon., *Narrow Waters*, 11; and scores of others.
36. See e.g. Mary Craddock, *A North Country Maid* (1960), 38 ff.; G. V. Holmes, *The Likes of Us* (1948), 18; Edward Dent quoted in Pamela Horn, *Education in Rural England 1800–1914* (1978), 263–4.
37. Willis, *101 Jubilee Road*, 76–7.
38. Stride, *Memoirs of a Street Urchin*, 34.
39. Jim Flowers, quoted in Stephen Humphries, *Hooligans or Rebels?* (1981), 44.
40. Both quoted in ibid. 43.
41. S. J. Colledge, 'The Study of History in the Teacher Training College', *History of Education Society Bulletin*, 36 (1985), reproduces some examination 'howlers' on p. 46. Clara E. Grant, *Farthing Bundles* (n.d. [1931]), 31, states that the only history she remembered from her training college (probably in the 1880s) was the story about Wolfe saying that he would rather have written Gray's Elegy than take Quebec.
42. The five 'schemes', recommended by the Board of Education in 1906, covered (1) Henry VII to Oliver Cromwell; (2) the Stuarts to Queen Anne; (3) George I to 1832, 'and a detailed study of the Expansion of England'—that is the imperial one; (4) the history of labour and industrial relations; and (5) a comparative study of

constitutional history and social reform in Britain, France, and the USA from 1832: ibid. 48. *Board of Education Regulations* (1906).

43. Stephen Heathorn, *For Home, Country and Race: Constructing Gender, Class, and Englishness in the Elementary School, 1880–1914* (Toronto, 2000), 12.
44. W. R. Lawson, *John Bull and His Schools* (Edinburgh, 1908), 217–18.
45. See Martin Lawn, *Servants of the State: The Contested Control of Teaching 1900–1930* (1987).
46. Colledge, 'Teacher Training College', 48.
47. R. J. W. Selleck, *The New Education 1870–1914* (1968), 247.
48. Walter Frewen Lord, 'The Creed of Imperialism', *Nineteenth Century and After*, 66 (1909), 33. Lord Meath's answer to the last objection—not enough room—was to scrap English, on the grounds that in his experience it made little difference anyway to the workers' diction and literacy. House of Lords, 12 May 1890, *Hansard*, 3rd ser., vol. 344, col. 646; 1 Aug. 1893, ibid., 4th ser., vol. 15, col. 985; 1 Dec. 1902, ibid., vol. 115, col. 818.
49. See e.g. Margaret Thatcher, *The Downing Street Years* (1993), 590, 595–6, and Richard Aldrich (ed.), *History in the National Curriculum* (1991), 95.
50. Forster's Preface to *The Citizen Reader* (*Cassell's Modern School Series*, [1886]), p. iv.
51. Lord Londonderry in House of Lords, 1 Dec. 1902, *Hansard*, 4th ser. vol. 115, col. 821 (italics added).
52. See Board of Education, *Suggestions for the Consideration of Teachers and Others Concerned in the Work of Public Elementary Schools* (1905), 61–3, proposing that 'the British Empire in some detail' might 'probably be found . . . the best subject' for final year geography in elementary schools; and that 'how the mother country . . . has founded daughter countries beyond the seas' could perhaps be covered in history lessons. In the latter case this was felt to be a way of teaching pupils 'something about their nationality which distinguishes them from the people of other countries'. There is a patriotic agenda implied there, but it is never spelled out. If it had been, the selection of the settlement (democratic) rather than the dependent (despotic) colonies as a defining characteristic of the British might have been significant. Elsewhere teachers are enjoined to avoid the more bellicose sorts of history: 'Care should . . . be taken that the lessons deal with the triumphs of peace', and 'in dealing with times of conflict with other peoples . . . do full justice to those who are national heroes in other countries'. That could have been a sop to anti-imperialists.
53. Board of Education, *Suggestions* (1905), 58; and see Aldrich and Dean, 'The Historical Dimension', 97–8.
54. Meath in House of Lords, 1 Dec. 1902, *Hansard*, 4th ser., vol. 115, col. 816.
55. Meath mentions it again in House of Lords, 1 Aug. 1893, ibid., vol. 15, col. 984. My own mother, born in 1912, remembers being taught nothing but 'the bloody Romans', over and over again.
56. See I. Steele, *Developments in History Teaching* (1976), for the 'regressive method'.
57. C. P. Lucas, 'Imperial Studies', *United Empire*, 6 (1915), quoted in James G. Greenlee, *Education and Imperial Unity, 1901–26* (1987), 103.
58. See e.g. the letter from A. H. P. Stoneham in *The Times*, 7 Feb. 1907, quoted in Greenlee, *Education and Imperial Unity*, 30–1. Stoneham (a Unionist parliamentary candidate) claimed that Leicestershire schools were entirely bereft of books and maps bearing on the empire and desperate for them, until he sent them material published by the 'League of the Empire', which they received, he wrote, 'with delight and enthusiasm'.

Since then he had been 'deluged with requests from schools and clubs all over the British Isles for similar materials'.

59. Edmond Holmes, quoted in Pamela Horn, *Education in Rural England 1800–1914* (1978), 252.
60. David Rubinstein, 'The London School Board 1870–1904', in Phillip McCann (ed.), *Popular Education and Socialization in the 19th Century* (1977), 242–3.
61. 'Common education is the true social leveller. Men and women who have been to school together, or who have been at schools of the same sort, will always understand each other.' Green, 'Lecture On the Work To Be Done By the New Oxford High School for Boys' (1882), quoted in R. J. W. Selleck, *The New Education 1870–1914* (1968), 168–9.
62. David Wardle, *The Rise of the Schooled Society* (1974), 103. The only real adjustments in this turn-of-the-century period were moves to provide secondary schools for working-class children in some progressive areas, and measures allowing for the transference of a minority of 'gifted' elementary-school children into middle-class schools (and therefore values) elsewhere. These could have functioned as safety-valves. Ibid. 103, 137; Stephen Humphries, ' "Hurrah for England": Schooling and the Working Class in Bristol', *Southern History*, 1 (1979), 204.
63. Quoted in Rubinstein, 'London School Board', 243.
64. M. L. V. Hughes, *Citizens to Be: A Social Study of Health, Wisdom and Goodness with Special Reference to Elementary Schools* (1915), 148–9, 208–9.
65. Paraphrased in Greenlee, *Education and Imperial Unity*, 104.
66. Meath in 1900, quoted in J. S. Hurt, 'Drill, Discipline and the Elementary School Ethos', in McCann, *Popular Education*, 187.
67. *The Citizen Reader*, 18, 165 (italics added).
68. Kimberley in House of Lords, 1 Aug. 1893, *Hansard*, 4th ser., vol. 15, col. 988.
69. Harold E. Gorst, 'The Blunder of Modern Education', *Nineteenth Century*, 49 (1901), 843; and see his *The Curse of Education* (1901).
70. [O. Eltzbacher, alias J. Ellis Barker], 'The Economic Decay of Great Britain.—II', *Contemporary Review*, 79 (1901), 787; and see his 'The Disadvantages of Education', *Nineteenth Century*, 53 (1903), 315.
71. Geoffrey Drage, *Eton and the Empire* (1890), 17. This view also had foreign support. See Pierre de Coubertin, 'Are the Public Schools a Failure? A French View', *Fortnightly Review*, 78 (1902), 886; and Edmond Demolins, *Anglo-Saxon Superiority: To What It Is Due* (1898), book I, ch. 3.
72. 'Calchas', 'Will England Last the Century?', *Fortnightly Review*, 75 (1901), 25–6. Cf. Charles Copland Perry, 'Our Undisciplined Brains—the War-Test', *Nineteenth Century*, 50 (1901), 895–901; Henry E. Armstrong, 'The Reign of the Engineer', *Quarterly Review*, 198 (1903), 463; Lord Avebury, 'On Education', in *Essays and Addresses 1900–1903* (1903), 237–60; Richard Burdon Haldane, *Education and Empire* (1902), Paper I; Lawson, *John Bull, passim.*
73. Lord Meath, 'Have We the "Grit" of Our Forefathers?', *Nineteenth Century*, 64 (1908), 427; and cf. Meath in House of Lords, 12 May 1890, *Hansard*, 3rd ser., vol. 344, col. 646.
74. *National Review*, 53 (1909), 302–3.
75. Ibid. The imperialist C. P. Lucas recommended packing all suffragettes off to Australia. Greenlee, *Education and Imperial Unity*, 104.

76. A. J. Berry, *Britannia's Growth and Greatness: A Historical Geography of the British Empire* (1913), 9–10.
77. Paraphrased in Greenlee, *Education and Imperial Unity*, 104.
78. See Reginald Horsman, 'Origins of Racial Anglo-Saxonism in Great Britain Before 1850', *Journal of the History of Ideas*, 37 (1976), 387–410.
79. One effect of this new slant was to downgrade the 'Ancient Britons', who in earlier texts had been portrayed as the original English, and contrasted with present-day Britons, with encouraging implications for other races at the same state of 'civilization' now as the Britons had been at then. But now they were sometimes treated more like native Americans and Australian aborigines: 'destined to be driven out, or extinguished, or absorbed', as one book put it, 'according to that apparently inevitable law of nature by which the weaker race disappears before the stronger': *The Young Student's English History Reading Book* (1881), 10, quoted in Heathorn, '"Let us remember..."', 402. That cannot have pleased the Welsh, Irish, and Gaelic Scots.
80. Heathorn, '"Let us remember..."', 402–7. The two quotations in this passage are both taken from this: the first (Scandinavian origins) is *Black's Story of the English People* (1905), 45–6, quoted on p. 405; the second (Queen Victoria's Saxon pedigree) is a *Raleigh History Reader* (1895), iv. 24, quoted on p. 420.
81. Above, p. 188.
82. Stanley in House of Lords, 21 Nov. 1906, *Hansard*, 4th ser., vol. 165, col. 762.
83. Meath and Lord Crewe in House of Lords, 21 Nov. 1906, ibid., vol. 165, cols. 760–2.
84. Some historians seem unaware of this; e.g. Horn, *Education in Rural England*, 254; and Avril M. C. Maddrell, 'Empire, Emigration and School Geography: Changing Discourses of Imperial Citizenship, 1880–1925', *Journal of Historical Geography*, 22 (1996), 379.
85. Delaney in Commons, 11 May 1908, *Hansard*, 4th ser., vol. 188, col. 739.
86. e.g. Horatio Myer in Commons, 18 Apr. 1907, ibid., vol. 172, col. 1171.
87. Asquith in Commons, 8 May 1913, ibid., 5th ser., vol. 52, col. 2220 (italics added). The date was chosen because it was the late queen's birthday.
88. Macveagh to Arnold-Foster in Commons, 15 June 1905, ibid., 4th ser., vol. 147, col. 700.
89. In Commons, 25 May 1907, ibid., vol. 174, col. 288.
90. In Commons, 11 May 1909, ibid., 5th ser., *Commons*, vol. 4, col. 1420.
91. In Commons, 19 Apr. 1910, ibid., vol. 16, col. 1898.
92. In Commons, 11 May 1909, ibid., vol. 4, col. 1420.
93. Dilke in Commons, 19 Apr. 1910, ibid., vol. 16, cols. 1897–8.
94. Dilke again, ibid.
95. Humphries, *Hooligans or Rebels?*, 135.
96. See John Springhall, 'Meath, Youth, and Empire', *Journal of Contemporary History*, 5 (1970), 109–10 (instancing Battersea and Derby); Horn, 'English Elementary Education', 48; Humphries, '"Hurrah for England": Schooling and the Working Class in Bristol' (where the idea of banning Empire Day on these grounds was 'ridiculed'), 202.
97. Ethel Mannin, *Confessions and Impressions* (1930), 45.
98. See Horn, 'English Elementary Education', 50; Humphries, *Hooligans or Rebels?*, 41; and the Bishop Auckland children's rhyme quoted in Iona and Peter Opie, *The Lore and Language of Schoolchildren* (Oxford, 1959), 263: 'Empire Day, Empire Day, If you don't give us a holiday We'll all run away.'

99. Above, p. 200. Cf. a Bristol contemporary, quoted in Humphries, '"Hurrah for England"', 184: 'It taught us we were the best nation in the world and must live up to it.' Humphries thinks this kind of imperial display appealed to these children 'because it reflected and reinforced a number of [their] cultural traditions, in particular the street gangs' concern with territorial rivalry and the assertion of masculinism': Humphries, *Hooligans or Rebels?* 41.
100. See M. L. V. Hughes, *Citizens To Be* (1915), 209.
101. Anne Bloomfield, 'Drill and Dance as Symbols of Imperialism', in J. A. Mangan (ed.), *Making Imperial Mentalities* (Manchester, 1990), 83–4. Bloomfield reads an imperialistic message into all of these, but there is no need to. 'Merrie England' in particular had a contemporary socialist resonance (after Robert Blatchford).
102. Humphries, *Hooligans or Rebels?* 42.
103. Harry Burton, *There Was a Young Man* (1958), quoted in Jonathan Rose, *The Intellectual Life of the British Working Classes* (New Haven, Conn., 2001), 348. The second part of this quotation is Rose's paraphrase.
104. Greenlee, *Education and Imperial Unity*, 82.
105. Robert Baden-Powell, *Scouting For Boys* (1908; 4th edn. 1911), ch. 9.
106. Allen Warren, '"Mothers for the Empire"? The Girl Guides Association in Britain, 1909–39', in Mangan (ed.), *Making Imperial Mentalities*, 101.
107. Ezard, *Battersea Boy*, 82–97.
108. On this see Springhall, 'Boy Scouts, Class and Militarism', 138–40.
109. William J Tucker, *Autobiography of an Astrologer* (1960), 17.
110. Humphries, *Hooligans or Rebels?*, 134–5; Tim Jeal, *Baden-Powell* (1989), 397; Ezard, *Battersea Boy*, 84.
111. Rose, *Intellectual Life*, 348.
112. Jeffrey Richards (ed.), *Imperialism and Juvenile Literature* (Manchester, 1989), Introduction, pp. 2, 9. The Victorian middle classes worried about the effect of trashy fiction on the working classes for much the same reason: 'Jack Sheppard' would turn them all into criminals. See Patrick Dunae, 'Penny Dreadfuls: Late Nineteenth Century Boys' Literature and Crime', *Victorian Studies*, 22 (1979); and W. Fraser Rae (1865), quoted in Natalie Houston's Introduction to Mary Braddon, *Lady Audley's Secret* (2003 edn.), 19: 'Into uncontaminated minds they [i.e. "sensational" novels] will instil false views of human conduct.'
113. Quoted in J. S. Bratton, *The Impact of Victorian Children's Fiction* (1981), 200. Richards also quotes this, but only the first half, to show how influential Henty was: 'With Henty to Africa', in Richards (ed.), *Imperialism and Juvenile Literature*, 73. John MacKenzie quotes the whole, but also claims that Taylor, as an 'intellectual', was atypical: *Propaganda and Empire: The Manipulation of British Public Opinion 1880–1960* (Manchester, 1984), 253.
114. Bratton, *Impact of Victorian Children's Fiction*, 199–200; and cf. Rose, *Intellectual Life*, 348–49.
115. The words are by A. C. Benson,and postdated the music. The tune itself has been used in other than imperial contexts; see Bernard Porter, 'Edward Elgar and Empire', *Journal of Imperial and Commonwealth History*, 29 (2001), 1–2, 11–12.
116. V. G. Kiernan, 'Working Class and Nation in Nineteenth-century Britain', in Maurice Cornford (ed.), *Rebels and their Causes* (1978), 130.

117. Richards (ed.), *Imperialism and Juvenile Literature*, 8.
118. Springhall, 'Healthy Papers', 114.
119. See above, p. 387 n. 82, for the sample on which this is based.
120. I have dipped into *Aly Sloper* and *Chums*. Apart from the occasional humorous 'darkie', I have found very few empire-related references.
121. See Rose, *Intellectual Life*, 367–71.
122. e.g. the *Illustrated Police News* (1864–1939), and *Illustrated Police Budget* (1871–1910).
123. See Rose, *Intellectual Life*, ch. 4 *et passim*.
124. These are taken from Frederick Willis, *101 Jubilee Road: A Book of London Yesterdays* (1948), 151. John Blake, *Memories of Old Poplar* (1977), 31–2, and A. S. Jasper, *A Hoxton Childhood* (1969), 47, also print lists of their favourite Edwardian plays, most of which are murder-melodramas
125. Looking for plays with imperially related titles in these years in lists like 'Plays Submitted to the Lord Chamberlain', and the one appended to Allardyce Nicoll, *A History of English Drama 1660–1900*, vol. 5 (1959), is like looking for the proverbial needle in a haystack. My findings are listed above, p. 386 n. 75; nearly all of them were directed at the 'lower' end of the market. I may have missed some, but they were clearly a tiny minority, even for the 'low' theatres, outnumbered by other themes—romance, crime, intrigue—by about 100–200 to 1. This does not even rate as a 'genre'.

    The same is true of the contemporary ('serious') concert programmes and criticism I have read, including Dan H. Laurence (ed.), *Shaw's Music: The Complete Musical Criticism of Bernard Shaw*, 3 vols. (1981), which covers the years 1876 to 1898 (effectively: Shaw gave up regular music criticism after then); although of course the fact that most music performed was (and is) either foreign or abstract, or both, makes it less significant—indeed, entirely unremarkable—that so little of it was on 'imperial' themes.
126. Rose, *Intellectual Life*, 324, 341. The quotation is from Robert Roberts.
127. Willis, *101 Jubilee Road*. 141.
128. Taken from the *Official Guide to the Imperial International Exhibition, White City* (1909). There is a picture of the 'Flip-Flap' in Willis, *101 Jubilee Road*, between pp. 112 and 113. To be fair, this was more of a pleasure gardens than most. Kiralfy's Indian Exhibition of 1895 was more focused on India, though not without its sensational attractions also, including a 'Himalayas Gravity Railway', a 'Nirvana Garden', and some 'Popular Entertainment Buildings'. *The Empire of India Exhibition 1895, Earl's Court, London. The Conception, Design and Production of Imre Kiralfy* (1895).
129. Willis, *101 Jubilee Road*, 143.
130. 'More precisely, my use of "popular" is to describe cultural vehicles which were accessible to, and consumed by, an educated middle and lower middle-class public with a general interest in the colonies . . . It is not, as so often the case with historical studies of popular culture, a short-hand term for working-class culture.' Annie E. Coombes, *Reinventing Africa: Museums, Material Culture and Popular Imagination in Late Victorian and Edwardian England* (New Haven, Conn., 1994), 3.
131. Examples (covering the relevant period) are George Acorn, *One of the Multitude* (1911); Thomas Burke, *Son of London* [1946]; Walter Citrine, *Men and Work* (1964); Frederick Rogers, *Labour, Life and Literature: Some Memories of Sixty Years* (1913); and Will Thorne, *My Life's Battles* [1925].

132. Arthur Newton, *Years of Change: An Autobiography of a Hackney Shoemaker* (1974), 11.
133. Anon., *Narrow Waters*, 33.
134. Willis, *101 Jubilee Road*, 79–81.
135. Charles Chaplin, *My Autobiography* (1964), 50.
136. W. H. Davies, *The Autobiography of a Super-Tramp* (1920), 156.
137. Tierl Thompson (ed.), *Dear Girl: The Diaries and Letters of Two Working Women 1897–1917* (1987), 25.
138. Which is not to say that Robert Noonan (his real name) was uninfluenced by his time there, according to Jonathan Hyslop, 'A Ragged Trousered Philanthropist and the Empire: Robert Tressell in South Africa', *History Workshop Journal*, 51 (2001). Hyslop argues persuasively that it was his South African experience that turned him into a socialist, and enabled him to see the British victims of capitalism more objectively. There is one imperial reference in the novel: India appears in a sermon recounted near the end of it (1993 edn., p. 477), as an example of capitalist exploitation.
139. e.g. Roberts, *A Ragged Schooling*. 125–6.
140. All London street references are taken from a current *A–Z Guide*. See David Young, 'East-End Street Names and British Imperialism', *The Local Historian*, 22 (1992), who also makes the point that it was the capitalist developers who did the naming, not the inhabitants. It could also be significant that most of London's Chamberlain, Milner, and Curzon streets—i.e. those named after imperial *rulers*—are in the posher West End. There are also at least two 'Kop ends' at football grounds (named after the battle of Spion Kop in the Boer War): see Denis Judd and Keith Surridge, *The Boer War* (2002), 131. (The other one is at Northampton Town—or, for Northampton readers, Liverpool.) Whether these really gave London's East Enders, or the Liverpool Kopites, warm imperial feelings as they walked or stood there must be doubtful. I used to live in an Edwardian 'Lansdowne Road'; I never—even as an imperial historian—remember connecting it at the time with the Indian viceroy and foreign secretary after whom it was obviously named.
141. 15 Labour candidates stood in 1900 (in 670 constituencies); 51 in 1906; 81 in February 1910; and 59 in December 1910. At that time just 27% of the adult population had the vote (58% of males). David Butler and Jennie Freeman, *British Political Facts 1900–1960* (1965), 122, 129.
142. Price, *Imperial War*, ch. 5; M. D. Blanche, 'British Society and the War', in Peter Warwick (ed.), *The South African War: The Anglo-Boer War 1899–1902* (1980).
143. Sydney Peel, *Trooper 8008 I.Y* (1901), quoted in Judd and Surridge, *The Boer War*, 77. Peel however was an 'Honourable', and his regiment (the Imperial Yeomanry) a famously upper-middle-class one.
144. This is Lord Meath, asking 'whether it is not a fact that surrenders to the enemy without serious loss of life took place during the Boer war more frequently than it is agreeable to the patriot to hear about?' 'Have we Lost the "Grit" of our Forefathers', *Nineteenth Century*, 64 (1908), 423.
145. Letter in *Club News*, 11 Mar. 1899, quoted in Price, *An Imperial War*, 67; and ibid., ch. 2, *passim*.
146. Roberts, *Classic Slum*, 113.
147. There are exceptions, whose testimony has often been saved for us by 'aural' historians, such as John Burnett, *Useful Toil* (1974), containing reminiscences from

27 working men; Raphael Samuel (ed.), *East End Underworld: Chapters in the Life of Arthur Harding* (1981), from taped interviews; and (for a slightly later period) Worker's Educational Association, South-East Scotland District, *Friday Night Was Brasso Night* (1987), and John Halstead, Royden Harrison, and John Stevenson, 'The Reminiscencres of Sid Elias', *Bulletin of the Society for the Study of Labour History*, 38 (1979); most of which, however, have even fewer imperial references than the others, perhaps partly because of the questions the aural historians have asked.

148. See e.g. the problems that the politically aware hero of Robert Tressell's *The Ragged-Trousered Philanthropists* (1914) has with his reactionary fellow workers.

149. See Bernard Porter, *Critics of Empire: British Radical Attitudes to Colonialism in Africa, 1895–1914* (1968), ch. 4.

150. Ibid. 108.

151. See Burns's speech on the Fashoda crisis reported in *The Times*, 14 Nov. 1898, and William Kent, *John Burns, Labour's Lost Leader* (1950). 88. Another prominent working-class politician with imperialistic tendencies—consistently supporting the government on the Boer War, for example—was Joseph Havelock Wilson, MP for Middlesborough. 'I do believe in upholding the integrity of the British Empire. I am a British patriot above all things.' Speech in House of Commons, 6 Feb. 1900, *Hansard*, 4th ser., vol. 78, cols. 798–800.

152. Price, *An Imperial War*, 78.

153. For Sussex, 1863–4, as a right-hand middle-order batsman, making 309 runs in all (highest score 64) at an average of 16.26. Benny Green, *Wisden Book of Obituaries* (1986), under 'Hyndman'. His 'wobble' was his decision to support World War I, against the majority of his British Socialist Party, which he was consequently forced to leave.

154. Porter, *Critics of Empire*, 105–6, 137.

155. See e.g. J. A. Hobson, *Imperialism: A Study* (1902; 3rd edn. 1938), 142.

156. Examples of socialists attacking *Jewish* capitalist imperialism are quoted in Porter, *Critics of Empire*, 103, 128, 129 n., and pictured in two cartoons taken from the *Labour Leader* and reproduced between pp. 184 and 185. Hobson himself cannot be absolved of blame for this. Though he never showed any other signs of anti-Semitism, he did become convinced of the existence of a specifically Jewish conspiracy to drag Britain into war with the Boers when he visited Johannesburg for the *Manchester Guardian* just before the war broke out: see his letter to C. P. Scott (the editor), 2 Sept. 1899, quoted in *Critics of Empire*, 201–2. In *Imperialism: A Study* the references are usually to 'cosmopolitan finance', which is code for Jews. One or two contemporaries picked him up on this; e.g. the pro-war Congregationalist minister J. Guinness Rogers, in 'The Churches and the War', *Contemporary Review*, 77 (1900), 616–17.

157. More than 120,000 entered Britain in the 1890s and 1900s, fleeing pogroms in Russia, Poland, and the Baltic States. Thousands of these settled in the Whitechapel and surrounding areas of east London, which became the centre of a short-lived popular racist movement, led by Arnold White's 'British Brothers League'. (White, incidentally, was also an active propagandist for imperialism.) This was one factor leading to the passage of Britain's first effective 'Aliens' (or Immigration) Act for 80 years, in 1905. See Bernard Gainer, *The Alien Invasion: The Origins of the Aliens Act of 1905* (1972), chs. 4–5.

158. Hardie in House of Commons, 13 Dec. 1900, *Hansard*, 4th ser., vol. 88, col. 758.

159. Labour MPs asked 18 Parliamentary questions on the South African Chinese labour issue from May 1903 to July 1905.
160. It would be tedious to list these; but Joseph Pointer's Commons speech on the Colonial Office vote, 27 June 1912, is a broad treatment of these questions empire-wide: *Hansard*, 5th ser., vol. 40, cols. 577–81.
161. Ibid., col. 581.
162. B. R. Mitchell and Phyllis Deane, *Abstract of British Historical Statistics* (Cambridge, 1962), 344, 64–5. There are no reliable figures for unemployment, but the best we have (based on trade-union returns) suggest that the mid-1890s and 1902–10 were particularly bad years.
163. e.g. Arthur Newton remembered bands of children marching around his school playground in the 1910s singing 'Eight hours work, eight hours play, eight hours sleep, and eight bob a day'. *Years of Change*, 24.
164. Basil Thomson, *Queer People* (1922), 265. Thomson was not known for his good judgement, however, to put it kindly. See the references to him in my *Plots and Paranoia: A History of Political Espionage in Britain, 1790–1988* (1989).
165. Bernard Porter, *The Origins of the Vigilant State: The London Metropolitan Police Special Branch Before the First World War* (1987), 169.
166. On this see Paul Kennedy, *The Rise of the Anglo-German Antagonism 1860–1914* (1980), ch. 12 (which deals with colonial rivalries), *et passim*; and David French, 'Spy Fever in Britain, 1900–1915', *Historical Journal*, 21 (1978).
167. The gross figures (including Ireland) are: 1881–90: 3,259,000; 1891–1900: 2,149,000; 1901–10: 3,150,000; 1911–20: 2,587,000. William Woodruff, *Impact of Western Man: A Study of Europe's Role in the World Economy 1750–1960* (1966), 106. The USA/empire balance is spelled out in Mitchell and Deane, *Abstract*, 50. In 1891 four times as many emigrants were making for the USA as went to all the colonies combined; by 1913 twice as many were going to the colonies as to the USA. The turning-point was 1903 (124,000 to America, 122,000 to the major colonies).
168. Andrew Hassam, *Through Australian Eyes: Colonial Perceptions of Imperial Britain* (Melbourne, 2000), is based on the diaries and letters of a number of returnees, most of whom, however, were—either originally, or having worked their way up to that station in Australia—middle class.
169. e.g. Walter Southgate, *That's the Way it Was: A Working-Class Autobiography 1890–1950* (1982), 13, mentions the emigration of a friend. One or two authors had either considered emigrating: e.g. Acorn, *One of the Multitude*, 145; or did in fact emigrate and then returned: Sir Readers Buller, *The Camels Must Go: An Autobiography* (1961), 19 (this was when he was a baby, and was taken to Canada by his dock-labourer father); and W. H. Davies, *The Autobiography of a Super-Tramp* (1920).
170. Clara E. Grant, *Farthing Bundles* (n.d. [1931]), 116.
171. For emigration figures, see Mitchell and Deane, *Abstract*, 50–2.
172. 5,774 (men *and* officers) were killed in total: Chris Cook and John Stevenson, *The Longman Handbook of Modern British History 1714–1980* (1983), 214. A number of others settled in South Africa after the war.
173. Rose, *Intellectual Life*, 336. Rose's charwoman was Margaret Powell, *My Mother and I* (1972), 50. Alice Linton, *Not Expecting Miracles* (1982), 4, boasts of a father who served in India.

174. Edward Ezard, *Battersea Boy* (1979), 78, 36–7.
175. Anon., *Narrow Waters*, 16.
176. Samuel, *East End Underworld*, 50, 55, 56.
177. Roberts, *The Classic Slum*, 145. See also Rose, *Intellectual Life*, 337–8.
178. 'When They Found I Was a soldier', sung by Fred Earle; words by Harry Wincott, music by Joseph Tabrar and Wincott; from Max Tyler's collection.
179. Francis Younghusband, 'The Emerging Soul of England', *National Review*, 55 (1910), 66.
180. J. L. Garvin, 'The Falsehood of Extremes', *National Review*, 50 (1907), 556.
181. T. Evan Jacob, 'A Little Cloud like a Man's Hand', *Westminister Review*, 166 (1906), 637.
182. C. P. Lucas, 1916, quoted in Greenlee, *Education and Imperial Unity*, 103.
183. e.g. Edward Dicey, 'Liberalism In Extremis', *Fortnightly Review*, N.S., 76 (1901), 210; Horace G. Garrod, 'The Break-Up of the Party System', *Westminster Review*, 155 (1901), 216; Dudley S. A. Cosby, 'The Conservative Disaster', ibid. 165 (1906), 237; 'Calchas', 'The Ebbing Tide of Liberalism', *Fortnightly Review*, 88 (1907),178; William Barry, 'Forecasts of Tomorrow', *Quarterly Review*, 209 (1908), 27; and Walter Frewen Lord, 'The Creed of Imperialism', *Nineteenth Century*, 66 (1909), 35. All these predicted a future political line-up where an 'Imperialist' party—usually the Conservative party, or a merger between Conservatives and Liberal Imperialists—would face a Socialist—or socialized 'New Liberal'—party over the floor of the House of Commons.
184. e.g. Garvin, 'The Falsehood of Extremes', 556; and see above, pp. 190–1.
185. e.g. Geoffrey Drage, 'The Progress of British Imperialism', *Fortnightly Review*, O.S., 86 (1906), 68.
186. Norman Chamberlain, 'The New Imperialism and the Old Parties', *National Review*, 51 (1908), 649.
187. Quoted in Julia Bush, *Edwardian Ladies and Imperial Power* (2000), 95.
188. Ibid., 94, 96. The 'servant's hall' description is her sister's, which she endorses.
189. Eliza Riedi, 'Imperialist Women in Edwardian Britain: The Victoria League 1899–1914', Ph.D. thesis, St Andrews University (1997), 47–8.
190. Will Thorne, *My Life's Battles* (n.d.), 56.
191. Andrew Thompson, *Imperial Britain: The Empire in British Politics c.1880–1932* (2000), 54.
192. Chamberlain, 'The New Imperialism', 650.
193. 1921, quoted in Anne Bloomfield, 'Drill and Dance as Symbols of Imperialism', in Mangan (ed), *Making Imperial Mentalities*, 80–1.
194. Greenlee, *Education and Imperial Unity*, 291.
195. Stride, *Memoirs of a Street Urchin*, 15.
196. Blake, *Memories of Old Poplar*, 18.
197. Stride, *Memoirs of a Street Urchin*, 30.
198. Scotland's education was less class-based, which may explain the broader spread of imperial commitment there.

CHAPTER 10

1. At least 50% of cabinet ministers between 1880 and 1905 were aristocrats, with most of the rest being pretty high-born. Chris Cook and Bendan Keith, *British Historical Facts 1830–1900* (1975), 33–47; David Butler and Jennie Freeman, *British Political Facts 1900–1960* (1963), 1–6.

2. See e.g. John Huntley Skrine, 'The Romance of School', *Contemporary Review*, 73 (1898), 432; J. E. C. Welldon, *Recollections and Reflections* (1915), 100; Horace Vachel's Harrow-based novel *The Hill* (1905), esp. the the 'blood sacrifice' undertones in the head's sermon at the end of it; and some of Henry Newbolt's poetry. On this topic generally, see P. J. Rich, *Elixir of Empire: The English Public Schools, Ritualism, Freemasonry, and Imperialism* (1989); Rich's chapter, 'Public-School Freemasonry in the Empire', in J. A. Mangan (ed.), *Benefits Bestowed? Education and British Imperialism* (Manchester, 1988), 248–54; and Geoffrey Best, 'Militarism and the Victorian Public School', in Brian Simon and Ian Bradley (eds.), *The Victorian Public School* (1975), 144–6.
3. Colonial examples are the killings after the battle of Omdurman in 1898; the Denshawi massacre in the Sudan in 1906; and of course the Amritsar massacre of 1919. In Britain men were shot by the military during the Featherstone strike of 1893, the Tonypandy riots of 1910, and the Liverpool disturbances of 1911.
4. See e.g. Welldon's farewell speech to Harrow, in the *Harrovian*, 11: 8 (Nov. 1898), 96.
5. Three examples out of many taken from school magazines are 'Hector' on 'Cheechee-stan', *Malvernian*, 180 (Nov. 1890), 78–80; 'A Trip to Cairo' *Brentwoodian* (July 1892), 1–3; and notes of the debate on Egypt in the *Wykehamist*, 286 (Mar. 1893), 327. See also Christopher Hollis, *Eton, a History* (1960); and, on other kinds of literature, Kathryn Castle, *Britannia's Children: Reading Colonialism through Children's Books and Magazines* (Manchester, 1996).
6. Quoted in C. L. R. Fletcher, *Edmond Warre* (1922), 255.
7. David Cannadine, *Ornamentalism: How the British Saw Their Empire* (2001).
8. On Mary Kingsley, see, among a clutch of biographies going back to the 1950s, Dea Birkett, *Mary Kingsley: Imperial Adventuress* (1992); Alison Blunt, *Travel, Gender, and Imperialism: Mary Kingsley and West Africa* (1994); Robert Desmond Pearce, *Mary Kingsley: Light at the Heart of Darkness* (Oxford, 1990); and her own *Travels in West Africa* (1897) and *West African Studies* (1899). For her influence on 'indirect rule' and radical critiques of imperialism, see Bernard Porter, *Critics of Empire: British Radical Attitudes to Colonialism on Africa 1895–1914* (1968), ch. 8.
9. The novels were by Frank Richards. A crueller version appeared regularly in *Punch* in the early 1900s. The title of this series is worth quoting in full: 'A Bayard from Bengal. Being some account of the Magnificent and Spanking Career of Chunder Bindabun Ghosh, Esq., B.A. Cambridge. By Baboo Hurry Bungsho Jabberjee, B.A. Calcutta University. (Author of "Jottings and Tittlings" &c., &c.)', *Punch*, 119 (1900), 12 Sept. 195.
10. e.g. Philip Woodruff, *The Men who Ruled India: The Guardians* (1954), 55–6.
11. See W. K. Hancock, *Survey of British Commonwealth Affairs*, vol. 2, part 2 (1942), 176–94 *passim*; Charles Wilson, *The History of Unilever: A Study in Economic Growth and Social Change*, vol. 1 (1954), ch. 11.
12. This refers to the involvement of Rhodes, and the controversy over the goldfields of the Witwatersrand, which were widely reported long before J. A. Hobson used the war to corroborate his general theory of capitalist imperialism.
13. Quoted (together with other similar opinions) in Dennis Judd and Keith Surridge, *The Boer War* (2002), 243–44, and see also chs. 12 and 16.
14. Campbell-Bannerman's 'methods of barbarism' charge was made in the House of Commons, 14 June 1901: see J. A. Spender, *The Life of the Right Hon. Sir Henry Campbell-Bannerman, G.C.B* (n.d.), i. 336. On 'chivalric' objections generally, see Paula Krebs,

'"The Last of the Gentlemen's Wars": Women in the Boer War Concentration Camp Controversy', *History Workshop Journal*, 33 (1992), and *Gender, Race, and the Writing of Empire: Public Discourse and the Boer War* (Cambridge, 1999), ch. 4 *passim*.

15. Quoted in Judd and Surridge, *Boer War*, 244.
16. See Peter Fraser, *Joseph Chamberlain* (1966), 50–1; and see p. 55 above for public schoolboys sniffing at his 'trade' origins.
17. See Hans-Christoph Schröder, *Imperialismus und Antidemokratishes Denken* (Wiesbaden, 1978).
18. See Walter Nimocks, *Milner's Young Men: The 'Kindergarten' in Edwardian Imperial Affairs* (1968).
19. See David Gilmour, *The Long Recessional: The Imperial Life of Rudyard Kipling* (2002).
20. 1906; quoted in Alexander C. May, 'The Round Table, 1910–66', D.Phil. thesis, Oxford University (1995), 127.
21. For a list of these see my *The Lion's Share: A Short History of British Imperialism 1850–1995* (3rd edn. 1996), 130–40 *passim*.
22. Cannadine, *Ornamentalism*.
23. Prof. J. A. Liebmann, quoted in *Proceedings of the Royal Colonial Institute 1894–95* (1895), 341.
24. M. Peterson, *Family, Love and Work in the Lives of Victorian Gentlewomen* (Bloomington, Ind., 1989), p. x; quoted in Julia Bush, *Edwardian Ladies and Imperial Power* (2000), 8.
25. J. G. Greenlee, 'Imperial Studies and the Unity of the Empire', *Journal of Imperial and Commonwealth History*, 7 (1979), 331.
26. Annie E. Coombes, *Reinventing Africa: Museums, Material Culture and Popular Imagination in Late Victorian and Edwardian England* (New Haven, Conn., 1994).
27. *Report of the Royal Commission for the Colonial and Indian Exhibition (London, 1886)* (1887), p. xlvii. Obviously allowance has to be made for multiple visits.
28. Arabella Buckley, *History of England for Beginners* (1887; repr. 1897), 363.
29. Richard Price, *An Imperial War and the British Working Class* (1972), ch. 4.
30. I am thinking in particular of the Epilogue to *The Banner of St George* (1897), lauding the 'race, whose empire of splendour, Has dazzled a wondering world!'; the Finale of his oratorio *Caractacus* (1898), which suddenly transplants us from ancient Rome to the modern British empire, bidding Britons be 'alert' to the dangers threatening it; the *Imperial March* of 1897; and A. C. Benson's words for *Pomp and Circumstance March No. 1* (1901): 'Wider still and wider, May thy bounds be set...'
31. Beatrice Webb, *Our Partnership*, ed. Barbara Drake and Margaret Cole (1948), 140.
32. See Andrew Porter, *The Origins of the South African War: Joseph Chamberlain and the Diplomacy of Imperialism, 1895–99* (Manchester, 1980), *passim*. The Selbourne quote is on p. 255.
33. Wemyss Reid, 'Last Month', *Nineteenth Century*, 52 (1902), 877.
34. Anon., 'England After War', *Fortnightly Review*, O.S., 78 (1902), 6.
35. J. L. Garvin, 'The Compulsion of Empire', *National Review*, 47 (1906), 503.
36. e.g. 'Episodes of the Month', ibid. 46 (1906), 772–4, 903.
37. 'Episodes of the Month', ibid. 49 (1907), 24.
38. Walter Frewen Lord, 'The Creed of Imperialism', *Nineteenth Century*, 66 (1909), 35.
39. Greenlee, 'Imperial Studies and the Unity of the Empire', 321.
40. See (on censorship) Kenneth Morgan, 'The Boer War and the Media (1899–1902)', in *20th Century British History*, 13 (2002), 2–5; and H. John Field, *Towards a Programme of*

Imperial Life: The British Empire at the Turn of the Century (Oxford, 1982), chs. 4–5. The *Manchester Guardian* was broadly pro-Boer, with J. A. Hobson one of its reporters in the field. In January 1901 the (London) *Daily News* was bought by the Quaker chocolate manufacturer George Cadbury and turned into a pro-Boer paper.

41. *Westminster Gazette*, 12 Oct. 1899.
42. 10 Nov. 1899, quoted in ibid. 75.
43. On the Boer War divisions see Porter, *Critics of Empire*, chs. 3–4; and Colin Matthew, *The Liberal Imperialists: The Ideas and Politics of a Post-Gladstonian Elite* (Oxford, 1973); and on the 1886 split, D. G. Hoskins, 'The Genesis and Significance of the 1886 "Home Rule" Split in the Liberal Party', Ph.D. thesis, Cambridge University (1963), ch. 1; and Peter Marshall, 'The Imperial Factor in the Liberal Decline, 1880–1885', in J. E. Flint and G. Williams (eds.), *Perspectives of Empire* (1973). The Home Rule split coincided roughly with Gladstone's failure to rescue Gordon from Khartoum in 1885, and his cave-in over Transvaal independence after the 'first' Boer War of 1881, which lost him popularity in some quarters.
44. See Henry Pelling, *Popular Politics and Society in Late Victorian Britain* (1968), 92–4.
45. See Brian Roberts, *Those Bloody Women: Three Heroines of the Boer War* (1991), on Emily Hobhouse, who publicized the conditions in the camps.
46. Most claimed either to have opposed the war at the time, which jars with most calculations that have been made of middle-class opinion; or else that they came to their senses shortly afterwards; e.g. Norman Angell, *After All* (1951), 86, which describes how the Hearst Press in America turned him against jingoism; G. K. Chesterton, *Autobiography* (1936), 110–15; Richard Church, *Over the Bridge: An Essay in Autobiography* (1955), referring to his father's 'pro-Boer' views; Helen Corke, *In Our Infancy: An Autobiography*, Part 1, *1882–1912* (Cambridge, 1975), 108; Philip Gibbs, *The Pageant of the Years* (1946), 26; Gilbert Thomas, *Autobiography* (1946), 48; and Eric Bligh, *Tooting Corner* (1946), 297.
47. Price, *An Imperial War*, ch. 4.
48. Andrew Thompson, 'Publicity, Philanthopy and Commemoration: British Society and the War', in David Omissi and Andrew Thompson (eds.), *The Impact of the South African War* (2002), 107. The 11-year-old Cécile de Banke was a collector, singing 'The Absent-Minded Beggar' outside posh hotels to raise money for the 'Widers and Orfins': the words she had written on her collecting tin. De Banke, *Hand over Hand* (1957), 105.
49. This was one of Keir Hardie's arguments against the war, for example, in the House of Commons, 7 Dec. 1900, *Hansard*, 4th ser., vol. 88, col. 303. See also Peter Struthers, 'South Africa and Imperialism', *Westminster Review*, 156 (1901), 117–19; and Anon., *Narrow Waters: The First Volume of the Life and Thoughts of a Common Man* (1935).
50. Peter Cain, 'British Radicalism, the South African Crisis, and the Origins of the Theory of Financial Imperialism', in Omissi and Thompson (eds.), *Impact of the South African War*, 186–9, and Iain R Smith, 'Capitalism and the War', in ibid. 61, both downplay this famous book's influence at the time, as against later (in Smith's case, much later). But contemporary reviews and ripostes show it to have been widely read and highly controversial, at the very least.
51. There is now an extensive Hobson bibliography, which effectively started with E. E. Nemmers, *Hobson and Underconsumption* (Amsterdam, 1956), Harvey Mitchell, 'Hobson Revisited', *Journal of the History of Ideas*, 26 (1965), and my own *Critics of Empire*

(1968), and at the time of writing has culminated in Peter Cain's *Hobson and Imperialism: Radicalism, New Liberalism, and Finance, 1887–1938* (2002), which also (pp. 296–9) lists the rest.

52. Augustine Birrell, 'Patriotism and Christianity', *Contemporary Review*, 87 (1905), 199–200. Other examples of anti-imperialist and 'pro-Boer' writings include F. Reginald Statham, *South Africa and the Transvaal: The Story of a Conspiracy* (1899); Robert Wallace, 'The Seamy Side of "Imperialism" ', *Contemporary Review*, 76 (1899); Morrison Davidson, *Africa for the Afrikanders: Why I am a Pro-Boer* (1902); F. W. Hirst *et al.*, *Liberalism and the Empire* (1900); C. F. G. Masterman *et al.*, *The Heart of the Empire* (1901); G. H. Perris, *Blood and Gold in South Africa* (1902); J. M. Robertson, *Patriotism and Empire* (1899) and *Wrecking the Empire* (1901); H. N. Brailsford, *The War of Steel and Gold* (1914); scores of articles in the (Liberal) *Westminster Review* throughout this period; and Hobson's other main contributions to this genre, *The War in South Africa: Its Causes and Effects* (1900) and *The Psychology of Jingoism* (1901).
53. Andrew Allan, 'The False Prophet', *Westminster Review*, 160 (1903), 144.
54. F. S. Oliver, 'From Empire to Union', in the (right-wing) *National Review*, 53 (1909), 34.
55. 'These domestic critics tended to be urban, middle class and intellectual': Cannadine, *Ornamentalism*, 136.
56. C. R. L. Fletcher was an Old Etonian and fellow and tutor in history at Magdalen College, Oxford, who authored a five-volume *Introductory History of England* (1904–24), and some ludicrous World War I propaganda (e.g. two pamphlets published by Oxford University Press in 1914: *Their Empire, and How They Have Made It*, and *Their Empire, and What They Covet*). He was also a delegate of the Clarendon Press (effectively OUP), which may explain why they published *A School History*. Later OUP had considerable reservations over it: see below, pp. 274–5.
57. Cuttings in the Oxford University Press (OUP) Archive.
58. Cuttings from the *Tablet* and the *Belfast News Letter*, in ibid.
59. See e.g. the *Sydney Sun*, which also claimed the book was inaccurate on points of Australian detail. Cutting in ibid.
60. This is the *Athenaeum*, which also praised the 'Imperialistic and patriotic spirit' of the book. Good reviews were also carried by the *Westminster Gazette* ('on the whole extremely sensible and fair'), *Blackwood's Magazine* ('On every page there shines the light of a wise and reasoned patriotism'), the *Daily Express*, the *Morning Post*, and the *Church Family Newspaper*. OUP Archive.
61. The OUP Archive prices it at 7*s.* 6*d.* for the main edition and 2*s.* 6*d.* for the School Edition, although some reviews quote it at 1*s.* 8*d.* In 1893–4 the Manchester School Board spent 2*s.* 7*d.* per pupil on new books (to cover all subjects), according to Stephen Heathorn, *For Home, Country and Race: Constructing Gender, Class, and Englishness in the Elementary School, 1880–1914* (Toronto, 2000), 13–14. Heathorn also makes the point about the unimportance of Fletcher and Kipling (p. 7).
62. The actual figures are: an initial printing of 55,000, then about 2,000–5,000 for each of the next 20 years, totalling 134,555 copies in all before it finally went out of print in 1954. OUP Archive. This was quite good, but not as good as one might expect, 'when you consider how well known the authors were', as a publisher who briefly toyed with the idea of reissuing it put it in 1975: Anthony Foster, Methuen, to the Copyright Department of OUP, 12 June 1975. J. R. Green's *A Short History of the English People*

outsold it by a ratio of 4 to 1, above, p. 349, n. 106; and many of the cheap 'Readers' by very much more than this. Heathorn, *For Home, Country and Race.*

63. Fletcher wrote the text, Kipling contributed 23 poems, though Fletcher claimed he influenced his text as well: Peter Sutcliffe, *The Oxford University Press: An Informal History* (1978), 161–2.
64. James Reid, *A Manual of Moral Instruction: A Graded Course of Lessons on Conduct Worked Out on the Concentric Plan* (1908), 198, 200 (italics added). The colonies are *incidentally* mentioned as a source of 'supplies' on p. 199; and the Indian Mutiny cited as an object lesson in the results of 'disobedience' on p. 176.
65. Cf. e.g. Cassell's fervently imperialistic *Citizen Reader* of 1886, which nonetheless climaxes with a chapter (21) on 'How our Freedom was Won'.
66. H. J. Mackinder, *The Nations of the Modern World: An Elementary Study in Geography* (n.d. [1911]), vol. 4, ch. 22, pp. 287–8.
67. S. R. Gardiner, *Outline of English History* (1888 edn.), 235. The context is Britain's dealings with 'men savage and ignorant' overseas.
68. Ibid. 490.
69. By 'strictly imperial' here I mean in terms of mere power.
70. Rare exceptions are J. Roscoe Mongan, *The Oxford and Cambridge British History for School Use* (1882), 214, and *Chambers's Geographical Readers, Standard IV* (1884), 98–9, which mentions the value of imperial trade; although in *Standard III* (1884), 170–1, a section on 'Things which contribute to England's wealth and greatness' omits all mention of colonies.
71. See e.g. Gardiner, *Outline of English History*, 181; *The Royal School Series: The Reign of Queen Victoria: A Reading Book of History for Schools* (1881), 84; *Gill's Imperial History of England* (1883), 370; Revd D Morris, *The History of England from the Accession of George III to the Present Time, Adapted to Standards VI and VII* (1883), 277; Arabella B. Buckley, *History of England for Beginners* (1887), 342; and many others.
72. From *The Banner of St George* (1897). Cf. the final chorus of *Caractacus* (1898): 'And where the flag of Britain, | In triple crosses rears, | No slave shall be for subject, | No trophy wet with tears . . . ', etc.
73. See Bernard Porter, 'Edward Elgar and Empire', *Journal of Imperial and Commonwealth History*, 29 (2001), 16–18; Robert Anderson, *Elgar and Chivalry* (2002).
74. Porter, 'Elgar and Empire', 9, 18.
75. See Bernard Porter, 'Hobson and Internationalism', in Michael Freeden (ed.), *Reappraising J. A. Hobson: Humanism and Welfare* (1990).
76. Idiosyncratic it may have been, but it went through eleven editions between June 1889 and October 1910. It is a version of the 18th-century 'noble savage' idea.
77. It was for this reason that I called my first book '*Critics* of Empire', rather than 'The Anti-Imperialists', the title I had in mind at the beginning of my research for it; because of this trace of what might be regarded as imperialist assumptions that I found at the bottom of all the ideas I studied.
78. J. A. Hobson, *Imperialism: A Study* (1902; 3rd edn. 1938), 227; but the argument appeared before this, in his article 'Ethics of Empire', *Progressive Review*, 2 (1897), 452; and *The Social Problem: Life and Work* (1901), 274.
79. It is precisely the same case put forward to justify imperialism by e.g. Benjamin Kidd in his *Social Evolution* (1894), 316–17, and *The Control of the Tropics* (1898), 51–3.

80. G. B. Shaw, *Fabianism and the Empire* (1900), 24, 46.
81. Ibid. 22.
82. Quoted in Porter, *Critics of Empire*, 119–20.
83. George Newman, *The Health of the State* (1907), quoted in Anna Davin, 'Imperialism and Motherhood', *History Workshop*, 5 (1978), 31.
84. The 'kangaroo' example comes in Percy F. Rowland, 'The Literature of Australia', *Nineteenth Century*, 51 (1902), 656. For other examples, see above, pp. 201, 233.
85. 1886; quoted in Richard Faber, *The Vision and the Need: Late Victorian Imperialist Aims* (1966), 64, where similar quotations from other imperialists can be found. Some others appear in my *The Lion's Share: A Short History of British Imperialism 1850–1995* (3rd edn. 1996), 130–4.
86. William D. Hamilton, 'Labour Questions and the Empire', *Westminster Review*, 156 (1901), 58.
87. *Magazine of Art* supplement, *Royal Academy Pictures 1899*. Peace is implied in the rural idylls, and made explicit in the title of WL Wyllie's *Peace and Plenty*: a harvest scene under a blue sky with a church spire behind. The two 'imperial' paintings are W. B. Wollen's *The 21st Lancers at Omdurman*, a huge battle-scene; and W. Frank Calderon's *A Son of the Empire*, depicting an urchin mimicking a soldier in front of some cavalry officers. As well as these there are a few portraits of military and naval officers, and of Dr Welldon, ex-head of Harrow and now bishop of Calcutta; a picture of 'Crusoe'; and a rare 'Orientalist' canvas by Walter C. Horsley, called *Arbitration*, showing an African potentate judging between two European women.
88. Wilfred Scawen Blunt, *Satan Absolved* (1899), in Chris Brooks and Peter Faulkner (eds.), *The White Man's Burdens: An Anthology of British Poetry of* the Empire (1966), 322.
89. Jeffrey Richards, *Imperialism and Music: Britain 1876–1953* (2001), ch. 5, pp. 359–60, 525.
90. There is also Shaw's fantastical *Back to Methuselah* (1921), which predicts the British empire's being run from Baghdad in the year 3,000 (part IV).
91. J. W. M. Hichberger, *Images of the Army: The Military in British Art, 1815–1914* (Manchester, 1988), 85.
92. Robert Buchanan, 'The Voice of "The Hooligan" ', *Contemporary Review*, 76 (Dec. 1899), 774–89; J. M. Robertson, *Patriotism and the Empire* (1899), 52–5.
93. Cecil Gray, *A Survey of Contemporary Music* (1924: 2nd edn. 1927), 79–80. But he was not quite consistent in this. He admitted, for example, that' 'nationalism has always been one of the most powerful of all external incentives to artistic creation'. The difference between this and imperialism was that the former had its 'roots in the very soil'. Ibid. 80.
94. Quoted in Tim Barringer, 'Not a "modern" as the word is now understood"? Byam Shaw and the Poetics of Professional Society', in David Peters Corbett and Lara Perry (eds.), *English Art 1860–1914*, (Manchester, 2000), 77.
95. Felix Barker and Ralph Hyde, *London As It Might Have Been* (1982), 149–53, which includes the architects' drawing. It was designed to be 'a worthy centre in the metropolis of the Empire "upon which the sun never sets." ' Many similar architectural commemorations of the empire also never came about. In 1910 the *Strand Magazine*, lamenting that the 'British Empire, the greatest and most opulent the world has ever seen, lodges its monarch . . . in a style befitting a third-rate Power', published some grandiose drawings of a huge new Buckingham Palace (vol. 40, pp. 592–7), which never left the drawing-board. Instead we have the present dull new front. Similarly with a

projected 'British Walhalla' of national heroes on the Thames; and a pyramid entered via a Stonehenge druidical arch in Hyde Park. Barker and Hyde, *London*.

96. Taken from the original programme of the occasion, at the Elgar Birthplace, Lower Broadheath, Worcester. Later, during World War I, his *Fringes of the Fleet* song cycle, with words by Kipling, received its premiere at the same venue, with the singers dressed in fishing boots and sou'westers. Jerrold Northrop Moore, *Edward Elgar: A Creative Life* (1984), 707–9.
97. Gilbert Thomas, *Autobiography 1891–1941* (1946), 230.
98. An example is William (Lord) Armstrong, the Newcastle armaments manufacturer, whose great gothic pile 'Cragside', near Rothbury in Northumberland, deliberately avoids, in its details, furnishings, and the artwork that used to fill it, anything pertaining to his business or war. See Bernard Porter, 'Cragside', *History Today*, 45: 1 (Jan. 1995), 46–52.
99. Dr Emil Reich, *Imperialism: Its Prices; its Vocation* (1905), 95.
100. Suspicions attach especially to Henry Lawrence, General Charles Gordon, Cecil Rhodes, Sir Robert Baden-Powell, and Lord Kitchener, though they may be baseless. See Ronald Hyam, *Empire and Sexuality: The British Experience* (1990).
101. See Porter, 'Elgar and Empire', 22–5.
102. Barringer, 'Not a "modern"', 67.
103. Jerrold Northrop Moore, *Edward Elgar*, 338–9.
104. e.g. the stanza of *The Music Makers* (1912), which begins 'With wonderful deathless ditties'; and 'Shakespeare's Kingdom', one of the songs in his *Pageant of Empire* music (1924).
105. This is argued at length in Porter, 'Elgar and Empire'.
106. His only Kipling settings are *The Fringes of the Fleet* (1917) and the song 'Big Steamers', added to the cycle in 1918. Kipling later withdrew permission for these settings, and the performances—highly lucrative for Elgar—had to be stopped. His distaste for certain of Kipling's stories, however, pre-dates this. See his letter to Frank Webb, 27 Mar. 1892: 'some are too awful to have ever been written.' Percy M. Young (ed.), *Letters of Edward Elgar and Other Writings* (1956), 55. The two scarcely knew one another socially.
107. Barringer, 'Not a "modern"', 80. The picture is in the Birmingham Art Gallery.
108. Hichberger, *Images of the Army*, 81–3.
109. Butler came from a genteel artistic family, and was brought up in Italy; her husband was General Sir William Butler, a famous soldier with widespread imperial experience.
110. Quoted in Faber, *The Vision and the Need*, 64.
111. See Bernard Porter, 'So Much to Hate', *London Review of Books*, 25 Apr. 2002, pp. 23–5.
112. See John and Joan Comaroff, *Ethnography and the Historical Imagination* (Boulder, Col., 1992), 183–4.
113. Ronald Hyam, *Empire and Sexuality*.

CHAPTER 11

1. Technically these were not supposed to be 'colonies', but territories 'mandated' to Britain on behalf of the new League of Nations; but no one in the government felt that made much difference. 'I do not think', the colonial under-secretary, Leopold

Amery, told the House of Commons on 30 July 1919, 'that the Mandate is likely to impose upon us any conditions which we would not impose upon ourselves or which we have not been in the habit of imposing upon ourselves whenever we dealt with subject peoples'. *Hansard*, 5th ser., vol. 118, col. 2175.

2. My own assessment of these repercussions is spelled out more fully in my *The Lion's Share: A Short History of British Imperialism 1850–1995* (3rd edn. 1996), ch. 7, and *Britannia's Burden: The Political Evolution of Modern Britain 1851–1990* (1994), ch. 14. See also Robert Holland, 'The British Empire and the Great War, 1914–1918', in Judith Brown and Wm. Roger Louis (eds.), *The Oxford History of the British Empire, vol. 4: The Twentieth Century* (1999), 114–37.
3. See e.g. J. C. Darracott and B. M. Loftus, *First World War Posters* (1972).
4. There are good general discussions of this in John Bourne, *Britain and the Great War 1914–1918* (1989), ch. 9; id., 'The British Working Man in Arms', in Hugh Cecil and Peter H Liddle (eds.), *Facing Armageddon: The First World War Experienced* (Barnsley, 1996); and Denis Winter, *Death's Men: Soldiers of the Great War* (1978), esp. 32–5. 228–34.
5. See Bernard Waites, *A Class Society at War: England 1914–1918* (Leamington Spa, 1987), 201–9; and Gloden Dallas and Douglas Gill, *The Unknown Army: Mutinies in the British Army in World War I* (1985).
6. e.g. at King's Cathedral School, Worcester: 'In memory of those who, having learnt in this place to play the game for their School, played it also for their Country during the years 1914–1919' (the school had used the money to build a new 'Memorial Pavilion'). C. F. Kernot, *British Public Schools War Memorials* (1927), 30.
7. Various enquiries, e. g. at the Imperial War Museum, have uncovered almost no references to the empire carved into World War I memorials, though as Angela Gaffney has told me (letter to author, 12 May 1997), it *was* sometimes referred to in speeches (usually by senior military men) at unveiling ceremonies. Even the Cenotaph in Whitehall does not mention it. Public-school memorials are similarly bereft of imperial allusions: see Kernot, *Public Schools War Memorials, passim.* One factor here (though this will not apply to the public-school examples) may have been the democratization of memorial sculpture generally from the Boer War onwards, with the sacrifices of ordinary soldiers being much more often commemorated than their leaders or causes: Allen Borg, *War Memorials from Antiquity to the Present* (1991), 107 ff.; Alex King, *Memorials of the Great War in Britain: The Symbolism and Politics of Remembrance* (1998), ch. 7. This would explain why the grandiose plans of the 'Empire War Memorial League', to rebuild most of central Westminster and several provincial cities as huge monuments to the war and the empire, never came to anything. King, *Memorials of the Great War*, 72–3.

   The main exception to this general rule is the Tomb of the Unknown Warrior in Westminster Abbey, dedicated to those who gave their lives 'For God, For King and Country, For loved ones, home and Empire, For the sacred cause of justice and freedom in the world'. Kipling had a hand in this. Angela Gaffney also cites Llanbradach in South Wales; and Kernot (above) quotes imperialist inscriptions on memorials at Auckland Grammar School and Waitaki High School (for the boys who fell 'In the high cause of Empire'), both in New Zealand (pp. 311–12). There are also monuments in Britain to the colonial dead, like the Cavalry Memorial in Hyde Park (a 'St George and the Dragon').

8. About 28,000 Indians served on the Western Front during the first year of the war, after which the infantry divisions among them were redeployed, either back home or in the Middle Eastern theatre, partly because of the effect it was feared the experience of being pummelled by the Germans might have on their respect for their British rulers. See Jeffrey Greenhut, 'The Imperial Reserve: The Indian Corps on the Western Front, 1914–15', *Journal of Imperial and Commonwealth History*, 12 (1983), 65; and David Omissi (ed.), *Indian Voices of the Great War: Soldiers' Letters, 1914–18* (1999), 1–4.
9. e.g. Louie Stride, who remembers her mother marrying a Canadian soldier billeted with her who turned out to be 'a hopeless alcoholic', and a neighbour sheltering an Australian deserter. *Memoirs of a Street Urchin* (Bath, n.d.), 15, 27.
10. Unless they were hospitalized in Britain. Omissi, *Indian Voices*, 18, 36 *et passim*.
11. Dominions support was made much of in the contemporary *Illustrated War News*, for example. A random sample of just four issues from 1915 (vol. 4, pts. 38–41) has the Canadians featured prominently in pt. 38, pp. 1–3; pt. 39, pp. 3, 5, 20–1; pt. 41, pp. 20–1; Australian and New Zealand regiments in p. 40, p. 10 and pt. 41, pp. 24–5; the Nigerians (in the Cameroons) in pt. 38, p. 19; an Indian war mule in pt. 38, p. 16; and—perhaps most telling of all—General Botha of South Africa in pt. 41, pp. 33–4: fighting for Britain now, as the caption points out, despite his fighting *against* her in the Boer War. Most pictures of dominions regiments, incidentally, are labelled 'Fighters for the freedom of Europe' (not for the empire). I am grateful to John Bourne for putting me on to this source.
12. P. J. Cain and A. G. Hopkins, *British Imperialism: Crisis and Deconstruction 1914–1990* (1993), 37, 45; Michael Barratt Brown, *After Imperialism* (2nd edn. 1970), 110.
13. B. R. Mitchell and Phyllis Deane, *Abstract of British Historical Statistics* (1962), 51. This is a *net* emigration figure: that is, after immigrants from the empire have been subtracted. During the same period around 335,000 Britons (net) migrated to the USA.
14. *Census of England and Wales 1931* (1950: *sic*), 168. This figure is for people *born* there; they could be visitors or immigrants, but will not include returning emigrants. Of these, 28,319 were from Australia, 32,001 from Canada, 23,814 from the Union of South Africa, and 86,963 from the Indian empire. The last figure will include Anglo-Indians.
15. www. imperial-airways.com/ops.
16. Before 1932 Indians used to play for the England team. One of them—the famous K. S. Ranjitsinhji—must have boosted popular awareness of India before the war considerably.
17. See Lawrence Le Quesne, *The Bodyline Controversy* (1983), 60. It may be significant that the England captain of the time, Douglas Jardine, was one of the imperialist elite, born in the Raj and with a notoriously patrician mien. His (working-class) bowlers apparently disliked his tactics, but had to obey his orders.
18. Gary Messinger, *British Propaganda and the State in World War I* (1992).
19. Stephen Constantine, '"Bringing the Empire Alive": The Empire Marketing Board and Imperial Propaganda, 1926–33', in John Mackenzie (ed.), *Imperialism and Popular Culture* (1986).
20. W. K. Hancock, *Survey of British Commonwealth Affairs*, vol. 2, *Problems of Economic Policy 1918–1939*, Part 2 (1942), 201–2. The National Museum of Australia in Canberra is still selling puddings made by this recipe in its gift shop, from the label of one of which the quotation is taken.

21. John MacKenzie, '"In Touch with the Infinite": The BBC and the Empire, 1923–53', in MacKenzie (ed.), *Imperialism and Popular Culture*, 168–71.
22. The Round Table movement originated in 1909–10, with some of Rhodes's money, as a means of promoting the empire and certain imperial causes, like federation. Between the wars its main efforts were directed towards the leaders and formers of opinion, rather than the broader public directly. See Alexander C May, 'The Round Table, 1910–66', D.Phil. thesis, Oxford University (1995), 230–6.
23. B. J. Elliott, 'History Examinations at Sixteen and Eighteen Years in England and Wales Between 1918 and 1939', *History of Education*, 20 (1991), 121.
24. The following (incomplete) list gives an idea of the quantity: A. D. Innes, *A History of England and the British Empire* (1915); C. B. Thurston, *An Economic Geography of the British Empire* (1916); E. A. Hughes, *Britain and Greater Britain in the Nineteenth Century* (1919); Ramsay Muir, *A Short History of the British Empire* (1920); J. C. Cunningham, *Products of the Empire* (1921); C. S. S. Higham, *History of the British Empire* (1921); W. R. Kermack, *The Expansion of Britain from the Age of Discoveries: A Geographical History* (1922); L. W. Lyde, *Commercial Geography of the British Empire* (1922); A. D. Innes, *A Classbook of the British Commonwealth* (1923); Sir Charles Lucas, *The Story of the Empire* (1924: this was commissioned by the management of the Wembley Exhibition); G. W. Morris and L. S. Wood, *The English-speaking Nations: A Study of the Commonwealth Ideal* (1924); A. J. Herbertson and R. L. Thompson, *The Geography of the British Empire* (1924); J. A. Williamson, *Builders of the Empire* (1925); R. M. Rayner, *Nineteenth Century England: A Political and Social History of the British Commonwealth* (1927); H. F. B. Wheeler, *Makers of the British Empire* (1927); F. W. Tickner, *Building the British Empire* (1929); A. P. Newton and J. Ewing, *The British Empire Since 1783: Its Political and Economic Development* (1929: commissioned by the Royal Empire Society); Ramsay Muir, *British History: A Survey of the History of All the British Peoples* (1929); J. A. Williamson, *A Short History of British Expansion* (2nd edn. 1930); R. A. F. Mears, *A Short History of the British Empire* (1931); J. Fairgrieve and E. Young, *Human Geography: The British Commonwealth* (1931); A. E. Hogan and Isabel Powell, *The Government of Great Britain in the Dominions and Colonies* (1934); J. A. Williamson, *The British Empire and Commonwealth: A History for Senior Forms* (1935); G. W. Morris, *The Building of the Commonwealth* (1936); C. B. Bowman, *Atlas of English and Empire History* (1937); T. Chadwick, *Practical Citizenship: An Introduction to Government in the British Empire* (1937); S. King-Hall, *The Empire Yesterday and Today* (1937); H. F. B. Wheeler, *Makers of the British Empire* (1937); M. M. B. and C. S. S. Higham, *Makers of the Commonwealth* (1939); and E. H. Short, *Living with History*, Book 3, *Building the Commonwealth* (1939). For an analysis of these, see below, pp. 274–7.
25. Innes, *Classbook of the British Commonwealth*, p. v.
26. John Springhall, 'Lord Meath, Youth, and Empire', *Journal of Contemporary History*, 5 (1970), 105.
27. These include *Livingstone* (M. A. Wetherell, 1925), *Sanders of the River* (Zoltan Korda, 1935), *Rhodes of Africa* (Michael Balcon, 1936), *The Drum* (Korda, 1936), and *The Four Feathers* (Korda, 1939). Among American films about the British empire are *Lives of a Bengal Lancer* (Henry Hathaway, 1935), *Wee Willie Winkie* (John Ford, 1937), and *Gunga Din* (George Stevens, 1939). See Jeffrey Richards, *Films and British National Identity: From Dickens to Dad's Army* (1997), ch. 2.
28. MacKenzie, '"In Touch with the Infinite"', 168–71.

29. Beginning with MacKenzie's *Propaganda and Empire: The Manipulation of British Public Opinion, 1880–1960* (Manchester, 1984), and continued in his Manchester University Press 'Studies in Imperialism' series.
30. All listed in Arthur Byron, *London Statues* (1981). The proportion of imperial (including military) to non-imperial statues for the 1917–68 period is 18 : 103.
31. Official Guide to the Exhibition, quoted in MacKenzie, *Propaganda and Empire*, 108.
32. Donald Maxwell, *Wembley in Colour* (1924), 55, 95. There are also good descriptions in James (Jan) Morris, *Farewell the Trumpets: An Imperial Retreat* (1978), 299–302, and MacKenzie, *Propaganda and Empire*, 108–12.
33. *Morning Post*, 24 Ap. 1924; cutting at the Elgar Birthplace Museum, Broadheath.
34. Jerrold Northrop Moore, *Edward Elgar: A Creative Life* (1984), 768–9.
35. MacKenzie, *Propaganda and Empire*, 112–13. This was a different exhibition—not the Wembley one transplanted.
36. John Foulds (1880–1939), whose music is reputed to have been effectively blacklisted because of his socialist beliefs, and whose love of Indian culture and sympathy with Indian national aspirations inspired him to move to and work in India. I have not heard any of his music, and so have no opinion as to whether his neglect is deserved or not. See Simon Heffer, 'A Genius Ignored For His Politics', *New Statesman*, 25 Dec. 2000, pp. 36–7; and Jeffrey Richards, *Imperialism and Music: Britain 1876–1953* (2001), 159–60.
37. I have found Margaret Meredith (née Elliot) elusive. She was born in 1865, and educated at Cheltenham College and (musically) under Danreuther and Ernst Pauer in Germany. She was the founder of the Independent Music Club for the Protection and Advancement of Art and Artists; and of its journal, the *Independent Musical World*. Her works (from the British Library's music catalogue) include a flood of patriotic pieces from the 1910s, including requiems for Queen Victoria and Edward VII, and a 'Song of the Flag'.
38. That is not to say that they do not betray imperialist attitudes, especially in the matter of race. To my mind Cary is the most problematical in this regard; but his anti-colonial credentials seem secure: see his *The Case for African Freedom*, with an introduction by George Orwell (1941).
39. Other reasons were: old age, the death of his wife, illness, and a depression that seems to have been chronic. Occasionally he roused himself to work on new substantial pieces (an opera, a symphony, and a piano concerto), but he could not sustain this sufficiently to complete any of them. A feeling of being passé undoubtedly contributed to this. The 'Third Symphony' was recently put together from sketches and other Elgar material by Anthony Payne.
40. Martin Seymour-Smith, *Rudyard Kipling* (1989), 337–9, 351; and see Charles Carrington, *Rudyard Kipling: His Life and Work* (1955), 487–8; John Raymond, 'The Last Phase', in John Gross (ed.), *Rudyard Kipling: The Man, His Work and His World* (1972), 148; Angus Wilson, *The Strange Ride of Rudyard Kipling* (1977), 299–301, 324; and David Gilmour, *The Long Recessional: The Imperial Life of Rudyard Kipling* (2002).
41. See Constance Babington Smith, *John Masefield: A Life* (1978). Masefield was a very British but never a particularly imperialist poet, even in his pre-war heyday.
42. Alfred Noyes, 'Britain—To the Empire' (1924), printed in *Collected Poems* (Edinburgh, 1927), 291.

43. B. J. Elliott, 'An Early Failure of Curriculum Reform: History Teaching in England 1918–1940', *Journal of Educational Administration and History*, 12 (1980), 39–45. Relativism was attacked by J. D. Mackie, 'The Teaching of History and the War', *History*, 25 (1940), 134–5: 'The past has no objective reality ... It is realised through the minds of historians. There are no absolute "facts".'
44. Celia Evans, 'Geography and World Citizenship', in *The Teaching of Geography in Relation to the World Community*, published for the League of Nations Union, Advisory Education Committee for Wales (Cambridge, 1933), 16, 18 (original italics).
45. The 1920s and '30s saw a spate of new textbooks on European and world history, or on Britain's history in relation to Europe. Gordon Batho's collection (see above, p. 343, n. 17) contains about 70 titles which suggest this focus (I have not read these; some may still take an imperialist line). Some examples are: F. J. C. Hearnshawe, *An Outline Sketch of the Political History of Europe in the 19th Century* and M. W. Keatinge and N. L. Frazer, *An Introduction to World History* (both 1920); Lucy Dale, *Stories from European History*; Lawrence H. Davison, *Movements in European History*, and J. E. Morris, *A History of Modern Europe from the Middle of the 16th Century* (1921); C. R. Beazley, *Nineteenth Century Europe and Britain*, A. Browning, *Britain as a European Power*, Muriel O. Davis, *Outlines of European History*, and L. C. Smith, *Main Currents in World History* (1922); Etheldreda M. Wilmot-Buxton, *Outlines of European History for the Middle Forms of Schools* and E. L. Hasluck, *A Short History of Modern Europe* (1923); F. J. C. Hearnshaw, *A First Book of World History*, J. S. Hoyland, *Modern European History*, and F. J. Weaver, *Europe and England 1494–1715* (1924); W. F. and T. F. Reddaway, *Modern European History: A General Sketch, 1492–1924* (1926); J. B. Newman, *The Beginner's History of the World from Earliest Times to the Present Day* (1927); D. K. Gordon, *A Junior History of Europe, 410–1927* (1928); R. B. Mowat, *A History of Europe and the Modern World* (1929); H. Cory, *The Story of Man (A Historical Concourse for Junior Schools)* (1930); A. D. Innes, *A Classbook of European History for Public and Secondary Schools* (1930); S. Reed Brett, *Europe Since the Renaissance* (1931); R. A. F. Mears, *Britain and Europe* (1933); S. Reed Brett, *Modern Europe: 1789–1914: A School Certificate Course* (1936); G. B. Smith, *Outlines of European History* (3rd edn. 1930); H. A. Davies, *An Outline History of the World* (1937); G. W. Southgate, *A Textbook of Modern European History 1830–1919* (1937); S. Reed Brett, *Modern Europe: 1789–1914 and After*; R. M. Rayner, *Britain and Europe 1815–1936*; D. Richards, *An Illustrated History of Modern Europe, 1789–1938* (1938); S. F. Woolley, *Modern Europe 1789–1939* (1939); H. R. Exelby, *A Modern English-European History*, 2 vols. (*c.*1939).

    Another comparatively new fashion was for economic and social histories of Britain. Gordon Batho's collection has around 25 of these from this inter-war period. One (by Eleanor Doorly) is suggestively titled *England in Her Days of Peace: An Introduction to Social and Industrial History* (1920).
46. Wheeler, *Makers of the British Empire*, 10; Williamson, *British Empire and Commonwealth*, 388; Mears, *Short History of the British Empire*, 5.
47. Mackie, 'The Teaching of History and the War', 138–9. Mackie was Professor of Scottish History at Glasgow University.
48. J. C. Stobart, 'The Child: The Empire', *United Empire*, 16 (1925), 174–6.
49. MacKenzie, '"In Touch with the Infinite"', 171–3.
50. Ibid. 173.
51. Richard Symonds, *Oxford and the Empire: The Last Lost Cause?* (1986), 22.

52. Quoted in Morris, *Farewell the Trumpets*, 304.
53. MacKenzie, *Propaganda and Empire*, 111; and cf. Jeffrey Richards, 'the empire was above all *the people*'s Empire', quoted above.
54. Ronald Taylor, 'Music in the Air: Elgar and the BBC', in Raymond Monk (ed.), *Edward Elgar: Music and Literature* (1993), 336; and see John Gardiner, 'The Reception of Sir Edward Elgar 1918–*c*.1934: A Reassessment', *Twentieth Century British History*, 9 (1998). On his recordings (most of which Elgar was actively involved in), see Jerrold Northrop Moore, *Elgar on Record: The Composer and the Gramophone* (Oxford, 1974).
55. This is taken from the *British Library Catalogue*. It excludes American editions and foreign translations, which greatly outnumbered British printings in this period.
56. G. A. Henty died in 1902, but many of his novels continued to be reprinted for 50 years afterwards, with an 'Omnibus' edition appearing in 1937 and a new collection in 1953. Stables did not weather quite so well, but there were new editions of batches of his books in 1925 (Blackie) and 1927 (Hulberts of Glasgow), and of individual titles up to *c*.1937.
57. Derek Winterbottom, *Henry Newbolt: The Spirit of Clifton* (1986), 74.
58. He never, so far as I know, disowned it, conducting it himself frequently in the 1920s (it was a nice little earner); but he was never happy about the original words, and expressed irritation in 1924 at the philistine King George V's forever demanding it, instead of any of his newer works. Michael Kennedy, *Portrait of Elgar* (1968), 251.
59. Coward, *This Happy Breed* (1943), quoted in Morris, *Farewell the Trumpets*, 302.
60. It amassed a debt of £600,000 in its first year, and more thereafter. MacKenzie, *Propaganda and Empire*, 111.
61. Amery, *My Political Life*, vol. 2 (1953), 340.
62. Elgar to Alice Stuart-Wortley, 26 Apr. 1924, in Percy M. Young, *Letters of Edward Elgar and Other Writings* (1956), 287.
63. The song is 'Shakespeare's Kingdom'.
64. Letter by Major Gordon Home to the Colonial Office, 11 Oct. 1921, in PRO CO 323/84; quoted in Finlay Murray, 'The Making of British Policy on Tropical Africa: Approaches To and Influences On Policy-making', Ph.D. thesis, University of Newcastle upon Tyne (2001), 81.
65. In the report of the AGM of the African Society in its *Journal*, 19 (1919–20), 102; quoted in ibid. 35.
66. Minute by J. E. W. Flood, 26 Mar. 1923, in PRO CO 323/916; in ibid. 83.
67. Ralph Furse, *Aucuparius: Memoirs of a Recruiting Officer* (Oxford, 1962), 225.
68. *Colonial Office Conference*, 1927, *Appendices*: Cmd. 2884, 14, quoted in Murray, 'Making of British Policy', 94.
69. Oldham to Curtis, 25 Feb. 1929, in Oldham Papers, 4/1/179, quoted in ibid. 57.
70. Quoted in Trevor Reese, *The History of the Royal Commonwealth Society 1868–1968* (1968), 156–7.
71. Shiels in Commons, 20 Feb. 1929: *Hansard*, 5th ser., vol. 219, col. 2681. I am grateful to Dr Finlay Murray for this reference.
72. See George H. Gallup, *The Gallup International Public Opinion Polls: Great Britain 1837–1975*, vol. 1, *1937–1964* (New York, n.d. [1976]), 10. A smaller majority said they would 'rather fight than hand them back'. 'Mass Observation' was a different method of eliciting public opinion in the 1930s (through interviews). It seems to have avoided

colonial issues too. See Charles Madge and Tom Harrison (eds.), *Britain by Mass-Observation* (Harmondsworth, 1939), *passim*; and Angus Calder and Dorothy Sheridan, *Speak for Yourself: A Mass-Observation Anthology, 1937–49* (1984), esp. 251–3, which is a list of the topics investigated by Mass Observation.

73. i.e. either during the war (26%), or just after (51%). Gallup, *The Gallup International Public Opinion Polls*, i. 25.
74. G. K. Evens, *Public Opinion on Colonial Affairs: A Survey Made in May and June, 1948, for the Colonial Office* (1948), ii–iii, 1–2, 6, 16 (italics added).
75. Christopher Andrew, *Secret Service: The Making of the British Intelligence Community* (1985), ch. 7; Bernard Porter, *Plots and Paranoia: A History of Political Espionage in Britain, 1790–1988* (1989), 142–4.
76. Chris Cook and John Stevenson, *The Longman Handbook of Modern British History 1714–1980* (1983), 68–9.
77. Ibid. 153.
78. Many of those in the forefront of anti-communist movements between the wars started off as imperialists: like Sir William Joynson-Hicks, home secretary during the General Strike; Admiral Reginald 'Blinker' Hall, the founder of the anti-Bolshevik 'Economic League'; Henry Page Croft, a tariff reformer turned undercover anti-communist; and Patrick Hannon, whose British Commonwealth Union (1915–?1926) was in fact a mainly pro-capitalist organization. On this general area, see G. C. Webber, *The Ideology of the British Right 1918–39* (1986).
79. Morris, *Farewell the Trumpets*, 304.
80. Sir Donald Maclean in the House of Commons, 30 July 1919; *Hansard*, 5th ser., vol. 118, col. 2186; and see above, n. 1.
81. This was in 1928. Murray, 'The Making of British Policy on Tropical Africa', 40. Much of the following is derived from Dr Murray's research.
82. McDonnell in the Commons, 13 July 1928, *Hansard*, 5th ser., vol. 219, col. 2655, quoted in ibid. 45.
83. Charles Ponsonby, *Ponsonby Remembers* (1965), 115, quoted in ibid. 40. This applies to colonial as distinct from Indian debates, where the faces were more numerous and often different.
84. Frank Melland, 'Eastern Africa—Our Opportunity', *Fortnightly Review*, 125 (1929), 505. I am grateful to Dr Murray for this reference.
85. Amery, *My Political Life*, ii. 212.
86. John Ramsden, *The Age of Balfour and Baldwin 1902–40* (1978), 212–13.
87. Thomas, 1924, quoted in Paul Ward, *Red Flag and Union Jack: Englishness, Patriotism and the British Left, 1881–1924* (1998), 185. He was ridiculed largely because of the delight he took in dressing up in court garb when he went to meet the king.
88. Partha Sarathi Gupta, *Imperialism and the British Labour Movement, 1914–1964* (1975), 27, 60, *et passim*. Labour accepted the idea of 'Colonial Development', however, partly on the grounds that as well as helping the colonies it would 'in turn provide work for our people in this country'; which may be thought implicitly to concede some of the Empire economic unionists' case. William Lunn, House of Commons, 17 July 1929, *Hansard*, 5th ser., vol. 230, col. 471.
89. These included a number of colonial nationalist organizations with a presence in Britain, like the Indian Home Rule League (founded at the end of the war), the India

League (founded 1930), and the Kikuyu Central Association (*c.*1930), together with the broader-based League Against Imperialism (1928), the British Centre Against Imperialism (1937), and the International Africa Service Bureau (1937). In 1939 some of these combined together in a submission to the Colonial Office, pledging not to 'rest until the crime of Empire is wiped off the earth'; sadly the Office did not think it worth even acknowledging. Memorial in PRO CO 323/1607/15; quoted in Murray, 'The Making of British Policy on Tropical Africa', 174.

90. P. J. Cain, *Hobson and Imperialism: Radicalism, New Liberalism, and Finance 1887–1938* (2002), 201, 231–2.
91. Imperialism, it said, tended 'to perpetuate the reign of capitalism, not only by increasing the power of wealth, but by neglecting the needs of the Home market, and leaving the natural resources of our own country undeveloped'. The first part of that is Lenin, the second Hobson. Gupta, *Imperialism and the British Labour Movement,* 29. The ILP was much more vigorously anti-imperialist, with Fenner Brockway taking a leading part. See e.g. *Report of the Annual Conference held at Leicester, April, 1927,* 9, 45, 84; and *Report of the Annual Conference held at Norwich, April, 1928,* 6–7, 35; but also below, p. 279.
92. Gupta, *Imperialism,* 41, 51.
93. Walter Citrine, *Men and Work: An Autobiography* (1964), 335.
94. Gupta, *Imperialism,* 227.
95. A cutting from the *Brighouse and Elland Echo* in the (Charles Roden) Buxton Papers, quoted in Murray, 'Making of British Policy', 38.
96. Ibid.
97. Ibid. 82.
98. Ibid.
99. Ibid. 83.
100. Minute by Cowell, 4 Aug. 1937, in PRO 323/1495/17 (italics added), in ibid. 194.
101. Ibid. 84.
102. Ibid. 61.
103. Furse, *Aucuparius,* 214; Robert Heussler, *Yesterday's Rulers* (1963), 37–43.
104. 'A Song of Union', from *Pageant of Empire* (1924). The 'Wider still' reference, of course, is from 'Land of Hope and Glory' (1902).
105. See Dennis Judd, *Empire: The British Imperial Experience, From 1765 to the Present* (1996), 215, for the origin of the word 'commonwealth' (in this context) in the 1880s. Nicholas Mansergh, *The Commonwealth Experience* (1969), 23–6, traces the 'idea' back to the Durham Report of 1839.
106. Ward, *Red Flag and Union Jack,* 185.
107. The others are (1) 'Shakespeare's Kingdom'; (2) 'The Islands: A Song of New Zealand'; (3) 'The Blue Mountains: A Song of Australia'; (4) 'The Heart of Canada'; (5) 'Sailing Westward' (on the Elizabethan explorers); (6) 'Merchant Adventurers'; and (7) 'The Immortal Legions' (commemorating the Great War dead).
108. It was banned in government schools in British Guiana in 1929, according to a cutting from the *Daily Sketch,* 25 Apr. 1929; and in India, according to a representative of the press in a letter to Fletcher, 28 May 1929: both in the OUP Archive.
109. See Kenneth Sisam (OUP) to Fletcher, 4 June 1929, in OUP Archive. He was also worried that teachers might infer that its publication by the Press gave the

University's imprimatur to its extreme views. This correspondence is about a new chapter Fletcher wished to add to the book, bringing it up to date. See also Peter Sutcliffe, *The Oxford University Press: An Informal History* (1978), 158–62.

110. W. P. Welpton, *The Teaching of Geography* (1923), 7 (italics added). See also Sir Ernest Simon and Eva M. Hubback, *Training For Citizenship* (1935), 8, 22, 25.
111. e.g. in E. C. T. Horniblow, *People and Children in Wonderful Lands*, the first volume in his or her *Lands and Life: Human Geographies* series (1927–32); and A. B. Archer and Helen G. Thomas, *Geography, First Series*, book I [1936], on 'the daily lives of Bimbo' (a West African) and others. See also D. M. Preece and H. R. B. Wood, *Modern Geography* [1938–9], for older students, which dwells on the 'backwardness' of the most 'primitive' 'races', but without the sensationalism of the pre-war texts, and with some positive judgements too: 'They are virile and courageous', 'their inherent knowledge of nature and of the sources of natural poisons is probably unsurpassed', and so on (book 1, pp. 257–8).
112. Lucas, *Story of the Empire*, 268.
113. King-Hall, *Empire Yesterday and Today*, 1. See also the incidence of 'Commonwealth' in the *titles* listed above, n. 24. Later the historian Nicholas Mansergh, albeit without denying the 'imperialism'of Britain's original imperialism, maintained that (in Ronald Robinson's précis) 'the ethic of Commonwealth was not only distinct from, but utterly opposed to, the ethic of empire'. Robinson, 'Oxford in Imperial Historiography', in Frederick Madden and D. K. Fieldhouse (eds.), *Oxford and the Idea of Commonwealth* (1982), 41.
114. Morris and Wood, *The English-Speaking Nations*, p. vii.
115. Higham and Higham, *Makers of the Commonwealth*; Short, *Building the Commonwealth*.
116. e.g. Innes, *A History of England and the British Empire*, and Tickner, *Building the British Empire*, do not mention tropical Africa, apart from a brief glance at Livingstone in the latter. One text that does dwell unusually on Africa and the 'native problem' is Morris, *The Building of the Commonwealth*, 88 ff. The Boer War could hardly be ignored entirely, of course—it was too recent and too famous—but the emphasis here now is on the concord between Briton and Boer that is supposed to have followed it, which fits in better with the new temper; e.g. Higham, *History of the British Empire*, 168; Morris, *Building of the Commonwealth*, 74; Higham and Higham, *Makers of the Commonwealth*, 251–2.
117. Lucas, *Story of the Empire*, 274–5.
118. Tickner, *Building the British Empire*, 134.
119. Williamson, *British Empire and Commonwealth*, 389.
120. Rayner, *Nineteenth Century England*, 332.
121. Morris and Wood, *English-Speaking Nations*, 357; and cf. Rayner, *Nineteenth Century England*, 332.
122. Short, *Building the Commonwealth*, 51.
123. Tickner, *Building the British Empire*, 7.
124. See e.g. Morris and Wood, *English-Speaking Nations*, 360, on Britain's treatment of native races: 'At best it has succeeded in inspiring actual love.'
125. Hughes, *Britain and Greater Britain*, 282; and cf. Morris and Wood, *English-Speaking Nations*, 360: 'the familiar comparison of the British Commonwealth to a family [is] no mere figure of speech.'
126. Norton and Ewing, *The British Empire Since 1783*, 272.

127. See also MacKenzie, *Propaganda and Empire*, 187. There are exceptions. One is Wheeler, *Makers of the British Empire* (1927), which prefaces its account of the empire with this onslaught on its new rival (pp. 7–8). 'Some people, who sleep when they are supposed to be awake and dream of an unpractical world-nation, would willingly surrender the British Empire in pursuance of their will-o'-the-wisp... This book is not for the would-be citizens of no country, whose blood is no thicker than water...'
128. Tickner, *Building the British Empire*, 152. Other kinds of books of the time make the same comparison; e.g. Edward Salmon and A. A. Longden, *The Literature and Art of the Empire* (1924), 2: 'this lesser League of Nations, the British Empire.'
129. Morris, *Building of the Commonwealth*, 113.
130. e.g. Morris and Wood, *English-Speaking Nations*, 371.
131. J. O. Springhall, 'The Boy Scouts, Class and Militarism in Relation to British Youth Movements 1908–1930', *International Review of Social History*, 16 (1971), 149–54.
132. Allen Warren. 'Mothers for the Empire? The Girl Guides Association in Britain, 1909–1939', in J. A. Mangan (ed.), *Making Imperial Mentalities* (1990), 106.
133. *Girl Guides Gazette*, 6 (1918–19), 28 (Lady B-P) and 65 (Meath).
134. Ibid. 121–23.
135. Warren, 'Mothers for the Empire?', 106.
136. Quoted in Paul Wilkinson, 'English Youth Movements, 1908–30', *Journal of Contemporary History*, 4 (1969), 16–17.
137. The rather cranky Kibbo Kift Kindred and the socialist Woodcraft Folk were founded in 1920 and 1925 respectively, the former by a defector from the Baden-Powell movement, John Hargrave. Their memberships were tiny by comparison with the latter: e.g. 4,521 Woodcraft Folk in 1938, as against 438,713 (UK) boy scouts. See J. O. Springhall, *Youth, Empire and Society: British Youth Movements, 1883–1940* (1977), ch. 7 and app. V; and Wilkinson, 'English Youth Movements', 18–20.
138. See Tammy M. Proctor, '(Uni)Forming Youth: Girl Guides and Boy Scouts in Britain, 1908–39', *History Workshop Journal*, 45 (1998), 106, 112–16.
139. Quoted in Ward, *Red Flag and Union Jack*, 185.
140. Or rather, the 'Sambo' image as mediated through its American versions. See above, p. 391, n. 137.
141. This is part of a resolution on 'Internationalism' proposed by the ILP at the Labour Women's Conference of 1927, printed in ILP, *Report of the Annual Conference, Leicester, April 1927*, 45. At a more particular level, the ILP concentrated on securing early self-rule for India, and calling for 'international supervision of all territories where a democratic constitution is not immediately practicable, with the object of preventing exploitation and developing self-government at the earliest possible moment'. Short of that, it also called for specific reforms *under* colonial rule. See ibid. 9, 84.
142. On all this see Anthony Clayton, '"Deceptive Might": Imperial Defence and Security, 1900–1968', in Brown and Louis, *Oxford History of the British Empire*, iv. 280–305; David Omissi, *Air Power and Colonial Control: The Royal Air Force, 1919–1939* (Manchester, 1990), chs. 1–3; David Anderson and David Killingray (eds.), *Policing the Empire: Government, Authority and Control, 1830–1940* (Manchester, 1991), and *Policing and*

Decolonisation: Nationalism, Politics and the Police, 1917–65 (Manchester, 1992); and Thomas R. Mockaitis, *British Counter-Insurgency, 1919–60* (1990).

143. Bruce Elder, *Blood on the Wattle: Massacres and Maltreatment of Australian Aborigines Since 1788* (Frenchs Forest, NSW, 1988), chs. 11–12.
144. Including my own; not because I was trying to hide it, but because I was unaware of it until recently.
145. The main exception, where there was a great deal of constructive effort, was an attempt to federate the British colonies north of the Limpopo River into one or two new 'Great White Dominions', i.e. dominated by the European settlers of Southern Rhodesia and Kenya. That failed in the end because of the adverse black–white ratio, anti-racist pressure on behalf of the Africans, and the complication of a separate Indian population in Kenya. The only change that came out of it was the effective devolution of government to the whites of Southern Rhodesia alone (later just 'Rhodesia', now Zimbabwe), in 1923.
146. 'The Islands', from *Pageant of Empire.*
147. Clayton, '"Deceptive Might"', 290.
148. Omissi, *Air Power,* 175–6.
149. Clayton, '"Deceptive Might"', 290.
150. See Derek Sayer, 'British Reaction to the Amritsar Massacre, 1919–1920', *Past and Present,* 131 (1991).
151. See Anderson and Killingray (eds.), *Policing the Empire,* esp. chs. 1–2; and *Policing and Decolonisation,* esp. ch. 1. Charles Smith's essay in the latter volume, however, 'Communal Conflict and Insurrection in Palestine, 1936–48', 79, shows how several ex-'Black-and-Tans' found their way to top policing jobs there.
152. Smith, 'Communal Conflict and Insurrection', 66–7.
153. Mockaitis, *British Counter-Insurgency, passim;* Richard J. Popplewell, *Intelligence and Imperial Defence: British Intelligence and the Defence of the Indian Empire 1904–1924* (1995), chs. 12–13.
154. Clayton, '"Deceptive Might"', 291.
155. e.g. the short-lived 'Anti-Waste League' which managed to get three of its candidates elected as MPs in by-elections in 1921, singled out the British occupation of Iraq as one burdensome responsibility that should be ditched. See Kenneth Morgan, *Consensus and Disunity: The Lloyd George Coalition Government* (1979), 98, 244–5. Labour attacked the Iraq mandate on exactly the same grounds: Gupta, *Imperialism and the British Labour Movement,* 29.
156. 'I have not become the King's First Minister in order to preside over the liquidation of the British Empire.' Churchill in *The Times,* 11 Nov. 1942, quoted in P. N. S. Mansergh, *Survey of British Commonwealth Affairs, 1939–1952* (1952), 192. The irony of this has been pointed out many times: that one of the most imperialist members of the political establishment should have been largely responsible for the empire's demise, through his resolute opposition to the policy that probably would have enabled Britain to hang on to it for at least a little while longer, namely 'appeasement'. See John Charmley, *Churchill: The End of Glory: A Political Biography* (1995).
157. Reported in Patrick Cosgrave, *The Lives of Enoch Powell* (1989), 115, which attributes the story, however, to R. A. Butler's high-table gossip at Trinity College Cambridge after he had become Master there: so it may not be reliable.

CHAPTER 12

1. Avner Offer, 'Costs and Benefits, Prosperity and Security, 1870–1914', in Andrew Porter (ed.), *The Oxford History of the British Empire, Vol. 3: The Nineteenth Century* (1999), 690–711.
2. See Mathew Thomson, *The Problem of Mental Deficiency: Eugenics, Democracy, and Social Policy in Britain, c. 1870–1959* (Oxford, 1998), 34 *et passim.*
3. Anna Davin, 'Imperialism and Motherhood', *History Workshop*, 5 (1978), *passim.*
4. Davin cites the example of the Ladies' Health Society of Manchester and Salford, which was offering 'home instruction in domestic hygiene' as early as the 1860s: ibid. 37.
5. e.g. Maurice Bruce, *The Coming of the Welfare State* (1961), section V, 'The Turning Point: Social Reform 1905–1914'; and Bentley B. Gilbert, *The Evolution of National Insurance* (1966), whose subtitle is 'The Origins of the Welfare State'.
6. Gilbert, *Evolution of National Insurance*, 89.
7. Davin, 'Imperialism and Motherhood', 17.
8. Above, n. 4.
9. Davin, 'Imperialism and Motherhood', 11.
10. e.g. J. A. Hobson, *Imperialism: A Study* (1902; this edn. 1938), 140 ff.
11. This is also the view of Geoffrey Searle, '"National Efficiency" and the "Lessons" of the War', in David Omissi and Andrew S. Thompson (eds.), *The Impact of the South African War* (2002), 198.
12. Jonathan Rose, *The Edwardian Temperament* (Athens, Ohio, 1986), 118.
13. See e.g. Kajsa Ohrlander, *I barnens och nationens intresse. Socialliberal reformpolitik 1903–1930* (Stockholm, 1992), esp. 62 ff., on 'Barnens fattigdom [poverty] och nationens intresse'. Sweden had just lost Norway, however (1905).
14. See Searle, '"National Efficiency" and the "Lessons" of the War', 203; and Andrew Porter, 'The South African War and Imperial Britain: A Question of Significance?', in Greg Cuthbertson, Albert Grundlingh, and Mary-Lynn Suttie, *Writing a Wider War: Rethinking Gender, Race and Identity in the South African War, 1899–1902* (Athens, Ohio, 2002).
15. e.g. Anon., 'England after War', *Fortnightly Review*, o.s., 78 (1902), 8; 'Vates', 'The Revenge for Fashoda', ibid. 79 (1903), 774.
16. C. W. Radcliffe-Cooke, 'The Invasion Scare—a New View', *Nineteenth Century*, 61 (1907), 402. Radcliffe-Cooke was an ex-Conservative MP.
17. Quoted in Helen Callaway and Dorothy O. Helly, 'Crusader for Empire', in Nupur Chaudhuri and Margaret Strobel (eds.), *Western Women and Imperialism* (Bloomington, Ind., 1992), 93. Other examples of imperialist anti-suffrage arguments can be found in Brian Harrison, *Separate Spheres: The Opposition to Women's Suffrage in Britain* (1978), 75–6.
18. Other prominent 'antis' were Joseph Chamberlain and Rudyard Kipling. See Harrison, *Separate Spheres*, 129. The NLOWS was founded in 1910.
19. Julia Bush, *Edwardian Ladies and Imperial Power* (Leicester: 2000), 171–3 and App. II; Eliza Riedi, 'Imperialist Women in Edwardian Britain: The Victoria League 1899–1914', Ph.D thesis, St Andrews University (1997), 211–12.
20. There were serious attempts to enfranchise women made in connection with the 1867 and 1884 Parliamentary Reform Bills. Other marks of progress before the turn of the

century were the Married Women's Property Act of 1870; the right to become Poor Law Guardians in 1875; the vote in the Isle of Man in 1881; and the right to vote in parochial council elections granted in 1894. All these, however, could be seen as consistent with women's 'separate' domestic sphere. There was a big gulf between these and national political participation.

21. Women's suffrage may have come close to being accepted by the Commons in 1912, when the government of the day accepted an amendment along these lines to a wider Franchise Bill, only to be stymied by the speaker, who ruled it was inadmissible.
22. See Harrison, *Separate Spheres*, 32.
23. Bush, *Edwardian Ladies*, esp. chs. 5, 8, and 9; and Eliza Riedi, 'Women, Gender and the Promotion of Empire: The Victoria League, 1901–1914', *Historical Journal*, 45 (2002), 578–92.
24. As Eliza Riedi has reminded me, this is not true in all cases. Violet Markham of the Victoria League wrote extensively on broader policy: see Riedi, 'Options For an Imperialist Woman: The Case of Violet Markham, 1899–1914', *Albion*, 32 (2000); as did Mary Kingsley, brilliantly, albeit deferentially, and Flora Shaw of *The Times* (later Lady Lugard).
25. Riedi, 'Women, Gender and the Promotion of Empire', 573.
26. She had made 'so admirable a speech against the enfranchisement of women that she nearly defeated her own cause', wrote *Truth* of Violet Markham in 1912; quoted in Riedi, 'Options For an Imperialist Woman', 80.
27. Bush, *Edwardian Ladies*, 172–3.
28. Clare Midgley, 'Ethnicity, "Race" and Empire', in June Parris (ed.), *Women's History: Britain 1850–1845* (1995), 264. Midgley is summarizing Antoinette Burton here.
29. Mary Ann Lind, *The Compassionate Memsahibs: Welfare Activities of British Women in India, 1900–1947* (New York, 1988).
30. Janice Brownfoot, 'Sisters Under the Skin: Imperialism and the Emancipation of Women in Malaya, *c.*1891–1941', in J. A. Mangan (ed.), *Making Imperial Mentalities* (1990), 67; and see the same author's 'Memsahibs in Colonial Malaya: A Study of European Wives in a British Colony and Protectorate 1900–1940', in Hilary Callan and Shirley Ardener (eds.), *The Incorporated Wife* (1984).
31. Mary A. Procida, *Married to the Empire: Gender, Politics and Imperialism in India, 1883–1947* (2002); Beverley Gartrell, 'Colonial Wives: Villains or Victims?', in Callan and Ardener (eds.), *The Incorporated Wife*. On the gendering of 'races' generally, see Mrinalini Sinha, *Colonial Masculinity. The 'Manly Englishman' and the 'Effeminate Bengali' in the Late Nineteenth Century* (Manchester, 1995); and cf. Mary Kingsley's characterization of Africans as a 'feminine race': above, pp. 229–30.
32. See Sir David Lean, 1985, quoted in Margaret Strobel, *European Women and the Second British Empire* (Bloomington, Ind., 1991), 1.
33. Antoinette Burton, *Burdens of History: British Feminists, Indian Women, and Imperial Culture, 1865–1915* (Chapel Hill, Calif., 1994), 4. See also (for an earlier period) Clare Midgley, 'Anti-Slavery and the Roots of "Imperial Feminism"', in Midgley (ed.), *Gender and Imperialism* (1998).
34. Procida, *Married to the Empire*, 12.
35. Ibid. 123. It went through several later editions, in 1905, 1907, and 1915 (British Library Catalogue). But it could still have appealed mainly to the Anglo-Indian market.

36. John Buchan, *John Macnab* (1925), 141.
37. Allen Warren, '"Mothers for the Empire?" The Girl Guides Association in Britain, 1909–1939', in Mangan (ed.), *Making Imperial Mentalities*; Mary Cadogan and Patricia Craig, *You're a Brick, Angela!* (1976), ch. 9. Not all imperialist women welcomed this; e.g. Violet Markham thought that 'Scouting for girls leads nowhere from the national point of view': letter in the *Spectator*, 103 (4 Dec. 1909), 942 (reference kindly provided by Eliza Riedi).
38. Brownfoot, 'Sisters Under the Skin', 46.
39. Antoinette Burton's word, in *Burdens of History*, 17.
40. Ashis Nandy, *The Intimate Enemy* (1993), quoted in Julie Codell and Dianne Sachko Macleod (ed.), *Orientalism Transposed: The Impact of Colonies on British Culture* (1998), 2.
41. e.g. John Galsworthy comments in *The Man of Property* (1906; this edn. 1965), 154, on 'the movement against generosity, which had at that time already [*c.*1880] commenced among the saner members of the community'; by which he means (ironically) the upper middle class.
42. On this see esp. Ronald Hyam, *Empire and Sexuality: The British Experience* (1990), 66–71.
43. On this whole question, see Jane Haggis, 'Gendering Colonialism or Colonising Gender? Recent Women's Studies Approaches to White Women and the History of British Colonialism', *Women's Studies International Forum*, 5 (1990); Malia B. Formes, 'Beyond Complicity Versus Resistance: Recent Work on Gender and European Imperialism', *Journal of Social History* (1995); Jonathan Rutherford, *Forever England: Reflections on Masculinity and Empire* (1997).
44. See Stanley H. Palmer, *Police and Protest in England and Ireland 1780–1850* (Cambridge, 1988).
45. See Chandak Sengoopta, *Imprint of the Raj: How Fingerprinting Was Born in Colonial India* (2003).
46. This is elaborated in Bernard Porter, *The Origins of the Vigilant State: The London Metropolitan Police Special Branch Before the First World War* (1987), chs. 1–5.
47. See J. A. Hobson, *Imperialism: A Study* (1902), part 2, chapter 1.
48. See Gordon Goodman, 'Liberal Unionism: The Revolt of the Whigs', *Victorian Studies*, 3 (1959); and W. H. G. Armitage, 'The Railway Rates Question and the Fall of the Third Gladstone Ministry, *English Historical Review*, 65 (1950).
49. John Rae, 'Teach British To Be Pirates, Not Prefects', in *Observer*, 6 Apr. 1980.
50. C. R. Attlee, *As It Happened* [n.d.], 19; and see above, p. 54.
51. See John Stuart Mill, *Autobiography* (1872; new edn., Oxford, 1979), 138; and *Principles of Political Economy* (2nd edn. 1849), book 2, ch. 1, sec. 3, which prepares the way for this volte-face: if capitalism *didn't* have the potential to make people more equal, he writes there, then 'Communism' *would* be preferable. By the 1870s he had become convinced that this was indeed the case.
52. Rhodesia (Zimbabwe) and Hong Kong. On the Falklands, see below, pp. 302–3.
53. The connection between an anti-capitalist culture and the decline of British capitalism is made by Martin J. Wiener, in his *English Culture and the Decline of the Industrial Spirit 1850–1980* (Cambridge, 1981), but he gives less of a role to the empire. Lord (David) Young, *The Enterprise Years: A Businessman in the Cabinet* (1990), 25–8, is an earlier potted version of almost exactly the same reading of modern British history as mine, with the empire's part included. Young was a businessman whom Thatcher recruited briefly to

her government in order to inject it with some business efficiency. The experiment is not generally reckoned to have been a success, which may support the point made above about the tensions between capitalism and government.

54. Peter Cain's phrase, in *Hobson and Imperialism: Radicalism, New Liberalism, and Finance 1887–1938* (Oxford, 2002), 209.
55. Aspects of this subject are discussed much more fully and adequately than they can be here in Stuart Ward (ed.), *British Culture and the End of Empire* (Manchester, 2001).
56. Examples are *Mogambo* (1953); *Storm over the Nile*—a remake of *The Four Feathers* (1955); *Bhowani Junction* (1956); *North-West Frontier* (1959); *Guns at Batasi* (1964); *Passage to India* (1984); *White Mischief* (1987); *Mister Johnson* (1990); and a highly distorted 'post-colonial' version, influenced by Said, of *Mansfield Park* (1999).
57. The most celebrated fictional series was ITV's *Jewel in the Crown* (1984). Recent examples of empire-based documentaries include Channel 4's *Baden-Powell: The Boy Man* (1995); BBC2's *Kitchener: The Empire's Flawed Hero* (1998); BBC2's *Windrush*, about West Indians in Britain (1998); Timewatch's *The British in India* and *The Boer War: The First Media War* (both 1998); the misconceived 'Omnibus' programme on the *Empire of the Nude* (2001)—see above, pp. 146–7; *Pukka Tales*, on Indian influences on Britain (2001); Channel 4's *Untold India* (2001); ITV's *The British Empire in Colour* (2002); BBC2's 'Correspondent' programme, *Kenya: White Terror* (2002); Simon Schama's 'The Empire of Good Intentions' episode of his *History of Britain* series (2002); and Niall Ferguson's *Empire* (2003).
58. The two major museums are the 'British in India Museum' in Colne, Lancashire, and the 'British Empire and Commonwealth Museum' in Bristol.
59. One of the first Indian restaurants in Britain was Veeraswami's, in London (1927), catering mainly for India hands and the rich: information from *Big Dreams: The Joy of Curry*, BBC2, 29 Oct. 2003.
60. See the Channel 4 *Pukka Tales* series (above); and David Burton, *The Raj at Table: A Culinary History of the British in India* (1993), p. vii, from which I have taken my list of words.
61. The post-1950 additions in London are General Gordon in Victoria Embankment Gardens (1953); David Livingston at the Royal Geographical Society (1953); Jan Smuts in Parliament Square (1956); Sir Walter Raleigh in Whitehall (1959); Captain John Smith, a 17th-century colonist, in Cheapside (1960); Lord Baden-Powell in Queen's Gate (1961); and a bust of Arthur Phillip, first governor of New South Wales, in Cannon Street (1968). Arthur Byron, *London Statues* (1981), *passim*.
62. A search on the internet reveals 'Imperial Hotels' in London (Russell Square), Blackpool, Harrogate, Llandudno, and Castle Douglas in Scotland (there are probably many more); but also in just about every other country of the world.
63. *Guardian G2*, 27 Nov. 2003, pp. 2–3.
64. Two mooted alternatives were the European Free Trade Association (EFTA), a kind of *salon des refusés* of the EEC, which Britain was a member of for a time; and a North Atlantic Free Trade Association (NAFTA), in which Britain would obviously have been dominated by the USA.
65. See Bernard Porter, '"Bureau and Barrack": Early Victorian Attitudes Towards the Continent', *Victorian Studies*, 27 (1984).
66. Rhodesia (Zimbabwe) and Hong Kong. Thatcher admits to a youthful, 'not very realistic' imperialism in *The Path to Power* (1995), 45. After the Falklands War much of

her patriotic rhetoric made reference to Britain's worldwide 'greatness' (under capitalism) in the 19th century; the period which she most of all wished to emulate.

67. Miles Taylor gives a very specific possible example: the part the colonies may have played as a safety-valve for Britain's revolutionaries, transported there after the 1848 disturbances. That could be one reason why she avoided the much greater contemporary ructions on the continent. (the authorities liked to think it was because she was better governed). 'The 1848 Revolutions and the British Empire', *Past and Present*, 169 (2000), 152. Avner Offer makes the daring point that another result of the settlement colonies' *not* being peopled by Chinese could have been, '(given these countries' democratic instincts and their internal stability) a loss to global welfare'. 'Costs and Benefits, Prosperity and Security', 710.

CHAPTER 13

1. J. K. Paasikivi, *Meine Moskauer Mission 1939–41* (1968), 243. I first came across this reference in Patrick Salmon, *Scandinavia and the Great Powers* (1997), 18–19.
2. I was recently sent the typescript of a dictionary of historical quotations, for example, where the editor had a single division for 'Imperialism and Racism'. It has now been changed.
3. The use of inverted commas here should not be taken to imply that these events were necessarily invented or misdescribed as 'massacres' and so on. Anti-colonial 'atrocities' were perpetrated. The significant point being made here is about the press's dwelling on these, to the virtual exclusion, often, of other aspects of these conflicts, and also—it could be added—Britain's own atrocious acts.
4. The League had only 2,000–3,000 members at its height. When it folded it merged with the British National Party. See George Theyer, *The British Political Fringe* (1965), ch. 3; and Roger Eatwell, *Fascism: A History* (1996), 265.
5. See Harold Macmillan, *Riding the Storm 1956–1959* (1971), 222–9.
6. See e.g. Ian Macleod, a progressive colonial secretary of the time, quoted in Nigel Fisher, *Ian Macleod* (1973), 142. Harold Macmillan's famous 'Wind of Change' speech to the South African parliament in February 1960 marked a key moment in the formulation of this attitude and policy.
7. Significant i.e. as a kind of empire-substitute, with Britain still wielding influence through it, which is what many Conservatives wanted. The fact that this ambition was disappointed—mainly by the other members' berating Britain on the issue of South African apartheid—does not mean that the Commonwealth cannot be regarded as 'significant' in other ways.
8. Martin Jacques, 'The age of selfishness', in the *Guardian*, 5 October 2002.
9. See for example Blair's speech to the Partnership Summit in Bangalore, 5 January 2002, arguing for Britain's new role as a 'pivotal partner' in a new international movement to bring 'good' to the world, for which she is particularly fitted 'by virtue of our history. Our past gives us huge, perhaps unparalleled connections with many different regions of the world.'
10. The comparison between Blair and Gladstone is a common one, based on their common religiosity as well as their moral-imperial policies. Two pre-Iraq war examples are Richard Shannon, 'History Lessons', in *Guardian*, 4 October 2001; and

Andrew Rawnsley in the *Observer*, 7 October 2001. A search on the internet under 'Blair+Gladstone+empire' throws up dozens of others, including 'M Blair un nouveau Gladstone' on www.stratisc.org. See also Steve Bell's cartoon in the *Guardian*, 19 March 1902, which has Blair dressed as Queen Victoria seeing off British redcoats in a desert war, with a quotation from Kipling.

11. E.g. Donald Rumsfeld, 'We don't do empire': reported in *Guardian*, 2 March 2003; Dick Cheney, 'If we were a true empire we would currently preside over a much greater piece of the earth's surface than we do. That's not the way we operate': reported in *New York Times*, 25 January; and George W. Bush, 'we have no desire to dominate, no ambitions of empire': reported in *Washington Post*, and reprinted in *Guardian Weekly*, 29 January 2004. Condoleeza Rice came close to breaking ranks once when she claimed that America was 'imperial but not imperialist': quoted in *Observer*, 22 September 2003. That is a valid distinction.
12. Above, pp. 303–4.
13. The well-known 'Project for the American Century' – easily accessible *via* the internet – preaches an overt imperialism; as do a number of neo-conservative journalists: e.g. Mark Steyn in *Chicago Sun-Times*, 14 October 2001; Charles Krauthammer quoted in *New York Times* 2 April 2002; David Frum quoted in *National Post* (Canada), 29 March 3003; and Max Boot, 'The Case for American Empire', in *Weekly Standard*, 15 October 2001.

Select Bibliography

PRIMARY SOURCES

Periodicals

Ainsworth's Magazine
All the Year Round
Aly Sloper
Band of Hope Review
Bentley's Miscellany
Blackwood's Magazine
Boys of England
Boys of the Empire
Boys' Own Paper
Brentwoodian
British Workman
Cassell's Illustrated Family Paper
Chambers's Edinburgh Journal
Chums
Cliftonian
Contemporary Review
Cornhill Magazine
Democratic Review
Eastern Counties Herald,
Edinburgh Review
Eliza Cook's Journal
Englishwoman's Domestic Magazine
Etonian
Fortnightly Review
Fraser's Magazine
Girl Guides Gazette
Girl's Own Paper
The Good Old Times!
Good Words
Grip
Haileyburian
Harmsworth Magazine
Harrovian
Household Words
Howitt's Journal
Hull Advertiser
Hull Packet
Hull Times
Hull and North Lincolnshire Times
Illustrated London News
Illustrated Police Budget
Illustrated Police News
Illustrated War News
Juvenile Missionary Magazine
Labour Leader
London Journal
Malvernian
Marlburian
Marvel
Missionary Herald
National Review
New Rugbeian
Nineteenth Century
Northern Star (The Star of Freedom)
Once a Week
Penny Magazine
Pluck
Proceedings of the Royal Colonial Institute
Progressive Review
Punch
Quarterly Review
Radleian
Reynolds's Magazine
Reynolds's Newspaper
Saturday Magazine
Strand Magazine
Temple Bar
The Times
Tit-Bits
Union Jack

United Empire
Welcome Guest
Wellingtonian
Wesleyan Juvenile Offering
Westminster Review
Windsor Magazine
The Working Man
Wykehamist

Government and Related Publications

Annual Abstract of Statistics.
Board of Education, *Suggestions for the Consideration of Teachers and Others concerned in the Work of Public Elementary Schools* (1905).
Board of Education Regulations, 1906.
Census Reports of England and Wales: 1851, 1861, 1891, 1911, 1931.
Census of Great Britain 1851. Religious Worship in England and Wales (1854).
Colonial Office Lists.
Hansard's Parliamentary Debates.
India Office Lists.
Official Descriptive and Illustrated Catalogue of the Great Exhibition of the Works of Industry of all Nations, 1851 [1851].
'Plays Submitted to the Lord Chamberlain', Catalogue in British Library (Manuscript Room).
Report of the Assistant Commissioners Appointed to inquire into the State of Popular Education in England ('Newcastle Commission'), 1861.
Report of the Royal Commission for the Colonial and Indian Exhibition (1887).
Schools Enquiry Commission, vol. 1, *Report of the Commissioners* (1867–8).

Memoirs

George Acorn, *One of the Multitude* (1911).
Ruth Adler, *A Family of Shopkeepers* (1973).
Eric Ambler, *Here Lies: An Autobiography* (1985).
Julian Amery, *Approach March: A Venture in Autobiography* (1973).
Leopold Amery, *My Political Life*, 3 vols. (1953).
Norman Angell, *After All* (1951).
Anon., *A Brief Memoir and Theatrical Career of Ira Aldridge, The African Tragedian* (n.d.).
—— *Narrow Waters, The First Volume of the Life and Thoughts of a Common Man* (1935).
Joseph Arch, *Joseph Arch, the Story of His Life, Told by Himself* (1898).
Eighth Duke of Argyll [George Douglas], *Autobiography and Memoirs*, ed. Dowager Duchess of Argyll, 2 vols. (1906).
Clement Attlee, *As it Happened* (n.d.).
Eileen Baillie, *The Shabby Paradise: The Autobiography of a Decade* (1958).
Arthur James Balfour, *Chapters of Autobiography* (1930).
Cécile de Banke, *Hand over Hand* (1957).
Tom Barclay, *Memoirs and Medleys: The Autobiography of a Bottle-Washer* (1934).
Ron Barnes, *Coronation Cups and Jam Jars: A Portrait of an East End Family through Three Generations* (1976).
Sir Thomas Beecham, *A Mingled Chime: Leaves from an Autobiography* (1944).
Arnold Bennett, *Sketches for Autobiography* ed. James Hepburn (1979).

Frank Berry, *Bench, Saw and Plane: A Cotswold Apprenticeship* (1988).
Field-Marshall Lord Birdwood, *Khaki and Gown: An Autobiography* (1941).
John Blake, *Memories of Old Poplar* (1977).
Eric Bligh, *Tooting Corner* (1946).
W. E. Bowen, *Edward Bowen, a Memoir* (1902).
Walter Brierley, *Means-Test Man* (1935).
Sir Readers Buller, *The Camels Must Go: An Autobiography* (1961).
Thomas Burke, *Son of London* [1946].
[James Dawson Burn], *Autobiography of a Beggar Boy* (1855).
John Burnett (ed.), *Useful Toil* (1974).
Pat Campbell, *Blade of Grass—The Life and Times of an Ordinary Man* (1986).
Robert Cecil, *A Great Experiment: An Autobiography* (1941).
Charles Chaplin, *My Autobiography* (1964).
G. K. Chesterton, *Autobiography* (1936).
Agatha Christie, *An Autobiography* (1977).
Richard Church, *Over the Bridge: An Essay in Autobiography* (1955).
Walter Citrine, *Men and Work: An Autobiography* (1964).
Max Cohen, *I Was One of the Unemployed* (1945).
R. G. Collingwood, *An Autobiography* (1939).
Jack Common, *Kiddar's Luck* (1951).
Cyril Connolly, *Enemies of Promise* (1938; 1948).
B. L. Coombes, *These Poor Hands: The Autobiography of a Miner Working in South Wales* (1939).
Duff Cooper, *Old Men Forget* (1953).
Helen Corke, *In Our Infancy: An Autobiography*. Part I, *1882–1912* (1975).
G. G. Coulton, *Fourscore Years: An Autobiography* (1944).
Noël Coward, *An Autobiography* (1986).
Mary Craddock, *A North Country Maid* (1960).
Hannah Cullwick, *The Diaries of Hannah Cullwick, Victorian Maidservant*, ed. Liz Stanley (1984).
W. H. Davies, *The Autobiography of a Super-Tramp* (1920).
Snowden Dunhill, *The Life of Snowden Dunhill, Written by Himself* (1834).
George Elson, *The Last of the Climbing Boys* (1900).
Edward Ezard, *Battersea Boy* (1979).
H. A. L. Fisher, *An Unfinished Autobiography* (1940).
Grace Foakes, *My Part of the River: Memories of People and Places in the East End of Edwardian London* (1972).
Charlie Framp, *Crimson Skies: The History of a Twentith-Century English Working Man* (1988).
Ralph Furse, *Aucuparius: Recollections of a Recruiting Officer* (1962).
Thomas Gautrey, *'Laus Mihi Laus': School Board Memories* (1937).
Philip Gibbs, *The Pageant of the Years. An Autobiography* (1946).
Willy Goldman, *East End My Cradle* (1940).
Stephen Graham, *A Private in the Guards* (1928).
Clara E. Grant, *Farthing Bundles* (n.d. [1931]).
G. B. Grundy, *Fifty-five Years at Oxford: An Unconventional Autobiography* (1945).
Sir H. Rider Haggard, *The Days of My Life: An Autobiography*, 2 vols. (1926).
Edith Hall, *Canary Girls and Stockpots* (1977).

John Halstead, Royden Harrison, and John Stevenson, 'The Reminiscences of Sid Elias', *Bulletin of the Society for the Study of Labour History*, 38 (1979).

[Arthur Harding], *East End Underworld: Chapters in the Life of Arthur Harding*, ed. Raphael Samuel (1981).

James Hawker, *A Victorian Poacher*, ed. Garth Christian (1961).

F. H. Hayward, *An Educational Failure: A School Inspector's Story* (1938).

Archie Hill, *A Cage of Shadows* (1973).

G. V. Holmes, *The Likes of Us* (1948).

George Jacob Holyoake, *Sixty Years of an Agitator's Life* (1900).

M. V. Hughes, *A London Family 1870–1900: A Trilogy* (1981).

Alaric Jacob, *Scenes from a Bourgeois Life* (1949).

Joe Jacobs, *Out of the Ghetto: My Youth in the East End: Communism and Fascism 1913–39* (1978).

A. S. Jasper, *A Hoxton Childhood* (1969).

Louise Jermy, *The Memoirs of a Working Woman* (1934).

Fred Kitchen, *Brother to the Ox: The Autobiography of a Farm Labourer* (1940).

Charles Knight, *Passages of a Working Life During Half a Century*, 3 vols. (1864).

Alice Linton, *Not Expecting Miracles* (1982).

Richard Lowry, 'Diary', MS in Tyne and Wear Record Office, Newcastle upon Tyre.

Basil Maine, *The Best of Me: A Study in Autobiography* (1937).

Ethel Mannin, *Confessions and Impressions* (1930).

Hugh Miller, *My Schools and Schoolmasters; or, the Story of My Education* (1855).

Arthur Newton, *Years of Change: Autobiography of a Hackney Shoemaker* (1974).

Thomas Okey, *A Basketful of Memories: An Autobiographical Sketch* (1930).

F. D. Ommanney, *The House in the Park* (1944).

George Orwell, *Such, Such were the Joys* (1957).

Mary Paget (ed.), *Man of the Valleys: The Recollections of a South Wales Miner* (1985).

Max Pemberton, *Sixty Years Ago and After* (1936).

J. B. Priestley, *A Chapter of Autobiography* (1937).

—— *Rain upon Godshill* (1939).

—— *Instead of Trees* (1977).

Arthur Quiller-Couch, *Memories and Opinions: An Unfinished Autobiography* (1944).

W. Pett Ridge, *A Story Teller: Forty Years in London* [1923].

Bob Roberts, *Coasting Bargemaster* (1949).

Robert Roberts, *The Classic Slum: Salford Life in the First Quarter of the Century* (1971).

—— *A Ragged Schooling: Growing Up in the Classic Slum* (1976).

Angela Rodaway, *A London Childhood* (1960).

Frederick Rogers, *Labour, Life and Literature: Some Memories of Sixty Years* (1913).

'C. H. Rolph', *Living Twice* (1974).

A. L. Rowse, *A Cornish Childhood* (1942).

[Charles Manby Smith], *The Working-Man's Way in the World, being the Autobiography of a Journeyman Printer* [1857].

Walter Southgate, *That's the Way it Was: A Working-Class Autobiography 1890–1950* (1982).

Carolyn Steadman (ed.), *The Radical Soldier's Tale* (1988).

Louie Stride, *Memoirs of a Street Urchin* (n.d.).

John Sturrock, *The Diary of John Sturrock, Millwright, Dundee, 1864–65*, ed. Christopher Whatley (1996).

Ben Thomas, *Ben's Limehouse: Recollections* (1987).
Gilbert Thomas, *Autobiography* (1946).
Tierl Thompson (ed.), *Dear Girl: The Diaries and Letters of Two Working Women 1897–1917* (1987).
Basil Thomson, *Queer People* (1922).
Will Thorne, *My Life's Battles* [1925].
Anthony Trollope, *An Autobiography* (1883).
William J. Tucker, *Autobiography of an Astrologer* (1960).
Frank Vernon, *Pride and Poverty: Memories of a Mexborough Miner* (Doncaster, 1984).
Jane Walsh, *Not Like This* (1953).
J. E. C. Welldon, *Recollections and Reflections* (1915).
—— *Forty Years On: Lights and Shadows* (1935).
H. G. Wells, *Experiment in Autobiography* (1934).
Edna Wheway, *Edna's Story: Memories of Life in a Children's Home and in Service, in Dorset and London* (1984).
Frederick Willis, *101 Jubilee Road: A Book of London Yesterdays* (1948).
Worker's Educational Association (South-east Scotland District), *Friday Night Was Brasso Night* (1987).

School Textbooks

These include a few history and geography texts that will not have been used in schools.

Anon., *The Good Old Times; or, The Poor Man's History of England* (1817).
—— *History of England*, reprinted from the *Cottager's Monthly Visitor* (*c.*1852).
—— *The History of England Mostly in Words of One Syllable* (*c.*1909).
A. B. Archer and Helen G. Thomas, *Geography, First Series*, 4 vols. (n.d. [1936?]).
H. O. Arnold-Forster, *The Citizen Reader*, Cassell's Modern School Series [1886].
'Edward Baldwin' [William Godwin], *The History of England, for the Use of Schools and Young Persons* (new edn., 1826).
Revd George Bartle, *A Synopsis of English History* (1865).
Dorothea Beale, *The Student's Text-Book of English and General History, from B.C. 100 to the Present Time* (1858).
A. J. Berry, *Britannia's Growth and Greatness: A Historical Geography of the British Empire* (1913).
Favell Lee Bevan, *Near Home; or, The Countries of Europe Described* (1850).
—— *Far Off; or Asia and Australia Described* (1852).
Thomas Birkby, *The History of England from the Roman Period to the Present Time* [1871?].
Arthur Bowes, *A Practical Synopsis of English History*, 4th edn. (1863).
C. B. Bowman, *Atlas of English and Empire History* (1937).
Caroline Bray, *The British Empire: A Sketch of the Geography, Growth, Natural and Political Features of the United Kingdom, its Colonies and Dependencies* (1863).
Revd Collingwood Bruce, *The Handbook of English History*, 4th edn. (1861).
Arabella B. Buckley [Mrs Fisher], *History of England for Beginners* (1887).
Thomas and Francis Bullock, *The Illustrated History of England* (1861).
Lady (Maria) Callcott, *Little Arthur's History of England* (1835 and subsequent editions).
T. Chadwick, *Practical Citizenship: An Introduction to Government in the British Empire* (1937).
Chambers's Educational Course, no. 21, *History and Present State of the British Empire* (1837).

Chambers's Geographical Readers of the Continents (1885–1902).
Chambers's Historical Readers, Book IV (1883).
Chambers's Preparatory History of England (1901).
Chambers's History of England (1901).
Chambers's Advanced History of England (1909).
Chambers's Stories From English History and *From British History* (several books, 1901–5).
H. Le M Chepmell, *A Short Course of History*, 2nd edn. (1849).
The Citizen Reader, Cassell's Modern School Series (1886).
William F. Collier, *History of the Nineteenth Century for Schools* (1869).
—— *The Great Events of History* (1889).
J. C. Cunningham, *Products of the Empire* (1921).
J. C. Curtis, *A School and College History of England* (1860).
C. S. Dawe, *King Edward's Realm: The Story of the Making of the Empire* (1902).
Charles Dickens, *A Child's History of England* (1853).
Eleanor Doorly, *England in Her days of Peace: An Introduction to Social and Industrial History* (1920).
[A. T. Drane], *A History of England for Family Use* (1873; new edn. 1881).
H. E. Egerton, *The Origin and Growth of the British Colonies* (1904).
—— *Historical Geography of the British Colonies* (1907–8).
J. Fairgrieve and E. Young, *Human Geography: The British Commonwealth* (1931).
Edward Farr, continued by Miss Corner, *Rodwell's Child's First Step to the History of England* (n.d. [1844]).
—— *The Manual of Geography, Physical and Political* (1861).
John Finnemore, *Famous Englishmen*, 2 vols. (1901–2).
Revd T. Flanagan, *A Short Catechism of English History, Ecclesiastical and Civil, for Children* (n.d. [1851]).
C. R. L. Fletcher and Rudyard Kipling, *A School History of England* (Oxford, 1911).
A. W. H. Forbes, *A History of the British Dominions Beyond the Seas* (1910).
S. R. Gardiner, *Outline of English History* (1881).
—— *Outline of English History: Second Period, 1603–1919* (new edn., 1920).
H. Gibbins, *Industrial History of England* (1890).
Gill's Imperial History of England, for School and College Use (1883).
Revd G. R. Gleig, *First Book of History: England* (1850).
—— *Second Book of History: The British Colonies*, 2nd edn. (1851).
Revd J. Goldsmith, *A Grammar of General Geography for the Use of Schools and Young Persons* (new edn., 1823).
J. R. Green, *A Short History of the English People* (1874).
Maria Hack, *Travels in Hot and Cold Lands* (1877).
A. Hassell, *The Making of the British Empire, 1714–1832* (1896).
A. J. Herbertson, *The Junior Geography* (1905).
—— and F. D. Herbertson, *Man and His Work: An Introduction to Human Geography* (1902).
—— and R. L. Thompson, *The Geography of the British Empire* (1924).
F. D. Herbertson, *The Junior Geography* (Oxford, 1905).
—— *The British Empire* (1910).
'J.H.' [James Hewitt], *Geography of the British Colonies and Dependencies* (1860).
C. S. S. Higham, *History of the British Empire* (1921).
—— and M. M. B. Higham, *Makers of the Commonwealth* (1939).

A. E. Hogan and Isabel Powell, *The Government of Great Britain in the Dominions and Colonies* (1934).
E. C. T. Horniblow, *Lands and Life: Human Geographies*, 6 vols. (1927–32).
E. A. Hughes, *Britain and Greater Britain in the Nineteenth Century* (1919).
David Hume, *History of England from the Invasion of Julius Caesar to the Revolution in 1688* (1754–61).
Henry Ince, *An Outline of English History . . . Designed for the Use of Schools* (1832).
A. D. Innes, *A History of England and the British Empire in Four Volumes* (1913–14).
—— *A Classbook of the British Commonwealth* (1923).
The Jack Historical Readers, 5 vols. (*c*.1905).
M. W. Keatinge and N. L. Frazer, *An Introduction to World History* (1920).
Thomas Keightley, *The History of England*, 2 vols. (1837/9).
W. R. Kermack, *The Expansion of Britain from the Age of Discoveries: A Geographical History* (1922).
P. H. and A. C. Kerr, *The Growth of the British Empire* (1911).
S. King-Hall, *The Empire Yesterday and Today* (1937).
Charles Knight, *The Popular History of England*, vol. 8 (1858).
J. S. Laurie (ed.), *Manual of English History Simplified; Or, our Country's Story, told by a Lady* (1866).
Revd W. E. Littlewood, *The Essentials of English History*, 2nd edn. (1865).
C. P. Lucas, *Introduction to a Historical Geography of the British Empire* (1887).
—— *Historical Geography of the British Colonies*, 4 vols. (1897).
—— (ed.), *An Historical Geography of the British Colonies*, 7 vols. (1888–1923).
—— *The Story of the Empire* (1924).
L. W. Lyde, *Commercial Geography of the British Empire* (1922).
Thomas (Lord) Macaulay, *The History of England* (1858 edn.).
H. J. Mackinder, *The Nations of the Modern World: An Elementary Study in Geography* (n.d. [1911]).
'Mrs Markham' [Elizabeth Penrose], *A History of England . . . for the Use of Young Persons* (1823; new edn., 1851).
R. A. F. Mears, *A Short History of the British Empire* (1931).
Lord Meath *et al.*, *Our Empire Past and Present* (1901).
J. M. D. Meiklejohn, *The British Empire* (1891).
J. Roscoe Mongan, *The Oxford and Cambridge British History for School Use* (1882).
Revd D. Morris, *The History of England from the Accession of George III to the Present Time, Adapted to Standards VI and VII* (1883).
—— *Third Historical Reader* (1883).
G. W. Morris and L. S. Wood, *The English-Speaking Nations: A Study of the Commonwealth Ideal* (1924).
—— *The Building of the Commonwealth* (1936).
Ramsay Muir, *A Short History of the British Empire* (1920).
—— *British History: A Survey of the History of All the British Peoples* (1929).
Revd J. M. Neale, *English History for Children* (1845).
[Nelson, publ.], *The World and its People. A New Series of Geography Readers* (1902).
A. P. Newton and J. Ewing, *The British Empire Since 1783: Its Political and Economic Development* (1929).
Revd C. H. S. Nicholls, *Outlines of English History, being a List of the most Remarkable Events in the History of England* (1850).
Charles and Mary Oman, *A Junior History of England* (1904).

George R. Parkin, *Round the Empire* (1892).
[G Philip], *The British Empire* (n.d.; *c*.1910).
Pinnock's Catechism of the History of England, from its Earliest Period to the Present Time. Written in Easy Language (1822).
D. M. Preece and H. R. B. Wood, *Modern Geography* [1938–9].
E. Protheroe, *Commercial Geography of the British Empire* (1902).
Cyril Ransome, *A Short History of England* (1887).
Mrs Cyril Ransome, *A First History of England* (1903).
R. M. Rayner, *Nineteenth Century England: A Political and Social History of the British Commonwealth* (1927).
James Reid, *Manual of Moral Instruction: A Graded Course of Lessons on Conduct Worked Out on the Concentric Plan* (1908).
Eleanor Richardson, *The Building of the British Empire: A Reading Book for Schools* (1913).
James Rowley, *The Settlement of the Constitution 1679–1784* (1903 edn.).
The Royal School Series: The Reign of Queen Victoria: A Reading Book of History for Schools (1881).
—— *Stories from English History Simply Told: A Reading Book for Standard III* (1886).
C. Bernard Rutley, *The British Commonwealth* (1948).
Edward Salmon, *The Story of the Empire* (1902).
Charles Selby, *Events to be Remembered in the History of England* (1852).
E. H. Short, *Living with History*, Book 3, *Building the Commonwealth* (1939).
Charles Selby, *Events to be Remembered in the History of England* (1852).
Tobias Smollett, *The History of England from the Revolution to the Death of George the Second*, 5 vol. (1763).
Revd Alexander Stewart, *A Compendium of Modern Geography* (1828; 35th edn., 1889).
J. H. Stocqueler, *A Familiar History of British India, from the Earliest Period to the Transfer of the Government of India to the British Crown in 1858* (n.d.).
Emily Taylor *et al.*, *Stories from History*(n.d. [1876?]).
Edith Thompson, *History of England* (1873).
C. B. Thurston, *An Economic Geography of the British Empire* (1916).
F. W. Tickner, *Building the British Empire* (1929).
Mrs [Sarah] Trimmer, *A Concise History of England, Comprised in a Set of Easy Lessons* (1816).
H. F. B. Wheeler, *Makers of the British Empire* (1927).
J. A. Williamson, *Builders of the Empire* (1925).
—— *A Short History of British Expansion*, 2nd edn. (1930).
—— *The British Empire and Commonwealth: A History for Senior Forms* (1935).
W. H. Woodward, *A Short History of the Expansion of the British Empire 1500–1902* (1899).

Other Books and Articles

Anon., *The Time and Affecting History of Henrietta Belgrave . . .* (n.d.).
Jane Austen, *Mansfield Park* (1814).
Lord Avebury, *Essays and Addresses 1900–1903* (1903).
Robert Baden-Powell, *Scouting for Boys* (1908).
R. M. Ballantyne, *The Coral Island* (1857).
Count Björnstjerna, *The British Empire in the East*, trans. H. Evans Lloyd (1840).
Wilfred Scawen Blunt, *Satan Absolved* (1899).

Mary Elizabeth Braddon, *Lady Audley's Secret* (1862).
H. N. Brailsford, *The War of Steel and Gold* (1914).
Brewer's Dictionary of Phrase and Fable, 'Classic Edition' (1894).
John Bright and Thorold Rogers (eds.), *Speeches on Questions of Public Policy by Richard Cobden* (1870).
Charlotte Brontë, *Jane Eyre* (1847).
John Buchan, *John Macnab* (1925).
—— *The Dancing Floor* (1926).
Joyce Cary, *Mister Johnson* (1939).
—— *The Case for African Freedom* (1941).
Thomas Carlyle, *Past and Present* (1843).
—— *Latter Day Pamphlets* (1850).
Centennial Survey of Foreign Missions (1902).
Chambers's Information for the People, 2 vols. (1841–2).
[Colonial; and Indian Exhibition], *Notes of Lectures given in the Conference Room of the Colonial and Indian Exhibition* (1886).
C. S. Cooper, *The Outdoor Monuments of London, Statues, Memorial Buildings, Tablets and War Memorials* (1928).
Lionel Cust, *A History of Eton College* (1899).
Morrison Davidson, *Africa for the Afrikanders: Why I am a Pro-Boer* (1902).
Revd Richard Dawes, *Suggestive Hints Towards Improved Secular Instruction* (1857).
Daniel Defoe, *The Life and Adventures of Robinson Crusoe* (1719).
—— *The Further Adventures of Robinson Crusoe* (1720).
Edmond Demolins, *Anglo-Saxon Superiority: To What It Is Due* (1898).
Charles Dickens, *American Notes* (1842).
—— *David Copperfield* (1849).
—— *Hard Times* (1851).
—— *A Tale of Two Cities* (1859).
—— *Great Expectations* (1861).
Sir Charles Dilke, *Greater Britain* (1868).
Samuel Dill, *Roman Society in the Last Century of the Western Empire* (1898).
Benjamin Disraeli, *Sybil, or The Two Nations* (1845).
Geoffrey Drage, *Cyril. A Romantic Novel* (1889).
—— *Eton and the Empire* (1890).
[A. O. Eltzbacher], *Drifting* (1901).
G. K. Evens, *Public Opinion on Colonial Affairs: A Survey made in May and June, 1948, for the Colonial Office* (1948).
Henry G. Farmer, *The Rise and Development of Military Music* (n.d. [1912]).
Frederic W. Farrar, *Eric, or Little by Little* (1858).
—— *'In the Days of Thy Youth': Sermons on Practical Subjects, preached at Marlborough College from 1871 to 1876*, 2nd edn. (1876).
J. G. Fitch, *Lectures on Teaching* (1881).
C. R. L. Fletcher, *Their Empire, and How They Have Made It* (1914).
—— *Their Empire, and What They Covet* (1914).
—— *Edmond Warre* (1922).
E. M. Forster, *A Passage to India* (1924).

Archibald Fox, *Public School Life: Harrow* (1911).
George MacDonald Fraser, *Flashman* (1969).
George H. Gallup, *The Gallup International Public Opinion Polls: Great Britain 1837–1975*, vol. 1, *1937–1964* (n.d. [1976]).
John Galsworthy, *The Man of Property* (1906).
—— *In Chancery* (1920).
Mary Gaskell, *North and South* (1855).
W. E. Gladstone, *Political Speeches in Scotland* (Edinburgh, 1879).
Lord Edward Gleichen, *London's Open-Air Statuary* (1928).
Mary Godolphin, *Robinson Crusoe in Words of One Syllable* (1868).
Harold E. Gorst, *The Curse of Education* (1901).
Edward Graham, *The Harrow Life of Henry Montague Butler* (1920).
Cecil Gray, *A Survey of Contemporary Music* (1924).
Earl Grey, *The Colonial Policy of Lord John Russell's Administration* (1853).
N. John Hall (ed.), *The Letters of Anthony Trollope* (1983).
Richard Burdon Haldane, *Education and Empire* (1902).
Martin Hardie (ed.), *The Pageant of Empire: Souvenir Volume* (1924).
F. J. C. Hearnshawe, *An Outline Sketch of the Political History of Europe in the 19th Century* (1920).
G. A. Henty, *With Roberts to Pretoria* (1902).
F. W. Hirst *et al.*, *Liberalism and the Empire* (1900).
J. A. Hobson, *The War in South Africa: Its Causes and Effects* (1900).
—— *The Psychology of Jingoism* (1901).
—— *The Social Problem: Life and Work* (1901).
—— *Imperialism: A Study* (1902).
W. B. Hockley, *Tales of the Zenana* (1827).
M. L. V. Hughes, *Citizens to Be: A Social Study of Health, Wisdom and Goodness with Special Reference to Elementary Schools* (1915).
Thomas Hughes, *Tom Brown's Schooldays* (1857).
—— *Tom Brown at Oxford* (1861).
[Imperial International Exhibition], *Official Guide to the Imperial International Exhibition, White City* (1909).
Independent Labour Party, *Report of the Annual Conference, Leicester, April 1927*.
George W. Joy, *The Work of George W. Joy, with an Autobiographical Sketch* (1904).
Benjamin Kidd, *Social Evolution* (1894).
—— *The Control of the Tropics* (1898).
Charles Kingsley, *Yeast* (1850).
—— *Westward Ho!* (1855).
Henry Kingsley, *The Recollections of Geoffrey Hamlyn* (Leipzig edn., 1864).
Mary Kingsley, *Travels in West Africa* (1897).
—— West African Studies (1899).
[Imre Kiralfy], *The Empire of India Exhibition 1895, Earl's Court, London. The Conception, Design and Production of Imre Kiralfy* (1895).
Imre Kiralfy and Angelo Venanzi, *India: An Operatic-Historical Production in Two Acts* (1909).
Rudyard Kipling, *Stalky and Co.* (1899).
John Alfred Langford, *Modern Birmingham and its Institutions: A Chronicle of Local Events, from 1841 to 1871* (1873).

Simon Laurie, *On Primary Instruction in Relation to Education* (1867).
'John Law' [Margaret Harkness], *In Darkest London: A New and Popular Edition of Captain Lobe: A Story of the Salvation Army* (this edn. 1891).
Dan H. Laurence (ed.), *Shaw's Music: The Complete Musical Criticism of Bernard Shaw*, 3 vols. (1981).
W. R. Lawson, *John Bull and His Schools* (1908).
League of Nations Union, Advisory Education Committee for Wales, *The Teaching of Geography in Relation to the World Community* (1933).
Alexandre Ledru-Rollin, *La Décadence d'Angleterre* (trans. as *The Decline of England*, 1850).
V. I. Lenin, *Imperialism: The Highest Stage of Capitalism* (1922).
Charles Lever, *The Dodd Family Abroad* (1853–4).
—— *A Day's Ride* (1863).
G. Cornewall Lewis, *An Essay on the Government of Dependencies* (1841).
London County Council, *Return of Outdoor Memorials in London* (1910).
[Peter Longueville], *The Adventures of Philip Quarll, the English Hermit; who was discovered by Mr. Dorrington on an Uninhabited Island where he had lived upwards of fifty years* [n.d.].
Thomas (Lord) Macaulay, *Essays and Lays of Ancient Rome*, Popular Edition (1897).
J. R. McCulloch, *A Statistical Abstract of the British Empire* (1837).
[Felix McDonagh], *The Hermit Abroad*, 4 vols. (1823).
J. D. Mackie, 'The Teaching of History and the War', *History* 25 (1940).
H. J. MacKinder, 'The Teaching of Geography from an Imperial Point of View', *The Geographical Teacher*, 6 (1911).
Charles Madge and Tom Harrison (eds.), *Britain by Mass-Observation* (1939).
Magazine of Art supplement, *Royal Academy Pictures 1899* (1899).
H. Major, *Standard Teaching Helps, illustrated by Model Lessons . . . for Boys', Girls', and Mixed Schools* (1889).
Bessie Marchant, *The Rajah's Daughter: or, the Half-Moon Girl* (1899).
—— *Held at Ransom: A Story of Colonial Life* (1901).
—— *The Captives of the Kaid* (1904).
—— *The Girl Captives: A Story of the Indian Frontier* (1906).
—— *The Deputy Boss: A Tale of British Honduras* (1910).
—— *Lesbia's Little Blunder* (1934).
C. F. G. Masterman *et al.*, *The Heart of the Empire* (1901).
Donald Maxwell, *Wembley in Colour* (1924).
Lord Meath *et al.*, *Essays on Duty and Discipline* (1910).
Hermann Melville, *Typee: A Peep at Polynesian Life* (1846).
John Stuart Mill, *Principles of Political Economy*, 2nd edn. (1849).
—— *Autobiography* (1872; new edn., Oxford, 1979).
J. G. Cotton Minchin, *Old Harrow Days* (1898).
Alfred Noyes, *Collected Poems* (1927).
George Orwell, *Burmese Days* (1934).
G. H. Perris, *Blood and Gold in South Africa* (1902).
W. M. Flinders Petrie, *Janus in Modern Life* (1907).
J. Enoch Powell, *Freedom and Reality*, ed. John Wood (1969).
Dr Emil Reich, *Imperialism: Its Prices; its Vocation* (1905).
G. W. M. Reynolds, *The Soldier's Wife* (1853).

G. W. M. Reynolds, *The Bronze Statue* (1854).
—— *The Loves of the Harem: A Tale of Constantinople* (1855).
Revd Legh Richmond, *The Negro Servant* (1876).
J. M. Robertson, *Patriotism and Empire* (1899).
—— *Wrecking the Empire* (1901).
Routledge One Shilling Guide to the Crystal Palace and Park at Sydenham (1854).
Rugby School Registers, vols. 1–3 (1886, 1891).
John Ruskin, *The Works of John Ruskin*, ed. E. T. Cook and Alexander Wedderburn (1905).
Bertrand Russell, *Education and the Social Order* (1932).
Edward Salmon, 'What the Working Classes Read', *Nineteenth Century*, 20 (1886).
—— *Juvenile Literature As It Is* (1888).
Sir Walter Scott, *Guy Mannering* (1815).
—— *The Surgeon's Daughter* (1827).
J. R. Seeley, *The Expansion of England, Two Courses of Lectures* (1883).
—— *Lectures and Essays* (1895).
G. B. Shaw, *Arms and the Man* (1894).
—— *Fabianism and the Empire* (1900).
—— Preface to *John Bull's Other Island* (1904).
—— *Captain Brassbound's Conversion* (1906).
—— *Back to Methuselah* (1921).
Sir Ernest Simon and Eva M. Hubback, *Training for Citizenship* (1935).
W. Shaw Sparrow (ed.), *The Spirit of the Age: The Work of Frank Brangwyn ARA* (1905).
—— *Frank Brangwyn and His Work* (1910).
Gordon Stables, *On War's Red Tide* (1900).
F. Reginald Statham, *South Africa and the Transvaal: The Story of a Conspiracy* (1899).
W. T. Stead, *The History of the Mystery; or, The Story of the Jameson Raid* (1896).
J. H. Stocqueler, *The Hand-book of India, A Guide to the Stranger and Traveller, and a Companion to the Resident* (1845).
—— *The Oriental Interpreter and Treasury of East India Knowledge* (1848).
—— *The Overland Companion: Being a Guide for the Traveller to India via Egypt* (1850).
—— *India: Its History, Climate, Productions, and Field Sports; with Notices of European Life and Manners, and of the various Travelling Routes* (1853).
'Hesba Stretton', *Lost Gip* (1873 edn.).
Philip Meadows Taylor, *Confessions of a Thug* (1839).
—— *Tipoo Sultaun: A Tale of the Mysore War* (1840).
W. M. Thackeray, *Vanity Fair* (1847–8).
Robert Tressell, *The Ragged-Trousered Philanthropists* (1914).
Anthony Trollope, *The West Indies and the Spanish Main* (1859).
—— *Tales of All Countries*, 2 vols. (1861, 1863).
—— *Phineas Finn* (1869).
—— *Australia and New Zealand* (1873).
—— *The Eustace Diamonds* (1875).
—— *The Way We Live Now* (1875).
—— *South Africa* (1877).
Horace Annesley Vachel, *The Hill: A Romance of Friendship* (1905).
Edouard de Warren, *L'Inde Anglaise en 1843–44*, 2 vols. (1844).

Beatrice Webb, *Our Partnership*, ed. Barbara Drake and Margaret Cole (1948).
W. P. Welpton, *The Teaching of Geography* (1923).
Virginia Woolf, *Night and Day* (1919).
—— *The Years* (1937).
World Atlas of Christian Missions (1911).
M. Digby Wyatt, *Views of the Crystal Palace and Park, Sydenham* (1854).
James Wyld, *Notes to Accompany Mr Wyld's Model of the Earth, Leicester Square* (1851).
Percy M. Young (ed.), *Letters of Edward Elgar and other Writings* (1956).
Israel Zangwill, *Children of the Ghetto* (1892).

SECONDARY SOURCES

Place of publication is London unless otherwise indicated.

R. J. Q. Adams, 'The National Service League and Mandatory Service in Edwardian England', *Armed Forces and Society*, 12 (1985).
Luis Ajagán-Lester, *'De Andra'. Afrikaner I svenska pedagogiska texter (1768–1965)* (Stockholm, 2000).
Richard Aldrich (ed.), *History in the National Curriculum* (1991).
Richard Altick, *The English Common Reader: A Social History of the Mass Reading Public 1800–1900* (Chicago, 1957).
—— *The Shows of London* (Cambridge, Mass., 1978).
Benedict Anderson, *Imagined Communities: Reflections on the Origin and Spread of Nationalism* (1983).
David Anderson and David Killingray (eds.), *Policing the Empire: Government, Authority and Control, 1830–1940* (Manchester, 1991).
—— *Policing and Decolonisation: Nationalism, Politics and the Police, 1917–65* (Manchester, 1992).
Robert Anderson, *Elgar and Chivalry* (Rickmansworth, 2002).
Jonathan Arac and Harriet Ritvo (eds.), *Macropolitics of Nineteenth-Century Literature: Nationalism, Exoticism, Imperialism* (Philadelphia, 1991).
David Arnold (ed.), *Imperial Medicine and Indigenous Societies* (Manchester, 1988).
Guy Arnold, *Hold Fast for England: G. A. Henty, Imperialist Boys' Writer* (1980).
Talal Asad (ed.), *Anthropology and the Colonial Encounter* (1973).
Jeffrey Auerbach, *The Great Exhibition of 1851: A Nation on Display* (New Haven, conn., 1999).
Peter Bailey, 'Custom, Capital and Culture in the Victorian Music Hall', in R. D. Storch (ed.), *Popular Culture and Class in Victorian England* (1982).
T. W. Bamford, *The Rise of the Public Schools* (1967).
—— 'Thomas Arnold and the Victorian Idea of a Public School', in Simon and Bradley (eds.), *The Victorian Public School* (1975).
Olive Banks, *Parity and Prestige in English Secondary Education: A Study in Educational Sociology* (1955).
Felix Barker and Ralph Hyde, *London As It Might Have Been* (1982).
Kathleen Barker, *Early Music Hall in Bristol* (Bristol, 1979).
John Barnes, *The Beginnings of the Cinema in England*, vols. 4–6 (1976).
—— *Filming the Boer War* (1992).
Correlli Barnett, *The Collapse of British Power* (1972).
—— *The Audit of War* (1986).

Tim Barringer and Tom Flynn (eds.), *Colonialism and the Object: Empire, Material Culture and the Museum* (1998).

—— 'The South Kensington Museum and the Colonial Project', in Barringer and Flynn (eds.), *Colonialism and the Object* (1998).

—— '"Not a 'modern' as the word is now understood"? Byam Shaw and the Poetics of Professional Society', in David Peters Corbett and Lara Perry (eds.), *English Art 1860–1914* (Manchester, 2000).

T. O. Beidelman, *Colonial Evangelism: A Socio-Historical Study of the East African Mission at the Grassroots* (Bloomington, Ind., 1982).

Morag Bell, Robin A. Butlin, and Michael Hefferman (eds.), *Geography and Imperialism, 1820–1940* (Manchester, 1995).

G. Bennett, *The Concept of Empire* (1953).

Geoffrey Best, 'Militarism and the Victorian Public School', in Simon and Bradley (eds.), *The Victorian Public School* (1975).

Raymond F. Betts, 'The Allusion to Rome in British Imperialist Thought of the Late Nineteenth and Early Twentieth Centuries', *Victorian Studies*, 15 (1971).

Homi K. Bhabha, 'The Other Question: Difference, Discrimination and the Discourse of Colonialism', in Francis Barker *et al.*, *Literature, Politics and Theory* (1986).

T. J. H. Bishop, *Winchester and the Public School Élite* (1967).

Jeremy Black, *Maps and History: Constructing Images of the Past* (New Haven, conn., 1997).

M. D. Blanch, 'Imperialism, Nationalism and Organized Youth', in John Clarke *et al.* (eds.), *Working-Class Culture: Studies in History and Theory* (1979).

—— 'British Society and the War', in Peter Warwick (ed.), *The South African War: The Anglo-Boer War 1899–1902* (1980).

Anne Bloomfield, 'Drill and Dance as Symbols of Imperialism', in Mangan (ed.), *Making Imperial Mentalities* (1990).

C. A. Bodelsen, *Studies in Mid-Victorian Imperialism* (1924; new edn. 1960).

Elleke Boehmer (ed.), *Empire Writing: An Anthology of Colonial Literature 1870–1918* (1998).

Christine Bolt, *Victorian Attitudes to Race* (Oxford, 1971).

Michael R. Booth, *Victorian Spectacular Theatre 1850–1910* (1981).

Allen Borg, *War Memorials from Antiquity to the Present* (1991).

John Bourne, *Britain and the Great War 1914–1918* (1989).

—— 'The British Working Man in Arms', in Hugh Cecil and Peter H Liddle (eds.), *Facing Armageddon: The First World War Experienced* (Barnsley, 1996).

David Bradby *et al.*, *Performance and Politics in Popular Drama ... 1800–1976* (Cambridge, 1980).

Patrick Brantlinger, *Rule of Darkness: British Literature and Imperialism, 1830–1914* (Ithaca, NY, 1988).

J. S. Bratton, *The Impact of Victorian Children's Fiction* (1981).

—— 'British Imperialism and the Reproduction of Femininity in Girls' Fiction, 1900–1930', in Richards (ed.), *Imperialism and Juvenile Literature* (1989).

—— *et al.*, *Acts of Supremacy: The British Empire and the Stage, 1790–1930* (Manchester, 1991).

Asa Briggs, 'Trollope the Traveller', in John Halperin (ed.), *Trollope Centenary Essays* (1982).

Joseph Bristow, *Empire Boys: Adventures in a Man's World* (1991).

Chris Brooks and Peter Faulkner (eds.), *The White Man's Burdens: An Anthology of British Poetry of the Empire* (Exeter, 1996).

B. H. Brown, *The Tariff Reform Movement in Great Britain 1881–1895* (Oxford, 1943).

Judith Brown and Wm. Roger Louis (eds.), *The Oxford History of the British Empire, Vol. 4: The Twentieth Century* (1999).

Michael Barratt Brown, *After Imperialism* (revised edn., 1970).

Janice Brownfoot, 'Memsahibs in Colonial Malaya: A Study of European Wives in a British Colony and Protectorate 1900–1940', in Callan and Ardener (eds.), *The Incorporated Wife* (1984).

—— 'Sisters Under the Skin: Imperialism and the Emancipation of Women in Malaya, *c*.1891–1941', in Mangan (ed.), *Making Imperial Mentalities* (1990).

Anthony Brundage, *The People's Historian: John Richard Green and the Writing of History in Victorian England* (Westport, conn., 1994).

Elizabeth Buettner, 'From Somebodies to Nobodies: Britons Returning Home from India', in Martin Daunton and Bernhard Rieger (eds.), *Meanings of Modernity: Britain from the Late-Victorian Era to World War II* (2001).

Peter Burke, 'The "Discovery" of Popular Culture', in Raphael Samuel (ed.), *People's History and Socialist Theory* (1981).

Peter Burroughs, 'Parliamentary Radicals and the Reduction of Imperial Expenditure in British North America, 1827–1834', *Historical Journal*, 11 (1968).

—— 'The Canadian Rebellions in British Politics', in J. E. Flint and G. Williams (eds.), *Perspectives of Empire* (1973).

—— 'John Robert Seeley and British Imperial History', *Journal of Imperial and Commonwealth History*, 1 (1973).

—— 'The Human Cost of Imperial Defence in the Early Victorian Age', *Victorian Studies*, 24 (1980).

—— 'Crime and Punishment in the British Army, 1815–1870', *English Historical Review*, 100 (1985).

Antoinette Burton, 'The White Woman's Burden', in Chaudhuri and Strobel (eds.), *Western Women and Imperialism* (1992).

—— *Burdens of History: British Feminists, Indian Women, and Imperial Culture, 1865–1915* (Chapel Hill, 1994).

—— 'Rules of Thumb: British History and "Imperial Culture" in Nineteenth- and Twentieth-century Britain', *Women's History Review*, 3 (1994), 483–5.

—— *At the Heart of the Empire: Indians and the Colonial Encounter in Late-Victorian Britain* (1998).

David Burton, *The Raj at the Table: A Culinary History of the British in India* (1993).

Barbara Bush, '"Britain's Conscience on Africa": White Women, Race and Imperial Politics in Inter-war Britain', in Midgley (ed.), *Gender and Imperialism* (1998).

Julia Bush, *Edwardian Ladies and Imperial Power* (Leicester, 2000).

Robin A. Butlin, 'Historical Geographies of the British empire, c. 1887–1925', in Bell, Butlin, and Hefferman (eds.), *Geography and Imperialism* (1995).

Arthur Byron, *London Statues: A Guide to London's Outdoor Statues and Sculpture* (1981).

Mary Cadogan and Patricia Craig, *You're a Brick, Angela! A New Look at Girl's Fiction from 1839 to 1975* (1976).

Peter Cain, 'Political Economy and Edwardian England: The Tariff-Reform Controversy', in Alan O'Day (ed.), *The Edwardian Age: Conflict and Stability* (1979).

—— 'British Radicalism, the South African Crisis, and the Origins of the Theory of Financial Imperialism', in Omissi and Thompson (eds.), *Impact of the South African War* (2001).

Peter Cain, *Hobson and Imperialism: Radicalism, New Liberalism, and Finance, 1887–1938* (2002).

—— and A. G. Hopkins, *British Imperialism: Innovation and Expansion 1688–1914*, and *Crisis and Deconstruction 1914–1990* (1993).

Angus Calder and Dorothy Sheridan, *Speak for Yourself: A Mass-Observation Anthology, 1937–49* (1984).

Hilary Callan and Shirley Ardener (eds.), *The Incorporated Wife* (1984).

Helen Callaway, *Gender, Culture and Empire: European Women in Colonial Nigeria* (Urbana, Ill., 1987).

—— and Dorothy O Helly, 'Crusader for Empire', in Chaudhuri and Strobel (eds.), *Western Women and Imperialism* (1992).

David Cannadine, 'The Context, Performance and Meaning of Ritual: The British Monarchy and the "Invention of Tradition", *c.*1820–1977', in Eric Hobsbawm and Terence Ranger (eds.), *The Invention of Tradition* (1983).

—— *The Decline and Fall of the British Aristocracy* (New Haven, Conn., 1990).

—— 'The Empire Strikes Back', *Past and Present*, 147 (1995).

—— *Ornamentalism: How the British Saw Their Empire* (2001).

Charles Carrington, *Rudyard Kipling: His Life and Work* (1955).

Kathryn Castle, 'The Imperial Indian: India in British History Textbooks for Schools 1890–1914', in Mangan (ed.), *The Imperial Curriculum* (1993).

—— *Britannia's Children: Reading Colonialism Through Children's Books and Magazines* (Manchester, 1996).

—— 'The Representation of Africa in Mid-Victorian Children's Magazines', in Gretchen Gerzina (ed.), *Black Victorians, Black Victoriana* (Brunswick, NJ, 2003).

Valerie Chancellor, *History for their Masters: Opinion in the English History Textbooks, 1800–1914* (Bath, 1970).

John Charmley, *Churchill: The End of Glory: A Political Biography* (1995).

Amal Chatterjee, *Representations of India, 1740–1840: The Creation of India in the Colonial Imagination* (1998).

Nupur Chaudhuri, 'Shawls, Jewelry, Curry, and Rice in Victorian Britain', in Chaudhuri and Strobel (eds.), *Western Women and Imperialism* (1992).

—— and Margaret Strobel (eds.), *Western Women and Imperialism: Complicity and Resistance* (Bloomington, Ind., 1992).

Susan Chitty, *The Beast and the Monk: A Life of Charles Kingsley* (1974).

Laura Chrisman, 'The Imperial Unconscious? Representations of Imperial Discourse', *Critical Quarterly*, 32 (1990).

F. G. Clarke, *The Land of Contrarieties: British Attitudes to the Australian Colonies 1828–1855* (Melbourne, 1977).

Anthony Clayton, '"Deceptive Might": Imperial Defence and Security, 1900–1968', in Brown and Louis (eds.), *Oxford History of the British Empire, vol. 4* (1999).

Julie Codell and Dianne Sachko Macleod (ed.), *Orientalism Transposed: The Impact of Colonies on British Culture* (1998).

S. J. Colledge, 'The Study of History in the Teacher Training College 1888–1914', *History of Education Society Bulletin*, 36 (Autumn 1985).

Linda Colley, *Britons: Forging the Nation, 1707–1837* (New Haven, Conn., 1992).

—— 'The Imperial Embrace', *Yale Review*, 81 (1993).

Brenda Colloms, *Charles Kingsley: The Lion of Eversley* (1975).

John and Joan Comaroff, *Ethnography and the Historical Imagination* (Boulder, Col., 1992).
Stephen Constantine, '"Bringing the Empire Alive": The Empire Marketing Board and Imperial Propaganda, 1926–33', in Mackenzie (ed.), *Imperialism and Popular Culture* (1986).
J. E. Cookson, *The British Armed Nation 1793–1815* (Oxford, 1997).
Annie E. Coombes, '"For God and for England": Contributions to an Image of Africa in the First Decade of the Twentieth Century', *Art History*, 8 (1985).
—— *Reinventing Africa: Museums, Material Culture and Popular Imagination in Late Victorian and Edwardian England* (New Haven, conn., 1994).
Frederick Cooper and Ann Laura Stoler (eds.), *Tensions of Empire: Colonial Cultures in a Bourgeois World* (Berkeley, 1997).
Patrick Cosgrave, *The Lives of Enoch Powell* (1989).
Helen I. Cowan, *British Emigration to British North America: The First Hundred Years* (Toronto, 1961).
Hugh Cunningham, 'Jingoism in 1877–78', *Victorian Studies*, 14 (1971).
—— 'The Language of Patriotism', in Raphael Samuel (ed.), *Patriotism: The Making and Unmaking of British National Identity*, vol. 1, *History and Politics* (1989).
Greg Cuthbertson, Albert Grundlingh, and Mary-Lynn Suttie, *Writing a Wider War: Rethinking Gender, Race and Identity in the South African War, 1899–1902* (Athens, Ohio, 2002).
Gloden Dallas and Douglas Gill, *The Unknown Army: Mutinies in the British Army in World War I* (1985).
Phillip Darby, 'Taking Fieldhouse Further: Post-Colonizing Imperial History', in Peter Burroughs and A. J. Stockwell (eds.), *Managing the Business of Empire* (1998).
J. C. Darracott and B. M. Loftus, *First World War Posters* (1972).
John Darwin, 'Imperialism in Decline? Tendencies in British Imperial Policy Between the Wars', in *Historical Journal*, 23 (1980).
—— 'The Fear of Falling: British Politics and Imperial Decline Since 1900', *Transactions of the Royal Historical Society*, 5th ser., 36 (1986).
Martin Daunton and Rick Halpern (eds.), *Empire and Others: British Encounters With Indigenous Peoples, 1600–1850* (1999).
J. H. Davidson, 'Anthony Trollope and the Colonies', *Victorian Studies*, 12 (1969).
Anna Davin, 'Imperialism and Motherhood', *History Workshop*, 5 (1978).
—— *Growing up Poor: Home, School and Street in London, 1870–1914* (1996).
Lance E. Davis and Robert A. Huttenback, *Mammon and the Pursuit of Empire: The Political Economy of British Imperialism* (Cambridge, 1986).
Ray Desmond, *The India Museum, 1801–1879* (1982).
Margarita Díaz-Andreu and Timothy Champion (eds.), *Nationalism and Archaeology in Europe* (1996).
Nicholas B. Dirks (ed.), *Colonialism and Culture* (Ann Arbor, Mich., 1992).
Maurice Willson Disher, *Victorian Song: From Dive to Drawing Room* (1955).
Felix Driver and David Gilbert (eds.), *Imperial Cities. Landscape, Display and Identity* (Manchester, 1999).
Patrick Dunae, 'Boy's Own Paper: Origins and Editorial Policies', *The Private Library*, 2nd ser., 9 (1976).
—— 'Boys' Literature and the Idea of Race: 1870–1900', *Wascana Review*, 12 (1977).
—— 'Penny Dreadfuls: Late Nineteenth-Century Boys' Literature and Crime', *Victorian Studies*, 22 (1979).

Patrick Dunae, 'Boys' Literature and the Idea of Empire, 1870–1914', *Victorian Studies*, 24: 4 (1980).

—— *Gentlemen Emigrants: From the British Public Schools to the Canadian Frontier* (Vancouver, 1981).

—— 'Education, Emigration and Empire: The Colonial College, 1887–1905', in Mangan, *Benefits Bestowed?* (1988).

Bruce Elder, *Blood on the Wattle: Massacres and Maltreatment of Australian Aborigines since 1788* (Frenchs Forest, NSW, 1988).

B. J. Elliott, 'An Early Failure of Curriculum Reform: History Teaching in England 1918–1940', *Journal of Educational Administration and History*, 12 (1980).

—— 'History Examinations at Sixteen and Eighteen Years in England and Wales between 1918 and 1939', *History of Education*, 20 (1991).

Richard Faber, *The Vision and the Need: Late Victorian Imperialist Aims* (1966).

J. Fabian, 'Religious and Secular Colonisation (1990)', in *Time and the Work of Anthropology: Critical Essays 1971–1991* (Chur, Switzerland, 1991).

C. R. Fay, *Palace of Industry 1851: A Study of the Great Exhibition and its Fruits* (Cambridge, 1951).

Geoffrey Field, 'Social Patriotism and the British Working Class: Appearance and Disappearance of a Tradition', *International and Working Class History*, 42 (1992).

H. John Field, *Towards a Programme of Imperial Life: The British Empire at the Turn of the Century* (Oxford, 1982).

David Fitzpatrick, *Oceans of Consolation: Personal Accounts of Irish Emigration to Australia* (Melbourne, 1995).

Malia B. Formes, 'Beyond Complicity Versus Resistance: Recent Work on Gender and European Imperialism', *Journal of Social History* (1995).

Wendy Forrester, *Great Grandmama's Weekly: A Celebration of the Girls's Own Paper 1880–1901* (1980).

Peter Forster, 'Empiricism and Imperialism: A Review of the New Left Critique of Social Anthropology', in Asad (ed.), *Anthropology and the Colonial Encounter* (1973).

Peter Fryer, *Staying Power: The History of Black People in Britain* (1984).

Tim Fulford and Peter J. Kitson (eds.), *Romanticism and Colonialism: Writing and Empire, 1790–1830* (Cambridge, 1998).

J. A. Gallagher and R. E. Robinson, 'The Imperialism of Free Trade', *Economic History Review*, 6 (1953).

Anna Gambles, *Protection and Politics: Conservative Economic Discourse, 1815–1852* (1999).

L. H. Gann and Peter Duignan, *The Rulers of British Africa 1870–1914* (1978).

John Gardiner, 'The Reception of Sir Edward Elgar 1918–*c*.1934: A Reassessment', *Twentieth Century British History*, 9 (1998).

Beverley Gartrell, 'Colonial Wives: Villains or Victims?', in Callan and Ardener (eds.), *The Incorporated Wife* (1984).

Bentley B. Gilbert, *The Evolution of National Insurance in Great Britain: The Origins of the Welfare State* (1966).

David Gilmour, *The Long Recessional: The Imperial Life of Rudyard Kipling* (2002).

Anne Godlewska and Neil Smith (eds.), *Geography and Empire* (Oxford, 1994).

J. M. Goldstrom, *The Social Content of Education 1808–1870: A Study of the Working Class School Reader in England and Ireland* (Shannon, 1972).

—— 'The Content of Education and the Socialization of the Working-Class Child 1830–1860', in McCann (ed.), *Popular Education and Socialisation* (1985).

Alfred Gollin, *Balfour's Burden: Arthur Balfour and Imperial Preference* (1965).

Jack Goody, *The East in the West* (Cambridge, 1996).

Corissa Gould, 'Edward Elgar, *The Crown of India*, and the Image of Empire', *Elgar Society Journal*, 13 (2003).

Andy Green, *Education and State Formation: The Rise of Education Systems in England, France and the USA* (1990).

E. H. H. Green, *The Crisis of Conservatism: The Politics, Economics and Ideology of the British Conservative Party, 1880–1914* (1995).

Martin Green, *Dreams of Adventure, Deeds of Empire* (New York, 1979).

—— 'The Robinson Crusoe Story', in Richards (ed.), *Imperialism and Juvenile Literature* (1989).

Allen J. Greenberger, *The British Image of India: A Study in the Literature of Imperialism* (1969).

Paul Greenhalgh, *Ephemeral Vistas: Expositions Universelles, Great Exhibitions and World's Fairs, 1851–1939* (Manchester, 1988).

Jeffrey Greenhut, 'The Imperial Reserve: The Indian Corps on the Western Front, 1914–15', *Journal of Imperial and Commonwealth History*, 12 (1983).

James G. Greenlee, '"A Succession of Seeleys": The "Old School" Re-examined', *Journal of Imperial and Commonwealth History*, 4 (1976).

—— 'The ABC's of Imperial Unity', *Canadian Journal of History*, 14 (1979).

—— 'Imperial Studies and the Unity of the Empire', *Journal of Imperial and Commonwealth History*, 7 (1979).

—— *Education and Imperial Unity, 1901–1929* (New York, 1987).

Breandan Gregory, 'Staging British India', in Bratton *et al.*, *Acts of Supremacy* (1991).

Inderpal Grewal, *Home and Harem: Nation, Gender, Empire and the Cultures of Travel* (Leicester, 1996).

Richard Grove, *Green Imperialism: Colonial Expansion, Tropical Island Edens and the Origins of Environmentalism, 1600–1860* (Cambridge, 1995).

Partha Sarathi Gupta, *Imperialism and the British Labour Movement, 1914–1964* (1975).

Jane Haggis, 'Gendering Colonialism or Colonising Gender? Recent Women's Studies Approaches to White Women and the History of British Colonialism', *Women's Studies International Forum*, 5 (1990).

Robert F. Haines, *Emigration and the Labouring Poor: Australian Recruitment in Britain and Ireland, 1831–60* (1997).

Catherine Hall, 'Going a-Trolloping: Imperial Man Travels the Empire', in Midgley (ed.), *Gender and Imperialism* (1998).

—— (ed.) *Cultures of Empire: Colonizers in Britain and the Empire in the Nineteenth and Twentieth Centuries: A Reader* (Manchester, 2000).

—— *Civilising Subjects: Metropole and Colony in the English Imagination 1830–1867* (2002).

John Halperin, *Trollope and Politics: A Study of the Pallisers and Others* (1977).

Gavin Hambly, 'Muslims in English-Language fiction', in Winks and Rush (eds.), *Asia in Western Fiction* (1990).

A. James Hammerton, *Emigrant Gentlewomen: Genteel Poverty and Female Emigration, 1830–1914* (1979).

W. K. Hancock, *Survey of British Commonwealth* Affairs, vol. 2, *Problems of Economic Policy 1918–1939*, Part 2 (1942).

Stuart Hannabuss, 'Ballantyne's Message of Empire', in Richards (ed.), *Imperialism and Juvenile Literature* (1989).

Freda Harcourt, 'Disraeli's Imperialism, 1866–68: A Question of Timing,' *Historical Journal*, 23 (1980).

Bob Harris, '"American Idols": Empire, War and the Middling Ranks in Mid-Eighteenth-century Britain', *Past and Present*, 150 (1996).

Brian Harrison, *Separate Spheres: The Opposition to Women's Suffrage in Britain* (1978).

Andrew Hassam, *Through Australian Eyes: Colonial Perceptions of Imperial Britain* (Melbourne, 2000).

Elizabeth Hay, *Sambo Sahib: The Story of Little Black Sambo and Helen Bannerman* (1981).

Daniel R. Headrick, *The Tools of Empire: Technology and European Imperialism in the Nineteenth Century* (Oxford, 1991).

—— *The Tentacles of Progress: Technology Transfer in the Age of Imperialism, 1850–1940* (Oxford, 1988).

Stephen Heathorn, '"Let us remember that we, too, are English": Constructions of Citizenship and National Identity in English Elementary School Reading Books, 1880–1914', *Victorian Studies*, 38 (1995).

—— *For Home, Country and Race: Constructing Gender, Class, and Englishness in the Elementary School, 1880–1914* (Toronto, 2000).

Michael Hechter, *Internal Colonialism: The Celtic Fringe in British National Development, 1536–1966* (Berkeley, 1975).

Robert Heussler, *Yesterday's Rulers: The Making of the British Colonial Service* (Syracuse, NY, 1963).

Christopher Heywood, 'Yorkshire Slavery in *Wuthering Heights*', *Review of English Studies*, N.S., 38 (1987).

J. W. M. Hichberger, *Images of the Army: The Military in British Art, 1815–1914* (Manchester, 1988).

Fred F. Hitchins, *The Colonial Land and Emigration Commission* (Philadelphia, 1931).

E. J. Hobsbawm, *Industry and Empire: An Economic History of Britain since 1750* (1968).

Robert Holland, 'The British Empire and the Great War, 1914–1918', in Brown and Louis (eds.), *Oxford History of the British Empire, vol. 4* (1999).

Christopher Hollis, *Eton, a History* (1960).

Richard Holt, *Sport and the British* (1989).

J. R. de S. Honey, *Tom Brown's Universe: The Development of the Victorian Public School* (1977).

Pamela Horn, *Education in Rural England 1800–1914* (1978).

—— 'English Elementary education and the Growth of the Imperial Ideal, 1880–1914', in J. A. Mangan, *Benefits Bestowed?* (1988).

Reginald Horsman, 'Origins of Racial Anglo-Saxonism in Great Britain before 1850', *Journal of the History of Ideas*, 37 (1976).

D. G. Hoskins, 'The Genesis and Significance of the 1886 "Home Rule" Split in the Liberal Party', Cambridge University Ph.D. dissertation (1963).

Stephen Howe, 'Labour Patriotism, 1939–83', in Samuel (ed.), *Patriotism* (1989).

—— *Anticolonialism in British Politics. The Left and the End of Empire, 1918–1964* (Oxford, 1993).

—— *Ireland and Empire: Colonial Legacies in Irish History and Culture* (Oxford, 2000).

S. Humphries, '"Hurrah for England": Schooling and the Working Class in Bristol, 1870–1914', *Southern History*, 1 (1979).

S. Humphries, *Hooligans or Rebels? An Oral History of Working-Class Childhood and Youth 1889–1939* (Oxford, 1981).

J. S. Hurt, 'Drill, Discipline and the Elementary School Ethos', in Phillip McCann (ed), *Popular Education and Socialisation in the Nineteenth Century* (1977).

—— *Elementary Schooling and the Working Classes1860–1918* (1979).

Ronald Hyam, *Empire and Sexuality: The British Experience* (1990).

—— 'The Study of Imperial and Commonwealth History at Cambridge, 1881–1981', *Journal of Imperial and Commonwealth History*, 29 (2001).

Ralph Hyde, *Panoramania! The Art and Entertainment of the 'All-Embracing' View* (1988).

William G. Hynes, *The Economics of Empire: Britain, Africa and the New Imperialism 1870–95* (1979).

Jonathan Hyslop, 'A Ragged Trousered Philanthropist and the Empire: Robert Tressell in South Africa', *History Workshop Journal*, 51 (2001).

Ronald Inden, *Imagining India* (Oxford, 1990).

Joseph E. Inikori, *Africans and the Industrial Revolution in England: A Study in International Trade and Economic Development* (Cambridge, 2002).

Louis James, 'Tom Brown's Imperialist Sons', *Victorian Studies*, 17 (1973).

Wendy James, 'The Anthropologist as Reluctant Imperialist', in Asad (ed.), *Anthropology and the Colonial Encounter* (1973).

Tim Jeal, *Baden-Powell* (1989).

D. H. Johnson, 'The Death of Gordon: A Victorian Myth', *Journal of Imperial and Commonwealth History*, 10 (1982).

H. J. M. Johnston, *British Emigration Policy 1815–1830: 'Shovelling out Paupers'* (Oxford, 1972).

Dennis Judd, *Empire: The British Imperial Experience, from 1765 to the present* (1996).

—— and Keith Surridge, *The Boer War* (2002).

Miles Kahler, *Decolonisation in Britain and France: The Domestic Consequences of International Relations* (1984).

John Kendle, *The Round Table Movement and Imperial Union* (Toronto, 1975).

Dane Kennedy, 'Imperial History and Post-Colonial Theory', *Journal of Imperial and Commonwealth History*, 24 (1996).

—— *Britain and Empire, 1880–1945* (2002).

Michael Kennedy, *Portrait of Elgar* (1968).

Stephen Kern, *The Culture of Time and Space 1880–1918* (Cambridge, Mass., 1983).

C. F. Kernot, *British Public Schools War Memorials* (1927).

Victor Kiernan, *The Lords of Human Kind: European Attitudes to the Outside World in the Imperial Age* (1969).

—— 'Working Class and Nation in Nineteenth-Century Britain', in Maurice Cornford (ed.), *Rebels and their Causes* (1978).

—— 'Tennyson, King Arthur, and Imperialism', in Raphael Samuel and Gareth Stedman Jones (eds.), *Culture, Ideology and Politics* (1982).

Dagmar Kift, *The Victorian Music Hall: Culture, Class and Conflict* (Cambridge, 1996).

David Killingray, 'The Empire Resources Development Committee and West Africa 1916–20', *Journal of Imperial and Commonwealth History*, 10 (1982).

Dennis Kincaid, *British Social Life in India, 1608–1937* (1938; 2nd edn. 1973).

Alex King, *Memorials of the Great War in Britain: The Symbolism and Politics of Remembrance* (1998).

Anthony Kirk-Greene, *Britain's Imperial Administrators 1858–1966* (2000).

Claudia Knapman, *White Women in Fiji, 1835–1930: The Ruin of Empire?* (Sydney, 1986).

B. A. Knox, 'Reconsidering Mid-Victorian Imperialism', *Journal of Imperial and Commonwealth History*, 1 (1973).

Richard Koebner, *Empire* (Cambridge, 1961).

—— and H. D. Schmidt, *Imperialism: The Story and Significance of a Political Word, 1840–1960* (Cambridge, 1964).

Stephen Koss, *The Rise and Fall of the Political Press in Britain*, vol. 1, *The Nineteenth Century* (1981).

R. W. Kostal, 'A Jurisprudence of Power: Martial Law and the Ceylon Controversy of 1848–51', *Journal of Imperial and Commonwealth History*, 28 (2000).

Paula Krebs, '"The Last of the Gentlemen's Wars": Women in the Boer War Concentration Camp Controversy', *History Workshop Journal*, 33 (1992).

—— *Gender, Race, and the Writing of Empire: Public Discourse and the Boer War* (Cambridge, 1999).

Lara Kriegel, 'Narrating the Subcontinent in 1851: India at the Crystal Palace', in Louise Purbrick (ed.), *The Great Exhibition of 1851: New Interdisciplinary Essays* (Manchester, 2001).

Loren Kruger, 'Attending (to) the National Spectacle: Instituting National (Popular) Theatre in England and France', in Arac and Ritvo (eds.), *Macropolitics of 19th Century Literature* (1991).

Henrika Kuklick, *The Savage Within: The Social History of British Anthropology, 1885–1945* (Cambridge, 1991).

Thomas Walter Laqueur, *Religion and Respectability: Sunday Schools and Working-Class Culture 1780–1850* (New Haven, Conn., 1976).

Martin Lawn, *Servants of the State: The Contested Control of Teaching 1900–1930* (1987).

Errol Lawrence, 'Just Plain Common Sense: The "Roots" of Racism', in Centre for Contemporary Cultural Studies, *The Empire Strikes Back: Race and Racism in 70s Britain* (1982).

Nigel Leask, *British Romantic Writers and the East: Anxieties of Empire* (Cambridge, 1992).

Alan J. Lee, *The Origins of the Popular Press 1855–1914* (1976).

Robert Leeson, *Reading and Righting: The Past, Present and Future of Fiction for the Young* (1985).

Donald Leinster-Murray, 'The Nineteenth-Century English Preparatory School: Cradle and Crèche of Empire?', in J. A. Mangan (ed.), *Benefits Bestowed?* (1988).

Robin Jared Lewis, 'The Literature of the Raj', in Winks and Rush (eds.), *Asia in Western Fiction* (1990).

T. Lilly, 'The Black African in Southern Africa: Images in British School Geography Books', in Mangan (ed.), *The Imperial Curriculum* (1993).

Mary Ann Lind, *The Compassionate Memsahibs: Welfare Activities of British Women in India, 1900–1947* (New York, 1988).

David N. Livingstone, 'Climate's Moral Economy: Science, Race and Place in Post-Darwinian British and American Geography', in Godlewska and Smith (eds.), *Geography and Empire* (1994).

D. A. Lorimer, *Colour, Class and the Victorians: English Attitudes to the Negro in the Mid-19th Century* (Leicester, 1978).

Kenneth Lunn, 'Reconsidering "Britishness": The Construction and Significance of National Identity in Twentieth-Century Britain', in Brian Jenkins and Spyros A. Sopos (eds.), *Nation and Identity in Contemporary Europe* (1996).

Anne McClintock, *Imperial Leather: Race, Gender and Sexuality in the Colonial Contest* (New York, 1995).

Norman McCord, 'Victorian Newcastle Observed: The Diary of Richard Lowry', *Northern History*, 37 (2000).

Robert H. MacDonald, *The Language of Empire: Myths and Metaphors of Popular Imperialism* (Manchester, 1994).
Colin MacInnes, *Sweet Saturday Night* (1967).
P. McIntosh, *Physical Education in England Since 1800* (1952).
E. C. Mack, *Public Schools and British Opinion, 1780–1860* (1938).
—— *Public Schools and British Opinion Since 1860* (New York, 1941).
John MacKenzie, *Propaganda and Empire: The Manipulation of British Public Opinion 1880–1960* (Manchester, 1984).
—— (ed.), *Imperialism and Popular Culture* (1986).
—— '"In Touch with the Infinite": The BBC and the Empire, 1923–53', in MacKenzie (ed.), *Imperialism and Popular Culture* (1986).
—— (ed.), *Imperialism and the Natural World* (Manchester, 1990).
—— (ed.), *Popular Imperialism and the Military* (Manchester, 1992).
—— 'Scotland and the Empire', *International History Review*, 14 (1993).
—— *Orientalism: History, Theory and the Arts* (Manchester, 1995).
—— 'Empire and Metropolitan Cultures', in Andrew Porter (ed.), *The Oxford History of the British Empire, vol. 3: The Nineteenth Century* (Oxford, 1999).
—— '"The Second City of the Empire": Glasgow—Imperial Municipality', in Driver and Gilbert (eds.), *Imperial Cities* (1999).
Frederick Madden and D. K. Fieldhouse (eds.), *Oxford and the Idea of Commonwealth* (1982).
—— 'The Commonwealth, Commonwealth History, and Oxford, 1905–1971', in Madden and Fieldhouse (eds.), *Oxford and the Idea of Commonwealth* (1982).
Avril M. C. Maddrell, 'Empire, Emigration and School Geography: Changing Discourses of Imperial Citizenship, 1880–1925', *Journal of Historical Geography*, 22 (1996).
Javed Majeed, *Ungoverned Imaginings: James Mill's* The History of British India *and Orientalism* (Oxford, 1992).
J. A. Mangan, 'Athleticism: A Case Study of the Evolution of an Educational Ideology', in Simon and Bradley (eds.), *The Victorian Public School* (1975).
—— 'Images of Empire in the Late Victorian Public School', *Journal of Educational Administration History*, 12: 1 (1980).
—— *Athleticism in the Victorian and Edwardian Public School* (1981).
—— *The Games Ethic and Imperialism* (1986).
—— (ed.), *Benefits Bestowed? Education and British Imperialism* (Manchester, 1988).
—— (ed.), *Pleasure, Profit, Proselytism: British Culture and Sport at Home and Abroad 1700–1914* (1988).
—— (ed.), *Making Imperial Mentalities* (Manchester, 1990).
—— (ed.), *The Cultural Bond: Sport, Empire, Society* (1992).
—— (ed.), *The Imperial Curriculum: Racial Images and Education in the British Colonial Experience* (1993).
Helen Taft Manning, 'Colonial Crises before the Cabinet, 1829–1835', *Bulletin of the Institute for Historical Research*, 30 (1957).
O. Mannoni, *Prospero and Caliban: The Psychology of Colonization* (1956).
Nicholas Mansergh, *Survey of British Commonwealth Affairs, 1939–1952* (1952).
—— *The Commonwealth Experience* (1969).
Shula Marks, 'History, the Nation and Empire: Sniping from the Periphery', *History Workshop*, 29 (1990), 112.

Bill Marsden, 'Politicization, Pedagogy, and the Educational Experience of English Children: 1850–1870', in Petter Aasen (ed.), *Proceedings of the Conference of Historical Perspectives on Childhood* (Trondheim, 1990).
Herbert Marshall and Mildred Stock, *Ira Aldridge: The Negro Tragedian* (1958).
Peter Marshall, 'The Imperial Factor in the Liberal Decline, 1880–1885', in J. E. Flint and G. Williams (eds.), *Perspectives of Empire* (1973).
—— 'Imperial Britain', in Peter Marshall (ed.), *The Cambridge Illustrated History of the British Empire* (1992).
—— 'Imperial Britain', *Journal of Imperial and Commonwealth History*, 23 (1995).
—— 'A Nation Defined by Empire, 1755–1776', in A. Grant and K. Stringer (eds.), *Uniting the Kingdom? The Making of British History* (1995).
Ged Martin, 'Was There a British Empire?', *Historical Journal*, 15: 3 (1972).
Arthur Marwick, 'Youth in Britain, 1920–1960: Detachment and Commitment', *Journal of Contemporary History*, 5 (1970).
Philip Mason, *Prospero's Magic: Some Thoughts on Class and Race* (1962).
Colin Matthew, *The Liberal Imperialists: The Ideas and Politics of a Post-Gladstonian Elite* (Oxford, 1973).
Alexander C. May, 'The Round Table, 1910–66', Ph.D. thesis, Oxford University (1995).
David Mayer, 'The World on Fire . . . Pyrodramas at Belle Vue Gardens, Manchester, *c*.1850–1950', in John MacKenzie (ed.), *Popular Imperialism and the Military* (1992).
Standish Meacham, *A Life Apart: The English Working Class 1890–1914* (1977).
Gary Messinger, *British Propaganda and the State in World War I* (1992).
Thomas R. Metcalf, *Ideologies of the Raj* (Cambridge, 1995).
Susan Meyer, 'Colonialism and the Figurative Strategy of *Jane Eyre*', *Victorian Studies*, 33 (1990).
Jeffrey Meyers, *Fiction and the Colonial Experience* (Ipswich, 1973).
Clare Midgley, 'Ethnicity, "Race" and Empire', in June Parris (ed.), *Women's History: Britain 1850–1845* (1995).
—— (ed.), *Gender and Imperialism* (1998).
—— 'Anti-slavery and the Roots of "Imperial Feminism"', in Midgley (ed.), *Gender and Imperialism* (1998).
Maria Mies, Veronika Bennholdt-Thomsen, and Claudia von Werlhof, *Women: The Last Colony* (1988).
Edward Miller, *That Noble Cabinet: A History of the British Museum* (1973).
S. Mills, *Discourses of Difference: An Analysis of Women's Travel Writing and Colonialism* (1991).
Sidney W. Mintz, *Sweetness and Power: The Place of Sugar in Modern History* (New York, 1985).
Harvey Mitchell, 'Hobson Revisited', *Journal of the History of Ideas*, 26 (1965).
Thomas R. Mockaitis, *British Counter-Insurgency, 1919–60* (1990).
Jerrold Northrop Moore, *Edward Elgar: A Creative Life* (1984).
Katharine Moore, 'The Pan-Britannic Festival: A Tangible but Forlorn Expression of Imperial Unity', in Mangan (ed.), *Pleasure, Profit, Proselytism* (1988).
—— '"The Warmth of Comradeship": The First British Empire Games and Imperial Solidarity', in Mangan (ed.), *The Cultural Bond* (1992).
Kenneth Morgan, *Consensus and Disunity: The Lloyd George Coalition Government* (1979).
—— 'The Boer War and the Media (1899–1902)', *20th Century British History*, 13 (2002).
Jan Morris, *Pax Britannica: The Climax of an Empire* (1968).

Jan Morris, *Farewell the Trumpets: An Imperial Retreat* (1978).

Richard Mullen with James Munson, *The Penguin Companion to Trollope* (Hamondsworth, 1996).

Finlay Murray, 'The Making of British Policy on Tropical Africa: Approaches to and Influences on Policy-making', Ph.D. thesis, University of Newcastle upon Tyne (2001).

—— 'School and Empire: British Imperial Service and the Public Schools Between the Wars', *Inklings* (2001).

Tom Nairn, *The Break-up of Britain* (1977).

—— *The Enchanted Glass: Britain and its Monarchy* (1988).

Ashis Nandy, *The Intimate Enemy: Loss and Recovery of Self under Colonialism* (Delhi, 1983).

Stephen Neill, *Colonialism and Christian Missions* (1966).

E. E. Nemmers, *Hobson and Underconsumption* (Amsterdam, 1956).

David Newsome, *Godliness and Good Learning* (1961).

—— *The Victorian World Picture: Perceptions and Introspection in an Age of Change* (1997).

Walter Nimocks, *Milner's Young Men: The 'Kindergarten' in Edwardian Imperial Affairs* (1968).

Jeff Nunokawa, 'For Your Eyes Only: Private Property and the Oriental Body in *Dombey and Son*', in Arac and Ritvo (eds.), *Macropolitics of Nineteenth Century Literature* (1991).

Patrick O'Brien, 'The Costs and Benefits of British Imperialism 1846–1914', *Past and Present*, 120 (1988).

Erin O'Connor, 'Preface for a Post-Colonial Criticism', *Victorian Studies*, 45 (2003).

Patrick O'Farrell, *The Irish in Australia* (Kensington, NSW, 1987).

Avner Offer, 'Costs and Benefits, Prosperity and Security, 1870–1914', in Andrew Porter (ed.), *The Oxford History of the British Empire, Vol. 3: The Nineteenth Century* (Oxford, 1999).

David Omissi, *Air Power and Colonial Control: The Royal Air Force, 1919–1939* (Manchester, 1990).

—— (ed.), *Indian Voices of the Great War: Soldiers' Letters, 1914–18* (1999).

—— and Andrew Thompson (eds.), *The Impact of the South African War* (2002).

Iona and Peter Opie, *The Lore and Language of Schoolchildren* (Oxford, 1959).

Christopher Parker, *The English Historical Tradition Since 1850* (1990).

Benita Parry, 'Problems in Current Theories of Colonial Discourse', *Oxford Literary Review*, 9 (1987).

R. D. Pearce, 'The Prep School and Imperialism: The Example of Orwell's St Cyprian's', *Journal of Educational Administration and History*, 23 (1991).

Ronald Pearsall, *Edwardian Popular Music* (1975).

Henry Pelling, *Popular Politics and Society in Late Victorian Britain* (1968).

Suventrini Perara, *Reaches of Empire: The English Novel from Edgeworth to Dickens* (New York, 1991).

Alicia Percival, *Very Superior Men: Some Early Public School Headmasters and their Achievements* (1973).

Jan Pieterse, *White on Black: Images of Africa and Blacks in Western Popular Culture* (New Haven, Conn., 1992).

Richard J. Popplewell, *Intelligence and Imperial Defence: British Intelligence and the Defence of the Indian Empire 1904–1924* (1995).

M. H. Port, *Imperial London: Civil Government Building in London 1850–1915* (New Haven, Conn., 1995).

Andrew Porter, *The Origins of the South African War: Joseph Chamberlain and the Diplomacy of Imperialism, 1895–99* (Manchester, 1980).

Andrew Porter (ed.), *The Oxford History of the British Empire*, Vol. 3: *The Nineteenth Century* (1999).

—— 'The South African War and Imperial Britain. A Question of Significance?', in Cuthbertson, Grundlingh and Suttie, *Writing a Wider War* (2002).

Bernard Porter, *Critics of Empire: British Radical Attitudes to Colonialism in Africa, 1895–1914* (1968).

—— *The Lion's Share: A Short History of British Imperialism 1850–1995* (1975; 3rd edn., 1996).

—— 'The Edwardians and their Empire', in Donald Read (ed.), *Edwardian England* (1982).

—— 'Hobson and Internationalism', in Michael Freeden (ed.), *Reappraising J. A. Hobson: Humanism and Welfare* (1990).

—— *Britannia's Burden: The Political Evolution of Modern Britain 1851–1990* (1994).

—— 'Cragside', *History Today*, 45 (1995).

—— 'Edward Elgar and Empire', *Journal of Imperial and Commonwealth History*, 29 (2001).

—— 'Empire and British National Identity, 1815–1914', in R. Phillips and H. Brocklehurst (eds.), *History, Nationhood and the Question of Britain* (2004).

Mary Louise Pratt, *Imperial Eyes: Travel Writing and Transculturation* (1992).

Rebecca Preston, ' "The Scenery of the Torrid Zone": Imagined Travels and the Culture of Exotics in Nineteenth-Century British Gardens', in Driver and Gilbert (eds.), *Imperial Cities* (1991).

Jacob M. Price, 'Who Cared About the Colonies? The Impact of the Thirteen Colonies on British Society and Politics, circa 1714–1775', in Bernard Bailyn and Philip D. Morgan (eds.), *Strangers Within the Realm: Cultural Margins of the First British Empire* (Chapel Hill, 1991).

Richard Price, *An Imperial War and the British Working Class: Working-Class Attitudes and Reactions to the Boer War 1899–1902* (1972).

Mary A. Procida, *Married to the Empire: Gender, Politics and Imperialism in India, 1883–1947* (2002).

Tammy M. Proctor, '(Uni)Forming Youth: Girl Guides and Boy Scouts in Britain, 1908–39', *History Workshop Journal*, 45 (1998).

Nicholas Pronay, 'The Political Censorship of Films in Britain Between the Wars', in N. Pronay and D. W. Spring (eds.), *Propaganda, Politics and Film, 1918–45* (1982).

Sam Pryke, 'The Popularity of Nationalism in the Early British Boy Scout Movement', *Social History*, 23 (1998).

Christopher Pulling, *They were Singing: And What They Sang About* (1952).

Eric Quayle, *Ballantyne the Brave: A Victorian Writer and His Family* (1967).

Carroll Quigley, *The Anglo-American Establishment* (1949; new edn., New York, 1981).

John Ramsden, *The Age of Balfour and Baldwin 1902–40* (1978).

Jonah Raskin, *The Mythology of Imperialism: Rudyard Kipling, Joseph Conrad, E. M. Forster, D. H. Lawrence and Joyce Cary* (New York, 1971).

John Raymond, 'The Last Phase', in John Gross (ed.), *Rudyard Kipling: The Man, His Work and His World* (1972).

W. J. Reader, *At Duty's Call: A Study in Obsolete Patriotism* (Manchester, 1988).

Christopher Redwood (ed.), *An Elgar Companion* (1982).

Trevor R. Reese, *The History of the Royal Commonwealth Society 1868–1968* (Oxford, 1968).

Paul B. Rich, *Race and Empire in British Politics* (Cambridge, 1986).

P. J. Rich, *Elixir of Empire: The English Public Schools, Ritualism, Freemasonry, and Imperialism* (1989).

P. J. Rich, 'Public-School Freemasonry in the Empire', in J. A. Mangan (ed.), *Benefits Bestowed?* (1988).

Jeffrey Richards, 'Boy's Own Empire: Feature Films and Imperialism in the 1930s', in Mackenzie (ed.), *Imperialism and Popular Culture* (1986).

—— (ed.), *Imperialism and Juvenile Literature* (Manchester, 1989).

—— 'With Henty to Africa', in Richards (ed.), *Imperialism and Juvenile Literature* (1989).

—— 'Popular Imperialism and the Image of the Army in Juvenile Literature', in MacKenzie (ed.), *Popular Imperialism and the Military* (1992).

—— *Films and British National Identity: From Dickens to Dad's Army* (1997).

—— *Imperialism and Music: Britain 1876–1953* (2001).

Thomas Richards, *The Imperial Archive: Knowledge and the Fantasy of Empire* (1993).

Jane Ridley, 'Edwin Lutyens, New Delhi, and the Architecture of Imperialism', *Journal of Imperial and Commonwealth History*, 26 (1998).

—— *The Architect and His Wife: A Life of Edwin Lutyens* (2002).

Eliza Riedi, 'Imperialist Women in Edwardian Britain: The Victoria League 1899–1914', Ph.D. thesis, St Andrews University (1997).

—— 'Options for an Imperialist Woman: The Case of Violet Markham, 1899–1914', *Albion*, 32 (2000).

—— 'Women, Gender and the Promotion of Empire: The Victoria League, 1901–1914', *Historical Journal*, 45 (2002).

Harriet Ritvo, *The Animal Estate: The English and other Creatures in the Victorian Age* (Cambridge, Mass., 1987).

John Roach, *A History of Secondary Education in England 1800–1870* (1986).

—— *Secondary Education in England 1870–1902: Public Activity and Private Enterprise* (1991).

Brian Roberts, *Those Bloody Women: Three Heroines of the Boer War* (1991).

Ronald Robinson, 'Oxford in Imperial Historiography', in Madden and Fieldhouse (eds.), *Oxford and the Idea of Commonwealth* (1982).

Jonathan Rose, *The Edwardian Temperament* (Athens, Ohio, 1986).

—— *The Intellectual Life of the British Working Classes* (New Haven, Conn., 2001).

Michael Rosenthal, 'Knights and Retainers: The Earliest Version of Baden-Powell's Boy Scout Scheme', *Journal of Contemporary History*, 15 (1980).

—— *The Character Factory: Baden-Powell and the Origin of the Boy Scout Movement* (1986).

Marlon B. Ross, 'Romancing the Nation-State: The Poetics of Romantic Nationalism', in Arac and Ritvo (eds.), *Macropolitics of Nineteenth-Century Literature* (1991).

David Rubinstein, 'The London School Board 1870–1904', in Phillip McCann (ed.), *Popular Education and Socialization in the 19th century* (1977).

W. D. Rubinstein, 'Education and the Social Origins of British Elites, 1880–1970', *Past and Present* 112 (1986).

Dave Russell, *Popular Music in England, 1840–1914: A Social History* (1987).

Jonathan Rutherford, *Forever England: Reflections on Masculinity and Empire* (1997).

Edward Said, *Orientalism* (1978).

—— 'Yeats and Decolonisation', in T. Eagleton, F. Jameson and E. Said (eds.), *Nationalism, Colonialism and Literature* (Minneapolis, 1990).

—— *Culture and Imperialism* (1993).

Raphael Samuel (ed.), *Patriotism: The Making and Unmaking of British National Identity*, Vol. 1, *History and Politics* (1989).

Raphael Samuel and Paul Thompson (eds.), *The Myths We Live By* (1990).
Alan Sandison, *The Wheel of Empire: A Study of the Imperial Idea in Some Late Nineteenth and Early Twentieth Century Fiction* (1967).
Derek Sayer, 'British Reaction to the Amritsar Massacre 1919–1920', *Past and Present*, 131 (1991).
Jonathan Schneer, *London 1900: The Imperial Metropolis* (New Haven, Conn., 1999).
Hans-Christoph Schröder, *Imperialismus und Antidemokratisches Denken* (Wiesbaden, 1978).
Joseph Schumpeter, *The Sociology of Imperialism* (first German edn. 1919; new edn. New York, 1955).
Bill Schwarz (ed.), *The Expansion of England: Race, Ethnicity and Cultural History* (1996).
Geoffrey Searle, *The Quest for National Efficiency: A Study in British Politics and British Political Thought 1899–1914* (1971).
—— 'Critics of Edwardian Society: The Case of the Radical Right', in Alan O'Day (ed.), *The Edwardian Age* (1979).
—— '"National Efficiency" and the "Lessons" of the War', in Omissi and Thompson (eds.), *The Impact of the South African War* (2002).
R. J. W. Selleck, *The New Education 1870–1914* (1968).
Bernard Semmel, *The Governor Eyre Controversy* (1962); published in USA as *Democracy versus Empire: The Jamaica Riots of 1865 and the Governor Eyre Controversy* (New York, 1969).
—— *The Rise of Free Trade Imperialism: Classical Political Economy the Empire of Free Trade and Imperialism 1750–1850* (Cambridge, 1970).
—— *Imperialism and Social Reform: English Social-Imperial Thought 1895–1914* (1960).
Laurence Senelick, 'Politics as Entertainment: Victorian Music-Hall Songs', *Victorian Studies*, 19 (1975–6).
Chandak Sengoopta, *Imprint of the Raj: How Fingerprinting Was Born in Colonial India* (2003).
Martin Seymour-Smith, *Rudyard Kipling* (1989).
Jenny Sharpe, *Allegories of Empire: The Figure of Woman in the Colonial Text* (Minneapolis, 1993).
Marika Sherwood, 'Race, Empire and Education: Teaching Racism', *Race and Class*, 42 (2001).
Colin Shrosbree, *Public Schools and Private Education: The Clarendon Commission 1861–64 and the Public School Acts* (Manchester, 1988).
Folarin Shyllon, *Black People in Britain 1555–1933* (1977).
Brian Simon, *Two Nations and the Educational Structure, 1780–1870* (1960).
—— *Education and the Labour Movement 1870–1920* (1965).
—— and Ian Bradley (eds.), *The Victorian Public School* (1975).
—— *The State and Educational Change: Essays in the History of Education and Pedagogy* (1994).
Mrinalini Sinha, *Colonial Masculinity: The 'Manly Englishman' and the 'Effeminate Bengali' in the Late Nineteenth Century* (Manchester, 1995).
Frank Smith, *A History of English Elementary Education* (1931).
Iain R. Smith, 'Capitalism and the War', in Omissi and Thompson (eds.), *Impact of the South African War* (2002).
Tori Smith, '"A Grand Work of Noble Conception': The Victoria Memorial and Imperial London', in Driver and Gilbert (eds.), *Imperial Cities* (1999).
Constance Babington Smith, *John Masefield: A Life* (1978).
R. Soloway, 'Counting the Degenerates: The Statistics of Race Deterioration in Edwardian England', *Journal of Contemporary History*, 17 (1982).

Gayatri Spivak, 'Imperialism and Sexual Difference', *Oxford Literary Review*, 8 (1986).
—— 'Three Women's Texts and a Critique of Imperialism', in Robyn Warhol and Diane Price Herndl (eds.), *Feminisms: An Anthology of Literary Theory and Criticism* (New Brunswick, NJ, 1991).
John Springhall, 'Lord Meath, Youth, and Empire', *Journal of Contemporary History*, 5 (1970).
—— 'Boy Scouts, Class and Militarism in Relation to British Youth Movements 1908–1930', *International Review of Social History*, 16 (1971).
—— *Youth, Empire and Society: British Youth Movements, 1883–1940* (1977).
—— *et al.*, 'Baden-Powell and the Scout Movement Before 1920: Citizen Training or Soldiers of the Future?', *English Historical Review*, 102 (1987).
—— 'Healthy Papers For Manly Boys: Imperialism and Race in the Harmsworths' Halfpenny Boys' Papers of the 1890s and 1900s', in Richards (ed.), *Imperialism and Juvenile Literature* (1989).
David Spurr, *The Rhetoric of Empire: Colonial Discourse in Journalism, Travel Writing, and Imperial Administration* (Durham, NC, 1993).
Gareth Stedman-Jones, 'Working Class Culture and Working Class Politics in London, 1870–1900', *Journal of Social History*, 7 (1974).
W. B. Stephens, *Education, Literacy and Society, 1830–70: The Geography of Diversity in Provincial England* (Manchester, 1987).
—— *Education in Britain 1750–1918* (1998).
Gordon T. Stewart, 'Tenzing's Two Wrist-Watches: The Conquest of Everest and Late Imperial Culture in Britain, 1921–1953', *Past and Present*, 149 (1995).
Eric Stokes, *The English Utilitarians and India* (Oxford, 1959).
D. R. Stoddart, *On Geography and Its History* (1986).
Anne Laura Stoler, 'Rethinking Colonial Categories: European Communities and the Boundaries of Rule', in Dirks (ed.), *Colonialism and Culture* (1992).
—— *Race and the Education of Desire. Foucault's* History of Sexuality *and the Colonial Order of Things* (Durham, NC, 1995).
—— and Frederick Cooper, 'Between Metropole and Colony: Rethinking a Research Agenda', in Cooper and Ann Laura Stoler (eds.), *Tensions of Empire* (1997).
Margaret Strobel, *European Women and the Second British Empire* (Bloomington, Ind., 1991).
Anne Summers, 'Edwardian Militarism', in Samuel (ed.), *Patriotism* (1989).
Peter Sutcliffe, *The Oxford University Press: An Informal History* (Oxford, 1978).
Gillian Sutherland, *Policy-Making in Elementary Education 1870–1895* (Oxford, 1973).
Cecillie Swaisland, *Servants and Gentlewomen to the Golden Land: The Emigration of Single Women from Britain to Southern Africa, 1820–1939* (Durban, 1993).
Richard Symonds, *Oxford and the Empire: The Last Lost Cause?* (1986).
Miles Taylor, 'Patriotism, History and the Left in Twentieth-Century Britain', *Historical Journal*, 33 (1990).
—— 'Imperium et Libertas? Rethinking the Radical Critique of Imperialism During the Nineteenth Century', *Journal of Imperial and Commonwealth History*, 19 (1991).
—— 'The 1848 Revolutions and the British Empire', *Past and Present*, 169 (2000).
—— 'Colonial Representation at Westminster, *c.*1800–65', in Julian Hoppit (ed.), *Parliament, Nations and Identities in Britain and Ireland, 1660–1850* (Manchester, 2003).
Ronald Taylor, 'Music in the Air: Elgar and the BBC', in Raymond Monk (ed.), *Edward Elgar: Music and Literature* (1993).

Imogen Thomas, *Haileybury 1806–1987* (Haileybury, 1987).
Nicholas Thomas, *Colonialism's Culture: Anthropology, Travel and Government* (Cambridge, 1994).
Andrew Thompson, 'Tariff Reform: An Imperial Strategy', *Historical Journal*, 40 (1997).
—— *Imperial Britain: The Empire and British Politics c.1880–1932* (2000).
—— 'Publicity, Philanthopy and Commemoration: British Society and the War', in Omissi and Thompson (eds.), *The Impact of the South African War* (2002).
E. P. Thompson, 'The Peculiarities of the English', *Socialist Register, 1965* (1965).
Lynne Thomson, ' "The Golden Thread of Empire": Women's Popular Education in the Lancashire Federation of Women's Institutes 1920–39', *Journal of Educational Administration and History*, 28 (1996).
Mathew Thomson, *The Problem of Mental Deficiency: Eugenics, Democracy, and Social Policy in Britain, c.1870–1959* (Oxford, 1998).
Susan Thorne, ' "The Conversion of Englishmen and the Conversion of the World Inseparable": Missionary imperialism and the Language of Class in Early Industrial Britain', in Cooper and Stoler (eds.), *Tensions of Empire* (1997).
—— *Congregational Missions and the Making of an Imperial Culture in 19th-Century England* (Stanford, Cal., 1999).
Kathryn Tidrick, *Empire and the English Character* (1990).
B. R. Tomlinson, 'The Contraction of England: National Decline and the Loss of Empire', *Journal of Imperial and Commonwealth History*, 11 (1982).
Luke Trainor, *British Imperialism and Australian Nationalism* (Cambridge, 1994).
David Trotter, 'Colonial Subjects', *Critical Quarterly*, 32 (1990).
Frank M. Turner, *Contesting Cultural Authority* (1993).
J. E. Tyler, *The Struggle for Imperial Unity 1868–1895* (1938).
David Vincent, *Bread, Knowledge and Freedom: A Study of Nineteenth-Century Working Class Autobiography* (1981).
Gauri Viswanathan, *Masks of Conquest* (1898).
Bernard Waites, *A Class Society at War: England 1914–1918* (Leamington Spa, 1987).
Paul Ward, *Red Flag and Union Jack: Englishness, Patriotism and the British Left, 1881–1924* (1998).
Stuart Ward (ed.), *British Culture and the End of Empire* (Manchester, 2001).
David Wardle, *The Rise of the Schooled Society: The History of Formal Schooling in England* (1974).
Allen Warren, 'Sir Robert Baden-Powell, the Scout movement and Citizen Training in Great Britain, 1900–1920', *English Historical Review*, 101 (1986).
—— 'Citizens of the Empire: Baden-Powell, Scouts and Guides, and an "Imperial Ideal" ', in Mackenzie (ed.), *Imperialism and Popular Culture* (1986).
—— ' "Mothers for the Empire"? The Girl Guides Association in Britain, 1909–39', in Mangan (ed.), *Making Imperial Mentalities* (1990).
George Watson, *The English Ideology* (1973).
M. S. Watts, *George Frederic Watts*, 3 vols. (1912).
R. K. Webb, *The British Working Class Reader 1790–1848: Literary and Social Tension* (1955).
G. C. Webber, *The Ideology of the British Right 1918–39* (1986).
Wendy Webster, *Imagining Home: Gender, 'Race' and National Identity, 1945–64* (1998).
James Whitehead, 'Thomas Hardy and the South African War', *The Hardy Review*, 1 (New Haven, Conn., 1998).
Martin J. Wiener, *English Culture and the Decline of the Industrial Spirit 1850–1980* (1981).

Paul Wilkinson, 'English Youth Movements, 1908–30', *Journal of Contemporary History*, 4 (1969).
Rupert Wilkinson, *The Prefects: British Leadership and the Public School Tradition* (1964).
Patrick Williams and Laura Chrisman (eds.), *Colonial Discourse and Post-Colonial Theory: A Reader* (Hemel Hempstead, 1993).
Angus Wilson, *The Strange Ride of Rudyard Kipling* (1977).
Kathleen Wilson, 'Empire, Trade and Popular Politics in Mid-Hanoverian Britain: The Case of Admiral Vernon', *Past and Present*, 121 (1988).
Judith Wilt, 'The Imperial Mouth: Imperialism, the Gothic and Science Fiction', *Journal of Popular Culture*, 14 (1981).
Donald Winch, *Classical Political Economy and the Colonies* (1965).
R. W. Winks and J. R. Rush (eds.), *Asia in Western Fiction* (1990).
Denis Winter, *Death's Men: Soldiers of the Great War* (1978).
J. M. Winter, *The Great War and the British People* (1985).
Derek Winterbottom, *Henry Newbolt: The Spirit of Clifton* (1986).
Philip Woodruff [Philip Mason], *The Men who Ruled India: The Guardians* (1954).
William Woodruff, *Impact of Western Man: A Study of Europe's Role in the World Economy 1750–1960* (1966).
Deborah Wormell, *Sir John Seeley and the Uses of History* (Cambridge, 1980).
Peter Yeandle, 'Lessons in Englishness and Empire, *c.*1880–1914: Further Thoughts on the English/British Conundrum', in R. Phillips and H. Brocklehurst (eds.), *History, Nationhood and the Question of Britain* (2004).
David Young, 'East-End Street Names and British Imperialism', *The Local Historian*, 22 (1992).
Percy Young, *Alice Elgar: Enigma of a Victorian Lady* (1978).
Robert J. C. Young, *Colonial Desire: Hybridity in Theory, Culture and Race* (1995).
Lynn Barry Zastoupil, 'J. S. Mill and the British Empire: An Intellectual Biography', Ph.D. dissertation, University of Minnesota (1985).
S. H. Zebel, 'Joseph Chamberlain and the Genesis of Tariff Reform', *Journal of British Studies*, 7 (1967).
Sue Zemka, 'The Holy Books of Empire: Translations of the British and Foreign Bible Society', in Arac and Ritvo (eds.), *Macropolitics of Nineteenth Century Literature* (1991).

Index

INDEX